Early Sunnī Historiography

Islamic History and Civilization

STUDIES AND TEXTS

VOLUME 157

The titles published in this series are listed at *brill.com/ihc*

Early Sunnī Historiography

A Study of the Tārīkh *of Khalīfa b. Khayyāṭ*

By

Tobias Andersson

BRILL

LEIDEN | BOSTON

Cover illustration: A copy of a page from the manuscript of the *Tārīkh* of Khalīfa b. Khayyāṭ, National Library of Morocco (Rabat), no. 199, p. 53. Photo by Tobias Andersson.

Library of Congress Cataloging-in-Publication Data

Names: Andersson, T. S. (Tobias Sahl), author.
Title: Early Sunni historiography : a study of the Tarikh of Khalifa b. Khayyat / by Tobias Andersson.
Description: Leiden ; Boston : Brill, 2018. | Series: Islamic history and civilization ; Volume 157 | Includes bibliographical references and index.
Identifiers: LCCN 2018035513 (print) | LCCN 2018040103 (ebook) | ISBN 9789004383173 (ebook) | ISBN 9789004383166 (hardback : alk. paper)
Subjects: LCSH: ʿUṣfūrī, Khalīfah ibn Khayyāṭ, -854. Tārīkh Khalīfah ibn Khayyāṭ. | Umayyad dynasty–History–Early works to 1800. | Islamic Empire–History–661-750–Early works to 1800.
Classification: LCC DS38.5.U743 (ebook) | LCC DS38.5.U743 A53 2018 (print) | DDC 956/.013–dc23
LC record available at https://lccn.loc.gov/2018035513

Typeface for the Latin, Greek, and Cyrillic scripts: "Brill". See and download: brill.com/brill-typeface.

ISSN 0929-2403
ISBN 978-90-04-38316-6 (hardback)
ISBN 978-90-04-38317-3 (e-book)

This book is printed on acid-free paper and produced in a sustainable manner.

Contents

Acknowledgements VII
Note on Conventions VIII

Introduction 1
1 Subject and Scope 1
2 Previous Studies on Khalīfa's *Tārīkh* 10
3 Manuscripts and Published Editions 13

1 **The Transmission of Khalīfa's *Tārīkh*** 15
1 Introduction 15
2 The Transmitters: Baqī b. Makhlad and Mūsā b. Zakariyyā al-Tustarī 16
3 Differences between the Recensions and the Question of Authorship 21
4 Missing Material in Baqī's Recension 28
5 Conclusion 44

2 **Khalīfa's Life and Works** 45
1 Introduction 45
2 Biography 45
3 Works 52
4 Scholarly Reputation 55
5 Khalīfa's *Tārīkh* in Later Scholarship 59
6 Conclusion 65

3 **Social and Intellectual Context** 67
1 Introduction 67
2 Social and Political Context 68
3 Intellectual Context 78
4 Historiographical Context 90
5 Conclusion 103

4 **Khalīfa's Sources** 105
1 Introduction 105
2 Main Direct Transmitters (20–110 Citations) 106
3 Less Frequently Cited Direct Transmitters (5–19 Citations) 112
4 Minor Direct Transmitters (1–4 Citations) 120

5 Major Indirect Sources 125
6 Analysis of Material 131
7 Conclusion 137

5 **Khalīfa's Methods** 139
1 Introduction 139
2 Epistemology of Historical Knowledge 140
3 System of Reference 151
4 Selection and Evaluation of Transmitters 158
5 Conclusion 164

6 **Structure and Arrangement of the *Tārīkh*** 166
1 Introduction 166
2 Concept of Chronography 166
3 General Structure: Annalistic and Caliphal Chronology 172
4 Structure of Individual Years and Lists 178
5 Conclusion 193

7 **Themes I: Prophethood, Community and Hegemony** 195
1 Introduction 195
2 Prophethood 196
3 Community 203
4 Hegemony 209
5 Conclusion 223

8 **Themes II: Leadership and Civil War** 225
1 Introduction 225
2 The Rāshidūn Period 226
3 The Umayyad Period 250
4 The ʿAbbāsid Period 275
5 Conclusion 279

Conclusion 283
1 Overview 283
2 Methods, Concerns and Contexts of the Early Historians 283
3 Chronography among the Early *Ḥadīth* Scholars 285
4 Articulations of Sunnī Views in the Early Historical Tradition 286

Appendix: Citations of Khalīfa in al-Bukhārī's *al-Jāmiʿ al-ṣaḥīḥ* 289
Bibliography 299
Index 317

Acknowledgements

I would like to thank my teachers, colleagues and friends for their support during the years spent writing this book. I am particularly grateful to Abdassamad Clarke and Abdussalaam Nordenhök for always providing excellent advice in all matters and for their wonderful company. I would also like to thank my PhD supervisor, Andrew Marsham, for his constant help and beneficial discussions of the thesis upon which this work is based. Lastly, I must thank my wife and family, who have offered their continual support throughout the composition of this book.

Note on Conventions

The dates in this book follow the Hijrī/Common Era format. Translations of Khalīfa's *Tārīkh* are my own, although I have based some parts on Wurtzel's translation of the section in Khalīfa's *Tārīkh* on the Umayyad period: *Khalifa ibn Khayyat's History on the Umayyad Dynasty* (Liverpool 2015). The phrase "may the peace and blessings of God be upon him (*ṣallā Allāhu ʿalayhi wa-sallam*)," which usually follows the Prophet Muḥammad's name in the Muslim sources, is abbreviated as (ṣ).

Introduction

1 Subject and Scope

This is a study of the oldest Islamic chronological history still extant: the *Tārīkh* ('Chronicle') of Khalīfa b. Khayyāṭ (d. 240/854).[1] Abū ʿAmr Khalīfa b. Khayyāṭ al-ʿUṣfurī—also known as Shabāb—was a *ḥadīth* scholar and historian who lived and worked in the large southern Iraqi city of Basra, which was one of the main centres of learning in the Muslim world at the time. The extant recension of the *Tārīkh* was transmitted from Khalīfa by the leading *ḥadīth* scholar of al-Andalus, Baqī b. Makhlad al-Qurṭubī (d. 276/889), during his travels in the East.[2] After an introductory section on calendar systems and chronography, Khalīfa's *Tārīkh* is arranged annalistically by years of the lunar Hijrī calendar (1–232/622–847 in Baqī b. Makhlad's recension). It covers the political and administrative history of the Muslim polity from its origins in Medina at the time of the Prophet Muḥammad and the first caliphs that succeeded him up to the Umayyad and ʿAbbāsid caliphates.

Despite its early date, Khalīfa's *Tārīkh* has received little attention in modern scholarship.[3] Previous works on Khalīfa's *Tārīkh* are only partial studies or general introductions, without any in-depth analysis of its sources, structures, content and underlying aims and methods.[4] These survey and textbook accounts tend to remark on its being the earliest surviving annalistic history in Arabic, in contrast to earlier single-subject texts and Prophetic biographies. Some modern historians have dismissed it as telling us little or nothing that is not known from the later historical tradition,[5] although others have pointed out

1 Another chronological history compiled around the same time that might be more or less complete in its extant recension is the *Tārīkh* of ʿAbd al-Malik b. Ḥabīb (d. 238/853). On the discussions about the state of the surviving version, see Aguadé's introduction to Ibn Ḥabīb, *Tārīkh* 77–108.

2 Another recension was transmitted from Khalīfa by Mūsā b. Zakariyyā al-Tustarī (d. before 300/912), but it survives only partially as scattered citations in later sources. On these two recensions, see Chapter 1.

3 Apart from this book, there are so far only a few partial studies. See Roberts, *Early Islamic historiography* 65–77; ʿĀṣī, *Khalīfa*; Nawas, An early Muslim philosopher of history; Robinson, *Islamic historiography* 77–79; Ṣaddām, *Tārīkh Khalīfa*; Wurtzel, *Khalifa ibn Khayyat's History*. The latter is based on Wurtzel's PhD thesis from 1977, *The Umayyads in the "History" of Khalīfa b. Khayyāṭ*, which was prepared for publication by Robert Hoyland. See also Andersson and Marsham, First Islamic chronicle.

4 See the review of previous studies below.

5 Robinson, *Islamic historiography* 77.

 DOI:10.1163/9789004383173_002

that it contains a good amount of unique and detailed information as well as somewhat different perspectives on certain events.[6] Khalīfa's *Tārīkh* was also compiled before the reorganisation and standardisation of historical knowledge that took place around the late third/ninth and early fourth/tenth centuries, when what Borrut has described as the most successful and enduring of the "early Islamic historiographical filters" was established.[7] However, it is not only the early date and some of the information that distinguish Khalīfa's *Tārīkh*; the selection and framing of the material (political-administrative history from an early Sunnī perspective) and the context of its compilation (the Basran *ḥadīth* circles) also set it apart from many other early histories. In that sense, Khalīfa's *Tārīkh* is itself a largely overlooked historical fact that helps us better understand the development of Islamic historical writing—especially in the early *ḥadīth* circles to which Khalīfa belonged and which were crucial in the articulation of Sunnism during the early third/ninth century.[8]

The purpose of the book is, accordingly, to reassess and reappraise Khalīfa's *Tārīkh* by means of a detailed analysis of both the text and the context of its compilation. Apart from the lack of detailed attention to Khalīfa's *Tārīkh* in modern scholarship, there are three principal reasons why this full-length study is important for the wider field of Islamic historiography. First, full-length studies on the works of some early historians have shown the importance of detailed examinations of specific historians for understanding their aims and methods of compilation. They also highlight the great diversity in the early historical tradition.[9] Because of Khalīfa's preoccupation with both *ḥadīth* transmission and history writing, his *Tārīkh* lends itself particularly well to an in-depth examination of the interaction between the two fields of *ḥadīth* and *akhbār* history, more specifically chronography (*tārīkh*), in the early third/ninth century.[10] Understanding the sources, methods and agendas

6 Wurtzel, *Khalifa ibn Khayyat's History* viii; Borrut, *Entre mémoire et pouvoir* 94–95. See also Andersson and Marsham, First Islamic chronicle 20–22.

7 Borrut, Vanishing Syria 44–45, *Entre mémoire et pouvoir* 97–108. See also his point regarding Khalīfa's *Tārīkh* as clearly distinguishable from the slightly later "historiographical vulgate" in *Entre mémoire et pouvoir* 94–95.

8 See Lucas, *Constructive critics* 21. See also Zaman, *Religion and politics* 208–213.

9 E.g. Khalidi, *Islamic historiography*; Shboul, *al-Masʿūdī and his world*; Sezgin, *Abū Mikhnaf*; Leder, *Das Korpus al-Haiṯam*; Shoshan, *Poetics*; Hirschler, *Medieval Arabic historiography*; Kennedy, *al-Ṭabarī*; Mårtensson, *Tabari*; Anthony, *Caliph and the heretic*; Lindstedt, *Transmission of al-Madāʾinī's material*; Bonner, *Historiographical study*.

10 There are some studies on the relation between *maghāzī-sīra* and *ḥadīth*, but fewer on the post-Prophetic *akhbār* tradition. For a recent example of the former, including a summary of previous studies, see Görke, Relationship between *maghāzī* and *ḥadīth*.

of these early historians is, of course, also important in order to avail oneself of them as sources in historical scholarship on early Islam.[11]

Second, some studies on Khalīfa's *Tārīkh* have acknowledged his role as a *ḥadīth* scholar,[12] but, unlike the present book, none of them have examined its implications for our understanding of Khalīfa's aims, methods and historical views. Chronography (*tārīkh*) is not usually associated with the early *ḥadīth* scholars, who generally were more concerned with the transmission and evaluation of reports as well as their application in core fields such as jurisprudence (*fiqh*) and credal beliefs (*ʿaqīda*).[13] Likewise, the two most common types of *ḥadīth* works until the mid-third/ninth century were *musnad* collections (arranged according to transmitters) and *muṣannaf* collections (arranged according to legal subjects).[14] As this book seeks to highlight, however, a few early chronological histories were compiled by *ḥadīth* scholars or *ḥadīth*-minded jurisprudents—including ʿAbd al-Malik b. Ḥabīb (d. 238/853), al-Fasawī (d. 277/890), Ibn Abī Khaythama (d. 279/892) and Abū Zurʿa al-Dimashqī (d. 282/895)—but they have been rather neglected in modern studies on the development of Islamic historical writing.[15] Importantly, these works were combined with, or compiled in close relation to, *ṭabaqāt* material ('prosopography arranged by generations'), which the *ḥadīth* scholars used as a part of the biographical study and evaluation of *ḥadīth* transmitters (*ʿilm al-rijāl*).[16] This book explores this type of historical writing among early *ḥadīth* scholars by focusing specifically on Khalīfa's *Tārīkh* as transmitted by Baqī b. Makhlad. Because of the link between *tārīkh* and *ṭabaqāt* writing, Khalīfa's *Ṭabaqāt* will be used in the analysis of the *Tārīkh* for information about Khalīfa's context, sources, methods and historical views.

---

11 As illustrated by a couple of recent historical studies that combine social and literary concerns: Savant, *New Muslims*; Clarke, *Muslim conquest*.

12 See al-ʿUmarī's introduction to Khalīfa b. Khayyāṭ, *Tārīkh* (1985) 5–16; Zakkār, Ibn Khayyāṭ al-ʿUṣfurī; Roberts, *Early Islamic historiography* 65; ʿĀṣī, *Khalīfa* 30–35; Wurtzel, *Khalifa ibn Khayyat's History* 10–16.

13 As Robinson summarises, "later chronography and non-Prophetic biography (including autobiography) were on the margins of their [i.e. the *ḥadīth* scholars'] programme." *Islamic historiography* 103.

14 For an overview of these formats, see Brown, *Hadith* 25–31.

15 Ibn Ḥabīb, *Tārīkh*; al-Fasawī, *Maʿrifa*; Ibn Abī Khaythama, *Tārīkh*; Abū Zurʿa al-Dimashqī, *Tārīkh*. For example, Khalidi mentions Khalīfa and Abū Zurʿa, but only as references or brief comments in the footnotes. *Arabic historical thought* 21, 23–24, 31–35, 45, 80. Besides Khalīfa, Robinson mentions the works of Ibn Ḥabīb and al-Fasawī, but only in a couple of sentences. *Islamic historiography* 59.

16 On biographical dictionaries, see al-Qāḍī, Biographical dictionaries.

Third, Khalīfa's *Tārīkh* is one of the earliest coherent chronographical articulations of early Sunnī historical views—in some ways, it is similar to the works of later Sunnī historians such as Ibn ʿAsākir (d. 571/1176), al-Dhahabī (d. 748/1348) and Ibn Kathīr (d. 774/1373), who made significant use of his material.[17] Khalīfa's early Sunnī orientation has been noted before,[18] but there are no detailed studies on how it is expressed in his selection of sources, in his structuring of the work or in his presentation of historical events. In this book, the term 'early Sunnī' designates those scholarly groups of the early third/ninth century that were characterised by transmission- and text-based approaches to *fiqh* and *ʿaqīda* (i.e. based on the Qurʾān, Prophetic *ḥadīth*s and reports from the Companions/Successors) in addition to a firm commitment to the collective authority of the Companions and the special merit of the first four caliphs.[19] Such ideas had become fundamental to *ḥadīth* scholarship and *ḥadīth*-based jurisprudence and were accordingly shared by most scholars in these fields.[20] This early Sunnī tradition cannot, however, be entirely equated with the broader classical Sunnī consensus of the fourth/tenth century onwards, although it constituted its basis. Other terms might be possible (e.g. 'proto-Sunnī' or *jamāʿī*), but 'early Sunnī' is clearer, and there is evidence for an early usage of the term *ahl al-sunna* or *ahl al-sunna wa-l-jamāʿa* ('People of the Prophetic Tradition and the Community').[21] Moreover, *ahl al-sunna* was the

---

17 See Chapter 2.

18 Wurtzel remarks that Khalīfa was "basically of orthodox religious outlook" and briefly discusses his religio-political views in *Khalifa ibn Khayyat's History* 3, 24–30.

19 Following Zaman, *Religion and politics* 1–2, 49–56; Lucas, *Constructive critics* 18–21. For a classical and more comprehensive definition, see Ibn Ḥazm's *al-Fiṣal* 2:271, where he says, "The *ahl al-sunna* that we mention are the people of truth (*ahl al-ḥaqq*) and those who oppose them are the people of innovation (*ahl al-bidʿa*). They are the Companions, may God be pleased with them, and all those who followed their way from the best of the Successors, may God Most High have mercy on them, then the people of *ḥadīth* (*aṣḥāb al-ḥadīth*) and the jurists (*fuqahāʾ*) who followed them, generation after generation until this day, as well as the common people (*ʿawāmm*) in the East and the West who followed their example, may God have mercy on them."

20 Lucas, *Constructive critics* 282–285.

21 E.g. Ibn Sīrīn's (d. 110/729) famous words, "In the early period they did not ask about the *isnād*, but when the civil war (*fitna*) occurred they said, 'Name for us your informants.' Thus, the *ahl al-sunna* could be looked at and their *ḥadīth*s accepted, and the *ahl al-bidaʿ* could be looked at and their *ḥadīth*s ignored." Muslim b. al-Ḥajjāj, *Ṣaḥīḥ* 8 (*muqaddima, bāb fī anna al-isnād min al-dīn*). There are also many reports mentioning *ahl al-sunna* attributed to individuals such as Ibn ʿAbbās (d. 68/687–688), Ayyūb al-Sakhtiyānī (d. 131/748), Sufyān al-Thawrī (d. 161/778), al-Fuḍayl b. ʿIyāḍ (d. 187/803), Abū ʿUbayd al-Qāsim b. Sallām (d. 224/838), Aḥmad b. ʿAbdallāh b. Yūnus (d. 227/842) and Aḥmad b. Ḥanbal (d. 241/855). See al-Lālakāʾī, *Sharḥ uṣūl iʿtiqād ahl al-sunna* 1:54–55, 60–61, 64, 66,

term that the third/ninth-century *ahl al-ḥadīth* ('Proponents of Ḥadīth'), with whom Khalīfa seems to have been associated, used to define themselves, often in contrast to opponents, whom they termed *ahl al-bidaʿ* ('People of Religious Innovations') or *ahl al-ahwāʾ* ('People of Heretical Inclinations').[22] Early Sunnī ideas were not limited to the *ahl al-ḥadīth*, but these scholars were leading proponents of early Sunnism in Iraq, especially in Basra, during Khalīfa's lifetime, and they are the main focus of this book. A number of studies have explored the importance of the *ḥadīth* scholars, the jurists (*fuqahāʾ*) and the theologians in the articulation of early Sunnism.[23] As these studies have shown, the disciplines of *ḥadīth* and *fiqh* were far more important in the articulation of early Sunnism than the collection of historical reports (*akhbār*), but some early Sunnī *ḥadīth* scholars, such as Khalīfa, nonetheless compiled works of *akhbār* articulating such ideas. This book explores these expressions of early Sunnī concerns and ideas in the field of *akhbār* history by focusing on Khalīfa's *Tārīkh* and comparing it with other early histories. Thereby it will also highlight an oft-neglected source of pre-classical Sunnī historical thought and compilation.[24]

These general concerns are treated in relation to more specific questions in the eight chapters of the book. Chapter 1 outlines the history of the transmission of Khalīfa's *Tārīkh*, with a focus on the extant recension of Baqī b. Makhlad and the now lost recension of Mūsā b. Zakariyyā al-Tustarī (d. before 300/912), which is only partially preserved in later sources. The chapter suggests that Khalīfa's *Tārīkh* was most likely transmitted on the basis of written notes of lectures that Baqī and al-Tustarī heard at different times, and edited into book form in slightly different ways, which would explain many of the relatively minor differences between the two recensions. On the basis of the overall correspondence between the material in the two recensions, the chapter argues

---

72; al-Ṭabarī, *Tahdhīb al-āthār* 3:660; Abū ʿUbayd al-Qāsim b. Sallām, *Kitāb al-Īmān* 9; Ibn Abī Yaʿlā, *Ṭabaqāt al-ḥanābila* 1:55, 65.

22 On the *ahl al-ḥadīth*, see below in the introduction and Chapter 3. Melchert notes regarding the early *ahl al-ḥadīth* that *ahl al-sunna* was "their usual term for themselves." Melchert, *Formation* 2. See also Zaman, *Religion and politics* 49–54. Ibn Qutayba (d. 276/889) mentions that "if someone asks to be shown the *ahl al-sunna*, people would lead them to the *aṣḥāb al-ḥadīth*." Ibn Qutayba, *Taʾwīl mukhtalif al-ḥadīth* 172.

23 E.g. Schacht, *Origins of Muhammadan jurisprudence*; Watt, *Formative period*; Hodgson, *Venture of Islam 1*; Ess, *Theologie und Gesellschaft*; Melchert, *Formation*; Zaman, *Religion and politics*; Rahman, *Revival and reform*; Lucas, *Constructive critics*; Hallaq, *Origins and evolution*.

24 Hagler, for instance, examines the historical memory of the Umayyad dynasty on the basis of a number of early histories and notes that these "earlier sources are decidedly pro-ʿAlid (as are most extant early histories)," but overlooks Khalīfa's *Tārīkh* as a possible source of comparison. Hagler, Repurposed narratives 2.

that Khalīfa was responsible for at least the general form and content of Baqī's extant recension. The chapter also examines the possibility that Baqī or someone else after him in the *isnād* of the extant recension omitted certain material for ideological reasons, as suggested in a recent study,[25] but it concludes that it is equally possible that the missing material in Baqī's recension was never a part of the version of the *Tārīkh* that Khalīfa transmitted to Baqī. The main implication of this for the study of Khalīfa's *Tārīkh* is that the possibility of occasional omissions and abridgements in the extant recension necessitates caution when analysing Khalīfa's arrangement of material and narration of historical events.

Chapter 2 outlines Khalīfa's biography and his role as a *ḥadīth* scholar of Basra, where he spent most of his life. On the basis of his students and teachers, it suggests that Khalīfa was associated with the *ahl al-ḥadīth*—the Proponents of Ḥadīth—who came to prominence in Iraq during the second/eighth century.[26] There has been some discussion about the diversity of the scholars associated with the *ahl al-ḥadīth* and to what extent they represented a consistent scholarly approach.[27] On the basis of their general commonality, however, the term usually refers to "those scholars who prioritized the derivation of norms from texts (*nuṣūṣ*) above consistency in legal analogy, selecting these proof texts through the emerging science of *ḥadīth* criticism (*jarḥ wa-taʿdīl*)."[28] Not all *ḥadīth* scholars (*muḥaddithūn*) belonged by definition to the *ahl al-ḥadīth* in the sense of a scholarly methodology, but many Iraqi *ḥadīth* scholars in the late second/eighth and early third/ninth centuries were associated with the *ahl al-ḥadīth* rather than with the different rationalist groups in their approach to *fiqh* and *ʿaqīda*.[29] This context of compilation is important as it helps to explain Khalīfa's methods in compilation, the distinctive content of his *Tārīkh* and its underlying historical perspective. The chapter also discusses the use of Khalīfa's *Tārīkh* in later scholarship and suggests that Khalīfa's scholarly agenda and

---

25 Ṣaddām, *Tārīkh Khalīfa* 9, 21–22.

26 Melchert, *Formation* 1–31, How Ḥanafism came to originate in Kufa, Traditionist-jurisprudents; Hallaq, *Origins and evolution* 74–78; Lucas, Where are the legal ḥadīth?; Spectorsky, *Ḥadīth*.

27 On the diversity of the early *ahl al-ḥadīth*, see the previous footnote and Brown, Did the Prophet say it or not? 260.

28 Brown, Did the Prophet say it or not? 260.

29 Melchert, *Formation* 2–3, Traditionist-jurisprudents 383–386. I avoid Makdisi's terms 'traditionist' for a *muḥaddith* and 'traditionalists' for *ahl al-ḥadīth*, and simply use '*ḥadīth* scholar' for *muḥaddith* and '*ahl al-ḥadīth*' for adherents of the scholarly approach. See Makdisi, Ashʿarī and the Ashʿarites 49. However, I sometimes use the adjective 'traditionist' in the sense of *ḥadīth*-related (as in 'traditionist methods') or *ḥadīth*-minded (as in 'traditionist historians').

early Sunnī perspective in the *Tārīkh* were indeed understood and appreciated by many later Sunnī scholars of similar scholarly and historical perspectives to Khalīfa.

Chapter 3 maps out Khalīfa's social, intellectual and historiographical context. First, it contextualises Khalīfa's career by summarising the major social and political trends in the early-to-mid ʿAbbāsid caliphate in general and the city of Basra in particular. Second, it outlines the different scholarly and religio-political groups in Basra, with special reference to the *ahl al-ḥadīth*. Third, it discusses the two forms of history that Khalīfa compiled: *tārīkh* ('chronography') and *ṭabaqāt* ('prosopography arranged by generations'). It suggests that these two formats were closely linked among the early *ḥadīth* scholars; a number of *tārīkh* works compiled by third/ninth-century *ḥadīth* scholars were combined with *ṭabaqāt* sections and thus linked to *ʿilm al-rijāl*. Since the biographies and evaluations of *ḥadīth* transmitters in these works were compiled for an audience of mainly *ḥadīth* scholars, the *tārīkh* sections were most probably written for the same audience. These points are important to the analysis of Khalīfa's *Tārīkh* since they highlight its close connection to his *Ṭabaqāt* and suggest that Khalīfa's fellow *ḥadīth* scholars were the main audience for both works.[30] The chapter also compares Khalīfa's *Tārīkh* with other surviving *tārīkh* works compiled by early Sunnī *ḥadīth*-minded scholars (especially the works of ʿAbd al-Malik b. Ḥabīb, al-Fasawī, Ibn Abī Khaythama and Abū Zurʿa al-Dimashqī) and highlights a number of commonalities in style, form, content and historical views. It thereby suggests that chronography (*tārīkh*) had its place in the *ḥadīth* circles, although it was not one of the main subjects, and that it was linked to *ʿilm al-rijāl* and *ṭabaqāt* compilation.

Chapter 4 examines Khalīfa's selection of sources in the *Tārīkh*, with a focus on the transmitters from whom he directly received his material. First, it demonstrates the preponderance of Basran transmitters and the large number of major *ḥadīth* scholars upon whom Khalīfa relied. Second, it clarifies Khalīfa's method of source selection by examining what types and amounts of material he cites from certain transmitters in relation to their scholarly occupations and reputations. The chapter thus contributes to our understanding of the origins of Khalīfa's material and his selection of sources, while also providing material for the examination of his methods of compilation.

30 This notion of Khalīfa's audience is corroborated by other aspects of the *Tārīkh*: Khalīfa's sources, his methods, his arrangement of the *Tārīkh*, the death notices of *ḥadīth* scholars in the work, his early Sunnī historical perspective and the later transmission of the work among *ḥadīth* scholars. See Chapters 2, 4–8.

Chapter 5 outlines some of the methods and scholarly conventions according to which Khalīfa compiled his *Tārīkh*, including his epistemology of historical knowledge, system of reference, and selection and evaluation of transmitters. In contrast to the view of the early *akhbār* narratives as mere political commentary,[31] it is argued that the early Sunnī view of history in Khalīfa's *Tārīkh* was legitimised by, and dependent upon, the claim to represent historical realities. This claim was, in turn, grounded in its agreement with the authoritative scholarly tradition of the *ḥadīth* scholars. The outline of Khalīfa's system of reference highlights his different usage of *isnād*s depending on the period and the historical importance of the event under discussion. The examination of Khalīfa's evaluation of transmitters shows that it differs according to subject matter: for controversial events, such as the early civil wars, or important historical details, such as the birth and death of the Prophet Muḥammad, Khalīfa relies mainly on well-known *ḥadīth* scholars, but he otherwise cites common *akhbār* compilers (*akhbārīyūn*) for the general chronological narrative. The chapter also outlines Khalīfa's usage of transmission formulas (e.g. *ḥaddathanā*—'He narrated to us') and shows that detailed formulas indicating direct transmission are more common in accounts of controversial or otherwise important events.

Chapter 6 examines the structure and arrangement of the *Tārīkh*, which highlights both Khalīfa's methods of arranging material and the narrative implications of this arrangement. It is argued that Khalīfa's model of chronography—sections of political history arranged annalistically combined with sections of administrative lists placed after each caliph's reign—not only accommodates the main objectives of political and administrative history respectively but also corresponds to Khalīfa's early Sunnī perspective by bringing the continuity of the caliphate and its institutions to the foreground. It also shows how Khalīfa sometimes arranges material in the annalistic sections by chronology and sometimes by other factors (e.g. themes, geography and historical importance).

Chapters 7 and 8 compare some of the main themes in Khalīfa's *Tārīkh* to other early historical works from the second/eighth and third/ninth centuries. The selection is based on Donner's identification of key themes in the early historical tradition: prophethood, community, hegemony and leadership (including civil war).[32] Donner is concerned primarily with how these themes developed among the early Muslims (until c. the mid-second/eighth century), but his outline is based mainly on third/ninth- and fourth/tenth-

31 El-Hibri, *Reinterpreting Islamic historiography* 216.

32 Donner, *Narratives* 147–202.

century works.[33] His outline is therefore useful for identifying major themes that the third/ninth-century historians continued to restructure, reinterpret and expand upon in new contexts, and gives focus to the comparison of Khalīfa's *Tārīkh* with other early histories. Both chapters illustrate Khalīfa's straightforward narrative style and his nearly exclusive focus on chronology and political-administrative history, which differs from many other early works and leads to quite different treatments of the aforementioned themes. The chapters also show Khalīfa's early Sunnī understanding of major events in the early Muslim community, such as successions to the caliphate and civil wars (*fitan* sing. *fitna*)—reflecting, for instance, the chronological ranking of the four rightly-guided caliphs (*al-khulafāʾ al-rāshidūn*), the probity of the Prophet's Companions and the importance of communal unity.[34] Such perspectives, which resemble later classical Sunnī ideas, can be found in other *tārīkh* works compiled by *ḥadīth* scholars and in sections on political history in *ḥadīth* collections, but they differ from some other *akhbār* histories, especially those compiled by early Shīʿī-inclined historians.

Altogether, the book shows how Khalīfa's early Sunnī perspective and his concerns as a *ḥadīth* scholar are reflected in the form and content of the *Tārīkh*, while also highlighting important similarities to other historical works compiled by *ḥadīth* scholars of the third/ninth century. In this sense, Khalīfa's *Tārīkh* is one of the earliest coherent chronographical presentations of Sunnī historical views. It therefore constitutes a key source for the study of the development of Islamic historical writing and early articulations of Sunnism.

---

33 As Donner acknowledges in *Narratives* 125.

34 From here on, when speaking of the first four caliphs in Khalīfa's *Tārīkh* and the works of other early Sunnī scholars, I use the terms 'Rāshidūn caliphs' and 'the Rāshidūn period', which reflect their views on these caliphs and their special status. It has been argued that this periodisation (i.e. the division of the early history into the Rāshidūn, Umayyad and ʿAbbāsid periods) was largely an ʿAbbāsid-era construct, which might be correct for some aspects, but, at least in the case of the first four caliphs, seems to ignore the numerous references in the *ḥadīth* literature and the early scholarly tradition. On the question of periodisation, see Borrut, Vanishing Syria. For the present purposes, it is enough to note that the idea of the special status of the first four caliphs was common among the early Sunnī scholars of the late second/eighth and early third/ninth centuries, although they might differ on some details, and to note that they themselves contributed actively to its further establishment and standardisation.

2 Previous Studies on Khalīfa's *Tārīkh*

Despite being one of the oldest surviving histories in Islam, Khalīfa's *Tārīkh* has attracted attention from modern historians mostly as a source for Islamic history that is complementary to better-known historians such as al-Balādhurī (d. 279/892) and al-Ṭabarī (d. 310/923). Its value as a source for understanding the development of early Islamic historiography has generally been disregarded. The earliest article on Khalīfa's *Tārīkh* is Schacht's short review from 1969, in which he describes the work as "the first completely preserved representative of the most archaic form of Muslim historiography" as it consists mainly of "dry enumerations of persons, of events, of appointments and dismissals, of deaths, etc., year by year."[35] More recent studies on early Islamic historiography and the appearance of new manuscripts of early works (e.g. Sayf b. ʿUmar's *Kitāb al-Ridda wa-l-futūḥ*) have raised questions about Schacht's initial views. Although Khalīfa's *Tārīkh* resembles in some respects the earlier *ḥadīth* tradition in style, other early historians (e.g. Sayf b. ʿUmar, Abū Mikhnaf, Ibn al-Kalbī, Ibn Isḥāq and Naṣr b. Muzāḥim) compiled a different type of more narrative history. However, only a few incomplete studies on Khalīfa's *Tārīkh* have appeared since Schacht's brief article.

Two general introductions are found in al-ʿUmarī's and Zakkār's editions of Khalīfa's *Tārīkh*, both of which discuss Khalīfa's life and works, his scholarly reputation and, briefly, his method of compilation.[36] In addition, al-ʿUmarī also lists Khalīfa's informants in the *Tārīkh* and discusses the most prominent among them.[37] Besides al-ʿUmarī's lists of informants, however, the two introductions only provide basic outlines of Khalīfa's biography and his *Tārīkh*, rather than any in-depth contextual or textual analysis of the work. Similar introductions are also found in their respective editions of Khalīfa's *Ṭabaqāt*.[38]

The fullest treatments of the *Tārīkh* are Wurtzel's PhD thesis on its Umayyad part (1977), Ḥusayn ʿĀṣī's general survey of both Khalīfa's *Tārīkh* and his *Ṭabaqāt* (1993) and Ṣaddām's study of material from Khalīfa's *Tārīkh* that is preserved in later sources but absent from the extant recension of Baqī b. Makhlad (2016).[39] Wurtzel's thesis was edited by Hoyland and published in 2015 as *Khalifa ibn Khayyat's History on the Umayyad Caliphate*. The main part of Wurtzel's work

35 Schacht, Kitāb al-tārīḫ 79.

36 See al-ʿUmarī's introduction in Khalīfa b. Khayyāṭ, *Tārīkh* (1985) 3–40, and Zakkār's in Khalīfa b. Khayyāṭ, *Tārīkh* (1993) 5–14.

37 Al-ʿUmarī's introduction to Khalīfa b. Khayyāṭ, *Tārīkh* (1985) 16–30.

38 Khalīfa b. Khayyāṭ, *Ṭabaqāt* (1967) 13–79; Khalīfa b. Khayyāṭ, *Ṭabaqāt* (1993) 7–17.

39 Wurtzel, *Umayyads*; ʿĀṣī, *Khalīfa*; Ṣaddām, *Tārīkh Khalīfa*.

consists of a translation of the part on the Umayyad caliphate (41–132/661–750). Wurtzel also provides a useful introduction to Khalīfa's biography and scholarly background, as well as to the informants cited in the Umayyad section of the *Tārīkh*.[40] Since the purpose of Wurtzel's work is not a detailed (textual or contextual) analysis, Wurtzel only provides cursory conclusions regarding the purpose of the *Tārīkh* and its context. Without much further discussion, he states, for instance, that the main purpose of the *Tārīkh* was "to fix the dates of events" and that Khalīfa "probably intended his work to be a sort of outline, or convenient handbook, in which historical data were presented for the sake of determining a date for every important event in the history of Islam."[41] Similarly, he concludes regarding the religio-political attitudes in the *Tārīkh* that its "general impression is one of detached neutrality and objectivity," but he notes elsewhere that Khalīfa himself was "basically of orthodox religious outlook, and possibly in the Ḥanbalite camp."[42] He provides some remarks about Khalīfa's attitude towards the Umayyads, ʿAlids and Khawārij in the *Tārīkh*, but not much more than in terms of positive or negative depictions.[43] The most important parts of Wurtzel's study are the sections on Khalīfa's biography, his sources on the Umayyad period and the use of the *Tārīkh* by later scholars.[44]

In his monograph on Khalīfa's *Tārīkh* and *Ṭabaqāt*, Ḥusayn ʿĀṣī surveys the context in which the two works were compiled.[45] However, his survey focuses more on the general development of Islamic historical writing in the first centuries AH than on Khalīfa's immediate political, social and scholarly context. Most useful are his remarks on Khalīfa's methods and sources.[46] It must be noted, however, that substantial parts of his work (about Khalīfa and his sources) are taken directly from al-ʿUmarī's introduction to his edition of Khalīfa's *Tārīkh*.[47]

Ṣaddām's monograph is a study of material from Khalīfa's *Tārīkh* that is preserved in later sources, especially Ibn ʿAsākir's *Tārīkh madīnat Dimashq*, but absent from the extant recension of Baqī b. Makhlad. After some introductory material on Khalīfa's own sources and the *isnād*s of the material preserved

40 Wurtzel, *Khalifa ibn Khayyat's History* 1–46.
41 Wurtzel, *Khalifa ibn Khayyat's History* 20.
42 Wurtzel, *Khalifa ibn Khayyat's History* 3, 24.
43 Wurtzel, *Khalifa ibn Khayyat's History* 24–30.
44 Wurtzel, *Khalifa ibn Khayyat's History* 1–16, 30–46.
45 ʿĀṣī, *Khalīfa* 14–28, 44–49.
46 ʿĀṣī, *Khalīfa* 49–68.
47 Cf. the discussion of Khalīfa's sources in ʿĀṣī, *Khalīfa* 49–63, and al-ʿUmarī's introduction to Khalīfa b. Khayyāṭ, *Tārīkh* (1985) 16–30.

in later sources, Ṣaddām collects 202 reports that are transmitted on Khalīfa's authority but missing in Baqī's recension—most of them from the (now lost) recension of Mūsā al-Tustarī. Based on these reports, he argues that Baqī b. Makhlad abridged substantial parts of Khalīfa's *Tārīkh* and omitted negative material about the Umayyads "because of his 'Uthmānī inclinations" and his close relation to the Umayyads in al-Andalus.[48] Although Ṣaddām is right in pointing out the differences between the two recensions and the active role of the transmitters, his conclusions regarding Baqī b. Makhlad and Baqī's editing of the *Tārīkh* are highly questionable in light of recent studies on the transmission of scholarly texts in early Islam. He assumes, for example, that Khalīfa had one fixed original version of the *Tārīkh* that he transmitted in the same way throughout his life. He thereby overlooks the possibility that Khalīfa transmitted slightly different versions of the *Tārīkh* at different times to different students, which could explain many of the differences between the recensions. These issues surrounding the transmission of Khalīfa's *Tārīkh* are examined in detail in Chapter 1.

Khalīfa's account of the Battle of the Camel is treated in a PhD thesis by Joseph B. Roberts (1986). Roberts highlights Khalīfa's assertion of the legitimacy of 'Alī's caliphate and points out some unusual aspects of Khalīfa's organisation of the material, but without analysing the work as a whole.[49] He also provides a sensible counterargument against Schacht's aforementioned views: none of the works attributed to other early historians (e.g. Abū Mikhnaf, Ibn al-Kalbī, Ibn Isḥāq and Naṣr b. Muzāḥim) resemble Khalīfa's work. Roberts notes that they all use a more narrative style than Khalīfa's *Tārīkh* and that the works attributed to these earlier historians were often single-subject histories rather than complete histories of the Muslim community.[50]

Another partial study is Nawas's brief article "An early Muslim philosopher of history" (1992) about the introductory section of Khalīfa's *Tārīkh*. Nawas suggests that Khalīfa "interjoins religion and history" in a way that "causes history to be subsumed under religion, hence giving history its status of a religious science."[51] However, Nawas's article lacks appreciation of Khalīfa's scholarly context, and Nawas's analysis of the introductory section overlooks its place in the narrative of the *Tārīkh* as a whole. For instance, the introductory section not only establishes the importance of dating and chronography (*tārīkh*)

48 Ṣaddām, *Tārīkh Khalīfa* 21–22.
49 Roberts, *Early Islamic historiography* 65–77.
50 Roberts, *Early Islamic historiography* 66–67.
51 Nawas, Early Muslim philosopher of history 165.

for Muslims and mankind in general but also outlines the scope (Hijrī calendar), subject (political-administrative history) and point of view (the Muslim community) upon which the *Tārīkh* is based.[52]

Another short assessment of some formal and structural features of Khalīfa's work is found in Robinson's *Islamic historiography* (2003), where Robinson briefly points out the accommodative nature of its annalistic scheme, "the early tradition's enthusiasm for lists," Khalīfa's use of collective *isnād*s and the technique of "emphasis through arrangement."[53] Contrary to the argument of the present book, however, Robinson also describes the work as "significant only because it is the earliest we possess; neither the author, who merits only two lines in Ibn al-Nadīm's *Fihrist*, nor his short book, which tells us little that we do not otherwise know from the later tradition, is noteworthy otherwise."[54]

What none of the existing studies have done is a full-length analysis of Khalīfa's *Tārīkh*, including the context of its compilation and its relation to the broader development of Islamic historical writing. In contrast to these previous studies, the present book seeks to demonstrate the distinctiveness and significance of the *Tārīkh* as an example of early annalistic historiography, compiled by a *ḥadīth* scholar at the beginning of the third/ninth century. Accordingly, the approach of this book is both textual and contextual: the text of the *Tārīkh* is analysed in relation to the context of the social and political world in which Khalīfa worked, the scholarly tradition in which he stood and the textual environment in which he compiled his work.[55] Thereby, it will reassess Khalīfa's *Tārīkh* and highlight its importance for the study of early Islamic historical writing, especially historical writing among the *ḥadīth* scholars.

3 Manuscripts and Published Editions

The extant manuscript of Baqī b. Makhlad's recension of Khalīfa's *Tārīkh* was copied in al-Andalus in 477/1084 by Aḥmad b. Muḥammad al-Ashʿarī.[56] It comprises a single volume of 168 folios (336 pages) written in clear Andalu-

52 See Chapter 6.
53 Robinson, *Islamic historiography* 77–79.
54 Robinson, *Islamic historiography* 77.
55 On these three aspects, see Hirschler, *Medieval Arabic historiography* 1–3.
56 The full chain of transmission of this version is Aḥmad b. Muḥammad al-Ashʿarī from Abū l-Walīd Hishām b. Aḥmad from Abū ʿUmar Aḥmad b. Muḥammad al-Ṭalamankī from Abū ʿAbdallāh Muḥammad b. Yaḥyā b. Mufarrij from Abū l-Qāsim Aḥmad b. ʿAbdallāh b. Muḥammad b. al-Mubārak b. Ḥabīb b. ʿAbd al-Malik b. al-Walīd b. ʿAbd al-Malik (the

sian/Maghribī script, and is held at the National Library in Rabat, Morocco.[57] The manuscript has been photocopied from the original microfilm and consulted throughout the study that forms the basis of this book, mainly in order to identify additions (such as headings or corrected spellings) by the editors of the published editions. The two main published editions of the *Tārīkh* were edited independently by Akram Ḍiyā' al-ʿUmarī (Baghdad 1967) and Suhayl Zakkār (Damascus 1967).[58] Al-ʿUmarī's edition was later republished by Dār Ṭayba (Riyadh) in 1985; Zakkār's edition was republished by Dār al-Fikr (Beirut) in 1993. Both have been used, but references in the footnotes are generally limited to al-ʿUmarī's edition, which has the advantage of better indexes and footnotes, useful introductory material and a more accessible layout. Similar to the *Tārīkh*, Khalīfa's *Ṭabaqāt* survives in one manuscript, held in the National Library in Damascus. It was transmitted from Khalīfa by Mūsā b. Zakariyyā al-Tustarī and corroborated, as noted in the manuscript, by another transmission from Khalīfa by ʿUmar b. Aḥmad al-Ahwāzī.[59] Because of the war in Syria, the manuscript has not been consulted. The *Ṭabaqāt* was edited independently by Zakkār (Damascus 1967) and al-ʿUmarī (Baghdad 1967). Both editions have been consulted, but the references are usually limited to Zakkār's edition (republished by Dār al-Fikr in 1993).

Umayyad caliph) from Baqī b. Makhlad. Khalīfa b. Khayyāṭ, *Tārīkh* (1985) 36–38; Khalīfa b. Khayyāṭ, *Tārīkh* (1993) 21–22.

57 See Khalīfa b. Khayyāṭ, *Tārīkh* (1985) 34–41; Khalīfa b. Khayyāṭ, *Tārīkh* (1993) 12–17.

58 There is also a third edition, published by Dār al-Kutub al-ʿIlmiyya (1995) and edited by M.N. Fawwāz and Ḥ.K. Fawwāz.

59 See al-ʿUmarī's introduction to Khalīfa's *Ṭabaqāt* (1967) 65–67, and Zakkār's introduction to Khalīfa's *Ṭabaqāt* (1993) 15–16.

CHAPTER 1

The Transmission of Khalīfa's *Tārīkh*

1 Introduction

The extant recension of Khalīfa's *Tārīkh* was transmitted by Baqī b. Makhlad al-Qurṭubī (d. 276/889). Another recension, transmitted by Mūsā b. Zakariyyā al-Tustarī (d. before 300/912), survives only partially as scattered citations in later sources. This chapter examines the transmission of Khalīfa's *Tārīkh* in detail with focus on Baqī's extant recension. First, it introduces the two main transmitters, Baqī b. Makhlad and Mūsā al-Tustarī, and their respective recensions. Second, it outlines the transmission of scholarly texts in early Islam and its implications for our understanding of the differences between the recensions of Baqī and al-Tustarī.[1] It is suggested that Khalīfa's *Tārīkh* was most likely transmitted on the basis of written notes of lectures that Baqī and al-Tustarī heard at different times and edited into book form in slightly different ways, which would explain many of the relatively minor differences between the recensions. It also discusses the question of authorship and, based on the overall correspondence between the two recensions, argues that Khalīfa was responsible for at least the general form and content of the extant recension. Third, it examines the citations of Khalīfa's *Tārīkh* that are preserved in later sources but absent from Baqī's recension, and discusses the claim that Baqī abridged or omitted certain reports because of Umayyad sympathies.[2] It suggests that, although it is possible that Baqī or someone after him in the *isnād* of the extant recension omitted material for ideological or scholarly reasons, it is equally possible that this material was never a part of the version of the *Tārīkh* that Khalīfa transmitted to Baqī. The chapter argues that Khalīfa was responsible for the overall form and content of the extant recension of the *Tārīkh*, although one must bear in mind that it was probably a series of lecture notes edited into book form by Baqī, so some alterations may well have occurred in the course of transmission.

1 Largely based on Schoeler's *Oral and the written* and *Genesis of literature in Islam*.
2 Ṣaddām, *Tārīkh Khalīfa* 21–22.

 | DOI:10.1163/9789004383173_003

2 The Transmitters: Baqī b. Makhlad and Mūsā b. Zakariyyā al-Tustarī

The two known transmitters of Khalīfa's *Tārīkh* are Baqī b. Makhlad al-Qurṭubī and Abū ʿImrān Mūsā b. Zakariyyā al-Tustarī.[3] Both of them transmitted Khalīfa's two works, the *Tārīkh* and the *Ṭabaqāt*, but only Baqī's transmission of the *Tārīkh* and al-Tustarī's transmission of the *Ṭabaqāt* have survived. Mūsā al-Tustarī presumably came from Tustar in southwestern Persia, but he took up residence in Basra.[4] Relatively little is known about him and, unlike Baqī b. Makhlad, he is not remembered as a major *ḥadīth* scholar. Al-Dhahabī (d. 748/1348) notes:

> Mūsā b. Zakariyyā al-Tustarī, who narrated from Shabāb al-ʿUṣfurī [Khalīfa b. Khayyāṭ] and the likes of him. Al-Dāraquṭnī spoke critically of him (*takallama fīhi*) and al-Ḥākim narrated from al-Dāraquṭnī that his transmission is abandoned (*matrūk*).[5]

However, al-Ṭabarānī (d. 360/971), Ibn Qāniʿ (d. 351/962) and al-Ḥākim al-Naysābūrī (d. 405/1014) narrate several reports from him, which suggests that he was at least a known transmitter in his time.[6] Al-Tustarī's recension of the *Tārīkh* was used by Ibn ʿAsākir (d. 571/1176), as indicated by the *isnāds* in his *Tārīkh madīnat Dimashq*, and most likely by other Syrian scholars such as al-Dhahabī (d. 748/1348) and Ibn Kathīr (d. 774/1373).[7] Ibn ʿAsākir is the historian who preserves most narrations from al-Tustarī's recension; Ṣaddām notes that he transmits in total 1,487 narrations from Khalīfa via al-Tustarī and that 165

---

3 On the approximate date of al-Tustarī's death ("before 300/912"), see al-Dhahabī, *al-Mughnī* 2:333.

4 See Ṣaddām, *Tārīkh Khalīfa* 19; al-Ṭabarānī, *al-Muʿjam al-ṣaghīr* 2:111.

5 Al-Dhahabī, *Mīzān* 4:399. See also Ibn Ḥajar, *Lisān* 8:198.

6 Ṣaddām, *Tārīkh Khalīfa* 19–20. See Ibn Qāniʿ, *Muʿjam al-ṣaḥāba* 1:96, 171, 306, 347, 2:112, 128, 217, 3:83; al-Ḥākim al-Naysābūrī, *al-Mustadrak* 1:283, 2:60, 3:246, 258, 265.

7 See Chapter 2. Al-Tustarī also transmitted the extant recension of Khalīfa's *Ṭabaqāt*, which he passed on to the leading *ḥadīth* scholar Abū l-Qāsim al-Ṭabarānī. The manuscript of this recension contains an alternative *isnād* corroborating al-Tustarī's transmission, which mentions that Khalīfa transmitted it to Abū Ḥafṣ ʿUmar b. Aḥmad al-Ahwāzī, who in turn transmitted it to another major *ḥadīth* scholar, Abū Bakr b. al-Muqriʾ al-Aṣbahānī (d. 381/991). Thus al-ʿUmarī suggests that the current recension of the *Ṭabaqāt* was likely written based on al-Tustarī's transmission (through al-Ṭabarānī) and then compared to al-Ahwāzī's transmission, whose *isnāds* were added to the first two (of five) parts of the *Ṭabaqāt*—in order to corroborate and strengthen al-Tustarī's transmission. See al-ʿUmarī's introduction to Khalīfa's *Ṭabaqāt* (1967) 65–67 and Zakkār's introduction to Khalīfa's *Ṭabaqāt* (1993) 15–16.

of these are not found in Baqī b. Makhlad's recension.[8] Al-Tustarī probably received the *Tārīkh* from Khalīfa around 238/853, which is the last date recorded in Ibn ʿAsākir's citations from al-Tustarī's recension.[9] Ibn al-ʿAsākir received this version of Khalīfa's *Tārīkh* from Abū Ghālib Muḥammad b. al-Ḥasan al-Māwardī (d. 525/1131),[10] who transmitted it from Abū l-Ḥasan Muḥammad b. ʿAlī b. Aḥmad al-Sīrāfī.[11] The latter transmitted it from Abū ʿAbdallāh Aḥmad b. Isḥāq al-Nihāwandī (d. 410/1019),[12] who transmitted from Abū l-Ḥasan Aḥmad b. ʿImrān b. Mūsā al-Ashnānī from Mūsā b. Zakariyyā al-Tustarī.[13] Four of these transmitters (Abū Ghālib al-Māwardī, Abū l-Ḥasan al-Sīrāfī, Aḥmad b. Isḥāq al-Nihāwandī and Mūsā al-Tustarī) are known to have resided in Basra at some points, and the fifth (Abū l-Ḥasan Aḥmad b. ʿImrān al-Ashnānī) likely also resided in the city, which would make al-Tustarī's transmission an entirely Basran recension of the *Tārīkh* until it reached the Damascene Ibn ʿAsākir.

Much more is known about the other transmitter of Khalīfa's *Tārīkh*, the leading *ḥadīth* scholar of Córdoba, Baqī b. Makhlad, who received it during his travels in the East—probably around 232/847, which is the last recorded date in his recension.[14] Besides the *Tārīkh*, he introduced Khalīfa's *Ṭabaqāt* (in a now lost recension) and a number of other famous works to al-Andalus, among them the *Risāla* of al-Shāfiʿī (d. 204/820) and the *Muṣannaf* of Ibn Abī Shayba (d. 235/849). He was a prominent *ḥadīth* scholar and, unlike the dominant group of Mālikī jurists in al-Andalus and North Africa, associated with the more exclusively *ḥadīth*-based approach of the *ahl al-ḥadīth*—similar to contemporaries such as Ibn Abī Shayba and Aḥmad b. Ḥanbal.[15] Thus Ibn Abī Yaʿlā (d. 526/1131) included him in *Ṭabaqāt al-ḥanābila*.[16] Along with Muḥammad b. Waḍḍāḥ (d. 287/900), Baqī played a key role in developing the study of

8 Ṣaddām, *Tārīkh Khalīfa* 22. Al-Daʿjānī also mentions that Ibn ʿAsākir cites 1,487 narrations from Khalīfa's *Tārīkh* in *Mawārid Ibn ʿAsākir* 1:118.

9 Ibn ʿAsākir, *Tārīkh madīnat Dimashq* 8:140.

10 Al-Dhahabī, *Siyar* 3388–3389.

11 Little is known about Abū l-Ḥasan al-Sīrāfī, but Ibn ʿAsākir mentions his full name and location in *Tārīkh madīnat Dimashq* 1:24, 2:101, 50:175, 61:159.

12 Al-Khaṭīb al-Baghdādī, *Tārīkh Baghdād* 5:61; al-Dhahabī, *Tārīkh al-Islām* 28:198.

13 For the full *isnād* see e.g. Ibn ʿAsākir, *Tārīkh madīnat Dimashq* 1:24, 2:101, 3:211, 4:256. See also al-Daʿjānī, *Mawārid Ibn ʿAsākir* 1:117–119; Ibn Ḥajar, *al-Muʿjam al-mufahras* 171.

14 Khalīfa b. Khayyāṭ, *Tārīkh* (1985) 480. For Baqī b. Makhlad's biography, see al-Dhahabī, *Siyar* 1215–1218, *Tadhkira* 629–631; Marín, Baqī b. Majlad; Nūrī, *Muḥammad b. Waḍḍāḥ al-Qurṭubī*; al-ʿUmarī, *Baqī b. Makhlad*; Ávila, Nuevos datos; Raisuddin, Baqī b. Makhlad; Fierro, Introduction of hadith in al-Andalus.

15 Ávila, Baqī b. Makhlad.

16 Ibn Abī Yaʿlā, *Ṭabaqāt al-ḥanābila* 1:320–323.

ḥadīth in al-Andalus.[17] His own works are lost, but the two most important were a commentary on the Qur'ān (*tafsīr*) and a massive *ḥadīth* collection, which combined the two formats of *musnad* (arrangement by Companions who narrated the *ḥadīths*) and *muṣannaf* (arrangement by subjects).[18]

Baqī transmitted the extant version of Khalīfa's *Tārīkh* to the Córdoba-based Umayyad descendent, Abū l-Qāsim Aḥmad b. ʿAbdallāh b. Muḥammad b. al-Mubārak b. Ḥabīb b. ʿAbd al-Malik b. al-Walīd b. ʿAbd al-Malik b. Marwān b. al-Ḥakam (d. 333/944), who also studied under other major *ḥadīth* scholars such as Muḥammad b. Waḍḍāḥ and whom Ibn al-Faraḍī (d. 403/1013) describes as inclined towards *akhbār* and *adab*.[19] He transmitted the *Tārīkh* to the prominent Cordovan judge, jurist and *ḥadīth* scholar, Abū ʿAbdallāh Muḥammad b. Aḥmad b. Muḥammad b. Yaḥyā b. Mufarrij (d. 380/990),[20] who then transmitted it to another prominent *ḥadīth* scholar of al-Andalus, Abū ʿUmar Aḥmad b. Muḥammad al-Ṭalamankī (d. 428–429/1036–1037).[21] The latter transmitted it to the jurist, philologist and grammarian from Toledo, Abū l-Walīd Hishām b. Aḥmad al-Waqqashī (d. 489/1096),[22] who transmitted it to Aḥmad b. Muḥammad al-Ashʿarī, who copied the extant manuscript in 477/1084. It is mentioned in the surviving manuscript that it was compared with another copy of Baqī b. Makhlad's recension, and the rare differences are noted in the margin.[23] During the transmission of Khalīfa's *Tārīkh*, Baqī b. Makhlad added some 55 reports to Khalīfa's text, all of which pertain to the Umayyad period from 58/677 to 61/681 and 64/683 to 75/695, besides one item added to year 231/845–846.[24] These

17 Al-Dhahabī, *Siyar* 1215. See also Ávila, Baqī b. Makhlad.

18 Ávila, Baqī b. Makhlad. Ibn Ḥazm (d. 456/1064) said about Baqī b. Makhlad's *Tafsīr*, "I assert with certainty that nothing like Baqī's *Tafsīr* has ever been compiled in Islam," and about his *Musnad*, "I do not know of this quality in anyone before him, in addition to his reliability (*thiqa*), accuracy (*ḍabṭ*), perfection (*itqān*) and great concern for collecting *ḥadīth*." Al-Dhahabī, *Siyar* 1216.

19 Ibn al-Faraḍī, *Tārīkh ʿulamāʾ al-Andalus* 1:77; al-Ḥumaydī, *Jadhwat al-muqtabis* 185; al-Ḍabbī, *Bughyat al-multamis* 1:231; al-Dhahabī, *Tārīkh al-Islām* 25:85–86. See also al-ʿUmarī's introduction to Khalīfa's *Tārīkh* (1985) 38.

20 Ibn al-Faraḍī, *Tārīkh ʿulamāʾ al-Andalus* 2:122–124; al-Ḥumaydī, *Jadhwat al-muqtabis* 61–62; al-Ḍabbī, *Bughyat al-multamis* 1:71–72; al-Dhahabī, *Siyar* 3272. See also al-ʿUmarī's introduction to Khalīfa's *Tārīkh* (1985) 37–38.

21 Al-Ḥumaydī, *Jadhwat al-muqtabis* 166–167; al-Ḍabbī, *Bughyat al-multamis* 1:205; al-Dhahabī, *Siyar* 987–988, *Tadhkira* 1098–1100. See also al-ʿUmarī's introduction to Khalīfa's *Tārīkh* (1985) 37.

22 Al-Ḍabbī, *Bughyat al-multamis* 2:653; al-Dhahabī, *Siyar* 4077. See also al-ʿUmarī's introduction to Khalīfa's *Tārīkh* (1985) 36–37.

23 See al-ʿUmarī's introduction to Khalīfa's *Tārīkh* (1985) 35 and his footnotes on pp. 160, 312, 385. See also Zakkār's introduction to Khalīfa's *Tārīkh* (1993) 13.

24 Khalīfa b. Khayyāṭ, *Tārīkh* (1985) 225–235, 253–271, 480.

reports are narrated in sequence, separate from Khalīfa's reports, and distinguished by Baqī's *isnāds*.[25] Baqī received these narrations from other scholars during his travels in the East, and they are divided among the three direct transmitters outlined below.[26]

1. Bakkār b. ʿAbdallāh (d. c. 251–260/865–874)—Damascus—c. 25 citations[27]

Baqī b. Makhlad uses the transmission formula *kataba ilayya* ('He wrote to me'), which indicates that he received Bakkār's material in written form.[28] Bakkār is mentioned in Ibn ʿAsākir's *Tārīkh madīnat Dimashq*, and Abū Ḥātim al-Rāzī declared him sincere (*ṣadūq*) in *ḥadīth* transmission.[29] Bakkār's information comes from the Syrian historian, *maghāzī* compiler and financial secretary Muḥammad b. ʿĀʾidh al-Dimashqī (d. 233–234/847–849), whom some of the early transmitter critics declared reliable (*thiqa*) or sincere (*ṣadūq*).[30] He is occasionally cited without mentioning Bakkār, but these reports presumably refer back to Bakkār's *isnāds*.[31] Muḥammad b. ʿĀʾidh, in turn, received his material from ʿAbd al-Aʿlā b. ʿAbd al-Aʿlā (d. 189/804–805), al-Wāqidī (d. 207/822), Ismāʿīl b. ʿAyyāsh (d. 181/797–798), al-Walīd b. Muslim al-Dimashqī (d. 195/810) and Marwān b. Muḥammad al-Ṭāṭarī (d. 210/825–826). The reports from Bakkār pertain mainly to the expeditions against the Romans and to the Umayyads in Syria.[32]

2. Yaḥyā b. ʿAbdallāh b. Bukayr al-Makhzūmī (d. 231/845)—Egypt—c. 20 citations

Baqī uses the transmission formula *quriʾa ʿalā ibn Bukayr wa-ana asmaʿu* ('It was read out to Ibn Bukayr while I listened'), which indicates that he attended ses-

25 E.g. Khalīfa b. Khayyāṭ, *Tārīkh* (1985) 225–227, 229–231, 234–235, 253–254, 261–262.
26 See also Wurtzel, *Khalifa ibn Khayyat's History* 38–39.
27 The number of citations is only a close approximation, because of occasional ambiguities as to whether certain citations belong to the same report or constitute separate reports.
28 On the transmission formulas in Khalīfa's *Tārīkh*, see Chapter 5.
29 Ibn ʿAsākir, *Tārīkh* 10:363–365; Ibn Abī Ḥātim, *al-Jarḥ wa-l-taʿdīl* 2:410. Al-Dhahabī places him in the generation that died around 251–260/865–874. *Tārīkh al-Islām* 19:95.
30 E.g. Yaḥyā b. Maʿīn and Ṣāliḥ b. Muḥammad Jazara considered him reliable (*thiqa*), ʿAbd al-Raḥmān b. Ibrāhīm Duḥaym considered him sincere (*ṣadūq*) and al-Nasāʾī said that there is no problem with him (*laysa bihi baʾs*). Al-Dhahabī, *Siyar* 3465; al-Mizzī, *Tahdhīb* 25:427–429; Ibn Ḥajar, *Tahdhīb* 3:599. Ibn Ḥibbān also included him in his *Kitāb al-Thiqāt* 9:75.
31 Khalīfa b. Khayyāṭ, *Tārīkh* (1985) 230–231, 254.
32 Khalīfa b. Khayyāṭ, *Tārīkh* (1985) 225, 227, 229–231, 235, 253–254, 261, 270–271.

sions where Ibn Bukayr's material was read aloud by his students. Ibn Bukayr was a *ḥadīth* narrator whom some critics considered reliable, although al-Nasāʾī declared him weak (*ḍaʿīf*).[33] He received his material from the leading Egyptian jurist and *ḥadīth* scholar in his day, al-Layth b. Saʿd (d. 175/791), who does not mention his own sources. His material pertains to pilgrimage leaders and events in Egypt, North Africa and Syria.[34] Baqī also narrates one report from Ibn Bukayr's son, ʿAbdallāh, about the date of his father's death in 231/845.[35]

3. Muḥammad b. ʿAbdallāh b. Numayr (d. 234/849)—Kufa—c. 10 citations

Baqī b. Makhlad transmits directly from Muḥammad b. ʿAbdallāh b. Numayr, as indicated by the formula *ḥaddathanā* ('He narrated to us'). Ibn Numayr was a leading Kufan *ḥadīth* scholar and widely regarded as reliable (*thiqa*).[36] His material consists of short pieces of information relating to the Umayyads, pilgrimage leaders and deaths of prominent individuals.[37]

The reports added by Baqī b. Makhlad comply with the content and narrative style of Khalīfa's material and reflect similar early Sunnī perspectives and traditionist methods of transmission.[38] Apart from the notes about pilgrimage leaders, Baqī's reports focus on events pertaining to the Syrian region during the second civil war (*fitna*) in 64–73/684–692 between the Zubayrids and the Umayyads.[39] Baqī's material provides details about the expeditions against the Romans and information about the Umayyads, such as ʿAbd al-Malik's observation of ʿĪd al-Aḍḥā ('the Festival of Sacrifice') in Damascus.[40] In addition to the general focus on the Umayyads, there are a few other indications of an Umayyad, or Syrian, perspective in some of the material: Ibn Bukayr's reports from al-Layth b. Saʿd call Yazīd, Marwān and ʿAbd al-Malik 'Commander of the Believers' (*amīr al-muʾminīn*), which is not the case for Ibn al-Zubayr, and Bakkār reports that al-Muhallab b. Abī Ṣufra said about ʿAbd al-Malik b. Marwān, "By God, if he becomes ruler [it would be fine]; he is a virtuous Muslim

33 Al-Dhahabī, *Siyar* 4182–4183, *Mīzān* 5:129; al-Mizzī, *Tahdhīb* 31:401–404; Ibn Ḥajar, *Tahdhīb* 4:368.

34 Khalīfa b. Khayyāṭ, *Tārīkh* (1985) 225, 227, 229, 235, 253, 261, 263–267, 270–271.

35 Khalīfa b. Khayyāṭ, *Tārīkh* (1985) 480.

36 Al-Dhahabī, *Siyar* 3536–3537; Ibn Ḥajar, *Tahdhīb* 3:618–619.

37 Khalīfa b. Khayyāṭ, *Tārīkh* (1985) 227, 231, 235, 254, 261, 270.

38 On Khalīfa's early Sunnī historical views, see esp. Chapter 8.

39 E.g. Khalīfa b. Khayyāṭ, *Tārīkh* (1985) 261, 265–267. On Khalīfa's account of the Zubayrid–Umayyad conflict, see Chapter 8.

40 Khalīfa b. Khayyāṭ, *Tārīkh* (1985) 253, 261, 263–267.

(*ʿafīf fī l-islām*) and one of the best of his kinsfolk."[41] Baqī might also have sought to correct some details in Khalīfa's text, such as the date of Muʿāwiya b. Abī Sufyān's death; Khalīfa says it occurred in Rajab 59/679, while Baqī reports that it occurred in Rajab 60/680.[42] However, the main purpose of Baqī b. Makhlad's additions seems to have been to add information and to complement Khalīfa's material, especially on the second *fitna*, with details about the Umayyads and the Greater Syrian region. Citations in later works show that Baqī b. Makhlad's recension of Khalīfa's *Tārīkh* began to circulate among the scholars of al-Andalus and north-west Africa, while al-Tustarī's recension circulated in Greater Syria and Egypt, but in all cases mainly among Sunnī *ḥadīth* scholars compiling chronological histories or biographical dictionaries.[43]

3 Differences between the Recensions and the Question of Authorship

Most previous studies on Khalīfa's *Tārīkh* have assumed that Baqī b. Makhlad and Mūsā b. Zakariyyā al-Tustarī transmitted their recensions from Khalīfa without significantly altering it.[44] In other words, Khalīfa has been seen as solely responsible for the form and content of the extant version of the *Tārīkh*. In the first major study of Khalīfa's *Tārīkh*, Wurtzel concluded that the recensions of Baqī b. Makhlad and Mūsā al-Tustarī "must have been practically identical, since the passages quoted by Ibn ʿAsākir duplicate almost literally the same passages in Baqī's version."[45] This position has recently been challenged by Ṣaddām, who suggests that Baqī b. Makhlad omitted and abridged substantial parts of Khalīfa's *Tārīkh*. Ṣaddām has gathered 202 narrations from Khalīfa, preserved by later historians (mainly Ibn ʿAsākir), that are not found in Baqī's recension of Khalīfa's *Tārīkh*. Most of these reports are transmitted by Mūsā al-Tustarī and were presumably found in his recension of the *Tārīkh*. Ṣaddām acknowledges that most of Ibn ʿAsākir's narrations from al-Tustarī's recension (1,322 of 1,487) correspond in both content and wording to their equivalents in Baqī's recension, but he nonetheless describes Baqī's version as "a deficient abridgement reflecting his lack of trustworthiness" and al-

41 Khalīfa b. Khayyāṭ, *Tārīkh* (1985) 253, 262, 264, 266–267, 271.
42 Khalīfa b. Khayyāṭ, *Tārīkh* (1985) 226, 228–231.
43 See Chapter 2 and Wurtzel, *Khalifa ibn Khayyat's History* 39–46.
44 See e.g. ʿĀṣī, *Khalīfa*; Wurtzel, *Khalifa ibn Khayyat's History*; Andersson and Marsham, First Islamic chronicle.
45 Wurtzel, *Khalifa ibn Khayyat's History* 40.

Tustarī's version as "more complete and detailed."[46] He also suggests that Baqī tends to remove, in particular, offensive material about the Umayyads "because of his ʿUthmānī inclinations" and his close relation to the Umayyads in al-Andalus, especially the *amīr* Muḥammad b. ʿAbd al-Raḥmān (r. 238–273/852–886), who actively supported him and his scholarship.[47]

While Ṣaddām is right in pointing out the differences between the two recensions and the active role of the transmitters, his conclusions regarding Baqī b. Makhlad and Baqī's editing of the *Tārīkh* are highly questionable. First, Ṣaddām assumes that there was one fixed original version of Khalīfa's *Tārīkh* that was transmitted in the same way to both Baqī b. Makhlad and Mūsā al-Tustarī. This is unlikely in the early period, when texts were usually transmitted aurally (through *samāʿ*) and often ascribed to authors (like Khalīfa), but compiled from lecture notes and edited into final form by their students (like Baqī and al-Tustarī).[48] Second, he assumes that Khalīfa did not transmit different versions of the *Tārīkh* at different times to different students. The last date in Baqī's recension is 232/847, while the last date in what Ibn ʿAsākir transmits from al-Tustarī's recension is 238/853. In light of this, one simple explanation for the differences between the recensions would be that Khalīfa himself edited his *Tārīkh* in this period and transmitted slightly different versions to Baqī and al-Tustarī, who then edited the received material into book form. Third, Ṣaddām takes for granted that Baqī abridged the *Tārīkh* and that al-Tustarī did not add to his recension material that he had received elsewhere from Khalīfa.

The following section proposes a more cautious approach, arguing that Khalīfa's *Tārīkh* was most likely a series of lecture notes transmitted at different times to Baqī b. Makhlad and Mūsā al-Tustarī, who edited them into book form and possibly made some (relatively minor) alterations to the material. Based on the overall correspondence between the recensions, it also argues that the general form and content of the extant recension belong to Khalīfa, although it is possible that Baqī (as well as al-Tustarī) abridged or removed some material that was originally transmitted by Khalīfa as a part of the *Tārīkh*. Hence this somewhat complicated transmission of Khalīfa's *Tārīkh* does not impede the analysis of Khalīfa's context of compilation, sources, methods, general arrangement of material, approach to key events and historical views. However, one must bear in mind that it was most likely a series of lecture notes edited into book form by his students, so some alterations may well have occurred in the course of transmission.

46 Ṣaddām, *Tārīkh Khalīfa* 21–22.

47 Ṣaddām, *Tārīkh Khalīfa* 21–22.

48 See the following pages below.

In addition to Ṣaddām's aforementioned challenges to the assumption that Khalīfa was solely responsible for the form and content of the *Tārīkh*, Lindstedt has suggested—based on analogies to other early works ascribed to 'authors' but compiled from lecture notes and edited into final form by their students—that Khalīfa's *Tārīkh* "seems to be a series of notes edited into a book form by Baqī b. Makhlad al-Qurṭubī."[49] This more cautious assessment seems appropriate; it is indeed likely that Khalīfa, similar to many other early scholars, transmitted his *Tārīkh* aurally through *samāʿ*—that is, lectures based on written notes (read out or recited from memory), which students listened to and put back into writing.[50] It is also likely that there was no definitive or fixed version of the *Tārīkh*, but rather a series of lecture notes that were changed slightly over time and that were transmitted at different occasions to Baqī and al-Tustarī, who then edited them into book form. That said, a number of factors support the attribution of the general content and structure of the extant recension to Khalīfa. These factors will be discussed after a brief outline of how *ḥadīth* and *akhbār* texts of this kind were transmitted in Khalīfa's time.

In his influential studies on scholarly transmission in early Islam, Schoeler suggests a model of combined oral and written transmission.[51] Although written material circulated widely in the scholarly circles of *ḥadīth, fiqh, akhbār* history and other disciplines before and during Khalīfa's lifetime (c. 160–240/776–854), simply copying texts only later became one of the main ways of transmitting them and, even then, combining oral and written transmission remained ideal.[52] In the second/eighth and third/ninth centuries, the two main ways of transmitting texts were listening to the teacher (*samāʿ*) and reading out/presenting to the teacher (*qirāʾa* or *ʿarḍ*), which took place in teaching sessions (*majālis*) or circles (*ḥuluqāt*).[53] This lecture-based transmission meant that material was presented orally by the teacher (or one of the students), but it was usually based on written records and often written down by the students.[54] Because of this supplementary relationship between oral and written transmis-

---

49 Lindstedt, Role of al-Madāʾinī's students 316.

50 On the transmission of early texts, see Schoeler, *Oral and the written* 28–61.

51 Schoeler, *Oral and the written*, *Genesis of literature in Islam*. See also Toorawa, *Ibn Abi Tahir Tayfur* 1–34; Borrut, *Entre mémoire et pouvoir* 14–26. For other earlier studies, see Sezgin, GAS I 53–84, 237–256; Abbott, *Historical texts* 6–31; Abbott, *Qur'anic commentary and tradition* 5–64; Aʿẓamī, *Studies in early ḥadīth literature* 1–211. In relation to Schoeler's *Oral and the written*, see also the review of the book in Haddad, Enduring myths of Orientalism.

52 See Schoeler, *Oral and the written* 30, 36–37; Lindstedt, Role of al-Madāʾinī's students 296.

53 Schoeler, *Oral and the written* 30. See also Ibn al-Ṣalāḥ, *ʿUlūm al-ḥadīth* 132–150; al-Sakhāwī, *Fatḥ al-Mughīth* 2:325–388.

54 Lindstedt, Role of al-Madāʾinī's students 296; Schoeler, *Oral and the written* 183n181.

sion, Schoeler proposes the term 'aural' transmission instead of oral.[55] Simple copying of notebooks (e.g. *wijāda, kitāba*) also existed early on, but it was considered inferior since the text in question had not been heard from, or read out to, the transmitting authority or compiler.[56]

As for transmission of compiled works, Schoeler suggests that the second/eighth- and third/ninth-century transmitters occasionally modified and rearranged the works they were passing on, including by adding or subtracting material, which can sometimes complicate the distinction between 'author/compiler/collector' and 'transmitter.'[57] As for the formation of different and divergent transmissions of certain works, Schoeler proposes the following factors: (1) the teacher may have presented material differently in different lectures, (2) the students would have produced different written records and (3) the students and their students transmitted the material differently, so other modifications of the text could have occurred during this process.[58] Overall, this model of complementary oral and written transmission has the advantage of considering and reconciling different types of evidence in the early sources: the emphasis on oral transmission, the references to written transmission and written sources (*kutub, dafātir, ṣuḥuf, qarāṭīs*) already in the first generations, the absence of book titles in the *isnād*s and the debate among some scholars whether 'to write or not to write.'[59] This way of transmitting texts—aurally in lecture settings, based on written compilations or lecture notes that students put back into writing—also seems to fit the way Khalīfa transmitted his *Tārīkh* to Baqī b. Makhlad, as indicated by (1) the citation of Khalīfa in third person at the beginning and in other parts of Baqī's recension,[60] (2) Baqī's additions of some of his own narrations to the text[61] and (3) the differences between Baqī's

---

55 Schoeler, *Genesis of literature in Islam* 8–9, 122–125.

56 Schoeler, *Oral and the written* 30. See also Ibn al-Ṣalāḥ, *'Ulūm al-ḥadīth* 173–174, 178–181; al-Sakhāwī, *Fatḥ al-Mughīth* 2:497–510, 520–530. Also, the second/eighth-century *ḥadīth* scholars of Basra, in particular, were known for emphasising oral transmission and lecturing from memory. See Schoeler, *Oral and the written* 68, 114–116, 125–127.

57 Schoeler, *Oral and the written* 36–37. See also Haddad, Enduring myths of Orientalism, where he proposes an intermediary category of 'critical transmitters' who "narrate with an eye for an original design of substance (e.g. *fiqh*) or standard (e.g. authenticity) legible to posterity as being *also theirs*, a typical case being Muḥammad ibn al-Ḥasan's *Muwaṭṭa'*."

58 Schoeler, *Oral and the written* 45.

59 Schoeler, *Oral and the written* 40–42; Lindstedt, Role of al-Madā'inī's students 297. On the reluctance to write down *ḥadīth* among some early scholars, see Cook, Opponents of the writing of tradition, and the clarifications in Haddad, Enduring myths of Orientalism.

60 See Khalīfa b. Khayyāṭ, *Tārīkh* (1985) 49–54.

61 See Section 2 above. See also Wurtzel, *Khalifa ibn Khayyat's History* 38–39.

recension and the lost recension of al-Tustarī, as cited in later sources.[62] With this in mind, however, there are a number of reasons for attributing the general content and structure of Baqī's recension of the *Tārīkh* to Khalīfa.

First, most citations of Khalīfa's *Tārīkh* in later sources relying on the (now lost) recension of Mūsā al-Tustarī are more or less identical to Baqī b. Makhlad's recension.[63] As discussed above, Ṣaddām has shown that there were some discrepancies between the recensions of Baqī and al-Tustarī, but he also notes that only about 11 per cent (165 of 1,487) of Ibn 'Asākir's narrations from Khalīfa do not correspond to the material in Baqī's recension.[64] Such a percentage is certainly sufficient to establish that there were some differences between the two recensions, but it still shows that most material (1,322 of 1,487 narrations) was more or less the same in both wording and content. This suggests that the general content, as narrated by Baqī, indeed belongs to Khalīfa. In order to explain the differences between the two recensions, it makes sense to consider a combination of several possible factors. Besides the possibilities that Baqī abridged or omitted material and that al-Tustarī added extra material that was not originally a part of the *Tārīkh*, one must consider that the two recensions were transmitted at different times; the last date in Baqī's recension is 232/847, while the last date in al-Tustarī's material is 238/853. It is thus likely that Khalīfa himself edited and altered his work to some extent between 232/847 and 238/853. Moreover, as discussed above, Khalīfa's *Tārīkh* was probably transmitted on the basis of written notes of lectures that Baqī and al-Tustarī heard separately and, in slightly different ways, edited into book form. Altogether, the differences

62 Discussed by al-'Umarī in his introduction to Khalīfa's *Tārīkh* (1985) 35–36; Wurtzel, *Khalīfa ibn Khayyat's History* 39–40; Ṣaddam, *Tarikh Khalīfa* 57–133.

63 See e.g. the following citations of Khalīfa's *Tārīkh* in the first ten volumes of Ibn 'Asākir's *Tārīkh madīnat Dimashq*, with the page numbers in al-'Umarī's edition of Khalīfa's *Tārīkh* within brackets: 1:24–25 (49–50), 35–36 (50), 2:80 (119), 101 (120), 111–112 (125–126), 114 (126), 139 (129–130), 142 (130), 180 (126), 251 (300); 3:76 (53), 121 (147), 146 (92, 94), 149 (92), 152 (65), 154 (93), 159–160 (96), 199 (65), 200 (225), 203 (66), 206 (66), 214–215 (149), 220 (224), 225 (218), 235 (86), 238 (135); 4:256 (60), 298 (156), 333–334 (99); 6:137 (97, 131), 139 (120), 157 (336), 446 (446); 7:37 (313), 154 (340), 165 (457), 169 (470), 170 (473), 247 (369), 249 (369), 250 (374), 260–261 (337–343), 261 (357), 266 (362), 347 (167); 8:64–65 (100), 86 (335), 231 (224), 255 (421), 267 (440), 315 (338, 358–359), 317 (347), 322 (350), 335 (321), 390 (395), 440 (323); 9:25 (417, 420, 431), 62 (264), 98 (149), 136 (193), 144 (199), 166 (281), 295 (292), 299 (392–393), 323 (337), 370 (259), 377 (265), 383 (306); 10:24 (324), 36 (354), 127 (410), 149 (195, 218), 234 (326), 235 (330, 334), 255 (268, 271, 294), 264 (273), 269 (309, 313), 388 (371), 395 (355), 428 (227), 479 (149), 512 (361), 522 (196). See also Wurtzel, *Khalifa ibn Khayyat's History* 40; Ṣaddām, *Tārīkh Khalīfa* 22.

64 Ṣaddām, *Tārīkh Khalīfa* 22. My own comparison between Baqī's recension and Ibn 'Asākir's transmission from al-Tustarī's recension also suggests a divergence of about 11 per cent and a correspondence of about 89 per cent.

between the recensions are probably due to a combination of (1) the absence of a fixed 'original' version of the *Tārīkh*, (2) Khalīfa's own changes to his material, (3) the different occasions of transmission to different students, (4) the way it was edited into book form by the students after being transmitted aurally based on lecture notes and (5) further alterations, such as abridgements or omissions of reports, that might have occurred in the course of transmission.

Another indication that the general content belongs to Khalīfa is that Baqī clearly distinguishes his added reports from Khalīfa's material by his *isnād*s, which suggests that the rest of the material belongs to Khalīfa.[65] On the basis of Baqī's additions, Lindstedt suggests that there are "probably also other interpolations by Baqī that are not explicitly stated by the *isnād*s," but provides no evidence apart from an analogy to the transmission of Ibn Shabba's *Tārīkh al-Madīna* and Ibn Sa'd's *Ṭabaqāt*.[66] The beginning and end of Baqī b. Makhlad's additions are clearly marked in the text of the *Tārīkh*, and his material is easily distinguishable from Khalīfa's by his introductory phrases of "Baqī said" and "Khalīfa said." This is also supported by the coherence of Khalīfa's own sources and their material. They differ completely from Baqī b. Makhlad's additions, which are attributed to other sources and pertain mainly to the Syrian region and the Umayyads in the period 58–75/677–695.[67] Thus one cannot be certain that Baqī did not add other material, but his systematic use of *isnād*s and the clear differences in sources and content suggest that the remaining material belongs to Khalīfa, although it is possible that Baqī (or someone else in the *isnād*) abridged or otherwise altered some of it.

Third, there are also some internal indicators that Khalīfa was responsible for the general content and structure. Khalīfa introduces the work with the words, "This is the Book of Chronography (*hādhā kitāb al-tārīkh*)," which suggests that Khalīfa had at least ordered written material in what may be termed a *kitāb*—that is, according to the *Tahdhīb al-lugha* of Abū Manṣūr al-Azharī (d. 370/980), "something put together [in one place] in writing (*mā kutiba majmū'an*)."[68] Khalīfa also refers to previous sections in the *Tārīkh* in several places by the formula "and we have previously written" (*wa-qad katabnā*), which supports the notion that the transmission was based on a written record and that Khalīfa was responsible for the basic structure of the work.[69] More

65 E.g. Khalīfa b. Khayyāṭ, *Tārīkh* (1985) 225–227, 229–231, 234–235, 253–254, 261–262.

66 Lindstedt, Role of al-Madā'inī's students 316.

67 On Baqī's additions, see Section 2 above. On Khalīfa's sources, see Chapter 4.

68 Al-Azharī, *Tahdhīb al-lugha* 10:151 (s.v. *kitāb*). See also Ibn Manẓūr, *Lisān* 1:698 (s.v. *kitāb*); Sellheim, Kitāb.

69 Khalīfa b. Khayyāṭ, *Tārīkh* (1985) 123, 155, 178, 179, 202, 435, 442, 464.

generally, the annalistic structure of the *Tārīkh* corresponds to Khalīfa's own wording, his selection of material and his systematic focus on chronology. This is reflected in the material transmitted by both Baqī and al-Tustarī. In his transmission from al-Tustarī's recension, Ibn ʿAsākir sometimes refers to Khalīfa's lists (*tasmiyāt* sing. *tasmiya*) of certain caliphs' governors ("Khalīfa mentioned in the list of so-and-so's governors"), and the same material is found in the list sections in Baqī's recension, which indicates that the annalistic structure with list sections at the end of each caliph's reign was inherent to Khalīfa's own material.[70] Altogether, this strongly suggests that the general structure and arrangement of the text indeed belong to Khalīfa, although some parts might have been abridged and restructured in the course of transmission.

Fourth, Khalīfa's direct students and later writers unanimously attribute the *Tārīkh* to him without reservations.[71] Both Baqī b. Makhlad and al-Tustarī received the *Tārīkh* from Khalīfa and attributed it to him without any indications of rearrangement—apart from Baqī b. Makhlad's added reports, which are clearly distinguished from Khalīfa's. The *Tārīkh* is likewise attributed to Khalīfa by all later writers. This not only confirms its attribution to Khalīfa but also suggests that he, rather than his students, was responsible for the basic content and the structure of the work.[72]

These four points strongly suggest that at least the general content and structure of Baqī's extant recension of the *Tārīkh* belong to Khalīfa. It is, however, important to bear in mind that it was probably transmitted aurally based on lecture notes (through *samāʿ* or *ʿarḍ*) and that Baqī b. Makhlad edited it into book form, which means that parts of Khalīfa's original material may have undergone some abridgement and restructuring in the course of transmission. This possibility of alteration necessitates caution when analysing specific aspects of the content or structure of the *Tārīkh*, but there seems to be no reason to doubt the attribution of its general content and overall structure to Khalīfa. Moreover, even if Baqī abridged or omitted certain material, his recension would still reflect Khalīfa's selection of sources, his general methods of compilation, his structuring of the work and his historical perspective on events. In order to further understand Baqī's transmission of Khalīfa's material, it is necessary to

---

70 E.g. Ibn ʿAsākir, *Tārīkh* 4:333–334 (99); 6:137 (97), 446 (446); 8:86 (335), 440 (323); 10:235 (334), 388 (371). See Khalīfa's material in al-ʿUmarī's edition within brackets.

71 On the later writers, see Chapter 2.

72 Melchert also notes about Khalīfa's work, "I have observed no internal evidence by which to assign the *Tārīkh* to a later date." He also argues that the content of the *Tārīkh* and the *Ṭabaqāt* fits the political and scholarly climate of their time. Melchert, How Ḥanafism came to originate in Kufa 322, 339–340.

examine in detail the citations of Khalīfa's *Tārīkh* that are preserved in later sources but missing in Baqī's recension, and to discuss the claim that Baqī omitted certain material for ideological reasons.

4 Missing Material in Baqī's Recension

Similar to Khalīfa, both Baqī b. Makhlad and Mūsā al-Tustarī can be described as early Sunnīs. Ṣaddām describes Khalīfa, Baqī and al-Tustarī as ʿUthmānīs with Umayyad sympathies and suggests that these leanings are reflected in both Baqī's and al-Tustarī's recensions of the *Tārīkh*.[73] In the case of Baqī's recension, however, Ṣaddām also argues that Baqī removed offensive material about the Umayyads "because of his ʿUthmānī inclinations" and his close ties with the Umayyads in al-Andalus, especially the *amīr* Muḥammad b. ʿAbd al-Raḥmān (r. 238–273/852–886), who protected him and supported his scholarship.[74] A close examination suggests that Baqī may have omitted some of this material for ideological or scholarly reasons but also that Khalīfa may equally have transmitted slightly different versions of the *Tārīkh* at different times, so that it was never a part of the version that Khalīfa transmitted to Baqī. It is also difficult to exclude the possibility that someone after Baqī in the *isnād* of the extant recension omitted certain material or that al-Tustarī added material that he had received elsewhere (not as a part of the *Tārīkh*) from Khalīfa. Thus, in the absence of definitive evidence, all these possibilities have to be considered. The following section examines the reports in Ṣaddām's collection of material from Khalīfa that is preserved in later sources but absent in Baqī's recension, and discusses the possible reasons for their absence.

4.1 *The Prophetic Period*

Ten reports from Khalīfa, not found in Baqī's recension, pertain to the Prophetic period, although some of these might have been transmitted as separate *ḥadīth*s, not as parts of the *Tārīkh*.[75] The content of some reports is also found

73 Ṣaddām, *Tārīkh Khalīfa* 21–22, 54. Ṣaddām seems to define 'Umayyad sympathies' as the acceptance of the legal validity of the Umayyad caliphate. On the terms 'early Sunnī' and "Uthmānī', see Chapter 3.

74 Ṣaddām, *Tārīkh Khalīfa* 21–22.

75 See, in part., nos. 3, 5, 9 in Ṣaddām, *Tārīkh Khalīfa* 57–60; al-Bukhārī, *Ṣaḥīḥ* 5:99 (*kitāb al-maghāzī, bāb thumma anzala ʿalaykum min baʿd al-ghamm amana*), 5:112 (*kitāb al-maghāzī, bāb marjaʿ al-nabī ṣallā Allāhu ʿalayhi wa-sallam min al-aḥzāb*); Ibn ʿAsākir, *Tārīkh madīnat Dimashq* 4:186.

in Baqī's recension.[76] The reports that are absent from Baqī's recension are short narrations about the Prophet's marriage to Zaynab bt. Jaḥsh, the Battle of Uḥud, the birth of al-Ḥusayn b. ʿAlī b. Abī Ṭālib, the date palms that used to be assigned to the Prophet before the conquest of Banū Qurayẓa and Banū l-Naḍīr, the death of ʿAbdallāh b. ʿUthmān b. ʿAffān and the Prophet wearing his ring on his left hand.[77] The only slightly longer report is the one about the date palms (about half a page in print), which al-Bukhārī also narrates from Khalīfa in his *Ṣaḥīḥ*,[78] but reports of this length are not unusual in the extant recension of Khalīfa's *Tārīkh*. There is no pattern in what is missing from Baqī's recension regarding the Prophetic period that would indicate that he omitted it for ideological reasons.

4.2 *The Rāshidūn Period*

There are 38 reports on the Rāshidūn period (11–40/632–661) that are not found in Baqī's recension. Two brief reports concern the caliphate of Abū Bakr (r. 11–13/632–634); the first pertains to Abū Bakr's death, the date of his oath of allegiance (*bayʿa*) and his lineage, while the latter pertains to the death of Fāṭima, the Prophet's daughter.[79] The same information is found in Baqī's recension.[80] There are twelve reports on the caliphate of ʿUmar (r. 13–23/634–644). These pertain, respectively, to the date of the Battle of Marj al-Ṣuffar (13/634), Abū Bakr's *muʾadhdhin*, Abū ʿUbayda's appointment of Khālid b. al-Walīd as governor of Damascus, the Battle of al-Yarmūk (15/636, four reports), the Battle of al-Qādisiyya (15/636), the plague of ʿAmwās, the death of ʿAbdallāh b. Ḥudhāfa al-Sahmī, the succession of governors in Syria and the expedition of Iṣṭakhr (23/643–644).[81] They resemble the narrative style in Baqī's recension, and some of the content is also found in Baqī's recension.[82] There are eight reports on the caliphate of ʿUthmān (r. 23–35/644–656): on the succession of governors in

76 See nos. 2, 7, 8, 10 in Ṣaddām, *Tārīkh Khalīfa* 57–60; Khalīfa b. Khayyāṭ, *Tārīkh* (1985) 66, 79, 86, 92, 94–95; Ibn ʿAsākir, *Tārīkh madīnat Dimashq* 3:146, 203, 16:229, 21:178.

77 Ibn ʿAsākir, *Tārīkh madīnat Dimashq* 3:152, 211, 4:186, 14:115; al-Bukhārī, *Ṣaḥīḥ* 5:99, 112; Abū Yaʿlā al-Mawṣilī, *Musnad* 7:122–123; Ṣaddām, *Tārīkh Khalīfa* 57–60.

78 No. 10 in Appendix.

79 Ibn ʿAsākir, *Tārīkh madīnat Dimashq* 3:159–160, 30:451; Ṣaddām, *Tārīkh Khalīfa* 60–61.

80 Khalīfa b. Khayyāṭ, *Tārīkh* (1985) 96, 100, 121.

81 Ibn ʿAsākir, *Tārīkh madīnat Dimashq* 2:101, 142, 19:146–147, 47:247, 59:110–111, 67:269–270; Ibn ʿAbd al-Barr, *al-Istīʿāb* 2:594, 3:891; al-Dhahabī, *Tārīkh al-Islām* 3:232, *Siyar* 4279–4280; al-Ḥākim al-Naysābūrī, *al-Mustadrak* 3:308; Abū Nuʿaym al-Aṣbahānī, *Maʿrifat al-ṣaḥāba* 5:2583; Ṣaddām, *Tārīkh Khalīfa* 61–66.

82 See nos. 14, 16, 17, 22, 23 in Ṣaddām, *Tārīkh Khalīfa* 62–66; Khalīfa b. Khayyāṭ, *Tārīkh* (1985) 123, 130–131, 142, 155–156.

Kufa, the deaths of Abū l-Dardā', Ka'b al-Ḥabr, Abū Sufyān b. Ḥarb and al-'Abbās b. 'Abd al-Muṭṭalib, 'Uthmān's pilgrimages, a message from 'Uthmān to 'Alī and the killing of 'Uthmān.[83] Similar to the aforementioned reports, the narrative style resembles Baqī's transmission, and some of the same information is also found in Baqī's recension; the report on the assassination of 'Uthmān, for example, corresponds almost exactly in wording, except that it is narrated as two reports with the same *isnād* in Baqī's recension.[84]

Finally, there are 16 reports on the caliphate of 'Alī b. Abī Ṭālib (r. 35–40/655–661) that are not found in Baqī's recension. They pertain to Marwān b. al-Ḥakam's killing of Ṭalḥa b. 'Ubaydallāh, names of generals during the Battle of Ṣiffīn (seven reports), the fighting for the watering place at the Euphrates before the Battle of Ṣiffīn, the succession of governors in Egypt, the name of the one who killed 'Ammār b. Yāsir, Khuzayma b. Thābit's death at Ṣiffīn (two reports), Qays b. Makshūḥ al-Murādī's death at Ṣiffīn, Ḥābis b. Sa'd al-Ṭā'ī's death at Ṣiffīn, Abū l-'Āliya's avoidance of fighting at Ṣiffīn and the first Khawārij.[85] The style resembles Baqī's recension, and much of the same information is also found in Baqī's recension, including the material about Marwān's killing of Ṭalḥa.[86] The material that could suggest an ideologically motivated omission is the report about the succession of governors in Egypt, narrated by Ibn 'Abd al-Barr (d. 463/1070) in *al-Istī'āb*:

> Khalīfa b. Khayyāṭ said: 'Alī b. Abī Ṭālib appointed Muḥammad b. Abī Ḥudhayfa as governor of Egypt, but then dismissed him and appointed Qays b. Sa'd b. 'Ubāda. He then dismissed him and appointed al-Ashtar Mālik b. al-Ḥārith al-Nakha'ī, but he died before reaching Egypt. 'Alī then appointed Muḥammad b. Abī Bakr, but he was killed there and 'Amr b. al-'Āṣ took control over Egypt.
>
> Muḥammad b. Abī Ḥudhayfa had been the one who incited most against 'Uthmān. 'Amr b. al-'Āṣ, after his dismissal as governor of Egypt, similarly used all his stratagems (*ḥiyal*) to malign 'Uthmān and incite

83 Ibn 'Asākir, *Tārīkh madīnat Dimashq* 23:438, 35:244, 39:208–209, 366, 411, 47:201, 50:175, 63:236; Ibn 'Abd al-Barr, *al-Istī'āb* 2:817; Ṣaddām, *Tārīkh Khalīfa* 67–69.

84 See nos. 25, 28, 29, 30, 32 in Ṣaddām, *Tārīkh Khalīfa* 67–69; Khalīfa b. Khayyāṭ, *Tārīkh* (1985) 157–160, 166, 168, 174–175, 178.

85 Ibn 'Asākir, *Tārīkh madīnat Dimashq* 10:522, 11:351, 353, 12:87, 16:370, 18:182, 25:62, 27:102, 31:271, 49:497, 65:106; Ibn al-'Adīm, *Bughyat al-ṭalab* 4:1912; Ibn 'Abd al-Barr, *al-Istī'āb* 3:1369–1370; al-Ḥākim al-Naysābūrī, *al-Mustadrak* 3:448; Ṣaddām, *Tārīkh Khalīfa* 69–75.

86 See nos. 33, 34, 35, 36, 37, 38, 39, 40, 46, 48 in Ṣaddām, *Tārīkh Khalīfa* 69–75; Khalīfa b. Khayyāṭ, *Tārīkh* (1985) 181, 185, 192–196. Baqī preserves four reports in his recension describing how Marwān killed Ṭalḥa. See Khalīfa b. Khayyāṭ, *Tārīkh* (1985) 181, 185.

> against him. ʿUthmān had taken responsibility to provide for Muḥammad b. Abī Ḥudhayfa after the death of his father, Abū Ḥudhayfa, and for many years he continued to support him and provide for him. Then, when people arose against ʿUthmān, Muḥammad b. Abī Ḥudhayfa was one of those who aided, incited and agitated the Egyptians against him. After the assassination of ʿUthmān, he fled to Syria where Rishdīn, the *mawlā* of Muʿāwiya, found him and killed him.[87]

The first part is also found in Baqī's recension in the section on the governors of ʿAlī b. Abī Ṭālib,[88] but the second part—about the young Companion, Muḥammad b. Abī Ḥudhayfa, and the more senior Companion, ʿAmr b. al-ʿĀṣ—is missing. The possible ideological motivation would be to omit the negative depiction of Muḥammad b. Abī Ḥudhayfa and ʿAmr b. al-ʿĀṣ in order to relieve these two Companions of blame for involvement in the conflicts that eventually led to the killing of ʿUthmān, although a few other somewhat negative reports about ʿAmr b. al-ʿĀṣ were still preserved in Baqī's recension.[89] However, it is very unlikely that Baqī b. Makhlad omitted the second half of the report, since Ibn ʿAbd al-Barr makes clear in the introduction that he received Khalīfa's *Tārīkh* with two *isnād*s—both containing three intermediary transmitters—from Baqī b. Makhlad, not Mūsā al-Tustarī.[90] There are thus four main possibilities why the second half is not found in the extant recension: (1) that Ibn ʿAbd al-Barr received it as an individual report from Khalīfa via someone other than Baqī, (2) that it was originally a part of Baqī's recension of the *Ṭabaqāt* rather than the *Tārīkh*, (3) that someone else after Baqī in the *isnād* of the extant recension omitted it or (4) that the second half is Ibn ʿAbd al-Barr's own unreferenced words and that Khalīfa's words end in the same way as in Baqī's extant recension ("and ʿAmr b. al-ʿĀṣ took control over Egypt").[91] The two latter

87 Ibn ʿAbd al-Barr, *al-Istīʿāb* 3:1369–1370; Ṣaddām, *Tārīkh Khalīfa* 72.

88 Khalīfa b. Khayyāṭ, *Tārīkh* (1985) 201.

89 See in part. the reports about ʿAmr's execution of the young Companion, Muḥammad b. Abī Bakr. Khalīfa b. Khayyāṭ, *Tārīkh* (1985) 192–193.

90 The first *isnād* is Abū ʿUmar Aḥmad b. ʿAbdallāh b. Muḥammad b. ʿAlī—his father—ʿAbdallāh b. Yūnus—Baqī b. Makhlad; the second is Abū l-Qāsim Khalaf b. Saʿīd—Abū Muḥammad ʿAbdallāh b. Muḥammad b. ʿAlī—ʿAbdallāh b. Yūnus—Baqī b. Makhlad. Ibn ʿAbd al-Barr, *al-Istīʿāb* 1:22. Compare with the *isnād* of the extant version of Baqī's recension: Aḥmad b. Muḥammad al-Ashʿarī—Abū l-Walīd Hishām b. Aḥmad—Abū ʿUmar Aḥmad b. Muḥammad al-Ṭalamankī—Abū ʿAbdallāh Muḥammad b. Yaḥyā b. Mufarrij—Abū l-Qāsim Aḥmad b. ʿAbdallāh b. Muḥammad b. al-Mubārak b. Ḥabīb b. ʿAbd al-Malik b. al-Walīd b. ʿAbd al-Malik (the Umayyad caliph)—Baqī b. Makhlad.

91 Ibn ʿAbd al-Barr also states something similar, in his own words, about ʿAmr b. al-ʿĀṣ elsewhere in *al-Istīʿāb* 3:919.

possibilities are the most likely, although one cannot entirely rule out the other possibilities. In any case, the absence of this material in Baqī's extant recension does not challenge the attribution of the form and content of the *Tārīkh* to Khalīfa, since some alterations in the course of transmission are not unusual for this type of text. The differences between the two recensions in the material on the Rāshidūn period are no more than one might expect from different recensions transmitted to different students at different times, and there is no clear evidence to suggest that Baqī b. Makhlad omitted material regarding this period for ideological reasons.

4.3 *The Umayyad Period*

There are 109 reports on the Umayyad caliphate in Ṣaddām's collection of material not found in Baqī's recension. These are examined below, caliph by caliph. Because Ṣaddām claims that Baqī b. Makhlad omitted material that could be considered offensive to the Umayyads, it is particularly important to examine these reports in detail. Twenty-three pertain to the caliphate of Muʿāwiya b. Abī Sufyān (r. 41–60/661–680). Their subjects are a winter expedition of Busr b. Arṭā, the governorship of al-Mughīra b. Shuʿba, brief biographical details about al-Ḥasan b. ʿAlī, the pilgrimage and charity of al-Ḥasan b. ʿAlī,[92] the date of Busr b. Arṭā's death, an expedition of Yazīd b. Shajara, the date of ʿUqba b. ʿĀmir al-Juhanī's death, the death and funeral of ʿĀʾisha bt. Abī Bakr, the death of Maslama b. Mukhallad and some information about Muʿāwiya's governors (14 short reports).[93] The style resembles that of Baqī's recension, and much of the same information is likewise found in Baqī's recension.[94] The main difference is the absence of material about Muʿāwiya's governors (and some material about his judges) in Baqī's recension, although some of the information is found in the year sections rather than the list sections in Baqī's recension. The

---

92 The report on al-Ḥasan's pilgrimage and his charity is narrated by Ibn ʿAsākir from Khalīfa via Aḥmad b. Sahl b. Ayyūb (d. 291/904), not via Mūsā al-Tustarī. Considering the narrator (not known to have transmitted the whole *Tārīkh*) and the content of the report (typical *faḍāʾil* material that is unusual in Khalīfa's *Tārīkh*), it was probably transmitted as a separate report and not as a part of the *Tārīkh*. The biographical details are transmitted by al-Tustarī, and they are the same as in Baqī's recension, except that the date of al-Ḥasan's death differs: 49/669 in Baqī's recension and 50/670 in al-Tustarī's. Ibn ʿAsākir, *Tārīkh madīnat Dimashq* 13:244, 303; Khalīfa b. Khayyāṭ, *Tārīkh* (1985) 203.

93 Ibn ʿAsākir, *Tārīkh madīnat Dimashq* 7:360, 8:231, 10:149, 11:415–416, 13:244, 303, 16:10, 19:170, 22:461, 26:165, 29:283, 31:271–272, 38:268, 40:22–23, 49:378, 58:63–64, 60:3–4, 62:431, 65:233, 67:295; Ibn ʿAbd al-Barr, *al-Istīʿāb* 3:1073, 4:1885; al-Ḥākim al-Naysābūrī, *al-Mustadrak* 3:683; al-Khaṭīb al-Baghdādī, *Tārīkh Baghdād* 1:551; Ṣaddām, *Tārīkh Khalīfa* 75–83.

94 See nos. 49, 51, 54, 55, 57, 59 in Ṣaddām, *Tārīkh Khalīfa* 75–83; Khalīfa b. Khayyāṭ, *Tārīkh* (1985) 197, 203, 205, 210, 223–225, 227.

reason seems to be that the list of Muʿāwiya's governors and parts of the list of his judges are missing from Baqī's recension. However, there is no particular reason to think that Baqī or someone else intentionally omitted this material for any ideological, scholarly or other reason; the material preserved in Mūsā al-Tustarī's recension resembles Khalīfa's usual lists and contains no negative material about the Umayyads. It may never have been a part of the *Tārīkh* that Baqī received from Khalīfa, or it might have disappeared in the course of transmission, but it seems unlikely that it was removed for ideological reasons.

There are seven reports on the reign of Yazīd b. Muʿāwiya (r. 60–64/680–683), pertaining to the date of Maslama b. Mukhallad's death, the governors of Medina, the death of ʿUqba b. Nāfiʿ and Yazīd's governors (four reports),[95] although three of the reports on Yazīd's governors repeat parts of the same report (two narrated by Ibn ʿAsākir and one by Ibn al-ʿAdīm).[96] Some of the same information is found in Baqī's recension.[97] The main reason for the differences seems to be that the list of Yazīd's governors is missing from Baqī's recension. There is, however, nothing negative about the Umayyads in the material, and thus nothing that would indicate that Baqī or someone else omitted this material for ideological reasons—if it was actually a part of the *Tārīkh* as Baqī received it from Khalīfa. There are also two very brief reports on the reign of Muʿāwiya b. Yazīd (r. 64/684), pertaining to the name of his mother and the length of his reign, which are not found in Baqī's recension. Nine short reports pertain to the reign of Marwān b. al-Ḥakam (r. 64–65/684–685) and the Battle of Marj Rāhiṭ (three reports), the situation in Iraq after Yazīd's death, the army of Ḥubaysh b. Dulja sent towards Medina by Marwān b. al-Ḥakam (two reports), the escape of Zufar b. al-Ḥārith, the death of al-Nuʿmān b. Bashīr and the death of ʿAlqama b. Qays.[98] All of these brief reports resemble the narrative style of Baqī's recension and contain nothing that would suggest an ideologically motivated omission.

There are 36 reports on the caliphates of ʿAbdallāh b. al-Zubayr (r. 64–73/684–692) and ʿAbd al-Malik b. Marwān (r. 65–86/685–705). They pertain to Ibn al-Zubayr's imprisonment of Muḥammad b. al-Ḥanafiyya, the killing of al-Mukhtār al-Thaqafī, the killing of ʿUmar b. Saʿd b. Abī Waqqāṣ, the Battle of

---

95 Ibn ʿAsākir, *Tārīkh madīnat Dimashq* 18:247–248, 34:371, 40:23–24, 534, 61:377–378; al-Ḥākim al-Naysābūrī, *al-Mustadrak* 3:565; Ibn al-ʿAdīm, *Bughyat al-ṭalab* 5:2236; Ṣaddām, *Tārīkh Khalīfa* 83–85.

96 See nos. 75, 77, 78 in Ṣaddām, *Tārīkh Khalīfa* 84–85.

97 See nos. 73, 74, 76 in Ṣaddām, *Tārīkh Khalīfa* 83–85; Khalīfa b. Khayyāṭ, *Tārīkh* (1985) 236, 251.

98 Ibn ʿAsākir, *Tārīkh madīnat Dimashq* 7:36, 11:183, 12:89, 19:210–211, 33:35, 41:190, 49:310, 62:127, 63:109; Ṣaddām, *Tārīkh Khalīfa* 86–88.

Khāzir, the fighting between the armies of al-Mukhtār and Muṣʿab b. al-Zubayr, the attack of ʿAmr b. al-Zubayr against his brother ʿAbdallāh b. al-Zubayr, Ibn al-Zubayr's governors of Iraq (two reports), Ibn al-Zubayr's governors of Medina, the death of al-Aḥnaf b. Qays, the death of Jābir b. ʿAbdallāh (two reports), the death of ʿAbd al-Raḥmān b. Ḥāṭib b. Abī Baltaʿa, the death of Qabīṣa b. Jābir, the fighting between the armies of ʿAbd al-Malik and Muṣʿab b. al-Zubayr (four reports), the pilgrimage in 72/692, the army of ʿUmar b. ʿUbaydallāh b. Maʿmar sent by ʿAbd al-Malik b. Marwan, the expeditions of Ḥassān b. al-Nuʿmān al-Ghassānī in North Africa (two reports), the death of ʿAbdallāh b. ʿUmar, al-Ḥajjāj's arrival in Kufa and his infamous *khuṭba*, al-Ḥasan al-Baṣrī's advice to not revolt against al-Ḥajjāj, ʿAbd al-Malik's *khuṭba* in Mecca in 75/695, the deaths of al-ʿIrbāḍ b. Sāriya and Thābit b. al-Ḍaḥḥāk, the career of al-Muhallab b. Abī Ṣufra, ʿAbd al-Malik's governors of Khurāsān and Sijistān, the death of Umayya b. ʿAbdallāh b. Khālid b. Asīd, the death of Busr b. Arṭā, some poetry of ʿAbdallāh b. al-Zabīr al-Asadī, ʿAbd al-Malik's commander of the security forces (*shuraṭ*), the governorship of Bishr b. Marwān and his death in Basra, the pilgrimage leaders during ʿAbd al-Malik's caliphate and the death of ʿAbdallāh b. Jaʿfar b. Abī Ṭālib.[99] The narrative style resembles Baqī's transmission, and much of the same information is also found in Baqī's recension.[100] There is no particular pattern in the missing material that would suggest that Baqī or someone else omitted it because of Umayyad sympathies. Mūsā al-Tustarī preserves from Khalīfa some historically noteworthy reports, such as an early account of al-Ḥajjāj's *khuṭba* in Kufa and some details about the revolt of al-Mukhtār al-Thaqafī, the Zubayrid–Umayyad conflict and al-Muhallab b. Abī Ṣufra's career, which are not found in Baqī's recension. One reason for their absence in Baqī's recension might be that Baqī omitted or abridged them, but it is equally possible that Khalīfa transmitted slightly different versions of the *Tārīkh* to Baqī and Mūsā al-Tustarī. However, the possibility that Baqī (or someone else) omitted or abridged this material necessitates caution in the analysis of Khalīfa's approach to these events and underlines the importance of taking Mūsā al-Tustarī's transmission into consideration.

---

99 Ibn ʿAsākir, *Tārīkh madīnat Dimashq* 6:155, 9:293, 295, 10:156, 264, 11:239, 443–444, 12:127, 177, 451, 15:178, 27:297, 28:263, 34:286, 37:135, 462, 40:190, 45:58, 291, 46:8–9, 52:132, 54:337–338, 58:115, 218–219, 232–234, 65:366; al-Dhahabī, *Tārīkh al-Islām* 5:67, 196, 209, 443; al-Ḥākim al-Naysābūrī, *al-Mustadrak* 3:642; Ṣaddām, *Tārīkh Khalīfa* 88–105.

100 See nos. 90, 91, 92, 93, 99, 100, 104, 107, 110, 113, 116, 117, 118, 119, 120, 122, 124, 125 in Ṣaddām, *Tārīkh Khalīfa* 88–105; Khalīfa b. Khayyāṭ, *Tārīkh* (1985) 206, 262–265, 269, 271, 273, 277, 280, 292, 294–295, 299.

There are three brief reports on the caliphate of al-Walīd b. ʿAbd al-Malik (r. 86–96/705–715), pertaining to ʿUmar b. ʿAbd al-ʿAzīz leading the pilgrimage thrice, the date of Abū l-ʿĀliya's death and ʿAbd al-ʿAzīz b. al-Walīd's leadership of the pilgrimage and of an expedition against the Romans.[101] There is one report on the caliphate of Sulaymān b. ʿAbd al-Malik (r. 96–99/715–717), pertaining to the length of his reign and the date of Nāfiʿ b. Jubayr b. Muṭʿim's death, and one report on the caliphate of ʿUmar b. ʿAbd al-ʿAzīz (r. 99–101/717–720), pertaining to the length of his reign.[102] Ṣaddām also collects five reports on the caliphate of Yazīd b. ʿAbd al-Malik (r. 101–105/720–4), pertaining to the deaths of Mālik b. Mismaʿ, Yazīd b. ʿAbdallāh b. al-Aṣamm, Ḥassān b. Thābit and Abān b. ʿUthmān, as well as to an expedition of al-Jarrāḥ b. ʿAbdallāh.[103] Much of the same information is found in Baqī's recension, and there are no indications in the missing material that Baqī or someone else would have intentionally omitted it.[104]

Seven reports pertain to the caliphate of Hishām b. ʿAbd al-Malik (r. 105–125/724–43) and the deaths of Sālim b. ʿAbdallāh b. ʿUmar, Muʿāwiya b. Qurra al-Muzanī, Muḥammad b. Wāsiʿ, al-Ḥakam b. ʿUtayba, ʿAlī b. ʿAbdallāh b. ʿAbbās and Iyās b. Muʿāwiya b. Qurra al-Muzanī, the revolt of Zayd b. ʿAlī b. al-Ḥusayn and the birth of ʿAbdallāh b. al-Mubārak.[105] Some of the same information is found in Baqī's recension,[106] but the missing report about the uprising of Zayd b. ʿAlī is noteworthy. The event is recounted with utmost brevity in Baqī's recension: "In it [122/740]: Zayd b. ʿAlī b. Ḥusayn b. ʿAlī b. Abī Ṭālib was killed in Kufa."[107] The account in al-Tustarī's recension, as preserved by Ibn ʿAsākir and Ibn al-ʿAdīm, is more detailed:

> Mūsā b. Zakariyyā said: Khalīfa narrated to us; he said: Abū l-Yaqẓān narrated to me from Juwayriya b. Asmāʾ and others: Zayd b. ʿAlī went to Yūsuf b. ʿUmar at al-Ḥīra. He gave him gifts and treated him kindly. Then he went to Medina. Some people from Kufa approached him and said to him, "Go

101 Ibn ʿAsākir, *Tārīkh madīnat Dimashq* 18:191, 36:372, 45:140; Ṣaddām, *Tārīkh Khalīfa* 106.

102 Ibn ʿAsākir, *Tārīkh madīnat Dimashq* 49:208–209, 61:409; Ṣaddām, *Tārīkh Khalīfa* 106–107.

103 Ibn ʿAsākir, *Tārīkh madīnat Dimashq* 6:157, 34:301, 56:499, 65:122; al-Azdī, *Tārīkh al-Mawṣil* 23; Ṣaddām, *Tārīkh Khalīfa* 107–108.

104 See nos. 126, 128, 129, 130, 131, 132, 134, 135 in Ṣaddām, *Tārīkh Khalīfa* 106–108; Khalīfa b. Khayyāṭ, *Tārīkh* (1985) 301, 303, 306, 309, 311–312, 316–317, 321–322, 325–326, 330–331, 336.

105 Ibn ʿAsākir, *Tārīkh madīnat Dimashq* 10:36, 20:73, 32:400, 43:53, 59:274–275; Ibn al-ʿAdīm, *Bughyat al-ṭalab* 9:4049; al-Dhahabī, *Tārīkh al-Islām* 8:261; Ṣaddām, *Tārīkh Khalīfa* 108–110.

106 See nos. 136, 140, 142 in Ṣaddām, *Tārīkh Khalīfa* 108–110; Khalīfa b. Khayyāṭ, *Tārīkh* (1985) 338, 346, 349, 354.

107 Khalīfa b. Khayyāṭ, *Tārīkh* (1985) 353.

> back! Yūsuf is worth nothing. We will seize Kufa for you." He went back and many people pledged allegiance to him. Then he revolted and many people joined his revolt. They fought and Zayd was killed in that year, that is, in 122/740.[108]

Baqī or someone after him in the *isnād* may have omitted or abridged this report—if it was ever a part of the *Tārīkh* that Khalīfa transmitted to Baqī—a possible ideological motivation being to tone down the special role of the ʿAlid uprisings and martyrdoms, since there is nothing particularly negative about the Umayyads in the report; in fact, it blames the revolt and its outcome on the early Shīʿī factions of Kufa. Along with the missing reports about al-Mukhtār's revolt, this material could partially challenge the notion that the lack of information about the ʿAlid family and their partisans distinguishes Khalīfa's *Tārīkh*.[109] However, even with these additional reports from al-Tustarī's recension, the scarcity of information about the ʿAlids and their uprisings remains a distinct feature of the work. As noted above, the absence of this material in Baqī's recension underlines the importance of being cautious when analysing details of Khalīfa's approach or historical views due to the possibility of some later abridgement or omission.

There are four reports on the reign of al-Walīd (II) b. Yazīd (125–126/743–744), pertaining to the leaders of the pilgrimage, the date of Sulaymān b. Ḥabīb's death, al-Walīd b. Yazīd's chamberlain (*ḥājib*) and the date of Khālid al-Qasrī's death.[110] There are also two reports on the reign of Yazīd (III) b. al-Walīd (r. 126/744), pertaining to a short letter he sent to Marwān b. Muḥammad and the participation of Mālik b. al-Walīd al-Mizzī in Yazīd b. al-Walīd's seizure of Damascus, although the latter narration is most likely Ibn ʿAsākir's own words, not Khalīfa's.[111] Some of the information is also found in Baqī's recension, and there are no indications in the missing material that Baqī or someone else would have intentionally omitted it, since most of it consists of brief administrative or chronological information.[112]

Finally, there are nine reports on the caliphate of Marwān b. Muḥammad (r. 127–132/744–750), pertaining to the oath of allegiance to ʿAbdallāh b. Muʿāwiya, the date of Saʿd b. Ibrāhīm b. ʿAbd al-Raḥmān b. ʿAwf's death, the date of

108 Ibn ʿAsākir, *Tārīkh madīnat Dimashq* 19:478; Ibn al-ʿAdīm, *Bughyat al-ṭalab* 9:4049.
109 Wurtzel, *Khalifa ibn Khayyat's History* 29.
110 Ibn ʿAsākir, *Tārīkh madīnat Dimashq* 16:162, 22:212, 45:115, 48:6.
111 Ibn ʿAsākir 56:507–508; Ibn ʿAbd Rabbih, *al-ʿIqd al-farīd* 1:48.
112 See nos. 144 and 145 in Ṣaddām, *Tārīkh Khalīfa* 111; Khalīfa b. Khayyāṭ, *Tārīkh* (1985) 347, 360, 368.

Wakīʿ b. al-Jarrāḥ's birth, the *khuṭba* of the Khārijī leader Abū Ḥamza al-Azdī in Mecca, the battles of Ibn Hubayra's army, some pro-ʿAbbāsid revolts in Basra, the exhumation of the Umayyad caliphs and the deaths of Yaḥyā b. Yaḥyā al-Ghassānī and al-Nuʿmān b. al-Mundhir al-Ghassānī.[113] Some of the information is also found in Baqī's recension, including the oath of allegiance to Muʿāwiya b. ʿAbdallāh and the revolts in Basra,[114] but two missing reports stand out: a long version of Abū Ḥamza's *khuṭba* in Mecca, which is more detailed than the one in Baqī's recension, and a report about the exhumation of the Umayyad caliphs, which is completely missing from Baqī's recension. Both reports are found in *Tārīkh al-Mawṣil* of Yazīd b. Muḥammad al-Azdī (d. 334/946), but he does not specify from whom he received them; he simply says that "it was narrated to me from Khalīfa b. Khayyāṭ (*ḥuddithtu ʿan Khalīfa b. Khayyāṭ*)" and "I was informed on the authority of Khalīfa b. Khayyāṭ (*ukhbirtu ʿan Khalīfa b. Khayyāṭ*)."[115] Elsewhere in *Tārīkh al-Mawṣil*, however, he transmits from Khalīfa via Ibn Muḥammad b. Isḥāq, who might be the source of the other narrations.[116] It is possible that al-Azdī had a copy of Khalīfa's *Tārīkh*, which he might have received from Ibn Muḥammad b. Isḥāq, but it is also possible that al-Azdī only had access to a number of individual reports from Khalīfa, not the entire *Tārīkh*. Baqī or someone else might have omitted these reports, but it is just as possible that these two reports were never a part of Khalīfa's *Tārīkh* (whether in Baqī's transmission or al-Tustarī's) and that Khalīfa transmitted them separately from his *Tārīkh*.

In contrast to most of the other missing material in Baqī's recension, however, there would be a clear ideological reason to omit these two reports. Therefore, Ṣaddām suggests that Baqī "omitted everything pertaining to the exhumation of the Umayyad caliphs just as he omitted all the accusations against the Umayyads in Abū Ḥamza's *khuṭba*", because of his "ʿUthmānī inclinations" and "his close ties with the Umayyad authorities in al-Andalus."[117] This is the only possibility Ṣaddām considers and, as with his conclusions in general, this notion is based on the questionable assumption that Khalīfa had one fixed version of the *Tārīkh* that he transmitted to all his students at all times. It is equally possible that these two reports are absent because Khalīfa transmit-

113 Ibn ʿAsākir, *Tārīkh madīnat Dimashq* 15:337, 20:225, 33:215, 63:65, 65:62; al-Azdī, *Tārīkh al-Mawṣil* 103–106, 117, 138; al-Dhahabī, *Tārīkh al-Islām* 8:554; Ṣaddām, *Tārīkh Khalīfa* 112–117.

114 See nos. 149, 150, 152, 153, 154 in Ṣaddām, *Tārīkh Khalīfa* 112–117; Khalīfa b. Khayyāṭ, *Tārīkh* (1985) 375, 382, 385–387, 397, 402–403.

115 Al-Azdī, *Tārīkh al-Mawṣil* 103–106, 138; Ṣaddām, *Tārīkh Khalīfa* 113–115, 117.

116 Al-Azdī, *Tārīkh al-Mawṣil* 188–189.

117 Ṣaddām, *Tārīkh Khalīfa* 21.

ted slightly different versions at different times to different students or because someone else, after Baqī in the *isnād* of the extant recension, omitted them. It is also quite possible that al-Azdī received these two reports as individual narrations that Khalīfa transmitted separately, not as a part of the *Tārīkh*. Moreover, it must be noted that other quite negative reports about certain Umayyad caliphs (such as Marwān b. al-Ḥakam, Yazīd b. Muʿāwiya and al-Walīd b. Yazīd, as well as, to some extent, Muʿāwiya b. Abī Sufyān) were preserved in the extant version of Baqī's recension.[118] The version of Abū Ḥamza's *khuṭba* in Baqī's recension still contains many accusations against the Umayyads for unlawfully seizing wealth, ruling tyrannically and judging by other than God's revealed law.[119] However, the first half of the *khuṭba* (as transmitted by al-Azdī) in which Abū Ḥamza enumerates the past caliphs and heavily criticises all of them, except Abū Bakr and ʿUmar, is absent in Baqī's recension. A similar, but slightly different, long version is also transmitted by Khalīfa's Basran contemporary, al-Jāḥiẓ (d. 255/868–869), in *al-Bayān wa-l-tabyīn* without mentioning the source of the *khuṭba*.[120] This might suggest that the *khuṭba* was well-known in the intellectual circles of Basra at the time. A shorter unreferenced version, resembling the one in Baqī's recension, is found in Ibn ʿAbd Rabbih's (d. 328/940) *al-ʿIqd al-farīd*.[121] He also narrates a second longer *khuṭba* that Abū Ḥamza delivered in Medina, which contains some sentences that are found in Baqī's recension, but there in the context of the Meccan *khuṭba*. After citing this material, Ibn ʿAbd Rabbih interestingly adds:

> We have left out the vilifications of the caliphs found in this *khuṭba*, since Abū Ḥamza slandered ʿUthmān and ʿAlī b. Abī Ṭālib, may God be pleased with them, as well as ʿUmar b. ʿAbd al-ʿAzīz. He did not exempt any of the caliphs except Abū Bakr and ʿUmar. He declared all caliphs after them unbelievers. May God curse him![122]

It is possible that Baqī or someone after him in the *isnād* of the extant recension similarly omitted the passage with vilifications of the caliphs. It could perhaps explain why Baqī's version is unreferenced after Khalīfa, while al-Azdī's longer version is narrated from Khalīfa on the authority of al-Madāʾinī narrating from Abū l-Layth al-Khurāsānī. The personal attacks on the Umayyad caliphs were

---

118 See Chapter 8, Section 3.

119 Khalīfa b. Khayyāṭ, *Tārīkh* (1985) 385–387.

120 Al-Jāḥiẓ, *al-Bayān* 2:122–125.

121 Ibn ʿAbd Rabbih, *al-ʿIqd al-farīd* 4:228–231; Khalīfa b. Khayyāṭ, *Tārīkh* (1985) 386–387.

122 Ibn ʿAbd Rabbih, *al-ʿIqd al-farīd* 4:230.

probably a lot more controversial under Umayyad rule in Baqī's al-Andalus than under ʿAbbāsid rule in Khalīfa's Basra, although Khalīfa clearly agreed neither with Abū Ḥamza's accusations of unbelief (*takfīr*) nor with his general historical views—especially on the Companions ʿUthmān, ʿAlī and Muʿāwiya. The report about the exhumation of the Umayyads reads as follows:

> I was informed on the authority of Khalīfa [who narrated] from Abū l-Dhayyāl, who said: When ʿAbdallāh b. ʿAlī had defeated Marwān, he and Ṣāliḥ agreed to seize Damascus. He took Yazīd b. Muʿāwiya b. Marwān and ʿAbdallāh b. ʿAbd al-Jabbār b. Yazīd b. ʿAbd al-Malik b. Marwān and sent them to Abū l-ʿAbbās, who crucified them. He then desecrated the graves of the Umayyads and burned them with fire.
>
> It is said (*wa-qīla*) that he appointed ʿAmr b. Tammām to exhume the graves. ʿAmr said, "I opened Hishām's grave and took out his body, which was intact. He flogged his corpse and it fell apart, after which he burned it with fire. Then we exhumed Sulaymān, but we only found his spine, head and ribs. Then we exhumed Maslama at Qinnasrīn, but we only found a skull and burned it. Then we came to al-Walīd's grave in Damascus, but we only found half of his head. Then we went to Muʿāwiya's grave and opened it, but we only found one bone in it. Then we went to the grave of Yazīd b. Muʿāwiya, but all we found was disintegrated fragments and a furrow as if he had turned into ashes. Then we continued and did the same to the rest of their graves."[123]

It is not hard to see why this material would have been considered offensive to the Umayyads in al-Andalus, and it is possible that Baqī omitted it from Khalīfa's *Tārīkh*, but it is not the only possibility. As with the long version of Abū Ḥamza's *khuṭba*, it is equally possible that this material was never a part of the *Tārīkh* as Baqī received it from Khalīfa, and perhaps not even a part of Mūsā al-Tustarī's recension, since al-Azdī seemed to have received Khalīfa's material from other sources.[124] These reports from Khalīfa might have been separate narrations that al-Azdī received on Khalīfa's authority and, as such, they might not have been a part of the *Tārīkh* at all. Moreover, if one assumes that the reports were omitted for ideological reasons, they could have been omitted by someone else after Baqī in the *isnād* of the extant recension—such as the Marwānid descendant Abū l-Qāsim Aḥmad b. ʿAbdallāh. One might also question

123 Al-Azdī, *Tārīkh al-Mawṣil* 138.

124 Ibn ʿAsākir also reports about the exhumation, but not with material from Khalīfa. See *Tārīkh madīnat Dimashq* 53:126–127.

if the second part of the above citation ("It is said that he appointed ʿAmr b. Tammām") really belongs to Khalīfa, or if Khalīfa's report is supposed to end with "He then desecrated the graves of the Umayyads and burned them with fire." It would certainly make the report a lot milder, although one would still need to explain why it is not found in Baqī's recension. Altogether, the possibility that Baqī or someone else omitted these two reports calls for caution when analysing details of Khalīfa's approach to the Umayyads in the *Tārīkh*. However, these two reports are not enough to claim that Baqī substantially abridged the *Tārīkh* for ideological reasons, especially not when considering other possibilities, such as Khalīfa's transmitting different versions of the *Tārīkh* to different students at different times or al-Azdī's receiving these reports as individual narrations from Khalīfa rather than as parts of the *Tārīkh*.

4.4 *The ʿAbbāsid Period*

There are 45 reports on the ʿAbbāsid period in Ṣaddām's collection of material not found in Baqī's recension. Three short reports pertain to the caliphate of Abū l-ʿAbbās al-Saffāḥ (r. 132–136/750–754) and the subjects of Abū Muslim sending Marrār b. Anas al-Ḍabbī to kill Abū Salama al-Khallāl and the dates of the deaths of ʿUbaydallāh b. Abī Jaʿfar (the *mawlā* of Banū Umayya) and ʿAlī b. Badhīma.[125] This information is not found in Baqī's recension of the *Tārīkh*,[126] but there is nothing in these brief reports that would suggest that they were omitted for ideological reasons.

There are 19 reports on the caliphate of Abū Jaʿfar al-Manṣūr (r. 136–158/754–775), pertaining to the appointment of Mūsā b. Muṣʿab as governor of al-Jazīra, the execution of Abū Muslim, the conquest of Ṭabaristān, the uprising of Ibrāhīm b. ʿAbdallāh (the brother of Muḥammad al-Nafs al-Zakiyya) in Basra, the views of Shuʿba b. al-Ḥajjāj, Hishām b. Ḥassān and Saʿīd b. Abī ʿArūba on joining the revolt of Ibrāhīm b. ʿAbdallāh, the encouragement of Abū Ḥanīfa and al-Aʿmash to join Ibrāhīm's uprising, the dismissal of ʿĪsā b. Mūsā and the appointment of Muḥammad b. Sulaymān b. ʿAlī as governor of Kufa, the governorship of Mosul, the leaders of the pilgrimage and the deaths of Khuṣayf b. ʿAbd al-Raḥmān (two reports), ʿAbdallāh b. ʿAlī b. ʿAbdallāh b. ʿAbbās, ʿAmr b. Muhājir, Mūsā b. ʿUqba, Ibrāhīm b. ʿUqba, ʿAmr b. al-Ḥārith b. Yaʿqūb, ʿUthmān b. Abī l-ʿĀtika (the *mawlā* of ʿUmar b. al-Khaṭṭāb), Abū ʿAmr b. al-ʿAlāʾ and Abū Sufyān b. al-ʿAlāʾ.[127] Some of the same information is found in Baqī's recen-

125 Ibn ʿAsākir, *Tārīkh madīnat Dimashq* 14:413–414, 37:414, 41:279; Ṣaddām, *Tārīkh Khalīfa* 118.

126 The date of ʿAlī b. Badhīma's death is mentioned in al-Tustarī's recension of Khalīfa's *Ṭabaqāt* (1993) 586.

127 Al-Azdī, *Tārīkh al-Mawṣil* 188–189, 226, 228; Ibn ʿAsākir, *Tārīkh madīnat Dimashq* 16:396–

sion, and the narrative style likewise resembles Baqī's recension,[128] but there are three noteworthy reports on the Basran uprising of Ibrāhīm b. ʿAbdallāh, the brother of Muḥammad al-Nafs al-Zakiyya, in 145/762. These reports are found in *Tārīkh al-Mawṣil* of al-Azdī, who received them from Ibn Muḥammad b. Isḥāq. Khalīfa's account of the uprising in Baqī's recension is fairly detailed in comparison to other events in the ʿAbbāsid period, but it focuses on chronology and main events. By contrast, al-Azdī's material describes how contemporaneous scholars viewed and supported the revolt. The first report describes Ibrāhīm's reaction as he received the news of his brother's death and then mentions a number of Iraqi scholars who joined the uprising. The second report mentions that Abū Ḥanīfa and al-Aʿmash actively encouraged people to join the uprising, and the third contains the following dialogues:

> Ibn Muḥammad informed me on the authority of Khalīfa; he said: Maysara b. Bakr said: I heard ʿAbd al-Wārith say: When Ibrāhīm revolted, we went to Shuʿba and said, "What do you think about joining his uprising?" He said, "I think you should join his uprising and support him." We went to Hishām b. [Ḥassān], Abū ʿAbdallāh, but he did not reply at all and then left us and entered his house. We went to Saʿīd b. Abī ʿArūba, who said, "I don't see anything wrong with a man who stays in his house and then fights back if someone enters it." Ḥammād b. Zayd said, "There was no one left from the people of Basra during the days of Ibrāhīm except Ibn ʿAwn."[129]

Besides describing these scholars' views on the uprising, the reports seem to justify it in light of the numerous scholars who supported Ibrāhīm and joined his uprising—similar to Khalīfa's account of Ibn al-Ashʿath's revolt in Baqī's recension.[130] It is possible that these reports were omitted by Baqī or someone else, but it is also quite possible that they were not a part of the version of the *Tārīkh* that Khalīfa transmitted to Baqī. The fact that Khalīfa's source, Maysara b. Bakr, is not mentioned in the *isnād*s in Baqī's recension might also

---

397, 31:68, 35:418, 38:397, 45:468, 46:406, 48:18–19, 51:229–230, 60:467–468, 67:119; al-Ṭabarī, *Tārīkh* 3:136–137; Ṣaddām, *Tārīkh Khalīfa* 118–126. However, Ṣaddām repeats two reports that are only narrated once in the original sources, which makes the total number of reports 17 rather than 19. See al-Azdī, *Tārīkh al-Mawṣil* 189; Ibn ʿAsākir, *Tārīkh madīnat Dimashq* 48:18–19; Ṣaddām, *Tārīkh Khalīfa* 123–124 (nos. 170, 172, 173, 174).

128 See nos. 161, 162, 166, 168, 173, 176, 178, 179 in Ṣaddām, *Tārīkh Khalīfa* 118–126; Khalīfa b. Khayyāṭ, *Tārīkh* (1985) 415–416, 418–419, 423, 425, 427, 433, 438–439, 441, 450.

129 Al-Azdī, *Tārīkh al-Mawṣil* 189.

130 Khalīfa b. Khayyāṭ, *Tārīkh* (1985) 280–289.

indicate that the report was not a part of the *Tārīkh*, or at least did not form part of the version that Khalīfa transmitted to Baqī. The subsequent name in the aforementioned *isnād*, ʿAbd al-Wārith b. Saʿīd b. Dhakwān, is also not found in Khalīfa's *isnād*s in Baqī's recension, although the date of his death is noted in 180/796.[131] Altogether, it is possible that this material about Ibrāhīm's uprising was omitted or that it was never a part of the *Tārīkh* as Khalīfa transmitted it to Baqī, but it is nonetheless important to take into consideration when analysing Khalīfa's accounts of revolts in the *Tārīkh*.

There is one short report on the caliphate of al-Mahdī (r. 158–169/775–785), about the date of ʿIsā b. Mūsā's death, which is not found in Baqī's recension.[132] There are eight reports on the caliphate of Hārūn al-Rashīd (r. 170–193/786–809), pertaining to the death of Muḥammad b. Sulaymān b. ʿAlī, Hārūn al-Rashīd's governors of Medina (two reports), the Khārijī rebellion of al-Faḍl al-Rādānī, the death of Yūnus b. Ḥabīb, the birth and death of al-ʿAbbās b. Muḥammad b. ʿAlī, the death of Abū Isḥāq al-Fazāzī and the death of Sulaym b. ʿĀmir al-Ḥanafī.[133] Two reports pertain to the caliphate of al-Amīn (r. 193–198/809–813) and the deaths of ʿAbd al-Malik b. Ṣāliḥ b. ʿAlī and Wakīʿ b. al-Jarrāḥ.[134] Most of this information is not found in Baqī's recension, although it resembles it in style, but there is nothing in the material that would suggest that Baqī or someone else omitted it for ideological reasons.[135]

There are four short reports on the caliphate of al-Maʾmūn (r. 198–218/813–833), pertaining to al-Maʾmūn's governors of Medina and the deaths of Sulaymān b. Abī Jaʿfar, Isḥāq b. ʿIsā b. ʿAlī and Abū l-Bukhtarī Wahb b. Wahb.[136] This information is not found in Baqī's recension, but there is nothing that would suggest that Baqī or someone else deliberately omitted it. Finally, there are eight reports on the caliphate of al-Mutawakkil (r. 232–247/847–861). One report pertains to al-Mutawakkil's abolition of the *miḥna* ('inquisition'); the rest are short notices about the deaths of Muḥammad b. ʿAbd al-Malik al-Zayyāt (233/847), Yaḥyā b. Maʿīn (233/848), Sulaymān b. Dāwūd al-Shādhakūnī (234/849), Sulaymān b. ʿAbdallāh b. Sulaymān b. ʿAlī b. ʿAbdallāh b. ʿAbbās (234/848), ʿAbdallāh b. Muḥammad al-Nufaylī (234/848), Manṣūr b. al-Mahdī (236/850–851) and

131 Khalīfa b. Khayyāṭ, *Tārīkh* (1985) 451, *Ṭabaqāt* (1993) 387; Ibn Saʿd, *Ṭabaqāt* 9:290; al-Dhahabī, *Siyar* 2595–2596.

132 Ibn ʿAsākir, *Tārīkh madīnat Dimashq* 48:19; Ṣaddām, *Tārīkh Khalīfa* 126.

133 Al-Azdī, *Tārīkh al-Mawṣil* 275; Ibn ʿAsākir, *Tārīkh madīnat Dimashq* 7:121–122, 26:401, 53:139, 348, 63:408; al-Dhahabī, *Tārīkh al-Islām* 12:179, 481; Ṣaddām, *Tārīkh Khalīfa* 126–128.

134 Ibn ʿAsākir, *Tārīkh madīnat Dimashq* 37:33–34, 63:106; Ṣaddām, *Tārīkh Khalīfa* 128–129.

135 See no. 181 in Ṣaddām, *Tārīkh Khalīfa* 126; Khalīfa b. Khayyāṭ, *Tārīkh* (1985) 448.

136 Ibn ʿAsākir, *Tārīkh madīnat Dimashq* 8:269, 22:337–338, 61:236, 63:422.

Isḥāq b. Rāhawayh (238/853).[137] This information is not found in Baqī's recension, which ends in 232/847, but they are important for two reasons in particular. First, the dates of these individuals' deaths suggest that al-Tustarī's recension of the *Tārīkh* was transmitted approximately six years after Baqī received his version of the *Tārīkh*.[138] The last date in Ibn ʿAsākir's material from Khalīfa via al-Tustarī is 238/853, while the last date in Baqī's recension is 232/847. This is significant as it could explain many of the differences between the two recensions; Khalīfa may well have edited and to some extent altered the *Tārīkh* in these years, although the main content and general structure must have been the same.

Second, the report about al-Mutawakkil's abolition of the *miḥna*, preserved by al-Dhahabī in his *Siyar aʿlām al-nubalāʾ*, clearly illustrates Khalīfa's early Sunnī orientation:

> Khalīfa b. Khayyāṭ said: al-Mutawakkil succeeded as caliph and affirmed the Sunna. He spoke about it at his court and wrote to the different regions about lifting the *miḥna*, spreading the Sunna and supporting its people.[139]

This citation probably comes from al-Tustarī's recension, which most likely was al-Dhahabī's source for Khalīfa's material. It is missing in Baqī's recension most likely because Baqī received the *Tārīkh* from Khalīfa around 232/847, which would be before, or at the very beginning of, the gradual lifting of

137 Al-Dhahabī, *Siyar* 1316; Ibn ʿAsākir, *Tārīkh madīnat Dimashq* 8:140, 22:334–335, 32:354–355, 41:271–272, 54:141, 60:354, 65:39; Ṣaddam, *Tarīkh Khalīfa* 131–133.

138 The last date recorded in al-Tustarī's recension of the *Ṭabaqāt* is 236/850–851, and it is possible that he received both works around 238/853, but also possible that he received them at different times. See Khalīfa b. Khayyāṭ, *Ṭabaqāt* (1993) 400.

139 Al-Dhahabī, *Siyar* 1316. This is probably the end of al-Dhahabī's citation of Khalīfa, although Ṣaddām also includes the following passage: "Al-Mutawakkil came to Damascus in Ṣafar year 244/858. It pleased him and he decided to stay there. He moved the royal registries (*dawāwīn al-mulk*) to the city and gave orders for building there. He gave orders for the Turks to be given wealth that would please them and constructed a large palace at Dārayyā, near al-Mizza." Since Khalīfa most likely died in 240/854, and this report mentions events taking place in 244/858, it might be al-Dhahabī's own words or a paraphrase of other material, although one cannot exclude the possibility that Khalīfa actually died later than conventionally accepted. Al-Dhahabī himself says about Khalīfa in the same work, "Muṭayyan and others said: He died in 240/854. I say: He was in his eighties. Whoever said that he died in 246/860 made a mistake. His grandfather died in 160/777." Al-Dhahabī, *Siyar* 1632. See the discussion about Khalīfa's birth and death in Chapter 2. On al-Mutawakkil's time in Damascus, see al-Ṭabarī, *Tārīkh* 3:1436; Cobb, al-Mutawakkil's Damascus.

the *miḥna* between 232/847 and 237/852.[140] The ongoing *miḥna* at the time of transmission might also explain why it is not mentioned in Baqī's recension. It is unlikely that Baqī—as an early Sunnī *ḥadīth* scholar and student of Aḥmad b. Ḥanbal among others—would have omitted this material about al-Mutawakkil's lifting of the *miḥna* for ideological, scholarly or other reasons.

5 Conclusion

This chapter has outlined the transmission history of Khalīfa's *Tārīkh* and has suggested that it was most likely transmitted on the basis of written notes of lectures that Baqī and al-Tustarī heard at different times and edited into book form in slightly different ways, which would explain many of the differences between the two recensions. That said, the differences seem to be relatively minor, and the overall correspondence between the two recensions strongly suggests that Khalīfa was responsible for at least the general form and content of Baqī's extant recension. The chapter also examined the content of the material that is preserved in later sources but absent from Baqī's recension. It suggested that, although Baqī (or someone after him in the *isnād* of the extant recension) may have abridged or omitted certain material, it is equally possible that this material was never a part of the version of the *Tārīkh* that Khalīfa transmitted to Baqī. It is also possible that some of this material was abridged or omitted and that some of it was not a part of the version of the *Tārīkh* that Baqī received. Altogether, the main implication for the study of Khalīfa's *Tārīkh* is that the possibility of occasional omission and abridgement in the extant recension necessitates caution when analysing Khalīfa's arrangement of material and narration of historical events. Although Khalīfa was responsible for the general form and content of the extant recension, some alterations of individual reports and their arrangement may well have occurred in the course of transmission; it was, after all, most likely a series of lecture notes edited into two slightly different versions by his two students, Baqī b. Makhlad and Mūsā al-Tustarī.

---

140 Hinds, Miḥna; Zaman, *Religion and politics* 106–118; Melchert, Religious policies 320–326, *Ahmad* 8–16; Lucas, *Constructive critics* 192–202.

CHAPTER 2

Khalīfa's Life and Works

1 Introduction

This chapter outlines Khalīfa's biography, education and works. It also discusses Khalīfa's reputation among the early and later scholars, and the usage of his *Tārīkh* in later Muslim scholarship. Besides surveying the available biographical material about Khalīfa, the purpose is to locate him in his social and intellectual context: the *ḥadīth* circles of Basra in the late second/eighth and early third/ninth centuries. It thereby provides a basis for the subsequent inquiry into the context in which the *Tārīkh* was compiled and circulated. The survey of the later usage of the *Tārīkh* also shows that it was mainly used by Sunnī scholars, most of them *ḥadīth* experts, which suggests that Khalīfa's scholarly agenda and early Sunnī perspective were indeed understood and appreciated by many later scholars.[1] Most information about Khalīfa is found in various biographical dictionaries and works of *ḥadīth* transmitter criticism. However, despite the number of sources, little is known about Khalīfa's life besides his preoccupation with *ḥadīth* scholarship and *akhbār* history. Most sources are brief and seldom provide more than his name, a list of teachers and students, the year of his death, statements about his reliability as a *ḥadīth* transmitter and, occasionally, a comment on his knowledge of history, genealogy and *ʿilm al-rijāl*. For present purposes, however, this type of information is valuable in order to outline the scholarly milieu in which Khalīfa was active.

2 Biography

2.1 *Name and Genealogy*

There are some disagreements in the earliest biographical notices on Khalīfa's name and lineage.[2] Three of his direct students—Mūsā b. Zakariyyā al-Tustarī, Muḥammad b. Ismāʿīl al-Bukhārī (d. 256/870) and Baqī b. Makhlad—all provide slightly different information. In al-Tustarī's recension of Khalīfa's *Ṭabaqāt*, his name is recorded as Khalīfa b. Khayyāṭ al-Shaybānī al-Dhuhlī with

1 Khalīfa's early Sunnī historical views are outlined in Chapters 3–8.

2 See Wurtzel, *Khalifa ibn Khayyat's History* 7–9.

 | DOI:10.1163/9789004383173_004

the *kunya* Abū ʿAmr and the *laqab* Shabāb.[3] Al-Bukhārī omits the *nisba* al-Shaybānī al-Dhuhlī but adds al-ʿUṣfurī and the name of Khalīfa's grandfather and great-grandfather: Khalīfa b. Khayyāṭ b. Khalīfa b. Khayyāṭ al-ʿUṣfurī Abū ʿAmr.[4] In his transmission of the *Tārīkh*, Baqī b. Makhlad only cites him as Khalīfa or Khalīfa b. Khayyāṭ, although the names of his grandfather and great-grandfather are written on the title page.[5] The main *nisba* in later biographical dictionaries is al-ʿUṣfurī.[6] Al-Samʿānī, Ibn al-Athīr and Ibn Khallikān maintain that this *nisba* derives from the Arabic word for safflower (*ʿuṣfur*) and thus refers to some involvement in the safflower trade.[7] Al-Mizzī cites al-Khaṭīb al-Baghdādī, who says that *ʿuṣfur* refers to a certain subtribe of the Arabs (*fakhdh min al-ʿarab*), but this might refer to *ʿuṣfūr* and the *nisba* al-ʿUṣfūrī, which is different from Khalīfa's al-ʿUṣfurī.[8]

Khalīfa does not mention his own full lineage in the *Ṭabaqāt*, despite listing his own grandfather, Abū Hubayra Khalīfa b. Khayyāṭ (d. 160/777),[9] who was also a prominent *ḥadīth* transmitter, whom Yaḥyā b. Maʿīn and Ibn Ḥibbān considered reliable (*thiqa*).[10] Khalīfa's father, Khayyāṭ b. Khalīfa b. Khayyāṭ, is not mentioned in the *Ṭabaqāt*, but he was also a *ḥadīth* transmitter, although less prominent than his father and son.[11] The exact social position of Khalīfa's father and grandfather is unclear, but the biographical notices about them show that Khalīfa came from a Basran family involved in *ḥadīth* scholarship.

2.2 *Birth and Death*

Khalīfa was born in Basra around 160/776.[12] The earliest dates of the deaths of those he transmitted from also confirm that he cannot have been born much later.[13] According to al-Dhahabī, Khalīfa was about 80 years old when he

3 Khalīfa b. Khayyāṭ, *Ṭabaqāt* (1967) 2; Khalīfa b. Khayyāṭ, *Ṭabaqāt* (1993) 25.
4 Al-Bukhārī, *Tārīkh* 3:193.
5 See Khalīfa b. Khayyāṭ, *Tārīkh* (1985) 41.
6 See Ibn Ḥibbān, *Thiqāt* 8:233; Ibn Khallikān, *Wafayāt* 2:243; al-Dhahabī, *Siyar* 1631; Ibn Ḥajar, *Tahdhīb* 1:551; al-Samʿānī, *al-Ansāb* 8:467–468; al-Mizzī, *Tahdhīb* 8:314–319.
7 Al-Samʿānī, *al-Ansāb* 8:467; Ibn al-Athīr, *al-Lubāb* 2:344; Ibn Khallikān, *Wafayāt* 2:243; al-ʿUmarī's introduction to Khalīfa b. Khayyāṭ, *Tārīkh* (1985) 5.
8 Al-Mizzī, *Tahdhīb* 8:314. On the *nisba* al-ʿUṣfūrī, see al-Samʿānī, *al-Ansāb* 8:470–471.
9 Khalīfa b. Khayyāṭ, *Ṭabaqāt* (1993) 382.
10 Al-Bukhārī, *Tārīkh* 3:191; Ibn Abī Ḥātim, *al-Jarḥ wa-l-taʿdīl* 3:378; Ibn Ḥibbān, *Thiqāt* 6:269; Ibn Ḥajar, *Tahdhīb* 1:551. See also Ibn Khallikān, *Wafayāt* 2:244.
11 Al-Bukhārī, *Tārīkh* 3:229; Ibn Abī Ḥātim, *al-Jarḥ wa-l-taʿdīl* 3:405; Wurtzel, *Khalifa ibn Khayyat's History* 9.
12 Wurtzel, *Khalifa ibn Khayyat's History* 1; Zakkār, Ibn Khayyāṭ al-ʿUṣfurī.
13 See the list of Khalīfa's teachers below. Also noted by Wurtzel in *Khalifa ibn Khayyat's History* 1.

died in 240/854.[14] Although the biographical sources offer three different dates for Khalīfa's death (230/845, 240/854, 246/860),[15] the majority of classical and modern scholars consider 240/854 to be the most likely year of his death.[16]

2.3 *Education and Teachers*

In the latter half of the second/eighth century, Basra was one of the main cultural and scholarly centres of the Islamic world. Numerous leading scholars hailed from Basra in this period, including experts in *ḥadīth, fiqh* and other fields. Since both Khalīfa's father and grandfather were *ḥadīth* transmitters and involved in the scholarly circles of Basra, Khalīfa likely received education in such fields from an early age. However, there is no information on Khalīfa's having travelled to study outside Basra. He is not, for example, mentioned in al-Khaṭīb al-Baghdādī's *Tārīkh Baghdād* or Ibn ʿAsākir's *Tārīkh madīnat Dimashq*.[17] On the basis of his sources in the *Tārīkh*, it is also clear that he received most of his material from Basran transmitters.[18] The only evidence of Khalīfa's having left Basra is one report in *Akhbār al-quḍāt* of Wakīʿ (d. 306/917), according to which Khalīfa and other prominent Basrans (*wujūh ahl al-Baṣra*) accompanied the Basran judge Aḥmad b. Riyāḥ (who had been accused by the Muʿtazila) during the *miḥna* to the court of al-Wāthiq (r. 227–232/842–847), presumably in Samarra or Baghdad.[19]

Because of Khalīfa's involvement in *ḥadīth* transmission, the biographical entries include lists of the authorities from whom he transmitted. The vast majority of these authorities were natives of Basra or residents in the city. Many of them are cited in the *Tārīkh* with formulas such as *ḥaddathanā* ('He narrated

---

14 Al-Dhahabī, *Siyar* 1632.

15 Ibn Khallikān, *Wafayāt* 2:244.

16 The year 230/845 is contradicted by information in the *Tārīkh* and the *Ṭabaqāt*, both of which record later events, while the year 246/860 appears only from an unnamed source. The year 240/854, on the other hand, is the date given by Khalīfa's contemporary, Muṭayyan Muḥammad b. ʿAbdallāh (d. 297/909–910), quoted by al-Dhahabī and Ibn Ḥajar, and conventionally accepted by most later writers. Al-Dhahabī states in his *Siyar*, "Muṭayyan and others said: He died in 240/854. I say: He was in his eighties. Whoever said that he died in 246/860 made a mistake." See Khalīfa b. Khayyāṭ, *Tārīkh* (1985) 479–480; al-Dhahabī, *Siyar* 1631–1632; Ibn Ḥajar, *Tahdhīb* 1:551; Ibn Khallikān, *Wafayāt* 2:244; al-Mizzī, *Tahdhīb* 8:319. See also al-ʿUmarī's introduction to Khalīfa's *Tārīkh* (1985) 13–14; Wurtzel, *Khalifa ibn Khayyat's History* 3; Zakkār, Ibn Khayyāṭ al-ʿUṣfurī.

17 See Zakkār's introduction to Khalīfa's *Ṭabaqāt* (1993) 7; Wurtzel, *Khalifa ibn Khayyat's History* 1.

18 See Chapter 4.

19 Wakīʿ, *Akhbār al-quḍāt* 347.

to us') or *akhbaranī* ('He informed me'), indicating direct transmission.[20] The most complete list of teachers, based on earlier sources, is found in al-Mizzī's (d. 742/1341) *Tahdhīb al-kamāl*:[21]

1. Ibrāhīm b. al-Ḥajjāj al-Nīlī (d. 232/846–847)
2. Ibrāhīm b. Ṣāliḥ b. Dirham al-Bāhilī
3. Aḥmad b. Mūsā al-Muqri' (d. c. 191–200/807–816)
4. Isḥāq b. Idrīs (d. c. 201–210/816–826)
5. Abū 'Ubayda Ismā'īl b. Sinān al-'Uṣfurī
6. Ismā'īl b. 'Ulayya (d. 193/809)
7. Ashhal b. Ḥātim (d. 208/823–824)
8. Unays b. Sawwār al-Jarmī
9. Bishr b. al-Mufaḍḍal (d. 187/802–803)
10. Bakr b. Sulaymān (d. c. 191–200/807–816)
11. Bakr b. 'Aṭiyya
12. Ja'far b. 'Awn (d. 206–207/821–822)
13. Ḥātim b. Muslim (d. c. 150/767?)
14. Abū Ṣakhr Ḥashraj b. 'Abdallāh b. Ḥashraj al-Muzanī
15. Ḥammād b. Salama (d. 167/783)[22]
16. Khālid b. al-Ḥārith (d. 186/802)
17. Khayyāṭ b. Khalīfa b. Khayyāṭ (his father)
18. Durust b. Ḥamza
19. Rawḥ b. 'Ubāda (d. 205/820)
20. Rayḥān b. 'Iṣma
21. Ziyād b. 'Abdallāh al-Bakkā'ī (d. 183/799)
22. Sufyān b. 'Uyayna (d. 196/811)
23. Sulaymān b. Ḥarb (d. 224/839)
24. Abū Dāwūd Sulaymān b. Dāwūd al-Ṭayālisī (d. 204/819)
25. Shu'ayb b. Ḥayyān
26. Ṣafwān b. 'Īsā (d. 200/815–816)
27. Abū 'Āṣim al-Ḍaḥḥāk b. Makhlad (d. 212/828)
28. 'Āmir b. Abī 'Āmir al-Khazzāz (d. c. 191–200/807–816)

---

20 See Chapter 5. These formulas were sometimes used for 'giving permission' (*ijāza*) and 'handing over' (*munāwala*), not just 'listening' (*samā'*) and 'reading out to the teacher' (*'arḍ*), but they still indicate that Khalīfa met the individuals from whom he is known to have transmitted. See al-Sakhāwī, *Fatḥ al-Mughīth* 2:483–496.

21 Al-Mizzī, *Tahdhīb* 8:314–316. The dates of death are based on Ibn Sa'd, *Ṭabaqāt*; al-Bukhārī, *Tārīkh*; al-Dhahabī, *Siyar*, *Mīzān*, *Tārīkh al-Islām*; al-Mizzī, *Tahdhīb*; Ibn Ḥajar, *Tahdhīb*.

22 Al-Dhahabī remarks that this is a mistake and that Khalīfa did not transmit from Ḥammād b. Salama. He suggests that the intended narrator might be the Kufan *ḥadīth* transmitter Ḥammād b. Usāma (d. 201/817). Al-Dhahabī, *Siyar* 1632, *Tārīkh al-Islām* 17:152.

29. ʿAbdallāh b. Bakr al-Sahmī (d. 208/823)
30. ʿAbdallāh b. Dāwūd al-Khuraybī (d. 213/828)
31. ʿAbdallāh b. Rajāʾ al-Ghudānī (d. 219–220/834–835)
32. ʿAbdallāh b. Maslama al-Qaʿnabī (d. 221/836)
33. ʿAbdallāh b. al-Mughīra
34. ʿAbdallāh b. Maymūn
35. ʿAbd al-Aʿlā b. ʿAbd al-Aʿlā al-Sāmī (d. 189/805)
36. Abū Baḥr ʿAbd al-Raḥmān b. ʿUthmān al-Bakrāwī (d. 195/810)
37. ʿAbd al-Raḥmān b. Mahdī (d. 198/814)
38. Abū Ẓafar ʿAbd al-Salām b. Muṭahhar (d. 224/839)
39. ʿAbd al-Malik b. Qurayb al-Aṣmaʿī (d. 213/828)
40. ʿAbd al-Wahhāb al-Thaqafī (d. 194/809–810)
41. ʿUbaydallāh b. ʿAbdallāh b. ʿAwn
42. ʿUbaydallāh b. Mūsā (d. 213/829)
43. ʿAththām b. ʿAlī al-ʿĀmirī (d. 194–195/810–811)
44. ʿUthmān b. al-Haytham (d. 220/835)
45. ʿAlī b. ʿĀṣim (d. 201/816)
46. ʿAlī b. ʿAbdallāh al-Madīnī (d. 234/849)
47. Abū l-Ḥasan ʿAlī b. Muḥammad al-Madāʾinī (d. c. 228/843)
48. ʿAmmār b. ʿAmr b. Abī l-Mukhtār
49. ʿUmar b. Abī Khalīfa al-ʿAbdī (d. 189/805)
50. ʿUmar b. ʿAlī al-Muqaddamī (d. 190/806)
51. Ghassān b. Muḍar (d. 184/800)
52. Abū Nuʿaym al-Faḍl b. Dukayn (d. 219/834)
53. Al-Faḍl b. al-ʿAlāʾ (d. 191–200/807–816)
54. Al-Fuḍayl b. Sulaymān (d. 183/799–800)
55. Kathīr b. Hishām (d. 207/822–823)
56. Kahmas b. al-Minhāl
57. Abū Ghassān Mālik b. Ismāʿīl (d. 219/834)
58. Muḥammad b. Jaʿfar Ghundar (d. 193/809)
59. Muḥammad b. al-Ḥasan Maḥbūb (d. c. 201–210/816–26)
60. Muḥammad b. Ḥumrān (d. c. 181–190/797–806)
61. Muḥammad b. al-Zubayr
62. Muḥammad b. Sawāʾ (d. 187/803)
63. Muḥammad b. ʿAbdallāh al-Anṣārī (d. 215/830)
64. Muḥammad b. ʿUthmān al-Qurashī
65. Muḥammad b. Abī ʿAdī (d. 194/810)
66. Muḥammad b. ʿUmar al-Wāqidī (d. 207/822)
67. Muḥammad b. Muʿāwiya
68. Marḥūm b. ʿAbd al-ʿAzīz al-ʿAṭṭār (d. 188/804)

69. Mu'ādh b. Mu'ādh al-'Anbarī (d. 196/811–812)
70. Mu'ādh b. Hishām al-Dastuwānī (d. 200/815)
71. Mu'tamir b. Sulaymān (d. 187/803)
72. Abū Salama Mūsā b. Ismā'īl (d. 223/838)
73. Nūḥ b. Qays al-Ḥuddānī (d. 183–184/799–801)
74. Hārūn b. Dīnār
75. Hubayra b. Ḥudayr al-'Adawī
76. Abū l-Walīd Hishām b. 'Abd al-Malik al-Ṭayālisī (d. 227/841)
77. Wakī' b. al-Jarrāḥ (d. 197/813)
78. Al-Walīd b. Hishām al-Qaḥdhamī (d. 222/836–837)
79. Wahb b. Jarīr b. Ḥāzim (d. 206/822)
80. Abū Ayyūb Yaḥyā b. Abī l-Ḥajjāj al-Khāqānī
81. Yaḥyā b. Sa'īd al-Qaṭṭān (d. 198/813)
82. Yaḥyā b. 'Abbād al-Ḍuba'ī (d. 198/813–814)
83. Yaḥyā b. 'Abd al-Raḥmān
84. Yaḥyā b. Muḥammad al-Ka'bī al-Madanī (d. c. 200/815)
85. Yazīd b. Zuray' (d. 182/798)
86. Yazīd b. Hārūn (d. 206/821)
87. Ya'lā b. 'Ubayd al-Ṭanāfisī (d. 209/825)
88. Yūsuf b. Khālid al-Samtī (d. 189/805)
89. Abū Sa'īd the *mawlā* of Banū Hāshim (d. 197/812–813)
90. Abū l-Yaqẓān al-'Ujayfī (d. 190/806).

Whether or not Khalīfa left Basra to study, this list shows that he received most of his knowledge in Basra from Basran scholars. Moreover, the number of major *ḥadīth* scholars among these teachers confirms his close affiliation with the Basran *ḥadīth* circles.[23] Besides Khalīfa's expertise in *ḥadīth* and *akhbār*, Ibn al-Jazarī (d. 833/1429) mentions him as a transmitter of Qur'ān readings (*qirā'āt*), which he must also have studied in Basra.[24]

2.4 *Students*

Khalīfa not only transmitted from numerous prominent *ḥadīth* scholars but also passed on his material to major scholars in the generation after him. Again, al-Mizzī provides the most complete list of those who transmitted *ḥadīth* from Khalīfa:[25]

1. Muḥammad b. Ismā'īl al-Bukhārī (d. 256/870)
2. Ibrāhīm b. 'Abdallāh b. al-Junayd al-Khuttalī (d. c. 270/883–884)

---

23 For more details on Khalīfa's sources, see Chapter 4.

24 Ibn al-Jazarī, *Ghāyat al-nihāya* 1:248–249.

25 Al-Mizzī, *Tahdhīb* 8:316–317.

3. Ibrāhīm b. Fahd al-Sājī
4. Ibrāhīm b. Muḥammad b. al-Ḥārith b. Nā'ila al-Aṣbahānī (d. 291/903–904)
5. Aḥmad b. Bashīr al-Ṭayālisī (d. 295/908)
6. Aḥmad b. al-Ḥusayn b. Naṣr al-Ḥadhdhā' al-Baghdādī
7. Abū Ya'lā Aḥmad b. 'Alī b. al-Muthannā al-Mawṣilī (d. 307/919)
8. Aḥmad b. 'Alī al-Abbār (d. 290/903)
9. Abū Bakr Aḥmad b. 'Amr b. Abī 'Āṣim al-Nabīl (d. 287/900)
10. Aḥmad b. Yazīd al-Ḥulwānī (d. c. 250/864)
11. Baqī b. Makhlad (d. 276/889)
12. Ḥarb b. Ismā'īl al-Kirmānī (d. 280/893)
13. Al-Ḥasan b. Isḥāq al-'Aṭṭār (d. 272/885)
14. Al-Ḥasan b. Sufyān al-Shaybānī (d. 303/916)
15. Al-Ḥasan b. Shujā' al-Balkhī (d. 244/859)
16. Al-Ḥasan b. 'Alī b. Shabīb al-Ma'marī (d. 295/907)
17. Al-Ḥusayn b. 'Alī al-'Aṭṭār al-Miṣṣīṣī
18. Al-Ḥusayn b. Muḥammad al-Ḥurānī (d. 318/930)
19. 'Abdallāh b. Aḥmad b. Ḥanbal (d. 290/903)
20. 'Abdallāh b. 'Abd al-Raḥmān al-Dārimī (d. 255/869)
21. 'Abdallāh b. Muḥammad b. Nājiya (d. 301/914)
22. 'Abd al-Raḥmān b. Ma'dān b. Jum'a al-Lādhiqī (d. c. 281–290/894–903)
23. 'Abdān al-Ahwāzī (d. 306/919)
24. Abū Zur'a 'Ubaydallāh b. 'Abd al-Karīm al-Rāzī (d. 264/878)
25. 'Alī b. Zakariyyā al-Qaṭī'ī al-Tammār (d. 267/880–881)
26. 'Umar b. Aḥmad al-Ahwāzī
27. 'Umar b. Abī 'Umar al-Balkhī
28. Abū Ḥātim Muḥammad b. Idrīs al-Rāzī (d. 277/890)
29. Muḥammad b. Isḥāq al-Ṣāghānī (d. 270/883)
30. Muḥammad b. Bishr b. Maṭar (d. 285/898)
31. Muḥammad b. Bakr b. 'Amr b. Rufay'
32. Muḥammad b. 'Abdūs al-Ahwāzī al-Ṣā'igh
33. Muḥammad b. Ghālib b. Ḥarb Tamtām (d. 283/896)
34. Muḥammad b. Yazīd al-Mustamlī (d. c. 251–260/865–874)
35. Mūsā b. Zakariyyā al-Tustarī (d. before 300/912)
36. Ya'qūb b. Shayba al-Sadūsī (d. 262/875)

In addition to these scholars who transmitted *ḥadīth* from Khalīfa, Ibn al-Jazarī mentions that Aḥmad b. Ibrāhīm b. 'Uthmān al-Warrāq and al-Mughīra b. Ṣadaqa studied Qur'ān readings under Khalīfa.[26] The above list includes many

26 Ibn al-Jazarī, *Ghāyat al-nihāya* 1:248–249.

major *ḥadīth* scholars and well-known representatives of the *ahl al-ḥadīth*, such as al-Bukhārī, al-Dārimī, Baqī b. Makhlad, Abū Ḥātim al-Rāzī, Abū Zurʿa al-Rāzī, ʿAbdallāh b. Aḥmad b. Ḥanbal, Ḥarb b. Ismāʿīl al-Kirmānī, al-Ḥasan b. Shujāʿ al-Balkhī, Muḥammad b. Isḥāq al-Ṣāghānī and al-Ḥasan b. ʿAlī b. Shabīb al-Maʿmarī. The scholarly affiliations of these students indicate that Khalīfa, too, was associated with the *ahl al-ḥadīth*.

3 Works

A number of compilations are ascribed to Khalīfa in the biographical notices. The earliest reference is found in *al-Jarḥ wa-l-taʿdīl* of Ibn Abī Ḥātim (d. 327/938), in which he cites his father, who mentions a *musnad* (*ḥadīth* collection arranged by transmitters) belonging to Khalīfa.[27] The earliest writer to mention the *Tārīkh* and the *Ṭabaqāt* is Ibn ʿAdī (d. 365/975), who also adds that Khalīfa knew a lot of *ḥadīth*.[28] In the *Fihrist*, Ibn al-Nadīm (d. 385/995 or 388/998) lists the following compilations:[29]

1. *Al-Ṭabaqāt* ('The Book of Generations')
2. *Al-Tārīkh* ('The Chronicle')
3. *Ṭabaqāt al-qurrāʾ* ('The Generations of the Qurʾān Reciters')
4. *Tārīkh al-zamnā wa-l-ʿurjān wa-l-marḍā wa-l-ʿumyān* ('The History of the Chronically Ill, the Lame, the Diseased and the Blind')
5. *Ajzāʾ al-Qurʾān wa-aʿshāruhu wa-asbāʿuhu wa-ayātuhu* ('The Thirtieths, Tenths, Sevenths and Verses of the Qurʾān')

Zakkār suggests that *Ṭabaqāt al-qurrāʾ* is the same as the extant *Ṭabaqāt*.[30] The only references to *Ṭabaqāt al-qurraʾ* in later works appear to be a few narrations in Ibn ʿAsākir's *Tārīkh madīnat Dimashq* and al-Mizzī's and Ibn Ḥajar's biographical entries on Saʿīd b. Abī l-Ḥasan al-Baṣrī, where they state that "Khalīfa b. Khayyāṭ mentioned him in the second generation of the Basran Qurʾān reciters (*al-ṭabaqat al-thāniya min qurrāʾ ahl al-Baṣra*)."[31] In addition to Ibn al-Nadīm's list, Ismāʿīl Pāshā al-Baghdādī (d. 1339/1920) mentions a *musnad* collection of *ḥadīth* among Khalīfa's compilations, which might be based

27 Ibn Abī Ḥātim, *al-Jarḥ wa-l-taʿdīl* 3:378.

28 Ibn ʿAdī, *Kāmil* 3:935.

29 Ibn al-Nadīm, *Fihrist* 2:111.

30 Zakkār, Ibn Khayyāṭ al-ʿUṣfurī.

31 Al-Daʿjānī, *Mawārid Ibn ʿAsākir* 1:439–440; al-Mizzī, *Tahdhīb* 10:386; Ibn Ḥajar, *Tahdhīb* 2:12. Noted by al-ʿUmarī in his introduction to Khalīfa's *Tārīkh* (1985) 13. Khalīfa lists the same person in the third generation of Basrans in the *Ṭabaqāt* (1993) 360.

on Abū Ḥātim's aforementioned reference to a *musnad*.[32] Most later sources, however, only mention the *Tārīkh* and the *Ṭabaqāt*, which are Khalīfa's most famous works by far.[33] It is therefore worth discussing these two works in some detail and, in particular, their value as sources for Khalīfa's scholarly activities.

3.1 Al-Ṭabaqāt

Khalīfa's *Ṭabaqāt* is one of the oldest biographical dictionaries of *ḥadīth* transmitters still extant—perhaps only preceded by the *Ṭabaqāt* of his contemporary, Muḥammad b. Saʿd (d. 230/845).[34] The extant recension was transmitted from Khalīfa by Mūsā b. Zakariyyā al-Tustarī towards the end of Khalīfa's life (the last recorded date of a death is 236/850–851). It contains biographies of approximately 3,375 individuals—mostly men, but also a section of 129 women—who had been cited in *ḥadīth* scholarship down to Khalīfa's own time. The *Ṭabaqāt* is structured according to three principles of arrangement: genealogy, generations and locations. Khalīfa begins with the Prophet Muḥammad, followed by his uncle al-ʿAbbās, and then the rest of the Companions from Banū Hāshim, then Banū Umayya and then from the other Arab tribes. Thereafter, he lists the major cities and regions in which the Companions settled: Kufa, Basra, Medina, Mecca, Egypt, Syria and so forth. He continues with the Successors and the following generations in each of the different cities and lists them according to genealogy and generations. The work concludes with a section on the female Companions who transmitted *ḥadīth*s from the Prophet. The biographical entries are very brief, and Khalīfa seldom provides more information than name, location and occasionally a date of birth and death—apart from some extra information on certain Companions and Successors, such as what *ḥadīth*s they were known to have transmitted. However, unlike Ibn Saʿd and some other later *ḥadīth* scholars who compiled *ṭabaqāt* collections, Khalīfa does not include transmitter criticism (*jarḥ wa-taʿdīl*).[35]

In relation to the issue of Khalīfa's context and scholarly activity, Khalīfa evidently compiled the *Ṭabaqāt* for an audience of *ḥadīth* scholars. After tracing the Prophet's lineage, for example, Khalīfa continues with the biographical entries of "his Companions, from whom *ḥadīth*s have been preserved, who

---

32 Ismāʿīl Pāshā al-Baghdādī, *Hadiyyat al-ʿārifīn* 1:350.

33 Ibn ʿAdī, *Kāmil* 3:935; Ibn Khallikān, *Wafayāt* 2:243; al-Dhahabī, *Siyar* 1631; Ibn Ḥajar, *Tahdhīb* 1:551.

34 On the transmission history of Ibn Saʿd's *Ṭabaqāt* and the later additions to the text, see Atassi, Transmission of Ibn Saʿd's biographical dictionary.

35 See also the comparison between the *ṭabaqāt* works of Ibn Saʿd, Khalīfa and Muslim b. al-Ḥajjāj in the editor Abū ʿUbayda Mashhūr b. Ḥasan's introduction to Muslim, *Ṭabaqāt* 33–55.

stayed in Medina or went elsewhere."[36] Similarly, Khalīfa introduces the section on women as a "list of the women whose *ḥadīths* from the Prophet (ṣ) have been preserved."[37] Moreover, Khalīfa sometimes points out what *ḥadīths* certain transmitters were known for, usually by citing the first words of the *ḥadīth* or by referring to its content. For example:

> **26. ʿUbayd the *mawlā* of the Messenger of God (ṣ)**
> His *ḥadīth* is: "The Messenger of God (ṣ) used to order us to pray [optional prayers] between the sunset prayer (*al-maghrib*) and the evening prayer (*al-ʿishāʾ*)." He also narrated other *ḥadīths*.
>
> **27. Abū ʿUbayd the servant of the Messenger of God (ṣ)**
> His *ḥadīth* is: "I once cooked a pot [of meat] for the Messenger of God (ṣ) and he said, 'Pass me the foreleg.'"
>
> **28. Abū ʿAsīb the *mawlā* of the Messenger of God (ṣ)**
> He narrated two *ḥadīths* [not cited in the *Ṭabaqāt*].[38]

In the sections on the Successors, Khalīfa sometimes mentions from which Companions they narrated *ḥadīth* and, in the sections on later generations, he sometimes remarks on certain tribes among whom there were no known *ḥadīth* transmitters (*laysa fīhim aḥad*).[39] This focus on *ḥadīth* transmission, alongside the references to specific *ḥadīths*, indicates not only an extensive preoccupation with *ḥadīth* scholarship but also a high level of expertise in both *ḥadīth* and *ʿilm al-rijāl*.[40] It is also worth noting that, as with the *Tārīkh*, Khalīfa mainly narrates from Basran transmitters in the *Ṭabaqāt*, which confirms the Basran *ḥadīth* circles as the main context of his scholarly activities.[41] The relatively limited attention Khalīfa pays to Ḥanafī, Mālikī and Shāfiʿī scholars in the *Ṭabaqāt*, or at least the absence of focus on one particular legal school (*madhhab*), might also indicate an affiliation to the Iraqi *ahl al-ḥadīth*.[42]

---

36 Khalīfa b. Khayyāṭ, *Ṭabaqāt* (1993) 29.

37 Khalīfa b. Khayyāṭ, *Ṭabaqāt* (1993) 619.

38 Khalīfa b. Khayyāṭ, *Ṭabaqāt* (1993) 34.

39 Khalīfa b. Khayyāṭ, *Ṭabaqāt* (1993) 333, 407, 430.

40 Melchert also highlights Khalīfa's interest in *ḥadīth*. How Ḥanafism came to originate in Kufa 323.

41 See Khalīfa's list of his transmitters in the *Ṭabaqāt* (1993) 25.

42 See Melchert, How Ḥanafism came to originate in Kufa 323–324. Ibn al-Nadīm also counts Khalīfa among the *aṣḥāb al-ḥadīth* rather than any of the other legal schools. *Fihrist* 2:111.

3.2 Al-Tārīkh

Khalīfa's *Tārīkh* is the oldest Islamic chronicle still extant.[43] Some earlier historians are credited with caliphal or annalistic chronicles, but none of these earlier works has survived.[44] The surviving recension of the *Tārīkh* was transmitted by Baqī b. Makhlad al-Qurṭubī. It is arranged chronologically, beginning, after a short introduction, with 1/622 and ending with 232/847. It covers the political and administrative history of the Muslim polity, from its origins in Medina at the time of the Prophet, via the first caliphs that succeeded him, to the Umayyad and ʿAbbāsid caliphates. In relation to the question of Khalīfa's own biography and scholarly context, the *Tārīkh* shows, first, that Khalīfa received most of his historical reports from Basran transmitters, many of whom were prominent *ḥadīth* scholars.[45] Second, Khalīfa's scholarly methods, selection of reports and historical perspective in the *Tārīkh* show that he not only frequented the Basran *ḥadīth* circles but also shared the *ḥadīth* scholars' early Sunnī approach and historical views.[46] These aspects of the *Tārīkh* will be discussed in detail in the following chapters, but they are worth noting here as they confirm that Khalīfa's occupation was with *ḥadīth* scholarship and that the Basran *ḥadīth* circles were the main audience for the *Tārīkh* and the *Ṭabaqāt*.

4 Scholarly Reputation

4.1 *Third/Ninth- and Fourth/Tenth-Century Scholars*

The earliest transmitter critics of the third/ninth and fourth/tenth centuries generally focus on Khalīfa's *ḥadīth* transmission, while later sources also discuss his knowledge of history, genealogy and *ʿilm al-rijāl*. The early critics differ in their opinions about Khalīfa's status as transmitter—some criticising his transmission, and others considering him reliable (*thiqa*) or sincere (*ṣadūq*)—but their remarks altogether indicate that he was a known *ḥadīth* scholar associated with the *ahl al-ḥadīth*. His association with the *ahl al-ḥadīth* is corroborated by Ibn al-Nadīm's *Fihrist*, in which Khalīfa is counted among the 'traditionist jurisprudents and *aṣḥāb al-ḥadīth*' (*fuqahāʾ al-muḥaddithīn wa-aṣḥāb*

43 One might also include the *Tārīkh* of ʿAbd al-Malik b. Ḥabīb (d. 238/853), which must have been compiled at a similar time, although there has been some discussion whether the extant version is complete or not. See Chapter 3 and Aguadé's introduction to Ibn Ḥabīb, *Tārīkh* 77–108.

44 Robinson, *Islamic historiography* 47.

45 See Chapter 4.

46 See Chapters 5–8.

al-ḥadīth) rather than among the 'historians and genealogists' (*al-akhbārīyūn wa-l-nassābūn*) or the scholars of the other legal schools (*madhāhib*).[47]

A few negative remarks about Khalīfa's status as *ḥadīth* transmitter are narrated from third/ninth-century critics who were his contemporaries.[48] 'Alī b. al-Madīnī (d. 234/849) is reported to have stated, "If Shabāb [i.e. Khalīfa] had not transmitted *ḥadīth*, it would have been better for him."[49] Similarly, Yaḥyā b. Maʿīn (d. 233/848) is reported to have said that Khalīfa, Ibn Abī Samīna and 'Ubaydallāh b. Muʿādh b. Muʿādh al-ʿAnbarī "were not specialists in *ḥadīth* (*laysū aṣḥāb ḥadīth*)."[50] Other criticism of Khalīfa is found in Ibn Abī Ḥātim's *al-Jarḥ wa-l-taʿdīl*. He narrates that his father, Abū Ḥātim al-Rāzī (d. 277/890), said about Khalīfa, "I do not transmit from him; he is not strong (*ghayr qawī*)."[51] He also relates that Abū Zurʿa al-Rāzī (d. 264/878) refrained from reading out *ḥadīth*s that he had received from Khalīfa.[52] Al-ʿUqaylī (d. 322/934) likewise included Khalīfa in his work on weak transmitters, *Kitāb al-Ḍuʿafāʾ al-kabīr*.[53]

Some early critics were more positive about Khalīfa's capacity as a *ḥadīth* transmitter. The earliest is al-Bukhārī (d. 256/870), who cites Khalīfa 21 times in *al-Jāmiʿ al-ṣaḥīḥ*.[54] However, Ibn Ḥajar points out that al-Bukhārī's narrations from Khalīfa in his *Ṣaḥīḥ* usually corroborate, and are corroborated by, parallel *isnād*s, and when he narrates from Khalīfa alone, he 'suspends' his narrations (*ʿallaqa aḥādīthahu*) and simply introduces them with "Khalīfa said to me" (*qāla lī Khalīfa*) rather than with "He narrated to me" (*ḥaddathanī*).[55]

47 Ibn al-Nadīm, *Fihrist* 2:111.

48 On the terminology of the *ḥadīth* transmitter critics, see al-Sakhāwī, *Fatḥ al-Mughīth* 2:277–301; al-Laknawī, *al-Rafʿ wa-l-takmīl* 129–186 (with 'Abd al-Fattāḥ Abū Ghudda's footnotes); al-Ghawrī, *Muʿjam* 129–698.

49 Ibn ʿAdī, *Kāmil* 3:935.

50 Ibn al-Junayd al-Khuttalī, *Suʾālāt* 290–291.

51 Ibn Abī Ḥātim, *al-Jarḥ wa-l-taʿdīl* 3:378. Al-Dhahabī notes that "when Abū Ḥātim says, 'He is not strong (*laysa bi-l-qawī*),' he means that this *shaykh* did not reach the level of the strong and firmly reliable (*darajat al-qawī al-thabt*)." Al-Dhahabī, *al-Mūqiẓa* 83.

52 Ibn Abī Ḥātim, *al-Jarḥ wa-l-taʿdīl* 3:378–379.

53 Al-ʿUqaylī, *al-Ḍuʿafāʾ* 2:22.

54 For the citations of Khalīfa in al-Bukhārī's *Ṣaḥīḥ*, see Appendix. See also al-ʿUmarī's introduction to Khalīfa b. Khayyāṭ, *Tārīkh* (1985) 8–9.

55 Ibn Ḥajar, *Tahdhīb* 1:551. See also al-Bājī, *al-Taʿdīl wa-l-tajrīḥ* 2:570. For a discussion about al-Bukhārī's 'suspended' narrations (*muʿallaqāt*) and his use of different transmission formulas (*ḥaddathanī, qāla lī* etc.), see Ibn Ḥajar, *al-Nukat* 599–601. There is one instance in the *Ṣaḥīḥ* where al-Bukhārī uses the formula "Khalīfa narrated to me" (*ḥaddathanī Khalīfa*) without corroboration, but that report is a short non-Prophetic report (i.e. not a Prophetic *ḥadīth*) about a Companion, Abū Zayd, and his participation in the Battle of Badr. See no. 7 in Appendix.

This indicates that al-Bukhārī considered Khalīfa's transmission acceptable for corroboration of other narrations, but not on the same level as the main reliable authorities (*thiqāt*) from whom he narrated without corroboration in his *Ṣaḥīḥ*.[56]

An explicit defence of Khalīfa's status as a reliable transmitter is found in *al-Kāmil fī ḍuʿafāʾ al-rijāl* of Ibn ʿAdī (d. 365/976). Ibn ʿAdī dismisses the report about Ibn al-Madīnī's criticism of Khalīfa on grounds that its transmitter, Muḥammad b. Yūnus al-Kudaymī (d. 286/899), was unreliable and even accused of lying and forging *ḥadīth*,[57] and argues that Ibn al-Madīnī would not have said such things about Khalīfa. He then adds:

> Shabāb was among the observant *ḥadīth* transmitters (*mutayaqqiẓī ruwāt al-ḥadīth*) and had numerous *ḥadīth*s as well as an excellent work on chronography (*tārīkh ḥasan*) and a work on the generations of transmitters (*ṭabaqāt fī l-rijāl*). How could anyone believe this story of what ʿAlī [b. al-Madīnī] supposedly said about him when he was one of ʿAlī's companions (*aṣḥāb*)?

Ibn ʿAdī concludes that Khalīfa was upright in *ḥadīth* transmission and sincere (*mustaqīm al-ḥadīth ṣadūq*).[58] Khalīfa is likewise counted among the reliable narrators in *Kitāb al-Thiqāt* of Ibn Ḥibbān (d. 354/965), who adds that he was accurate (*mutqin*) and particularly knowledgeable about history and genealogy (*ʿālim bi-ayyām al-nās wa-ansābihim*).[59] Moreover, Ibn Ḥibbān narrates three reports with *isnād*s going through Khalīfa in his *Ṣaḥīḥ*.[60] Maslama b. al-Qāsim al-Andalusī (d. 353/964) also said about Khalīfa, "There is no problem with him (*lā baʾs bihi*)."[61]

Altogether, it is clear that there were some discussions and disagreements regarding Khalīfa's status as a *ḥadīth* transmitter among the early critics. Some prominent third/ninth-century scholars were critical of his *ḥadīth* transmission, although al-Bukhārī considered Khalīfa's narrations acceptable and at least good enough to cite in corroboration of other narrations in his *Ṣaḥīḥ*. In the fourth/tenth century, a couple of generations after Khalīfa, there were oth-

---

56 See al-ʿUmarī's discussion in his introduction to Khalīfa's *Tārīkh* (1985) 8–9.

57 Ibn ʿAdī, *Kāmil* 6:2294–2296. See also al-Dhahabī, *Siyar* 3787–3788; Ibn Ḥajar, *Tahdhīb* 3:741–743.

58 Ibn ʿAdī, *Kāmil* 3:935.

59 Ibn Ḥibbān, *Thiqāt* 8:233.

60 Ibn Ḥibbān, *Ṣaḥīḥ* 1:281, 3:160, 12:12.

61 Mughalṭāy, *Ikmāl* 4:215; Ibn Ḥajar, *Tahdhīb* 1:551.

ers who came to regard him as reliable (*thiqa*) or sincere (*ṣadūq*), including Ibn Ḥibbān and Ibn ʿAdī. However, as both Ibn Ḥibbān and Ibn ʿAdī indicate in their biographical notices, Khalīfa's main accomplishment as a scholar was not his *ḥadīth* transmission but rather his two outstanding compilations of history and *ʿilm al-rijāl*: the *Tārīkh* and the *Ṭabaqāt*.[62] This was also what Khalīfa would be remembered for among later Sunnī scholars.

4.2 *Later Scholars*

Later assessments of Khalīfa's status are found in a wide range of works, including biographical dictionaries, works of transmitter criticism and texts on specific subjects. Most of these sources praise Khalīfa especially for his erudition in the fields of history, genealogy and *ʿilm al-rijāl*. For instance, the Andalusian Ibn ʿAbd al-Barr (d. 463/1070) includes him among the most important scholars of history (*tawārīkh*), biography (*siyar*) and genealogy (*ansāb*).[63] Another Andalusian scholar, Abū Bakr b. al-ʿArabī al-Maʿāfirī (d. 543/1148), mentions Khalīfa in *al-ʿAwāṣim min al-qawāṣim* as one of the *imāms* of historical knowledge to be relied upon (in that specific case, regarding the Battle of Ṣiffīn).[64] Among the scholars in Greater Syria, Ibn al-Athīr (d. 630/1233) praises Khalīfa's knowledge of history and also mentions the disagreements about his reliability as a *ḥadīth* transmitter.[65] Yaḥyā b. Sharaf al-Nawawī (d. 676/1277), says about Khalīfa in his biographical dictionary, *Tahdhīb al-asmāʾ wa-l-lughāt*:

> As for the names and the states of their people, I have only transmitted from the books of the leading scholars of outstanding mastery and knowledge (*al-aʾimmat al-ḥuffāẓ al-aʿlām*), who are well-known for their precedence (*imāma*) in this field and those relied-upon by all scholars—such as the *tārīkh* works of al-Bukhārī, Ibn Abī Khaythama and Khalīfa b. Khayyāṭ, known as Shabāb.[66]

Al-Nawawī's mentioning of Khalīfa, next to al-Bukhārī and Ibn Abī Khaythama, as one of the most important scholars of *ʿilm al-rijāl* again shows his high rank in this field in the eyes of later Sunnī scholars. Similarly, Ibn Khallikān (d. 681/1282) praises Khalīfa for his memorisation and knowledge of history

62 Ibn ʿAdī, *Kāmil* 3:935.
63 Ibn ʿAbd al-Barr, *al-Istīʿāb* 1:20, 22.
64 Ibn al-ʿArabī, *al-ʿAwāṣim* 308.
65 Ibn al-Athīr, *al-Lubāb* 2:344.
66 Al-Nawawī, *Tahdhīb al-asmāʾ* 1:6.

(*kāna ḥāfiẓan ʿārifan bi-l-tawārīkh wa-ayyām al-nās*), and lists a few major *ḥadīth* scholars who transmitted from him.[67] According to al-Dhahabī (d. 748/1348), Khalīfa was sincere (*ṣadūq*) in his transmission and especially knowledgeable about genealogy and history.[68] He also mentions that some of the earlier critics declared him reliable (*waththaqahu baʿḍuhum*), while others, without proof, declared him 'lenient' (*layyanahu baʿḍuhum bi-lā ḥujja*).[69] Al-Mizzī and Mughalṭāy b. Qalīj (d. 762/1361) also note the differences of opinion among earlier critics regarding Khalīfa's status as transmitter, but without explicitly providing any definitive opinion on his transmission.[70] Ibn Ḥajar al-ʿAsqalānī says about Khalīfa, "He was sincere (*ṣadūq*), but sometimes made mistakes (*rubbamā akhṭaʾa*), and he was a very learned historian (*akhbārī ʿallāma*)."[71]

5 Khalīfa's *Tārīkh* in Later Scholarship

A clear indication of Khalīfa's prominence among later scholars in the fields of history and biography are the citations of him in their works. This section discusses the usage of Khalīfa's *Tārīkh* in scholarship between the fourth/tenth and ninth/fifteenth centuries. The purpose is not to compare individual citations in different works as others have done,[72] but to outline which scholars used the *Tārīkh* and for what purposes. This shows that Khalīfa's *Tārīkh* was used mainly for biographical and chronological information, but also for some political history, in al-Andalus, Greater Syria and Egypt by Sunnī scholars of similar scholarly and historical outlook to Khalīfa.[73]

After the transmission from Khalīfa, Baqī b. Makhlad's recension of the *Tārīkh* began to circulate among the scholars of al-Andalus and north-west Africa, while al-Tustarī's recension circulated in Greater Syria and Egypt.[74] In

67 Ibn Khallikān, *Wafayāt* 2:243.
68 Al-Dhahabī, *Siyar* 1632.
69 Al-Dhahabī, *Siyar* 1632. On the term *layyin*, see al-Sakhāwī, *Fatḥ al-Mughīth* 2:295; al-Laknawī, *al-Rafʿ wa-l-takmīl* 143–146, 154, 182–183; al-Ghawrī, *Muʿjam* 594.
70 Al-Mizzī, *Tahdhīb* 8:317–318; Mughalṭāy, *Ikmāl* 2:215–217.
71 Ibn Ḥajar, *Taqrīb* 301. See also his *Tahdhīb* 1:551.
72 As Wurtzel did in *Khalifa ibn Khayyat's History* 39–46, based on the annotations of Zakkār and al-ʿUmarī in their respective editions. The following discussion is based on Wurtzel's results.
73 On Khalīfa's views, see Chapters 3–8.
74 Wurtzel, *Khalifa ibn Khayyat's History* 39–46.

addition, a few passages from Khalīfa's *Tārīkh* are found in the works of early scholars such as Yazīd b. Muḥammad al-Azdī (d. 334/946), Abū l-Shaykh al-Aṣbahānī (d. 369/979) and Abū Nuʿaym al-Aṣbahānī (d. 430/1039), but it is not clear from where they received their information.[75] However, all of them were Sunnī scholars of *ḥadīth*, which is evidence that, from an early date, Khalīfa's *Tārīkh* was transmitted and used mainly among Sunnī scholars, many of them experts in *ḥadīth*.[76]

5.1 *Al-Andalus*

The earliest known citations of Baqī b. Makhlad's transmission of the *Tārīkh* are found in *al-ʿIqd al-farīd* of the Andalusian poet and littérateur Ibn ʿAbd Rabbih (d. 328/940). He cites Khalīfa a number of times, sometimes just in a couple of sentences and sometimes longer passages, but overall in a manner very close to Baqī's extant recension of the *Tārīkh*, apart from some paraphrases and summaries.[77] Ibn ʿAbd Rabbih's work is an encyclopaedic *adab* compilation of literature and general cultural knowledge with material drawn from the works of al-Jāḥiẓ, Ibn Qutayba and other *adab* compilers—in other words, quite different from Khalīfa's *Tārīkh*. It shows that Khalīfa's *Tārīkh* was known outside *ḥadīth* circles, but, as outlined below, that it nonetheless circulated mainly among *ḥadīth* scholars.

A minor citation from Baqī's recension is also found in *Riyāḍ al-nufūs* of the North African Mālikī scholar Abū Bakr ʿAbdallāh b. Muḥammad al-Mālikī (d. after 453/1061), in which he combines small portions from Khalīfa's *Tārīkh* dealing with an expedition in North Africa.[78] Otherwise, one of the Andalusian scholars who used Baqī's recension the most was the *ḥadīth* master and Mālikī jurist Ibn ʿAbd al-Barr, who lists Khalīfa among his sources in *al-Istīʿāb fī*

75 Wurtzel, *Khalifa ibn Khayyat's History* 40–42. Al-Azdī cites some of Khalīfa's material on the authority of Ibn Muḥammad b. Isḥāq, who might have transmitted the *Tārīkh* to al-Azdī, but it is also possible that the latter had access only to some individual reports from Khalīfa, not the entire *Tārīkh*. See Al-Azdī, *Tārīkh al-Mawṣil* 188–189. Abū l-Shaykh al-Aṣbahānī cites a passage that is found in Khalīfa's *Tārīkh*, but he does not specify how he received it from Khalīfa. See Abū l-Shaykh al-Aṣbahānī, *Ṭabaqāt al-muḥaddithīn* 1:256; Khalīfa b. Khayyāṭ, *Tārīkh* (1985) 161. Abū Nuʿaym also cites a passage in *Dhikr akhbār Aṣbahān* that is found in Khalīfa's *Tārīkh*, but he does not specify how he received it from Khalīfa. See Abū Nuʿaym al-Aṣbahānī, *Dhikr akhbār Aṣbahān* 1:61; Khalīfa b. Khayyāṭ, *Tārīkh* (1985) 161.

76 On these three, see al-Dhahabī, *Tadhkira* 894–895, 945–947, 1092–1098.

77 Wurtzel, *Khalifa ibn Khayyat's History* 41.

78 Al-Mālikī, *Riyāḍ al-nufūs* 11; Khalīfa b. Khayyāṭ, *Tārīkh* (1985) 159; Wurtzel, *Khalifa ibn Khayyat's History* 42.

maʿrifat al-aṣḥāb.[79] He also mentions that he read the *Tārīkh* in two narrations from Baqī b. Makhlad—one of which, as Wurtzel points out, may refer to the *Ṭabaqāt*.[80]

Another leading Andalusian scholar of *fiqh* and *ḥadīth* who used Khalīfa's *Tārīkh* is Abū Bakr b. al-ʿArabī.[81] He narrates two paragraphs from the *Tārīkh*, regarding the Battle of Ṣiffīn and the subsequent arbitration, in *al-ʿAwāṣim min al-qawāṣim*. The material is an abridgement of a part of Khalīfa's account of the battle, which Ibn al-ʿArabī introduces by stating, "What is correct about this is what the *imām*s, such as Khalīfa b. Khayyāṭ and al-Dāraquṭnī, have said about it."[82] Apart from this instance, he does not cite Khalīfa by name, although other material seems to be derived from Khalīfa's *Tārīkh*.[83] The single citation and appraisal of Khalīfa is significant, however, as Ibn al-ʿArabī is well-known for his unabashedly Sunnī historical views. Ibn al-ʿArabī's use of Khalīfa corresponds to his attempt to defend the early generations of Muslims from Shīʿī accusations and to establish a Sunnī perspective on the early conflicts based on what he deemed the most reliable reports. This indicates that Khalīfa's early Sunnī perspective on these events was indeed appreciated and understood by at least some Andalusian Sunnī scholars, for whom Khalīfa was, as Abū Bakr b. al-ʿArabī puts it, one of the *imām*s of historical knowledge.[84]

5.2 *Greater Syria and Egypt*

Al-Tustarī's transmission of Khalīfa's *Tārīkh* became popular in Greater Syria and Egypt, where many scholars used it in historical and biographical works. One of those who used it most was Ibn ʿAsākir, in his *Tārīkh madīnat Dimashq*, where he cites Khalīfa numerous times on the authority of al-Tustarī. Most texts from Khalīfa are identical or very close to the extant recension transmitted by Baqī b. Makhlad and are only occasionally paraphrased or abridged.[85] However, there are also a number of narrations that are not found in Baqī's recension, which suggests that Khalīfa transmitted slightly different versions of the *Tārīkh* at different times to different students and that some changes might have occurred in the course of transmission.[86] Similar to the Andalusian schol-

79 Ibn ʿAbd al-Barr, *al-Istīʿāb* 1:20.

80 Ibn ʿAbd al-Barr, *al-Istīʿāb* 1:22; Wurtzel, *Khalifa ibn Khayyat's History* 43.

81 Al-Dhahabī, *Tadhkira* 1294–1298; Ibn Khallikān, *Wafayāt* 4:296–297. See also Robson, Ibn al-ʿArabī.

82 Ibn al-ʿArabī, *al-ʿAwāṣim* 308.

83 See e.g. Khalīfa b. Khayyāṭ, *Tārīkh* (1985) 213–217; Ibn al-ʿArabī, *al-ʿAwāṣim* 327–332.

84 See also Ibn ʿAbd al-Barr's words about Khalīfa in *al-Istīʿāb* 1:20, 22.

85 Wurtzel, *Khalifa ibn Khayyat's History* 43; Judd, Ibn ʿAsākir's sources 86. See also Chapter 1.

86 See Chapter 1.

ars, Ibn ʿAsākir was a major Sunnī scholar of *ḥadīth*, who used Khalīfa's *Tārīkh*, alongside his *Ṭabaqāt*, as a key source of early Islamic history. As Judd notes, Ibn ʿAsākir's preference for Khalīfa over al-Ṭabarī suggests that he understood the agendas of the earlier historians and chose material that fitted his particular needs.[87]

A few citations of the *Tārīkh* are found in the *Muʿjam al-buldān* of Yāqūt al-Ḥamawī (d. 626/1229),[88] who frequented the Syrian region throughout his life and died in Aleppo.[89] He cites Khalīfa three times by name, but Wurtzel notes that he might have cited him elsewhere without mentioning the source.[90] Unlike most other Syrians mentioned here, Yāqūt was known not as a scholar of *ḥadīth* but rather as a biographer and geographer. As with the citations by Ibn ʿAbd Rabbih, this shows that Khalīfa's *Tārīkh* was known outside *ḥadīth* circles but that it was still used mainly by *ḥadīth* scholars.

Another Sunnī *ḥadīth* scholar and historian who seems to have used Khalīfa's *Tārīkh* is Ibn al-Athīr, who was born in Mosul but stayed at times in Aleppo and Damascus.[91] Ibn al-Athīr does not mention Khalīfa's name, but many passages appear to be taken from the *Tārīkh*. Wurtzel concludes that if these passages are not from Khalīfa, they at least derive from a common source.[92] Most of that material concerns the Khazar wars and expeditions in the Transcaucasus, North Africa and the Roman frontiers, but there are also some passages about Muʿāwiya and ʿAbd al-Malik b. Marwān.[93]

The leading Syria-based *faqīh* and *muḥaddith*, Yaḥyā b. Sharaf al-Nawawī, cites Khalīfa's *Tārīkh* a few times in his biographical dictionary *Tahdhīb al-asmāʾ wa-l-lughāt*.[94] As noted above, he also praises Khalīfa as an important scholar of *ʿilm al-rijāl*.[95] It is thus clear that al-Nawawī refers to Khalīfa's knowledge of the biographies of *ḥadīth* transmitters—which is what he cites him for in the *Tahdhīb*—rather than political history. Al-Nawawī's contemporary, Ibn Khallikān, who was based in Damascus and Cairo, also used Khalīfa's *Tārīkh* as a source and cites it several times in his biographical dictionary *Wafayāt*

87 Judd, *Religious scholars* 28. See also Judd, Ibn ʿAsākir's sources 93–99.
88 Wurtzel, *Khalifa ibn Khayyat's History* 43.
89 Gilliot, Yāqūt al-Rūmī.
90 Wurtzel, *Khalifa ibn Khayyat's History* 43.
91 Rosenthal, Ibn al-Athīr.
92 Wurtzel, *Khalifa ibn Khayyat's History* 44.
93 Wurtzel, *Khalifa ibn Khayyat's History* 44.
94 E.g. al-Nawawī, *Tahdhīb al-asmāʾ* 1:77, 312; 2:355; Khalīfa b. Khayyāṭ, *Tārīkh* (1985) 135, 225, 352. See also Wurtzel, *Khalifa ibn Khayyat's History* 44.
95 Al-Nawawī, *Tahdhīb al-asmāʾ* 1:6.

al-aʿyān.[96] He is known mostly as a biographer and historian, but he was a prominent Sunnī scholar and was employed as chief judge (*qāḍī al-quḍāt*) in Damascus.[97] Similarly to al-Nawawī, Ibn Khallikān cites Khalīfa for biographical details.

Someone who relied more upon the political history in Khalīfa's *Tārīkh* is the great *ḥadīth* scholar of Damascus, Shams al-Dīn al-Dhahabī.[98] In the introduction to his monumental history, *Tārīkh al-Islām*, al-Dhahabī mentions Khalīfa's *Tārīkh* and *Ṭabaqāt* among the sources that he used and cites them often for the early periods.[99] The citations range from brief statements about pilgrimage leaders and dates of deaths to entire passages cited word for word and abridgements of year sections. As Wurtzel notes, however, al-Dhahabī does not always mention Khalīfa as the source of these passages, although the corresponding order of unrelated reports indicates that the material comes from Khalīfa's *Tārīkh*. Al-Dhahabī also used Khalīfa's two works in his biographical dictionary *Siyar aʿlām al-nubalāʾ*—mostly for the dates of individuals' deaths.[100] Al-Dhahabī's citations of Khalīfa, especially in *Tārīkh al-Islām*, show that later Sunnī scholars cited him not only for biographical material but also for the political history of the Muslim community.

One of al-Dhahabī's most famous students, Ibn Kathīr (d. 774/1373), also relied on Khalīfa's *Tārīkh*, and occasionally the *Ṭabaqāt*, in his massive history, *al-Bidāya wa-l-nihāya*.[101] Similar to other scholars mentioned above, Ibn Kathīr singles out Khalīfa as one of the *imām*s of history (*aḥad aʾimmat al-tārīkh*).[102] Another example is the Egyptian Ibn Ḥajar al-ʿAsqalānī, perhaps the foremost of the later *ḥadīth* scholars, who cites Khalīfa several times in his *Tahdhīb al-tahdhīb* and sometimes in *al-Iṣāba fī tamyīz al-ṣaḥāba*.[103] He cites both the *Tārīkh* and the *Ṭabaqāt*, but most citations are brief notes concerning dates of death and dates of other events. The citations reflect Khalīfa's authority with

96 Ibn Khallikān, *Wafayāt* 6:306, 308–309, 314, 321; Khalīfa b. Khayyāṭ, *Tārīkh* (1985) 325, 382, 402; Wurtzel, *Khalifa ibn Khayyat's History* 44.

97 Fück, Ibn Khallikān.

98 On al-Dhahabī's scholarship, see Lucas, *Constructive critics* 40–47.

99 Al-Dhahabī, *Tārīkh al-Islām* 1:23; Wurtzel, *Khalifa ibn Khayyat's History* 44–45.

100 Wurtzel, *Khalifa ibn Khayyat's History* 44–45.

101 E.g. Ibn Kathīr, *al-Bidāya* 3:380; 6:150; 8:107, 117, 118, 242, 256, 279, 315; 9:472, 505, 546, 584; 10:171, 305, 339; 11:335, 642; 12:347, 555; 13:127; Khalīfa b. Khayyāṭ, *Tārīkh* (1985) 53–54, 60, 66, 92, 94–95, 107, 115, 125–126, 130, 152, 156, 170, 175–176, 221, 225, 227, 286–287, 325, 354. Wurtzel, *Khalifa ibn Khayyat's History* 45.

102 Ibn Kathīr, *al-Bidāya* 14:372.

103 Wurtzel, *Khalifa ibn Khayyat's History* 45.

respect to chronology and biographical information about *ḥadīth* transmitters, similar to the citations found in the works of Ibn ʿAbd al-Barr, al-Nawawī and Ibn Khallikān.

More extensive citations of the political history in Khalīfa's *Tārīkh* are found in the chronicle *al-Nujūm al-zāhira fī mulūk Miṣr wa-l-Qāhira* of the Egyptian courtier and historian Ibn Taghrībirdī (d. 875/1470).[104] He cites Khalīfa by name a few times,[105] but Wurtzel concludes that other parts of Ibn Taghrībirdī's history also derive from Khalīfa's *Tārīkh* through al-Dhahabī's *Tārīkh al-Islām*.[106] Like Ibn ʿAbd Rabbih and Yāqūt, Ibn Taghrībirdī was not known primarily as a *ḥadīth* scholar, although he is said to have studied under both Badr al-Dīn al-ʿAynī (d. 855/1451) and Ibn Ḥajar al-ʿAsqalānī.[107]

The leading Egyptian scholar of most Islamic sciences, Jalāl al-Dīn al-Suyūṭī (d. 911/1505), only cites Khalīfa twice by name in his *Tārīkh al-khulafāʾ*,[108] but he includes several passages that are in all likelihood derived from Khalīfa's *Tārīkh* through other works.[109] These passages probably come from Ibn ʿAsākir, al-Dhahabī and Ibn Kathīr, whom al-Suyūṭī cites extensively. The material in al-Suyūṭī's work that resembles Khalīfa's *Tārīkh* includes statements by caliphs, biographical information about the Umayyads and dates of conquests during their reigns.[110] Two lengthy unsourced passages that seem to be derived from Khalīfa's *Tārīkh*, although they are abridged in some places, are on Muʿāwiya's pilgrimage in 51/671 to take the pledge of allegiance for Yazīd and the inaugural *khuṭba* of Yazīd (III) b. al-Walīd.[111]

Altogether, the above outline shows that Khalīfa was remembered in later Sunnī scholarship mainly as an expert in history and biography rather than in *ḥadīth* transmission—as indicated by the statements of Ibn ʿAbd al-Barr, Abū Bakr b. al-ʿArabī, al-Nawawī, Ibn Kathīr and others. Many later scholars used Khalīfa's *Tārīkh* and *Ṭabaqāt* primarily for biographical information. However, some scholars used his political history, and those who did (e.g. Abū Bakr b. al-ʿArabī, Ibn ʿAsākir and al-Dhahabī) were also staunch upholders of Sunnī histor-

---

104 Wurtzel, *Khalifa ibn Khayyat's History* 45–46.

105 Ibn Taghrībirdī, *al-Nujūm al-zāhira* 1:7, 168, 210, 234, 235, 236, 281, 367, 386; 2:42, 61, 149, 172.

106 Wurtzel, *Khalifa ibn Khayyat's History* 45.

107 Popper, Abū ʾl-Maḥāsin Djamāl al-Dīn Yūsuf b. Taghrībirdī.

108 Al-Suyūṭī, *Tārīkh al-khulafāʾ* 104, 204.

109 Wurtzel, *Khalifa ibn Khayyat's History* 46. For a discussion about al-Suyūṭī's *Tārīkh al-khulafāʾ* and the context of its compilation, see the translator's introduction to al-Suyūṭī, *History of the Umayyad caliphs* xiii–xxiv.

110 Wurtzel, *Khalifa ibn Khayyat's History* 46.

111 Al-Suyūṭī, *Tārīkh al-khulafāʾ* 326–327, 408–409; Khalīfa b. Khayyāṭ, *Tārīkh* (1985) 213–214, 365.

ical views. This suggests that Khalīfa's scholarly agenda in the *Tārīkh* was indeed appreciated by later Sunnī scholars, confirming Judd's notion that "later historians, especially Ibn ʿAsākir, appear to have preferred Khalīfa to al-Ṭabarī, suggesting that they understood the agendas of their sources and chose material that fit their own needs."[112] Because of the often concise and non-judgemental style of Khalīfa's reports, however, later scholars seldom used the *Tārīkh* on its own for purposes of historical argument. Rather, they used it mainly as a reliable source for chronological information and outlines of events to be complemented by other sources and more detailed reports.

6 Conclusion

After this overview of Khalīfa's life and works, it is worth reiterating the most important points for the contextual and textual analysis in the following chapters. Khalīfa came from a Basran family with a tradition of *ḥadīth* scholarship; both his father and grandfather had been transmitters of *ḥadīth* and post-Prophetic history. He was born around 160/776 and probably died in 240/854, which would mean that he lived during the reigns of ʿAbbāsid caliphs from al-Mahdī (r. 158–169/775–85) to al-Mutawakkil (r. 232–247/847–61). Khalīfa studied under many leading *ḥadīth* scholars of his time, most of whom were natives of, or residents in, Basra. He likewise taught and transmitted *ḥadīth* to a number of major *ḥadīth* scholars in the generations after his own, the most famous being Muḥammad b. Ismāʿīl al-Bukhārī. Khalīfa's teachers and students, as well as the early critics' statements and Ibn al-Nadīm's inclusion of him among the traditionist jurisprudents (*fuqahāʾ al-muḥaddithīn*) and *aṣḥāb al-ḥadīth*, indicate that he was associated with the *ahl al-ḥadīth*.

Some leading third/ninth-century transmitter critics were critical of Khalīfa's *ḥadīth* transmission, although al-Bukhārī regarded Khalīfa's narrations as acceptable and at least good enough to cite in corroboration of other narrations in his *Ṣaḥīḥ*. Among the fourth/tenth-century scholars, a couple of generations after Khalīfa, there were others who came to regard him as reliable (*thiqa*) or sincere (*ṣadūq*), including Ibn Ḥibbān and Ibn ʿAdī. However, the early discussions and disagreements about his reliability at least show that he was a well-known scholar in Basran *ḥadīth* circles. This is also confirmed by the prominence of his teachers and students, as well as by his own expertise in *ʿilm al-rijāl*, as is evident from the *Ṭabaqāt*.

112 Judd, *Religious scholars* 28.

His two main works, the *Tārīkh* and the *Ṭabaqāt*, earned him a reputation as a distinguished scholar of history, biography and genealogy—especially among later scholars of the fourth/tenth century onwards. These later scholars praise Khalīfa mainly for his erudition in these fields, although some of them (e.g. al-Dhahabī and Ibn Ḥajar) also discuss and evaluate his reliability as a *ḥadīth* transmitter. From the fourth/tenth century onwards, Khalīfa's *Tārīkh* was used mainly by Sunnī *ḥadīth* scholars compiling biographical dictionaries or chronological histories. Their using it suggests that Khalīfa's scholarly agenda and early Sunnī perspective were understood and appreciated by later Sunnī scholars of a similar historical and scholarly orientation to Khalīfa.

CHAPTER 3

Social and Intellectual Context

1 Introduction

This chapter outlines the social and intellectual context in which Khalīfa compiled the *Tārīkh*. It is divided into three parts: (1) social and political context, (2) intellectual context and (3) historiographical context. The first part seeks to contextualise Khalīfa's career by summarising the major social and political trends in the early and middle ʿAbbāsid caliphates in general and the city of Basra in particular. Although this cannot in itself explain the content of the *Tārīkh*, it provides an important context for the discussion of Khalīfa's intellectual milieu.

The second part outlines Khalīfa's religio-political and scholarly milieu in Basra, with special reference to the 'Proponents of Ḥadīth' (*ahl al-ḥadīth*)—the group of *ḥadīth* scholars and 'traditionist jurisprudents' to which Khalīfa seems to have belonged. This context is important for understanding Khalīfa's methods and historical perspectives in the *Tārīkh*, as well as in the *Ṭabaqāt*, both of which reflect early Sunnī notions of scholarship and the history of the Muslim community.

The third part discusses Khalīfa's two forms of historical writing: *tārīkh* ('chronography') and *ṭabaqāt* ('prosopography arranged by generations'). Among early *ḥadīth* scholars, these two formats seem to have been linked; a number of surviving *tārīkh* works compiled by early *ḥadīth* scholars were combined with *ṭabaqāt* material. Since the biographies and evaluations of *ḥadīth* transmitters in these works were clearly compiled for an audience of *ḥadīth* scholars, one can assume that the *tārīkh* sections were written for the same audience. This notion of the audience for Khalīfa's *Tārīkh* is substantiated by several other factors: his sources, his methods, his arrangement of the *Tārīkh*, the prominent necrologies of *ḥadīth* transmitters in the text, his early Sunnī historical perspective and the transmission of the work among later *ḥadīth* scholars.[1] This is important for the analysis of Khalīfa's *Tārīkh*, since it highlights its close connection to the *Ṭabaqāt* and suggests that Khalīfa's fellow *ḥadīth* scholars were the main audience for both works.

1 See Chapters 2, 4–8.

 | DOI:10.1163/9789004383173_005

The third section also compares Khalīfa's *Tārīkh* with other works by early *ḥadīth* scholars that combine the *tārīkh* and *ṭabaqāt* formats. It highlights certain commonalities in form, content and religio-political views, which are found to a greater extent in these works than in the wider *akhbār* tradition. The scarcity of such *tārīkh* works suggests that they were unusual, but their close link to *ʿilm al-rijāl* and *ṭabaqāt* literature, as well as their circulation among *ḥadīth* scholars, is important for understanding the characteristics and audiences of these works.

2 Social and Political Context

2.1 *Early ʿAbbāsid Politics*

Khalīfa was born in Basra around 160/776 and grew up in the last quarter of the second/eighth century, under the third, fourth and fifth ʿAbbāsid caliphs: al-Mahdī (r. 158–169/775–785), al-Hādī (r. 169–170/785–786) and Hārūn al-Rashīd (r. 170–193/786–809). He would have been in his thirties during the civil war in 195–198/811–813 between Hārūn's two sons, al-Amīn and al-Maʾmūn. When Khalīfa died in 240/854—probably in his late seventies or early eighties—this was about eight years after the accession of al-Mutawakkil (r. 232–247/847–861). Hence his lifetime spans two periods, commonly known as the early and middle ʿAbbāsid caliphate. The first encompasses the consolidation of ʿAbbāsid authority until the fourth *fitna* after Hārūn al-Rashīd's death in 193/809. The latter is characterised by governmental changes, such as the replacement of Iraqi ʿAbbāsids with local non-ʿAbbāsid rulers during the reign of al-Maʾmūn, followed by al-Muʿtaṣim's relocation of the capital to Samarra in 221/836 and the new systematic recruitment of Turkish slave soldiers.

It is significant, however, that Khalīfa lived before the disastrous decade of anarchy in 247–256/861–870, which precipitated the political decline of the ʿAbbāsid caliphate. This period after Khalīfa's death and the subsequent decades was marked by the loss of central ʿAbbāsid authority, systemic financial problems and the appearance of independent local dynasties.[2] Although some of these developments began earlier, Khalīfa's *Tārīkh* was compiled before the results became visible. His *Tārīkh*, therefore, reflects a unique moment in Arabic historical writing; his view on the development of Islamic politics was based on the ideal of a strong, united and centrally governed caliphate—an ideal that to a certain extent corresponded to actual political conditions in his time.

2 See Kennedy, Decline 7–27.

This is not to say that other annalistic works were not compiled around this time; the type of history that Khalīfa compiled had precursors in both caliphal and annalistic chronography.[3] However, Khalīfa's *Tārīkh* is the only surviving chronicle (other than Prophetic histories and single-subject texts) composed in the early third/ninth century. One might also include the *Tārīkh* of ʿAbd al-Malik b. Ḥabīb (if the surviving version is more or less complete), which must have been compiled at a similar time, but under Umayyad rule in al-Andalus.[4]

In retrospect, the ʿAbbāsid caliphate might be seen as already in decline in Khalīfa's time. The fourth *fitna* and its aftermath (195–204/811–819) inflicted significant damage on ʿAbbāsid authority, which until then had remained fairly intact since the consolidation under al-Manṣūr and al-Mahdī (136–169/754–785).[5] However, the disintegration of ʿAbbāsid power began in earnest only after the so-called anarchy in Samarra (247–256/861–870), from which the caliphate never entirely recovered.[6] The ʿAbbāsids initially retrieved some of their power, but a second crisis in the early fourth/tenth century put an end to their centralised rule, and the caliphate disintegrated into various successor states.[7] When the *Tārīkh* was composed and circulated in Basra, however, the results of these political and economic problems were all in the future. Unified ʿAbbāsid rule, centred on Baghdad, had been restored by al-Maʾmūn in 204/819, and the idea of a centrally governed caliphate under a single Qurashī ruler corresponded more or less to the actual political conditions, although the Umayyads in al-Andalus and the Aghlabids in North Africa had already carved out their own emirates.[8]

It is true that after the victory of al-Maʾmūn's Khurāsānī troops in the fourth *fitna*, the ʿAbbāsid family were replaced by local rulers in the provinces, and the descendants of the revolutionary army (*al-abnāʾ*) lost much of their authority as Turkish slave soldiers were recruited, especially under al-Muʿtaṣim (r. 218–

---

3 Donner, *Narratives* 182–183, 230–231; Robinson, *Islamic historiography* 47.

4 Muranyi, ʿAbd al-Malik b. Ḥabīb. On the surviving version, see Aguadé's introduction to Ibn Ḥabīb, *Tārīkh* 77–108.

5 Some centrifugal developments had begun already under Hārūn al-Rashīd's rule, but ʿAbbāsid central authority was still strong compared to later times. See Kennedy, *Prophet and the age of caliphates* 132–147; El-Hibri, Empire in Iraq 269–284.

6 See Kennedy, *Prophet and the age of caliphates* 169–175; Gordon, *Breaking of a thousand swords* 90–104; Bonner, Waning of empire 308–322.

7 Kennedy, *Prophet and the age of caliphates* 196–198, Reign of al-Muqtadir 33–47; Bonner, Waning of empire 332–359.

8 On the memory of the period before al-Mutawakkil's death as a "golden age of unity and prosperity", see Bonner, Waning of empire 306–307.

227/833–842).[9] In the long run, this development imposed financial demands that proved difficult to meet, but, in the short run, it served to reinforce ʿAbbāsid central authority. Indeed, caliphs such as al-Muʿtaṣim and al-Mutawakkil, towards the end of Khalīfa's life, may in some respects have enjoyed a degree of absolute authority that even their predecessors had lacked.[10] It was not until the time of their successors, in the second half of the third/ninth century, that the internal political and economic problems became more apparent. Thus throughout Khalīfa's lifetime, the unified caliphate was still the model of Muslim politics and likewise the ideal for most religio-political factions—certainly for the *ḥadīth* scholars of Sunnī orientation.

Khalīfa's *Tārīkh* was probably composed over a period of several decades. The lifespans of some of his direct transmitters suggest that he must have begun collecting material around 180–190/796–805, perhaps even earlier.[11] The last year covered in the extant version of the *Tārīkh* is 232/847, which gives an approximate end date for its compilation and transmission to Baqī b. Makhlad: at the very beginning of al-Mutawakkil's reign (232–247/847–861) and before his abolishing the *miḥna* (in stages between 232/847 and 237/852).[12] The importance of this time frame is not so much the details of single events, but the larger political and cultural context. Khalīfa's *Tārīkh* was compiled before the reorganisation and standardisation of historical knowledge that took place "in the aftermath of the abandonment of Samarra and the return of the caliphate to Baghdad after 279/892."[13] The *Tārīkh* also reflects a time when the ideal of a unified and centrally governed caliphate corresponded more or less to the actual political conditions—before independent polities appeared in increasing numbers during the course of the third/ninth century. It does not mean, however, that Khalīfa toed the line with the ʿAbbāsid dynasty and its religious policies, which often, as we shall see below, differed from Khalīfa's own early Sunnī orientation.

---

9 This new military organisation also included some commanders of "aristocratic Transoxanian or Central Asian background … who brought with them their personal military retinues (*chākars*)." El-Hibri, Empire in Iraq 296; Kennedy, *Prophet and the age of caliphates* 157–159; De la Vaissière, *Sogdian traders* 285.

10 Kennedy, Decline 16.

11 See Chapter 4.

12 Hinds, Miḥna; Zaman, *Religion and politics* 106–118; Melchert, Religious policies 320–326, *Ahmad* 8–16; Lucas, *Constructive critics* 192–202.

13 Borrut, Vanishing Syria 44–45, *Entre mémoire et pouvoir* 94–95, 97–108.

2.2 *ʿAbbāsid Religious Policies*

The reorientation of the ʿAbbāsid dynasty, away from the early Shīʿī milieu in which their movement originated towards the broader early Sunnī community, is often said to have begun properly under the third caliph, al-Mahdī (158–169/775–785), although the exact nature of this reorientation remains unclear.[14] Some historical reports also suggest that Hārūn al-Rashīd's reign witnessed an endorsement of the ranking of the first four caliphs in chronological order (sometimes referred to as the 'four caliph thesis') represented by many early *ḥadīth* scholars.[15] In any case, the relationship between the ʿAbbāsid caliphs and the early Sunnī scholars seems to have been one of mutual dependence, even though they may not necessarily have agreed on issues of law, theology and politics.[16] What can be said is that the early ʿAbbāsid caliphs styled themselves as charismatic world-rulers and generally received critical but loyal support from the *ḥadīth* scholars.[17] An exception is the revolt of Muḥammad b. ʿAbdallāh al-Nafs al-Zakiyya in 145/762, which is said to have received support from many major scholars of *fiqh* and *ḥadīth*.[18] The early ʿAbbāsid caliphs supported some *ḥadīth* scholars and 'traditionist jurisprudents' by patronage,[19] but they also had a more or less systematic programme of appointing Ḥanafī, or otherwise rationalist-inclined, judges—especially in the eastern regions, where their authority was strongest.[20]

The most famous ʿAbbāsid intervention in religious life is al-Maʾmūn's *miḥna* ('inquisition'), but it was not the first. Some decades earlier, al-Mahdī had launched an organised persecution of individuals accused of *zandaqa*—an ambiguous term that initially denoted pre-Islamic Manichaean beliefs but that was then also applied to hypocrites (*munāfiqūn*) and others with heretical beliefs or practices.[21] Al-Mahdī even introduced the administrative office of the *ṣāḥib al-zanādiqa*, charged with pursuing and persecuting the *zanādiqa* (sing.

---

14 Zaman, *Religion and politics* 45–56; Crone, *God's rule* 93.

15 Zaman, *Religion and politics* 56–59.

16 Zaman, *Religion and politics* 208, *passim*.

17 See Zaman, *Religion and politics* 70–101, 208–212; Crone, *God's rule* 135–141.

18 Among them Mālik b. Anas, Abū Ḥanīfa, Abū Bakr b. Sabra, Shuʿba b. al-Ḥajjāj, Hushaym b. Bashīr, ʿAbbād b. al-ʿAwwām and Yazīd b. Hārūn. Zaman, *Religion and politics* 73–76; Ahmed, *Religious elite* 157–158; Abou El Fadl, *Rebellion* 75–79; Elad, *Rebellion* 363–373.

19 Zaman, *Religion and politics* 147–166; Crone and Hinds, *God's caliph* 83–90; Marsham, *Rituals* 186.

20 Tsafrir, *History of an Islamic school of law* 116–119. On Basran judges, see Melchert, *Formation* 43–47.

21 Zaman, *Religion and politics* 63–69; Mahmood, Religious inquisition; Turner, *Inquisition* 26–27; Abou El Fadl, *Rebellion* 79–80.

zindīq).[22] A function of the policies may well have been to strengthen the credentials of the ʿAbbāsid dynasty as defenders of orthodoxy, but the vigour of the persecution had already abated by the time of Hārūn al-Rashīd.[23]

While the reigns of al-Mahdī and Hārūn al-Rashīd witnessed a move away from the early Shīʿī milieu, with a greater appeal to the early Sunnī scholarly majority, al-Maʾmūn moved to a rationalist, or Muʿtazilī, position and became more tolerant of Shīʿī tendencies. In 201/817, in the midst of the lingering conflict between Khurāsān and Iraq, including a number of Shīʿī revolts, al-Maʾmūn proclaimed ʿAlī b. Mūsā al-Kāẓim (known as ʿAlī al-Riḍā) successor to the caliphate.[24] He was a descendant of the Prophet, via Fāṭima and ʿAlī, and considered to be the *imām* by some ʿAlid sympathisers. At the same time, al-Maʾmūn changed the ceremonial clothing of the caliphate from black to green, thus abandoning the colour of the revolution that had brought the ʿAbbāsids to power. The appointment of ʿAlī al-Riḍā as successor has led to a wide range of interpretations: weakness in al-Maʾmūn's authority,[25] eschatological expectations,[26] strengthening of his position vis-à-vis the scholars,[27] assertion of caliphal authority,[28] ʿAlid sympathies at al-Maʾmūn's court[29] and an attempt to assimilate the ʿAlids within the broader Hāshimī claim to the caliphate.[30] In any case, the succession was terminated by ʿAlī's death in Ṭūs in 203/818.

The main intervention in religious life was the *miḥna* that al-Maʾmūn set in motion shortly before he died in 218/833. It took the form of imposing the doctrine of the 'createdness of the Qurʾān'—a doctrine associated with various rationalists, especially the Muʿtazila.[31] It may have been an attempt to pro-

---

22 Al-Ṭabarī, *Tārīkh* 3:499, 519–520, 522; Chokr, *Zandaqa* 22–23; Zaman, *Religion and politics* 67.

23 Zaman, *Religion and politics* 64.

24 Marsham, *Rituals* 262.

25 Tor, Historiographical re-examination 127–128.

26 Madelung, New documents 339–345. For a refutation of Madelung's evidence, see Bayhom-Daou, al-Maʾmūn's alleged apocalyptic beliefs.

27 Abou El Fadl, *Rebellion* 88.

28 Crone and Hinds, *God's caliph* 93–95; Kimber, al-Maʾmūn and Baghdad; Abou El Fadl, *Rebellion* 88.

29 Gabrieli, *al-Maʾmūn*.

30 Chejne, *Succession* 115–116; Sourdel, Politique religieuse; Zahniser, Insights from the ʿUthmāniyya; Nagel, *Rechtleitung und Kalifat* 414–424; Crone, *God's rule* 93; Marsham, *Rituals* 262–263.

31 This doctrine was also associated with others, such as the Ḥanafī and Murjiʾī scholar Bishr al-Marīsī (d. 218/833), but nonetheless one that the Muʿtazila came to agree upon and promote. See Zaman, *Religion and politics* 106–118; Melchert, *Ahmad* 8–16; Lucas, *Constructive critics* 192–202; Turner, *Inquisition* 2–4; Abou El Fadl, *Rebellion* 89–96; Hinds, Miḥna.

mote *kalām* (speculative or dialectic theology) and to claim authority over Islamic orthodoxy, but it disturbed only temporarily relations between caliphs and scholars.[32] The *miḥna* might have been directed mainly at scholars in Baghdad and those performing official functions for the ʿAbbāsid government, but it nonetheless reached the local communities and led to the punishment, imprisonment and even death of a number of scholars.[33] Khalīfa himself is reported to have accompanied Aḥmad b. Riyāḥ, a Basran judge accused by the Muʿtazila, to the court of al-Wāthiq (r. 227–232/842–847).[34] The case against Ibn Riyāḥ was dismissed, but the story suggests, as al-ʿUmarī points out, that Khalīfa took a clear stance against the Muʿtazila of his time.[35]

The historical tradition sometimes depicts al-Maʾmūn as one of the more competent ʿAbbāsid rulers—apart from the *miḥna* and his support for the Muʿtazila—which might suggest that some material was shaped by Maʾmūnid propaganda and produced by affiliates of the ruling dynasty, possibly scribes.[36] This tendency is reflected in Baqī b. Makhlad's recension of Khalīfa's *Tārīkh*, which was transmitted around 232/847, when al-Maʾmūn's policies, including the *miḥna*, were still upheld. Khalīfa ignores the *miḥna* and takes a seemingly pro-Maʾmūnid stance in the fourth *fitna*: the defeated al-Amīn is named al-Makhlūʿ ('the Deposed'), while al-Maʾmūn is referred to as the Commander of the Believers, even during al-Amīn's lifetime.[37] There is, however, no indication of any relationship between Khalīfa and the ʿAbbāsid court, let alone patronage. This distinguishes Khalīfa from some later historians, such as al-Balādhurī and al-Yaʿqūbī, who were both trained scribes associated with the courts (ʿAbbāsids and Ṭāhirids).[38] Al-Mutawakkil gradually abolished the *miḥna* between 232/847 and 237/852—before Khalīfa's death, but probably after he had transmitted the *Tārīkh* to Baqī. By contrast, Mūsā al-Tustarī seems to have received his recension of the *Tārīkh* from Khalīfa around 238/853, after the end of the *miḥna*. Al-Dhahabī narrates, presumably from that recension of al-Tustarī, that Khalīfa said, "Al-Mutawakkil succeeded as caliph and affirmed the Sunna. He spoke about it at his court and wrote to the differ-

32 Zaman, *Religion and politics* 11, 106–118; Lucas, *Constructive critics* 198–202. For a summary of previous interpretations of the *miḥna*, see Turner, *Inquisition* 14–22.
33 Lucas, *Constructive critics* 192–202; Turner, *Inquisition* 13–14.
34 Wakīʿ, *Akhbār al-quḍāt* 347.
35 Wakīʿ, *Akhbār al-quḍāt* 347; al-ʿUmarī's introduction to Khalīfa's *Tārīkh* (1985) 7–8.
36 El-Hibri, *Reinterpreting Islamic historiography* 95–126; Cooperson, *Classical Arabic biography* 40–69; Kennedy, Caliphs and their chroniclers.
37 Khalīfa b. Khayyāṭ, *Tārīkh* (1985) 466–468.
38 Zaman, al-Yaʿqūbī; Becker and Rosenthal, al-Balādhurī.

ent regions about lifting the *miḥna*, spreading the Sunna and supporting its people."[39] This report clearly illustrates Khalīfa's early Sunnī orientation and his stance against the *miḥna*. It also suggests that the absence of any mentioning of the *miḥna* in Baqī's recension could be explained by the political situation—the *miḥna* was still underway when Khalīfa transmitted the *Tārīkh* to Baqī.

2.3 *Basra in the First Centuries* AH

To further understand Khalīfa's own context, it is necessary to look at the specific developments in Basra before and during his lifetime. Basra was originally founded as a military camp by ʿUtba b. Ghazwān during the early conquests at the time of ʿUmar b. al-Khaṭṭāb (r. 13–23/634–644). Located 15 kilometres from the Shaṭṭ al-ʿArab, by the marshlands of lower Iraq, Basra provided a base for further expeditions and facilitated control of the important trade routes of the Gulf.[40] In addition to its military importance, Basra soon became a major economic centre, with wealth derived from the commerce with the Gulf region and Sind as well as from the agricultural lands.[41] In the conquest period, Basra was divided into five tribal sectors (*khums*, pl. *akhmās*): Ahl al-ʿĀliya, Tamīm, Bakr b. Wāʾil, ʿAbd Qays and Azd. There were also many non-Arab immigrants and *mawālī* (clients), including Persians, Indians, Malays and sub-Saharan Africans (Zanj).[42] The city's population increased rapidly after its establishment and seems to have reached at least 250,000 by the late second/eighth century.[43] As with the two other major cities of Iraq, Kufa and Baghdad, this remarkable urban growth was, according to Kennedy, the result of four major political, social and economic factors:

> The first was the agricultural potential of the lands of Greater Mesopotamia, a potential that was largely unrealized until activated by man-made irrigation systems. The second was the river system, which permitted the transport of large quantities of grain and other foodstuffs. The third was the social and fiscal structure of the early Islamic state, which led to the emergence of a large body of people who were paid cash salaries by the administration and as such generated demand for supplies of all sorts.

---

39 Al-Dhahabī, *Siyar* 1316. See Chapter 1.
40 Pellat, *Le milieu basrien* 2–6; Kennedy, Feeding of the five thousand 182.
41 Kennedy, *Early Abbasid caliphate* 19–20; Kennedy, Feeding of the five hundred thousand.
42 Pellat, *Le milieu basrien* 23, 34–42; Picken, *Spiritual purification* 23–24.
43 Kennedy, Feeding of the five hundred thousand 177.

> The fourth and final element was the working out of a legal framework for landownership, which gave individuals security of tenure (at least in theory) and encouraged them to invest in projects of agricultural expansion.[44]

Basra in the late second/eighth century had become a commercial centre, with caravans meeting at al-Mirbad outside the city and ships arriving at the river port, al-Kallāʾ, a financial centre with Jewish, Christian and non-Arab communities, an industrial centre with significant arsenals and an agricultural centre with its date production.[45] The location near the Shaṭṭ al-ʿArab also enabled good communications and commercial exchange with the nearby cities of Kufa and Baghdad.[46]

At the time of the Umayyads, Basra—often paired with Kufa and ruled at times from Wāsiṭ or al-Ḥīra—functioned as a semi-independent governorate under a number of prominent governors, among them Ziyād b. Abīhi (r. 45–53/665–673), ʿUbaydallāh b. Ziyād (r. 54–67/674–686), al-Ḥajjāj b. Yūsuf (r. 75–95/694–714), Khālid b. ʿAbdallāh al-Qasrī (r. 106–120/724–738) and Yūsuf b. ʿUmar al-Thaqafī (r. 120–126/738–744). Under the early ʿAbbāsids from the time of al-Manṣūr, the proximity to the new capital of Baghdad might have reduced Basra's political importance. However, the foundation of Baghdad contributed to the commercial prosperity of Basra, as goods from Indian Ocean trade passed into Iraq, especially to Baghdad, via Basra and al-Ubulla. It was probably towards the late second/eighth century that Basra reached its zenith as both a commercial and intellectual centre.[47] This is also reflected in the remarkable concentration of leading *ḥadīth* authorities in Basra by the late second/eighth century, before Baghdad increasingly took over as the intellectual centre of Iraq.[48]

From its foundation, Basra also witnessed continuing sociopolitical upheaval—perhaps reinforced by the mix of recently sedentarised Arab tribes with a long history of mutual animosity, in addition to an increasing number of non-Arab peoples.[49] In 36/656, the city became the stage for the Battle of the

44 Kennedy, Feeding of the five hundred thousand 177.

45 Pellat and Longrigg, Baṣra 51.

46 On the Basra–Baghdad route, see Agius, *Classic ships of Islam* 67–69.

47 Pellat and Longrigg, Baṣra 50–51; Donner, Basra. See also Kennedy, Feeding the five hundred thousand 177; Lucas, *Constructive critics* 359–360.

48 See Ibn Saʿd, *Ṭabaqāt* 9:273–311; Lucas, *Constructive critics* 359–366.

49 On the sedentarisation of nomadic Arab tribes in Basra, see Bulliet, Sedentarization of nomads 36–46.

Camel, in which parts of the population participated.[50] Yet, the city was already less associated than the nearby city of Kufa with ʿAlid partisanship and the various early Shīʿī causes. The following year, many Basrans kept away from the Battle of Ṣiffīn, while others fought on the side of ʿAlī. Some were also recruited into al-Ḥarūriyya—known as the first Khawārij—who seceded from ʿAlī's army after Ṣiffīn and were defeated at al-Nahrawān in 38/658.[51]

A number of revolts occurred in Basra during the Umayyad period, many of which, as is evident from Khalīfa's *Tārīkh*, were important in the memory of later generations of scholars. Apart from the caliphate of ʿAbdallāh b. al-Zubayr, which controlled Basra from around 64/684 to 72/691, and the recurring Khārijī revolts,[52] the most important uprisings were those of Ibn al-Ashʿath (80–83/699–702) and Yazīd b. al-Muhallab (101–102/720). Both were ultimately unsuccessful and put down by the Umayyads. Unlike many contemporaneous revolts elsewhere, these Basran revolts were devoid of ʿAlid or Shīʿī rhetoric. More specifically, the uprisings of both Ibn al-Ashʿath and Yazīd b. al-Muhallab indicate the importance of military and tribal factions within the caliphate, in addition to religio-political ones.[53]

The first major revolt with ʿAlid rhetoric, besides the Shīʿī elements of the ʿAbbāsid Revolution, came in the early ʿAbbāsid period.[54] In 145/762–763, the revolt of Muḥammad b. ʿAbdallāh al-Nafs al-Zakiyya, a descendant of al-Ḥasan b. ʿAlī b. Abī Ṭālib, reached Basra under the command of his brother Ibrāhīm b. ʿAbdallāh but was quickly suppressed.[55] Thereafter, Basra seems to have experienced a period of relative calm throughout the reigns of al-Mahdī and Hārūn al-Rashīd. Apart from the rapid succession of governors—perhaps as a result of a policy to prevent accumulation of authority—the sources are quiet about the political history of Basra until the fourth *fitna*.[56]

In 196/812, about a year into the conflict between al-Amīn and al-Maʾmūn, the Basran elite and its governor, Manṣūr b. al-Mahdī, surrendered to al-Maʾ-

50 According to Khalīfa's *Tārīkh*, 2,500 Basrans from Banū Azd and 800 from Banū Ḍabba were killed fighting against ʿAlī. Khalīfa b. Khayyāṭ, *Tārīkh* (1985) 186. See also Pellat, *Le milieu basrien* 5; Morony, *Iraq after the Muslim conquest* 250.

51 Pellat, al-Baṣra.

52 Wellhausen, *Religio-political factions* 39–88; Crone, *God's rule* 55–56.

53 Hawting, *First dynasty of Islam* 67–70, 73–76; al-Faruque, Revolt of Ibn al-Ashʿath; Veccia Vaglieri, Ibn al-Ashʿath; Crone, Muhallabids.

54 On Basra (and Kufa) during the ʿAbbāsid Revolution, see Sharon, *Black banners* 54–71, *Revolt* 205–221.

55 On the revolt, see Elad, *Rebellion* 145–230.

56 Kennedy, *Early Abbasid caliphate* 118; Khalīfa b. Khayyāṭ, *Tārīkh* (1985) 423–466; al-Ṭabarī, *Tārīkh* 3:451–764.

mūn's forces.[57] After the fall of Baghdad and the death of al-Amīn in 198/813, the city was subsumed under the control of al-Ḥasan b. Sahl, on behalf of al-Ma'mūn.[58] However, the upheaval in Iraq continued during the first years of al-Ma'mūn's reign, when he was still ruling from Marw in Khurāsān. The ʿAlid revolt of Ibn Ṭabāṭabā, led by his military commander, Abū l-Sarāyā, took control of Basra in 199/815.[59] The ʿAbbāsids soon suppressed the revolt and restored their authority in Basra, but revolts and internal power struggles continued throughout al-Ma'mūn's reign.

A group that caused much trouble for ʿAbbāsid control of Basra in the early third/ninth century were the Zuṭṭ, a people from north-western India originally brought to the Gulf under the Sāsānids and later, in the Umayyad period, as military reinforcement.[60] They were settled in the marshlands (*baṭā'iḥ*) of lower Iraq and may have increased in number during the early ʿAbbāsid period, when they began to challenge the authorities. In 205/815, al-Ma'mūn appointed commanders to suppress the Zuṭṭ, whose activities had damaged Basra's economy and at times cut it off from Baghdad. Their apparently prolonged uprising culminated in 219/834, when al-Ma'mūn's successor, al-Muʿtaṣim, sent the commander ʿUjayf b. ʿAnbasa in a massive campaign that finally subdued them. It is reported that 27,000 of the Zuṭṭ, including 12,000 fighting men, were brought to Baghdad in 220/835 and then deported to Khāniqīn and further to ʿAyn Zarba, on the Roman frontiers.[61] The exact results of the Zuṭṭ upheavals remain unclear, but for 15 years they challenged ʿAbbāsid authority in Basra. After 220/835, the sources are quiet about the political developments in Basra; some conflicts are said to have broken out after Muhammad b. Rajā became governor in 239/853–854, but otherwise the city seems to have witnessed a period without major upheaval until the Zanj revolt in 255–270/869–883.[62] These events, however, began after Khalīfa's lifetime and certainly after the transmission of the *Tārīkh* to Baqī b. Makhlad (c. 232/847).

From this overview, it is clear that Basra remained prosperous and relatively peaceful until the end of Hārūn al-Rashīd's reign (193/809). From the time of

57 Kennedy, *Early Abbasid caliphate* 143; Khalīfa b. Khayyāṭ, *Tārīkh* (1985) 467; al-Ṭabarī, *Tārīkh* 3:857.

58 Kennedy, *Early Abbasid caliphate* 151–152.

59 Kennedy, *Early Abbasid caliphate* 152; Khalīfa b. Khayyāṭ, *Tārīkh* (1985) 469–470.

60 Al-Balādhurī, *Futūḥ* 522–523; Pellat, *Le milieu basrien* 37–40. Al-Zuṭṭ, as they are known in the Muslim sources, is an Arabisation of the Indian ethnic term Jhāt, referring to a people from the north-western regions of India. See Bosworth, al-Zuṭṭ; Bazmee Ansari, Djāṭ.

61 Al-Ṭabarī, *Tārīkh* 3:1044–1045, 1166–1170; al-Balādhurī, *Futūḥ* 523; Bosworth, al-Zuṭṭ.

62 Al-Aʿẓamī, *Mukhtaṣar* 72; Ibn al-Jawzī, *al-Muntaẓam* 12:86–87.

the civil war between al-Amīn and al-Maʾmūn, Basra might have lost some of its commercial and political importance. Throughout Khalīfa's lifetime, however, Basra remained one of the most important cities of the Muslim world—not only historically but also in contemporary scholarship, politics and commerce. That said, Khalīfa may have belonged to one of the last few generations of Basran scholars for whom this was the case; the political and commercial importance of Basra gradually diminished from the late third/ninth century—its population, for example, would reach the same levels again only in the second half of the twentieth century.[63]

3 Intellectual Context

As one of the major cities of the Muslim world, most famous religio-political and scholarly groups were present in Basra. Besides the *ahl al-ḥadīth* ('Proponents of Ḥadīth') with whom Khalīfa seems to have been affiliated, these groups included the Khawārij, the early Shīʿīs and the various rationalist trends. They differed from each other to various extents in their beliefs, scholarly methods and historical views, as well as in their views on religious and political authority in the Muslim community. Although these groups contained internally diverse subfactions, sometimes in opposition to each other, these categories nonetheless serve the purpose of mapping out the religio-political landscape in Basra. It is, however, important to point out that this overview focuses on scholars and political activists—partly because these groups are most relevant for Khalīfa's intellectual context and partly because of the scarcity of information about the general population of Basra.

3.1 *Khawārij*

From the mid-first/seventh century, Basra was one of the most important bases of the Khawārij.[64] Four of the most important subsects of the Khawārij are said to have originated in the city around the time of the second *fitna* (60–73/680–692): the Azāriqa, the Najdiyya, the Ibāḍiyya and the Ṣufriyya.[65] The Khawārij became known for declaring those who commit major sins (*kabāʾir*) unbeliev-

63 Kennedy, Feeding of the five hundred thousand 177.

64 Wellhausen, *Religio-political factions* 39–42.

65 See Pellat, *Le milieu basrien* 209–211; Lewinstein, *Studies in Islamic heresiography* 55–154, Azāriqa 252, Making and unmaking a sect 77–84; Robinson, *Empire and elites* 110–114; Crone, *God's rule* 55; Gaiser, Source-critical methodologies; Wilkinson, *Ibâḍism* 104–112, 122–160.

ers and, with respect to the early history, for considering Abū Bakr and ʿUmar legitimate caliphs, unlike ʿUthmān and ʿAlī, who they thought had lost their status as caliphs and as Muslims by violating the revealed laws. In their view, the supporters of ʿUthmān and ʿAlī had likewise become unbelievers; the only Muslims left were the Khawārij, and the only legitimate leaders of the Muslim community were their own. In effect, all caliphs after Abū Bakr and ʿUmar were considered illegitimate kings (*mulūk*) and tyrants (*jabābira*), which necessitated emigration and/or revolts to re-establish righteous governance—based exclusively on merit rather than on descent or military force. Although these views were modified over time in the various subsects, the different Khārijī groups until the mid-third/ninth century at least shared these historical notions and this aversion to contemporary caliphs. By the early ʿAbbāsid period, the militant Khawārij had begun to disappear from Basra and the other urban centres in Iraq. Some smaller groups lingered in the city, but larger groups of militant Khawārij survived only elsewhere—mainly in North and East Africa, eastern Arabia and Sīstān.[66] However, the idea of Khārijism and the Khawārij as a historical and sectarian phenomenon remained important in the scholarly discourse, in particular as a part of the self-definition of other groups.[67]

3.2 *Early Shīʿa*

Basra was less associated than Kufa with the different Shīʿī movements that appeared in Iraq during the first/seventh and second/eighth centuries. These groups maintained that the family of the Prophet Muḥammad, whether defined as ʿAlids or Hāshimites, had exclusive rights to the caliphate and to religious authority in general. As noted above, some ʿAlid revolts reached Basra in the early ʿAbbāsid period, including the uprising of Muḥammad al-Nafs al-Zakiyya's brother, Ibrāhīm b. ʿAbdallāh, in 145/762–763 and that of Abū l-Sarāyā, on behalf of Ibn Ṭabāṭabā, in 199/815. Both insurgencies were, however, short-lived, and there is little to suggest any deep-rooted attachment to specific ʿAlid or Shīʿī causes—in fact, al-Nafs al-Zakiyya's revolt is said to have been supported by many early Sunnī scholars in different cities.[68] By Khalīfa's time, the majority of those designated as early Shīʿīs among the scholars and activists were probably either Zaydīs, who generally accepted the legitimacy of Abū Bakr

66 Levi Della Vida, Khāridjites; Crone, *God's rule* 52, 55–56, 97.

67 Hagemann, *History and memory* 256–261. See also Lewinstein, Azāriqa, Making and unmaking a sect.

68 See Sections 2.2 and 2.3. On Basra during al-Nafs al-Zakiyya's revolt, see Elad, *Rebellion* 137–141.

and ʿUmar, or Imāmīs (also known as Rāfiḍa—'Rejecters'), who rejected the legitimacy of the first three caliphs and the authority of most Companions.

Other scholars had less defined 'moderate Shīʿī tendencies' (*tashayyuʿ*), preferring ʿAlī to ʿUthmān while still considering Abū Bakr and ʿUmar superior to both of them.[69] These scholars are usually included among the *ahl al-sunna*, as long as they accepted both ʿUthmān and ʿAlī as legitimate caliphs, although their opinion on the issue of ranking differed from the majority opinion that the best of the community after the Prophet is Abū Bakr, then ʿUmar, then ʿUthmān and then ʿAlī.[70] They were thus inclined to the idea of the ongoing righteousness of the majority community and, unlike the extreme Shīʿīs (like the Imāmiyya/Rāfiḍa), more accepted in the *ḥadīth* circles.[71] Such *tashayyuʿ* existed among some jurisprudents and *ḥadīth* scholars but was overall less prevalent in Basra than in Kufa.[72] Besides these, there are accounts of various minority Shīʿī sects—usually termed 'extremists' (*ghulāt*) in the sources—in Basra during the early ʿAbbāsid period, such as the Manṣūriyya, Mughīriyya, Kāmiliyya, Kaysāniyya and Nāwūsiyya.[73] These groups may have contributed to some disturbance in the city, but they were nonetheless minorities and not represented in scholarly circles.

3.3 Ahl al-Ḥadīth

During Khalīfa's lifetime (c. 160–240/776–854), Basra was one of the foremost centres of *ḥadīth* scholarship and home to numerous leading *ḥadīth* scholars.[74] Many of them were also associated with the text-based approach to *fiqh* and *ʿaqīda* of the *ahl al-ḥadīth*. In modern scholarship, there is some discus-

69 Ibn Ḥajar notes that, "*Tashayyuʿ* in the terminology of the early scholars (*ʿurf al-mutaqaddimīn*) refers to the belief that ʿAlī is better than ʿUthmān and that ʿAlī was correct in his wars and that his opponents were wrong, while still preferring the two shaykhs [Abū Bakr and ʿUmar] and considering them better than both of them. Some of them might also have believed that ʿAlī was the best of all people after the Messenger of God (ṣ)." Ibn Ḥajar, *Tahdhīb* 1:53. Al-Dhahabī also mentions that, "Preferring ʿAlī [to ʿUthmān] is neither *rafḍ* nor *bidʿa*, for several of the Companions and the Successors did that. ... However, the vast majority of the community agree to give precedence to ʿUthmān over Imam ʿAlī and that is our position. It is a simple matter and there is no doubt that the two shaykhs [Abū Bakr and ʿUmar] are better than both of them. Whoever differs with this is a hardened Shīʿī." Al-Dhahabī, *Siyar* 2818.

70 See Ibn Taymiyya's summary in *al-ʿAqīdat al-Wāsiṭiyya* 117–118.

71 Melchert, *Ahmad* 97; Lucas, *Constructive critics* 322–323.

72 Ibn Taymiyya, *Minhāj al-sunna* 8:224–225; Ibn Ḥajar, *Fatḥ al-Bārī* 6:221. See also Melchert, *Ahmad* 97.

73 Pellat, *Le milieu basrien* 199–206.

74 Lucas, *Constructive critics* 187–188, 359–360.

sion as to what extent all those early scholars associated with the *ahl al-ḥadīth* represented a consistent scholarly approach.[75] On the basis of their general commonality, however, the term usually refers to "those scholars who prioritized the derivation of norms from texts (*nuṣūṣ*) above consistency in legal analogy, selecting these proof texts through the emerging science of *ḥadīth* criticism (*jarḥ wa-taʿdīl*)."[76] Not all *ḥadīth* scholars (*muḥaddithūn*) belonged by definition to the *ahl al-ḥadīth*, in the sense of a scholarly methodology, but at least most Iraqi *ḥadīth* scholars in the late second/eighth and early third/ninth centuries were associated with the broadly defined *ahl al-ḥadīth* in *fiqh* and *ʿaqīda*—rather than the rationalist-inclined scholars of the *ahl al-raʾy* ('Proponents of Individual Legal Reasoning').[77]

When responding to legal issues for which the Qurʾān and the well-known narrations from the Prophet and the Companions provided no clear answer, the *ahl al-raʾy*, like the Kufan Abū Ḥanīfa (d. 150/767) and his followers, relied on their own interpretations of these sources. By contrast, the *ahl al-ḥadīth* preferred less well-established narrations from the Prophet and the opinions of the earliest generations to their own independent reasoning.[78] For this reason, legal opinions from Companions and senior Successors, in addition to Prophetic reports, were important in traditionist jurisprudence.[79] One of the most famous representatives of the *ahl al-ḥadīth* in Iraq, Aḥmad b. Ḥanbal (d. 241/855), articulated this text-based approach in his words: "You hardly see anyone applying reason (*raʾy*) [to issues of law and belief] except that there is corruptness (*daghal*) in his heart. A weak narration [i.e. a *ḥadīth* not fulfilling all the conditions for being *ṣaḥīḥ*] is thus dearer to me than the use of reason."[80] In this way, the *ahl al-ḥadīth* sought to preserve the authenticity of Islam by holding on to the ways of the Prophet and the early Muslim community as preserved in the transmitted texts. This strictly text-based approach to law distinguished the Iraqi *ahl al-ḥadīth* from the *ahl al-raʾy*. The *ahl al-ḥadīth* also

75 See Brown, Did the Prophet say it or not? 260; Melchert, Traditionist-jurisprudents; Spectorsky, *Ḥadīth*; Lucas, Where are the legal ḥadīth?

76 Brown, Did the Prophet say it or not? 260. See also Brown, *Hadith* 17–18; Dickinson, *Development* 2–5; Hallaq, *Origins and evolution* 74; Melchert, Traditionist-jurisprudents 383.

77 Melchert, *Formation* 2–3; Melchert, Traditionist-jurisprudents 383–386. While valid for the Iraqi *ahl al-ḥadīth* at the time of Khalīfa, the division is problematic for the Medinan tradition of Mālik b. Anas and his followers, which represented a slightly different approach to *ḥadīth* and *raʾy*. See Wymann-Landgraf, *Mālik and Medina* 8–11.

78 Brown, *Canonization* 49–50.

79 Melchert, *Formation* 13–18; Melchert, Traditionist-jurisprudents; Lucas, Principles of traditionist jurisprudence, Where are the legal ḥadīth?

80 Al-Sakhāwī, *Fatḥ al-Mughīth* 1:147. Also cited by Brown in *Canonization* 50.

represented a similar transmission-based approach to matters of belief and generally rejected the early discipline of *kalām* and its associates, in particular the Muʿtazila.[81]

Important terms in the earliest sources, referring to *ḥadīth* scholars of such inclinations, are *ṣāḥib sunna* and *ṣāḥib ḥadīth*. These two terms largely overlapped, but they were perhaps not necessarily interchangeable: a *ṣāḥib sunna* could be a weak transmitter, and a *ṣāḥib ḥadīth*, at least theoretically, could adhere to some religious innovations (*bidaʿ*).[82] In practice, however, most *ahl al-ḥadīth* in the late second/eighth and early third/ninth centuries espoused views that can be characterised as 'early Sunni', since ideas such as the collective authority of the Companions had become foundational to early *ḥadīth* scholarship.[83] The labels *ṣāḥib sunna* and *ṣāḥib ḥadīth* are fairly frequent in the early biographical dictionaries, but far from applied to all scholars associated with *ahl al-ḥadīth*. It is noteworthy, however, that these two terms refer mostly to *ḥadīth* scholars of Basra, Kufa and Baghdad who were active from the late second/eighth century onwards, which indicates their significance in the scholarship of the Iraqi region.[84]

In this book, as discussed in the introduction, the religio-political outlook of these scholars is termed 'early Sunnī', which refers to those second/eighth- and third/ninth-century groups—including the *ahl al-ḥadīth*, but not exclusively them—that were characterised by an increasingly transmission-based approach to *fiqh* and *ʿaqīda*, in addition to a firm commitment to the collective authority of the Prophet's Companions and the special merit of the first four caliphs. The term *ahl al-sunna* ('People of the Prophetic Tradition') was, moreover, used by early Sunnīs such as the *ahl al-ḥadīth* to define themselves, often in contrast to opponents termed *ahl al-bidaʿ* ('People of Religious Innovations') or more specific groups such as the Murjiʾa and the Muʿtazila.[85]

In terms of contemporary politics, many of the *ahl al-ḥadīth* upheld a pragmatic policy of critical loyalty to political authorities in order to preserve stability and order, although some are said to have supported the uprising of, for example, Muḥammad al-Nafs al-Zakiyya in the early ʿAbbāsid period.[86] They

---

81 See e.g. Melchert's discussion of Aḥmad b. Ḥanbal's beliefs in *Ahmad* 83–93.

82 Lucas, *Constructive critics* 323–325; Zaman, *Religion and politics* 52; Juynboll, Sunna. See also Ibn al-Ṣalāḥ, *Fatāwā* 1:213. Al-Khallāl (d. 311/923) ascribes to Aḥmad b. Ḥanbal the opinion that *ṣāḥib sunna* refers to those who ranked Abū Bakr, ʿUmar, ʿUthmān and ʿAlī in chronological order. See al-Khallāl, *al-Sunna* 1:408.

83 Lucas, *Constructive critics* 18–21, 282–285.

84 Lucas, *Constructive critics* 323–325.

85 See Introduction.

86 See Sections 2.2 and 2.3.

might have measured contemporary rulers critically against the Prophetic tradition and the standards of the first four caliphs, but at the same time they maintained loyalty by urging people to refrain from revolts and to preserve stability and communal unity as far as possible. Generally speaking, for the *ahl al-ḥadīth* the proper response to oppression was patience and endurance, since intra-Muslim fighting (*fitna*) was considered worse for the community, in terms of lives, property and violations of God's law, than oppressive leadership. Moreover, these scholars regarded religious authority as based solely on knowledge of the Qurʾān and the Prophetic Sunna, which placed it in the hands of the scholarly collective rather than in those of rulers or charismatic leaders. In this way, as with later Sunnīs, they made themselves in some sense independent of the ruler: the Muslim community was meant to unite around a common scheme of law and belief, regardless of current political policies.[87] By the early third/ninth century, when Khalīfa compiled his *Tārīkh*, this combination of critical political loyalty and text-based religious authority had become fundamental to many early Sunnī scholars' world view.

Another term used for certain early *ḥadīth* scholars is "Uthmānī.' A number of Basran *ḥadīth* scholars in the early ʿAbbāsid period are said to have held ʿUthmānī views.[88] By the late second/eighth century, it probably referred to (some of) those who ranked ʿUthmān above ʿAlī in general or who said that the best of the community after the Prophet is Abū Bakr, then ʿUmar, then ʿUthmān and then were silent about ʿAlī, although they would still maintain that ʿAlī was one of the greatest Companions.[89] The four positions on this

87 Melchert, *Ahmad* 93.

88 See e.g. Ibn Saʿd, *Ṭabaqāt* 9:125, 261, 287, 290–291. See also Crone, *God's rule* 128; Crone, ʿUthmāniyya.

89 Al-ʿIjlī mentions regarding Ṭalḥa b. Muṣarrif al-Yāmī that he was "a reliable (*thiqa*) Kufan Successor, who considered *nabīdh* forbidden and who was an ʿUthmānī who ranked ʿUthmān above ʿAlī (*kāna ʿuthmāniyyan yufaḍḍilu ʿUthmān ʿalā ʿAlī*)." Al-ʿIjlī, *Maʿrifat al-thiqāt* 1:479. See also al-Fasawī, *Maʿrifa* 2:678. Another example is Muḥammad b. ʿUbayd al-Ṭanāfisī (d. 204–205/819–821), whom al-ʿIjlī describes as "a reliable Kufan who was ʿUthmānī" and about whom Ibn Saʿd says, "He was reliable, had numerous *ḥadīth*s and was a *ṣāḥib sunna wa-jamāʿa*." Muḥammad b. ʿUbayd himself is reported to have said, "The best of this community after its Prophet is Abū Bakr, then ʿUmar and then ʿUthmān. Beware so that these Kufans do not deceive you!" Yaʿqūb b. Shayba al-Sadūsī (d. 262/875) also said about him, "He was one of those who ranked ʿUthmān above ʿAlī and this position is unusual among the Kufans." Al-ʿIjlī, *Maʿrifat al-thiqāt* 2:247; Ibn Saʿd, *Ṭabaqāt* 8:520; al-Dhahabī, *Siyar* 3552; Ibn Ḥajar, *Tahdhīb* 3:640. There is also a passage in al-Bukhārī's *Ṣaḥīḥ* that reads, "from Abū ʿAbd al-Raḥmān who was ʿUthmānī; he said to Ibn ʿAṭiyya, who was ʿAlawī, 'I know very well what encouraged your leader (i.e. ʿAlī) to shed blood.'" Al-Bukhārī, *Ṣaḥīḥ* 4:76 (*kitāb al-jihād, bāb idhā uḍṭurra al-rajul ilā-l-naẓar fī shuʿūr ahl al-dhimma* …)

issue among the early Sunnīs in general and the *ḥadīth* scholars in particular were (1) those who ranked the four Rāshidūn caliphs in chronological order beginning with Abū Bakr, then ʿUmar, then ʿUthmān and then ʿAlī, (2) those who ranked the first three in chronological order and then were silent about ʿAlī, (3) those who avoided the question of ʿUthmān's and ʿAlī's relative merits by simply noting that the two of them were the best after Abū Bakr and ʿUmar, and (4) those who ranked ʿAlī above ʿUthmān while still acknowledging the legitimacy of ʿUthmān's caliphate, although this latter position was often described as a moderate expression of *tashayyuʿ*.[90] In other words, the early Sunnīs agreed on the legitimacy of the caliphates of Abū Bakr, ʿUmar, ʿUthmān and ʿAlī, as well as on the precedence of Abū Bakr and ʿUmar in merit, but differed regarding the relative merit of ʿUthmān and ʿAlī. This point is also asserted by the summary of the acceptable views among the early *ḥadīth* scholars attributed to Khalīfa's contemporary, the leading *ḥadīth* authority Yaḥyā b. Maʿīn (d. 233/848):

> I asked Yaḥyā [b. Maʿīn], "What about one who says Abū Bakr and ʿUmar and ʿUthmān?" He replied, "He is correct. And one who says Abū Bakr and ʿUmar and ʿUthmān and ʿAlī is also correct. He who says Abū Bakr and ʿUmar and ʿAlī and ʿUthmān is a Shīʿī, but one who says Abū Bakr and ʿUmar and ʿUthmān, and stops at that, is correct." Yaḥyā added, "I say Abū Bakr and ʿUmar and ʿUthmān and ʿAlī. This is our view and our position."[91]

In the course of the third/ninth and fourth/tenth centuries, however, most Sunnīs came to agree upon the position that the best of the community after the Prophet are the four Rāshidūn caliphs and that their relative merits correspond to the order of their succession (Abū Bakr, then ʿUmar, then ʿUthmān and then ʿAlī). By the time Khalīfa compiled the *Tārīkh*, the views that ranked ʿUthmān as the third after Abū Bakr and ʿUmar (whether or not explicitly mentioning ʿAlī as the fourth) were most common in Basra, while the view that ranked ʿAlī above ʿUthmān was more prevalent in Kufa.[92] It is possibly this chrono-

---

Regarding this, Ibn Ḥajar says, "His words 'who was ʿUthmānī' mean that he ranked ʿUthmān above ʿAlī in merit … and his words 'who was ʿAlawī' mean that he ranked ʿAlī above ʿUthmān in merit and that is a well-known position (*madhhab mashhūr*) of a group from *ahl al-sunna* in Kufa." Ibn Ḥajar, *Fatḥ al-Bārī* 6:221.

90 See Ibn Taymiyya, *al-ʿAqīdat al-Wāsiṭiyya* 117–118. On *tashayyuʿ*, see Section 3.2.

91 Ibn Maʿīn, *Tārīkh* 3:465. Cited in Zaman, *Religion and politics* 52.

92 Ibn Taymiyya, *Minhāj al-sunna* 8:224–225; Ibn Ḥajar, *Fatḥ al-Bārī* 6:221. Abū Nuʿaym narrates that Sufyān al-Thawrī (d. 161/778) used to relate material about the merits of ʿAlī when

logical ranking of the Rāshidūn caliphs—including the ranking of ʿUthmān above ʿAlī and the objection to the idea of ʿAlī's superiority and unique right to leadership—to which Khalīfa's Basran contemporary al-Jāḥiẓ (d. 255/868–869) referred when he observed that the ʿUthmāniyya are "more numerous and have the most *fuqahāʾ* and *muḥaddithūn*."[93]

Given the infrequent usage of the term ʿUthmānī in third/ninth-century biographical dictionaries, it was probably not widely used by the *ḥadīth* scholars themselves. However, it is noteworthy that the ʿUthmānīs identified in Ibn Saʿd's *Ṭabaqāt* are found in Khalīfa's *isnād*s in the *Tārīkh*: ʿAbdallāh b. Shaqīq al-ʿUqaylī, Ibn ʿAwn, Ḥammād b. Zayd, Yazīd b. Zurayʿ and Bishr b. al-Mufaḍḍal.[94] On the basis of these associations, especially the link to Yazīd b. Zurayʿ, Zakkār and Wurtzel suggest that Khalīfa might have been ʿUthmānī.[95] There are, however, no references to such ʿUthmānī views in the sources, and it is not entirely clear what these ʿUthmānī views would have entailed. If one equates the ʿUthmāniyya with those who ranked ʿUthmān as the third and then were silent about ʿAlī, there is nothing that particularly suggests any differentiation of ʿAlī from the earlier caliphs in Khalīfa's *Tārīkh*; his accounts of the battles of the Camel and Ṣiffīn, for example, both emphasise ʿAlī's legitimacy as caliph and rather seem to fit the classical Sunnī position of the four Rāshidūn caliphs ranked in chronological order.[96] And if one equates it with the classical Sunnī position, then one might simply use 'early Sunnī' instead. Moreover, the term *ahl al-sunna* (or 'early Sunnī') in itself contains all these different positions regarding the ranking of the Rāshidūn caliphs that existed among the early Sunnīs, although the majority eventually agreed upon the ranking of the four Rāshidūn caliphs in chronological order. Thus, for the sake of clarity, the present book refers to Khalīfa's religio-political orientation as 'early Sunnī' and his scholarly community as the Basran *ḥadīth* scholars.

The same can be said about Wurtzel's speculation that Khalīfa "may have sympathized" with the so-called Nābita, whom he describes as "a school of Umayyad defenders" that was criticised by al-Jāḥiẓ in his *Risāla fī l-Nābita*.[97]

he entered Basra and material about the merits of ʿUthmān when he entered Kufa. Sufyān al-Thawrī is also reported to have said, "When you are in Syria, mention the merits of ʿAlī and when you are in Kufa, mention the merits of Abū Bakr and ʿUmar." Abū Nuʿaym al-Aṣbahānī, *Ḥilyat al-awliyāʾ* 7:26–27.

93 Al-Jāḥiẓ, *ʿUthmāniyya* 176.

94 Ibn Saʿd, *Ṭabaqāt* 9:125, 261, 287, 290–291. See also Lucas, *Constructive critics* 320.

95 Zakkār, Ibn Khayyāṭ al-ʿUṣfurī; Wurtzel, *Khalifa ibn Khayyat's History* 12.

96 See Chapter 8.

97 Wurtzel, *Khalifa ibn Khayyat's History* 3; al-Jāḥiẓ, *Rasāʾil* 2:7–22.

In al-Jāḥiẓ's usage, however, 'Nābita' seems to have been a pejorative term for the opponents of the Muʿtazila in certain matters of creed, so it probably tells us more about how al-Jāḥiẓ and his fellow Muʿtazila viewed their intellectual opponents than what these opponents actually believed.[98] Al-Jāḥiẓ might have referred to some *ḥadīth*-minded scholars like Khalīfa, but 'Nābita' was not a term that these scholars would have used for themselves, nor was it a term by which they became known in the heresiographical literature.[99] Besides the fact that there are no textual references to Nābita sympathies in relation to Khalīfa, the speculative description of him as possibly having sympathised with the 'group' that al-Jāḥiẓ called Nābita would not add much to our understanding of Khalīfa's views and scholarly environment, although it is correct that he opposed the Muʿtazila. Again, it is preferable to describe Khalīfa's religio-political orientation as early Sunnī and his scholarly community as *ḥadīth* scholars, rather than adopting a term that some intellectual opponents might have used for scholars like him.

In light of Khalīfa's known scholarly affiliates, from whom he transmitted *ḥadīth* and *akhbār*, he probably considered himself one of the *ahl al-ḥadīth* in terms of *fiqh* and *ʿaqīda*. Thus Ibn al-Nadīm counts Khalīfa among the 'traditionist jurisprudents' (*fuqahāʾ al-muḥaddithīn*) and *aṣḥāb al-ḥadīth* rather than other legal schools (*madhāhib*) such as the Mālikiyya, Ḥanafiyya and Shāfiʿiyya.[100] This affiliation is also indicated by Khalīfa's own students, who include many scholars from the *ahl al-ḥadīth*.[101] It is likewise indicated by Khalīfa's *Ṭabaqāt*, which focuses on the generations of *ḥadīth* transmitters, and by the necrologies in his *Tārīkh*, which primarily focus on prominent *ḥadīth* transmitters.[102] Khalīfa's somewhat limited attention to Mālikī, Ḥanafī and Shāfiʿī scholars might also suggest an affiliation to the Iraqi *ahl al-ḥadīth* rather than to any other legal school.[103] Since no legal works or opinions of Khalīfa are known, nothing more specific can be said regarding his legal views. It is clear, however, that Khalīfa's historical and political views in the *Tārīkh* correspond to those upheld by many of the *ahl al-ḥadīth* and by the early Sunnīs in general—for instance, the ranking of the Rāshidūn caliphs in chronological order, the probity of the Prophet's Companions and the critical loyalty towards political

---

98 See al-Qāḍī, Earliest "Nābita" 57. See also Pellat, Nābita.
99 See al-Qāḍī, Earliest "Nābita" 57–60.
100 Ibn al-Nadīm, *Fihrist* 2:111.
101 See Chapters 2 and 4.
102 See Chapter 6.
103 See Melchert, How Ḥanafism came to originate in Kufa 323–324.

authorities.[104] The narrations from Khalīfa in *Ṣaḥīḥ al-Bukhārī* also pertain to foundational beliefs among the *ahl al-ḥadīth*, such as the questioning in the grave, the night journey and the ascension (*al-isrāʾ wa-l-miʿrāj*), the Prophet's miracles, the Prophet's intercession on the Day of Judgement and the attributes of God as established in the revealed texts.[105] All of this suggests that Khalīfa and the *ahl al-ḥadīth* had much in common in the fields of *ʿaqīda* and possibly *fiqh* as well.

3.4 Ahl al-Raʾy *and the Rationalist Trends*

Besides the *ahl al-ḥadīth* in Iraq, other early Sunnī groups also based their *fiqh* mainly on textual sources, but with a little more reliance on reason in working with the texts—such as the early Mālikiyya and Shāfiʿiyya (both of whom are usually categorised among the *ahl al-ḥadīth* as opposed to *ahl al-raʾy*).[106] However, the main contrast to the *ahl al-ḥadīth* in Iraq was the so-called *ahl al-raʾy* ('Proponents of Individual Legal Reasoning'), headed by the early Ḥanafīs, who distinguished themselves by their more rationalist approach to jurisprudence.[107] The idea of a complete regional and methodological division between *ahl al-ḥadīth* and *ahl al-raʾy* might be misleading for the general development of Islamic jurisprudence,[108] but it was ideologically important in early third/ninth-century Iraq, as is evident from the negative connotations of the concept of *raʾy* (lit. 'view' or 'opinion') among the *ahl al-ḥadīth* at the time.[109] These *ahl al-raʾy* were particularly prominent in Iraq, where they constituted the main scholarly trend alongside the *ahl al-ḥadīth* in the late second/eighth and early third/ninth centuries. Some proponents of *raʾy*, as opposed to the *ahl al-ḥadīth*, were also associated with theological views such as those of the Murjiʾa and the Muʿtazila, which was also probably an important factor in the split. In general, however, the main difference between the *ahl al-ḥadīth* and the early Ḥanafīs were their disagreements in *fiqh* and *uṣūl al-fiqh*. Moreover, many third/ninth-century Ḥanafīs explicitly

104 See Chapters 7–8.

105 Appendix, nos. 1, 3, 4, 5, 13, 14, 18, 21.

106 Melchert, *Formation* 68–80, 164–177. See also Wymann-Landgraf, *Mālik and Medina* 8–16.

107 On the "Basran school of *raʾy*" in the late second/eighth and early third/ninth centuries, see Melchert, *Formation* 41–47. On *raʾy* in general, see Melchert, *Formation* 1–13; Hallaq, *Origins and evolution* 74–76; El Shamsy, *Canonization of Islamic law* 22–28; Wymann-Landgraf, *Mālik and Medina* 141–145.

108 Wymann-Landgraf, *Mālik and Medina* 8–11; Melchert, How Ḥanafism came to originate in Kufa 346.

109 See Melchert, *Formation* 1–7; Hallaq, *Origins and evolution* 74–76.

distanced themselves and their school from the connections of some earlier scholars with the Murji'a and the Muʿtazila.[110]

The Murji'a generally stood for a deferring of judgement to God on the early intra-Companion conflicts and held that belief (*īmān*) consists solely of affirmation in the heart and declaration by the tongue to the exclusion of actions—in contrast to the *ahl al-ḥadīth*, who held that true belief consists of affirmation in the heart, declaration with the tongue and actions by the limbs.[111] The Murji'a also held that belief does not increase or decrease, while the *ahl al-ḥadīth* held that it increases with obedience to God and decreases with disobedience. The Murji'a were severely opposed by the *ahl al-ḥadīth*, and Murjiʾī views were thus more common among early scholars associated with *ahl al-ra'y*.[112]

The most prominent theological adversary of the *ahl al-ḥadīth* in Iraq was the loose association of rationalist theologians known as the Muʿtazila. As noted above, one of the main debates in the early third/ninth century concerned the Muʿtazilī doctrine of the 'createdness of the Qur'ān,' which was imposed on ʿAbbāsid officials and scholars during the *miḥna* that began in 218/833. The Muʿtazila became known for their 'five principles' (*al-tawḥīd, al-ʿadl, al-waʿd wa-l-waʿīd, al-manzila bayna l-manzilatayn* and *al-amr bi-l-maʿrūf wa-l-nahy ʿan al-munkar*) and their particular understanding thereof, which included ideas such as humans' absolute free will and denial of God's attributes. At this early stage, however, the Muʿtazila were characterised by a diversity of doctrines and were mainly unified in their rationalist approach and methodology; the classical Basran and Baghdadi schools came together later in the third/ninth century.[113]

Other theological parties rejected by the *ahl al-ḥadīth* were the Qadariyya, who believed in humans' free will independent of God's will, and the so-called Jahmiyya (named after Jahm b. Ṣafwān, d. 128/746), who, similar to the

---

110 Melchert calls this the "traditionalization of Ḥanafī theology." *Formation* 8–13, 54–60. For an early *ʿaqīda* text (agreed upon by all Sunnīs) by a Ḥanafī scholar, see al-Ṭaḥāwī's (d. 321/933) *al-ʿAqīdat al-Ṭaḥāwiyya*.

111 Ibn Ḥajar said in *Hady al-Sārī*, "*Irjā'* has the sense of delaying (*ta'khīr*) and is of two types among the scholars: (1) some mean by it the delaying in declaring one's position on which of the two warring factions after [the death of] ʿUthmān was in the right and (2) some mean by it the delaying in declaring that the one who commits major sins and abandons obligations enters the Fire, on the basis that belief, according to them, consists of assertion (*iqrār*) and conviction (*iʿtiqād*) and that avoiding actions [in accordance with the commands and prohibitions] does not harm it." Cited by ʿAbd al-Fattāḥ Abū Ghudda in the footnotes to al-Laknawī, *al-Rafʿ wa-l-takmīl* 352n1.

112 Melchert, *Formation* 56–58; Zaman, *Religion and politics* 211.

113 Gimaret, Muʿtazila.

Muʿtazila, are associated with the doctrine of the 'createdness of the Qurʾān' and the negation of God's attributes, among other things.[114] All these theological parties became important in the heresiographical discourse of the *ahl al-ḥadīth* and as points of contrast in their definitions of their own creed.

In terms of politics, the *ahl al-ḥadīth* and the *ahl al-raʾy*—unlike the Khawārij and the Shīʿī factions—shared the appreciation of communal togetherness. Despite their disagreements on some issues, they preferred unity and refused to create separatist communities under their own leaders, although they might consider the ruling dynasty unjust and oppressive.[115] This broad, non-separatist community is sometimes referred to as *jamāʿī*.[116] Although there is minor support in the early sources for the adjective *jamāʿī* as the opposite of Khārijī, it was not widely used by the Muslims themselves.[117] It does, however, highlight the minimum political ideal that the broad, non-separatist proto-Sunnī community (including both *ahl al-ḥadīth* and *ahl al-raʾy*) had in common, before the later formulations of classical Sunnism. It also included many of those 'moderate' Shīʿī or ʿAlid sympathisers who inclined to the majority community and did not promote active rebellion (like some of the Zaydiyya) or rejection of the first caliphs and most Companions (like the Rāfiḍa or Imāmiyya). Altogether, the *ahl al-ḥadīth* and the *ahl al-raʾy* remained within the majority community and generally accepted the current political order under ʿAbbāsid rule, although they might have been critical of specific rulers and their policies.

114 See Aḥmad b. Ḥanbal's rejected theological groups in Ibn Abī Yaʿlā, *Ṭabaqāt al-ḥanābila* 1:65–74, and Melchert's notes on these groups in *Ahmad* 89–93. See also Montgomery Watt, Djahmiyya.

115 Crone, *God's rule* 28. As the Ḥanafī jurist and *ḥadīth* scholar al-Ṭaḥāwī (d. 321/933) states in his well-known *ʿaqīda* text, "We do not accept any rebellion against our leaders or the administrators of our public affairs, even if they are oppressive. We also do not pray for evil to befall any one of them or withdraw our allegiance from them. We consider our civic duty to them concordant with our duty to God, the Sublime and Exalted, and legally binding on us, unless they command us to the immoral. We pray for their probity, success, and welfare." Al-Ṭaḥāwī, *al-ʿAqīda* 24, trans. Yusuf in *The creed of Imam al-Ṭaḥāwī* 70. See also Ibn Abī l-ʿIzz, *Sharḥ al-ʿaqīdat al-Ṭaḥāwiyya* 540–544.

116 Hodgson originally used the adjective *jamāʿī-sunnī*, but Crone (and others) have limited it to *jamāʿī*. See Hodgson, *Venture of Islam* 1 278; Crone, *God's rule* 28–29.

117 E.g. al-Yaʿqūbī, *Kitāb al-Buldān* 352. Al-Dhahabī also narrates that al-Jāḥiẓ said about Abū ʿUbayda Maʿmar b. al-Muthannā (d. c. 210/825), "There was no *jamāʿī* or *khārijī* on earth more knowledgeable in all the sciences than Abū ʿUbayda." Al-Dhahabī, *Siyar* 3913.

4 Historiographical Context

4.1 *Forms of Historical Writing:* Tārīkh *and* Ṭabaqāt

The formative period of Islamic historical writing took place from the mid-second/eighth to mid-third/ninth centuries, during which time chronography, biography and prosopography emerged in forms that remained familiar throughout the classical period.[118] Khalīfa's *Tārīkh* and *Ṭabaqāt* correspond to the forms of *tārīkh* ('chronography') and *ṭabaqāt* ('prosopography arranged by generations'). Although they differ from many early works, there are a few other surviving chronological works that contain *ṭabaqāt* material and that were compiled by *ḥadīth* scholars or *ḥadīth*-minded jurisprudents—among them the *tārīkh* works of ʿAbd al-Malik b. Ḥabīb, al-Fasawī, Ibn Abī Khaythama and Abū Zurʿa al-Dimashqī. Based on these works and historical sections in some early *ḥadīth* collections (e.g. Ibn Abī Shayba's *Muṣannaf*), one may discern some patterns in the way third/ninth-century *ḥadīth* scholars compiled history. Although not representing a well-defined genre, these works share some important characteristics in terms of form, content, historical perspective and context. Before turning to these works, however, it is useful to look at the development of the two general types of *tārīkh* and *ṭabaqāt* compilation.[119]

4.1.1 *Tārīkh*

The second/eighth century saw an expanding corpus of historical material put down in writing and the development of new frameworks to structure that material.[120] The main narrative units within these frameworks were the *akhbār* (sing. *khabar*)—that is, reports about past events consisting of a chain of transmission (*isnād*) and a text (*matn*), which usually ranges from one line to about half a page in length and sometimes more. While the *ḥadīth* compilers arranged their material according to legal subjects (in *muṣannaf* collections) or according to transmitters (in *musnad* collections), the *akhbār* compilers constructed narrative frameworks proper—whether as single-subject texts or as large-scale

118 See Robinson, *Islamic historiography* 24–30.

119 These two categories might not have been as distinct and solidified in the early centuries AH as generally assumed, and the works of the aforementioned *ḥadīth*-minded scholars, including Khalīfa, likely contributed to shaping them in the course of the third/ninth century. Yet, some categorisation is necessary in order to discuss the two general forms of compilation that these scholars adopted. Moreover, in the case of Khalīfa's two works, there is clear evidence for a division of material into chronography (as in the *Tārīkh*) and prosopography (as in the *Ṭabaqāt*), although other third/ninth-century scholars combined the two forms of compilation in their works.

120 Robinson, *Islamic historiography* 24.

chronicles. Generally speaking, the *ḥadīth* scholars focused mainly on the lifetime of the Prophet and the Companions, while the *akhbār* compilers took an interest in a much longer historical period. But even when they treated the same periods, such as the Prophetic period, their different interests, aims and methods led to different treatments of the material. The *ḥadīth* compilers were concerned primarily with the transmission and authentication of individual reports and their application in *fiqh, ʿaqīda* and other sciences. They generally selected and presented reports one by one, introduced by (ideally) complete *isnād*s; establishing chronological sequences of historical material was not a primary concern at the stage of compilation, although the material was occasionally arranged chronologically.[121] The *ḥadīth* scholars were, after all, experts primarily in collecting, transmitting and authenticating material—besides using it in *fiqh, ʿaqīda* or other scholarly fields.

By contrast, the *akhbār* compilers, or *akhbārīyūn*, were not specialists in authentication of material, but concerned themselves with contextualisation and chronology. Broadly speaking, they were also more interested in political, administrative and cultural subjects than in the *ḥadīth* scholars' core subjects of legal rulings and credal beliefs. Key questions for the *akhbārīyūn* were when a certain event occurred, where it occurred, what caused it, who were involved and its relation to other events.[122] This contextual information could generally not be derived from individual *ḥadīth*s, but required other types and combinations of material. Thus, while *ḥadīth* works are largely limited to *isnād*-equipped reports, works of *akhbār* history tend to include a wider range of material, such as Qurʾānic verses, poems, lists, documents and even comments or longer narratives by the compiler himself.[123] As free-standing textual units, the *akhbār* in themselves could sometimes be disconnected, chronologically or geographically, from their original context.[124] By providing chronological frameworks and other forms of narrative schemes, the *akhbār* compilers sought to furnish reports with context and thereby created narratives that could differ substantially from one another.

It is evident from the later biographical dictionaries and works of transmitter criticism that the *ḥadīth* scholars distinguished themselves from the *akhbārīyūn*, whose interests, methods and works they considered unsound for the subjects of law and belief, or simply tangential to them. Already in the

121 Zaman, *Maghāzī* and the *muḥaddithūn* 3–4.

122 Görke, Relationship between *maghāzī* and *ḥadīth* 175.

123 Watt, Materials 24–31, Reliability 31–43; Leder, Literary use of the *khabar* 309–310; Görke, Relationship between *maghāzī* and *ḥadīth* 173–174.

124 Donner, *Narratives* 260–263.

first two centuries AH, *ḥadīth* scholarship seems to have been distinguished from *akhbār* history—the former based on *ḥadīth* methods and often (but not exclusively) legal concerns, and the latter based on less rigorous methods and wider 'historical' concerns.[125] Although some scholars transmitted both types of material (Ibn Isḥāq being one of the most obvious examples), a *ḥadīth* work of the late second/eighth and early third/ninth centuries would be distinguished from other types of historical compilation.[126] Henceforth, however, the primary concern is *akhbār* history and, more specifically, chronography.

Besides the more complex Prophetic biographies—like Ibn Isḥāq's *Sīra*—most early works of *akhbār* history from the mid-to-late second/eighth century are texts on single subjects, which may or may not have been parts of larger compilations.[127] For example, the two *akhbār* compilers Abū Mikhnaf (d. 157/774) and Sayf b. ʿUmar (d. c. 180/796) are credited with numerous titles on different subjects.[128] However, towards the end of the second/eighth century, with compilers such as al-Wāqidī (d. 207/822), al-Haytham b. ʿAdī (d. 207/822) and al-Madāʾinī (d. c. 228/843), more synthetic forms of historiography appeared, in which chronology became increasingly important.

The form of chronography that Khalīfa compiled had its precursors in caliphal and annalistic chronography, the former of which appeared first and may have been the basis for the latter.[129] Both Ibn Isḥāq (d. c. 150/767) and Abū Maʿshar (d. 170/787) are credited with caliphal chronicles (*tārīkh al-khulafāʾ*) before the earliest known annalist, al-Haytham b. ʿAdī.[130] It is possible, as some modern historians have suggested, that these forms of Arabic chronography developed initially under influence from non-Arabic historical traditions (especially Syriac historical writing),[131] but, by the late second/eighth and early third/ninth centuries, they were nonetheless well-known ways of compiling history among Arabic-speaking Muslim scholars. However, Khalīfa and his likes must have been important for the further establishment and development of these forms of chronography in scholarly circles.

125 See Landau-Tasseron, Sayf ibn ʿUmar 9; Zaman, *Maghāzī* and the *muḥaddithūn* 13; Görke, Relationship between *maghāzī* and *ḥadīth* 185.

126 Zaman, *Maghāzī* and the *muḥaddithūn* 13.

127 Donner, *Narratives* 302–306.

128 Robinson, *Islamic historiography* 28.

129 Donner, *Narratives* 182–183, 230–231; Robinson, *Islamic historiography* 47. See also Rosenthal, *History of Muslim historiography* 71–93.

130 Robinson, *Islamic historiography* 47. On al-Haytham b. ʿAdī, see Leder, *Das Korpus al-Haiṯam*.

131 See Rosenthal, *History of Muslim historiography* 71–81; Hoyland, Arabic, Syriac and Greek historiography; Robinson, *Islamic historiography* 43–50.

Besides Khalīfa's *Tārīkh*, the earliest surviving annalistic work is the *Tārīkh* of the Andalusian Mālikī jurist ʿAbd al-Malik b. Ḥabīb (d. 238/853). There has been some discussion about the ascription to Ibn Ḥabīb and the completeness of the surviving recension, but Aguadé reasonably argues that the general content can be ascribed to Ibn Ḥabīb. It was, however, subjected to some glosses and interpolations in the centuries after its compilation.[132] Although Ibn Ḥabīb's work is shorter than Khalīfa's, it covers the period from the Creation to the Muslim conquest of al-Andalus and concludes with a *ṭabaqāt* section on jurisprudents (*fuqahā*ʾ). A similar but more extensive work from the generation after Khalīfa is *al-Maʿrifa wa-l-tārīkh* of the Basran *ḥadīth* scholar Yaʿqūb b. Sufyān al-Fasawī (d. 277/890), which begins with a chronological section (of which only the period 135–242/752–857 survives) and continues with biographical accounts of *ḥadīth* transmitters. Other similar works by third/ninth-century scholars, containing both *tārīkh* and *ṭabaqāt* material, are the Baghdadi *ḥadīth* scholar Ibn Abī Khaythama's (d. 279/892) *al-Tārīkh al-kabīr* and the Syrian *ḥadīth* scholar Abū Zurʿa al-Dimashqī's (d. 282/895) *Tārīkh*.[133]

Apart from these combined *tārīkh* and *ṭabaqāt* works, the mid-to-late third/ninth century witnessed the emergence of large-scale synthetic histories, such as the 'universal' chronicles of al-Dīnawarī (d. c. 282/895), al-Yaʿqūbī (d. c. 292/905), al-Ṭabarī (d. 310/923) and al-Masʿūdī (d. 345/956). These works are exclusively devoted to chronological history, without any *ṭabaqāt* material. Moreover, while the works of, for example, Khalīfa and al-Fasawī seem to have been compiled primarily for an audience of *ḥadīth* scholars, many later universal chronicles were circulated in other contexts. This is reflected in the fact that al-Dīnawarī, al-Yaʿqūbī and al-Masʿūdī all eschew the *isnād* system—which had become the hallmark of traditionist scholarship—in favour of synthetic, continuous narratives. Also, some universal histories from the later third/ninth century onwards were compiled under patronage or in close proximity to the ʿAbbāsids or their successor dynasties.[134]

4.1.2 *Ṭabaqāt*

Ṭabaqāt refers to a particular type of Arabic prosopography: biographical dictionaries primarily organised by generations. Whereas biography is about distinctive individuals, prosopography "compiles and organizes those items of biographical data that mark an individual's belonging to a group."[135] In the early

132 See Aguadé's introduction to Ibn Ḥabīb, *Tārīkh* 77–108; Clarke, *Muslim conquest* 29.
133 On all these works, see below.
134 On universal history and patronage, see Marsham, Universal histories 445–452.
135 Robinson, *Islamic historiography* 66.

period, these works were compiled about distinct groups, such as those who possessed special merits (e.g. the Companions of the Prophet) or who were involved in particular fields of learning (e.g. *ḥadīth* transmitters, jurisprudents or Qur'ān reciters). They reflect the important place of lists in early Islamic literature, which is also a defining characteristic of Khalīfa's two works.[136] In addition to the generation-based *ṭabaqāt* format, alphabetically arranged biographical dictionaries appeared in the third/ninth century. An example of this is al-Bukhārī's alphabetically arranged catalogue of *ḥadīth* transmitters, known as *al-Tārīkh al-kabīr*.[137]

Both *ṭabaqāt* works and alphabetically arranged dictionaries became popular among early *ḥadīth* transmitter critics in their effort to identify, classify and evaluate transmitters (in the discipline known as *ʿilm al-rijāl*). In fact, most surviving early *ṭabaqāt* works were compiled by *ḥadīth* scholars, among them Ibn Saʿd, Khalīfa, Muslim b. al-Ḥajjāj, al-Fasawī and Ibn Abī Khaythama.[138] The *ṭabaqāt* format also resembles to some extent the *musnad* form of *ḥadīth* collection that was arranged by transmitters.[139] It is thus clear that *ḥadīth* transmitter criticism gave an important impetus to the development of early *ṭabaqāt* writing.[140] Our concern here, however, is not the origins of the *ṭabaqāt* format, nor the *ṭabaqāt* literature as a whole, but specifically the format's importance among the *ḥadīth* scholars of the third/ninth century.

The *ḥadīth* scholars compiled *ṭabaqāt* works that served the needs of their discipline. Their methods of authenticating *ḥadīth* were based primarily on the evaluation of the *isnād*—the chain of transmitters that, for a report to be considered sound (*ṣaḥīḥ*), had to stretch back from their own time to the Prophet and his Companions.[141] In general, this *isnād* evaluation consisted of two main elements: first, to establish whether the transmitters in the *isnād* had (or at least could have) met each other and, second, to establish the reliability of each link in the *isnād* by examining its 'uprightness' (*ʿadāla*) and 'accuracy' (*ḍabṭ*).[142] Both elements are reflected in the scope of the *ṭabaqāt* works, which

136 On the lists in Khalīfa's *Tārīkh*, see Ch. 6.

137 See Robinson, *Islamic historiography* 68–72.

138 See Gilliot, Ṭabakāt.

139 Makdisi, Ṭabaqāt 376.

140 Robinson, *Islamic historiography* 67.

141 On the *ḥadīth* scholars' evaluations of the content of *ḥadīths*, see Brown, How we know early ḥadīth critics.

142 Besides these two elements, the *ḥadīth* scholars also add that for a *ḥadīth* to be considered *ṣaḥīḥ* it must not be 'anomalous' (*shādhdh*) or 'defective' (*muʿallal*). See e.g. Ibn al-Ṣalāḥ, *ʿUlūm al-ḥadīth* 11–14; al-Sakhāwī, *Fatḥ al-Mughīth* 1:23–29. See also Brown, *Hadith* 77–92.

identify transmitters and locate them in the scholarly networks, as well as providing material regarding their capacity and reputation as transmitters. Not all *ṭabaqāt* compilers, however, included evaluations of transmitters. Some works, like Khalīfa's *Ṭabaqāt*, are restricted to basic biographical information. Other works, like Ibn Saʿd's *Ṭabaqāt*, contain material on the subjects' abilities as narrators, including both opinions attributed to other scholars and the compilers' own judgements. In either case, however, these biographical works became crucial in the science of *ḥadīth* transmitter criticism (*al-jarḥ wa-l-taʿdīl*), by which scholars evaluated the uprightness and accuracy of the transmitters and, by extension, the evidential value of their reports in the different scholarly fields.[143]

Much of the above also pertains to the alphabetically arranged dictionaries, which gradually took over as the dominant form of compilation for transmitter critics. In terms of compilation and arrangement, however, the *ṭabaqāt* format involved a greater concern than the alphabetic format for chronology, geography and genealogy. Thus, in addition to their role as reference works, the *ṭabaqāt* works could (and often did) make more explicit claims about history. An example is the role of *ṭabaqāt* literature in the formation of the legal schools from the late third/ninth century onwards. In this period of increasing rivalry between schools, all major schools had *ṭabaqāt* works compiled about their associates. Besides identifying the scholars, these works set down the school's past and defined and contrasted it with other schools.[144] The inclusion/exclusion and evaluation of transmitters in the early *ṭabaqāt* works of *ḥadīth* transmitters had similar functions of identifying the inheritors and transmitters of the Prophetic tradition and classifying their scholarly authority.[145] These compilations of the generations of transmitters also highlighted the continuity between the past (the Prophetic and Rāshidūn periods) and the scholars' own time. For early Sunnī scholars, across the legal schools, authentic accounts of the Prophetic tradition constituted the main source of guidance alongside the Qur'ān. The tradition of *isnād* criticism that developed to authenticate these accounts required righteous, honest and accurate transmitters in each generation, which these *ṭabaqāt* works helped to clarify and determine.[146] In this way, *ʿilm al-rijāl* in general, and *ṭabaqāt* works in particular, affirmed the unbroken link and continuity with the Prophet and his Companions. This common

143 See e.g. Ibn Ḥajar, *Nuzhat al-naẓar* 286–288.
144 See Makdisi, Ṭabaqāt 385–387; Robinson, *Islamic historiography* 73.
145 Makdisi, Ṭabaqāt 373.
146 See Judd, *Religious scholars* 25.

understanding of the continuity of the Prophetic tradition through the transmission of *ḥadīth* was fundamental to the articulation of early Sunnism.[147]

Some early *ṭabaqāt* works also suggest a relation to chronography and the subject of political history, which is not usually associated with the early *ḥadīth* scholars.[148] In the *ḥadīth* collections, establishing chronology was not the primary concern, and compilation of political history usually took the form of sections on military expeditions (*maghāzī*) and, occasionally, civil wars (*fitan*).[149] Instead, a number of surviving examples of annalistic chronography (*tārīkh*), compiled by *ḥadīth* scholars, were combined with, or closely related to, *ṭabaqāt* material and the discipline of *ʿilm al-rijāl*.

The first examples are Khalīfa's *Tārīkh* and *Ṭabaqāt*, which were transmitted alongside each other by both Baqī b. Makhlad and Mūsā b. Zakariyyā al-Tustarī. These two works were also available to many later scholars citing Khalīfa.[150] There is some overlap between the material on the births and deaths of prominent individuals in the *Tārīkh* and the *Ṭabaqāt*.[151] More important, they seem to complement each other and reflect different but related aspects of Khalīfa's scholarly interests. The *Tārīkh*, on the one hand, outlines the political and administrative chronology of the Muslim polity from its origin in Medina and identifies the key dates, events, personalities and institutions. The *Ṭabaqāt*, on the other hand, identifies and organises the distinctive members of the Muslim community by generation, genealogy and location—focusing on *ḥadīth* transmitters—from the Prophet and his Companions in Medina to the other urban centres of the Muslim world. Taken together, in addition to their roles as chronological and biographical reference books, they represent an early Sunnī *ḥadīth* scholar's vision of the defining political and scholarly constituents of the Muslim community.

Another early scholar who combined the formats of *tārīkh* and *ṭabaqāt* was the Andalusian Mālikī jurist ʿAbd al-Malik b. Ḥabīb. Most of his short *Tārīkh* (only 179 pages in the published edition) consists of a chronology of mankind from the Creation, via the Prophet Muḥammad's lifetime and the subsequent caliphs, to the Muslim conquest of al-Andalus. After that, Ibn Ḥabīb outlines the generations of jurisprudents (*fuqahāʾ*) in a brief *ṭabaqāt* section (about a tenth of the total work), arranged according to generations and locations (Med-

147 Lucas, *Constructive critics* 18.

148 See Robinson, *Islamic historiography* 103.

149 See ʿAbd al-Razzāq, *Muṣannaf* 5:313–492; Ibn Abī Shayba, *Muṣannaf* 12:5–59, 13:5–79, 196–503, 14:5–311.

150 See Chapter 2.

151 See Chapter 6. Also noted by Judd in *Religious scholars* 28.

ina, Mecca, Iraq, Syria, Egypt and al-Andalus).[152] In the chronological section, Ibn Ḥabīb includes some standard material on the earlier Prophets, the Prophet Muḥammad and the caliphs, but also a good amount of anecdotes, prophecies and exhortatory stories.[153] Although these latter aspects of Ibn Ḥabīb's chronological section differ from Khalīfa's straightforward and rather dry narrative, Ibn Ḥabīb's work illustrates the link between *tārīkh* and *ṭabaqāt* compilation. It also highlights the potential use of *ṭabaqāt* for defining groups—in this case, the *fuqahāʾ* of the Muslim community.

The third combined *tārīkh-ṭabaqāt* work is *al-Maʿrifa wa-l-tārīkh* of the Basran *ḥadīth* scholar al-Fasawī, who is said to have studied under Khalīfa.[154] Judging from what survives in later sources and the form of what survives, the *tārīkh* section seems to have begun with the Meccan period of the Prophet's life and to have continued to the mid-third/ninth century.[155] The extant annalistic section covers the period from 135/752–753 to 242/856–857. It might have contained an account of the Creation, but the surviving reports suggest that al-Fasawī, similar to Khalīfa, focused mainly on the period from the Prophet's lifetime onwards, although al-Fasawī's scope seems to have extended beyond Khalīfa's strict focus on politics and administration—including, for instance, the Meccan period, some 'proofs of prophethood' (*dalāʾil al-nubuwwa*) and the virtues of certain Companions.[156] Al-Fasawī is particularly concerned with the dates of birth and death of scholars, especially *ḥadīth* scholars, which dominate many of the year sections in his work. The focus on chronology and dates, as well as the structure and style of the year sections, resembles Khalīfa's *Tārīkh*, although it lacks Khalīfa's separate list sections.[157] In terms of historical views, al-Fasawī's accounts imply an early Sunnī perspective on the history of the Muslim community, similar to the aforementioned works of Khalīfa and Ibn Ḥabīb.[158] The *ṭabaqāt* section is arranged initially by generations and names but then proceeds without any clear structure, which might suggest that al-Fasawī read it out from notebooks to his students.[159] Unlike Khalīfa in his

152 Ibn Ḥabīb, *Tārīkh* 156–178.

153 See Clarke, *Muslim conquest* 29.

154 See al-ʿUmarī's introduction to al-Fasawī's *Maʿrifa* 1:88.

155 Al-Fasawī, *Maʿrifa* 1:115–213, 3:248–454.

156 Al-Fasawī, *Maʿrifa* 3:248–454.

157 Al-Fasawī, *Maʿrifa* 1:115–213.

158 See e.g. al-Fasawī, *Maʿrifa* 3:398–409. Melchert notes that al-Fasawī "seems to represent a strand of Basran Sunnism." Melchert, al-Fasawī, Yaʿqūb b. Sufyān.

159 See al-ʿUmarī's introduction to al-Fasawī, *Maʿrifa* 1:52–53; Melchert, How Ḥanafism came to originate in Kufa 332; Melchert, al-Fasawī, Yaʿqūb b. Sufyān.

Ṭabaqāt, al-Fasawī also includes material on subjects pertaining to their scholarly networks and qualities.

A fourth work that combines *tārīkh* and *ṭabaqāt* is *al-Tārīkh al-kabīr* of Aḥmad b. Abī Khaythama (d. 279/892), an associate of Aḥmad b. Ḥanbal active in Baghdad.[160] Unlike the others, Ibn Abī Khaythama's chronological sections only pertain to the Prophet's lifetime and are placed inside the *ṭabaqāt* structure. Thus the Meccan chronology precedes the *ṭabaqāt* of the Meccan Companions, and the Medinan chronology precedes that of the Medinan Companions.[161] Most similar to Khalīfa's *Tārīkh* in terms of form and content is the annalistic chronology of the Medinan period, which is divided into year sections.[162] The rest of Ibn Abī Khaythama's work is structured according to cities and the *ḥadīth* transmitters in them.

A fifth work is the *Tārīkh* of the Syrian *ḥadīth* scholar Abū Zurʿa al-Dimashqī (d. 282/895), who is also known to have compiled an independent (now lost) *Ṭabaqāt*.[163] The beginning of the extant recension of his *Tārīkh* consists of a chronological biography of the Prophet Muḥammad and short sections for the reigns of Abū Bakr, ʿUmar and ʿUthmān, followed by even briefer accounts of the Umayyads and ʿAbbāsids until Hārūn al-Rashīd. The remaining parts contain historical and biographical material pertaining to Syria, including some descriptions of the Companions there and a section on al-Awzāʿī (d. 157/774).[164] The chronological material at the beginning of Abū Zurʿa's *Tārīkh* is sparser than the other works discussed here, and its overall structure is less systematic. Moreover, the biographical material is not structured according to the *ṭabaqāt* format. Abū Zurʿa's *Tārīkh* is worth considering, however, in relation to the other works because of its similarity in style (short chronological reports), its combination of chronological and biographical material, and its possible relation to his now lost *Ṭabaqāt*. Abū Zurʿa was a prominent *ḥadīth* scholar whose teachers included Aḥmad b. Ḥanbal, Yaḥyā b. Maʿīn and many followers of al-Awzāʿī. He has been described as Ḥanbalī or Mālikī but might have been affiliated with the legal school of al-Awzāʿī. His writings also include some hostile statements about the Qadariyya and Abū Ḥanīfa, which resemble the stances

160 Al-Dhahabī, *Siyar* 782.

161 Ibn Abī Khaythama, *Tārīkh* 1:152–181, 365–392; 2:5–41.

162 Ibn Abī Khaythama, *Tārīkh* 1:365–392, 2:5–41.

163 On his *Ṭabaqāt*, see Gerhard, Das Kitāb al-Ṭabaqat. See also Judd, Abū Zurʿa al-Dimashqī; Borrut, *Entre mémoire et pouvoir* 56.

164 For a summary of Abū Zurʿa's work, see al-Qawjānī's introduction to Abū Zurʿa al-Dimashqī, *Tārīkh* 107–110.

of al-Awzāʿī and Aḥmad b. Ḥanbal.[165] In addition, his *Tārīkh* might reflect the position of those who ranked Abū Bakr, then ʿUmar and then ʿUthmān as the best of the community after the Prophet and who then were silent about ʿAlī: it contains separate sections for the reigns of the first three caliphs, while ʿAlī's reign is ignored and simply described as a five-year *fitna* "until the community united under Muʿāwiya in the year 40/661, which they called the year of unity (*sanat al-jamāʿa*)."[166]

To the above works, one could add Ibn Saʿd's *Ṭabaqāt*, which begins with a partially chronological biography of the Prophet, before *ṭabaqāt* sections on the Companions and the later generations in the different cities.[167] Some later works by major *ḥadīth* scholars also combine the *tārīkh* and *ṭabaqāt* formats, but they were compiled after the third/ninth century—for example, al-Azdī's (d. 334/945) *Tārīkh al-Mawṣil*, which might have been combined with his (now lost) *Ṭabaqāt muḥaddithī al-Mawṣil*, and Ibn Ḥibbān's (d. 354/965) *Kitāb al-Thiqāt*, which begins with a chronological history (Prophetic to ʿAbbāsid period) and continues with generations of *ḥadīth* transmitters.[168]

Taken together, the above-mentioned works indicate some relationship between *tārīkh* and *ṭabaqāt*: the former was unusual in the early *ḥadīth* circles, but when it was compiled, it was often in relation to the latter and with a concern for *ʿilm al-rijāl*. Some *ḥadīth* scholars also compiled independent *ṭabaqāt* works without any concern for chronography, such as Muslim b. al-Ḥajjāj in his *Ṭabaqāt*.[169] However, the above examples suggest some links between the two formats, links that are worth examining further in order to understand the historiographical tradition in which Khalīfa compiled his works.

4.2 Tārīkh *Works Compiled by Early* Ḥadīth *Scholars*

On the basis of the above outline of combined *tārīkh* and *ṭabaqāt* writing among third/ninth-century *ḥadīth* scholars, this section highlights what their works have in common. The main examples are Khalīfa's *Tārīkh*, Ibn Ḥabīb's *Tārīkh*, Ibn Saʿd's *Ṭabaqāt*, al-Fasawī's *al-Maʿrifa wa-l-tārīkh*, Ibn Abī Khaythama's *Tārīkh* and Abū Zurʿa al-Dimashqī's *Tārīkh*.[170] The section outlines

165 Judd, Abū Zurʿa al-Dimashqī.

166 Abū Zurʿa al-Dimashqī, *Tārīkh* 1:187–188.

167 Ibn Saʿd, *Ṭabaqāt* 1:4–436, 2:5–288.

168 Rosenthal, al-Azdī; al-Azdī, *Tārīkh al-Mawṣil*; Ibn Ḥibbān, *Thiqāt*. On the dating of al-Azdī's work, see Robinson, Local historian's debt 523–524.

169 Muslim b. al-Ḥajjāj, *Ṭabaqāt*.

170 Now lost *tārīkh* and *ṭabaqāt* works are attributed to *akhbārīyūn* in the generation before Khalīfa, among them al-Wāqidī and al-Haytham b. ʿAdī, but their compilers were not major

six commonalities that are more prominent in these works than in the wider *akhbār* tradition, relating to their (1) authors, (2) sources, (3) form, (4) content, (5) historical perspective and (6) relation to *ḥadīth* scholarship. More details on how these aspects are expressed in Khalīfa's *Tārīkh* are found in Chapters 4–8.

First, the authors of these works were *ḥadīth* scholars and associated with the *ahl al-ḥadīth* or similar text-based approaches to *fiqh* and *ʿaqīda*.[171] Even the Mālikī *faqīh* Ibn Ḥabīb, who was criticised for his own handling of *ḥadīth*, was known among Mālikīs for his strict adherence to *ḥadīth* in legal matters.[172] This traditionist background is less common in the wider *akhbār* tradition—especially among the authors of the later universal chronicles (e.g. al-Dīnawarī, al-Yaʿqūbī and al-Masʿūdī), but also among earlier *akhbārīyūn* (e.g. Abū Mikhnaf, Sayf b. ʿUmar, Naṣr b. Muzāḥim, Hishām b. al-Kalbī, al-Haytham b. ʿAdī and al-Madāʾinī). These compilers might have narrated *ḥadīth* material, but they were considered weak by the transmitter critics and not associated with *ḥadīth*-minded scholarship.[173] An exception among the later chroniclers is al-Ṭabarī, who was a major *ḥadīth* scholar, although his 'semi-rationalist' approach to *fiqh* differed from that of the Iraqi *ahl al-ḥadīth*.[174]

Second, although the works contain reports from transmitters common in the wider *akhbār* tradition, they also comprise a great number of citations from well-known *ḥadīth* authorities—as one would expect from their scholarly affiliations. This is most evident in the source selection of Khalīfa,[175] al-Fasawī,[176]

ḥadīth scholars or critics. A few other works entitled *tārīkh* are attributed to third/ninth-century scholars associated with *ḥadīth* scholarship, but, apart from those mentioned, the rest seem to be either lost or simply biographical dictionaries. See Ibn al-Nadīm, *Fihrist* 1:308, 312–313; 2:97, 101, 104–106, 115.

171 See their biographies in al-Dhahabī's *Siyar* 782, 1631–1632, 2200–2201, 2564–2566, 4246–4247.

172 E.g. Al-Dhahabī narrates that Abū ʿUmar al-Ṣadafī said about Ibn Ḥabīb, "He narrated much, gathered many narrations and based his *fiqh* on following *ḥadīth* (*yaʿtamidu ʿalā al-akhdh bi-l-ḥadīth*), but he did not distinguish them and was unaware of the transmitters, although he was an expert in legal issues (*faqīh fī l-masāʾil*)." Al-Dhahabī, *Siyar* 2565. See also ʿIyāḍ b. Mūsā al-Yaḥṣubī, *Tartīb al-madārik* 4:122–142; Ibn Ḥajar, *Tahdhīb* 2:610–611, *Lisān* 5:255–259; Muḥammad Makhlūf, *Shajarat al-nūr* 1:111–112; Wuld Abāh, *Madkhal ilā uṣūl al-fiqh al-mālikī* 81.

173 On the first three, see Zaman, al-Yaʿqūbī; Lewin, al-Dīnawarī; Pellat, al-Masʿūdī. On the last six, see Ibn al-Nadīm, *Fihrist* 1:291–295, 301–307, 311–313, 315–323; al-Dhahabī, *Mīzān* 2:236–237, 3:163, 413, 5:17, 60–61, 76.

174 Melchert, *Formation* 191–197.

175 See Chapter 4.

176 See al-ʿUmarī's introduction to al-Fasawī, *Maʿrifa* 1:42–51.

Ibn Abī Khaythama[177] and Abū Zurʿa.[178] In the case of Ibn Ḥabīb, he relies heavily on *akhbārīyūn* such as al-Wāqidī and often provides incomplete *isnād*s, but he also cites several Mālikī authorities from al-Ḥijāz and Egypt.[179] Another example is the Prophetic biography in Ibn Saʿd's *Ṭabaqāt*, where he relies on al-Wāqidī, Hishām b. al-Kalbī and other *akhbārīyūn* but at the same time refers frequently to well-known *ḥadīth* authorities.[180] The proportion of *ḥadīth* scholars among the sources differs from the slightly later universal chroniclers—many of whom eschewed the *isnād* system altogether—again with the exception of al-Ṭabarī and to some extent al-Balādhurī. It also differs from the earlier tradition of single-subject texts, with compilers such as Abū Mikhnaf,[181] Sayf b. ʿUmar,[182] Naṣr b. Muzāḥim[183] and al-Madāʾinī,[184] whose works in general contain a lesser range of *ḥadīth* scholars. This comparison is somewhat complicated by the limited scope of the latter historians' works and their earlier context; however, Khalīfa and the aforementioned *ḥadīth* scholars clearly had access to a wider range of *ḥadīth* authorities, whom they accordingly cited in their works.

Third, the form of chronography compiled by these *ḥadīth* scholars is characterised by short reports with *isnād*s and brief statements by the compilers themselves, pieced together in an overall chronological sequence.[185] Compared both to many earlier histories and to later universal chronicles, these works are generally less synthetic and less continuous in their narrative style. They are largely limited to straightforward, chronological sequences of *akhbār*, along

---

177 See Halal's introduction to Ibn Abī Khaythama's *Tārīkh* and, e.g., the narrators in the first two years AH in the *Tārīkh* 1:29–30, 365–392.

178 On Abū Zurʿa's sources, see al-Qawjānī's introduction to Abū Zurʿa's *Tārīkh* 1:119–125. For some examples, see his *isnād*s in the section for the Prophet's life, 1:141–169.

179 Aguadé's introduction to Ibn Ḥabīb, *Tārīkh* 104–107.

180 See e.g. Ibn Saʿd's direct transmitters in the first section of the *Ṭabaqāt*, which contains several major *ḥadīth* authorities. Ibn Saʿd, *Ṭabaqāt* 1:4–9.

181 On Abū Mikhnaf's *isnād*s, see Sezgin, *Abū Mikhnaf* 66–98.

182 Most of Sayf's named sources are unknown to both modern and classical scholars. Anthony, *Caliph and the heretic* 22.

183 See e.g. Naṣr b. Muzāḥim's direct transmitters in the first section to his *Waqʿat Ṣiffīn* 17–84. See also Petersen, *ʿAlī and Muʿāwiya* 101–109.

184 Al-Madāʾinī studied under some major *ḥadīth* scholars of Iraq, but, as Lindstedt puts it, "analyzing the names of his authorities found in the *isnād*s in the surviving historical works, one finds a rather different set of names, for instance al-Mufaḍḍal al-Ḍabbī and many figures that were affiliated with the Umayyad and ʿAbbāsid court." Lindstedt, Life and deeds 238.

185 Abū Zurʿa's *Tārīkh* contains large amounts of unorganised material, but the beginning of his work is chronological. Abū Zurʿa al-Dimashqī, *Tārīkh* 1:141–196.

with short statements or summaries by the compilers themselves.[186] The annalistic structure of their works, or parts of them, also reflects a particular concern for establishing chronology and fixing the dates of events, although the annalistic format is not exclusive to them. In addition to the chronological sequence of *akhbār*, Khalīfa's *Tārīkh* also contains administrative list sections, which are not common in the works of the other *ḥadīth* scholars. Instead, similar but shorter lists are found in the works of al-Yaʿqūbī and al-Ṭabarī.[187]

Fourth, the content and scope of the *tārīkh* works compiled by these scholars are focused on the affairs of the Muslim community—in particular political, military and to some extent legal history, but also the prophethood of the Prophet Muḥammad and the virtues of his Companions. This is not unusual in the earlier or later *akhbār* tradition, but the limited interest in non-Muslim cultures differs from the later universal chronicles of al-Yaʿqūbī, al-Dīnawarī, al-Ṭabarī and al-Masʿūdī. The exception is Ibn Ḥabīb, who includes a substantial amount of pre-Islamic material. The *tārīkh* works of Khalīfa and al-Fasawī also reflect a particular concern for recording the dates of scholars' deaths.

Fifth, these works are all characterised by an underlying early Sunnī vision of Islamic history, as is evident in the treatment of the Prophet's Companions, the Companion-caliphs and early intra-Muslim conflicts. This is the case for Khalīfa, Ibn Ḥabīb, al-Fasawī, Ibn Abī Khaythama and Abū Zurʿa, as well as for Ibn Saʿd in his *Ṭabaqāt*, although they might differ in details and in their approaches to these issues.[188] Other historians compiled favourable narratives about the Companions, among them Sayf b. ʿUmar in the second/eighth century and al-Ṭabarī in the third/ninth, but the *akhbār* tradition also include many Shīʿī historians—both early ones (e.g. Abū Mikhnaf and Naṣr b. Muzāḥim) and later ones (e.g. al-Yaʿqūbī and al-Masʿūdī). In other words, the early Sunnī perspective is a defining characteristic of the *tārīkh* works compiled by early *ḥadīth* scholars, but it is not exclusive to them.

Sixth, these *tārīkh* works were compiled and transmitted in close relation to *ḥadīth* scholarship in general and *ʿilm al-rijāl* in particular—often combined with *ṭabaqāt* material or transmitted alongside it. This point distinguishes

186 E.g. Khalīfa b. Khayyāṭ, *Tārīkh* (1985) 49–54; Ibn Ḥabīb, *Tārīkh* 82–97; al-Fasawī, *Maʿrifa* 1:115–136; Abū Zurʿa al-Dimashqī, *Tārīkh* 1:142–167; Ibn Abī Khaythama, *Tārīkh* 1:365–375.

187 See Chapter 6.

188 As for the accusation of *tashayyuʿ* against al-Fasawī, the editor al-ʿUmarī dismisses this, as did al-Dhahabī and Ibn Kathīr before him. Al-Fasawī, *Maʿrifa* 1:14–17. Melchert notes that "there is no sign of Shīʿism in al-Fasawī's choice of *ḥadīth* to relate in *al-Maʿrifa*." He also concludes that al-Fasawī "seems to represent a strand of Basran Sunnism". Melchert, al-Fasawī, Yaʿqūb b. Sufyān.

them from earlier and later stand-alone histories, including al-Ṭabarī's *Tārīkh*, which otherwise shares some of the characteristics listed above. Although Khalīfa divided the *tārīkh* and *ṭabaqāt* material into two works, they seem to have been compiled in close relation to each other and were transmitted as a pair by both Baqī b. Makhlad and Mūsā b. Zakariyyā al-Tustarī.[189] This is important for understanding the audience of these chronographies compiled by *ḥadīth* scholars. The biographies and evaluations of *ḥadīth* transmitters in the *ṭabaqāt* sections suggest that these works were compiled primarily for other *ḥadīth* scholars—with the exception of Ibn Ḥabīb's *Tārīkh*, which reflects broader and more *adab*-oriented concerns. Because these *ṭabaqāt* sections were combined with *tārīkh* sections, the *tārīkh* material likely was also compiled for, and transmitted to, the same audience of mainly *ḥadīth* scholars.

5 Conclusion

This chapter has outlined the sociopolitical, intellectual and historiographical context in which Khalīfa compiled his *Tārīkh*. It has shown, first, that Khalīfa's *Tārīkh* was compiled before the major political and cultural transitions in the Islamic world of the mid-to-late third/ninth and early fourth/tenth centuries. In this way, the *Tārīkh* reflects a unique moment in Arabic chronicle writing, before the increasing disintegration of ʿAbbāsid political authority and the rise of independent, non-Arab dynasties. While this context cannot in itself explain the content of the *Tārīkh*, it is important for understanding Khalīfa's outlook on politics, which, as discussed in the following chapters, differs in some respects from later chronographies compiled in other contexts.

Second, the chapter has outlined Khalīfa's scholarly milieu in Basra and has located him among the Basran *ḥadīth* scholars, many of whom adhered to the approach of the *ahl al-ḥadīth* in *fiqh* and *ʿaqīda*. This context is important for the subsequent analysis of the *Tārīkh* because it helps to explain and contextualise Khalīfa's selection of sources, his choice of material and, in particular, his early Sunnī views on the history of the Muslim community.

Third, the chapter has discussed *tārīkh* and *ṭabaqāt* writing among the early *ḥadīth* scholars and has highlighted the close links between these two formats of historical writing; a number of surviving *tārīkh* works compiled by third/ninth-century *ḥadīth* scholars were combined with *ṭabaqāt* sections of *ḥadīth* transmitters and compiled in close relation to *ʿilm al-rijāl*. Thereby, it is

---

189 See Chapters 1–2.

possible to discern an early type of chronography that was compiled by a few *ḥadīth* scholars, primarily for other *ḥadīth* scholars, and that reflects early Sunnī perspectives on Islamic history. This is important for the analysis of Khalīfa's *Tārīkh* and *Ṭabaqāt*, which were often transmitted as a pair. Rather than reflecting different audiences and markets,[190] Khalīfa's two works seem to reflect different interests and needs among the same audience of mainly *ḥadīth* scholars. This is substantiated by the later transmission of Khalīfa's *Tārīkh* among *ḥadīth* scholars and by other aspects of the work: his sources, his methods, his arrangement of material, the content (e.g. death notices of *ḥadīth* scholars) and his early Sunnī perspective. These aspects are examined in the following chapters, beginning with a survey of the transmitters from whom Khalīfa received his historical material.

---

190 As Judd suggested in *Religious scholars* 28.

CHAPTER 4

Khalīfa's Sources

1 Introduction

This chapter examines Khalīfa's sources in Baqī b. Makhlad's recension of the *Tārīkh*. Section 2 outlines the nine main direct transmitters (each cited 20–110 times), including their locations, scholarly affiliations and reputations and the subjects of their material. It shows that eight of the nine were Basrans, that most of them were authorities in *akhbār* history rather than *ḥadīth*, and that they were often criticised by the *ḥadīth* transmitter critics. Section 3 examines the next most-cited group, of twenty-three transmitters (each cited 5–19 times), most of whom are reputable Basran *ḥadīth* scholars. Section 4 looks at the geographical locations of the remaining seventy-three transmitters (each cited fewer than five times), which confirms the connection to Basra and its *ḥadīth* circles. Section 5 discusses the main sources from whom Khalīfa did not transmit directly but whose material is central to Khalīfa's narrative—such as the *sīra* compiler Muḥammad b. Isḥāq. Section 6 discusses the results of the preceding survey and highlights five distinct features of Khalīfa's selection of sources: (1) the preponderance of Basran transmitters, (2) the difference in what Khalīfa cites from *akhbārīyūn* and *muḥaddithūn* respectively, (3) the exclusion of popular Kufan and Shīʿī transmitters, (4) the large number of reputable *ḥadīth* scholars and (5) the possibility that Khalīfa had access to official documents and written sources.

Khalīfa's sources in the *Tārīkh* have been treated elsewhere with a focus on the main transmitters' material,[1] but this chapter examines all direct transmitters and also looks at their scholarly reputations, affiliations and locations. The chapter thereby seeks to demonstrate the preponderance of Basran transmitters and the number of well-known *ḥadīth* scholars among Khalīfa's direct transmitters, which confirms Basra and its *ḥadīth* circles as the context of compilation. It also aims to clarify Khalīfa's method of source selection by examining what types and amounts of material he cites from certain transmitters in relation to their scholarly occupations and reputations. This shows a consistent approach to what material is cited from what type of transmitter: Khalīfa

1 See al-ʿUmarī's introduction to Khalīfa's *Tārīkh* (1985) 16–30; ʿĀṣī, *Khalīfa* 49–63; Wurtzel, *Khalifa ibn Khayyat's History* 30–38; Ṣaddām, *Tārīkh Khalīfa* 34–49.

 | DOI:10.1163/9789004383173_006

relies mainly on well-known *ḥadīth* scholars for subjects of religio-political controversy (e.g. civil wars and revolts) or particular historical importance (e.g. the birth and death of the Prophet), but he otherwise cites common *akhbār* transmitters, such as Ibn Isḥāq and al-Madāʾinī, for the general chronological narrative. Hence the chapter prepares for the examination of Khalīfa's methods in Chapter 5.

The purpose of this chapter, however, is not to evaluate the strength or reliability of Khalīfa's reports by means of transmitter criticism (*jarḥ wa-taʿdīl*), which would require an examination of all names in the *isnād*s and comparisons to similar reports elsewhere. It only seeks to outline the direct transmitters from whom Khalīfa received his material, in order to make clear his scholarly affiliations and selection of sources. Likewise, the purpose is not to arrive at definitive judgements on the status of individual transmitters—such as 'reliable' (*thiqa*) and 'weak' (*ḍaʿīf*)—but simply to present some of the early transmitter critics' views on them and thereby highlight their scholarly reputations.[2]

2 Main Direct Transmitters (20–110 Citations)

Many of Khalīfa's informants were major *ḥadīth* authorities, such as Yazīd b. Zurayʿ, ʿAbd al-Raḥmān b. Mahdī, Abū Dāwūd al-Ṭayālisī, Yaḥyā b. Saʿīd al-Qaṭṭān, Ghundar, Wahb b. Jarīr and Ismāʿīl b. ʿUlayya. The prominence of *ḥadīth* scholars is evident when looking at all Khalīfa's direct transmitters in total, but a different picture emerges if one examines only the nine transmitters cited more than twenty times. Eight are Basrans, but only one was a prominent *ḥadīth* scholar. The others are remembered as either weak transmitters or authorities in other disciplines, such as *maghāzī-sīra*, post-Prophetic history and genealogy. This reveals a pattern in Khalīfa's selection of sources: he relies on a rather limited number of *akhbāriyūn* for the main body of his work but refers to well-known *muḥaddithūn* when it comes to historiographically controversial subjects.[3]

The citations of the nine main transmitters listed below comprise about half of all citations in the *Tārīkh* (c. 450 of 900). Because of occasional ambiguities in Khalīfa's citation—whether certain citations belong to the same or differ-

---

2 On the terminology of the *ḥadīth* transmitter critics, see al-Sakhāwī, *Fatḥ al-Mughīth* 2:277–301; al-Laknawī, *al-Rafʿ wa-l-takmīl* 129–186 (with ʿAbd al-Fattāḥ Abū Ghudda's footnotes); al-Ghawrī, *Muʿjam* 129–698.

3 Discussed further in Sections 6.1 and 6.2 below.

ent reports—the numbers and percentages are only close approximations, but they nonetheless clarify the distribution of reports. The names listed below are direct transmitters with whom Khalīfa had personal contact, as indicated by the transmission formulas (e.g. *ḥaddathanī*, 'He narrated to me'; or *akhbaranī*, 'He informed me') and biographical sources mentioning that Khalīfa transmitted from these individuals.[4]

The list contains information about the transmitters' reputations and scholarly activities, derived from biographical dictionaries and works of *ḥadīth* transmitter criticism—both contemporaneous to Khalīfa, like Ibn Saʿd's *Ṭabaqāt*, and later works, like those of al-Dhahabī and Ibn Ḥajar. The main reason for consulting later works is that they contain material from earlier sources (usually verbatim citations) and provide information from now lost works.[5] They are thus primarily consulted for locations, biographical material and opinions of third/ninth- and fourth/tenth-century critics. Also, as Lucas has demonstrated, there was a high degree of consensus among contemporary *ḥadīth*-transmitter critics at the time of Khalīfa; they often agreed in their assessments and classifications of transmitters, although their terminologies sometimes differed.[6]

1. ʿAlī b. Muḥammad al-Madāʾinī (d. c. 228/843)—Basra and Baghdad—c. 107 citations (12%)

Al-Madāʾinī is the most frequent direct transmitter in the *Tārīkh* and the main source for the Prophetic period alongside Khalīfa's indirect source for the same period, Ibn Isḥāq. He is also a major source for later history, including subjects such as the *ridda* wars, the conquest of Persia, the civil wars during ʿAlī's caliphate, Ibn al-Ashʿath's revolt and the Khārijī revolts in the Umayyad and ʿAbbāsid periods. Although al-Madāʾinī was born in Basra, he also resided in Baghdad. He studied under many well-known *ḥadīth* scholars of his time,

4 See Chapter 5. These formulas were sometimes used for 'giving permission' (*ijāza*) and 'handing over' (*munāwala*), not only for 'listening' (*samāʿ*) and 'reading out to the teacher' (*ʿarḍ*), but they still indicate that Khalīfa met these individuals from whom he transmitted, and this is further supported by the biographical sources mentioning that Khalīfa narrated from them. See al-Sakhāwī, *Fatḥ al-Mughīth* 2:483–496.

5 Motzki, *Origins* 286.

6 Lucas, *Constructive critics* 287–326. Lucas examines the opinions of Ibn Saʿd, Aḥmad b. Ḥanbal and Ibn Maʿīn. He concludes that they were concerned with grading quite different pools of transmitters, but he shows (by bilateral comparisons) a more than 85 per cent consensus between Ibn Maʿīn and Ibn Saʿd, and between Ibn Ḥanbal and Ibn Saʿd.

among them Shuʿba b. al-Ḥajjāj, Juwayriya b. Asmāʾ and Ḥammād b. Salama. He is credited with numerous compilations on a wide range of historical subjects, but he was mainly known as an authority in *maghāzī-sīra*, history and genealogy—not in *ḥadīth*.[7] As Ibn ʿAdī remarks, "He is not strong in *ḥadīth*; he is a compiler of *akhbār*."[8] There has been some speculation regarding al-Madāʾinī's supposed Shīʿī inclinations, but it is not mentioned in the works of transmitter criticism.[9] Whatever his religio-political affiliations were, there seem to be no indications of any particular Shīʿī tendencies in the citations in Khalīfa's *Tārīkh*.

2. Abū l-Yaqẓān Suḥaym b. Ḥafṣ (d. 190/806)—Basra—c. 56 citations (6%)

Abū l-Yaqẓān is a major source in both the *Tārīkh* and the *Ṭabaqāt*.[10] His reports pertain to the eastern conquests, the Battle of the Camel, the Battle of Dayr al-Jamājim, the administration in Iraq and various events in the Umayyad period. He is also cited for the lifespans of the caliphs until the early ʿAbbāsid period and their births and deaths. Abū l-Yaqẓān was considered not a *ḥadīth* transmitter but rather an authority on genealogy (*nasab*) and history (*akhbār*), which is reflected in Khalīfa's use of him as a source for chronology and basic post-Prophetic information.[11]

3. Al-Walīd b. Hishām al-Qaḥdhamī (d. 222/836–837)—Basra—c. 56 citations (6%)

The material from al-Walīd b. Hishām pertains mainly to the eastern conquests, the administration of Iraq and the deaths of Umayyad caliphs. He is also cited for a few reports about the conquests of Syria and Egypt. Most of al-Walīd's *isnāds* are traced via his father to his grandfather, Qaḥdham b. Sulaymān b. Dhakwān, the *mawlā* of Abū Bakra al-Thaqafī.[12] His grandfather was also secretary of finance (*kātib al-kharāj*) under the Umayyad governor Yūsuf b. ʿUmar al-Thaqafī (r. 120–126/738–744) in Iraq.[13] The reliance on al-Walīd b. Hishām and the narrations from his grandfather corresponds to Khalīfa's concern for the

7 Lindstedt, Life and deeds 242–263; al-Dhahabī, *Siyar* 2840.
8 Ibn ʿAdī, *Kāmil* 5:1855.
9 See Lindstedt, Life and deeds 241.
10 Khalīfa b. Khayyāṭ, *Ṭabaqāt* (1993) 25.
11 Ibn al-Nadīm, *Fihrist* 1:298; Yāqūt al-Ḥamawī, *Muʿjam* 3:1342.
12 Khalīfa b. Khayyāṭ, *Tārīkh* (1985) 162.
13 Khalīfa b. Khayyāṭ, *Tārīkh* (1985) 368.

administrative history of the caliphate in general and of Iraq in particular. He was a Basran transmitter who was mainly known for narrating post-Prophetic *akhbār* and whom Ibn Ḥibbān included in *Kitāb al-Thiqāt*.[14]

4. Abū ʿUbayda Maʿmar b. al-Muthannā (d. c. 210/825)—Basra—c. 44 citations (5%)

Abū ʿUbayda is an important source of information about the eastern conquests and the activities of the Khawārij. His reports also include information about the Persian calendar system, the deaths of Persian leaders, the Prophet's lifetime, the *ridda* wars and various events in the Umayyad period. Khalīfa usually introduces the reports by "Abū ʿUbayda said," but he sometimes mentions that he received them from Muḥammad b. Muʿāwiya.[15] He is also one of Khalīfa's main sources in the *Ṭabaqāt*.[16] Abū ʿUbayda was considered not a *ḥadīth* scholar but mainly an expert in philology and grammar.[17] He is also credited with many compilations in genealogy and history, including a book about the Khawārij—a subject that seems to have interested him to such a degree that he is said to have held Khārijī views.[18] Khalīfa may have consulted a written source for Abū ʿUbayda's material.[19] Like most of the main transmitters, Abū ʿUbayda is an important source in Khalīfa's general narrative but is not one of the scholars that Khalīfa cites for particularly controversial subjects.

5. Bakr b. Sulaymān al-Aswārī (d. c. 191–200/807–816)—Basra—c. 43 citations (5%)

Khalīfa only cites Bakr b. Sulaymān as one of the two transmitters of Ibn Isḥaq's *Sīra* and the only transmitter of Ibn Isḥāq's material on the Rāshidūn period. He is cited by name about 43 times, but many other references to Ibn Isḥāq without *isnād* presumably refer to Bakr b. Sulaymān's transmission. He was a minor Basran narrator, mainly known for his transmission from Ibn Isḥāq.[20] Ibn Ḥib-

14 See Ibn Ḥibbān, *Thiqāt* 7:555–556; al-Bukhārī, *Tārīkh* 8:157; Ibn Abī Ḥātim, *al-Jarḥ wa-l-taʿdīl* 9:20; al-Dhahabī, *Mīzān* 5:95; Ibn Ḥajar, *Lisān* 8:393.

15 Khalīfa also mentions that he received some of Abū ʿUbayda's material directly and some from Muḥammad b. Muʿāwiya in his *Ṭabaqāt* (1993) 25.

16 Khalīfa b. Khayyāṭ, *Ṭabaqāt* (1993) 25.

17 Al-Dhahabī, *Siyar* 3912–3913. See also Lecker, Biographical notes on Abū ʿUbayda.

18 Ibn al-Nadīm, *Fihrist* 1:149–152; al-Dhahabī, *Siyar* 3912–3913; Ibn Ḥajar, *Tahdhīb* 4:126–127; Lecker, Biographical notes on Abū ʿUbayda 94–97.

19 Wurtzel, *Khalifa ibn Khayyat's History* 33.

20 Al-Bukhārī, *Tārīkh* 2:90.

bān included him in his *Kitāb al-Thiqāt*, and Abū Ḥātim al-Rāzī declared his status unknown (*majhūl*).[21] Al-Dhahabī includes him among those who died between 191/807 and 200/816.[22]

6. Abū Khālid al-Baṣrī (d. 189/805)—Basra—c. 42 citations (4.5%)

His full name is Yūsuf b. Khālid al-Samtī, but Khalīfa refers to him as Abū Khālid. Most of his reports pertain to the Transcaucasus and North Africa in the Umayyad period. He received much of his material from Abū l-Barā' al-Numayrī and Abū l-Khaṭṭāb al-Asadī. Much of Abū Khālid's information is found only in Khalīfa's *Tārīkh*.[23] He was active in Basra and studied under many prominent scholars, including the Medinan *maghāzī* compiler Mūsā b. 'Uqba (d. 141/758). He was known for his knowledge of legal opinions and verdicts (*al-ra'y wa-l-fatwā*), but critics considered him weak in *ḥadīth* transmission, in some cases even accusing him of lying.[24] His reputation might explain why Khalīfa mainly cites him for the history of regions far from the centre of events in the Umayyad period.

7. Hishām b. Muḥammad al-Kalbī (d. 204/819)—Kufa—c. 35 citations (4%)

Khalīfa cites Hishām b. al-Kalbī for accounts of the encounters between the Muslims and the Romans between 13/634 and 117/735. Khalīfa might have taken these reports from a written work of Ibn al-Kalbī, since they are cited without indicating direct transmission ("Ibn al-Kalbī said") and without mentioning Ibn al-Kalbī's own sources.[25] Khalīfa mentions only once that he received material directly from Ibn al-Kalbī: "according to what Ibn al-Kalbī narrated to me (*fīmā ḥaddathanī Ibn al-Kalbī*)."[26] Ibn al-Kalbī compiled books on various subjects, but he was most known for his works on genealogy.[27] He lived and died

21 Ibn Ḥibbān, *Thiqāt* 8:148; Ibn Abī Ḥātim, *al-Jarḥ wa-l-ta'dīl* 2:387; al-Dhahabī, *Mīzān* 1:321–322; Ibn Ḥajar, *Lisān* 2:343–344. On Abū Ḥātim's usage of 'unknown' (*majhūl*), see al-Laknawī, *al-Raf' wa-l-takmīl* 229–256.

22 Al-Dhahabī, *Tārīkh al-Islām* 13:133.

23 Wurtzel, *Khalifa ibn Khayyat's History* 33.

24 Ibn Sa'd, *Ṭabaqāt* 9:293–294; al-Bukhārī, *Tārīkh* 8:388; Ibn Abī Ḥātim, *al-Jarḥ wa-l-ta'dīl* 9:221–222; Ibn 'Adī, *Kāmil* 7:2616–2619; al-Dhahabī, *Mīzān* 5:188–189; Ibn Ḥajar, *Tahdhīb* 4:454–455.

25 Al-'Umarī's introduction to Khalīfa's *Tārīkh* (1985) 20.

26 Khalīfa b. Khayyāṭ, *Tārīkh* (1985) 160.

27 Ibn Ḥanbal, *Mawsū'a* 4:45–46; al-Bukhārī, *Tārīkh* 8:200; Ibn al-Nadīm, *Fihrist* 1:301–307; Ibn 'Adī, *Kāmil* 7:2568; Ibn Abī Ḥātim, *al-Jarḥ wa-l-ta'dīl* 9:69.

in Kufa, but he was also active in Baghdad. He is described as Shīʿī, as was his father, but he was and has remained one of the main authorities in genealogy across the scholarly traditions, despite harsh criticism from *ḥadīth* scholars.[28] Ibn al-Kalbī is also one of Khalīfa's sources in the *Ṭabaqāt*.[29] Khalīfa's citations of Ibn al-Kalbī in the *Tārīkh* show that Khalīfa considered Ibn al-Kalbī acceptable as a narrator of reports on the expeditions against the Romans, but also that he preferred other transmitters for more controversial subjects.

8. ʿAbdallāh b. al-Mughīra—Basra—c. 34 citations (4%)

ʿAbdallāh b. al-Mughīra's reports come from his father who, judging from the material he conveys, might have been involved in the Iraqi administration, so might have had access to government records.[30] Most reports pertain to the government of Iraq under the Umayyads and the dates of births and deaths of Umayyad and ʿAbbāsid caliphs. He also narrates a few accounts of the conquests of Syria, Egypt and the East. He is not mentioned in the works of transmitter criticism, not even Khalīfa's *Ṭabaqāt*, but he was probably a local Basran informant.

9. Wahb b. Jarīr b. Ḥāzim (d. 206/822)—Basra—c. 34 citations (4%)

Wahb b. Jarīr b. Ḥāzim is cited many times in the *Tārīkh*, often with full *isnāds* through his father or Juwayriya b. Asmāʾ. He is one of the two transmitters of Ibn Isḥāq's *Sīra*, but he also transmits reports from others, on, for example, the Battle of the Camel, the Khawārij in Iraq and the conflicts between the Umayyads and the people of al-Ḥijaz. He was a prominent Basran *ḥadīth* scholar whom Ibn Saʿd, Ibn Maʿīn, al-ʿIjlī and others considered reliable (*thiqa*).[31] Ibn Ḥanbal describes him as *ṣāḥib sunna*, which indicates his early Sunnī outlook and affiliation with the *ahl al-ḥadīth*.[32] Wahb is the only well-known *ḥadīth* scholar

28 Al-Dhahabī, *Mīzān* 5:60–61, *Siyar* 4095; Ibn Ḥajar, *Lisān* 8:339–340; Atallah, al-Kalbī; Khalidi, *Arabic historical thought* 50–54.

29 Khalīfa b. Khayyāṭ, *Ṭabaqāt* (1993) 25.

30 Al-ʿUmarī's introduction to Khalīfa's *Tārīkh* (1985) 22; Wurtzel, *Khalifa ibn Khayyat's History* 32. As Wurtzel notes, ʿAbdallāh b. ʿUmar b. ʿAbd al-ʿAzīz, who served as governor of Iraq in the late Umayyad period, had a secretary named al-Mughīra b. ʿAṭiyya who might have been the father of ʿAbdallāh. See al-Jahshiyārī, *Kitāb al-Wuzarāʾ* 49.

31 Ibn Saʿd, *Ṭabaqāt* 9:299; al-ʿIjlī, *Maʿrifat al-thiqāt* 2:344; Ibn Ḥibbān, *Thiqāt* 9:228; Ibn Abī Ḥātim, *al-Jarḥ wa-l-taʿdīl* 9:28; al-Dhahabī, *Siyar* 4137–4138, *Tadhkira* 336–337; Ibn Ḥajar, *Tahdhīb* 4:329–330.

32 Ibn Ḥanbal, *Mawsūʿa* 4:98. On this term see Chapter 3.

among the major transmitters in the *Tārīkh*, and many of his reports pertain to important or controversial subjects.

3 Less Frequently Cited Direct Transmitters (5–19 Citations)

Section 2 showed that Khalīfa relies for much of his narrative on Basran *akhbār* transmitters who were not prominent *ḥadīth* scholars. But a different pattern is found among the less frequently cited direct transmitters: 18 of the 23 transmitters cited 5–19 times in the *Tārīkh* were known *ḥadīth* transmitters, and all, except one, were based in Basra. The following list outlines these 23 transmitters and their material. It shows that Khalīfa cites these *ḥadīth* scholars mainly for controversial episodes or important historical details. This illustrates Khalīfa's use of different sources for different subjects and confirms his affiliation with the Basran *ḥadīth* scholars.

10. Ismāʿīl b. Ibrāhīm al-Shuʿayrāwī al-ʿAtakī—Basra—c. 18 citations (2%)

Ismāʿīl b. Ibrāhīm's reports pertain to Syria, Iraq and al-Jazīra. They include details about the third *fitna* at the time of al-Walīd (II) b. Yazīd, some lines of poetry, the text of Yazīd (III) b. al-Walīd's *khuṭba* and information about the revolt of ʿAbdallāh b. Muʿāwiya and some of the Khawārij. He is not mentioned in the biographical dictionaries, but he was probably a local Basran informant. Apart from the statistical likelihood, the tribal affiliation (al-ʿAtakī) might indicate Basra: Banū ʿAtīk refers to a branch of al-Azd, one of the main tribes that settled in Basra, and other Basrans also have the same *nisba*.[33]

11. Yazīd b. Zurayʿ (d. 182/798)—Basra—c. 15 citations (1.5%)

The material of Yazīd b. Zurayʿ pertains mostly to the lifetime of the Prophet, including an explanation of a Qurʾānic verse, the length of the Prophet's time in Mecca and Medina, the change of the *qibla*, the number of martyrs at Uḥud, the Treaty of Ḥudaybiya and the age of the Prophet. He is also cited regarding the Battle of al-Qādisiyya, Anas b. Mālik's statement about the missed prayer during the siege of Tustar and the conquest of Adharbayjān. Ibn Zurayʿ was a leading Basran *ḥadīth* scholar whose father had been governor of al-Ubulla, pre-

33 Al-Samʿānī, *al-Ansāb* 8:387–391; Ibn al-Athīr, *al-Lubāb* 2:322.

sumably under the Umayyads.[34] He was widely regarded as a reliable authority; Ibn Saʿd, for example, describes him as "reliable, authoritative and abundant in *ḥadīth* (*thiqa ḥujja kathīr al-ḥadīth*)."[35] He is also described as ʿUthmānī.[36] As with other *ḥadīth* authorities in the *Tārīkh*, Khalīfa often cites Ibn Zurayʿ for material with religious implications—for example, commentary on the Qurʾān, the Prophet's time in Mecca and Medina, and Anas b. Mālik's words about the prayer.

12. Muḥammad b. Jaʿfar, Ghundar (d. 193/809)—Basra—13 citations (1.5%)

Ghundar's reports pertain to the conquest of Iraq, the assassination of ʿUthmān, the Battle of the Camel, the killing of Muḥammad b. Abī Bakr, the Zubayrid–Umayyad conflict and Ibn al-Ashʿath's revolt. He was a prominent Basran *ḥadīth* scholar considered reliable (*thiqa*).[37] He was particularly known for his exceptional knowledge of the *ḥadīth* corpus of Shuʿba b. al-Ḥajjāj (d. 160/776).[38] The subjects of Ghundar's reports correspond to Khalīfa's citation of well-known *ḥadīth* scholars for important or controversial topics.

13. ʿAbd al-Wahhāb b. ʿAbd al-Majīd (d. 194/809–810)—Basra—11 citations (1%)

Seven of ʿAbd al-Wahhāb b. ʿAbd al-Majīd's reports pertain to the lifetime of the Prophet, including his time in Mecca and Medina, the change of the *qibla*, the Prophet's marriage to Juwayriya bt. al-Ḥārith, the Treaty of al-Hudaybiya and three reports about the Prophet's age. The other four concern Abū Bakr's decision to fight those who refused to pay the *zakāt*, Abū Bakr's age, al-Hurmuzān's dialogue with ʿUmar and the assassination of ʿUthmān. ʿAbd al-Wahhāb was a prominent Basran *ḥadīth* scholar considered reliable (*thiqa*).[39] It is also said

---

34 Ibn Ḥibbān, *Thiqāt* 7:632; Ed., Yazīd b. Zurayʿ.

35 Ibn Saʿd, *Ṭabaqāt* 9:290; Ibn Ḥanbal, *Mawsūʿa* 4:148–149; al-ʿIjlī, *Maʿrifat al-thiqāt* 2:363; Ibn Abī Ḥātim, *al-Jarḥ wa-l-taʿdīl* 9:263–265; al-Dhahabī, *Siyar* 4221–4222; Ibn Ḥajar, *Tahdhīb* 4:411–412.

36 Ibn Saʿd, *Ṭabaqāt* 9:290. On the term ʿUthmānī, see Chapter 3.

37 Ibn Saʿd, *Ṭabaqāt* 8:297; Ibn Ḥanbal, *Mawsūʿa* 3:247–249; al-ʿIjlī, *Maʿrifat al-thiqāt* 2:235; al-Bukhārī, *Tārīkh* 1:57–58; al-Dhahabī, *Siyar* 3375–3376; Ibn Ḥajar, *Tahdhīb* 3:531–532.

38 Ibn Saʿd, *Ṭabaqāt* 8:297; al-Dhahabī, *Siyar* 3375–3376; Ibn Ḥajar, *Tahdhīb* 3:351–352.

39 Ibn Saʿd, *Ṭabaqāt* 9:290–291; Ibn Ḥanbal, *Mawsūʿa* 2:397–398; al-ʿIjlī, *Maʿrifat al-thiqāt* 2:108; Ibn Ḥibbān, *Thiqāt* 7:132–133; al-Dhahabī, *Siyar* 2600–2601, *Tadhkira* 321; Ibn Ḥajar, *Tahdhīb* 2:638.

that he used to distribute all his annual revenues (40–50,000 dirhams) among the *aṣḥāb al-ḥadīth*, which indicates his scholarly associations.[40]

14. Abū Dāwūd al-Ṭayālisī (d. 204/819)—Basra—11 citations (1%)

Abū Dāwūd al-Ṭayālisī's reports pertain to the Prophet's time in Mecca and Medina, the date of the Battle of Badr, the Night of Glory (*laylat al-qadr*) at Badr, the change of the *qibla*, the Prophet's age, Abū Bakr's age, ʿUmar's age, the killing of ʿUthmān and the Battle of the Camel. He was a highly regarded Basran *ḥadīth* scholar and widely considered reliable (*thiqa*).[41] He also compiled a *musnad* collection of *ḥadīth*, arranged in the conventional way according to the names of the transmitters—beginning with Abū Bakr, ʿUmar, ʿUthmān, ʿAlī and then the other Companions among the ten promised Paradise, which clearly shows his early Sunnī orientation.[42]

15. Yaḥyā b. Muḥammad al-Kaʿbī (d. c. 200/815)—Medina and Basra—11 citations (1%)

Yaḥyā b. Muḥammad's reports pertain to mankind's systems of dating, those who died in Ibn al-Ashʿath's revolt and the births and deaths of prominent individuals. He was a Medinan and later Basran narrator, whose transmission some critics considered weak and others considered sufficiently acceptable to be written down.[43]

16. Yaḥyā b. Saʿīd al-Qaṭṭān (d. 198/813)—Basra—11 citations (1%)

Yaḥyā al-Qaṭṭān's reports pertain to the change of the *qibla*, Khālid b. al-Walīd's mission to destroy the idol al-ʿUzzā, the Prophet's death, Abū Bakr's decision to fight those who held back the *zakāt*, Abū Bakr's death, the conquest of Tustar, Saʿd b. Abī Waqqāṣ's question about the 'Fear Prayer' (*ṣalāt al-khawf*) during a campaign, the killing of ʿUthmān and the Battle of the Camel. Only two reports are cited as direct transmission (*ḥaddathanā*) and one without specification of

40 Al-Khaṭīb al-Baghdādī, *Tārīkh Baghdād* 12:274.

41 Ibn Saʿd, *Ṭabaqāt* 9:299; Ibn Ḥanbal, *Mawsūʿa* 2:91–92; al-ʿIjlī, *Maʿrifat al-thiqāt* 1:427; Ibn Ḥibbān, *Thiqāt* 8:275–276; al-Dhahabī, *Tadhkira* 351–352; Ibn Ḥajar, *Tahdhīb* 2:90–92.

42 Al-Ṭayālisī, *Musnad* 1:3–196.

43 Al-Bukhārī, *Tārīkh* 8:304; Ibn Abī Ḥātim, *al-Jarḥ wa-l-taʿdīl* 9:184; al-Dhahabī, *Mīzān* 5:140–141; Ibn Ḥajar, *Tahdhīb* 4:386.

transmission (*qāla*),[44] while his other reports are transmitted through others. Yaḥyā b. Saʿīd al-Qaṭṭān was a leading *ḥadīth* scholar based in Basra and widely considered reliable (*thiqa*).[45] His status as *ḥadīth* scholar also corresponds to Khalīfa's citation of him for the above-mentioned subjects, which relate to legal issues and controversial historical episodes.

17. ʿAbd al-Raḥmān b. Mahdī (d. 198/814)—Basra—8 citations (1%)

ʿAbd al-Raḥmān b. Mahdī's reports pertain to the *ridda* wars, the assassination of ʿUthmān, the appointment of Yazīd b. Muʿāwiya, the Umayyad–Zubayrid conflict and Ibn al-Ashʿath's revolt. ʿAbd al-Raḥmān b. Mahdī is known as one of the pioneers of *ḥadīth* transmitter criticism and was considered a reliable transmitter (*thiqa*).[46] This is reflected in Khalīfa's citation of him regarding the aforementioned subjects, which were all important in the historical tradition.

18. Abū ʿĀṣim al-Ḍaḥḥāk b. Makhlad (d. 212/828)—Basra—8 citations (1%)

Abū ʿĀṣim's material pertains to the Prophet's time in Mecca and Medina, the change of the *qibla*, the Prophet's death, Fāṭima's death, the conquest of al-Ubulla and al-Ahwāz, the killing of ʿUthmān, and ʿAbd al-Malik b. Marwan's speech after Ibn al-Zubayr's death. He was a major Basran *ḥadīth* authority and widely recognised as a reliable narrator (*thiqa*), which explains Khalīfa's citation of him.[47]

19. Kahmas b. al-Minhāl—Basra—8 citations (1%)

Seven of Kahmas's reports pertain to the assassination of ʿUthmān and one to the Battle of the Camel. His reports are narrated on the authority of the Basran *ḥadīth* scholar Saʿīd b. Abī ʿArūba (d. 155–159/771–776). As was the case

44 Khalīfa b. Khayyāṭ, *Tārīkh* (1985) 88, 146, 166.

45 Ibn Saʿd, *Ṭabaqāt* 9:294; Ibn Ḥanbal, *Mawsūʿa* 4:114–120; al-Bukhārī, *Tārīkh* 8:276–277; al-ʿIjlī, *Maʿrifat al-thiqāt* 2:353; Ibn Abī Ḥātim, *al-Jarḥ wa-l-taʿdīl* 9:150–151; Ibn Ḥibbān, *Thiqāt* 7:611–612; al-Dhahabī, *Siyar* 4165–4168; Ibn Ḥajar, *Tahdhīb* 4:357–359; Lucas, *Constructive critics* 149–151.

46 Ibn Saʿd, *Ṭabaqāt* 9:299; Ibn Ḥanbal, *Mawsūʿa* 2:345–351; al-Dhahabī, *Siyar* 2242–2246, *Tadhkira* 329–332; Ibn Ḥajar, *Tahdhīb* 2:556–557; Lucas, *Constructive critics* 149–151; Brown, *Hadith* 80.

47 Ibn Saʿd, *Ṭabaqāt* 9:296; Ibn Ḥanbal, *Mawsūʿa* 2:183–184; Ibn Abī Ḥātim, *al-Jarḥ wa-l-taʿdīl* 4:463; Ibn Ḥibbān, *Thiqāt* 6:483–484; al-Dhahabī, *Siyar* 2043–2044, *Tadhkira* 366–367; Ibn Ḥajar, *Tahdhīb* 2:225–226.

with Saʿīd b. Abī ʿArūba, Kahmas was accused of Qadarī beliefs.[48] Ibn Ḥibbān included him in *Kitāb al-Thiqāt*, and Abū Ḥātim declared him sincere (*maḥalluhu al-ṣidq*), but al-Bukhārī included him in his *Kitāb al-Ḍuʿafāʾ*.[49] His material on ʿUthmān's death and the Battle of the Camel reflects early Sunnī views, which might explain Khalīfa's citing him.

20. Muʿādh b. Hishām (d. 200/815)—Basra—8 citations (1%)

Muʿādh b. Hishām's reports contain brief information about the age of the Prophet, the date of the Battle of Jalūlāʾ, the conquest of al-Jazīra and the deaths of ʿUmar and ʿUthmān. He was a Basran *ḥadīth* scholar whom some accused of Qadarī beliefs. Ibn Maʿīn declared him "sincere but not authoritative (*ṣadūq wa-laysa bi-ḥujja*)"; Ibn ʿAdī said that he was, hopefully, sincere (*arjū annahu ṣadūq*); and Ibn Ḥibbān included him in *Kitāb al-Thiqāt*.[50] As with other *ḥadīth* scholars, Khalīfa cites him for details about the Prophet and the Rāshidūn caliphs.

21. Muḥammad b. Muʿāwiya—Basra?—8 citations (1%)

Muḥammad b. Muʿāwiya transmits three reports from Abū ʿUbayda Maʿmar b. al-Muthannā, three from Bayhas b. Ḥabīb and two from a certain Sufyān (al-Thawrī or Ibn ʿUyayna). The reports from Bayhas pertain to the fall of the Umayyads. Bayhas had been an officer in the army of Ibn Hubayra in the late Umayyad period and had direct experience of the ʿAbbāsid Revolution. Khalīfa often cites Bayhas without mentioning Muḥammad b. Muʿāwiya, but he likely received these narrations from Muḥammad b. Muʿāwiya or from a written compilation.[51] The other reports pertain to the Persian calendar system, Fāṭima's death, the conquest of Ḥulwān, Abū Mūsā's suppression of a rebellion in al-Rayy and the number of men killed with al-Ḥusayn at Karbalāʾ. The exact identity of Muḥammad b. Muʿāwiya is unclear; the biographical dictionaries mention a few Iraqi scholars with the same name and similar scholarly affili-

48 Al-Dhahabī, *Mīzān* 2:143, 3:410; Raven, Saʿīd b. Abī ʿArūba.

49 Al-Bukhārī, *Tārīkh* 7:240, *Ḍuʿafāʾ* 101; Ibn Ḥibbān, *Thiqāt* 9:27–28; Ibn Abī Ḥātim, *al-Jarḥ wa-l-taʿdīl* 7:171; al-Dhahabī, *Mīzān* 3:410; Ibn Ḥajar, *Tahdhīb* 3:476–477. On the term *maḥalluhu al-ṣidq*, see al-Sakhāwī, *Fatḥ al-Mughīth* 2:282; al-Laknawī, *al-Rafʿ wa-l-takmīl* 138, 149; al-Ghawrī, *Muʿjam* 632–633.

50 Ibn Ḥanbal, *Mawsūʿa* 3:367; al-Bukhārī, *Tārīkh* 7:366; Ibn Ḥibbān, *Thiqāt* 9:176–177; Ibn ʿAdī, *Kāmil* 6:2426–2427; al-Dhahabī, *Siyar* 3876, *Tadhkira* 325, *Mīzān* 4:346–347; Ibn Ḥajar, *Tahdhīb* 4:102.

51 Khalīfa b. Khayyāṭ, *Tārīkh* (1985) 398, 400–402; Wurtzel, *Khalifa ibn Khayyat's History* 35.

ations.[52] In any case, Khalīfa also cites him in the *Ṭabaqāt* as a narrator from Abū ʿUbayda Maʿmar b. al-Muthannā.[53]

22. Abū Nuʿaym al-Faḍl b. Dukayn (d. 219/834)—Kufa—7 citations (1%)

Abū Nuʿaym's material includes one report on the date of the Battle of Badr, two reports about the Battle of the Camel and four reports about the dates of certain Companions' and Successors' deaths. He was a leading Kufan *ḥadīth* scholar considered reliable (*thiqa*). He was also praised for not complying with the *miḥna* and widely respected as a *ḥadīth* authority, although he is said to have had some light *tashayyuʿ* (*tashayyuʿ khafīf*), as al-Dhahabī puts it.[54]

23. Ismāʿīl b. ʿUlayya (d. 193/809)—Basra and Baghdad—7 citations (1%)

Khalīfa cites Ibn ʿUlayya once regarding the Battle of al-Yamāma, once regarding ʿUmar's death and five times regarding the assassination of ʿUthmān. He was a leading Basran *ḥadīth* scholar and was widely considered reliable (*thiqa*).[55] He was also put in charge of the *ṣadaqāt* (wealth tax) in Basra and later the *maẓālim* (court of grievances) in Baghdad towards the end of Hārūn al-Rashīd's reign.[56] His reports on the killing of ʿUthmān fit Khalīfa's early Sunnī perspective, which, in addition to his reputation, explains why he is cited in the *Tārīkh*.

24. Muḥammad b. ʿAbdallāh al-Anṣārī (d. 215/830)—Basra—7 citations (1%)

Al-Anṣārī's reports pertain to the Battle of al-Yamāma, Abū Bakr's governors, the Battle of Nihāwand and the siege against Ibn al-Zubayr in Mecca. He was a prominent Basran scholar of *ḥadīth* and *fiqh* who was twice appointed judge in Basra and who held other official positions under the ʿAbbāsids. His trans-

52 See al-Dhahabī, *Mīzān* 4:272–274; al-Mizzī, *Tahdhīb* 26:475–482; Ibn Ḥajar, *Tahdhīb* 3:704–705.

53 Khalīfa b. Khayyāṭ, *Ṭabaqāt* (1993) 25.

54 Ibn Saʿd, *Ṭabaqāt* 8:523–524; Ibn Ḥanbal, *Mawsūʿa* 3:151–154; Ibn Ḥibbān, *Thiqāt* 7:319; Ibn Abī Ḥātim, *al-Jarḥ wa-l-taʿdīl* 7:61–62; al-Dhahabī, *Siyar* 3031–3034, *Tadhkira* 372–373; Ibn Ḥajar, *Tahdhīb* 3:387–390. See also Rosenthal, Abū Nuʿaym al-Faḍl b. Dukayn al-Mulāʾī.

55 Ibn Saʿd, *Ṭabaqāt* 9:327–328; Ibn Ḥanbal, *Mawsūʿa* 1:94–99; al-Bukhārī, *Tārīkh* 1:342; Ibn Ḥibbān, *Thiqāt* 6:44–45; al-Dhahabī, *Siyar* 1092–1095, *Tadhkira* 322–323, *Mīzān* 1:217–220; Ibn Ḥajar, *Tahdhīb* 1:140–142.

56 Ibn Saʿd, *Ṭabaqāt* 9:327.

mission seems to have been considered sincere (*ṣadūq*) or reliable (*thiqa*), and many scholars transmitted *ḥadīth* from him.[57]

25. Muʿtamir b. Sulaymān (d. 187/803)—Basra—7 citations (1%)

All Muʿtamir's reports pertain to the assassination of ʿUthmān, except one about Shabath b. Ribʿī, the leader of al-Ḥarūriyya (who are known as the first Khawārij). Muʿtamir b. Sulaymān was a Basran *ḥadīth* scholar considered reliable (*thiqa*).[58] His subjects and status as transmitter conform to Khalīfa's standard of citing *ḥadīth* scholars for controversial subjects.

26. Umayya b. Khālid (d. 201/816–817)—Basra—7 citations (1%)

Umayya b. Khālid's reports pertain to the siege of al-Ṭāʾif in the Prophetic period, ʿUmar's pilgrimages and appointees, and Ibn al-Ashʿath's revolt (four reports). He was a Basran *ḥadīth* scholar whom Abū Zurʿa al-Rāzī, Abū Ḥātim and others considered reliable (*thiqa*).[59] Khalīfa cites Umayya, among other *ḥadīth* scholars, on Ibn al-Ashʿath's revolt, which indicates its importance for Khalīfa and the Basran scholars. He is one of Khalīfa's main sources in the *Ṭabaqāt*.[60]

27. Abū l-Dhayyāl Zuhayr b. Hunayd al-ʿAdawī—Basra—6 citations (0.5%)

One of Abū l-Dhayyāl's reports pertains to the conquest of al-Madāʾin; the rest, to events in the late Umayyad period. Khalīfa quite likely did not transmit directly from Abū l-Dhayyāl; four reports are narrated with one intermediary narrator, and two are introduced directly by "Abū l-Dhayyāl said." Little is known about Abū l-Dhayyāl, but he was a Basran narrator of *ḥadīth* and *akhbār* whom Ibn Ḥibbān included in *Kitāb al-Thiqāt*.[61]

---

57 Ibn Saʿd, *Ṭabaqāt* 9:296; Ibn Ḥanbal, *Mawsūʿa* 3:280; al-Bukhārī, *Tārīkh* 1:132; al-Dhahabī, *Siyar* 3523–3525, *Mīzān* 4:163–164; Ibn Ḥajar, *Tahdhīb* 3:614–615.

58 Ibn Saʿd, *Ṭabaqāt* 9:291–292; Ibn Ḥanbal, *Mawsūʿa* 3:373–375; Ibn Ḥibbān, *Thiqāt* 7:521–522; Ibn Abī Ḥātim, *al-Jarḥ wa-l-taʿdīl* 8:402–403; al-Dhahabī, *Tadhkira* 266–267; Ibn Ḥajar, *Tahdhīb* 4:117.

59 Ibn Saʿd, *Ṭabaqāt* 9:302; Ibn Ḥanbal, *Mawsūʿa* 1:127; al-Bukhārī, *Tārīkh* 2:10; al-ʿIjlī, *Maʿrifat al-thiqāt* 1:236; Ibn Abī Ḥātim, *al-Jarḥ wa-l-taʿdīl* 2:302–303; al-Dhahabī, *Mīzān* 1:263; Ibn Ḥajar, *Tahdhīb* 1:188.

60 Khalīfa b. Khayyāṭ, *Ṭabaqāt* (1993) 25.

61 Ibn Ḥibbān, *Thiqāt* 8:256. See also al-Bukhārī, *Tārīkh* 3:429; Ibn Abī Ḥātim, *al-Jarḥ wa-l-taʿdīl* 3:590–591; Ibn Ḥajar, *Tahdhīb* 1:641.

28. Ismāʿīl b. Isḥāq—Basra?—6 citations (0.5%)

Ismāʿīl b. Isḥāq's reports pertain to revolts in the late Umayyad period, including the text of Abū Ḥamza's *khuṭba* in Mecca and a report about the appearance of Abū Muslim in Khurāsān. His reports resemble those of Ismāʿīl b. Ibrāhīm b. Isḥāq, which led Wurtzel to suggest that they might have been the same person and that Khalīfa confused the names of Ismāʿīl's father and grandfather.[62] In any case, he does not seem to be identified by name in the major biographical dictionaries.

29. ʿAbd al-Aʿlā b. ʿAbd al-Aʿlā (d. 189/805)—Basra—5 citations (0.5%)

ʿAbd al-Aʿlā b. ʿAbd al-Aʿlā is cited about the origin of the Hijrī calendar, the revelation of Sūrat al-Tawba, the killing of ʿUthmān, the Battle of Ṣiffīn and the conquest of North Africa. ʿAbd al-Aʿlā was a Basran *ḥadīth* scholar whom Ibn Maʿīn, al-ʿIjlī and Abū Zurʿa al-Rāzī considered reliable (*thiqa*), although Ibn Saʿd remarked that "he was not strong (*lam yakun bi-l-qawī*)." He was also accused of Qadarī beliefs.[63] The subjects of his reports resemble those which Khalīfa cites from other *ḥadīth* scholars.

30. ʿAbd al-Malik b. Qurayb al-Aṣmaʿī (d. 213/828)—Basra—5 citations (0.5%)

Al-Aṣmaʿī reports about the date of Abū l-Haytham b. al-Tayyihān's death, the conquest of Hamadhān, the conquest of Aṣbahān, al-Shaʿbī's interaction with al-Ḥajjāj and the death of ʿUmar b. ʿAbd al-ʿAzīz. He was a leading philologist and one of the main figures of the Basran school of grammar. His contemporaries and later biographers described him as adhering to the Sunna—perhaps in contrast to some other language specialists with Muʿtazilī, Qadarī or Shīʿī inclinations. Although he was respected for his transmission, he was mainly known for his expertise in Arabic.[64]

---

62 Wurtzel, *Khalifa ibn Khayyat's History* 36.

63 Ibn Maʿīn, *Tārīkh* 4:84; Ibn Saʿd, *Ṭabaqāt* 9:291; Ibn Ḥanbal, *Mawsūʿa* 2:306–307; al-Bukhārī, *Tārīkh* 6:73; al-ʿIjlī, *Maʿrifat al-thiqāt* 2:68; Ibn Ḥibbān, *Thiqāt* 7:130–131; al-Dhahabī, *Siyar* 2135–2136, *Mīzān* 2:471–472; Ibn Ḥajar, *Tahdhīb* 2:465.

64 Ibn Ḥanbal, *Mawsūʿa* 2:389–390; Ibn Ḥibbān, *Thiqāt* 8:389; Ibn Abī Ḥātim, *al-Jarḥ wa-l-taʿdīl* 5:363; al-Dhahabī, *Siyar* 2579–2580; Ibn Ḥajar, *Tahdhīb* 2:622–623. See also Lewin, al-Aṣmaʿī; Lecker, Biographical notes on Abū ʿUbayda 94.

31. Abū Qutayba Salm b. Qutayba (d. 200/815–816)—Basra—5 citations (0.5%)

Abū Qutayba's short reports pertain to the Prophet's death, Abū Bakr's death, ʿUmar's death, the killing of ʿUthmān and ʿAbdallāh b. Ghālib's death during Ibn al-Ashʿath's revolt. He was a *ḥadīth* scholar whom Abū Zurʿa, Abū Dāwūd and Ibn Maʿīn considered reliable. Abū Ḥātim said about him, "He is acceptable, but made many mistakes; his *ḥadīth*s are written down (*laysa bihi baʾs kathīr al-wahm yuktabu ḥadīthuhu*)."[65] Most of the reports are very brief and only concern the deaths of prominent individuals, but his report on the assassination of ʿUthmān, in which ʿĀʾisha reproaches those who killed him, clearly reflects an early Sunnī perspective.[66]

32. Mūsā b. Ismāʿīl al-Tabūdhakī (d. 223/838)—Basra—5 citations (0.5%)

Al-Tabūdhakī's reports provide information about the army of Usāma b. Zayd, the apostasy of Banū Sulaym, the Battle of al-Yamāma, ʿUmar's appointment of Abū ʿUbayda over the Syrian army and the Battle of Nihāwand. He was a Basran *ḥadīth* scholar widely considered reliable (*thiqa*).[67] Unlike many other *ḥadīth* scholars in the *Tārīkh*, al-Tabūdhakī's reports do not pertain to the Prophet's life or early intra-Muslim conflicts, but they nonetheless relate to key episodes in the Rāshidūn period.

4 Minor Direct Transmitters (1–4 Citations)

Sections 2 and 3 have shown, first, that Khalīfa relies mainly on Basran *akhbārīyūn* for the basic chronological narrative and, second, that he cites many well-known *ḥadīth* authorities for particularly controversial or important information (especially relating to the Prophet Muḥammad and to intra-Muslim conflicts). The next step is to examine the remaining 73 transmitters, who are each cited fewer than five times. The results confirm both the preponderance of Bas-

65 Ibn Saʿd, *Ṭabaqāt* 9:303; Ibn Ḥanbal, *Mawsūʿa* 2:75; Ibn Abī Ḥātim, *al-Jarḥ wa-l-taʿdīl* 4:266; Ibn Ḥibbān, *Thiqāt* 8:297; al-Dhahabī, *Siyar* 1865, *Mīzān* 2:174; al-Mizzī, *Tahdhīb* 11:232–235; Ibn Ḥajar, *Tahdhīb* 2:66–67.

66 Khalīfa b. Khayyāṭ, *Tārīkh* (1985) 175–176.

67 Ibn Saʿd, *Ṭabaqāt* 9:307; al-ʿIjlī, *Maʿrifat al-thiqāt* 2:303; Ibn Abī Ḥātim, *al-Jarḥ wa-l-taʿdīl* 8:136; Ibn Ḥibbān, *Thiqāt* 9:160; al-Dhahabī, *Siyar* 3976–3977, *Tadhkira* 394–395; Ibn Ḥajar, *Tahdhīb* 4:169–170.

ran transmitters and the high number of *ḥadīth* authorities. The transmitters from whom Khalīfa indicates that he received direct transmission are marked with an asterisk (*); the remaining transmitters are those from whom he transmits without intermediary narrators, but without indicating direct transmission. It is possible that Khalīfa did not have personal contact with some of them and received their reports through others, but they are included here because they nonetheless reflect his selection of sources. The known transmitters are arranged according to the cities in which they were active; the others, who have not been identified in the biographical dictionaries, are listed at the end.

TABLE 1 Minor transmitters in Khalīfa's *Tārīkh*

Name of transmitter		Location
33.	Muḥammad b. Saʿd	Baghdad
34.	Kathīr b. Hishām*	Baghdad and Raqqa
35.	ʿAbdallāh b. Dāwūd al-Khuraybī*	Basra
36.	ʿAbd al-Raḥmān b. ʿUthmān	Basra
37.	ʿAbd al-Salām b. Muṭahhar*	Basra
38.	Abū Bakr al-Kalbī*	Basra
39.	Abū Wahb al-Sahmī*	Basra
40.	Abū l-Walīd Hishām b. ʿAbd al-Malik al-Ṭayālisī*	Basra
41.	Abū l-Yamān al-Nabbāl*	Basra
42.	Aḥmad b. ʿAlī*	Basra
43.	ʿĀmir b. Ṣāliḥ b. Rustum*	Basra
44.	ʿAmr b. al Mankhal al-Sadūsī*	Basra
45.	Ashhal b. Ḥātim*	Basra
46.	ʿAwn b. Kahmas b. al-Ḥasan*	Basra
47.	Azhar b. Saʿd*	Basra
48.	Bishr b. al-Mufaḍḍal*	Basra
49.	Ghassān b. Muḍar*	Basra
50.	Ḥammād b. Zayd	Basra
51.	Ibrāhīm b. Ṣāliḥ b. Dirham*	Basra
52.	Ibn Abī ʿAdī*	Basra
53.	Isḥāq b. Idrīs*	Basra
54.	Ismāʿīl b. Sinān*	Basra
55.	Khālid b. al-Ḥārith*	Basra
56.	Khayyāṭ b. Khalīfa b. Khayyāṭ*	Basra
57.	Marḥūm b. ʿAbd al-ʿAzīz	Basra
58.	Muʿādh b. Muʿādh*	Basra

TABLE 1 Minor transmitters in Khalīfa's *Tārīkh* (*cont.*)

Name of transmitter		Location
59.	Muḥammad b. Muʿādh*	Basra
60.	Muḥammad b. Saʿīd al-Bāhilī*	Basra
61.	Muslim b. Ibrāhīm al-Farāhīdī	Basra
62.	Naḍla*	Basra
63.	Rawḥ b. ʿUbāda*	Basra
64.	Ṣafwān b. ʿĪsā	Basra
65.	Sahl b. Bakkār*	Basra
66.	Sahl b. Yūsuf*	Basra
67.	Shuʿayb b. Ḥayyān*	Basra
68.	Sulaymān b. Ḥarb*	Basra
69.	ʿUbaydallāh b. ʿAbdallāh b. ʿAwn*	Basra
70.	ʿUmar b. Abī Khalīfa*	Basra
71.	ʿUmar b. ʿAlī*	Basra
72.	ʿUthmān al-Qurashī*	Basra
73.	ʿUthmān b. ʿUthmān al-Ghaṭafānī*	Basra
74.	Yaḥyā b. Abī l-Ḥajjāj (Abū Ayyūb al-Khāqānī)*	Basra
75.	ʿAbdallāh b. Maslama b. Qaʿnab*	Basra and Medina
76.	Al-ʿAlāʾ b. Burd b. Sinān al-Dimashqī*	Basra and Damascus
77.	Yaḥyā b. ʿAbd al-Raḥmān*	Basra or Kufa?
78.	ʿAlī b. ʿAbdallāh (b. al-Madīnī?)*	Basra?
79.	Muḥammad b. ʿAbdallāh al-Zubayrī*	Kufa
80.	Abū Ghassān Mālik b. Ismāʿīl*	Kufa
81.	ʿAththām b. ʿAlī	Kufa
82.	Jaʿfar b. ʿAwn*	Kufa
83.	ʿUbaydallāh b. Mūsā*	Kufa
84.	Wakīʿ b. al-Jarrāḥ*	Kufa
85.	Ziyād b. ʿAbdallāh al-Bakkāʾī*	Kufa
86.	Abū ʿAmr al-Shaybānī	Kufa and Baghdad
87.	Muḥammad b. ʿUmar al-Wāqidī*	Medina and Baghdad
88.	ʿAlī b. ʿĀṣim*	Wāsiṭ
89.	Yazīd b. Hārūn*	Wāsiṭ
90.	ʿAbdallāh b. Maymūn*	–
91.	ʿAbd al-Aʿlā b. al-Haytham*	–
92.	Abū l-ʿAbbās*	–
93.	Abū ʿAbd al-Raḥmān al-Qurashī*	–
94.	Abū Madyan	–

TABLE 1 Minor transmitters in Khalīfa's *Tārīkh* (*cont.*)

Name of transmitter		Location
95.	Abū Marwān al-Bāhilī*	–
96.	Abū Usāma	–
97.	'Amr b. 'Ubayda*	–
98.	Bakr b. 'Aṭiyya*	–
99.	Bishr b. Yasār*	–
100.	Al-Ḥasan b. Abī 'Amr*	–
101.	Maslama b. Thābit	–
102.	Muḥammad b. 'Amr	–
103.	Shihāb*	–
104.	Yaḥyā b. Arqam*	–
105.	Yasār b. 'Ubaydallāh*	–

This list shows that Khalīfa had access to and consulted many sources apart from his main transmitters. It contains many well-known Basran *ḥadīth* narrators, among them Bishr b. al-Mufaḍḍal (d. 186/802), Khālid b. al-Ḥārith (d. 186/802), Mu'ādh b. Mu'ādh (d. 196/811–812), Sulaymān b. Ḥarb (d. 224/839), Rawḥ b. 'Ubāda (d. 205/820), Muslim b. Ibrāhīm al-Farāhīdī (d. 222/837) and 'Abdallāh b. Maslama b. Qa'nab (d. 221/836).[68] Some non-Basran transmitters, such as Yazīd b. Hārūn (d. 206/821) of Wāsiṭ and Wakī' b. al-Jarrāḥ (d. 197/813) of Kufa, were also prominent *ḥadīth* scholars.[69] The percentage of Basran transmitters among the minor transmitters is about 60 per cent in total (44 of 73), but most of the unknown transmitters likely were also Basrans. If they were included, the percentage of Basrans would reach about 82 per cent (60 of 73). In any case, the list confirms that Khalīfa seldom cites non-Basran sources and that many of the non-Basrans were reputable *ḥadīth* scholars.[70]

A few names are important in relation to *akhbār* scholarship, in particular al-Wāqidī and Ibn Sa'd. Khalīfa cites al-Wāqidī once about the conquest

68 Al-Dhahabī, Siyar 1209–1210, 1592–1593, 1701–1702, 1901–1902, 2533–2535, 3834–3835, 3875–3876.

69 Al-Dhahabī, *Siyar* 4121–4128, 4232–4235; Ibn Sa'd, *Ṭabaqāt* 8:517; 9:316.

70 E.g. Ja'far b. 'Awn (Kufa), Ḥammād b. Usāma (Kufa), 'Ubaydallāh b. Mūsā (Kufa), 'Aththām b. 'Alī (Kufa), Kathīr b. Hishām (Baghdad), Muḥammad b. Sa'd (Baghdad), Wakī' b. al-Jarrāḥ (Kufa), Yazīd b. Hārūn (Wāsiṭ). For their biographies, see Ibn Ḥajar, *Tahdhīb* 1:309–310, 477; 3:28–29, 55, 466–467, 571; 4:311–314, 431–433.

of al-Madāʾin and indicates that he received the report by direct transmission (*ḥaddathanā*).[71] He also cites Ibn Saʿd once about the spoils of war after Ibn Abī Sarḥ's first raid in North Africa, but without indicating direct transmission.[72] Al-Wāqidī was a well-known compiler of *maghāzī* and *futūḥ* material. He was much cited by Ibn Saʿd, Ibn Ḥabīb, al-Balādhurī, al-Ṭabarī and others, but he was criticised by many *ḥadīth* scholars.[73] It is, therefore, noteworthy that Khalīfa cites al-Wāqidī only once in the *Tārīkh* but six times in the *Ṭabaqāt*.[74] It suggests that he knew of some of his material but preferred information from a different pool of transmitters. The citation of Ibn Saʿd is perhaps less significant, since he was less controversial than al-Wāqidī in *ḥadīth* circles. It is also unlikely that Khalīfa had personal contact with Ibn Saʿd; the latter does not include an entry on Khalīfa in his *Ṭabaqāt*, but he narrates one report about the *ridda* wars (found in the *Tārīkh*) and seven Prophetic *ḥadīth*s on Khalīfa's authority with the expression, "I was informed on the authority of (*ukhbirtu ʿan*) Khalīfa b. Khayyāṭ."[75] Ibn Saʿd probably received the material from Khalīfa's students or possibly from the *musnad* ascribed to Khalīfa.[76]

Other well-known scholars among the minor transmitters include Abū ʿAmr al-Shaybānī (d. 210/825), the grammarian, lexicographer and collector of poetry based in Kufa and Baghdad. He was also a respected transmitter from whom Aḥmad b. Ḥanbal and others narrated.[77] Thus Khalīfa transmits from three of the leading grammarians of the time: Abū ʿUbayda Maʿmar b. al-Muthannā, al-Aṣmaʿī and Abū ʿAmr al-Shaybānī. It shows Khalīfa's interaction with scholars of various disciplines, although he mainly narrates from those known as *muḥaddithūn* and *akhbāriyūn*.

As for the transmitters not identified in the biographical dictionaries, it is statistically likely that many of them were based in Basra. The unidentified *kunyas* (e.g. Abū Madyan, Abū l-ʿAbbās) might also refer to other authorities listed above under their full names. Altogether, the list of minor transmitters confirms that the bulk of Khalīfa's transmitters were Basrans and that many of them were known *ḥadīth* scholars. It also shows that Khalīfa had access to

71 Khalīfa b. Khayyāṭ, *Tārīkh* (1985) 133.

72 Khalīfa b. Khayyāṭ, *Tārīkh* (1985) 160.

73 Ibn Saʿd, *Ṭabaqāt* 9:336–337; Ibn Abī Ḥātim, *al-Jarḥ wa-l-taʿdīl* 8:20–21; Ibn ʿAdī, *Kāmil* 6:2245–2247; al-Dhahabī, *Mīzān* 4:218–221; Ibn Ḥajar, *Tahdhīb* 3:656–659.

74 Khalīfa b. Khayyāṭ, *Ṭabaqāt* (1993) 165, 466, 552, 553, 558.

75 Ibn Saʿd, *Ṭabaqāt* 9:74–77, 86–87; Khalīfa b. Khayyāṭ, *Tārīkh* (1985) 117–118.

76 Wurtzel, *Khalifa ibn Khayyat's History* 40–41.

77 Yāqūt al-Ḥamawī, *Muʿjam* 625–628; Ibn Khallikān, *Wafayāt* 1:201–202. Troupeau, Abū ʿAmr al-Shaybānī.

material from other cities and from specialists in other disciplines—probably through travelling scholars and possibly from circulating books—but nonetheless based his *Tārīkh* mostly on Basran *ḥadīth* and *akhbār* transmitters.

5 Major Indirect Sources

Besides Khalīfa's direct sources, there are a few particularly prominent names among the indirect transmitters from whom Khalīfa transmitted through one intermediary narrator. The following section discusses the indirect transmitters cited more than ten times in the *Tārīkh*. The list is limited to those from whom Khalīfa transmitted through one intermediary narrator and excludes earlier generations, such as Companions and Successors. The reason for examining these names in particular rather than all the names in Khalīfa's *isnād*s is not merely practical; these closer narrators are also more relevant for mapping the immediate scholarly tradition and network upon which Khalīfa based his *Tārīkh*.

1. Muḥammad b. Isḥāq (d. c. 150/767)—Medina and Baghdad—c. 130 citations (14%)

Ibn Isḥāq is Khalīfa's main source for the Prophet's lifetime alongside al-Madā'inī and is also an important source for the Rāshidūn period until ʿUmar's death in 23/644. It is possible that the post-Prophetic reports come from the *Tārīkh al-khulafā'* attributed to him.[78] Khalīfa does not transmit directly from Ibn Isḥāq, but via Bakr b. Sulaymān and Wahb b. Jarīr b. Ḥāzim from his father—both among the lesser-known transmitters of Ibn Isḥāq's *Sīra*.[79] In the section on the Prophet's lifetime, Khalīfa narrates from one or both of them, but in the Rāshidūn period, except for two instances, he only narrates from Bakr b. Sulaymān. In addition, Khalīfa often cites Ibn Isḥāq without complete *isnād*s ("Ibn Isḥāq said"), but these citations refer back to Bakr b. Sulaymān or Wahb b. Jarīr.

---

78 See al-ʿUmarī's introduction to Khalīfa b. Khayyāṭ, *Tārīkh* (1985) 17.

79 The more well-known include Ziyād b. ʿAbdallāh al-Bakkā'ī (d. 183/799), Yūnus b. Bukayr (d. 199/815) and Salama b. al-Faḍl (d. 191/806–807). It is noteworthy that Khalīfa does not narrate any accounts from Ibn Isḥāq through the Kufan transmitter al-Bakkā'ī, the source of Ibn Hishām's recension, although he narrates one report directly from him from Ḥajjāj from Nāfiʿ from Ibn ʿUmar. See Khalīfa b. Khayyāṭ, *Tārīkh* (1985) 54. On other transmitters of Ibn Isḥāq's *Sīra*, see Guillaume, *Life of Muḥammad* xxx–xxxiii; Schoeler, *Biography of Muḥammad* 31–32.

Early opinions about Ibn Isḥāq's status as a *ḥadīth* transmitter differ.[80] Many early critics considered him reliable (*thiqa*) or sincere (*ṣadūq*), although some declared him weak. Some also accused him of *tashayyuʿ* and Qadarī views.[81] Ibn Isḥāq is said to have written his famous *Sīra* for the ʿAbbāsid caliph al-Manṣūr (r. 136–158/754–775).[82] By the time of Khalīfa, Ibn Isḥāq was widely recognised as an authority on *maghāzī-sīra*. Khalīfa's reliance on Ibn Isḥāq for chronological information and short summaries of events resembles the approach of later Sunnī scholars, who considered him an authority on *maghāzī-sīra*, and crucial as a source of chronology, but less authoritative in the transmission of individual *ḥadīths*.[83] This can be seen in Khalīfa's systematic citing Ibn Isḥāq for basic chronological information but citing other *ḥadīth* authorities for events or details of particular importance (such as the Prophet's birth and death, and the change of the *qibla*).[84]

2. Hishām b. Qaḥdham b. Sulaymān—Basra—c. 48 citations (5%)

Hishām b. Qaḥdham b. Sulaymān is the father and main source of the aforementioned al-Walīd b. Hishām, who is the third most-cited direct transmitter in the *Tārīkh*. His father, Qaḥdham b. Sulaymān b. Dhakwān, was secretary of finance (*kātib al-kharāj*) under the Umayyad governor Yūsuf b. ʿUmar al-Thaqafī (r. 120–126/738–744) in Iraq.[85] Ibn Ḥibbān includes him in *Kitāb al-Thiqāt* but notes that he made mistakes in his transmission (*kāna yukhṭiʾu*).[86]

80 Ibn Ḥibbān, *Thiqāt* 7:380–385.

81 Ibn Maʿīn, *Tārīkh* 3:225; Ibn Saʿd, *Ṭabaqāt* 9:323–324; Ibn Ḥanbal, *Mawsūʿa* 3:235–240; al-Bukhārī, *Tārīkh* 1:40; al-ʿIjlī, *Maʿrifat al-thiqāt* 2:232; Ibn Abī Ḥātim, *al-Jarḥ wa-l-taʿdīl* 7:380–385; Ibn Ḥibbān, *Thiqāt* 7:380–385; Ibn ʿAdī, *Kāmil* 6:2116–2125; Ibn al-Nadīm, *Fihrist* 1:289–290; Ibn Sayyid al-Nās, *ʿUyūn al-athar* 1:54–67; al-Dhahabī, *Siyar* 3314–3320, *Tadhkira* 172–174; Ibn Ḥajar, *Tahdhīb* 3:504–507.

82 Al-Khaṭīb al-Baghdādī, *Tārīkh Baghdād* 2:16–17; Yāqūt al-Ḥamawī, *Muʿjam* 2419; Schoeler, *Biography of Muḥammad* 28.

83 E.g. al-Dhahabī, *Siyar* 3314–3320. Al-Dhahabī also states about Ibn Isḥāq, "More than one declared him reliable and others declared him weak. He is good enough in his *ḥadīth* transmission (*ṣāliḥ al-ḥadīth*). There is nothing wrong with him, in my view, except the unacceptable unreferenced things (*al-ashyāʾ al-munkarat al-munqaṭiʿa*) and the fabricated poetry (*al-ashʿār al-makhdhūba*) that he added to his *Sīra*." *Mīzān* 4:46.

84 Khalīfa b. Khayyāṭ, *Tārīkh* (1985) 52–54, 64–65, 94–96.

85 Khalīfa b. Khayyāṭ, *Tārīkh* (1985) 162, 368.

86 Ibn Ḥibbān, *Thiqāt* 7:571.

3. Al-Mughīra (Abū ʿAbdallāh)—Basra—c. 34 citations (4%)

Al-Mughīra is the father and main source of the aforementioned ʿAbdallāh b. al-Mughīra. Nothing is known about him, but, as noted above, he might have been involved in the administration of Iraq. As with his son, he is not found in the biographical dictionaries, but he was probably a local informant in Basra.

4. Jarīr b. Ḥāzim (d. 170/786–787)—Basra—c. 29 citations (3%)

Jarīr b. Ḥāzim is the father and main source of the aforementioned Wahb b. Jarīr. He transmitted Ibn Isḥāq's *Sīra* alongside a few reports on the Battle of the Camel, the Khawārij and conflicts in the early Umayyad period. As with his son, he was a Basran *ḥadīth* scholar, considered reliable (*thiqa*) by many critics and described by Aḥmad b. Ḥanbal as *ṣāḥib sunna*.[87]

5. Ḥātim b. Muslim (d. c. 150/767)—Basra—c. 25 citations (3%)

Ḥātim b. Muslim's reports pertain to Fāṭima's death, conquests in different regions, captives from the Battle of Jalūlāʾ, ʿUmar's appointment of Zayd b. Thābit over Medina, the Battle of the Camel, ʿAlī's death, the administration under some Umayyad caliphs, deaths of Umayyad caliphs, the killing of Yazīd b. Abī Muslim, deaths of prominent individuals and the administration under al-Mahdī. Although Khalīfa cites Ḥātim b. Muslim with formulas indicating direct transmission (e.g. *haddathanī*), there might not have been any personal contact between them, since Ḥātim seems to have died before Khalīfa's birth. According to al-Dhahabī, Ḥātim b. Muslim "died around the year 150/767."[88] However, the first report is transmitted through the Basran *ḥadīth* transmitter Abū Wahb ʿAbdallāh b. Bakr al-Sahmī (d. 208/823),[89] who might be Khalīfa's source for the other citations. Ḥātim b. Muslim was a Basran *ḥadīth* scholar considered reliable by many early critics.[90]

87 Ibn Saʿd, *Ṭabaqāt* 9:278; Ibn Ḥanbal, *Mawsūʿa* 1:189–192; al-ʿIjlī, *Maʿrifat al-thiqāt* 1:267; Ibn Abī Ḥātim, *al-Jarḥ wa-l-taʿdīl* 2:504–505; al-Mizzī, *Tahdhīb* 4:524–531; al-Dhahabī, *Siyar* 1285–1286; Ibn Ḥajar, *Tahdhīb* 1:294–296.

88 Al-Dhahabī, *Tārīkh al-Islām* 9:95.

89 Khalīfa b. Khayyāṭ, *Tārīkh* (1985) 96. On Abū Wahb al-Sahmī's reputation as a reliable transmitter, see al-Dhahabī, *Siyar* 2358; Ibn Ḥajar, *Tahdhīb* 2:309–310.

90 Ibn Saʿd, *Ṭabaqāt* 9:270; Ibn Ḥibbān, *Thiqāt* 6:236; al-Dhahabī, *Siyar* 1346; al-Mizzī, *Tahdhīb* 5:194–195; Ibn Ḥajar, *Tahdhīb* 1:324.

6. Sa'īd b. Abī 'Arūba (d. 155–159/771–776)—Basra—c. 17 citations (2%)

Sa'īd b. Abī 'Arūba's reports pertain to commentary on the Qur'ān, the Prophet's time in Mecca and Medina, the date of the Battle of Badr, the changing of the *qibla*, the martyrs at Uḥud, Anas b. Mālik's words about the missed prayer at Tustar, the date of 'Umar's death, the assassination of 'Uthmān and the Battle of the Camel. Khalīfa received most of Sa'īd's reports from Yazīd b. Zuray', Kahmas b. al-Minhāl and Ibn 'Ulayya. Sa'īd b. Abī 'Arūba was a major Basran *ḥadīth* scholar and was known as one of the first *ḥadīth* compilers of works in the *muṣannaf* format.[91] Critics of transmitters generally considered him reliable, although he is said to have become "confused" (*ikhtalaṭa*) some ten years before his death. It is also mentioned that he held Qadarī beliefs.[92] The subjects of his reports correspond to Khalīfa's transmission from well-known *ḥadīth* authorities regarding controversial or otherwise important subjects.

7. Ḥammād b. Salama (d. 167/783)—Basra—c. 15 citations (1.5%)

Ḥammād b. Salama's reports pertain to the Prophet's time in Mecca and Medina, his marriage to Ṣafiyya, the conquest of Mecca, the spoils of Ḥunayn, the Prophet's death, the *ridda* wars, 'Umar's appointment of Abū 'Ubayda over Syria, 'Umar's seeking council from al-Hurmuzān, the Battle of Ṣiffīn and Ibn al-Zubayr's caliphate. Khalīfa received his reports through the Basran transmitters Abū 'Ubayda Ma'mar b. al-Muthannā, al-Madā'inī, Mūsā al-Tabūdhakī and Ismā'īl b. Sinān. Ḥammād b. Salama was one of the leading Basran *ḥadīth* scholars and was widely considered reliable (*thiqa*).[93] His prominence as a *ḥadīth* scholar is also reflected in Khalīfa's citing him for important subjects pertaining to the Prophet and the early caliphs.

8. Shu'ba b. al-Ḥajjāj (d. 160/776)—Basra—c. 15 citations (1.5%)

Shu'ba's reports pertain to the Battle of Badr, the changing of the *qibla*, the conquest of al-Ṭā'if, the conquest of Iraq, the killing of 'Uthmān, the Battle of the Camel, the killing of Muḥammad b. Abī Bakr, the Battle of Ṣiffīn and

91 Raven, Sa'īd b. Abī 'Arūba.

92 Ibn Sa'd, *Ṭabaqāt* 9:273; Ibn Ḥanbal, *Mawsū'a* 2:39–43; al-Dhahabī, *Siyar* 1813–1815; Ibn Ḥajar, *Tahdhīb* 2:33–35.

93 Ibn Sa'd, *Ṭabaqāt* 9:282; Ibn Ḥanbal, *Mawsū'a* 1:297–302; al-Bukhārī, *Tārīkh* 3:22–23; al-Dhahabī, *Siyar* 1555–1558; Ibn Ḥajar, *Tahdhīb* 1:481–483.

Ibn al-Ashʿath's revolt. Khalīfa received his reports from Abū Dāwūd al-Ṭayālisī, Ghundar and Umayya b. Khālid. Shuʿba b. al-Ḥajjāj was one of the greatest early Basran *ḥadīth* scholars, widely considered reliable (*thiqa*).[94] His prominence in *ḥadīth* scholarship corresponds to Khalīfa's citation of him for controversial and important subjects.

9. ʿAbdallāh b. ʿAwn (d. 151/768)—Basra—c. 15 citations (1.5%)

Ibn ʿAwn's reports pertain to the *ridda* wars, ʿUmar's appointment of Abū ʿUbayda over Syria, the conquests of Iraq and Iran, the killing of ʿUthmān, the Battle of the Camel, Ibn al-Zubayr's caliphate and Ibn al-Ashʿath's revolt. Khalīfa received his material through the Basran narrators Muʿādh b. Muʿādh, Muḥammad b. ʿAbdallāh al-Anṣārī, al-Walīd b. Hishām, Ibn ʿUlayya and Ashhal. ʿAbdallāh b. ʿAwn was a Basran *ḥadīth* authority deemed reliable (*thiqa*).[95] Ibn Saʿd mentions that he had ʿUthmānī tendencies, which might be reflected in his material on the killing of ʿUthmān.[96]

10. ʿAbd al-ʿAzīz b. ʿImrān (d. 197/812–813)—Medina—c. 15 citations (1.5%)

ʿAbd al-ʿAzīz b. ʿImrān's reports pertain to the pre-Islamic systems of dating and the births and deaths of prominent individuals. It is unlikely that Khalīfa had personal contact with ʿAbd al-ʿAzīz: nine reports are transmitted through Yaḥyā b. Muḥammad al-Kaʿbī and six without intermediary transmitters, but without formulas indicating direct transmission. ʿAbd al-ʿAzīz b. ʿImrān was a Medinan *akhbār* and *ḥadīth* transmitter whom the early critics declared weak (*ḍaʿīf*) or rejected (*matrūk*).[97] However, Ibn Maʿīn said that he was a scholar not of *ḥadīth* but rather of genealogy and poetry.[98] This expertise in genealogy, rather than *ḥadīth*, might also explain Khalīfa's citing him mainly for the births and deaths of the caliphs.

94 Ibn Saʿd, *Ṭabaqāt* 9:280–281; Ibn Ḥanbal, *Mawsūʿa* 2:144–155; al-Bukhārī, *Tārīkh* 4:244–245; al-Dhahabī, *Siyar* 1980–1987; Ibn Ḥajar, *Tahdhīb* 2:166–170.

95 Ibn Saʿd, *Ṭabaqāt* 9:261–268; Ibn Ḥanbal, *Mawsūʿa* 2:272–274; al-Bukhārī, *Tārīkh* 5:163; al-Dhahabī, *Siyar* 2451–2454; Ibn Ḥajar, *Tahdhīb* 2:398–399.

96 Ibn Saʿd, *Ṭabaqāt* 9:261.

97 Ibn Saʿd, *Ṭabaqāt* 7:614; al-Bukhārī, *Ḍuʿafāʾ* 78; Ibn Abī Ḥātim, *al-Jarḥ wa-l-taʿdīl* 5:390–391; al-Dhahabī, *Mīzān* 2:552; al-Mizzī, *Tahdhīb* 18:178–181; Ibn Ḥajar, *Tahdhīb* 2:591–592.

98 Al-Mizzī, *Tahdhīb* 18:180.

11. Dāwūd b. Abī Hind (d. 139/756–757)—Basra—c. 10 citations (1%)

Dāwūd b. Abī Hind's reports pertain to the deaths of the Prophet, Abū Bakr and ʿUmar, the *ridda* wars, the conquests of Iraq and Iran, the Battle of the Camel and the killing of Yazīd b. Abī Muslim. Khalīfa received these reports through Ibn Abī ʿAdī, al-Madāʾinī and Abū l-Yaqẓān. Dāwūd b. Abī Hind was a Basran *ḥadīth* transmitter considered reliable (*thiqa*) by the early critics.[99]

12. ʿAbdallāh b. Lahīʿa (d. 174/790)—Egypt—10 citations (1%)

Ibn Lahīʿa's reports pertain to the conquests of Egypt and North Africa. Khalīfa received his material from anonymous sources (*man samiʿa Ibn Lahīʿa*) reporting directly from Ibn Lahīʿa or via his students. Ibn Lahīʿa lived in Egypt and was appointed judge during the caliphate of al-Manṣūr.[100] He was a famous *ḥadīth* transmitter but was criticised and considered weak by several early critics.[101] He is said to have had some Shīʿī tendencies; Ibn ʿAdī even describes him as extreme in his *tashayyuʿ* (*shadīd al-ifrāṭ fī l-tashayyuʿ*).[102] Since Ibn Lahīʿa's reports pertain mainly to his homeland Egypt, it may be that Khalīfa had no access to other sources and/or considered him an acceptable authority on Egyptian history.

13. Abū Maʿshar al-Sindī (d. 170/787)—Medina and Baghdad—10 citations (1%)

Khalīfa cites Abū Maʿshar three times on the authority of al-Madāʾinī. The other seven references—short statements introduced as "Abū Maʿshar said"—refer back to al-Madāʾinī's transmission. His material pertains to Abū Bakr's preparation for the *ridda* wars, the martyrs at the Battle of al-Yamāma (eight short citations) and the date of ʿUthmān's death. Khalīfa possibly took this material from the *Kitāb al-Maghāzī* ascribed to Abū Maʿshar,[103] which he could have

99 Ibn Saʿd, *Ṭabaqāt* 9:254; al-ʿIjlī, *Maʿrifat al-thiqāt* 1:342; Ibn Abī Ḥātim, *al-Jarḥ wa-l-taʿdīl* 3:411–412; al-Dhahabī, *Siyar* 1653–1654; Ibn Ḥajar, *Tahdhīb* 1:572.

100 Al-Kindī, *Kitāb al-Wulāt* 368–370; al-Dhahabī, *Siyar* 2463.

101 Ibn Maʿīn, *Tārīkh* 4:481; Ibn Saʿd, *Ṭabaqāt* 9:524; al-Bukhārī, *Tārīkh* 5:182–183; Ibn Abī Ḥātim, *al-Jarḥ wa-l-taʿdīl* 5:145–148; Ibn ʿAdī, *Kāmil* 4:1462–1472; al-Dhahabī, *Tadhkira* 237–239, *Siyar* 2462–2467, *Mīzān* 2:426–432; Ibn Ḥajar, *Tahdhīb* 2:411–414.

102 Ibn Qutayba, *al-Maʿārif* 624; Ibn ʿAdī, *Kāmil* 2:856. See also Zaman, *Religion and politics* 201; Ess, *Theologie und Gesellschaft* 2:717; Madelung, Sufyānī 36; Khoury, *ʿAbd Allāh ibn Lahīʿa* 46.

103 Al-ʿUmarī's introduction to Khalīfa's *Tārīkh* (1985) 18; Ibn al-Nadīm, *Fihrist* 1:290–291.

received from al-Madāʾinī. Abū Maʿshar was criticised by the early critics: al-Bukhārī, for example, states that his *ḥadīth* transmission is rejected (*munkar al-ḥadīth*), while Ibn Saʿd, Ibn Maʿīn, Abu Dāwūd and al-Nasāʾī declared him weak (*ḍaʿīf*).[104] Abū Maʿshar was mostly known for his knowledge of the Prophet's biography, but, as with many other *akhbārīyūn*, he was criticised for his transmission.[105] Khalīfa's citations of Abū Maʿshar confirm his tendency to cite such *akhbārīyūn* mainly for basic chronological information—in this case, regarding those who were killed at the Battle of al-Yamāma.

6 Analysis of Material

From the above survey of Khalīfa's sources, a few patterns are worth highlighting and discussing in more detail: (1) the prominence of Basran transmitters; (2) the reliance on *akhbārīyūn* for the basic chronology and on *muḥaddithūn* for particularly important events; (3) the limited citation of Kufans, Shīʿīs and certain popular *akhbār* authorities; (4) the prominence of Basran *ḥadīth* scholars and reputable transmitters; and (5) Khalīfa's possible access to official Umayyad/ʿAbbāsid material and written compilations.

6.1 *Basran Transmitters*

To illustrate the predominance of Basrans among Khalīfa's direct transmitters Tables 2 and 3 show, first, the locations of the 32 transmitters cited more than 5 times and, second, the locations of all direct transmitters in the *Tārīkh*. Some transmitters are known to have been active in different cities—such as al-Madāʾinī in both Basra and Baghdad—but each city's percentage is calculated here separately in relation to the total number of transmitters in order to give a more precise account of the geographical spread (the total percentage therefore exceeds 100).

Table 2 shows that 94 per cent (30 of 32) of the transmitters cited more than five times were for some or most of their lives based in Basra. These findings are confirmed by the second table of all direct transmitters, which shows that 70 per cent were Basrans (74 of 105). It must be added that most unknown transmitters (15 per cent) were probably active in Basra as well.

104 Ibn Saʿd, *Ṭabaqāt* 7:597; al-Bukhārī, *Ḍuʿafāʾ* 119, *Tārīkh* 8:114; al-Dhahabī, *Siyar* 4008–4009.

105 See Ibn Ḥanbal, *Mawsūʿa* 4:10–11; Ibn Abī Ḥātim, *al-Jarḥ wa-l-taʿdīl* 8:493–495; Ibn ʿAdī, *Kāmil* 7:2516–2519; al-Dhahabī, *Siyar* 4008–4009; Ibn Ḥajar, *Tahdhīb* 4:214–215.

TABLE 2 Locations of the 32 major direct transmitters

Location	Percentage
Basra	94% (30 of 32)
Baghdad	6% (2 of 32)
Kufa	6% (2 of 32)
Medina	3% (1 of 32)

TABLE 3 Locations of all direct transmitters

Location	Percentage
Basra	70% (74 of 105)
Unknown	15% (16 of 105)
Kufa	10% (11 of 105)
Baghdad	6% (6 of 105)
Medina	3% (3 of 105)
Wāsiṭ	2% (2 of 105)
Damascus	1% (1 of 105)
Raqqa	1% (1 of 105)

During Khalīfa's lifetime, historical reports were circulated widely between the cities by travelling scholars and the dissemination of written compilations. Khalīfa's *isnād*s show that his transmitters received their information from other cities—for example, a large number of *isnād*s for the earliest history are traced back to Medinan Companions and Successors (such as ʿĀʾisha, Saʿīd b. al-Musayyib and al-Zuhrī). However, in comparison to later and more widely travelled compilers, the pool of direct transmitters is very local; there are, for example, relatively few direct transmitters from the nearby city of Kufa, which by the second/eighth century had become a centre of historiographical activity.[106] In addition to the tables above, this can be seen in the list of major

106 Donner, *Narratives* 222.

indirect transmitters, cited more than ten times with one intermediary transmitter: 70 per cent (9 of 13) are Basrans.

Only two direct transmitters of more than five reports were non-Basrans (Ibn al-Kalbī and Abū Nuʿaym al-Faḍl b. Dukayn), and a similar pattern can be found among the less frequently cited transmitters. Since Khalīfa mainly drew upon these Basran transmitters, the *Tārīkh* can be expected to reflect their Basran perspective on the early history of Islam—largely corresponding to early Sunnī ideas, common among the *ḥadīth* scholars, and different from the early Shīʿī-inclined historical tradition associated with the nearby city of Kufa. This heavy reliance on Basran transmission is one of the most distinguishing features of Khalīfa's *Tārīkh*. The main reason is that Khalīfa spent most of his life in Basra and accordingly transmitted from the sources available to him. However, the Basran selection of sources also reflects Khalīfa's scholarly preferences: as a Basran who spent most of his life in his native city, Khalīfa knew the Basran transmitters and their capacities better than transmitters from other places. Moreover, as discussed further below, Basra was known for its *ḥadīth* scholars of early Sunnī orientation, whom Khalīfa accordingly preferred. The presence of non-Basran reports shows that Khalīfa was not averse in principle to transmitting from non-Basrans, but his use of such outside sources evidently was minimal.

6.2 *Different Subjects of the* Akhbār *and* Ḥadīth *Scholars*

The first list of Khalīfa's main direct transmitters (cited 20–110 times) and their material shows that Khalīfa relies heavily on *akhbār* authorities—usually not considered reliable *ḥadīth* transmitters—for basic chronological information and less controversial events, such as conquests and appointments or deaths of caliphs. This stands in contrast to the list of transmitters cited 5–19 times, which includes many prominent Basran *ḥadīth* scholars, cited for controversial or otherwise important information—in particular, details about the Prophet and intra-Muslim conflicts.

On the one hand, this pattern suggests some division of labour between *akhbārīyūn* and *muḥaddithūn*—the former more concerned with chronology and political history, and the latter with independent Prophetic/Companion/Successor reports mainly on subjects of law and belief (including the early intra-Muslim conflicts). On the other hand, Khalīfa's systematic reliance on *ḥadīth* authorities regarding controversial subjects such as the civil wars, which the popular *akhbārīyūn* are known to have transmitted, suggests that Khalīfa deliberately selected the *ḥadīth* scholars' material for such subjects. Since this point will be further examined in Chapter 5, which is devoted to Khalīfa's methods, it is enough here to note the pattern in Khalīfa's citation of *akhbārīyūn* for basic narrative information and of *ḥadīth* scholars for more important or controversial episodes.

6.3 *Exclusion of Sources: Kufans, Shīʿīs and Popular* Akhbārīyūn

Many transmitters in the *Tārīkh* are found in the works of later historians, but, unlike them, Khalīfa studied directly under these transmitters and frequented the same scholarly circles. More significant is Khalīfa's exclusion, or limited citation, of many popular but controversial transmitters found in other sources. Particularly striking is the low number of Kufans and transmitters with Shīʿī affiliations or tendencies. Khalīfa does not, for example, transmit any reports from Abū Mikhnaf (d. 157/774), the early Shīʿī *akhbārī* of Kufa who became a major source for many other third/ninth-century historians but who was completely rejected by *ḥadīth* scholars.[107] Moreover, many Kufans among Khalīfa's direct transmitters are described as reliable *ḥadīth* scholars in the works of transmitter criticism—except Hishām b. al-Kalbī, who was also known for his Shīʿī inclination.

It is also noteworthy that Sayf b. ʿUmar (d. c. 180/796) is only cited thrice (indirectly), for brief information regarding the Battle of Jalūlāʾ.[108] Sayf was another contested Kufan source, heavily criticised by the transmitter critics, but frequently cited by al-Ṭabarī and others.[109] He was not accused of Shīʿī tendencies, but rather maintained the legitimacy of the first caliphs and the probity of the Companions in his works—similarly to the *ahl al-ḥadīth*.[110] In that, some of Sayf's views may have resembled Khalīfa's, but his synthetic narrative style and embellished reports differ markedly from Khalīfa's *Tārīkh*.[111] The three citations in the *Tārīkh* show that Khalīfa knew about some of Sayf's material but limited the citation of him. Khalīfa possibly did not have access to more of Sayf's material, but the exclusion of his synthetic and elaborated accounts nevertheless illustrates Khalīfa's general preference for concise reports and reputable transmitters—at least regarding the early intra-Muslim conflicts.

According to many third/ninth-century transmitter critics, sectarian affiliations (i.e. non-Sunnī beliefs) did not necessarily preclude quality transmission,

---

107 Ibn Abī Ḥātim, *al-Jarḥ wa-l-taʿdīl* 7:182; Ibn ʿAdī, *Kāmil* 6:2110; al-Dhahabī, *Mīzān* 3:413; Ibn Ḥajar, *Lisān* 6:430–431.

108 Khalīfa b. Khayyāṭ, *Tārīkh* (1985) 137.

109 Al-Bukhārī, *Ḍuʿafāʾ* 187; Ibn Abī Ḥātim, *al-Jarḥ wa-l-taʿdīl* 4:278; Ibn ʿAdī, *Kāmil* 3:1271–1272; al-Dhahabī, *Mīzān* 2:236–237; Ibn Ḥajar, *Tahdhīb* 2:144. On Sayf b. ʿUmar in general, see Landau-Tasseron, Sayf ibn ʿUmar.

110 See Crone, Review of Samarrai's edition of Sayf b. ʿUmar.

111 See Chapter 8. On Sayf b. ʿUmar's views on the first *fitna*, see Anthony, *Caliph and the heretic* 9–138.

unless the transmitters propagated their own ideologies.[112] If, however, Khalīfa was constructing a narrative about the first two hundred years of Islam from an early Sunnī perspective, the absence of clearly Shīʿī narrators is no surprise.[113] In that, his selection corresponds to the ideal not to narrate from heretical transmitters who openly promoted sectarian beliefs, which would have been the case with explicit Shīʿī reports regarding intra-Companion conflicts. This absence of Shīʿī narrators and reports distinguishes Khalīfa's *Tārīkh* from many other early historical works. It is most apparent in Khalīfa's sections on controversial events such as the civil wars (*fitan*) and the killings of prominent ʿAlids, about which many *maqtal* works (pl. *maqātil*) circulated in the first centuries AH.[114] As discussed in more detail in the following chapters, the content of the *Tārīkh* represents an early Sunnī view on these events and excludes material with clear Shīʿī tendencies.

6.4 *Basran* Ḥadīth *Scholars and Reliable Transmitters*

The list of direct transmitters cited 5–19 times demonstrates Khalīfa's reliance upon Basran *ḥadīth* scholars. Moreover, his citation of them regarding important or controversial events shows that Khalīfa actively selected their material and, by extension, their historical perspectives on these defining moments for the early Muslim community. As discussed in Chapter 3, important ideas in early Sunnism, such as the collective authority of the Companions, were dominant among the third/ninth-century *ḥadīth* scholars, especially in Basra. The idea of local historiographical schools, originally proposed by Wellhausen, and its use as a source-critical tool for evaluating the historical reliability of accounts has been criticised. However, taking into account the local and scholarly contexts is nonetheless important for understanding the types and themes of history that developed in different scholarly circles during the first two centuries AH—located in different cities but not necessarily limited to them.[115] Khalīfa's nearly exclusive reliance on Basran *ḥadīth* scholars for particularly important or controversial events confirms his affiliation to the Basran *ḥadīth* circles and suggests that his *Tārīkh* was a critical collection of historical mate-

112 Ibn Ḥajar, *Nuzhat al-naẓar*, 211–214; al-Sakhāwī, *Fatḥ al-Mughīth* 2:220–235; Lucas, *Constructive critics* 320–325; Brown, *Hadith* 83–84.

113 Among the main direct transmitters, Hishām b. al-Kalbī is the only one well-known for Shīʿī views, although al-Faḍl b. Dukayn is said to have had some light tendencies of *tashayyuʿ* (*tashayyuʿ khafīf*). See al-Dhahabī, *Siyar* 3033.

114 On *maqātil* works, see Robinson, *Islamic historiography* 34; Günther, *Maqātil* literature.

115 Donner, *Narratives* 214–228; Wellhausen, Prolegomena 4–7, Arab kingdom vii–xv; Noth, Der Charakter der ersten großen Sammlungen; Noth and Conrad, *Early Arabic* 4–17. See also Dūrī's *Rise of historical writing*; Borrut, *Entre mémoire et pouvoir* 33–37.

rial prevalent in these circles. In this sense, Khalīfa's *Tārīkh* can be seen as a Basran history compiled in accordance with the historical views and concerns of the *ḥadīth* scholars, upon whose transmission he based his work. Such views and concerns were not limited to the *ḥadīth* scholars of Basra, but Khalīfa's general perspective and focus, as well as his selection of sources, give it a distinct Basran character. Thus, rather than local historiographical schools, it might be more useful to discuss the various types of historiography that developed in the first centuries AH in terms of different scholarly traditions and networks (located in urban centres but not necessarily limited to them), in addition to local concerns that shaped the specific expressions of these scholarly traditions.

It is also noteworthy that many of Khalīfa's main direct transmitters (cited more than five times) were, according to both contemporaneous and later transmitter critics, considered reliable (*thiqa*) or sincere (*ṣadūq*) as transmitters. Many such transmitters are also found among those cited less than five times. This fairly consistent citation of well-known *ḥadīth* scholars, especially regarding important or controversial events, is a distinguishing feature of Khalīfa's *Tārīkh*. Moreover, his exclusion of Shīʿī (often Kufan) sources and other popular but criticised transmitters indicates a concern for selecting reliable sources. A number of Khalīfa's informants were declared weak or not considered *ḥadīth* transmitters, but many of these were authorities in other genres or subjects—such as al-Madāʾinī and Abū l-Yaqẓān in *akhbār* history, Abū ʿUbayda in grammar and Hishām b. al-Kalbī in genealogy. Their authority in these fields and their concern for chronology and political-administrative information might explain why Khalīfa relied on them for much of his narrative.

6.5 *Umayyad/ʿAbbāsid Officials and Written Sources*

Besides Khalīfa's scholarly affiliations and selection of sources, the *isnād*s provide some clues about the source of the administrative material in the *Tārīkh*. A few of Khalīfa's main transmitters (and possibly some of the minor transmitters) had links to the Umayyad or ʿAbbāsid administration, either through their own appointments or through official appointees among their informants. The main ones are al-Walīd b. Hishām b. Qaḥdham, whose grandfather had been secretary of finance (*kātib al-kharāj*) under Yūsuf b. ʿUmar in Iraq; ʿAbdallāh b. al-Mughīra, whose father might have been involved in the Iraqi administration in the Umayyad period; and Bayhas b. Ḥabīb, who served as officer in the Umayyad army. Their material corresponds to their appointments: both al-Walīd b. Hishām and ʿAbdallāh b. al-Mughīra are cited regarding the administration of Iraq and the deaths of caliphs, while Bayhas b. Ḥabīb is cited regarding battles in the late Umayyad period. Moreover, in the list section concluding al-Walīd b. ʿAbd al-Malik's reign, Khalīfa explicitly states, "All of this was narrated to me by al-Walīd [b. Hishām] from his father from his grandfather and from ʿAbdallāh b. al-Mughīra from his father and from others."[116] It is possible that they were Khalīfa's sources for other lists and administrative material. In addition, there are a few examples of transmitters with ʿAbbāsid affiliations through appointments to judicial positions, Muḥammad b. ʿAbdallāh al-Anṣārī, Ibn ʿUlayya and Ibn Lahīʿa among the main ones. It is thus possible that some of the lists and administrative material in the *Tārīkh* derived from administrative sources and informants with access to such information.

For more general historical information, Khalīfa may also have consulted written compilations, as is suggested by some of the recurring statements introduced by "so-and-so said" without complete *isnāds*—for example, from Ibn Isḥāq, Ibn al-Kalbī and Abū ʿUbayda Maʿmar b. al-Muthannā. Some of Khalīfa's transmitters are credited with historical compilations that might have circulated in some form (lecture notes or books) at Khalīfa's time.[117] It is thus possible that he consulted written sources besides what he received by transmission and that he received written texts with authorisation (*ijāza*) from his direct transmitters. Moreover, the patterns in the relationship between subjects and informants show that some transmitters specialised in particular areas, which also helps to explain Khalīfa's reliance on certain transmitters regarding specific subjects—for example, on Ibn Isḥāq and al-Madāʾinī regarding *maghāzī-sīra* and on Abū ʿUbayda regarding the Khawārij.

7 Conclusion

The examination of Khalīfa's sources in the *Tārīkh* has highlighted a number of important points regarding Khalīfa's scholarly affiliations, his selection of sources and his methods of compilation. First, it has established Khalīfa's nearly exclusive reliance on Basran *ḥadīth* and *akhbār* transmitters in the *Tārīkh*, which shows the scholarly context in which it was compiled and originally circulated. Second, it has shown that Khalīfa transmitted directly from many well-known Basran *ḥadīth* scholars, in particular regarding important or controversial historical events. This confirms Khalīfa's affiliation with the Basran *ḥadīth* circles and the early Sunnī tradition upon which he based his *Tārīkh*. Third, the examination of major and minor sources has shown that Khalīfa

116 Khalīfa b. Khayyāṭ, *Tārīkh* (1985) 312.

117 On lecture notes and books in this period, see Schoeler, *Genesis of literature in Islam* 68–81.

relied on a rather limited number of *akhbārīyūn* for basic historical information in his work. These main transmitters were regarded as authorities not in *ḥadīth* but in other fields, such as post-Prophetic history or genealogy, and were seldom considered reliable narrators by the transmitter critics. At the same time, Khalīfa systematically cites prominent *ḥadīth* authorities for details of particular importance (e.g. information about the Prophet Muḥammad) or controversy (e.g. early intra-Muslim conflicts). These aspects of Khalīfa's selection of sources and material will be further explored in Chapter 5, which examines his methods.

CHAPTER 5

Khalīfa's Methods

1 Introduction

Despite modern historians' interest in early Islamic historical writing, there are relatively few detailed studies on specific works that deal with the methods of transmission and compilation among early *akhbār* historians.[1] It is, for example, known that the science of *ḥadīth* was crucial in shaping the development of *akhbār* history,[2] but questions remain as to how the early *akhbārīyūn* adopted and adapted the *ḥadīth* conventions. The present chapter seeks to provide some answers with respect to Khalīfa's *Tārīkh* as transmitted by Baqī b. Makhlad. Because of Khalīfa's preoccupation with both *ḥadīth* scholarship and *akhbār* history, his *Tārīkh* also lends itself to an examination of the interaction between these two fields. The chapter is divided into three sections, on different aspects of the work: (1) epistemology, (2) system of reference and (3) selection and evaluation of transmitters. Section 2 argues, in contrast to the view of the early *akhbār* narratives as mere political commentary and non-factual stories,[3] that the early Sunnī historical perspective in Khalīfa's *Tārīkh* was legitimised by, and dependent on, the claim that it overall represented historical realities. This claim was, in turn, based on the authoritative tradition of the *ḥadīth* scholars and transmission from *muhaddithūn* and *akhbārīyūn* within the past scholarly collective, which for Khalīfa was the primary source of reliable historical knowledge. Section 3 outlines Khalīfa's system of reference and highlights how he uses *isnād*s differently depending on the period (Prophetic, Rāshidūn, Umayyad or ʿAbbāsid) and on the historical importance of the event under discussion. Section 4 examines Khalīfa's evaluation of transmitters and shows that he narrates from different types of transmitters depending on the subject—for example, reliable *ḥadīth* transmitters regarding civil

1 Some examples are Mårtensson's introduction to al-Ṭabarī's life and works (mainly the *Tārīkh*), which deals with epistemology and methodology, and the extensive material on Ibn Isḥāq, which treats some aspects of *akhbār* transmission and compilation. See Mårtensson, *Tabari*; Guillaume, *Life of Muḥammad* xiii–xliii; Sellheim, Prophet, Chalif und Geschichte; al-Samuk, *Die historischen Überlieferungen*; Jarrar, *Prophetenbiographie*; Görke and Schoeler, *Die ältesten Berichte*; Schoeler, *Biography of Muḥammad*.

2 See e.g. Khalidi, *Arabic historical thought* 17–82; Donner, *Narratives* 255–260; Robinson, *Islamic historiography* 85–97.

3 El-Hibri, *Reinterpreting Islamic historiography* 216.

 | DOI:10.1163/9789004383173_007

wars and other controversial issues, and less reputable *akhbārīyūn* for basic outlines of events and chronology. It also examines Khalīfa's usage of transmission formulas (e.g. *ḥaddathanā*—'He narrated to us') and demonstrates the correspondence between certain formulas and the importance or controversy of the subject in question.

2 Epistemology of Historical Knowledge

The complex relationship between claims to historical truth and rhetorical strategies in early Islamic historiography has been discussed before.[4] However, there are few attempts to approach the issue from an angle of epistemology—in the sense of how the early historians themselves viewed the process of acquiring historical knowledge, the different types and uses of such knowledge and the value of their accounts in terms of accuracy and authenticity. This lack is, of course, related to the scarcity of material about the historians' own views on their works, but, in the case of Khalīfa, some conclusions may be drawn on the basis of the form and content of his *Tārīkh* as well as his background as both *ḥadīth* scholar and *akhbār* historian.

This section discusses a few aspects of Khalīfa's epistemology, which might differ from that of some modern historians: the claim to veracity on the basis of transmission and authoritative tradition, transmitted information as the primary source of historical knowledge, the acceptance of multiform transmission and the different criteria of authenticity depending on subject matter. In contrast to a view that sees early Islamic historiography as mere didactics and political commentary, it is contended that Khalīfa sought to compile a generally accurate history of the Muslim community, with the reservation that individual facts, statements or reports may well be questioned. Hence the early Sunnī understanding and the religio-political views expressed in Khalīfa's *Tārīkh* were legitimised by, and dependent on, this claim to convey a generally reliable historical account, which in turn was based on transmission from authorities within the past scholarly collective of *muḥaddithūn* and *akhbārīyūn*.

This argument may seem fairly straightforward, but some studies have confused the question of 'facts vs political commentary' and have made far too sweeping generalisations about the diverse tradition of *akhbār* history. Based on the rhetorical appearance of some early works, mainly al-Ṭabarī's *Tārīkh*, El-Hibri has argued that the early histories "were originally intended to be

4 Shoshan, *Poetics* 3–60; Hoyland, History, fiction and authorship. See also Leder, Literary use of the *khabar*; Beaumont, Hard-boiled.

read not for facts, but for their allusive power."[5] In his view, the purpose of these works was not the representation of historical realities but theological polemics, political commentary and parabolic narratives. Though this may be true for some works, or parts of some works, it is a generalisation that fails to recognise the differences in aims, contexts and audiences of the early historians. This view also disregards the claim to truth and to represent historical realities, which constitutes an intrinsic part of most historians' rhetoric.[6] Sayf b. 'Umar, for instance, who tried to resolve the intra-Companion conflicts with the story of the Saba'iyya, certainly presented his narrative *as if* it were true and presumably regarded it as representative of historical realities.[7] The severe criticism against some *akhbārīyūn* indicates that at least the scholarly audience (especially *ḥadīth* scholars) expected their works to uphold some standards of historical representation, although it was usually expressed in the language of *isnād* criticism.[8] Thus, to avoid confusion over the purposes behind the compilation and circulation of the early histories, in this case Khalīfa's *Tārīkh*, it is necessary to examine some of their underlying epistemological notions. It must be kept in mind, however, that the following discussion focuses on Khalīfa and his context rather than on the whole tradition of *akhbār* history, although some notions might be more widely applicable.

2.1 *The Authoritative Tradition of the* Ḥadīth *Scholars*

In some ways similar to historians of other pre-modern societies,[9] early Muslim historians judged historical accuracy according to criteria that might differ from those claimed by many modern ones. Besides conformity to empirical evidence and documents, it was also judged by its conformity to universal truths (e.g. revelation), its conformity to authoritative tradition (e.g. transmitted words of prior generations or consensus in certain communities), its conformity to similar cases (cf. the legal use of *qiyās* or analogy) and its conformity

5 El-Hibri, *Reinterpreting Islamic historiography* 216, see also 13–15, 21, 33, 35, 54, 57–58, 63, 75; *Parable and politics* 63, 92, 127, 237.

6 Shoshan, *Poetics* 6, 3–8.

7 On Sayf's corpus as 'theology as history', see Anthony, *Caliph and the heretic* 107–109.

8 Robinson, *Islamic historiography* 87–88. Ibn 'Adī, for example, states that al-Wāqidī's weakness as a transmitter is obvious and that the textual content (*mutūn*) of his *akhbār*, as with his *ḥadīths*, is regarded as neither reliable nor properly preserved (*ghayr maḥfūẓa*). Ibn 'Adī, *Kāmil* 6:2247. For other samples of criticism against historians in a later source, see al-Sakhāwī, *al-I'lān* 86–106. On the early *ḥadīth* scholars' content criticism 'concealed' in the language of *isnād* criticism, see Brown, How we know early ḥadīth critics.

9 See e.g. Given-Wilson, *Chronicles* 1–20; Cubitt, Introduction.

to plausibility.[10] In relation to Khalīfa's *Tārīkh*, conformity to authoritative tradition is particularly important, since the work seems to have been compiled as a critical and relatively concise history for his fellow *ḥadīth* and *akhbār* scholars. Regarding authority in early Islamic historiography, al-Azmeh has argued that "although veracity was put forward as the cause and guardian of authority, it appears in fact that authority is the main ground for the assertion of veracity."[11] Similarly, Robinson notes that the historians worked in an emerging culture of traditionalism, in which the most authoritative historical knowledge was preserved knowledge from the past scholarly collective.[12] By contrast, Mårtensson argues that the view of al-Azmeh and Robinson is a discursive construction "that opposes Islamic history to modern history: the former fabricating historical facts for the sake of authority and legitimacy, and the latter searching facts for the sake of disinterested knowledge."[13] She rightly points out that 'traditionalism' and reliance on authority, in this case, is simply a recognition that "the only way to know what happened in the past is through statements or other kinds of documentation pertaining to that particular time and event."[14] However, setting aside the comparison of pre-modern and modern historical scholarship, it is clear that many early Muslim scholars (including Khalīfa) preferred sources from their own scholarly community (e.g. early Sunnī *ḥadīth* scholars) and that their works derived legitimacy from reliance on, and transmission from, this authoritative tradition—in their understanding, the best-preserved and most reliable documentation of the past.

One must remember that assertion of veracity by means of authoritative tradition was not something that neither these scholars, nor their listeners or readers, would have regarded as opposed to critical scholarship or historical fact. Indeed, reliance on reputable authorities was seen as an indication of discernment and trustworthiness; choosing the right authorities, after sifting through the available ones and distinguishing the reliable from the weak, was a sign of critical scholarship. Early historians of traditionist persuasion, like Khalīfa, depended on what they considered authoritative tradition and authoritative transmitters for measuring the veracity of historical accounts. For Khalīfa, this meant, in particular, knowledge preserved and cultivated among *ḥadīth* scholars, which, as we shall see below, shaped his narrative along the lines of their scholarly concerns, views and conventions. This is to say not that Khalīfa wrote

10 See Ward, *History and chronicles* 13–14.
11 Al-Azmeh, *Arabic thought* 163, 161–166.
12 Robinson, *Islamic historiography* 83–102.
13 Mårtensson, Discourse 295.
14 Mårtensson, Discourse 294.

history for the sake of legitimising or strengthening the authority of his own scholarly community but that his claim to convey overall accurate historical information depended on their authority and their transmission.

2.2 *Transmission as the Primary Source of Historical Knowledge*

Khalīfa does not explicate any epistemological positions in the *Tārīkh* or the *Ṭabaqāt*, but presumably his views were similar to other *ḥadīth* scholars and *akhbār* historians of his time. Despite varying criteria and demands of authentication, both disciplines preferred transmission, textual evidence and primary sources to speculative reasoning. According to this notion, past events are known through transmitted information pertaining to those events—that is, through eyewitness accounts or other kinds of primary sources.[15] Al-Ṭabarī expresses these views in the introduction to his *Tārīkh*:

> For knowledge of the history of past men and of recent men cannot be attained by those who did not observe them and did not live in their times, but only through the information of informants (*ikhbār al-mukhbirīn*) and the transmission of transmitters (*naql al-nāqilīn*). Such knowledge cannot be brought out by reason or deduced by internal thought processes.[16]

Khalīfa, as a Basran *ḥadīth* and *akhbār* scholar, also favoured transmission-based knowledge. As noted above, Khalīfa worked in a culture where authoritative historical knowledge was transmitted and preserved knowledge from the past scholarly collective, in particular the *ḥadīth* scholars.[17] It means not that Khalīfa and scholars like him were opposed to framing the tradition in new ways, adapting transmitted knowledge to new circumstances or critically evaluating different accounts, but rather that they adhered to a position that preferred transmission from trusted authorities to reasoning as the principal source of historical knowledge.[18] It is thus clear that the early *ḥadīth* and *akhbār* scholars agreed on information transmitted by reliable narrators as the ideal sources, but what were their views on the veracity of their material and the material transmitted from less reliable, weak transmitters?

---

15 Mårtensson, Discourse 294.

16 Al-Ṭabarī, *Tārīkh* 1:6–7. Modified version of Rosenthal's translation in al-Ṭabarī, *History* 1:170.

17 See Robinson, *Islamic historiography* 83–102.

18 See Mårtensson, Discourse 294.

The early third/ninth-century *ḥadīth* scholars of Khalīfa's time divided reports into sound (*ṣaḥīḥ*) and weak (*ḍaʿīf*).[19] For a report to be considered sound it required a continuous, unbroken *isnād* in which all transmitters were known for their uprightness (*ʿadāla*) and accuracy (*ḍabṭ*), while also being free from irregularities (*shudhūdh*) in the textual content and hidden defects (*ʿilla*) in the *isnād*.[20] They would also acknowledge that there were different levels of soundness and that some sound reports were sounder (*aṣaḥḥ*) than others, depending on the variations in the aforementioned conditions.[21] In short, the early *ḥadīth* scholars regarded sound *āḥād ḥadīth*s (that is, *ḥadīth*s transmitted by one or a limited number of *isnād*s) as accurate and reliable historical representations of the Prophet's teachings, including his words and actions, but admitted the possibility of occasional mistakes or changes in the course of transmission—unless they could be corroborated by narrations from other transmitters or by other types of complementary evidence that would make them yield certain knowledge.[22] Therefore, as Brown notes, some of them admitted that "although a *ḥadīth* might be an entirely authentic representa-

19 Or sometimes, as with al-Tirmidhī (d. 279/892), into sound, fair (*ḥasan*) and weak. Al-Tirmidhī is known as the one who introduced the term *ḥasan* into technical usage, although there has been some discussion in modern scholarship whether or not he was really the first to use it in the sense of an intermediary term between *ṣaḥīḥ* and *ḍaʿīf*. See the summary and sources in Brown, Did the Prophet say it or not? 278n89.

20 Ibn al-Ṣalāḥ, *ʿUlūm al-ḥadīth* 11–12; Ibn Ḥajar, *Nuzhat al-naẓar* 111–116; al-Sakhāwī, *Fatḥ al-Mughīth* 1:23–25.

21 See e.g. al-Dhahabī, *al-Mūqiẓa*, 24–26, 32–33; Ibn Ḥajar, *Nuzhat al-naẓar* 117–121; Brown, Did the Prophet say it or not? 275–276.

22 The classical Sunnī legal theorists of the fourth/tenth century onwards differentiated between texts that are unquestionably established in their transmission (*qaṭʿī al-wurūd* or *qaṭʿī al-thubūt*)—such as the Qurʾān or mass-transmitted (*mutawātir*) *ḥadīth*s—and texts that are 'probabilistically' established in their transmission (*ẓannī al-wurūd* or *ẓannī al-thubūt*)—such as sound *āḥād ḥadīth*s. Many would also add that some sound *āḥād ḥadīth*s could be considered unquestionably established (*qaṭʿī*) if corroborated by circumstantial evidence, such as them being included in the *ṣaḥīḥ* collections of al-Bukhārī and Muslim. Within each of the two aforementioned categories, the legal theorists would then distinguish between texts that are unequivocal as evidence or 'certain in meaning' (*qaṭʿī al-dalāla*) and texts that are probabilistic as evidence (*ẓannī al-dalāla*). However, this epistemological terminology of *qaṭʿī* and *ẓannī* was adopted later and not used among the *ḥadīth* scholars of Khalīfa's time, although they were aware of the distinction between sound *ḥadīth*s yielding certain knowledge (by corroborative evidence) and sound *ḥadīth*s not yielding certain knowledge but nonetheless having enough preponderant strength to be used as evidence in matters of law and belief. See Ibn al-Ṣalāḥ, *ʿUlūm al-ḥadīth* 13–14, 28; Ibn Ḥajar, *Nuzhat al-naẓar*, 95–103; al-Sakhāwī, *Fatḥ al-Mughīth* 1:29–30, 92–95; ʿItr, *Manhaj al-naqd* 244–247, 291–294; Keller, *Reliance of the traveller* 20–22; Brown, Did the Prophet say it or not?; al-ʿAwnī, *al-Yaqīnī wa-l-ẓannī* 81–129.

tion of the Prophet's teachings, one could not swear that he actually said those words."[23] They also maintained that weak (*ḍaʿīf*) reports that did not fulfil the criteria for sound (*ṣaḥīḥ*) narrations could accurately reflect historical realities, especially if corroborated by alternative reports, although the transmission of the individual reports themselves was much less reliable than the sound ones.[24]

As a *ḥadīth* scholar, Khalīfa was well aware that his *Tārīkh* contained both sound reports, transmitted through reliable *isnād*s, and weak reports, transmitted through unreliable *isnād*s. His selection of sources shows that he included material from transmitters widely considered reliable (*thiqāt*, sing. *thiqa*) by the *ḥadīth* transmitter critics, as well as from transmitters known to be weak or unreliable (*ḍuʿafāʾ*, sing. *ḍaʿīf*).[25] Thus, compiled in a genre with considerably less stringent requirements of authenticity than core subjects such as *fiqh* and *ʿaqīda*, Khalīfa's *Tārīkh* was most likely an attempt, based on the available material, to accurately outline the chronology and political-administrative history of the Muslim community—with the reservation that the authenticity or correctness of individual facts, statements and reports may well be questioned, criticised or dismissed. However, the fact that Khalīfa understood that not everything in his *Tārīkh* was historically certain or accurate does not mean that he was not concerned with historical accuracy; it simply means that he upheld a realistic view on historical knowledge, influenced by the *ḥadīth* scholars of his time, and applied it in the less strict field of *akhbār* history. He knew that his work contained sound and reliable reports as well as weak and unreliable ones, but he considered the general historical outline accurate and left the individual reports or facts to be judged according to their *isnād*s and their correspondence to other material elsewhere.

---

23 Brown, Did the Prophet say it or not? 271–275, 285. E.g. Abū Bakr al-Athram (d. 273/886) narrates that his teacher, Aḥmad b. Ḥanbal, said, "If a *ḥadīth* comes from the Prophet (ṣ) via a *ṣaḥīḥ isnād* and contains a ruling or obligation, I act according to that, and I profess it by God Most High, but I do not testify that the Prophet (ṣ) said it." Abū Yaʿlā b. al-Farrāʾ, *al-ʿUdda* 3:898, cited in Brown, Did the Prophet say it or not? 273.

24 Those who eventually added an intermediary category of fair (*ḥasan*) reports regarded these as acceptable reports that did not reach the same level of soundness as the *ṣaḥīḥ* reports but that nonetheless could be used as scholarly evidence. See Ibn al-Ṣalāḥ, *ʿUlūm al-ḥadīth* 29–40; Ibn Ḥajar, *Nuzhat al-naẓar* 129–132; al-Sakhāwī, *Fatḥ al-Mughīth* 1:116–170; ʿItr, *Manhaj al-naqd* 263–268. ʿItr, following Ibn Ḥajar, defines *ḥasan* as "a *ḥadīth* with an unbroken *isnād* that is transmitted by an upright person (*ʿadl*) with slightly less accuracy (*khaffa ḍabṭuhu*) and that is free from irregularities and hidden defects (*ghayr shādhdh wa-lā muʿallal*)." *Manhaj al-naqd* 264.

25 See Chapter 4.

2.3 *Multiform Transmission and Differing Reports*

Because the works of *akhbār* history at the time of Khalīfa were produced in a context of combined oral and written transmission, historians were aware of the potential problems of transmission and were used to some degrees of fluidity. Multiform transmission was commonly accepted without necessarily impinging on perceptions of accuracy or reliability.[26] Long before that, the ancient Greek historian Thucydides (d. c. 395 BCE), who himself heard some of the speeches recorded in his history of the Peloponnesian War, admitted:

> It was in all cases difficult to carry them word for word in one's memory, so my habit has been to make the speakers say what was in my opinion demanded of them by the various occasions, of course adhering as closely as possible to the general sense of what they really said.[27]

Historians have long accepted such notions of a certainty of approximation and a creative recollection in spoken history.[28] Thucydides went much further than the early Muslim scholars would allow, but many second/eighth- and third/ninth-century *ḥadīth* scholars accepted the practice of transmitting the general meanings of *ḥadīth*s (*al-riwāya bi-l-maʿnā*) for scholars as long as they knew the intended meanings and the original wordings were not specified as parts of acts of worship or from among the Prophet's concise and comprehensive expressions (*jawāmiʿ al-kalim*).[29] Needless to say, this practice was also accepted in the transmission of post-Prophetic *akhbār* history. Thus, when speaking of Khalīfa's claim to convey generally accurate historical information in the *Tārīkh*, it is not to be understood as a claim to always provide literal records of statements, exact imitations of what happened or even correct information in all cases. Rather, it refers to his claim to accurately recount historical events and developments in general, although he was well aware that particular statements or facts might not be historically, let alone literally, accurate. Moreover, like many other *ḥadīth* scholars and *akhbār* historians, Khalīfa sometimes narrates different versions of statements and events, which show an acceptance of multiform transmission and an awareness of its dependence on human perception and memory.[30] One should also remember that the use

26 See also Dutton, Orality.

27 Thucydides, *Peloponnesian war* 14. Cited in Brown, Did the Prophet say it or not? 265.

28 Brown, Did the Prophet say it or not? 265. See also Fornara, *Nature of history* 145.

29 Ibn Ḥajar, *Nuzhat al-naẓar*, 205–206; ʿItr, *Manhaj al-naqd* 227–230; Brown, Did the Prophet say it or not? 274.

30 See the discussion about multiple versions of events below.

of the *isnād* system placed the responsibility on the *isnād*s and allowed *akhbār* historians like Khalīfa to narrate weaker reports, whose value was to be judged according to the strength of the *isnād*—sometimes to show different versions of events, sometimes to illustrate different opinions among the earlier generations, sometimes to add details and sometimes because no stronger reports were available.

A characteristic of early *akhbār* histories is that they often contain different reports for each event, which might repeat, supplement, overlap or sometimes even contradict one another.[31] This is important for understanding the early historians' views on historical knowledge. It corresponds to the early compilers' emphasis on transmitted knowledge and the acceptance of some approximation and 'creative' recollection in spoken history, which sometimes led to divergent accounts. Khalīfa applies a similar format in the *Tārīkh*, although he generally cites reports that supplement other reports rather than repeating or contradicting them. The exceptions are conflicting dates for major events—especially in the Prophetic and Rāshidūn periods, such as the Prophet's birth, his time in Mecca and Medina and his age when he died—which shows a particular concern for these details and for precision in chronology.[32] Also, some reports differ about events during the early intra-Muslim conflicts, and some statements differ regarding, for instance, who was appointed to what position, who conquered what land and how many individuals were killed in certain battles.[33] Thus Khalīfa generally presents a more or less single narrative, with relatively few differing or contradictory reports. The different reports about some events, however, suggest a concern for representing historical realities, rather than indifference or manipulation, and it certainly had the effect of signifying credibility. For example:

> In this year—which is year 2/623–624—the direction of the prayer (*al-qibla*) was changed. God says to His Prophet Muḥammad (ṣ), "We have seen you looking up into heaven, turning this way and that, so We will turn you towards a direction (*qibla*) which will please you. Turn your face, therefore, towards the Sacred Mosque (*al-masjid al-ḥarām*)." (Q 2:144)
>
> He said: Abū Dāwūd narrated to us; he said: al-Masʿūdī narrated to us from ʿAmr b. Murra from Ibn Abī Laylā from Muʿādh b. Jabal that the Messenger of God (ṣ) prayed towards Jerusalem for 16 months after his arrival

31 Humphreys, *Islamic history* 73.
32 Khalīfa b. Khayyāṭ, *Tārīkh* (1985) 52–54, 94–96.
33 E.g. Khalīfa b. Khayyāṭ, *Tārīkh* (1985) 98–99, 122–123, 127–128, 134, 151, 184–186. On the intra-Muslim conflicts, see Chapter 8.

> in Medina. Then God revealed, "We have seen you looking up into heaven, turning this way and that, so We will turn you towards a direction which will please you." (Q 2:144)
>
> Abū Dāwūd narrated to us; he said: Shuʿba narrated to us from Abū Isḥāq from al-Barāʾ b. ʿĀzib; he said: The Messenger of God (ṣ) prayed towards Jerusalem for 16 months after his arrival in Medina.
>
> Yazīd b. Zurayʿ narrated the same to us from Saʿīd from Qatāda.
>
> He said: I heard ʿAbd al-Wahhāb b. ʿAbd al-Majīd say: I heard Yaḥyā b. Saʿīd say: I heard Saʿīd b. al-Musayyib say: The Messenger of God (ṣ) prayed towards Jerusalem for 16 months. He changed the direction two months before the battle of Badr.
>
> Al-Ḍaḥḥāk b. Makhlad narrated to us; he said: ʿUthmān b. Saʿd al-Kātib narrated to us from Anas b. Mālik; he said: The Messenger of God (ṣ) changed the direction from Jerusalem after nine or ten months. During the noon prayer (*al-ẓuhr*) in Medina, he prayed two prayer-units (*rakʿatayn*) towards Jerusalem and then turned his face to the Kaʿba. The fools said, "What has made them turn away from the direction (*qibla*) they used to face?"
>
> Abū l-Walīd narrated to us from Zāʾida from Simāk from ʿIkrima from Ibn ʿAbbās: After 16 months.
>
> Bakr narrated to us from Ibn Isḥāq and Wahb from his father from Ibn Isḥāq; he said: The *qibla* was changed in Rajab, 17 months after his arrival.
>
> Ibn Abī ʿAdī narrated to us from Ashʿath from al-Ḥasan; he said: The Messenger of God (ṣ) prayed two years towards Jerusalem and was then ordered to change the *qibla*.[34]

In this case, Khalīfa takes the position that the *qibla* was changed after 16 months, which is what he narrates from most Companions and Successors. However, his inclusion of different reports shows an understanding of historical knowledge as dependent on perception, memory and transmission, which meant that some differences could occur in the reports when several narrators transmitted information about the same events.[35]

2.4 *Different Criteria of Authenticity Depending on Subject Matter*

Although the *ḥadīth* scholars criticised many *akhbār* historians' handling of the *isnāds*, they usually accepted their practice as long as it did not impinge on core

---

34 Khalīfa b. Khayyāṭ, *Tārīkh* (1985) 63–65.

35 See also Mårtensson, Discourse 297.

subjects such as legal rulings and credal beliefs.[36] The usage of weak (*ḍaʿīf*) *ḥadīth*s—that is, reports that did not meet all the conditions for being considered sound (*ṣaḥīḥ*)—in second/eighth- and third/ninth-century scholarship may illustrate these attitudes. For instance, the early Basran *ḥadīth* critic and teacher of Khalīfa, ʿAbd al-Raḥmān b. Mahdī (d. 198/814), is reported to have said:

> If reports are related to us from the Prophet (ṣ) concerning rulings and what is permitted and prohibited, we are severe with the *isnād*s and criticise the transmitters. If, however, reports are related concerning the virtues of actions, rewards, punishments, permissible things or invocations, we are lax with the *isnād*s.[37]

Thus many early *ḥadīth* scholars had different standards of strictness and verification depending on the subject matter—just as Khalīfa had different standards depending on the event and type of information in question.[38] In fact, Khalīfa's strictness when it comes to particularly important or controversial events—such as the early intra-Muslim conflicts, which related to theological debates—clearly shows a differentiation between those subjects that required more rigorous authentication and those which allowed for some leniency. None of the early Sunnī *ḥadīth* scholars allowed the use of *ḥadīth*s they acknowledged to be very weak or forgeries.[39] However, many made room for weak reports in certain fields (outside *fiqh* and *ʿaqīda*) by, for instance, placing the responsibility on the *isnād*s or euphemising them through ambiguous citation (e.g. *ruwiya ʿan*).[40] One must also remember that the primary reason for declaring a *ḥadīth* weak were flaws in its *isnād*; weak *ḥadīth*s could be accepted as historically representative if bolstered by other narrations or, in legal matters, the practice of the Muslim scholars.[41] For Khalīfa, in the field of history, a report with weak transmitters or a broken *isnād* would have meant not that it was necessarily historically inaccurate but that it was not securely transmitted and thus

---

36 See Brown, Even if it's not true it's true.

37 Al-Ḥākim al-Naysābūrī, *al-Mustadrak* 1:666. A similar statement is narrated from Aḥmad b. Ḥanbal in al-Khaṭīb al-Baghdādī, *al-Kifāya* 134. See Brown, Even if it's not true it's true 7. See also ʿItr, *Manhaj al-naqd* 291–296.

38 See sections 3 and 4 below.

39 Brown, Even if it's not true it's true 15. See also ʿItr, *Manhaj al-naqd* 291–296.

40 Brown, Did the Prophet say it or not? 285.

41 Brown, Did the Prophet say it or not? 277–279. For example, when asked about acting upon a certain *ḥadīth*, Aḥmad b. Ḥanbal is reported to have said, "We only declare its *isnād* weak, but it is acted on (*al-ʿamal ʿalayhi*)." Abū Yaʿlā b. al-Farrāʾ, *al-ʿUdda* 3:938.

unreliable—unless it could be supported by other, alternative reports. As noted above, the use of the *isnād* also placed the responsibility for inaccuracies on the transmitters or the cited *akhbārīyūn* and left the criticism of the content and the transmitters to the reader or listener.

The views expressed in the above citation of ʿAbd al-Raḥmān b. Mahdī were common in Khalīfa's time. As Brown notes, "Early Sunnis allowed ḥadīths whose authenticity they doubted into discourse on manners, preaching and history because they saw these subjects as falling outside the true purviews of religion: law and ritual."[42] This includes *akhbār* pertaining to *maghāzī-sīra* and, even more so, to political events in the Rāshidūn, Umayyad and ʿAbbāsid periods; these subjects were important and potentially controversial, especially the early intra-Muslim conflicts, but not on the same level as legal rulings and credal beliefs. Historians were thus able to set aside the strictest requirements for authentication while still employing the *isnād* system. As noted above, however, Khalīfa is particularly careful with the *isnād*s when it comes to details about the Prophet and important or controversial events in the historical tradition, such as the early intra-Muslim conflicts (which of course related to the *ʿaqīda* debates over the status of the Companions), while showing more leniency in the general chronological narrative. It is thus clear that one cannot reduce all early historical works, especially not the likes of Khalīfa's carefully compiled *Tārīkh*, to mere storytelling in the way of the *qiṣaṣ* tradition.

Many early *ḥadīth* scholars criticised the storytellers (*quṣṣāṣ*, sing. *qāṣṣ*) in the mosques because of their lack of properly authenticated material, especially their use of fabricated *ḥadīths*.[43] However, the exhortatory and dissuasive tales of these storytellers are altogether different from the form of history that Khalīfa compiled. The form, content and context of circulation show that his *Tārīkh* was not compiled as a collection of allusive tales, moral stories or court entertainment. Instead, Khalīfa's *Tārīkh* resembles in different ways the historical material compiled by other *ḥadīth* scholars such as Ibn Abī Shayba, al-Fasawī, Abū Zurʿa al-Dimashqī and others.[44] These works represent certain scholarly and religio-political stances, but such stances depended on their agreement with the authoritative tradition of the early Sunnī *ḥadīth* scholars and their attempt to provide more or less accurate representations of historical realities.

42 Brown, Even if it's not true it's true 50.

43 Brown, Did the Prophet say it or not? 284.

44 On the history sections in the *ḥadīth* collections of ʿAbd al-Razzāq and Ibn Abī Shayba, see Zaman, *Maghāzī* and the *muḥaddithūn*. On the other compilers, see Chapter 3.

It is also worth noting that Khalīfa does not explicitly argue against the historical views of the non-traditionists in Basra, such as the prominent rationalists, who may have held other views, although his *ḥadīth*-minded method of compilation, his sources and his early Sunnī historical understanding of controversial events can be seen as a general argument against those who would have taken other positions. Unlike, for example, the slightly later Basra-born Sunnī theologian Abū l-Ḥasan al-Ashʿarī (d. 324/935–936), who defended the Sunnī beliefs and countered the Muʿtazila by making use of their own rationalist methods, Khalīfa adheres strictly to the methods and material of his own scholarly circles, whereby he establishes his narrative of the early history of the Muslim community. This further suggests that his fellow *ḥadīth* scholars and *akhbār* historians were not only the main sources of his historical information but also the main audience of both his *Tārīkh* and *Ṭabaqāt*.

In conclusion, as a historian active in the *ḥadīth* circles of Basra, with an audience of like-minded scholars, Khalīfa compiled his *Tārīkh* as an attempt to outline the chronology and political-administrative history of the Muslim community as accurately as possible based on the information available to him—with the reservation that the accuracy of individual statements and facts (in particular reports with weak *isnād*s) may well be questioned, criticised and dismissed. Later transmissions and evaluations of Khalīfa's *Tārīkh* also show that its audience received it as an overall reliable compilation of historical information and as particularly useful for matters relating to chronology.[45] His *Tārīkh* was, in this sense, transmitted and circulated as a work of historical fact, not merely a political commentary, although his narrative sometimes had this function as well.[46]

3 System of Reference

The material in Khalīfa's *Tārīkh* can be divided into two broad categories: (1) referenced material, with *isnād*s of varying length and completeness, and (2) unreferenced material. The former consists of reports traced back with *isnād*s to primary sources or secondary authorities. The second consists of unreferenced summaries or statements of varying length, and list entries. Examining Khalīfa's use of the *isnād* in different parts of the *Tārīkh*, and his use of it in relation to different subjects, reveals that his approach differs depending on

45 See Chapter 2.
46 See Chapter 8.

the period (Prophetic, Rāshidūn, Umayyad or 'Abbāsid) and on the historical importance of the event under discussion. For example, Khalīfa is more concerned with *isnāds* for the Prophetic and Rāshidūn periods than for the Umayyad and 'Abbāsid periods, but he increases the amount of referenced reports in the later periods for controversial events such as revolts and civil wars. The *isnāds* therefore indicate the importance Khalīfa attached to certain periods in general and certain events in particular.

3.1 *Material with* Isnāds

The *isnād*-equipped material in Khalīfa's *Tārīkh* divides into (1) reports traced back to eyewitnesses or contemporaries of events and (2) reports traced back to secondary authorities. A substantial amount of material in the *Tārīkh* is traced back to contemporaries—for example, to Companions for reports about the Prophetic and Rāshidūn periods, and to Successors for the Umayyad period. But not all *isnāds* go back to such primary authorities; Khalīfa often traces material only to secondary authorities, whether direct transmitters (such as al-Madā'inī and Abū l-Yaqẓān) or earlier authorities cited through intermediary transmitters (such as Ibn Isḥāq). However, the division between these types of sources is complicated by the occasional ambiguity as to whether certain narrators are cited as contemporaries of events or as secondary authorities. The *isnād*-equipped material in Khalīfa's *Tārīkh* is therefore treated here as one single category and examined in relation to the Prophetic, Rāshidūn, Umayyad and 'Abbāsid periods.[47]

3.1.1 Prophetic Period

Most material in the Prophetic period consists of *isnād*-equipped reports, apart from some short notes that certain events occurred ('In this year this-and-that happened').[48] Approximately a third of the reports are traced back to Companions, though they might not have been eyewitnesses to all events. Most of these Companion-reports are short and pertain to non-military history, such as the Prophet's birth and death, his arrival in Medina, his marriages and the change of the *qibla*.[49] The remaining reports are cited on the authority of either Successors, such as 'Urwa b. al-Zubayr and al-Zuhrī, or later scholars, such as Ibn Isḥāq and al-Madā'inī, without indication of the sources of their information. In the Prophetic period and in the rest of the *Tārīkh*, Khalīfa also combines

47 These periods are not named by Khalīfa in the *Tārīkh*, but they are nonetheless formally and thematically discernible. See Chapter 6.

48 E.g. Khalīfa b. Khayyāṭ, *Tārīkh* (1985) 56, 65–66, 76, 79, 86.

49 Khalīfa b. Khayyāṭ, *Tārīkh* (1985) 52–55, 64–65, 80, 86, 94–95.

information about one topic from two or more sources and cites the different *isnāds* joined by "and" (*wa*)—for example, "Bakr narrated to us from Ibn Isḥāq and Wahb from his father from Ibn Isḥāq from al-Zuhrī, Yazīd b. Rūmān and others that the Messenger of God (ṣ) …"[50]

3.1.2 Rāshidūn Period

The referenced material in the section for the Rāshidūn period (11–40/632–661) resembles the section for the Prophet's lifetime, in that most of it consists of *isnād*-equipped reports, although Khalīfa's own summaries and necrologies become a bit more frequent.[51] About three-fifths of the referenced material are cited from Companions and Successors. Such reports are especially prominent in sections on controversial events such as the killing of ʿUthmān and the civil wars during ʿAlī's caliphate. Some of the younger Successors, however, were not eyewitnesses or even contemporaries to these events (e.g. Qatāda b. Diʿāma and al-Zuhrī). The remaining material with *isnāds* is attributed to later authorities, from whom Khalīfa transmitted directly (such as al-Madāʾinī) or through an intermediary transmitter (such as Ibn Isḥāq).

3.1.3 Umayyad Period

In the section for the Umayyad period (41–132/661–750), Khalīfa continues to include material from possible contemporaries of events—Successors and Successors of the Successors (*atbāʿ al-tābiʿīn*). Most of these reports pertain to caliphal successions and revolts, but some also pertain to military expeditions, the administration of Iraq and the births and deaths of Umayyad caliphs.[52] In comparison to the Rāshidūn section, which consists mostly of *isnād*-equipped reports, the proportion of referenced material decreases substantially in favour of Khalīfa's own summaries, which outnumber the *isnād*-equipped material. About a third of the total number of reports and statements in the Umayyad period are referenced with *isnāds*, and the rest are Khalīfa's own short summaries. This shows Khalīfa's slightly different approach to the Prophetic and Rāshidūn periods and the Umayyad and ʿAbbāsid periods—the former requiring more rigour and referenced reports than the latter.

50 Khalīfa b. Khayyāṭ, *Tārīkh* (1985) 67.

51 Khalīfa b. Khayyāṭ, *Tārīkh* (1985) 116, 122–123, 129, 135, 141, 149, 152, 158–159, 163, 166, 168.

52 Khalīfa b. Khayyāṭ, *Tārīkh* (1985) 213–218, 232–239, 273, 280–286, 292, 308–309, 317, 321–322, 327–328, 331, 335, 342, 363–365, 368, 372–404, 408.

3.1.4 ʿAbbāsid Period

In the section for the ʿAbbāsid period (132–232/750–847), Khalīfa summarises most of the history in his own words, apart from some 20 reports narrated on the authority of others, often contemporaries of events. There is a correspondence between referenced reports and major events in the ʿAbbāsid period, but it is less apparent than the earlier periods since many major events also lack referenced reports.[53] Instead, Khalīfa summarises most events himself, usually introduced by "In this year," especially those within his own lifetime (from c. 160/776).

3.2 *Material without* Isnāds

The material without *isnād*s is found in (1) the list sections and (2) in Khalīfa's own summaries in the year sections. List sections are found throughout the work, but they vary in length depending on the length of the caliph's reign and the number of administrative posts. The proportion of Khalīfa's summaries in each year increases as the chronology proceeds, especially from the caliphate of Muʿāwiya. These two types of unreferenced material in the *Tārīkh* are outlined separately below, followed by a brief discussion about the reasons for the absence of *isnād*s for this material.

3.2.1 Lists

The list sections conclude the reigns of each caliph and a few prominent governors of Iraq and the East.[54] They contain information about administrative appointees during each caliph's (or governor's) reign, including posts such as provincial governors, pilgrimage leaders, judges, scribes, guards, chamberlains, treasurers, secretaries of the seal, tax administrators and commanders of security forces (*shuraṭ*).[55] Besides these lists at the end of reigns, the year sections also contain shorter lists of prominent people who died in each year, and occasionally lists of deaths in major battles. The lists of governors and judges are the longest and are followed by shorter lists of other administrative posts. The list

53 The subjects of the referenced reports are the succession of Abū l-ʿAbbās al-Saffāḥ, the births and deaths of the ʿAbbāsid caliphs, the death of Abū Muslim, a naval attack against Basra by al-Maydh and the revolts of Ibrāhīm b. ʿAbdallāh (the brother of Muḥammad al-Nafs al-Zakiyya), ʿAbd al-Salām al-Yashkurī and Jurāsha b. Shaybān. Khalīfa b. Khayyāṭ, *Tārīkh* (1985) 409–410, 412, 416–417, 422, 426, 429, 439, 443, 446, 454, 460, 465. Al-Dhahabī describes al-Maydh as Indians (*hunūd*) in his *Tārīkh al-Islām* 9:10.

54 See the sections for Ziyād b. Abīhi, al-Ḥajjāj, Yazīd b. al-Muhallab, Ibn Hubayra, Khālid al-Qasrī, Yūsuf b. ʿUmar, ʿAbdallāh b. ʿUmar b. ʿAbd al-ʿAzīz and Yazīd b. ʿUmar b. Hubayra. Khalīfa b. Khayyāṭ, *Tārīkh* (1985) 211–212, 308–312, 317, 335, 350–351, 368, 382–383.

55 For a more detailed discussion about the content of these lists, see Chapter 6.

sections consist mainly of unreferenced list-like summaries of appointed and dismissed governors, judges and other officials. Referenced material is unusual in the caliphal list sections,[56] but some material with *isnāds* appears in the sections for appointees under prominent governors of Iraq such as Ziyād b. Abīhi, al-Ḥajjāj b. Yūsuf and Yazīd b. al-Muhallab.[57]

The other type of list enumerates participants in major events, mostly people killed in battles. Similar lists are found in other early *akhbār* works.[58] The main examples of such lists in the *Tārīkh* are the lists of martyrs in the military expeditions of the Prophet, those whose hearts were reconciled after the conquest of Mecca (*al-muʾallafat qulūbuhum*), the martyrs in the Battle of al-Yamāma, those killed in the Battle of the Camel, those killed in the Battle of al-Ḥarra, the participants in Ibn al-Ashʿath's revolt and those killed in the Battle of Qudayd.[59] There are also shorter lists of prominent people who died in certain years or during certain reigns, but these lists comprise usually only about five to ten names.[60]

3.2.2 Unreferenced Summaries and Statements

The second type of unreferenced material are Khalīfa's own summaries and statements of various lengths. Some examples of these are:

> [1.] In it [10/632]: The Messenger of God (ṣ) made the Farewell Pilgrimage.
>
> [2.] In it [25/646]: The people of Alexandria revolted and ʿAmr b. al-ʿĀṣ attacked them as the governor of Egypt. He killed and took captives. Then ʿUthmān returned the captives to their *dhimmī*-status.
>
> [3.] In it [60/680]: al-Ḥusayn b. ʿAlī b. Abī Ṭālib sent his cousin, Muslim b. ʿAqīl b. Abī Ṭālib, to the people of Kufa to make them pledge allegiance to him and many people did so. Yazīd b. Muʿāwiya united the governance of

56 For some exceptions, see Khalīfa b. Khayyāṭ, *Tārīkh* (1985) 123, 154, 180, 324, 465. Another exception is the list of al-Walīd b. ʿAbd al-Malik's appointees, which Khalīfa concludes by stating, "All of this was narrated to me by al-Walīd from his father from his grandfather and from ʿAbdallāh b. al-Mughīra from his father and from others." *Tārīkh* (1985) 312.

57 Khalīfa b. Khayyāṭ, *Tārīkh* (1985) 211–212, 308, 310–312, 317, 335, 350, 368, 382.

58 See e.g. Ibn Isḥāq's *Sīra* as transmitted in Ibn Hishām, *Sīra* 2:90–92, 99–108, 305–306, 321–357, 3:86–92, 202–203, 291–292.

59 Khalīfa b. Khayyāṭ, *Tārīkh* (1985) 59–61, 68–73, 83–84, 90–92, 111–115, 187–190, 240–250, 286–287, 392–393.

60 E.g. *Tārīkh* (1985) 129, 149–150, 166–168, 226, 264–266, 279, 291–292, 300, 336, 348–350, 417–420.

> Iraq under ʿUbaydallāh b. Ziyād. The people of Iraq revolted.[61] Muslim b. ʿAqīl and Hanīʾ b. ʿUrwa al-Murādī were killed.
>
> [4.] In it [201/817]: al-Maʾmūn took the oath of allegiance for ʿAlī b. Mūsā b. Jaʿfar to the caliphate after him and removed al-Qāsim b. Hārūn, the son of the Commander of the Believers, from the succession. He also gave orders about the black [ceremonial clothing], which was taken off and green began to be worn.[62]

This type of material appears both as introductions to year sections (1 and 4 above) or as parts of longer sequences of reports (2 and 3). In the Prophetic and early Rāshidūn periods, until the end of ʿUmar's reign (13–23/634–644), Khalīfa's entries are often short introductions to subsequent reports. For example:

> In it [year 14/635]: Damascus was conquered. Abū ʿUbayda b. al-Jarrāḥ set out accompanied by Khālid b. al-Walīd. He besieged them and they made a treaty with him and then opened the Jābiya Gate for him. Khālid opened another gate by force (*ʿanwatan*) and Abū ʿUbayda included them in the treaty (*al-ṣulḥ*). Al-Walīd b. Hishām narrated to me ...[63]

Summaries are common throughout the *Tārīkh*, but they become a bit more prominent from the caliphate of ʿUthmān and even more so from the caliphate of Muʿāwiya, when the proportion of reports decreases in favour of Khalīfa's own entries. An example of Khalīfa's summary year entries is year 43/663–664, Muʿāwiya's third year as caliph:

> In it: ʿAbd al-Raḥmān b. Samura conquered al-Rukhkhaj and Zābulistān in the region of Sijistān.
>
> In it: ʿUqba b. Nāfiʿ al-Fihrī raided and conquered districts in the region of al-Sūdān. He also conquered Waddān in the territory of Barqa. All of these places are in Ifrīqiya.
>
> In it: Busr b. Arṭā conducted a winter expedition in the Roman lands.
>
> In it: Muʿāwiya appointed ʿAbdallāh b. Sawwār al-ʿAbdī over Mukrān.

---

61 The same report is transmitted by Ibn ʿAsākir via al-Tustarī in *Tārīkh madīnat Dimashq* 73:168–169, but there it reads, "He went to Kufa (*fa-kharaja ilā l-Kūfa*)," instead of, "The people of Iraq revolted (*fa-kharaja ahl al-ʿIrāq*)." Al-ʿUmarī corrects the manuscript wording and suggests, "He went with the people of Iraq (*fa-kharaja bi-ahl al-ʿIrāq*)."

62 Khalīfa b. Khayyāṭ, *Tārīkh* (1985) 94, 158, 231, 470.

63 Khalīfa b. Khayyāṭ, *Tārīkh* (1985) 125–126.

> In it: ʿAmr b. al-ʿĀṣ died in Egypt on the Day of Breaking the Fast (*yawm al-fiṭr*). It is also said that he died in year 42/662–663. Muḥammad b. Maslama al-Anṣārī and ʿAbdallāh b. Salām also died. Marwān b. al-Ḥakam led the pilgrimage.[64]

The exceptions to this are years of major events, when the number of *isnād*-equipped reports increases—for example, 51/671 (when Muʿāwiya appointed his son Yazīd as successor), which contains seven lengthy and detailed reports with *isnāds*.[65] A similar pattern of an increased proportion of referenced reports in years of major events is found throughout the Prophetic, Rāshidūn and Umayyad periods, but it is less apparent in the ʿAbbāsid period, where *isnād*-reports are overall rare.

3.2.3 Reasons for the Absence of *Isnāds*

A few factors might explain why some, and not other, material is cited without *isnāds*. First, some of Khalīfa's unreferenced material are introductions to more detailed sequences of *isnād*-equipped reports, so would not require *isnāds* in themselves. For example: "In it [year 12/633–634]: Abū Bakr sent Khālid b. al-Walīd to the land of Basra, which used to be called the land of India (*arḍ al-Hind*). ʿAwn b. Kahmas b. al-Ḥasan narrated to us [about the conquest of Iraq] …"[66]

Second, some of the non-*isnād* material was probably considered common knowledge, so acceptable without *isnāds*, among the scholars. This is especially pertinent to Khalīfa's own short summaries and introductions to subjects, which generally do not contain much detail, dialogues or other information that would have required *isnāds* (ideally traced back to eyewitnesses or contemporaries).[67]

Third, it is possible that no other summaries corresponding to the form and scope of Khalīfa's *Tārīkh* were available. Similar summary entries for Umayyad and ʿAbbāsid history are transmitted from earlier historians—among them al-Wāqidī and Hishām b. al-Kalbī—but Khalīfa's summaries are often briefer and systematically structured according to the formula of 'In this year, this-and-that occurred.'[68] Although Khalīfa must have based his summaries on earlier

64 Khalīfa b. Khayyāṭ, *Tārīkh* (1985) 205–206. See Wurtzel, *Khalifa ibn Khayyat's History* 55–56.

65 Khalīfa b. Khayyāṭ, *Tārīkh* (1985) 213–218.

66 Khalīfa b. Khayyāṭ, *Tārīkh* (1985) 117.

67 See Beaumont, Hard-boiled 10, 18, 23; Görke, Relationship between *maghāzī* and *ḥadīth* 175.

68 For al-Wāqidī, see al-Ṭabarī, *Tārīkh* 2:180, 223, 399, 472, 783, 818, 1039–1040, 1063, 1085, 1127,

material, he might have found it necessary to rework it in order to fit the format of the *Tārīkh* and therefore did not attribute it to others. Moreover, similar unreferenced material is attributed to other early historians, which suggests that *isnād*s were less common for such general summaries of political history than for more detailed reports.[69]

Fourth, administrative material and dates of births and deaths might have been considered less susceptible to forgery and alteration than political history or at least less controversial in the historical tradition than, for example, the early intra-Muslim conflicts.[70] This is also indicated by Khalīfa's greater concern for *isnād*s in his *Tārīkh* than in his *Ṭabaqāt*, where he lists his main sources in the introduction but thereafter rarely provides *isnād*s.[71] Moreover, transmission of biographical material without *isnād*s was an accepted practice among the *ḥadīth* scholars at the time, as is evident from the *ṭabaqāt* collections of Khalīfa, Ibn Saʿd and Muslim b. al-Ḥajjāj.[72]

Fifth, some administrative material may have been taken from administrative records or other types of documentation. Some *isnād*s contain appointees within the Umayyad administration, who might have provided such information.[73] It is thus possible, but difficult to prove, that Khalīfa had access to 'official' information through these or other administrative sources, which he considered acceptable to transmit without *isnād*s. Altogether, Khalīfa's use of references in the *Tārīkh* reveals a systematic approach to what material does or does not require *isnād*s—depending on the period and on the level of detail and importance or controversy of the event under discussion.

4 Selection and Evaluation of Transmitters

There is only one explicit evaluation of a transmitter in the *Tārīkh*, transmitted by both Baqī and al-Tustarī, but Khalīfa's concern for it is indicated by

---

1182, 1185, 1197, 1254–1255, 1740, 1942. For Ibn al-Kalbī, see al-Ṭabarī, *Tārīkh* 2:1740, 1875; 3:88, 451, 526, 579, 739.

69 In addition to al-Wāqidī and Ibn al-Kalbī above, see Ibn Isḥāq's material in Ibn Hishām's *Sīra*, e.g. 2:19, 67, 71, 86, 99, 117, 215, 233–234, 240–243, 249. Such unreferenced material is also provided by al-Ṭabarī himself throughout his *Tārīkh*, e.g. 2:1063, 1085, 1127, 1182, 1234–1235, 1255, 1269, 1305, 1314, 1336, 1346–1347, 1359, 1394, 1436, 1461, 1487, 1506, 1526, 1530, 1562, 1635, 1666–1667, 1698.

70 See al-ʿUmarī's introduction to Khalīfa's *Tārīkh* (1985) 15–16; ʿĀṣī, *Khalīfa* 66–67.

71 Khalīfa b. Khayyāṭ, *Ṭabaqāt* (1993) 25.

72 See the editor's introduction to Muslim, *Ṭabaqāt* 33–55.

73 See Chapter 4.

three characteristics of his work.[74] First, many of Khalīfa's direct transmitters were considered reliable (*thiqa*) among the early *ḥadīth* transmitter critics. Second, the relationship between selection of sources and subject matter shows that the level of concern for reputable transmitters corresponds to the degree of importance, controversy or complexity of the subject under discussion. Third, the patterns in Khalīfa's use of transmission formulas (e.g. *ḥaddathanā, akhbaranī, ruwiya ʿan*) show different levels of strictness and detail, depending on the subject matter under discussion.

4.1 *Selection of Reliable Transmitters*

As shown in Chapter 4, many of Khalīfa's main direct transmitters were considered reliable (*thiqa*) or sincere (*ṣadūq*) by the early transmitter critics. For example, 18 of 23 transmitters cited 5–19 times in the *Tārīkh* were well-known *ḥadīth* transmitters, whom Khalīfa cites mostly for controversial episodes or important details in the Prophetic, Rāshidūn and Umayyad periods. Khalīfa's reliance on these transmitters for such information—instead of popular but criticised *akhbāriyūn* such as Abū Mikhnaf, Sayf b. ʿUmar and al-Wāqidī—suggests that he selected transmitters on the basis of their scholarly reputations and qualities. The selection also reflects Khalīfa's own scholarly preferences: most transmitters are Basran narrators (whose abilities he knew well), and many are associated with *ḥadīth* scholarship. Their material in the *Tārīkh* also agrees with Khalīfa's own early Sunnī perspective on the early history of Islam. Such early Sunnī views were generally more common in Basra than in the nearby city of Kufa, where various forms of early Shīʿism were popular.[75] Thus, besides Khalīfa's access to these Basran *ḥadīth* scholars and his knowledge about them, he might also have preferred them because their material fitted his own historical understanding.

4.2 Isnād*s and Controversial Subject Matters*

The second indication of an underlying transmitter criticism in the *Tārīkh* is the correspondence between the citation of transmitters considered reliable in the early *ḥadīth* circles and the importance or controversy of the subject matter

74 In Baqī's recension: "ʿImrān b. Abī ʿĀtika, the *mawlā* of ʿUmar b. al-Khaṭṭāb, [died in 155/771–772]; he was reliable in *ḥadīth* (*kāna thiqa fī l-ḥadīth*)." Ibn ʿAsākir transmits via Mūsā al-Tustarī that Khalīfa said: "In 155/771–772 ʿUthmān b. Abī l-ʿĀtika, the *mawlā* of ʿUmar b. al-Khaṭṭāb, died and he was reliable in *ḥadīth* (*wa-kāna thiqat al-ḥadīth*)." Khalīfa b. Khayyāṭ, *Tārīkh* (1985) 427; Ibn ʿAsākir, *Tārīkh madīnat Dimashq* 38:397; al-Mizzī, *Tahdhīb* 19:400.

75 See Ibn Taymiyya, *Minhāj al-sunna* 8:224–225.

TABLE 4 Direct transmitters in the first eleven years of ʿUthmān's caliphate

Name	Grade in Ibn Saʿd's *Ṭabaqāt*
1. Yaḥyā b. Saʿīd al-Qaṭṭān	*thiqa-maʾmūn-rafīʿ-ḥujja* ('reliable-secure-elevated-authority')
2. Azhar b. Saʿd	*thiqa* ('reliable')
3. Ḥātim b. Muslim	*thiqa in shāʾ Allāh* ('reliable, if God wills')
4. Abū Khālid Yūsuf b. Khālid	*ḍaʿīf* ('weak')
5. Ibn al-Kalbī	– (not graded)
6. Muḥammad b. Saʿīd al-Bāhilī	–
7. ʿUthmān al-Qurashī	–
8. Abū l-Yaqẓān	–
9. Al-Walīd b. Hishām	–
10. Muḥammad b. Saʿd	–
11. Muḥammad b. Muʿāwiya	–
12. Al-Aṣmaʿī	–
13. Abū ʿUbayda Maʿmar b. al-Muthannā	–
14. Al-Madāʾinī	–
15. Abū ʿAmr al-Shaybānī	–
16. Unknown (from Ibn Lahīʿa)	–

in question. This can be illustrated by Khalīfa's account of ʿUthmān's caliphate (23–35/644–656) in the *Tārīkh*. Besides Khalīfa's own summary entries, the sections for ʿUthmān's first 11 years as caliph (24–34/644–655) are based on reports from 16 direct transmitters, and most *isnād*s are incomplete (only containing one or two names). By contrast, the final year of ʿUthmān's reign (35/655–656) contains reports from 24 transmitters, many of them prominent *ḥadīth* authorities, with more or less complete *isnād*s. Table 4 shows the transmitters for ʿUthmān's first eleven years as caliph; Table 5, the transmitters for his last year.

Table 5 shows that many of Khalīfa's transmitters on ʿUthmān's last year as caliph were reputable *ḥadīth* scholars.[76] This stands in contrast to the narrators on the earlier years of ʿUthmān's reign: only three are described as reliable by Ibn Saʿd, and most others are authorities in disciplines other than *ḥadīth*—for example, Abū l-Yaqẓān and Ibn al-Kalbī in history/genealogy, and Abū ʿUbayda,

76 On the reputations of some of Ibn Saʿd's ungraded transmitters, see Chapter 4.

TABLE 5 Direct transmitters in the last year of ʿUthmān's caliphate

	Name	Grade in Ibn Saʿd's *Ṭabaqāt*
1.	Ibn ʿUlayya	*thiqa-thabt-ḥujja* ('reliable-firm-authority')
2.	Muʿtamir b. Sulaymān	*thiqa* ('reliable')
3.	Yazīd b. Hārūn	*thiqa*
4.	Khālid b. al-Ḥārith	*thiqa*
5.	Abū ʿĀṣim al-Ḍaḥḥāk b. Makhlad	*thiqa*
6.	ʿAbd al-Raḥmān b. Mahdī	*thiqa*
7.	Rawḥ b. ʿUbāda	*thiqa in shāʾ Allāh* ('reliable, if God wills')
8.	Ghundar	*thiqa in shāʾ Allāh*
9.	Abū Dāwūd al-Ṭayālisī	*thiqa wa-rubbamā ghaliṭa* ('reliable, but sometimes made mistakes')
10.	ʿAbd al-Wahhāb b. ʿAbd al-Majīd	*thiqa wa-fīhi ḍaʿf* ('reliable with some weakness')
11.	ʿAbd al-Aʿlā b. ʿAbd al-Aʿlā	*lam yakun bi-l-qawī* ('not strong')
12.	ʿAbd al-Aʿlā b. al-Haytham	– (not graded)
13.	Abū Bakr al-Kalbī	–
14.	Abū Qutayba Salm b. Qutayba	–
15.	Abū l-Yaqẓān	–
16.	Kahmas b. al-Minhāl	–
17.	Al-Madāʾinī	–
18.	Muʿādh b. Hishām	–
19.	Muḥammad b. ʿAmr	–
20.	ʿUbaydallāh b. ʿAbdallāh b. ʿAwn	–
21.	ʿUmar b. Abī Khalīfa	–
22.	Yaḥyā b. Abī l-Ḥajjāj	–
23.	Yaḥyā b. Muḥammad	–
24.	Unknown (from al-Aʿmash)	–

al-Aṣmaʿī and Abū ʿAmr al-Shaybānī in grammar. Other examples of such major events with a wider and more critical selection of transmitters are the Battle of the Camel, the Battle of Ṣiffīn, the Battle of al-Ḥarra and Ibn al-Ashʿath's revolt.[77] The great number of reports from Basran *ḥadīth* authorities for such

77 Khalīfa b. Khayyāṭ, *Tārīkh* (1985) 180–196, 236–250, 280–288.

topics might also indicate the concern for these controversial events among the *ḥadīth* scholars in Khalīfa's context.

4.3 *Transmission Formulas and Subject Matters*

Khalīfa's different formulas of transmission generally correspond to the importance or controversy of the subject matter under discussion. Expressions of direct transmission indicate stricter transmission and treatment of the *isnāds*—for example, 'So-and-so narrated to me' (*ḥaddathanī*), or 'So-and-so narrated to us' (*ḥaddathanā*). These formulas are particularly common in accounts of controversial events, while the rest of the *Tārīkh* often contain formulas that indicate some laxity—for example, 'It was narrated from' (*ruwiya ʿan*), 'It was narrated to us from' (*ḥuddithnā ʿan*) or simply, 'So-and-so said' (*qāla*).[78] There are also slightly more ambiguous formulas such as 'from so-and-so' (*ʿan*), which probably refers to direct transmission if it can be established elsewhere that Khalīfa met (or at least could have met) these transmitters.[79] As Khalidi points out, similar patterns in the relation between transmission formulas and subject matters can be observed in the works of al-Wāqidī and al-Balādhurī.[80]

In the case of Khalīfa, the correspondence between controversial events and well-defined transmission formulas in his *Tārīkh* suggests a consistent approach; the *isnāds* are generally detailed, complete and explicit for controversial events but often vaguer or abbreviated for more mundane events. One way of illustrating this is to look at the year sections when major events occurred. Returning to ʿUthmān's caliphate (23–35/644–656), divided into the first eleven years of his reign and the last year, Tables 6 and 7 show Khalīfa's use of more detailed and explicit formulas for the last year than for the first eleven years.[81]

It is also noteworthy that 89 per cent of the reports (42 of 47) on ʿUthmān's last year contain three or more names in the *isnāds*, while only 45 per cent of the reports (21 of 47) in the prior years have three or more names in the *isnāds*. This shows that Khalīfa preferred material with complete *isnāds*, and generally provided such *isnāds*, for particularly controversial events. A similar

---

78 See al-ʿUmarī's introduction to Khalīfa b. Khayyāṭ, *Tārīkh* (1985) 15–16; ʿĀṣī, *Khalīfa* 67. For some examples, see Khalīfa b. Khayyāṭ, *Tārīkh* (1985) 118, 132–134, 137–138, 143–144, 146, 151–154, 181, 186, 190, 281, 283, 287.

79 Ibn al-Ṣalāḥ, *ʿUlūm al-ḥadīth* 61–67; Ibn Ḥajar, *Nuzhat al-naẓar* 268; al-Sakhāwī, *al-Fatḥ al-Mughīth* 1:286–302; Brown, *Hadith* 90.

80 Khalidi, *Arabic historical thought* 48, 60–61.

81 Khalīfa b. Khayyāṭ, *Tārīkh* (1985) 156–168, 168–177.

TABLE 6 Formulas for the first eleven years of 'Uthmān's caliphate

Transmission formula	Amount	Percentage
He said (*qāla*)	31	66%
He narrated to me (*ḥaddathanī*)	7	15%
No formula	5	11%
He narrated to us (*ḥaddathanā*)	3	6%
I heard (*samiʿtu*)	1	2%

TABLE 7 Formulas for the last year of 'Uthmān's caliphate

Transmission formula	Amount	Percentage
He narrated to us (*ḥaddathanā*)	26	55%
He said (*qāla*)	9	19%
He narrated to me (*ḥaddathanī*)	5	11%
No formula	4	9%
I heard so-and-so (*samiʿtu*)	1	2%
He informed me (*akhbaranī*)	1	2%
It was narrated to us (*ḥuddithnā ʿan*)	1	2%

pattern to that of 'Uthmān's caliphate is found in the sections for the reigns of ʿAlī, Muʿāwiya, Yazīd b. Muʿāwiya and ʿAbd al-Malik b. Marwān; the accounts of major events contain more reports with complete *isnād*s and defined transmission formulas than the remaining year sections. Tables 8 and 9 show the formulas in the sections for ʿAbd al-Malik's caliphate—divided into the years of Ibn al-Ashʿath's revolt (81–82/699–701) and the remaining years of his caliphate (65–80/685–699, 83–86/702–705).[82]

These tables show Khalīfa's use of more precise and detailed transmission formulas for controversial events such as revolts and civil wars than for the remaining narrative. There is thus a clear correspondence between reputable transmitters and controversial events in the *Tārīkh*, as well as between formulas of direct transmission and controversial events. More generally, these results underline the importance of paying attention to the *isnād*s in the study of early

82 Khalīfa b. Khayyāṭ, *Tārīkh* (1985) 261–293, 280–288.

TABLE 8 Formulas for Ibn al-Ashʿath's revolt (81–82/699–701)

Transmission formula	Amount	Percentage
He narrated to me (*ḥaddathanī*)	20	74%
He said (*qāla*)	5	19%
It was narrated to me (*ḥuddithtu ʿan*)	1	3.5%
No formula	1	3.5%

TABLE 9 Formulas for ʿAbd al-Malik's caliphate (65–80/685–699, 83–86/702–705)

Transmission formula	Amount	Percentage
He said (*qāla*)	15	68%
He narrated to me (*ḥaddathanī*)	6	27%
He narrated to us (*ḥaddathanā*)	1	5%

works of *akhbār* history; rather than being merely automated conventions, the *isnād* and the formulas of transmission were essential parts of the historians' methods and the meanings these historians were conveying.

5 Conclusion

This chapter has outlined some of the methods by which Khalīfa selected and presented the material at his disposal. It has sought to show how Khalīfa adopted certain *ḥadīth* conventions in compiling his *Tārīkh*, which sheds some light on the relationship between the methods of the *muḥaddithūn* and the *akhbārīyūn*. In relation to the question of epistemology and Khalīfa's views on historical knowledge, it has been suggested that Khalīfa compiled his *Tārīkh* as an attempt to outline the chronology and political-administrative history of the Muslim community as accurately as possible, based on the scholarly tradition of the early Sunnī *ḥadīth* scholars and *akhbār* historians before him—with the reservation that the accuracy of specific statements, facts and reports (especially weak narrations) may well be questioned, criticised or dismissed. The *Tārīkh* was, in this sense, transmitted and circulated as a critical chronology of historical facts and not merely a political commentary.

Similar to the early *ḥadīth* scholars, Khalīfa accepted some leniency with the *isnād*s in historical scholarship that did not pertain to core subjects such as *fiqh* and *ʿaqīda*. Thus he generally allowed for broken *isnād*s in the basic chronological narrative, while providing full *isnād*s and precise transmission formulas, indicating direct transmission, for subjects of particular importance or controversy (especially details about the Prophet and intra-Muslim conflicts). The main types of material that entirely lack *isnād*s are the administrative lists and Khalīfa's own shorter summaries. Khalīfa's selection of sources also indicates that he evaluated transmitters based on the tradition of the *ḥadīth* scholars. Although Khalīfa accepts reports from weak transmitters in the *Tārīkh*, he tends to select mainly reputable transmitters, especially Basrans, for important details or controversial events. The predominance of Basrans can be explained by the fact that Khalīfa spent most of his life in Basra, but it also reflects his scholarly preferences (he knew the capacities of the Basrans better than transmitters from other places) and his historical views (these Basran *ḥadīth* scholars generally shared his early Sunnī outlook). In addition to the aspects discussed above, other characteristics of Khalīfa's methods of compiling history are outlined in Chapter 6, which examines the structure of the *Tārīkh* and its different levels of arrangement in the year and list sections.

CHAPTER 6

Structure and Arrangement of the *Tārīkh*

1 Introduction

This chapter examines the structure and arrangement of Khalīfa's *Tārīkh* as transmitted by Baqī b. Makhlad. First, it discusses the concept of chronography (*tārīkh*) in the work, mainly based on an analysis of the title and the introductory section. It is suggested that the title and introduction, on the one hand, announce the form and scope of the work and, on the other hand, justify the practice of chronography to an audience of mainly *ḥadīth* scholars. Second, the chapter outlines the general structure of the *Tārīkh* and Khalīfa's combination of annalistic and caliphal chronography in the year and list sections. It is suggested that this framework not only fits the political-administrative scope of the *Tārīkh* but also corresponds to Khalīfa's early Sunnī perspective by foregrounding the continuity of the caliphate and its institutions. Third, the chapter examines the structure of individual year and list sections, which shows how the material in the year sections is sometimes arranged by chronology and sometimes by other factors (e.g. themes, geography and historical importance).

2 Concept of Chronography

2.1 Tārīkh *as Title*

The first indication of the chronological framework of Khalīfa's work is its title, *Kitāb al-Tārīkh* ('the Book of Chronography') or simply *al-Tārīkh* ('the Chronicle'), which literally means 'recording dates.'[1] 'Title' is to be understood not in the modern sense of a publication title but rather as the name by which the work was known during its early circulation and transmission. Many works were known by different titles, sometimes longer ones given by compilers and shorter ones by which they were commonly referred to—for instance, al-Bukhārī's *al-Jāmiʿ al-musnad al-ṣaḥīḥ al-mukhtaṣar min umūr rasūl Allāh* (*ṣ*) *wa-sunanihi wa-ayyāmihi*, which became known as *al-Jāmiʿ al-ṣaḥīḥ* or simply *al-Ṣaḥīḥ*. In the case of Khalīfa's work, *al-Tārīkh* or *Kitāb al-Tārīkh* seems to have been his own title. This impression is reinforced by its opening line: "Khalīfa b.

1 On the term *tārīkh* (also spelt *ta'rīkh*), see Lane, *Arabic-English lexicon* s.v.; De Blois, Ta'rīkh.

 | DOI:10.1163/9789004383173_008

Khayyāṭ said: This is *Kitāb al-Tārīkh*."[2] Moreover, the earliest notices about the work refer to it in the indefinite form as a *tārīkh* or in the definite form as *Kitāb al-Tārīkh*, and no other title for it is known.[3]

This usage of *tārīkh* is important as it indicates the genre in which Khalīfa compiled: annalistic chronography of events. In the third/ninth century, *tārīkh* was mainly used as a title for chronographies (including annalistic and caliphal histories) and for biographical dictionaries of *ḥadīth* transmitters.[4] Although Khalīfa's *Tārīkh* contains many dates of *ḥadīth* scholars' deaths, it is clearly an event-based chronography, while the *Ṭabaqāt* is a dictionary of transmitters.[5] Other third/ninth-century *ḥadīth* scholars also compiled chronological material entitled *tārīkh*—among them al-Fasawī, Ibn Abī Khaythama and Abū Zurʿa al-Dimashqī. However, they combine chronological sections with biographical sections in the same works. By contrast, Khalīfa clearly separates *tārīkh* from *ṭabaqāt* in his two works, although they were transmitted as a pair by both Baqī b. Makhlad and Mūsā b. Zakariyyā al-Tustarī. In that regard, Khalīfa's distinction between *tārīkh* and *ṭabaqāt* makes the chronological scope of the *Tārīkh* even clearer than these other *tārīkh* works: *Kitāb al-Tārīkh* on the political-administrative chronology of the Muslim community and *Kitāb al-Ṭabaqāt* on the generations of *ḥadīth* transmitters.

As for the wider tradition of *akhbār* history, most known histories from before the early third/ninth century are texts on single subjects such as Prophetic biography (*maghāzī-sīra*), the merits of certain people (*faḍāʾil*), conquests (*futūḥ*), civil wars (*fitan*) and killings/martyrdoms (*maqātil*).[6] In contrast to these single-subject texts (seldom entitled *tārīkh*), the title and opening sentence of Khalīfa's work announce its chronological structure and wider scope—not limited to single episodes or subjects, but considering the whole Hijrī chronology of the Muslim polity from its establishment in Medina in 1/622.

2.2 *The Introduction: Chronography, Dating and the Hijrī Calendar*

After introducing the title, Khalīfa outlines the chronological scope in his brief introduction, which is a bit more than one folio, or two pages, in the manuscript

2 Khalīfa b. Khayyāṭ, *Tārīkh* (1985) 49.

3 Ibn ʿAdī, *Kāmil* 3:935; Ibn al-Nadīm, *Fihrist* 2:111.

4 Some linguistic and technical definitions of *tārīkh*, based on and reflective of earlier *ḥadīth* scholarship, can be found in al-Sakhāwī, *al-Iʿlān* 16–19.

5 Similar to the *Tārīkh*, the *Ṭabaqāt* is consistently labelled as such (*al-Ṭabaqāt* or *Kitāb al-Ṭabaqāt*) in the early sources. See Ibn ʿAdī, *Kāmil* 3:935; Ibn al-Nadīm, *Fihrist* 2:111.

6 Robinson, *Islamic historiography* 24–30, 39. See also Donner's list of early texts and their titles in *Narratives* 299–306.

and three pages in the modern editions. It is comprised of Qur'ān citations and historical reports that address three main themes: (1) the importance of recording dates and chronography, (2) mankind's previous systems of dating and (3) the origins of the Hijrī calendar.[7] Besides presenting the scope of the *Tārīkh*, the introduction also justifies the practice of chronography (*tārīkh*). It begins with some Qur'ānic verses about measuring time:

> In the name of God, the Merciful, the Compassionate. May the peace and blessings of God be upon Muḥammad and his family.
>
> Khalīfa b. Khayyāṭ said: This is the Book of Chronography (*kitāb al-tārīkh*). By means of assigning dates (*tārīkh*), people know about the matter of their pilgrimage and their fasting, the end of the waiting-periods of their women and the due dates of their debts. God—Blessed and Exalted—says to His Prophet Muḥammad (ṣ), "They will ask you about the crescent moons. Say, 'They are set times for mankind and for the pilgrimage.'" (Q 2:189)
>
> Khalīfa said: Yazīd b. Zurayʿ narrated to us; he said: Saʿīd narrated to us from Qatāda about "They will ask you about the crescent moons." He said: They asked, "Why are these crescent moons made?" So God revealed what you hear: "They are set times for mankind and for the pilgrimage." God made them on account of the Muslims' fasting and the breaking of the fast, their pilgrimage and their rites during it, the waiting-periods of their women and the due dates of their debts among other things. God knows best what will set right His creation. He said, "We made the night and day two signs. We blotted out the sign of the night and made the sign of the day a time for seeing so that you can seek favour from your Lord and will know the number of years and the reckoning of time." (Q 17:12) He said in another verse, "It is He who appointed the sun to give radiance, and the moon to give light, assigning it phases so you would know the number of years and the reckoning of time. God did not create these things except with truth. He makes the signs clear for people who know." (Q 10:5)[8]

Thereby Khalīfa underlines the importance of chronography and measuring time with reference to fulfilling individual and communal duties—in the

7 See also Nawas, Early Muslim philosopher of history 165.

8 Khalīfa b. Khayyāṭ, *Tārīkh* (1985) 49–50.

sphere of worship as well as in social and economic transactions. The verses also point out the Qur'ānic basis for reckoning time by the phases of the moon, which constitute clear signs for people who know. In line with his scholarly orientation, Khalīfa begins with Qur'ānic citations and their explanations, before continuing with *isnād*-equipped reports from the Prophet and the early generations of Muslims.

The second theme is mankind's systems of dating. The practice of assigning dates and measuring time is said to be almost as old as mankind; people used to date from events in the lives of the Prophets Adam, Noah, Abraham and Ishmael. Khalīfa also notes that the Persian calendar began with the last Persian emperor, Yazdajird b. Shahrayār (r. 11–31/632–651), and that the Jews (Banū Isrā'īl) dated from the years of Dhū l-Qarnayn as named in the Qur'ān—understood as Alexander the Great and referring to the Seleucid era. He then outlines the calendar systems among the Arabs, culminating in the Muslims' dating from the Prophet Muḥammad's emigration from Mecca to Medina.[9] The references to calendars in previous communities highlight the relationship between calendars and communal identities—thereby further stressing the importance of chronography.[10] It also presents an understanding of the Muslim community as the religio-political successor to, and unifier of, the earlier Prophetic communities from Adam to Moses as well as the Persian Empire and pre-Islamic Arabia.[11] In this sense, Khalīfa's introduction reflects universal concerns, in line with the universal message of Islam, although the temporal and geographical scope of his *Tārīkh* is, strictly speaking, not universal.[12] The focus on time, prophethood and righteous community also bears some resemblance to Christian historiography from the same period.[13] However, the specific content, concerns, structures and scholarly methods underlying the *Tarıkh* are nonetheless particular to the Islamic tradition and, more specifically, reflect Khalīfa's background as an early Sunnī *ḥadīth* and *akhbār* scholar. Khalīfa then outlines 'Umar's introduction of the Hijrī calendar:

9 Khalīfa b. Khayyāṭ, *Tārīkh* (1985) 50.

10 In relation to the history of the Islamic calendar, Stowasser notes that the new chronology established by 'Umar b. al-Khaṭṭāb (r. 13–23/634–644) "affirmed the self-identity of the Islamic commonwealth as much as it obliterated access to the old Arabian tribal past. In its global and universalist thrust, the new Islamic calendar was a fitting symbol for the culture and the age that produced it." *Day begins at sunset* 16.

11 See Chapter 7.

12 On Islamic universal histories, see Radtke, *Weltgeschichte*; Robinson, *Islamic historiography* 134–138; Di Branco, Rose in the desert?; Marsham, Universal histories.

13 See Marsham, Universal histories.

ʿAbdallāh b. Maslama b. Qaʿnab and Isḥāq b. Idrīs narrated to us; they both said: ʿAbd al-ʿAzīz b. Abī Ḥāzim narrated to us from his father from Sahl b. Saʿd al-Sāʿidī; he said: People made mistakes about the reckoning of years. Then they did not reckon from the beginning of the Prophetic mission of God's Messenger (ṣ) nor from his death, but only from his arrival in Medina.

He said: ʿAbd al-Aʿlā b. ʿAbd al-Aʿlā reported to us; he said: Qurra b. Khālid narrated to us from Muḥammad b. Sīrīn; he said: An administrator (*ʿāmil*) said to ʿUmar b. al-Khaṭṭāb, "Do you not reckon the dates?" For they wanted to reckon the dates. They said, "From the beginning of the Prophetic mission of God's Messenger (ṣ) or from his death?" Then they agreed to begin from his emigration. They wanted to begin with the month of Ramaḍān, but then they decided to set it in al-Muḥarram.

Kathīr b. Hishām narrated to us; he said: Jaʿfar b. Burqān narrated to us from Maymūn b. Mihrān; he said: The Companions of God's Messenger (ṣ) consulted together about how they should record the dates. Some of them said, "We record it from the birth of the Messenger of God (ṣ)." Others said, "From when he received the first revelation." Others said, "From his emigration, in which he emigrated from the abode of idolatry to the abode of belief." Then they agreed that they should record the dates from his emigration.

Muḥammad b. ʿAbdallāh b. al-Zubayr narrated to us; he said: Ḥabbān narrated to us from Mujālid from ʿĀmir; he said: Abū Mūsā al-Ashʿarī wrote to ʿUmar, "Letters are reaching us the dates of which we do not know." So ʿUmar consulted the Companions of God's Messenger (ṣ). Some of them said, "From the beginning of the Prophetic mission", and others said, "From his death." Then ʿUmar said, "Reckon the dates from his emigration, for it distinguished between truth and falsehood."

Khalīfa narrated to us; he said: Isḥāq b. Idrīs narrated to us; he said: ʿAbd al-ʿAzīz b. Muḥammad narrated to us; he said: ʿUthmān b. ʿUbaydallāh narrated to us from Saʿīd b. al-Musayyib; he said: ʿUmar gathered the Muhājirūn and the Anṣār and said, "From when should I record the dates?" ʿAlī replied to him, "From that the Messenger of God (ṣ) departed from the land of idolatry, which is the day he emigrated." So ʿUmar b. al-Khaṭṭāb recorded from that.[14]

---

14 Khalīfa b. Khayyāṭ, *Tārīkh* (1985) 51.

These accounts resemble other sources, apart from Khalīfa's placing of them at the beginning of his work.[15] He thereby anticipates the arrangement and scope of the *Tārīkh*: a Hijrī chronology of the political and administrative development of the Muslim community. As the accounts suggest, the *hijra* was seen as the social and political establishment of the Muslim community, marked by the relocation from the abode of idolatry in Mecca to the abode of belief in Medina. Thus the first year of the Hijrī calendar is the beginning of Khalīfa's main narrative, apart from some accounts on the Prophet's birth and the length of his time in Mecca before the emigration.[16]

Khalīfa's introduction reflects his background as a *ḥadīth* scholar. It asserts the primacy of the Qurʾānic revelation and transmission-based scholarship, as well as the legitimacy of chronicle writing (*tārīkh*) on the basis of precedents that his fellow scholars would have recognised. Moreover, the *isnād*s contain the names of many major *ḥadīth* authorities, many of them Basrans. This supports the notion that Khalīfa's main audience were his fellow *ḥadīth* scholars. Chronography and post-Prophetic chronicles are usually not associated with the early *ḥadīth* scholars.[17] Besides some exceptions, as noted in Chapter 3, most compilations of political history by third/ninth-century *ḥadīth* scholars are sections on *maghāzī-sīra* (or similar subjects) in *ḥadīth* collections. Although *ḥadīth* scholars occasionally arranged material chronologically in their *ḥadīth* collections, establishing chronological sequences of events was not the primary concern at the stage of compilation.[18] The scarcity of chronological compilation among early *ḥadīth* scholars, and perhaps their potential criticism of *akhbār* history, may partially explain the justifications for chronography in Khalīfa's introduction—besides the primary purpose of outlining the approach and subject of the work.[19]

A similar but longer introduction to chronography is found in al-Ṭabarī's *Tārīkh*.[20] Similar to Khalīfa, al-Ṭabarī describes how God created the sun and the moon so that humans would be able to distinguish day from night—that is, measure time—both for acts of worship and for interpersonal transactions ("settling their debts and their claims").[21] Unlike Khalīfa, who then discusses mankind's previous systems of dating, al-Ṭabarī follows this with an outline of

15 E.g. Ibn Ḥabīb, *Tārīkh* 103–104; Ibn Shabba, *Tārīkh al-Madīna* 758–759; al-Ṭabarī, *Tārīkh* 1:1250–1255. See also Ibn al-Jawzī, *al-Muntaẓam* 4:226–229; Ibn Kathīr, *al-Bidāya* 4:510–513.

16 Khalīfa b. Khayyāṭ, *Tārīkh* (1985) 52–54.

17 See Robinson, *Islamic historiography* 103.

18 Zaman, *Maghāzī* and the *muḥaddithūn* 3–4.

19 For some *ḥadīth* scholars' criticism against historians see al-Sakhāwī, *al-Iʿlān* 86–106.

20 Al-Ṭabarī, *Tārīkh* 1:1–29. On al-Ṭabarī's introduction, see Mårtensson, *Tabari* 65–70.

21 Al-Ṭabarī, *Tārīkh* 1:3–4.

the two principal human responses to God's blessings: gratitude (*shukr*) and ingratitude (*kufr*). On this basis, al-Ṭabarī presents his aim to record "the dates of past kings … and summaries of their history, the times of the Messengers and Prophets and how long they lived, the days of the early caliphs and some of their biographical data, and the extent of the territories under their control, as well as the events that took place in their age."[22] Khalīfa does not state the aim and scope of his work, but the intention to compile a chronology of the Muslim polity is implied from the discussion about systems of dating and the Hijrī calendar. Moreover, Khalīfa includes nothing like al-Ṭabarī's methodological remarks about historical knowledge.[23] Although Khalīfa applies similar methods, he does not explicate his principles, which perhaps reflects the earlier context in which Khalīfa worked—even *ḥadīth* collections prior to Khalīfa lacked methodological introductions (the first one is in the *Ṣaḥīḥ* of Muslim b. al-Ḥajjāj).[24] Moreover, unlike al-Ṭabarī, who worked at a time when other forms of history (without *isnād*s) had become popular, Khalīfa worked in a traditionist milieu where *isnād*-based compilation of *akhbār* seems to have been the only acceptable method of writing history. In summary, the main functions of Khalīfa's introduction are, first, to introduce and justify chronography as a scholarly occupation and, second, to present the form and scope of his *Tārīkh*—that is, a political and administrative chronology of the Muslim community according to the Hijrī calendar.

3 General Structure: Annalistic and Caliphal Chronology

Khalīfa deploys two types of chronology in the *Tārīkh*: annalistic, according to the Hijrī calendar (in the year sections) and caliphal, according to the reigns of caliphs (in the administrative list sections concluding each reign). The main structure of Khalīfa's text is clearly annalistic, and his work is an annalistic history (*tārīkh ʿalā al-sinīn*) rather than a caliphal history (*tārīkh al-khulafāʾ*), but there are also some tendencies of a caliphal chronology and a 'dynastic' periodisation within that overall annalistic structure.[25] These two types of structure in Khalīfa's *Tārīkh* are examined below, concluded by a discussion about their narrative functions.

---

22 Al-Ṭabarī, *Tārīkh* 1:6. Trans. Rosenthal in al-Ṭabarī, *History* 1:169.

23 Al-Ṭabarī, *Tārīkh* 1:6–7.

24 E.g. Mālik b. Anas's *Muwaṭṭaʾ* and Ibn Abī Shayba's *Muṣannaf*.

25 On the distinction between 'annalistic history' (*tārīkh ʿalā al-sinīn*) and 'caliphal history' (*tārīkh al-khulafāʾ*), see Robinson, *Islamic historiography* 75.

3.1 *Annalistic Chronology*

Although Khalīfa's introduction discusses *tārīkh* in the sense of recording dates and calendar systems, Khalīfa applies *tārīkh* in the technical sense of annalistic chronography. After a short section on the birth of the Prophet and his time in Mecca and Medina, the structure of the *Tārīkh* is strictly annalistic. It is divided into year sections, of varying length, from 1/622 to 232/847 in the extant recension of Baqī b. Makhlad. Each section contains information limited to events in that year, which are often linked by phrases such as 'In this year (*fī hādhihi l-sana*)' or simply 'In it (*fīhā*).' The year sections are composed of three types of material: (1) transmitted reports with *isnād*s, (2) Khalīfa's own summaries or statements and (3) the names of prominent people who were born or died in each year. The sections occasionally contain longer lists of people who died or participated in major battles and revolts.[26] Although Khalīfa is strict with the annalistic chronology, a few occasional reports in the year sections extend to the future or refer to future events—for instance, the death of a person under discussion, the return of a military expedition or the duration of a governorship.[27] Some entries also refer to past years, but this is more common in the lists of governors and administrators at the end of caliphal reigns, as outlined below.

Similar to other early Islamic chronicles, the length of the year sections in the *Tārīkh* decreases towards the end of the work—closer to the time of the compiler himself.[28] About a third of the *Tārīkh*, as transmitted by Baqī, pertains to the Prophetic and Rāshidūn periods (1–41/622–661) and almost half to the Umayyad (41–132/661–750), but only a sixth to the ʿAbbāsid period (132–232/750–847). This imbalance between past and contemporary history reflects the scholarly context in which Khalīfa worked and its dedication to the early foundational periods of the Prophet, the Companions and the Successors.[29] If Khalīfa's principal aim was to outline the chronology and political-administrative development of the Muslim community from its roots in Medina—in a way that would be useful for his fellow *ḥadīth* scholars in par-

26 E.g. Khalīfa b. Khayyāṭ, *Tārīkh* (1985) 59–61, 187–190, 240–251, 286–287.

27 An example is the death of al-Ḥasan b. ʿAlī (d. 49/669), which is mentioned in 41/611, when he transferred the caliphate to Muʿāwiya. Another example is ʿAbbād b. Ziyād, who from 53/672 "remained as governor of Sijistān until Muʿāwiya died" in 60/680. Khalīfa b. Khayyāṭ, *Tārīkh* (1985) 203, 219.

28 Robinson, *Islamic historiography* 94–95. See also Donner's discussion of the most prominent themes in Islamic historical writing until the early third/ninth century, which reflect a limited interest in contemporary history. Donner, *Narratives* 141–202.

29 See Robinson, *Islamic historiography* 96.

ticular—the earlier foundational history from the Prophetic to the mid/late Umayyad period (the time of the Companions and the Successors) was naturally prioritised over the ʿAbbāsid period that included his own lifetime.

3.2 *Caliphal Chronology*

In addition to the general annalistic structure, Khalīfa also deploys some elements of a caliphal chronology. Its most explicit expression is in the list sections that conclude the reigns of all caliphs and a few Umayyad-era governors of Iraq and the East, containing names of governors, judges and other administrative appointees.[30] Most material in these sections pertains to administration during the whole reign, but Khalīfa occasionally adds new information within a caliphal, rather than annalistic, framework—mainly lists of people who died at the time of certain caliphs or governors.[31] The beginnings and ends of the caliphal reigns are also marked in the text by other means. At a new caliph's succession, Khalīfa mentions the pledge of allegiance, followed by the caliph's paternal and maternal lineages.[32] At the caliph's death, Khalīfa usually states the length of his reign and place of birth.[33] Examples of this demarcation of reigns are the entries at the beginning and end of the reign of Sulaymān b. ʿAbd al-Malik. First in 96/715:

> Then Sulaymān b. ʿAbd al-Malik b. Marwān received the oath of allegiance. His mother was Wallāda bt. al-ʿAbbās, who was also the mother of al-Walīd b. ʿAbd al-Malik.[34]

And then in 99/717:

> In it: Sulaymān b. ʿAbd al-Malik died at Dābiq.
>
> Al-Walīd b. Hishām narrated to me from his father from his grandfather and ʿAbdallāh b. al-Mughīra from his father; they both said: Sulaymān died in Dābiq on Friday, when ten days had passed of Ṣafar, in year 99/717. He was 43 years old. ʿUmar b. ʿAbd al-ʿAzīz led the funeral prayers for him.
>
> ʿAbd al-ʿAzīz said: He died at the age of 33.

30 The governors are Ziyād b. Abīhi, al-Ḥajjāj b. Yūsuf, Yazīd b. al-Muhallab, Ibn Hubayra, Khālid al-Qasrī, Yūsuf b. ʿUmar, ʿAbdallāh b. ʿUmar b. ʿAbd al-ʿAzīz and Yazīd b. ʿUmar b. Hubayra. Khalīfa b. Khayyāṭ, *Tārīkh* (1985) 211–212, 308–313, 317, 335, 350–351, 368, 382–383.

31 E.g. Khalīfa b. Khayyāṭ, *Tārīkh* (1985) 300, 363. On the death notes in the *Tārīkh*, see section 4.1 below.

32 E.g. Khalīfa b. Khayyāṭ, *Tārīkh* (1985) 100, 122, 156, 180, 203, 299–300, 447, 460.

33 E.g. Khalīfa b. Khayyāṭ, *Tārīkh* (1985) 122, 153, 199, 292, 331, 429, 446.

34 Khalīfa b. Khayyāṭ, *Tārīkh* (1985) 309.

Ḥātim b. Muslim said: He was 45 years old.

His reign lasted two years and ten and a half, or nine and a half, months.

Sulaymān was born in the house of ʿAbd al-Malik in Medina in the quarter of Banū Ḥudayla. He died in Dābiq in the district of Qinnasrīn.

Then ʿUmar b. ʿAbd al-ʿAzīz b. Marwān received the oath of allegiance. His mother was Umm ʿĀṣim bt. ʿĀṣim b. ʿUmar b. al-Khaṭṭāb.[35]

The list sections and the repetitive accounts at the beginning and end of reigns provide a caliphal structure within the annalistic scheme. There are also some tendencies towards a division into periods; the sections for the Prophetic, Rāshidūn, Umayyad (including Zubayrid) and ʿAbbāsid periods are distinguished from each other by Khalīfa's different approach to them. The Prophetic and Rāshidūn periods are overall characterised by longer year sections, a larger proportion of *isnād*-equipped material and a greater concern for complete *isnāds* as well as reputable transmitters. Most major *ḥadīth* transmitters cited in the *Tārīkh* are found in these two periods.[36] The Umayyad section is longer than the Prophetic and Rāshidūn periods (about half of Baqī's recension of the *Tārīkh* as opposed to a third), but the year sections are altogether shorter (92 years as opposed to 40) and less based on *isnād*-equipped reports. The section for the ʿAbbāsid period is significantly shorter than the earlier sections and mainly comprised of Khalīfa's own brief summaries; it contains only some 20 reports with *isnāds*. The same pattern is found in the preserved material from al-Tustarī's recension, including the material that is absent in Baqī's recension.[37] Although Khalīfa's narrative highlights the continuity of the caliphate throughout the Rāshidūn, Umayyad and ʿAbbāsid periods,[38] his approach to them reflects a scholarly tradition that divided the past into periods of different importance, deserving different levels of attention and strictness in historical studies.

By the caliphal elements and division into periods discussed above, Khalīfa superimposes a caliphal structure on the annalistic chronology. This twofold structure corresponds to the two main themes of his *Tārīkh*: the political chronology in the year sections and the administrative chronology in the list sections. This combination of annalistic structure and concluding list sections

35 Khalīfa b. Khayyāṭ, *Tārīkh* (1985) 316–317. See Wurtzel, *Khalifa ibn Khayyat's History* 183, 192.

36 See Chapter 4.

37 See Ṣaddām, *Tārīkh Khalīfa* 118–133.

38 On succession and leadership in the *Tārīkh*, see Chapter 8.

bears some resemblance to the works of al-Yaʿqūbī and al-Ṭabarī.[39] However, Khalīfa's list sections are more prominent and, in contrast to al-Ṭabarī but similar to al-Yaʿqūbī, are systematically placed at the end of each caliphal reign. Khalīfa's lists also contain more details, names and posts than those of both al-Yaʿqūbī and al-Ṭabarī. Al-Yaʿqūbī, for example, focuses mainly on the leading jurisprudents (*fuqahāʾ*), "the persons with the greatest influence over the caliph" (*al-ghālib ʿalayhi*) and a few other minor posts, rather than the whole line-up of administrative appointees that is found in Khalīfa's *Tārīkh*. None of the surviving *tārīkh* works of Ibn Ḥabīb, al-Fasawī, Ibn Abī Khaythama and Abū Zurʿa al-Dimashqī combines an annalistic structure with list sections in the same way as Khalīfa. The most similar in content is al-Fasawī, but he seems to have mixed the two, including administrative information (e.g. governors and pilgrimage leaders) in his year sections.[40]

Lists are prominent components of many early works,[41] but Khalīfa's lengthy independent list sections within an annalistic structure are not found in the same way in other extant histories prior to him. For example, no surviving *akhbār* work from before Khalīfa—such as the material of Abū Mikhnaf, Sayf b. ʿUmar, Ibn al-Kalbī, Ibn Isḥāq, Naṣr b. Muzāḥim and al-Wāqidī—seems to have resembled his *Tārīkh* in structure and arrangement.[42] Thus the availability of other formats suggests that Khalīfa's annalistic-caliphal scheme was a deliberate choice among different alternatives.

3.3 *Functions of the Annalistic-Caliphal Structure*

Histories based on the two types of chronology that Khalīfa deploys in the *Tārīkh*—annalistic and caliphal—appeared well before his time. Caliphal histories are ascribed to both Ibn Isḥāq and Abū Maʿshar, while al-Haytham b. ʿAdī is the earliest known annalist.[43] As discussed below, Khalīfa's combination of these two already existing forms of chronography fits, on the one hand, the political-administrative scope of the *Tārīkh* and, on the other hand, his early Sunnī historical outlook.

39 See al-Yaʿqūbī, *Tārīkh* 2:26, 54–55, 74, 120–121, 150–154, 169, 187, 202–204, 215–216, 224–225, 235–236, 242–243, 259–261, 265–267, 281–282, 296–299, 329–333, 344–348, 351–352, 379–383, 395–396, 429, 439–440, 446; al-Ṭabarī, *Tārīkh* 2:752–753, 783, 796–797, 834–835, 853–854, 1063, 1085, 1127, 1182, 1234, 1255, 1269, 1305, 1314, 1336, 1346–1347, 1359, 1394, 1436, 1461, 1487, 1506, 1526, 1530, 1562, 1635, 1666–1667, 1698.

40 Al-Fasawī, *Maʿrifa* 1:115–213.

41 See Noth and Conrad, *Early Arabic* 96–104; Bray, Lists and memory.

42 See Roberts, *Early Islamic historiography* 66.

43 Robinson, *Islamic historiography* 47.

First, the annalistic-caliphal chronology corresponds to the political and administrative scope of the *Tārīkh*. The annalistic scheme of the year sections accommodates the basic objectives of political history: what, where and when events occurred, who was involved and the relationship between events. The caliphal scheme with concluding list sections accommodates the basic objectives of administrative history: who was appointed to and dismissed from what positions under each caliph. This combined structure facilitates a coherent narrative that would have been difficult with a singular annalistic or caliphal chronology. It also solves some of the difficulties associated with these two formats. Annalistic chronography posed the problem of determining the precise dates of all events, whether battles, deaths, appointments or other events. Caliphal chronography solved this by ordering such material by reign, but at the same time it lost some of the annalistic precision. Both types also faced the problem that events did not pause at the turn of years or at the succession of caliphs, but might begin in one year or reign and end in another.[44] These problems were partly solved by Khalīfa's annalistic-caliphal scheme, which divided political and administrative history into chronological year sections and caliphal list sections. Whether or not Khalīfa was the first to use this scheme, it was a choice that enabled him to clearly and coherently structure the political and administrative content of his work.

Second, the annalistic-caliphal scheme also fits Khalīfa's early Sunnī outlook in that it foregrounds the continuity of the caliphate and its institutions from the Medinan origins. It means not that Khalīfa's *Tārīkh* uncritically approves of all caliphs and their policies in the Umayyad and ʿAbbāsid periods but rather that it stresses the historical continuity of the caliphate and its institutions in general as well as the importance of communal unity under the current caliphs—even if their rule was at times unjust and far below the standard of the Rāshidūn caliphs.[45] In other words, for Khalīfa, the caliphate was not a

44 See Robinson, *Islamic historiography* 76.

45 On the issue of communal unity and obedience to political leaders, see e.g. al-Ṭaḥāwī's (d. 321/933) famous *ʿaqīda* text, in which he says, "We do not consider violence or coercive power against anyone from the community of Muḥammad (ṣ) acceptable, unless legislated [by sacred law, such as penal punishments or the suppression of rebellion]. We do not accept any rebellion against our leaders or the administrators of our public affairs, even if they are oppressive. We also do not pray for evil to befall any one of them or withdraw our allegiance from them. We consider our civic duty to them concordant with our duty to God, the Sublime and Exalted, and legally binding on us, unless they command us to the immoral. We pray for their probity, success, and welfare. We adhere to the Sunnah and the majority [of scholars], and we avoid isolated opinions, discord, and sectarianism. We love just and trustworthy people, and we loathe oppressive and treacherous

historical failure and an ongoing tragedy, as the Shīʿīs saw it, but rather a historical reality and ongoing form of government—with its periods of successful and less successful leadership. This historical continuity is emphasised by the repetitive list sections throughout the Prophetic, Rāshidūn, Umayyad (including Zubayrid) and ʿAbbāsid periods. Khalīfa systematically provides longer and much more detailed lists than al-Yaʿqūbī and al-Ṭabarī of the different administrative positions in the caliphate—from governors and judges to chamberlains, treasurers and financial secretaries.[46]

The annalistic structure and its chronological scope also shift focus from singular, controversial events such as civil wars (*fitan*) and killings of prominent individuals (*maqātil*)—favourite subjects of early single-subject Shīʿī texts[47]—to the long-term development of the Muslim polity and its political-administrative organisation. Details about the early intra-Muslim conflicts are important in Khalīfa's *Tārīkh*, but they are summarised and subsumed in the larger chronology. This is to say not that annalistic-caliphal chronography per se promotes early Sunnī views—al-Yaʿqūbī's Shīʿī-inclined history shows otherwise—but that Khalīfa uses it in a way that fits such views.[48] Similar to how the generation-based structure of Khalīfa's *Ṭabaqāt* emphasises the continuous transmission of the Prophetic tradition since the time of the Companions, the annalistic-caliphal structure of the *Tārīkh* emphasises the general continuity of the political and administrative organisation of the Muslim community since its foundation in Medina.

4 Structure of Individual Years and Lists

This section outlines the internal structure of individual year and list sections in Khalīfa's *Tārīkh*. It shows, first, that events in the year sections are sometimes arranged according to chronology and sometimes according to other factors (e.g. themes, geography and importance or controversy), which establish different relationships between events. In relation to the year sections, it also examines Khalīfa's lists of individuals who died in each year, which con-

---

people." Al-Ṭaḥāwī, *al-ʿAqīda* 24, trans. Hamza Yusuf in *Creed of Imam al-Ṭaḥāwī* 70. See also Ibn Abī l-ʿIzz, *Sharḥ al-ʿaqīdat al-Ṭaḥāwiyya* 539–548.

46 On the content of these lists, see Section 4.2.

47 See Robinson, *Islamic historiography* 24–30, 39.

48 On al-Yaʿqūbī's Shīʿism, see Anthony, Was Ibn Wāḍiḥ al-Yaʿqūbī a Shiʿite historian?, where he establishes that al-Yaʿqūbī was indeed a Shīʿī historian with 'rejectionist,' or Rāfiḍī, historical views.

sist mostly of *ḥadīth* transmitters (also listed in the *Ṭabaqāt*). It thereby confirms Khalīfa's particular concern for *ḥadīth* scholarship and his elevation of these scholars as the defining members of the Muslim community. Second, the section discusses the list sections, which complement the political narrative of the year sections with information about corresponding administrative developments in the caliphate. As discussed in Chapter 1, although Khalīfa must have been responsible for at least the general structure of these year and list sections in Baqī b. Makhlad's extant recension, it is possible that some parts of them were restructured, abridged or otherwise altered in the course of transmission. Even if that were the case, however, they would still reflect Khalīfa's own general arrangement of the material.

4.1 *Year Sections: Chronology, Themes and Regions*

The first question regarding the structure of the year sections concerns the relation between chronological arrangement and other types of arrangements (e.g. theme, geography and importance). Because of Khalīfa's slightly different approach to the Prophetic, Rāshidūn, Umayyad and ʿAbbāsid periods, each one is outlined separately.

4.1.1 The Prophetic Period

The year sections for the Prophet's lifetime are overall arranged chronologically and follow the dates provided by Khalīfa's two main sources: Ibn Isḥāq and al-Madāʾinī, who probably drew largely on Ibn Shihāb al-Zuhrī (d. 124/742).[49] Khalīfa provides exact dates for many of the Prophet's expeditions, but not for events such as deaths or conversions to Islam. Thus battles and military expeditions follow upon one another in the order in which they occurred, usually followed by notices at the end about minor events that occurred in the same year. The exceptions are some year sections where the expeditions in which the Prophet participated (*maghāzī*) are arranged separately from the military detachments that he sent out (*sariyya*, pl. *sarāyā*).[50] For instance, the structure of year 7/628–629:

1. The expedition of Khaybar (4 reports)
2. The treaty with the people of Fadak (3 reports)
3. List of martyrs at Khaybar

49 Donner, *Narratives* 246. See also Görke and Schoeler, *Die ältesten Berichte* 272–273; Jones, Chronology.

50 E.g. Khalīfa b. Khayyāṭ, *Tārīkh* (1985) 56–65, 79–82.

4. The siege of Wādī al-Qurā (1 report)
5. The treaty with the people of Fadak (1 report)
6. Detachments (*sarāyā*) that the Prophet sent out (1 report)
7. The *ʿumra* to make up for the missed *ʿumra* (1 report)
8. The Prophet's marriage to Maymūna (1 report)
9. Short notices about the Prophet consummating his marriage with Umm Ḥabība, Ḥāṭib b. Abī Baltaʿa's return from his visit to al-Muqawqis, Jaʿfar b. Abī Ṭālib's return from Abyssinia, the Prophet's marriage to Ṣafiyya bt. Ḥuyayy, Umm Kulthūm bt. ʿUqba's emigration and the acceptance of Islam by Abū Hurayra, ʿImrān b. Ḥuṣayn and Khālid b. al-Walīd.[51]

Besides the main narrative of the Muslim polity (1–7 above), other non-political or non-military events are narrated separately, without chronological sequence (8–9)—usually at the end of the year sections, but sometimes at the beginning or middle. Examples of such events are the change of the *qibla*, the Prophet's marriages, individuals who accepted Islam, the deaths and births of prominent people, and brief notes about the deaths and coronations of Persian rulers.[52] There are only 14 death notices in the Prophetic period (excluding martyrs in expeditions). Besides the Prophet Muḥammad, five pertain to his wives and children, five to Persian rulers, two to Companions and one to the Abyssinian ruler, or Negus (al-Najāshī), Aṣḥama b. Abjar.[53] The notices at the end of the year sections seem to be arranged according to importance, in so far as they begin with events pertaining directly to the Prophet, such as his marriages, and end with notes about other individuals and Persian rulers.[54]

4.1.2 The Rāshidūn Period

The sections for the Rāshidūn caliphs follow a similar structure as the Prophetic period. Political events are narrated chronologically, and non-military events such as deaths are usually placed at the end of year sections. Apart from those who died in battles, there are 59 death notices—all of them Companions, most of whom are also listed in Khalīfa's *Ṭabaqāt* (55 of 59).[55] In accordance with

51 Khalīfa b. Khayyāṭ, *Tārīkh* (1985) 82–86.

52 Khalīfa b. Khayyāṭ, *Tārīkh* (1985) 63–66, 79, 86, 92–94, 96.

53 Besides the Prophet Muḥammad, the other individuals are Abū Umāma Asʿad b. Zurāra, Ruqayya (the Prophet's daughter), ʿUthmān b. Maẓʿūn, Zaynab bt. Khuzayma (the Prophet's wife), Khusraw Parwīz, Shīrawayh, Zaynab (the Prophet's daughter), Aṣḥama al-Najāshī, Umm Kulthūm (the Prophet's daughter), Shahrbarāz, Ardashīr, Ibrāhīm (the Prophet's son) and Būrān bt. Kisrā.

54 E.g. Khalīfa b. Khayyāṭ, *Tārīkh* (1985) 65, 93, 94.

55 The individuals whose deaths are noted in the Rāshidūn period are Fāṭima (the Prophet's

the territorial expansion in all directions that took place in this period, Khalīfa is forced to sometimes arrange political events regionally within the overall chronological structure. Thus simultaneous conquests in Syria, Egypt, Persia and other places in one year are divided and narrated separately with their own chronologies. For example, 14/635–636 is structured as follows:

1. The conquest of Damascus (4 reports)
2. The Battle of Fiḥl (3 reports)
3. The conquest of Ḥimṣ and Baʿlbak (1 report)
4. The conquests around Basra and events related to Basra (11 reports)
5. The deaths and births of prominent people and notices about ʿUmar's establishment of the congregational night prayer in Ramaḍān, ʿAbd al-Raḥmān b. ʿAwf's pilgrimage with the Prophet's wives and ʿUmar's leading of the pilgrimage from 14/636 to his death in 23/644.[56]

In comparison to the Prophet's lifetime, there are fewer exact dates in the Rāshidūn period. Instead, chronological order is often established by the narrative sequence and by chronological indications in the reports—for example, "ʿAmr b. al-ʿĀṣ conquered Alexandria. He then went to Labda in the land of Tripoli (Aṭrābulus) and conquered it, and then returned in year 24/645."[57] Khalīfa occasionally introduces an event in its chronological sequence at the beginning of a year section and then returns to it in more detail, after having mentioned other events in the same year—for example, the Battle of the Camel

daughter), ʿAbdallāh b. Abī Bakr, Saʿd b. ʿUbāda al-Anṣārī, Abū l-ʿĀṣ b. al-Rabīʿ, Abu Bakr al-Ṣiddīq, al-Muthannā b. Ḥāritha, Abū Qaḥāfa ʿUthmān b. ʿAmr, Nawfal b. al-Ḥārith, Māriya al-Qibṭiyya, Abū ʿUbayda b. al-Jarrāḥ, Muʿādh b. Jabal, Yazīd b. Abī Sufyān, Shuraḥbīl b. Ḥasana, al-Ḥārith b. Hishām b. al-Mughīra, ʿIyāḍ b. Ghanam al-Fihrī, Ṣafiyya bt. ʿAbd al-Muṭṭalib, Bilāl b. Rabāḥ, Zaynab bt. Jaḥsh (the Prophet's wife), Usayd b. Ḥuḍayr, Abū l-Haytham b. al-Tayyihān, Khālid b. al-Walīd, ʿUmar b. al-Khaṭṭāb, Qatāda b. al-Nuʿmān al-Anṣārī, Rabīʿa b. al-Ḥārith b. ʿAbd al-Muṭṭalib, Abū Kabsha (the Prophet's *mawlā*), Rāfiʿ b. ʿUmar al-Ṭāʾī, Surāqa b. Mālik, Umm Ḥarām bt. Milḥān, Ḥāṭib b. Abī Baltaʿa, Abū Usayd al-Sāʿidī, Abū Sufyān b. Ḥarb, ʿAbd al-Raḥmān b. ʿAwf, ʿAbdallāh b. Masʿūd, ʿAbdallāh b. Zayd, Abū Ṭalḥa al-Anṣārī, Abū Dharr al-Ghifārī, Ubayy b. Kaʿb, al-ʿAbbās b. ʿAbd al-Muṭṭalib, al-Miqdād b. al-Aswad, ʿĀmir b. Rabīʿa, ʿUbāda b. al-Ṣāmit, Abū ʿAbs b. Jabr, ʿUthmān b. ʿAffān, al-Mughīra b. al-Akhnas b. Sharīq al-Thaqafī, Ḥudhayfa b. al-Yamān, Salmān al-Fārisī, Qudāma b. Maẓʿūn, Khabbāb b. al-Aratt, Muḥammad b. Abī Bakr, ʿAbdallāh b. Khabbāb b. al-Aratt, Sahl b. Ḥunayf, ʿAlī b. Abī Ṭālib, al-Ashʿath b. Qays, Muʿayqīb b. Abī Fāṭima, Muʿādh b. ʿAfrāʾ, Abū Masʿūd, Kaʿb b. Mālik, Abū Rāfiʿ and Ḥassān b. Thābit. The ones not listed in the *Ṭabaqāt* are Abū l-ʿĀṣ b. al-Rabīʿ, al-Muthannā b. Ḥāritha, al-Mughīra b. al-Akhnas and Muʿādh b. ʿAfrāʾ.

56 Khalīfa b. Khayyāṭ, *Tārīkh* (1985) 125–129. For another example, see the conquest of different regions between 29/649–650 and 34/654–655, pp. 161–168.

57 Khalīfa b. Khayyāṭ, *Tārīkh* (1985) 152.

in 36/656–657.[58] The exception to the strict chronological structure is the Battle of Ṣiffīn, which is introduced at the beginning of 37/657–658 but narrated in detail in 38/658–659, right before the Battle of al-Nahrawān.[59]

4.1.3 The Umayyad Period

The year sections for the Umayyad period are arranged according to chronology and themes or geography. Events pertaining to the same themes or regions are narrated in more or less chronological sequence, often separately from events of other regions. Apart from major events and deaths, there are few exact dates. Instead, chronology is established by narrative sequence or other chronological indications in the reports. The increasing use of the formula 'In this year' (*fī hādhihi l-sana* or *fīhā*) for the Umayyad period shows that Khalīfa's main concern was to place events in the year they occurred and often in their relative chronology, but not necessarily specifying exact dates. For example, the brief section for 42/662–663:

> In it: Ibn ʿĀmir sent ʿAbd al-Raḥmān b. Samura to Sijistān. He was accompanied on that expedition by al-Ḥasan b. Abī l-Ḥasan, al-Muhallab b. Abī Ṣufra and Qaṭarī b. al-Fujāʾa. He conquered Zaranj and other districts of Sijistān.
>
> In it: ʿUqba b. Nāfiʿ raided Ifrīqiya and conquered Ghadāmis, killing many and taking captives.
>
> In it: Ibn ʿĀmir appointed Rāshid b. ʿAmr al-Judaydī as commander over the frontier of al-Hind.
>
> Abū Khālid said: Abū l-Khaṭṭāb said: Rāshid remained there carrying out raids and penetrated deeply into the land of al-Sind.
>
> In it: Ḥabīb b. Maslama al-Fihrī died in Armenia. Ṣafwān b. Umayya, ʿUthmān b. Ṭalḥa and Rukāna b. ʿAbd Yazīd died in the beginning of Muʿāwiya's caliphate. Abū Burda b. Niyār and Rifāʿa b. Rāfiʿ died when Muʿāwiya first came to power. ʿAnbasa b. Abī Sufyān b. Ḥarb led the pilgrimage.[60]

In comparison to the Prophetic and Rāshidūn sections, non-political and non-military events (such as births and deaths) in the Umayyad period are a bit more integrated into the narrative sequence and not always placed at the end of years. This relates to the more frequent use of the 'In it' formula, by which

58 Khalīfa b. Khayyāṭ, *Tārīkh* (1985) 181–191.
59 Khalīfa b. Khayyāṭ, *Tārīkh* (1985) 191–198.
60 Khalīfa b. Khayyāṭ, *Tārīkh* (1985) 205. See Wurtzel, *Khalifa ibn Khayyat's History* 55–56.

otherwise unrelated (political and non-political) events are narrated in one sequence. However, a consistent feature is the notices about pilgrimage leaders at the end of the year sections, which correspond to the place of the pilgrimage in the Hijrī calendar: in the last month of the year, Dhū l-Ḥijja. Because of its close association with the caliph's political authority, the enumeration of pilgrimage leaders in the *Tārīkh* is important. Besides illustrating the caliph's authority and sometimes the factions opposing him,[61] it also shows how the caliph delegated the pilgrimage leadership to his family, governors and in many cases his heir to the caliphate.[62] A striking feature of the Umayyad year sections is the increasing amount of death notices—in total about five hundred, including Companions, Successors and especially *ḥadīth* transmitters. These are placed both at the end of each year section and at the end of some list sections (mentioning those who died during a certain reign). To illustrate the preponderance of *ḥadīth* transmitters, we may look at three years from the beginning, middle and end of the Umayyad period:

> [59/678–679] The following died at the end of Muʿāwiya's reign: Usāma b. Zayd, ʿAmr b. ʿAwf, Ṣafwān b. al-Muʿaṭṭal, ʿUthmān b. Ḥunayf, Mujammiʿ b. Jāriya, Abū Ḥumayd al-Sāʿidī, Khirāsh b. Umayya, Ibn Buḥayna, Qays b. Saʿd b. ʿUbāda, Abū Jahm b. Ḥudhayfa, Maslama b. Mukhallad, Bilāl b. al-Ḥārith al-Muzanī, al-Ḥārith b. al-Azmaʿ al-Hamdānī, Miḥjan b. al-Adraʿ, who lived until [the end of the reign of] Muʿāwiya, Faḍāla b. ʿUbayd and Shaddād b. Aws, who according to some died in 41/661–662.[63]

All except three (Khirāsh, Ibn Buḥayna and Abū Jahm) are also listed in the *Ṭabaqāt*, but Khalīfa only mentions the dates of death for four of them.[64] As corroborated below, it shows that most names in the death notices are found in both the *Tārīkh* and the *Ṭabaqāt*, although some names and dates of deaths are exclusive to the *Tārīkh*. It also shows that the death notices in the Umayyad period are longer than those in the Rāshidūn period, but they still contain

61 A clear example is the second *fitna*, during which Ibn al-Zubayr leads the pilgrimage in Mecca until his defeat, after which Khalīfa concludes, "And al-Ḥajjāj b. Yūsuf led the people in the pilgrimage in year 73/693." In 66/686, Khalīfa also mentions that, "Ibn al-Ḥanafiyya stood with his companions [at ʿArafa during the pilgrimage], Najda stood with his companions and Ibn al-Zubayr stood with the majority of the people (*jamāʿat al-nās*)." Khalīfa b. Khayyāṭ, *Tārīkh* (1985) 263, 270.

62 On the politics surrounding the pilgrimage, see Mcmillan, *Meaning of Mecca*.

63 Khalīfa b. Khayyāṭ, *Tārīkh* (1985) 226–227.

64 Khalīfa b. Khayyāṭ, *Ṭabaqāt* (1993) 32, 81, 101, 102, 149, 153, 154, 157, 167, 168, 181, 250.

mainly names of Companions (in the above example, only Companions).[65] As the chronology proceeds, the proportion of Companions decreases in favour of Successors:

> [93/711–712] In this year, the following died: Saʿīd b. al-Musayyib, ʿUrwa b. al-Zubayr, Abū Salama b. ʿAbd al-Raḥmān b. ʿAwf, Abū Bakr b. ʿAbd al-Raḥmān b. al-Ḥārith b. Hishām, Maḥmūd b. Labīd, Khubayb b. ʿAbdallāh b. al-Zubayr, Jābir b. Zayd in Basra, Tamīm b. Ṭarafa in Kufa and Ibrāhīm b. Yazīd al-Taymī in Wāsiṭ, imprisoned by al-Ḥajjāj. Some say Ibrāhīm died in 94/712–713.[66]

This list from the middle Umayyad period contains names of *ḥadīth* transmitters from the generation of the Successors (in addition to Maḥmūd b. Labīd, who was born during the Prophet's lifetime).[67] All names are also mentioned with their years of death in the *Ṭabaqāt*.[68]

> [130/747–748] In this year, which is 130/747–748, the following died: Muḥammad b. al-Munkadir in Medina, ʿAbdallāh [b. Abī Bakr b. Muḥammad] b. ʿAmr b. Ḥazm in Medina, Yazīd b. Rūmān, Abū l-Zinād and Ismāʿīl b. Abī Ḥakīm—all of them in Medina; Mālik b. Dīnār, Shuʿayb b. al-Ḥabḥāb, Yazīd al-Rishk, Abū l-Ṭayyāḥ, Kulthūm b. Jabr, Ḥabīb al-Muʿallim and Yaḥyā al-Bakkāʾ—all of them in Basra; ʿAbd al-ʿAzīz b. Ṣuhayb, ʿĀmir al-Aḥwal, ʿAlī b. al-Ḥakam al-Bunānī, Ḥumayd b. Qays al-Aʿraj, Yazīd b. ʿAbdallāh b. Qusayṭ in Medina and Abū Wajza al-Saʿdī.[69]

All names except two (Kulthūm and Abū Wajza) are mentioned in the *Ṭabaqāt*, and dates are given for the rest except four (Shuʿayb, Ḥabīb al-Muʿallim, ʿĀmir al-Aḥwal, ʿAlī b. al-Ḥakam), although they are of course listed in the generation to which they belonged.[70] Similar to the previous example, all individuals

---

65 See Ibn ʿAbd al-Barr, *al-Istīʿāb* 1:75, 183, 282, 2:445, 694, 725, 3:1033, 1196, 1262, 1289, 1348, 1362, 1363, 1397, 4:1623, 1633.

66 Khalīfa b. Khayyāṭ, *Tārīkh* (1985) 306.

67 See al-Mizzī, *Tahdhīb* 2:232–233; 4:331–332, 434–437; 8:223–227; 11:66–75; 20:11–25; 27:309–311; 33:112–118, 370–376.

68 Khalīfa b. Khayyāṭ, *Ṭabaqāt* (1993) 263, 268, 361, 415, 420, 421, 422, 425.

69 Khalīfa b. Khayyāṭ, *Tārīkh* (1985) 395.

70 Khalīfa b. Khayyāṭ, *Tārīkh* (1985) 369, 370, 371, 451, 452, 458, 459, 466, 495. Three dates (ʿAbdallāh b. ʿAmr b. Ḥazm, Yazīd b. ʿAbdallāh b. Qusayṭ and Muḥammad b. al-Munkadir) are different from those in the *Tārīkh*. See the *Ṭabaqāt* (1993) 458, 459, 466.

are known *ḥadīth* transmitters found in later biographical dictionaries.[71] In this way, Khalīfa focuses on the *ḥadīth* transmitters within the Muslim community, which shows his particular concern for *ḥadīth* scholarship. The examples above also show the overlap between the *Tārīkh* and the *Ṭabaqāt*, since most names and dates in the *Tārīkh* are also found in the *Ṭabaqāt*. The same is true for Khalīfa's death notices in the ʿAbbāsid period, as outlined below.

4.1.4 The ʿAbbāsid Period

The ʿAbbāsid section follows a pattern similar to the Umayyad one, although the year sections are much shorter. Another difference is that the 'In it' summaries and death notices in the ʿAbbāsid period are more prominent—in total about 350 names of scholars of *ḥadīth* and *fiqh*. For example, 187/802–803:

> ʿUbaydallāh b. al-ʿAbbās b. Muḥammad led the pilgrimage.
>
> In it, the following died: Muʿtamir b. Sulaymān al-Taymī in al-Muḥarram, Bishr b. al-Mufaḍḍal in Jumādā, ʿAlī b. Naṣr al-Jahḍamī and ʿAbd al-Salām b. Ḥarb in Kufa, ʿUmar b. ʿUbayd al-Ṭanāfisī and al-Fuḍayl b. ʿIyāḍ in Mecca.
>
> In it: The Commander of the Believers [Hārūn al-Rashīd] killed Jaʿfar b. Yaḥyā b. Khālid b. Barmak at al-Anbār in the first night of Ṣafar. He also killed Ibrāhīm b. ʿUthmān b. Nahīk in the same year.
>
> In it: The Commander of the Believers, Hārūn, sent his son al-Qāsim on the summer expedition against the Romans along with ʿAbd al-Malik b. Ṣāliḥ and the people of the frontiers. He entered by the pass of al-Ṣafṣāf and reached Qurra. Nikephoros sent a messenger to him offering him to hand over 320 Muslim captives if he would depart. He accepted it and departed.[72]

All those who died in this year except ʿAlī b. Naṣr are also listed in the *Ṭabaqāt*, and dates of death are mentioned for the rest except al-Fuḍayl b. ʿIyāḍ, which further demonstrates the overlap between the *Tārīkh* and the *Ṭabaqāt*.[73] Like the earlier examples, all individuals are *ḥadīth* transmitters.[74] In the ʿAbbāsid section, as in the earlier sections, related events that occurred after each other

---

71 Al-Mizzī, *Tahdhīb* 3:63–66; 5:412–413; 7:384–389; 12:509–511; 14:65–67, 349–352, 476–483; 18:147–149; 20:413–415; 24:200–201; 26:503–509; 27:135–138; 31:533–536; 32:109–112, 122–123, 160–161, 177–180, 201–205.

72 Khalīfa b. Khayyāṭ, *Tārīkh* (1985) 458.

73 Khalīfa b. Khayyāṭ, *Ṭabaqāt* (1993) 289, 387, 504.

74 Al-Mizzī, *Tahdhīb* 4:147–151; 18:66–70; 21:157–159, 454–457; 23:281–300; 28:250–256.

are grouped together and arranged more or less chronologically. Some sections begin with what seems to have been considered the most important political events (e.g. successions, depositions and revolts), but others simply begin with the pilgrimage leader or death notices—even if major revolts occurred.[75]

The above overview shows that the structure of individual year sections differs depending on the period under discussion. A striking difference is that the section for the Prophet's lifetime is based on exact dates to a larger extent than the sections for the subsequent caliphates, in which exact dates are less common (and are mainly found only for major events and deaths).[76] Moreover, the year sections for the post-Prophetic period—when major events occurred simultaneously in different regions—are sometimes thematically or geographically divided, although chronology is the main organisational principle throughout the work. Khalīfa does not systematically begin the year sections with the most important or controversial event of each year. Although some sections clearly begin with the most important events,[77] it is not uncommon that such events are preceded by earlier minor events. For example, the Battles of Badr and Uḥud, the Treaty of al-Ḥudaybiya, the conquest of Mecca and the Battles of al-Yamāma, al-Qādisiyya, Jalūlāʾ and Qudayd were all probably considered among the most important events in their respective years, but Khalīfa narrates them in chronological sequence, after other events that he knew occurred earlier.[78] He narrates, for example, about many minor expeditions before Badr and Uḥud, about the deaths of Persian leaders before the Treaty of al-Ḥudaybiya and about the plague in Syria, ʿUmar's dismissal of al-Mughīra b. Shuʿba and minor conquests in Iraq before the Battle of Jalūlāʾ. Hence the structure of individual year sections cannot be taken as a consistent indication of Khalīfa's ranking of events by importance. Instead, the main criterion of arrangement seems to be chronology (albeit sometimes divided into thematic or geographic subsections) and thereafter the relative importance of events—possibly if the chronology is unknown or less important for the relation between events.

75 E.g. Khalīfa b. Khayyāṭ, *Tārīkh* (1985) 451–456, 468.

76 See above.

77 See e.g. the Farewell Pilgrimage, the killing of ʿUthmān, the Battle of Ṣiffīn, the Battle of al-Ḥarra and the revolt of Ibn al-Ashʿath. Khalīfa b. Khayyāṭ, *Tārīkh* (1985) 94, 168–177, 191–192, 236–252, 280–288.

78 Khalīfa b. Khayyāṭ, *Tārīkh* (1985) 57–61, 67–73, 81–82, 87, 107–115, 131–132, 136–138, 391–393.

4.2 *List Sections: Structure and Development of the Caliphate*

This section discusses the list sections at the end of caliphal reigns. It is divided according to the different periods covered in the *Tārīkh*. It is suggested that the list sections had two important functions besides their main purpose of structuring available administrative material: first, to provide non-narrative data within a caliphal rather than annalistic framework and, second, to illustrate the continuity and coherence of the caliphal organisation over time. The section also compares Khalīfa's lists with those of al-Yaʿqūbī and al-Ṭabarī, which shows that Khalīfa's lists are more detailed and systematic than the others.

4.2.1 Prophetic Period

The list section for the Prophet's appointees sets the model for subsequent list sections. It begins by listing his deputies in Medina during various expeditions and continues with his governors and *zakāt* administrators in other places. The next entry lists his messengers (*rusul*, sing. *rasūl*) to various leaders of both Arab tribes and major polities, including the rulers of Persia (Kisrā), Rome (Qayṣar) and Abyssinia (al-Najāshī). Khalīfa then includes a separate list of other *zakāt* administrators who were made responsible for different tribes in Arabia and another list of the Prophet's scribes (*kuttāb*, sing. *kātib*). The list section concludes with a list of various appointees, including those in charge of the expenditures (*nafaqāt*) and the seal (*khātam*), as well as the Prophet's treasurer, his servants, his *muʾadhdhin*s and his guards.[79]

4.2.2 Rāshidūn Period

The sections for the Rāshidūn caliphs follow a similar pattern, but the number and types of appointments increase with the territorial expansion and institutional development of the caliphate. Governors and *zakāt* administrators are listed for the main conquered regions: at the time of Abū Bakr, in al-Baḥrayn, ʿUmān, Yemen, Mecca, al-Ṭāʾif, al-Yamāma and Syria; at the time of ʿUmar, in Mecca, Medina, Yemen, al-Baḥrayn, ʿUmān, Basra, al-Yamāma, al-Ṭāʾif, the Syrian regions, Egypt and al-Jazīra, including Armenia and Adharbayjān; at the time of ʿUthmān, in Mecca, Medina, Basra, Kufa, Egypt, Syria, Yemen, Khurāsān, Sijistān, al-Sind and al-Baḥrayn; and at the time of ʿAlī in Khurāsān, Sijistān, al-Sind, al-Baḥrayn, Yemen, al-Jazīra, Mecca, Medina, Egypt, Basra and Kufa. The lists of governors are usually followed by shorter lists of judges (*quḍāt*): at the time of Abū Bakr, in Medina (ʿUmar b. al-Khaṭṭāb being the only judge), and at the time of the subsequent three caliphs, in Basra and Kufa. In addi-

79 Khalīfa b. Khayyāṭ, *Tārīkh* (1985) 96–99.

tion to these, the sections also include a wide range of other appointments, a range that increases as the chronology proceeds: the scribe (*kātib*), chamberlain (*ḥājib*), treasurer (*ʿalā bayt al-māl*), secretary of the military registers (*dawāwīn*, sing. *dīwān*) of Basra and Kufa, commander of the summer campaign (*al-ṣāʾifa*) and commander of the security forces (*ṣāḥib al-shuraṭ*). Unlike the sections for ʿUmar, ʿUthmān and ʿAlī, the one on Abū Bakr's appointees also includes his *muʾadhdhin* and his "administrator of all his affairs" (*ʿalā amrihi kullihi*).[80] The order of these other appointments differs between the lists of each caliph.

It is noteworthy that the common notion in the historical tradition of ʿUmar as the economic and administrative organiser of the early Muslim polity is not very prominent in Khalīfa's *Tārīkh*.[81] Khalīfa reports about ʿUmar's introduction of the Hijrī calendar and briefly notes the *dīwān*s of Basra and Kufa, but otherwise Khalīfa's account of ʿUmar's reign is not much different in that respect from the accounts of other long-reigning caliphs. Rather, the regularity of the Rāshidūn list sections seems to assert the overall continuity throughout the reigns of Abū Bakr, ʿUmar, ʿUthmān and ʿAlī. This also stands in contrast to Shīʿī accusations of innovations and nepotism against ʿUthmān; although the list of ʿUthmān's governors in the *Tārīkh* notes that he appointed some of his relatives, Khalīfa does not explicitly highlight this point.[82] In terms of administrative practices, the reigns of the Rāshidūn caliphs are narrated in a mode of continuity, emphasising the gradual development of the Muslim polity from its Prophetic origins.

4.2.3 Umayyad Period

The Umayyad list sections contain a wider range of governorates and offices than previous sections. In addition to the regions listed from the time of ʿUthmān and ʿAlī, the list sections from ʿAbd al-Malik's time onwards also include North Africa, Armenia and Adharbayjān. The lists of judges, however, are limited to Basra, Kufa and Medina, except in the list section of ʿAbd al-Malik's judges, which includes his judge in Syria. The main difference from the Prophetic and Rāshidūn periods is the increasing number and types of offices in the Umayyad administration. In different variations and combinations, the new offices include correspondence (*al-rasāʾil*), commander of the guard (*ṣāḥib ḥaras*), the minor seal (*al-khātam al-ṣaghīr*), the caliphal seal (*khātam*

80 Khalīfa b. Khayyāṭ, *Tārīkh* (1985) 123.
81 On the image of ʿUmar in the early historical tradition, see El-Hibri, *Parable and politics* 77–121, 262–278. See also Noth and Conrad, *Early Arabic* 82–84.
82 See Khalīfa b. Khayyāṭ, *Tārīkh* (1985) 178.

al-khilāfa), finance and army rolls (*al-kharāj wa-l-jund*), multiple treasuries and storehouses (*buyūt al-amwāl wa-l-khazā'in*) and slaves (*al-raqīq*).[83] At the end of the Umayyad period, Khalīfa also begins to occasionally mention who was appointed to lead the prayers in Basra and Kufa.[84] In contrast to the Prophetic, Rāshidūn and 'Abbāsid sections, Khalīfa also includes a number of list sections for major Umayyad-era governors of Iraq and the East.[85] It is also worth noting that Khalīfa includes a list section for the appointees of 'Abdallāh b. al-Zubayr during his caliphate (r. 64–73/684–692), containing the names of his chamberlain (*ḥājib*) and his "administrator of all affairs" (*'alā amrihi kullihi*).[86]

4.2.4 'Abbāsid Period

The lists of 'Abbāsid governors cover more or less the same geographical range as the Umayyad section, and the lists of judges are similarly limited to Basra, Kufa and Medina. In the case of Hārūn al-Rashīd, the list of judges also includes his own chief judge.[87] The exceptions are the sections concluding the reigns of al-Amīn and al-Ma'mūn, which are considerably shorter than the earlier ones,[88] and the reigns of the last two caliphs in the *Tārīkh*, al-Mu'taṣim and al-Wāthiq, which lack lists altogether.[89] The lists in the 'Abbāsid period introduce a few new offices: 'conquest correspondence' (*rasā'il al-futūḥ*), 'register of the Khurāsānī army rolls and the state land and its boundaries' (*dīwān jund Khurāsān wa-ṣawāfī al-arḍ wa-aḥwāzihā*), 'register of the army rolls' (*zimām al-jund*) and different security forces (*al-aḥdāth, al-ma'ūna*) at the time of al-Manṣūr; the one in charge of the 'court of grievances' (*al-maẓālim*) at the time of al-Mahdī; and 'vizier and administrator of all affairs' (*wazīruhu ṣāḥib amrihi kullihi*) at the time of Mūsā al-Hādī.[90] The overall order of the offices follows the same pattern as the Umayyad period—beginning with pilgrimage and security forces, and ending with guards and chamberlains.

---

83 Khalīfa b. Khayyāṭ, *Tārīkh* (1985) 228, 299, 319, 351, 362.
84 Khalīfa b. Khayyāṭ, *Tārīkh* (1985) 294, 351, 358, 428, 432, 440.
85 Khalīfa b. Khayyāṭ, *Tārīkh* (1985) 211–212, 308–313, 317, 335, 350–351, 368, 382–383.
86 Khalīfa b. Khayyāṭ, *Tārīkh* (1985) 269–270. On Ibn al-Zubayr's caliphate in the *Tārīkh*, see Chapter 8.
87 Khalīfa b. Khayyāṭ, *Tārīkh* (1985) 464–465.
88 Khalīfa b. Khayyāṭ, *Tārīkh* (1985) 468, 475–476.
89 Ṣaddām's list of material that is preserved from al-Tustarī's recension, but absent in Baqī's, contains one report on al-Ma'mūn's governor of Medina, but no information about the governors of al-Amīn, al-Mu'taṣim, al-Wāthiq and al-Mutawakkil. Ṣaddām, *Tārīkh Khalīfa* 128–133.
90 Khalīfa b. Khayyāṭ, *Tārīkh* (1985) 419, 428, 432, 436, 440, 442, 447.

4.2.5 Discussion: Khalīfa and al-Yaʿqūbī

Khalīfa's list sections for the different periods are more regular than his year entries, which differ in length and form between the Prophetic, Rāshidūn, Umayyad and ʿAbbāsid periods. The types and number of offices naturally increase with the territorial expansion and development of the caliphate, but the overall arrangement of the list sections remains constant. This standardised structure of the list sections and the continuity between them foreground the regularity of the caliphal organisation over time; the lists remain roughly the same despite recurring civil wars and dynastic transitions.

Khalīfa's lists can be compared with al-Yaʿqūbī's administrative lists in his *Tārīkh*, which are also placed at the end of caliphal reigns.[91] In contrast to Khalīfa's lists, al-Yaʿqūbī's lists are shorter and are limited to 'the persons with the greatest influence over the caliph' (*al-ghālib ʿalayhi*), leading jurisprudents (*fuqahāʾ*), leaders of pilgrimage, chamberlains, commanders of the guard and commanders of the security forces. In the period of the first three caliphs, he also mentions local governors (*ʿummāl*) and, in the ʿAbbāsid period, he occasionally adds companions and courtiers (*summār wa-julāsāʾ*).[92] Al-Yaʿqūbī does not foreground the continuity of administrative offices from the time of the Prophet to the later caliphs to the same extent as Khalīfa. His lists at the end of the Prophetic period briefly mention his governors and *zakāt* administrators, but they focus more on other aspects, such as his scribes, wives, freed slaves, personal possessions, sermons, sayings, character and physical description, 'those who resemble him' (*al-mushbihūn bihi*) and ancestors.[93] By contrast, Khalīfa's lists pertain exclusively to the Prophet's appointees and follow the same pattern as the later lists, although some of the offices differ.[94] Moreover, it is not until Muʿāwiya's reign that al-Yaʿqūbī lists all the aforementioned six offices, which he then consistently lists in the Umayyad and ʿAbbāsid sections. Before that, the lists at the end of the reigns of Abū Bakr, ʿUmar and ʿUthmān are limited to governors, jurisprudents and pilgrimage leaders, as well as, in the case of Abū Bakr, his chamberlain and ʿUmar as the person with the greatest influence over him (*al-ghālib ʿalayhi*).[95] Unlike the lists of al-Yaʿqūbī, Khalīfa's lists establish a clear structure from the time of the Prophet and the

---

91 Al-Yaʿqūbī, *Tārīkh* 2:26, 54–55, 74, 120–121, 150–154, 169, 187, 202–204, 215–216, 224–225, 235–236, 242–243, 259–261, 265–267, 281–282, 296–299, 329–333, 344–348, 351–352, 379–383, 395–396, 429, 439–440, 446, 457–458.

92 Al-Yaʿqūbī, *Tārīkh* 2:26, 54–55, 74, 296, 330.

93 Al-Yaʿqūbī, *Tārīkh* 1:401–413, 446–453.

94 Khalīfa b. Khayyāṭ, *Tārīkh* (1985) 96–99.

95 Al-Yaʿqūbī, *Tārīkh* 2:25–26, 54–55, 74.

Rāshidūn caliphs that continues throughout the Umayyad and ʿAbbāsid periods, which highlights the continuous development from the origins in Medina. This corresponds to Khalīfa's early Sunnī perspective on the political history of Islam, especially the history of the first four caliphs, which can be contrasted with al-Yaʿqūbī's 'rejectionist,' or Rāfiḍī, Shīʿī historical views on this period.[96]

The regularity of Khalīfa's list sections also creates a causal narrative of the development of the caliphate from the relatively simple but well-organised polity in Medina to the massive polities of the Umayyads and the ʿAbbāsids: the foundational Medinan model was expanded, step-by-step and reign-by-reign, by the caliphs and their appointees. Within this scheme, the individual list entries outline the chronological succession of appointees to governorates, judiciaries and other posts. The list sections thereby complement the political history of the year sections and illustrate each caliph's governmental policies of appointments, dismissals and introductions of new administrative offices. For example, the lists of judges and various other offices at the end of Muʿāwiya's reign:

> **Judges during Muʿāwiya's caliphate**
> (Khalīfa said:)
>
> **Basra:** ʿUmayra b. Yathribī al-Ḍabbī was appointed by Ibn ʿĀmir. ʿImrān b. Ḥuṣayn was then appointed, but he asked to be discharged from his duties, so Ibn ʿĀmir dismissed him. Ziyād appointed ʿĀṣim b. Faḍāla, the brother of ʿAbdallāh b. Faḍāla al-Laythī, and Zurāra b. Awfā al-Ḥarashī. Shurayḥ served under Ziyād as judge of Basra for a year. During the caliphate of Muʿāwiya, Zurāra b. Awfā served as judge for ʿUbaydallāh b. Ziyād. ʿAbd al-Raḥmān b. Udhayna also served as judge for him.
>
> **Kufa:** Shurayḥ served as judge until Ziyād transferred him with himself to Basra. Masrūq b. al-Ajdaʿ served after Shurayḥ until he returned.
>
> **Medina:** Marwan appointed ʿAbdallāh b. Nawfal b. al-Ḥārith as judge and he served until Marwān's dismissal in 48/668–669. Saʿīd b. al-ʿĀṣ was then appointed governor and he appointed Abū Salama b. ʿAbd al-Raḥmān b. ʿAwf as judge. He served as judge until the dismissal of Saʿīd b. al-ʿĀṣ. Then Marwān b. al-Ḥakam was reappointed as governor in year 54/673–674 and he appointed Muṣʿab b. ʿAbd al-Raḥmān b. ʿAwf, who served as judge until the dismissal of Marwān in 57/677 at the end of Dhū

96 On al-Yaʿqūbī's Shīʿī historical views, see Anthony, Was Ibn Wāḍiḥ al-Yaʿqūbī a Shiʿite historian?

> l-Qaʿda. Then al-Walīd b. ʿUtba b. Abī Sufyān was appointed governor and he appointed Ibn Zamʿa al-ʿĀmirī, who served as judge until Muʿāwiya died.
>
> (Khalīfa said:)
>
> **His secretary of correspondence:** ʿUbayd b. Aws al-Ghassānī.
>
> **Administrator of the *dīwān* and all his affairs (*ʿalā al-dīwān wa-amrihi kullihi*):** Sarjūn b. Manṣūr al-Rūmī.
>
> **His chamberlain:** Abū Ayyūb, his *mawlā*.
>
> **Commander of the security forces:** Yazīd b. al-Ḥurr, his *mawlā*. He died and Qays b. Ḥamza al-Hamdānī was appointed, but later dismissed. Dhuhl b. ʿAmr al-ʿUdhrī was then appointed.
>
> Muʿāwiya was the first to create the office of the commander of the guard (*ṣāḥib ḥaras*) and the first to institute the *dīwān* of the seal (*al-khātam*).
>
> **Commander of the guard:** al-Mukhtār, a *mawlā* of Ḥimyar.
>
> **Secretary of the seal:** ʿAbdallāh b. ʿAmr al-Ḥimyarī.[97]

This example shows how Khalīfa's list sections complement the political narrative with information about the internal politics and developments in the caliphal administration—for instance, the frequent change of judges following the change of governors, and Muʿāwiya's introduction of two new offices. The list sections for the Umayyad period, in particular, are often lengthy and provide detailed narrations in themselves. An example is the account of governors of Khurāsān during ʿAbd al-Malik's reign:

> **Khurāsān:** In the year of Muṣʿab's death, ʿAbd al-Malik wrote to ʿAbdallāh b. Khāzim concerning his governorship over Khurāsān. He sent the letter with Sawra b. Abjar al-Dārimī. Ibn Khāzim said to him, "If I did not abhor sowing dissension between Banū Tamīm and Sulaym, I would kill you. Instead, I will force you to eat the letter." So he ate it. Then ʿAbd al-Malik wrote to Bukayr b. Wishāḥ al-Ṣarīmī, "If you kill him or expel him from Khurāsān, you shall be the new governor." Bukayr killed Ibn Khāzim and served as governor until the arrival of Umayya b. ʿAbdallāh b. Khālid b. Asīd, when he was dismissed. Umayya was appointed, but later dismissed. Then al-Muhallab b. Abī Ṣufra was appointed in 79/698–699, but died in 82/701–702. He designated his son Yazīd, who was retained by ʿAbd al-

97 Khalīfa b. Khayyāṭ, *Tārīkh* (1985) 227–228. See Wurtzel, *Khalifa ibn Khayyat's History* 88–89.

> Malik for two years or more. Then Khurāsān was added to the jurisdiction of al-Ḥajjāj and he appointed Qutayba b. Muslim, who arrived in 86/705 before the death of ʿAbd al-Malik.[98]

Such narrative accounts are found in many list sections, although their length depends on the length of the reign.[99] Unlike al-Yaʿqūbī, al-Ṭabarī and many other historians, Khalīfa narrates very little biographical material about the caliphs.[100] However, the list sections provide detailed accounts of the high-level governmental and administrative developments during their reigns. The list sections at the end of reigns also enabled Khalīfa to arrange historical material non-chronologically, thereby avoiding the problem of not knowing the exact dates of administrative appointments. Exact dates are therefore less common in the list sections than in the year sections. Instead, the sequences of successive appointments to various posts provide a relative chronology, as in the examples above.

5 Conclusion

This chapter has outlined three aspects pertaining to the structure and arrangement of Khalīfa's *Tārīkh* as transmitted by Baqī b. Makhlad: (1) the concept of chronography in its title and introduction, (2) the general structure of the work and (3) the internal structure of the year and list sections. It has been suggested, first, that Khalīfa's title and introduction serve two main purposes: to introduce and justify chronography as a scholarly occupation to an audience of mainly *ḥadīth* scholars and to outline the chronological format and political-administrative scope of the work.

Second, it has shown that although Khalīfa's *Tārīkh* is an annalistic history (*tārīkh ʿalā al-sinīn*), there are some tendencies to a caliphal chronology within the main annalistic structure of the text. It has been argued that this combined annalistic-caliphal chronology, most importantly, accommodates the main objectives of political and administrative history but at the same time foregrounds the continuity of the caliphate throughout the Rāshidūn, Umayyad and ʿAbbāsid periods—despite times of civil war and inadequate leadership. In contrast to al-Yaʿqūbī and al-Ṭabarī, who similarly add administrative material at the end of reigns and years respectively, Khalīfa provides

98 Khalīfa b. Khayyāṭ, *Tārīkh* (1985) 294–295. See Wurtzel, *Khalifa ibn Khayyat's History* 163.

99 E.g. Khalīfa b. Khayyāṭ, *Tārīkh* (1985) 153–156, 310–313, 317–319, 430–436.

100 See Chapter 7.

longer and much more detailed lists of the different administrative positions and traces their origins from the time of the Prophet Muḥammad in Medina. Moreover, this structural emphasis on continuity fits the rest of Khalīfa's narrative and his pragmatic perspective on the development of the caliphate, as discussed further in Chapters 7 and 8.

Third, the chapter has shown that events in the year sections are sometimes arranged according to chronology and sometimes according to themes, geography or importance. It has also shown that Khalīfa's death notices in the year sections are concerned primarily with *ḥadīth* transmitters, whom Khalīfa singles out as the defining members of the Muslim community. Moreover, it has discussed how the structure and repetitiveness of the list sections highlight the continuity of the caliphate over time and impose order upon the sometimes turbulent history of the early community—to a greater extent than al-Yaʿqūbī's similar list sections. The chapter has thereby provided a foundation for the examination in Chapters 7 and 8 of four major narrative themes in Khalīfa's *Tārīkh*: prophethood, community, hegemony and leadership.

CHAPTER 7

Themes I: Prophethood, Community and Hegemony

1 Introduction

The following two chapters examine some of the main themes in Khalīfa's *Tārīkh*, as transmitted by Baqī b. Makhlad, in comparison to other *akhbār* histories from the second/eighth and third/ninth centuries. This chapter treats the themes of prophethood, community and hegemony. Chapter 8 treats the themes of leadership and civil war (*fitna*). The selection is based on Donner's development of Noth's notion of themes in the early historical tradition, which refers to "those subjects about which a great number of accounts are collected."[1] Donner is concerned primarily with the four themes' origins and developments among the early Muslims (until c. the mid-second/eighth century), but his outline is mainly based on third/ninth- and fourth/tenth-century works.[2] It is, therefore, useful for identifying key subjects and areas of historical enquiry that remained important for the historians of the third/ninth centuries onwards.

The centrality of these themes in early Islamic historiography allows for broad comparisons between Khalīfa's *Tārīkh* and the wider historical tradition. This thematic approach to its content (as opposed to case studies of a few events) also facilitates an analysis of the work as a whole and the relations between its different sections.[3] Focus lies on Khalīfa's selection of content and presentation of key themes or episodes in the historical tradition. On this basis, the present chapter argues that Khalīfa's approach to these themes is mainly characterised by (1) the relatively concise chronological format, (2) the almost exclusive focus on politics and administration, (3) the caliphate-centred perspective and (4) the underlying Basran and early Sunnī historical outlook. These characteristics can be found to various degrees in other early histories, but taken together they are the main points that determine and distinguish Khalīfa's narration of the aforementioned themes. In other words, it is not

1 Noth and Conrad, *Early Arabic* 26–61; Donner, *Narratives* 127, 144–202.
2 As Donner acknowledges in *Narratives* 125.
3 Compare with the notion of al-Ṭabarī's *Tārīkh* a single narrative unit and its importance for analysing the work, as noted by El-Hibri, Unity of Tabari's chronicle; Donner, *Narratives* 127–131; Mårtensson, Discourse 297, *Tabari* 36–39.

 | DOI:10.1163/9789004383173_009

mainly the information that distinguishes Khalīfa's *Tārīkh* but rather Khalīfa's particular chronological presentation, his historical perspective and his exclusive focus on the political-administrative history of the Muslim community—at the expense of other common subjects in the wider historical tradition. Hence it seems that Khalīfa compiled the *Tārīkh* as a critical chronological handbook for his fellow *ḥadīth* scholars, many of whom already shared his early Sunnī outlook and, to various extents, also his interest in chronological information. Finally, it must be noted that this analysis is based on the notion of Khalīfa being responsible for at least the general form and content of Baqī b. Makhlad's extant recension of the *Tārīkh*, as discussed in Chapter 1, which also means acknowledging the possibility that some material was omitted, abridged or otherwise altered in the course of transmission—by Baqī or someone after him in the *isnād* of the extant recension.

2 Prophethood

The question of prophethood (*nubuwwa*) was one of the main themes that shaped the historical tradition.[4] By the late second/eighth century—some generations after *maghāzī-sīra* pioneers such as ʿUrwa b. al-Zubayr (d. 94/712–713) and al-Zuhrī (d. 124/742)—Muslim scholars had long concerned themselves with compiling accounts of the Prophet Muḥammad's life. This also involved the history of earlier Prophets and their communities, mentioned in the Qurʾān and explained or expanded upon in collections of *ḥadīth* and *tafsīr*.[5]

The theme of prophethood is important in Khalīfa's *Tārīkh*, but it is presented differently from most other early *ḥadīth* works and *akhbār* histories. Khalīfa focuses exclusively on the post-*hijra* political and administrative history of the Prophet's life. Thus the *Tārīkh* contains almost no material about Prophetic characteristics (*shamāʾil*), miracles (*muʿjizāt*), signs or proofs of prophethood (*dalāʾil al-nubuwwa*) or the long succession of Prophets and Messengers before the Prophet Muḥammad, which are common in the wider tra-

4 Donner, *Narratives* 147–159; Adang, *Muslim writers* 1–22, 139–191; Rubin, *Eye of the beholder* esp. 5–17, 103–124. The Islamic tradition usually differentiates between Prophets (*anbiyāʾ*, sing. *nabī*) and Messengers (*rusul*, sing. *rasūl*), depending on the type of their missions and revelations, but 'prophethood' is here used in the generic sense of receiving and conveying divine revelation. For a summary of some classical views, see ʿIyāḍ b. Mūsā al-Yaḥṣubī, *al-Shifā* 1:347–348.

5 Donner, *Narratives* 147–159; Horovitz, *Earliest biographies*; Kister, *Sīrah* literature; Jones, *Maghāzī* literature; Robinson, *Islamic historiography* 20–30; Schoeler, *Biography of Muḥammad* 20–37; Görke, Relationship between *maghāzī* and *ḥadīth*.

dition.[6] This does not mean, however, that Khalīfa lacked interest in these subjects; his *ḥadīths* in al-Bukhārī's *Ṣaḥīḥ* include narrations pertaining to beliefs, earlier Prophets, signs of prophethood and the hereafter.[7] Rather, the focus on the Prophet's role as political leader shows that Khalīfa differentiated *tārīkh* compilation from general *ḥadīth* transmission (including core subjects such as law and belief) and singled out politics and administration as the focus of his *Tārīkh*.

According to Donner, the early historical compilers dealt with prophethood by two main themes: (1) Qur'ān-related narratives about earlier Prophets and (2) accounts about the Prophet Muḥammad's status as a Prophet, the nature of his mission and his place in the long chain of God's Messengers.[8] The following sections compare Khalīfa's treatment of these themes with the wider tradition.

2.1 *Earlier Prophets and Communities*

Narratives of past Prophets and communities (mentioned in the Qur'ān) figure frequently in second/eighth- and third/ninth-century *akhbār* histories, although much of it was collected and used earlier as a part of *tafsīr*.[9] This material was later also collected in separate works on *qiṣaṣ al-anbiyā'* ('stories of the Prophets') or included in biographies of the Prophet Muḥammad and universal histories. Such narratives often involved material about pre-Islamic Arabia, which was important in articulating Arab identity and historical memory in the post-conquest societies.[10] In addition, at least by the late third/ninth century, many universal histories included stories about earlier kings and empires, in particular pre-Islamic Persian rulers.[11] Early *ḥadīth* collections also contain material about previous Prophets, but, unlike the *akhbār* histories, these accounts are generally shorter, transmitted separately and not synthesised to fit a certain narrative or chronology.[12] In both fields, however, these accounts

6 This is also the case for the material pertaining to the Prophetic period that Ibn 'Asākir transmits from Khalīfa and that is not found in Baqī's recension. See Ibn 'Asākir, *Tārīkh madīnat Dimashq* 3:152, 211, 4:186, 14:115; Ṣaddām, *Tārīkh Khalīfa* 57–60.

7 See Khalīfa's *ḥadīths* in al-Bukhārī's *Ṣaḥīḥ* in Appendix, nos. 1, 3, 4, 5, 13, 14, 18, 20, 21.

8 Donner, *Narratives* 147–159.

9 See Donner, *Narratives* 154.

10 E.g. Ibn Hishām, *Sīra* 1:11–127. See also Webb's *Creating Arab origins* 3, in which he tries to argue for "the likelihood that the pre-Islamic Arabian Peninsula was in fact 'Arab-less', and that Islam catalysed the formation of Arab identity as it is familiar today."

11 E.g. al-Ya'qūbī, *Tārīkh* 1:112–327; al-Dīnawarī, *al-Akhbār al-ṭiwāl* 2–111; al-Ṭabarī, *Tārīkh* 1:597–966. See also Savant, *New Muslims* 31–60, 137–169; Dūrī, *The rise of historical writing* 57–60; Noth and Conrad, *Early Arabic* 39.

12 See Ibn Abī Shayba, *Muṣannaf* 11:63–99, 12:133–152; al-Bukhārī, *Ṣaḥīḥ* 4:131–177, 6:16–181. Compare these with, e.g. al-Ṭabarī, *Tārīkh* 1:86–741.

indicate the Prophet Muḥammad's coming Prophetic mission, locate the Muslims in the longer chain of Prophetic communities, clarify Qur'ānic stories and provide guidance by the examples of earlier Prophets.[13]

These themes are less apparent in Khalīfa's *Tārīkh* than many other histories. The only accounts of pre-Islamic history in Khalīfa's *Tārīkh* are found in the introduction, where Khalīfa narrates four reports about calendar systems in earlier communities. According to the first report, mankind have always had some way of recording dates; the first people dated from Adam's descent from the Garden, then from Noah's Prophetic mission, then from the Flood, then from the attempt to burn Abraham and then the Children of Ishmael (Banū Ismāʿīl—i.e. the Arabs descending from Ishmael, the son of Abraham) dated from the building of the Kaʿba.[14] The first report thereby prepares for the Prophet Muḥammad and his community by referring to well-known events mentioned in the Qur'ān and by tracing the line of previous Prophetic communities—here, in relation to systems of dating, which is the main subject of the *Tārīkh*. In the second report, Khalīfa narrates:

> Muḥammad b. Muʿāwiya reported to me from Abū ʿUbayda Maʿmar b. al-Muthannā; he said: The Persians have always had a calendar system by which they know their affairs. The calendar system of their reckoning up until the present day is since Yazdajird b. Shahrayār became king, and that was in year 16/637 after the emigration of the Messenger of God (ṣ). It is the people's calendar system today.[15]

The scope is here extended to the Persians. While the other reports present the Muslim community as the religious successor to the earlier Prophetic communities, this report also highlight its political replacing of the Persian Empire of the Sāsānids. The theme of pre-Islamic Persia is prominent in the wider tradition, as noted above, but Khalīfa's references only concern chronology and the deaths or successions of leaders, in line with his particular concerns. The third report mentions that the Jews (Children of Israel—Banū Isrāʾīl) had another calendar based on the years of Dhū l-Qarnayn, as named in the Qur'ān, which thus refers to Alexander the Great and the Seleucid era.[16] It is noteworthy that there is no mention of the Christians' calendar system—possibly because there was no single 'Christian' calendar, but rather a range of different ones followed

13 Donner, *Narratives* 154–159.
14 Khalīfa b. Khayyāṭ, *Tārīkh* (1985) 50.
15 Khalīfa b. Khayyāṭ, *Tārīkh* (1985) 50.
16 Khalīfa b. Khayyāṭ, *Tārīkh* (1985) 50.

by Christian peoples such as the Seleucid era, the *anno mundi* and the regnal years of the Roman emperors.[17] The fourth report outlines the pre-Islamic Arabic calendar systems among the Children of Ishmael (Banū Ismāʿīl) until the Muslims began to reckon dates from the Prophet Muḥammad's emigration. It concludes with the notion that "the Arabs also had a calendar system (*wa-qad kāna lil-ʿarab ayḍan tārīkh*),"[18] which seems to reflect the genealogists' distinction between the northern tribes descended from Ishmael via ʿAdnān (also referred to as *al-ʿarab al-mustaʿriba* or 'the Arabised Arabs') and the southern tribes descended from Qaḥṭān (also referred to as *al-ʿarab al-ʿāriba* or 'the Arab Arabs').[19]

Altogether, Khalīfa's introduction emphasises the relationship of chronography and calendar systems to the identity of communities in a way that distinguishes the Muslim community from the earlier ones (with their own calendar systems) but that at the same time locates it as their successor. Khalīfa's pre-Islamic section is substantially shorter than the sections in 'world histories,' such as those of al-Dīnawarī, al-Yaʿqūbī and al-Ṭabarī. It is also shorter than Ibn Ḥabīb's extensive section (about a third of his *Tārīkh*) on pre-Islamic Prophets.[20] In contrast to these, Khalīfa's exclusive focus on calendar systems illustrates his particular concern with chronology, which is the only thing he reports about pre-Islamic history.

2.2 *The Prophethood of Muḥammad*

The second sub-theme is the prophethood of the Prophet Muḥammad. It addresses his status as a Prophet, the nature of his Prophetic mission and his place in the long chain of God's Prophets and Messengers.[21] Some examples of subjects on this theme are miracles (*muʿjizāt*), circumstances of revelation (*asbāb al-nuzūl*) and signs of prophethood (*dalāʾil al-nubuwwa*), all of which are found in different forms in early *ḥadīth* collections and *akhbār* histories.[22]

---

17 See al-Bīrūnī, *al-Āthār al-Bāqiya* 13–36; Palmer, *Seventh century* xxiii–xxxv; Debié, Syriac historiography esp. 99–103.

18 Khalīfa b. Khayyāṭ, *Tārīkh* (1985) 50.

19 See Fisher and Irvine, Kaḥṭān; Webb, *Creating Arab origins* 84–116. However, Khalīfa's *Ṭabaqāt* suggests that he held that all Arabs, including both ʿAdnānīs and Qaḥṭānīs, descend from Abraham and Ishmael, although the ʿAdnānīs and the Qaḥṭānīs constitute separate groups. See Webb's discussion in *Creating Arab origins* 103–104; Khalīfa b. Khayyāṭ, *Ṭabaqāt* (1993) 26, 125.

20 Ibn Ḥabīb, *Tārīkh* 17–75.

21 Donner, *Narratives* 149.

22 See e.g. the accounts of the first revelation in Ibn Abī Shayba, *Muṣannaf* 13:204–208; al-Bukhārī, *Ṣaḥīḥ* 1:6–10; Ibn Hishām, *Sīra* 1:263–274; al-Ṭabarī, *Tārīkh* 1:1146–1156.

Besides these, there are also accounts of the Prophet Muḥammad's legislative and political roles in the community, but they are treated below under the theme of community.

Khalīfa's *Tārīkh* contains no reports about the beginning of prophethood and the revelations in Mecca, unlike most early works with accounts of the life of the Prophet.[23] The only exception is a short section on the birth of the Prophet, his age at the first revelations and the length of his Prophetic mission in Mecca and Medina respectively.[24] Instead, the main narrative of Khalīfa's *Tārīkh* is limited to the years of the Hijrī calendar. This can be explained by Khalīfa's focus on the political and administrative history of the Muslim community, whose political organisation was established in 1/622–623 in Medina. The omission of the Meccan period thereby indicates that Khalīfa's main concern when compiling the *Tārīkh* was the history of the Muslim community as a political entity, rather than the complete history of Islam from its origins in Mecca. It also relates to Khalīfa's strict adherence to the Hijrī calendar and perhaps the absence of a consistent pre-*hijra* calendar system, which ran contrary to Khalīfa's concern with annalistic chronology.[25] Moreover, it is likely that information about the Medinan period and its chronology was practically more important than the Meccan period for the *ḥadīth* scholars and jurists (*fuqahāʾ*) in Khalīfa's immediate scholarly community, although that in itself might not be sufficient reason to omit it entirely. As a *ḥadīth* scholar with access to the *sīra* material of Ibn Isḥāq and others, Khalīfa did not omit the Meccan period from his *Tārīkh* because he lacked material; rather, it was probably a deliberate choice relating to his particular concern for chronology and political-administrative history in the *Tārīkh*. A few other extant early *akhbār* histories also begin with the emigration to Medina, but these focus mainly on the conquests that began in the Medinan period.[26] The conquests are also one of the main subjects in Khalīfa's *Tārīkh*, but its political and administrative scope is wider than the regular conquest histories. Thus Khalīfa's exclusive focus on post-*hijra* history distinguishes his *Tārīkh* from many other early historical works covering the life of the Prophet.

Similar to the wider *maghāzī-sīra* tradition, Khalīfa focuses mainly on military expeditions in the Medinan period. However, it is noteworthy that his

---

23 E.g. Ibn Hishām, *Sīra* 1:129–376; Ibn Saʿd, *Ṭabaqāt* 1:81–193; Ibn Ḥabīb, *Tārīkh* 79–85; al-Fasawī, *Maʿrifa* 3:250–271; Ibn Abī Khaythama, *Tārīkh* 1:152–181; al-Yaʿqūbī, *Tārīkh* 1:341–358; al-Ṭabarī, *Tārīkh* 1: 1146–1256; al-Masʿūdī, *Murūj* 2:265–278.

24 Khalīfa b. Khayyāṭ, *Tārīkh* (1985) 52–54.

25 Also noted by Webb in *Creating Arab origins* 55–56.

26 Al-Wāqidī, *al-Maghāzī* 1–2; al-Balādhurī, *Futūḥ* 8.

Tārīkh contains no accounts of common 'non-political' subjects such as the miracles of the Prophet, his characteristics, the signs and proofs of his prophethood or conversion stories about his Companions. Even accounts of circumstances of revelation (*asbāb al-nuzūl*) are few: the change of the *qibla* in 2/623–624, the slander against 'Ā'isha (*al-ifk*) in 6/627–628 and the revelation of Sūrat al-Tawba in 9/630–631.[27] Instead, the main narrative in the year sections concerns the chronology of the Prophet's expeditions and his role as the leader of the nascent community. This can be illustrated by year 2/623–624, which is the longest year section in the Prophetic period. It is structured as follows:

Year 2/623–624

1. The expedition of al-Abwā' (2 reports)
2. The expedition of Buwāṭ (2 reports)
3. The expedition of 'Ushayra (2 reports)
4. The expedition of Safawān (1 report)
5. The expedition to the region of Juhayna (1 report)
6. The Battle of Badr (6 reports)
7. The expedition of al-Kudr (3 reports)
8. The expedition of al-Sawīq (3 reports)
9. List of the martyrs at Badr
10. The military detachment (*sariyya*) of 'Ubayda b. al-Ḥārith (4 reports)
11. The military detachment of Ḥamza b. 'Abd al-Muṭṭalib (3 reports)
12. The military detachment of Sa'd b. Abī Waqqāṣ (2 reports)
13. The sending of 'Abdallāh b. Ghālib al-Laythī (2 reports)
14. The searching for news about Abū Sufyān's caravan (1 report)
15. The change of the *qibla* (8 reports)
16. The Prophet's consummation of the marriage to 'Ā'isha (2 reports)
17. Notes about the birth of 'Abdallāh b. al-Zubayr and al-Nu'mān b. Bashīr
18. The death of Ruqayya, the daughter of the Prophet (1 report)
19. Notes about 'Alī's marriage to Fāṭima, the revelation about fasting in Ramaḍān and the death of 'Uthmān b. Maẓ'ūn.[28]

Khalīfa focuses on subjects with direct chronological and political-administrative relevance. Although the same information is found in other works, Khalīfa is more exclusive in his focus on these chronological and political-administrative aspects of the life of the Prophet.[29] This focus is also evident

27 Khalīfa b. Khayyāṭ, *Tārīkh* (1985) 63–65, 80, 93.

28 Khalīfa b. Khayyāṭ, *Tārīkh* (1985) 56–65.

29 Compare with the accounts of year 2/623–624 in Ibn Hishām, *Sīra* 2:233–387, 3:5–8;

in what information Khalīfa selects about each event—for example, the conquest of Mecca in 8/630, which he narrates as follows:

> In this year, which is year 8/629–630, the Messenger of God conquered Mecca.
>
> Bakr narrated to us from Ibn Isḥāq from al-Zuhrī from ʿUbaydallāh b. ʿAbdallāh b. ʿUtba; he said: The Messenger of God (ṣ) set off for Mecca when ten days had passed of the month of Ramaḍān.
>
> ʿAlī b. Muḥammad narrated to me from Ḥammād b. Salama from ʿAlī b. Zayd from Saʿīd b. al-Musayyib; he said: The Messenger of God (ṣ) conquered Mecca in year eight after his emigration, in the month of Ramaḍān. He stayed 15 days and then left, appointing ʿAttāb b. Asīd over Mecca.
>
> Ibn Isḥāq said: He conquered it when ten days remained of Ramaḍān.[30]

This account shows Khalīfa's concern with chronology and concise political-administrative information.[31] His concern with the latter is also evident from his conclusion of the Prophetic period with lists of all the appointees of the Prophet—rather than descriptions of his characteristics, lists of his wives or other personal matters, as in many other Prophetic biographies and histories.[32] Altogether, the type of material that Khalīfa includes in the Prophetic period is distinguished by the near exclusive focus on chronology and political-administrative history at the expense of other material normally associated with *maghāzī-sīra* in *ḥadīth* collections, *sīra* works and *akhbār* histories. This includes the *maghāzī-sīra* material in the *tārīkh* works of Ibn Ḥabīb, Ibn Abī Khaythama and probably also al-Fasawī, which, unlike Khalīfa's *Tārīkh*, contain more material on 'non-political' subjects such as revelation, the establishment

---

al-Wāqidī, *al-Maghāzī* 9–182; Ibn Saʿd, *Ṭabaqāt* 2:5–28; Ibn Ḥabīb, *Tārīkh* 84; al-Fasawī, *Maʿrifa* 3:276–281; Ibn Abī Khaythama, *Tārīkh* 1:377–392; al-Yaʿqūbī, *Tārīkh* 1:361–365; al-Ṭabarī, *Tārīkh* 1:1270–367.

30 Khalīfa b. Khayyāṭ, *Tārīkh* (1985) 87.

31 For more detailed accounts, see al-Wāqidī, *al-Maghāzī* 780–871; Ibn Hishām, *Sīra* 4:29–69; al-Yaʿqūbī, *Tārīkh* 1:376–381; al-Fasawī, *Maʿrifa* 3:294–297; al-Ṭabarī, *Tārīkh* 1:1618–1647. A similar account exclusively about the chronology of the conquest of Mecca is found in Ibn Abī Khaythama's *Tārīkh* 2:20–21.

32 Ibn Hishām, *Sīra* 4:290–297; al-Fasawī, *Maʿrifa* 3:316–364; al-Yaʿqūbī, *Tārīkh* 1:446–453; al-Ṭabarī, *Tārīkh* 1:1766–1794. Ibn Saʿd and Ibn Ḥabīb also narrate the same type of material, but in the beginning or middle rather than the end of their sections on the Prophet's life. See Ibn Saʿd, *Ṭabaqāt* 1:309–436; Ibn Ḥabīb, *Tārīkh* 79–82.

of legal rulings, the family of the Prophet and his Companions, and his character and physical description.[33]

3 Community

Besides affirming the Prophet Muḥammad's prophethood, the early historians sought to show his establishment of the new community in Medina and demonstrate its continuity throughout the later periods. This section examines three sub-themes by which this concern with community was articulated: (1) the foundation of the community, (2) law and administration and (3) taxation.[34]

3.1 *Foundation*

Accounts of the establishment of the community in Medina treat subjects such as the Muslims' identity in contrast to other communities; the role of the Prophet as the model for the community's social, legal and ritual practices; and the communal unity during the military campaigns.[35] These themes were established by Khalīfa's time, but later compilers would continue to restructure and elaborate on them. A key event is the Prophet's arrival in Medina and the foundation of the Medinan polity, which is prominent in Khalīfa's *Tārīkh*. While such accounts are subsumed in the middle of most other works, it marks the actual beginning of Khalīfa's main narrative.[36] Khalīfa's account of the rest of the first year in Baqī's recension is brief and focused mainly on events pertaining to the foundation of the Muslim community in Medina (e.g. the founding of the Qubā' mosque, the first Friday prayer in Medina, the building of the Prophet's mosque and dwellings in Medina, and the first call to prayer, *adhān*).[37]

---

33 Ibn Ḥabīb, *Tārīkh* 77–98; al-Fasawī, *Maʿrifa* 3:250–364; Ibn Abī Khaythama, *Tārīkh* 1:152–181, 347–392; 2:5–41.

34 Donner calls the second sub-theme "cult and administration" and limits the former to ritual practices, which neglects the wider range of legal rulings (including, but not exclusive to, ritual practices) that were treated in the historical works—hence 'law' instead of 'cult'. See Donner, *Narratives* 160.

35 Donner, *Narratives* 160–164.

36 Khalīfa b. Khayyāṭ, *Tārīkh* (1985) 54–55; Ibn Hishām, *Sīra* 2:133–134; Ibn Saʿd, *Ṭabaqāt* 1:193–204; al-Yaʿqūbī, *Tārīkh* 1:360; Ibn Abī Khaythama, *Tārīkh* 1:365–366; Ibn Ḥabīb, *Tārīkh* 82–83; al-Ṭabarī, *Tārīkh* 1:1242–1243; al-Masʿūdī, *Murūj* 2:278. Two other works beginning with the *hijra* are al-Wāqidī's *Maghāzī* 1–2, and al-Balādhurī's *Futūḥ* 8.

37 Khalīfa b. Khayyāṭ, *Tārīkh* (1985) 55–56.

After the first year, Khalīfa focuses mainly on the series of military expeditions between 2/623 and 11/632—largely based on Ibn Isḥāq and al-Madāʾinī. Khalīfa's *maghāzī* narrative resembles other histories but is mostly limited to basic information about chronology, location, participants and outcome. Similar to the wider tradition, these *maghāzī* accounts underline the unity of the early community by outlining its collective and successful effort to defend and spread Islam.[38] This also includes accounts of the treaties that the Prophet made and the delegations that he sent to non-Muslim rulers in yet-to-be-conquered places, which also foreshadow the later conquests.[39] In line with Khalīfa's main focus in the *Tārīkh*—chronology and political-administrative history—these military aspects of the early community take up most of his year sections for the Prophetic period.

Another important function of the foundation narratives was defining the identity of the new Muslim community in contrast to others, but this is not particularly prominent in Khalīfa's *Tārīkh*. Apart from military confrontations with the Arab idolaters and the Jewish communities around Medina, there are no explicit reports contrasting the new Muslim society with the old Arab order or the Jewish and Christian communities—even the famous conversion stories of major Companions are absent in the *Tārīkh*.[40] The exceptions are the brief notices concerning the Muslims' new ritual practices and the destruction of the old Arab idols.[41] This exclusive focus on intra-Muslim affairs, as opposed to non-Muslim history or interreligious subjects, characterises Khalīfa's narrative throughout the *Tārīkh* and relates to his compilation of the text as a political-administrative chronology of the Muslim community rather than as a world history proper.

3.2 *Law and Administration*

In the early *akhbār* histories, the identity of the Muslim community is also outlined by its adherence to certain legal, administrative and organisational practices. By the time of Khalīfa, the establishment and continuation of these practices had become a historiographical theme that marked the identity of the

38 Donner, *Narratives* 163.

39 Khalīfa b. Khayyāṭ, *Tārīkh* (1985) 79, 83, 85, 92.

40 Khalīfa only notes, without any details, some of those who accepted Islam in the Medinan period, such as ʿAbdallāh b. Salām, Abū Hurayra, ʿImrān b. Ḥuṣayn and Khālid b. al-Walīd. Khalīfa b. Khayyāṭ. *Tārīkh* (1985) 56, 86. Compare this with the extensive accounts about, e.g. ʿAbdallāh b. Salām in Ibn Hishām, *Sīra* 2:158–159; Ibn Saʿd, *Ṭabaqāt* 5:377–386; al-Bukhārī, *Ṣaḥīḥ* 4:132.

41 E.g. Khalīfa b. Khayyāṭ, *Tārīkh* (1985) 55–56, 63–65, 88.

Muslim community. As the *Tārīkh* illustrates, it could also serve to emphasise the continuity of the Muslim polity from the foundation in Medina.[42]

3.2.1 Law and Legal Rulings

The early histories contain many accounts of law and legal rulings pertaining to both worship (*ʿibādāt*—e.g. prayer, fasting, *zakāt*, pilgrimage and *jihād*) and interpersonal transactions (*muʿāmalāt*—e.g. marriage, punishments and prohibitions).[43] They also contain many accounts that outline administrative practices in the early polity, including both descriptions of the evolution of administrative institutions (e.g. the treasury, stipend system and coinage) and lists of appointees (e.g. governors, military commanders, leaders of the pilgrimage, judges and scribes).[44] Such legal and administrative material is found to various extents in most *akhbār* histories.

In Khalīfa's *Tārīkh*, accounts of the establishment of laws pertaining to acts of worship (*ʿibādāt*) and interpersonal transactions (*muʿāmalāt*) are few in comparison to the accounts of administration. But there are some important examples of the former, such as the first Friday prayer in Medina (1/622), the first call to prayer (1/622), the change of the *qibla* (2/624), the obligation of fasting in Ramaḍān (2/624), the first prayer before an execution (3/625), the division of spoils and negotiation of treaties (6–7/627–628) and ʿUmar's establishment of the congregational night prayer in Ramaḍān (14/635).[45] However, these accounts are very brief; for example, "In this year [14/635], ʿUmar b. al-Khaṭṭāb ordered people to gather for the night prayer in the month of Ramaḍān."[46] It is thus evident that Khalīfa's main concern is chronology, not details of the legal rulings in themselves, as in the *ḥadīth* collections and Ibn Abī Khaythama's *Tārīkh*.[47]

The theme of law and legal precedents also relates partly to the subject of 'originators' or 'first instances' (*awāʾil*). These are found in many early works, including both in *ḥadīth* collections, such as the *Muṣannaf* of Ibn Abī Shayba, and in *akhbār* collections, such the *Maʿārif* of Ibn Qutayba (d. 276/889).[48] There are a few notes in Khalīfa's *Tārīkh* about *awāʾil*, but these mainly con-

---

42 Donner, *Narratives* 166–171. See also Noth and Conrad, *Early Arabic* 35–36, 48–53.

43 See, e.g. Ibn Abī Khaythama, *Tārīkh* 1:370–375, 379–385, 389–392; al-Ṭabarī, *Tārīkh* 1:1156–1159, 1281, 1333–1334, 1454–1455, 1517–1528, 1753–1756.

44 Donner, *Narratives* 167–171.

45 Khalīfa b. Khayyāṭ, *Tārīkh* (1985) 55–56, 63–65, 75, 80–85, 129.

46 Khalīfa b. Khayyāṭ, *Tārīkh* (1985) 129.

47 E.g. Ibn Abī Khaythama, *Tārīkh* 1:370–375, 389–392.

48 Ibn Abī Shayba, *Muṣannaf* 13:5–78; Ibn Qutayba, *al-Maʿārif* 551–558. Works entitled *Kitāb al-Awāʾil* are also ascribed to earlier *akhbār* compilers such as Hishām b. al-Kalbī and al-

cern military campaigns and administrative practices. In the Prophetic period, besides some remarks about the first instances of certain ritual practices,[49] Khalīfa specifically mentions the Prophet's first expedition, the first military detachment (*sariyya*) that he sent out, the first banner tied before an expedition and those he appointed to specific tasks or offices.[50] In the post-Prophetic period, most *awāʾil* concern administrative practices and, in particular, the introduction of new governmental offices. The exceptions are ʿUmar's congregational night prayers in Ramaḍān, the first child born in Basra, the first to organise the Ḥarūriyya (i.e. the first Khawārij), the first Arab to cross the Oxus, the first to walk in a funeral procession without a cloak (*ridāʾ*) and the first Khārijī to take the area of Ṭaff al-Baṣra as a place of *hijra*.[51] In relation to *awāʾil*, it is also worth noting that Khalīfa does not include narrations that attribute reprehensible innovations (*bidaʿ*) to ʿUthmān and the Umayyads, which can be found in some other works.[52] Rather, their 'innovations' or 'firsts' are introduced (if they are mentioned at all) in their chronological order or in the list sections, without highlighting them as bad innovations—for example, ʿUthmān's appointment of the first commander of the security forces (*ṣāḥib al-shuraṭ*) and Muʿāwiya's appointment of the first commander of the guard (*ṣāḥib al-ḥaras*).[53] This illustrates Khalīfa's tendency to avoid or de-emphasise certain controversial subjects in the historical tradition—in particular those including Shīʿī accusations against the Companions and the Successors—rather than to engage in apologetics or intricate narrative counterarguments in the way of, for example, Sayf b. ʿUmar.[54] Some material on such controversial subjects may have been omitted or toned down in the course of transmission, but this tendency very likely was inherent to Khalīfa's *Tārīkh* as he transmitted it to Baqī b. Makhlad and also as he transmitted it to Mūsā al-Tustarī.[55] However, not all controversial subjects are de-emphasised; the extant recension still contains detailed accounts of early intra-Muslim conflicts and caliphal successions that were fiercely debated in Khalīfa's time.[56]

Madāʾinī. See Ibn al-Nadīm, *Fihrist* 1:303–304, 321; Noth and Conrad, *Early Arabic* 104–108; Rosenthal, Awāʾil.

49 Khalīfa b. Khayyāṭ, *Tārīkh* (1985) 55–56, 63–65, 75.

50 Khalīfa b. Khayyāṭ, *Tārīkh* (1985) 56, 61–62, 96–99.

51 Khalīfa b. Khayyāṭ, *Tārīkh* (1985) 129, 192, 222, 264, 272.

52 For a compilation of such material about ʿUthmān, see Madelung, *Succession* 78–140; El-Hibri, *Parable and politics* 122–153.

53 Khalīfa b. Khayyāṭ, *Tārīkh* (1985) 179, 228.

54 See Anthony, *Caliph and the heretic* 19–103.

55 See Chapter 1.

56 See Chapter 8.

3.2.2 Administration

Accounts of administrative practices in the early Muslim polity are found in many early histories, including lists or notices about, for example, appointments of governors, commanders of military campaigns and leaders of the pilgrimage. Other accounts describe the origins or evolution of certain practices (e.g. the stipend system, the minting of coins and the office of the seal).[57] In general, the concern for administrative history distinguishes the early *akhbār* histories from *ḥadīth* collections, which are focused more, albeit not exclusively so, on matters pertaining to law and belief. However, the administrative material is proportionally more prominent in Khalīfa's *Tārīkh* than other surviving histories from the first centuries AH—including earlier ones like the works of Ibn Isḥāq, Sayf b. ʿUmar and al-Wāqidī, as well as contemporaneous or later ones like those of Ibn Saʿd, Ibn Ḥabīb, al-Fasawī, Ibn Abī Khaythama, al-Dīnawarī, al-Yaʿqūbī and al-Ṭabarī. The exceptions are a few later works specifically on governors and judges, such as the *Akhbār al-quḍāt* of Wakīʿ (d. 306/918) and *Kitāb al-Wulāt wa-kitāb al-quḍāt* of al-Kindī (d. 350/961).[58]

One of the most distinctive features of Khalīfa's *Tārīkh* is the administrative list sections, which conclude the reigns of each caliph and a few prominent governors of Iraq and the East. These list sections enumerate the appointees in the caliphal administration and outline the development of its offices. Their regularity affirms the administrative continuity of the Muslim polity from its origins at the time of the Prophet in Medina.[59] In this way, the list sections reflect Khalīfa's focus on chronology, politics and administration, as well as his pragmatic early Sunnī perspective on the history of the caliphs—accepting the Umayyads, Zubayrids and ʿAbbāsids as political authorities but distinguishing them from the first four rightly-guided caliphs, about whom the Prophet said, "Those of you who live after me will see many disagreements, so you must hold to my *sunna* and the *sunna* of the rightly-guided, upright caliphs (*al-khulafāʾ al-mahdiyīn al-rāshidīn*)."[60] As we shall see in Chapter 8, this outlook is even clearer in Khalīfa's narration of caliphal successions and civil wars in the Umayyad and ʿAbbāsid periods, which is critical of some caliphs but nonetheless upholds the continuity of the caliphate and the importance of communal unity under its leaders.

---

57 Donner, *Narratives* 167–171.

58 Wakīʿ, *Akhbār al-quḍāt*; al-Kindī, *Kitāb al-Wulāt*.

59 See Chapter 6.

60 Abū Dāwūd, *Sunan* 7:16–17 (*kitāb al-sunna, bāb fī luzūm al-sunna*); al-Tirmidhī, *al-Jāmiʿ* 4:408 (*abwāb al-ʿilm, bāb mā jāʾa fī l-akhdh bi-l-sunna …*); Ibn Ḥanbal, *Musnad* 28:367–375 (*al-ʿIrbāḍ b. Sāriya*).

The theme of administration also pervades the year sections, where Khalīfa provides much material related to administration (e.g. leaders of military campaigns, conquered territories, appointed governors and events in their regions, as well as the appointments of new caliphs and their oaths of allegiance). This focus on straightforward political and administrative facts is a distinguishing characteristic of Khalīfa's *Tārīkh*. At the same time, his narrative lacks information about general cultural developments and avoids lengthy accounts of intrigues, conspiracies, counter-conspiracies, betrayals, tribal rivalries and personal anecdotes.[61] Such material is common in the corpuses of many other early *akhbār* compilers (e.g. Sayf b. ʿUmar, Abū Mikhnaf, Naṣr b. Muzāḥim, al-Yaʿqūbī, al-Balādhurī, al-Ṭabarī and al-Masʿūdī).[62] Thus, although Khalīfa shares his interest in administrative history with many other early historians, his focus on this is much more exclusive; in addition to chronology, civil wars and military campaigns, administration is the most detailed subject in Khalīfa's *Tārīkh*.

3.3 *Taxation*

The theme of taxation, especially in relation to conquered territories, is common in the early tradition. Besides *akhbār* compilations, it is also found in legal treatises such as Abū Yūsuf's (d. 182/798) *Kitāb al-Kharāj*, Yaḥyā b. Ādam's (d. 203/818) *Kitāb al-Kharāj* and Abū ʿUbayd al-Qāsim b. Sallām's (d. 224/838) *Kitāb al-Amwāl*.[63] Many accounts on this theme are concerned with the question of the type of conquest (*ṣulḥan* or *ʿanwatan*—'by treaty' or 'by force') and related issues such as the status of conquered lands and peoples, and the extraction of taxes (*kharāj* and *jizya*). Such material seems to have been used for purposes of tax systematisation under the Umayyads and the ʿAbbāsids.[64] Khalīfa narrates many *ṣulḥ-ʿanwa* accounts in the Rāshidūn and Umayyad periods. For example:

> [**Year 26/646–647**] ʿAbdallāh b. al-Mughīra said: My father narrated to me: Abū ʿUbayda sent ʿAmr b. al-ʿĀṣ to Qinnasrīn after he was finished at al-Yarmūk. He made a treaty (*ṣālaḥa*) with the people of Aleppo, Manbij

---

61 Wurtzel, *Khalifa ibn Khayyat's History* 23.

62 See Chapter 8.

63 Noth and Conrad, *Early Arabic* 48–49; Donner, *Narratives* 171–173; Abū Yūsuf, *Kitāb al-Kharāj*; Yaḥyā b. Ādam, *Kitāb al-Kharāj*; Abū ʿUbayd al-Qāsim b. Sallām, *Kitāb al-Amwāl*.

64 Noth, 'Ṣulḥ'-''Anwa'-Traditionen; Donner, *Narratives* 172.

> and Antioch. The remaining land of Qinnasrīn was conquered by force (*ʿanwatan*).[65]

Similar accounts are found in other chronicles and conquest histories from the first centuries AH. As with Khalīfa's *maghāzī-sīra* accounts, however, his conquest accounts are relatively brief in comparison to many accounts elsewhere.[66] The *jizya* is mentioned by name a few times in the Prophetic, Rāshidūn, Umayyad and ʿAbbāsid periods,[67] but elsewhere it is indicated by the sums agreed upon in the treaties—for example, "Abū ʿUbayd entered Bārūsmā and Ibn al-Andarzaghar made a treaty with him of four dirhams per head."[68] The *kharāj* is a regular feature in the list sections and is also mentioned a few times in the year sections.[69] That said, taxation in itself is not one of the main themes in Khalīfa's *Tārīkh* as it is in some other works. It contains less detail and less focus on specific legal issues of conquest and taxation than some other specialised conquest histories (e.g. al-Balādhurī's *Futūḥ al-buldān*) and legal treatises (e.g. Abū Yūsuf's *Kitāb al-Kharāj*). Taxation in the *Tārīkh* pertains mainly to treaties during the conquests and, in that sense, forms a part of the broader theme of conquest and hegemony, as discussed below.

4 Hegemony

Another major theme in the early histories is the question of what Donner calls hegemony—here referring to the Muslims' military and political authority over non-Muslim peoples during and after the conquests. Donner divides the theme of hegemony into conquest (*futūḥ*) and caliphate (*khilāfa*): while the conquest theme served to outline the historical process by which the Muslim hegemony came about and thereby, among other things, demonstrate its legitimacy, the caliphate theme concerned the Muslim polity's hegemony in later years.[70] In addition, this section examines the *ridda* wars during Abū Bakr's caliphate, which also relate to the question of Muslim hegemony on the Arabian peninsula. It shows that the basic information in Khalīfa's con-

65 Khalīfa b. Khayyāṭ, *Tārīkh* (1985) 134–135.
66 Compare, e.g. the accounts of the conquest of Damascus in Khalīfa b. Khayyāṭ, *Tārīkh* (1985) 125–126; al-Balādhurī, *Futūḥ* 165–172; al-Ṭabarī, *Tārīkh* 1:2145–2155.
67 See Khalīfa b. Khayyāṭ, *Tārīkh* (1985) 93, 135, 136, 144, 328, 336, 459.
68 Khalīfa b. Khayyāṭ, *Tārīkh* (1985) 124.
69 See Khalīfa b. Khayyāṭ, *Tārīkh* (1985) 140, 164, 224, 436.
70 Donner, *Narratives* 174.

quest narrative is similar to other histories. The most distinguishing feature is the concise presentation and focus on basic facts of chronology, location, participation and outcome. Moreover, Khalīfa provides very little information about the conquered peoples before or after the conquests, unlike later historians such as al-Yaʿqūbī, al-Dīnawarī, al-Ṭabarī and al-Masʿūdī. Another distinct feature relating to the sub-theme of caliphate is the scarcity of biographical material about the caliphs and other individuals (other than dates of births and deaths). Thereby Khalīfa narrates his *Tārīkh* as a political-administrative history of the Muslim community as a single entity rather than as a history of particular groups or individuals within it.

4.1 *The* Ridda *Wars*

In the historical tradition, the wars of apostasy (*ḥurūb al-ridda*) refer to the revolts of certain Arab tribes against the Muslim polity after the Prophet's death in 11/632. Accounts on the theme of the *ridda* wars were often merged with those of conquests (*futūḥ*), so it is unclear when it arose as a separate historiographical theme, although it had certainly done so by the late second/eighth century.[71] Because the theme of the *ridda* wars related to conflicts about leadership, Donner treats it as a sub-theme of leadership.[72] However, it is treated here as a part of the theme of hegemony because it also outlined Muslim hegemony on the Arabian peninsula and prepared for the sub-themes of conquest and caliphate.[73]

Khalīfa's account of the *ridda* wars in Baqī's recension of the *Tārīkh* is relatively detailed and contains some 50 reports in total, most of them from Ibn Isḥāq and al-Madāʾinī.[74] The remaining direct transmitters of one or two reports include many major *ḥadīth* authorities, such as ʿAbd al-Raḥmān b. Mahdī, Ismāʿīl b. ʿUlayya, Muʿādh b. Muʿādh, Mūsā al-Tabūdhakī and ʿAbd al-Wahhāb b. ʿAbd al-Majīd. The widest range of transmitters is found in Khalīfa's section on the Battle of al-Yamāma: seven different transmitters in comparison

71 Donner, *Narratives* 200–202; Noth and Conrad, *Early Arabic* 28–30. Some of the earliest texts on *ridda* before Khalīfa's time are *Kitāb al-Ridda* of Abū Mikhnaf (d. 157/774), *Kitāb al-Futūḥ wa-l-ridda* of Sayf b. ʿUmar (d. c. 180/796) and *Kitāb al-Ridda* of Abū Ḥudhayfa (d. 206/821), which suggests its differentiation from *futūḥ* compilations such as those ascribed to al-Shaʿbī (d. 103/721), Ibn Isḥāq and Muḥammad b. ʿAbdallāh al-Azdī (d. c. 180/796–797).

72 Donner, *Narratives* 200–202.

73 Writing about the conquests, however, Donner treats the *ridda* wars as one of the "foundations of the Islamic conquest." *Early Islamic conquests* 82–90. See also Shoufani, *al-Riddah*.

74 There are no reports about the *ridda* wars in Ṣaddām's collection of material that is missing in Baqī's recension. See Ṣaddām, *Tārīkh Khalīfa* 60–61.

to the total of eleven transmitters in the whole section on the *ridda* wars. This probably reflects the importance of the Battle of al-Yamāma as the culmination of the *ridda* wars. The battle was also remembered as one of the first great traumas to afflict the Muslim community; it led to the death of numerous Companions and many who had memorised the Qurʾān, which is widely reported as the incentive for the first collection of the Qurʾānic text.[75] Khalīfa reports that 450 or 500 were killed on the day of al-Yamāma, among them 30 or 50 who had memorised the Qurʾān. He then lists the Muhājirūn and Anṣār who were martyred on that day and concludes that they were 58 in total (24 Muhājirūn and 34 Anṣār).[76] Besides the range of transmitters, the length of Khalīfa's Yamāma account (more than half of the whole section on the *ridda* wars) and the inclusion of a list of martyrs also indicate the special importance of the event.

Overall, Khalīfa's account of the *ridda* wars resembles those of historians such as al-Balādhurī and al-Ṭabarī, although it is more focused on straightforward facts of chronology, locations and the people involved.[77] After introducing the unrest among the Arab tribes and Abū Bakr's mobilisation, Khalīfa treats the *ridda* of particular leaders, tribes and locations: Ṭulayḥa al-Asadī, Banū Sulaym, Banū Tamīm, Musaylima (the Battle of al-Yamāma), al-Baḥrayn, ʿUmān and Yemen.[78] Khalīfa's account of these events highlights a couple of aspects in particular that are common in the wider historical tradition.

First, it outlines the definitive establishment of Muslim hegemony in Arabia by the suppression of alternative religious and political claims among the Arab tribes that had appeared after the death of the Prophet Muḥammad. This is illustrated by Abū Bakr's enforcement of *zakāt*-collection, the defeat of several false prophets (Ṭulayḥa, Musaylima and al-Aswad al-ʿAnsī) and the eventual subjection of all Arab tribes to Muslim rule, after which the apostates returned to Islam. The defeat of these tribal leaders and false prophets also stresses the replacement of pre-Islamic political and religious structures among the Arabs with the new, all-embracing Muslim community, united under the Qurashī caliph.

Second, Khalīfa's account emphasises the precedence of certain Arab tribes—especially Quraysh, but also the Medinan tribes of the Anṣār—who

75 See al-Bukhārī, *Ṣaḥīḥ* 6:71 (*kitāb al-tafsīr, sūrat barāʾa*), 6:183 (*kitāb faḍāʾil al-Qurʾān, bāb jamʿ al-Qurʾān*); al-Tirmidhī, *al-Jāmiʿ* 5:180–181 (*abwāb tafsīr al-Qurʾān, bāb wa-min sūrat al-tawba*); Ibn Saʿd, *Ṭabaqāt* 5:311.

76 Khalīfa b. Khayyāṭ, *Tārīkh* (1985) 111–115. One report from al-Madāʾinī from Abū Maʿshar mentions that 140 from the Muhājirūn and the Anṣār were martyred, but Khalīfa concludes in his own words, after listing them, that the martyrs among them were 58 in total.

77 Al-Balādhurī, *Futūḥ* 131–149; al-Ṭabarī, *Tārīkh* 1:1851–2012.

78 Khalīfa b. Khayyāṭ, *Tārīkh* (1985) 102–117.

remained loyal to Islam throughout its early days and fought for the Medinan polity when certain other tribes reneged. The unique position of Quraysh in the Muslim community was often dealt with in strictly genealogical terms—as reflected in Khalīfa's genealogically ordered lists in the *Tārīkh* and the overall structure of his *Ṭabaqāt*—but the *ridda* war accounts of Khalīfa and others show that *akhbār* history could have similar functions.[79] Another example is the list of martyrs at al-Yamāma, which is arranged according to tribes and begins with the martyrs from Quraysh (beginning with Banū ʿAbd Shams b. ʿAbd Manāf) and thereafter from the Anṣār.[80] This focus on the martyrs from the Muhājirūn and Anṣār, while also noting those who had memorised the Qurʾān, corresponds to Khalīfa's interests as a *ḥadīth* scholar; they were remembered not only as fighters for the sake of God but also as defenders and transmitters of the Prophetic tradition.

Third, Khalīfa's account highlights the importance of certain individuals who participated in defending Islam and the Muslim community at this critical stage, in particular Abū Bakr al-Ṣiddīq. It is narrated that some Companions advised Abū Bakr not to attack the tribes who refused to pay *zakāt*, to which he famously replied, "If they were to withhold even a hobbling-cord that they used to give to the Messenger of God, I would fight them."[81] He is then presented as the one who mobilises the Medinan army, appoints commanders over the expeditions and dispatches them, and instructs them how to deal with the enemy. This is not unusual in the historical tradition, especially not among the Sunnīs, but it nonetheless illustrates Khalīfa's perspective on Abū Bakr's special role and merits.[82] The clearest example is the concluding report about Abū Bakr's mobilisation before the *ridda* wars, narrated on the authority of the Basran *ḥadīth* expert ʿAbd al-Raḥmān b. Mahdī:

> ʿAbd al-Raḥmān b. Mahdī narrated to us; he said: ʿAbd al-ʿAzīz b. ʿAbdallāh b. Abī Salama reported to us from ʿAbd al-Wāḥid b. Abī ʿAwn from al-Qāsim b. Muḥammad from ʿĀʾisha; she said: The Messenger of God (ṣ) died and if that which fell upon my father had fallen on firm mountains,

79 See Donner, *Narratives* 201–202. On the *Ṭabaqāt*, see Chapter 2.

80 Khalīfa b. Khayyāṭ, *Tārīkh* (1985) 111–115.

81 Khalīfa b. Khayyāṭ, *Tārīkh* (1985) 101. See also Mālik b. Anas, *al-Muwaṭṭaʾ* 1:362 (*kitāb al-zakāt, bāb mā jāʾa fī akhdh al-ṣadaqāt wa-l-tashdīd fīhā*); al-Bukhārī, *Ṣaḥīḥ* 9:15 (*kitāb istitābat al-murtaddīn wa-l-muʿānidīn wa-qitālihim, bāb qatl man abā qabūl al-farāʾiḍ …*); Muslim b. al-Ḥajjāj, *Ṣaḥīḥ* 1:31 (*kitāb al-īmān, bāb al-amr bi-qitāl al-nās ḥattā yaqūlū …*).

82 See e.g. al-Ṭabarī's account in his *Tārīkh* 1:1851–2012. See also El-Hibri, *Parable and politics* 62–63. On Abū Bakr's merits in general, see Ibn Abī Shayba, *Muṣannaf* 11:100–110; Ibn Ḥanbal, *Faḍāʾil al-ṣaḥāba* 65–243; al-Bukhārī, *Ṣaḥīḥ* 5:4–10.

> it would have crushed them; hypocrisy raised its head in Medina and the Arabs reneged. By God, they did not disagree about any matter in Islam more serious than what my father had to deal with.[83]

In light of Abū Bakr's successful suppression of the renegade tribes, this report underlines his enormous importance for the early Muslim community. Moreover, right before the reports about the *ridda* wars, Khalīfa also narrates two reports about Abū Bakr's unwavering insistence on dispatching the large army of Usāma b. Zayd that the Prophet, before he died, had ordered to be sent against the Romans in Syria.[84] Besides Abū Bakr, Khālid b. al-Walīd is also given a central role in Khalīfa's account of the *ridda* wars, although Khalīfa does not censor the issues that arose—such as Khālid's disagreement with some of the Anṣār during the early campaigns and the controversial execution of Mālik b. Nuwayra. The latter case is especially noteworthy and illustrates Khalīfa's approach to the Companions. In the section on the *ridda* of Banū Tamīm, Khalīfa notes that Mālik and some of his men were killed on Khālid's orders, despite saying that they were Muslims. He then narrates:

> ʿAlī b. Muḥammad [al-Madāʾinī] narrated to us from Ibn Abī Dhiʾb from al-Zuhrī from Sālim from his father; he said: Abū Qatāda went to Abū Bakr and informed him about the execution of Mālik and his companions. Abū Bakr became very upset and wrote to Khālid. He came to him. Abū Bakr said, "Can it be more than that Khālid judged the situation but was mistaken (*taʾawwala fa-akhṭaʾa*)?" Then Abū Bakr sent Khālid back and paid the blood money for Mālik b. Nuwayra and returned all captives and wealth.
>
> Bakr from Ibn Isḥāq; he said: Khālid went to Abū Bakr and informed him about the events. He apologised to him and was excused.[85]

Khalīfa does not conceal the issue or the events that took place; he even transmits Abū Qatāda's eyewitness account that the people prayed and said that they were Muslims. Yet, the account cited above provides an explanation and excuse for Khālid's actions, based on the basic facts available. It is shorter

83 Khalīfa b. Khayyāṭ, *Tārīkh* (1985) 102. Also narrated by Ibn Abī Shayba in his *Muṣannaf* 13:473.

84 Khalīfa b. Khayyāṭ, *Tārīkh* 1985, 100–101.

85 Khalīfa b. Khayyāṭ, *Tārīkh* (1985) 104–105. Ibn ʿAsākir narrates the same reports in the same sequence (including the following lines of poetry) via al-Tustarī in Ibn ʿAsākir's *Tārīkh madīnat Dimashq* 16:256–257.

than al-Ṭabarī's more detailed account, which also contains reports in defence of Khālid.[86] Unlike some other historians, however, Khalīfa does not dwell on Khālid's motives or ʿUmar's harsh stance against Khālid.[87] Instead, Khalīfa avoids the points of dispute and speculation by leaving it at Abū Bakr's understanding that Khālid followed the best of his own case-based judgement or interpretation (*ta'wīl, ta'awwul*).[88] The notion of 'judgement' relates to the concept of *ijtihād* ('striving to the best of one's ability to arrive at the correct judgement in a non-definitive matter'): those qualified for *ijtihād* are entitled to God's reward for their efforts to reach the correct judgement, even if they happen to be mistaken.[89] As the Prophet said in a well-known *ḥadīth*, "When a judge passes a judgement, having exerted his efforts to judge correctly (*ijtahada*), and is right, he will have two rewards. When he passes a judgement, having exerted his efforts to judge correctly, and is wrong, he will have one reward."[90] Since the *mujtahid* is rewarded even if he is mistaken, and since the ultimate assessment of the correctness of the *ijtihād* is up to God, this notion helped to relieve the Companions (in this case Khālid) of blame among the early Sunnīs.[91]

---

86 Al-Ṭabarī, *Tārīkh* 1:1921–1929.

87 According to al-Yaʿqūbī, for example, Khālid executed Mālik because he wanted his wife. Al-Yaʿqūbī, *Tārīkh* 2:18. According to an account transmitted by al-Ṭabarī, the executors misunderstood Khālid's command to "keep your captives warm," because of different dialects and usages of words. Al-Ṭabarī, *Tārīkh* 1:1925–1926.

88 See also Ibn Taymiyya, *Minhāj al-sunna* 5:518–520.

89 On *ijtihād* in legal scholarship, see Ibn al-Ḥājib, *Mukhtaṣar* 2:1203–1247; al-Shawkānī, *Irshād al-fuḥūl* 2:1025–1080; al-Zuḥaylī, *Uṣūl al-fiqh* 2:325–399.

90 Al-Bukhārī, *Ṣaḥīḥ* 9:108 (*kitāb al-iʿtiṣām bi-l-kitāb wa-l-sunna, bāb ajr al-ḥākim idhā ijtahada*).

91 See e.g. Ibn Abī Zayd al-Qayrawānī's (d. 386/996) *ʿaqīda* section in his *Risāla*, where he states, "None of the Companions of the Messenger of God (ṣ) should be mentioned except in the best way, while refraining from the disagreements that broke out between them. They are the people who have the most right that one seeks a good interpretation for them and that one has the best opinion about them." ʿAbd al-Wahhāb al-Baghdādī, *Sharḥ ʿaqīdat Mālik al-ṣaghīr* 274–276. As for the concept of *ijtihād* in relation to the Companions, the later Sunnī *ḥadīth* master Ibn Ḥajar summarised, "The *ahl al-sunna* have agreed upon the obligation to refrain from accusing anyone among the Companions because of that which occurred between them, even if one knows who was in the right. The reason is that they did not fight in those wars except on the basis of *ijtihād* and God has pardoned the one who is mistaken in his *ijtihād*—in fact, it has been established that he is rewarded once, while the one who is correct is rewarded twice." Ibn Ḥajar, *Fatḥ al-Bārī* 13:37. For the specific issue of Khālid b. al-Walīd and Mālik b. Nuwayra, see Ibn Taymiyya, *Minhāj al-sunna* 5:518–520. In the section on year 21/641–642, Khalīfa says, "In it: Khālid b. al-Walīd died in Syria, may God have mercy on him." Khalīfa b. Khayyāṭ, *Tārīkh* (1985) 150.

Khalīfa's account highlights other prominent individuals in the *ridda* wars, especially the martyrs among the Muhājirūn and the Anṣār, but Abū Bakr and Khālid are the ones who stand out. The fact that this is indicative of Khalīfa's early Sunnī perspective is evident when one compares the accounts of the *ridda* wars of Sunnī-inclined historians (such as Khalīfa and al-Ṭabarī) with their Shīʿī counterparts (such as al-Yaʿqūbī and Ibn Aʿtham): the former present it in favour of the Companions as those who defended Islam upon the Prophet's death, while the latter tend to highlight transgressions and less favourable aspects of their involvement.[92] In that sense, Khalīfa's account of the *ridda* wars outlines not only the consolidation of Muslim hegemony in Arabia but also the merit and special standing of the Companions who participated in defending Islam.

4.2 *Conquests*

The theme of conquests (*futūḥ*) is the most obvious expression of Muslim hegemony in the historical tradition. Besides its basic purpose of outlining events and establishing chronological order, it also served to explain the establishment of Muslim authority in the conquered territories, to advance claims of individuals or groups, to provide historical lessons and to establish precedents for purposes of law and administration.[93] The earliest surviving *futūḥ* work is the *Tārīkh futūḥ al-Shām* of Muḥammad b. ʿAbdallāh al-Azdī (d. c. 180/796–797),[94] but earlier works on this theme are ascribed to al-Shaʿbī (d. 103/721), Ibn Isḥāq (d. c. 150/767) and Abū Mikhnaf (d. 157/774).[95] In the second/eighth and third/ninth centuries, the earlier circulating material was reworked and put into new frameworks by both compilers of history (e.g. al-Balādhurī and al-Ṭabarī) and compilers of legal treatises (e.g. Abū Yūsuf and Abū ʿUbayd al-Qāsim b. Sallām).

Conquest is one of the main themes in Khalīfa's *Tārīkh*. His account of the early conquests resembles other histories in terms of basic content. The main difference to other more detailed works is Khalīfa's relatively concise material and straightforward narrative style, although Wurtzel has pointed out that his work also contains some "unique and detailed information" about military

92 Al-Yaʿqūbī, *Tārīkh* 2:13–19; al-Ṭabarī, *Tārīkh* 1:1851–2012; Ibn Aʿtham al-Kūfī, *Futūḥ* 1:14–70.

93 Noth and Conrad, *Early Arabic* 31–33; Donner, *Narratives* 174–182; Robinson, *Empire and elites* 1–32.

94 Al-Azdī, *Futūḥ al-Shām*. On the dating of al-Azdī's death, see Scheiner, Grundlegendes 11–12, Writing the history of the *futūḥ* 162.

95 Donner, *Narratives* 175.

expeditions.[96] In addition to the material in Baqī's recension of the *Tārīkh*, later historians such as Ibn ʿAsākir preserve a few other conquest reports from Khalīfa via al-Tustarī and others, but they resemble the material in Baqī's recension in style and content.[97] The reason for their absence is probably that Khalīfa transmitted slightly different versions of the *Tārīkh* at different times to different students. Khalīfa's account of the conquests begins in 12/633–634, right after the *ridda* wars:

> **Year 12/633–634**
> In it: Abū Bakr sent Khālid b. al-Walīd to the land of Basra, which used to be called the land of India (*arḍ al-Hind*).
> ʿAwn b. Kahmas b. al-Ḥasan narrated to us; he said: ʿImrān b. Ḥudayr reported to us; he said: A man among us named Muqātil narrated to us from Quṭba b. Qatāda al-Sadūsī; he said: Khālid b. al-Walīd attacked us with his cavalry and we said, "We are Muslims." He let us be and we raided al-Ubulla with him and conquered it.[98]

Similarly, both al-Yaʿqūbī and al-Ṭabarī place Khālid b. al-Walīd's departure to Basra directly after al-Yamāma. However, Khalīfa's wording might be significant as the others do not single out Basra in the same way, but rather mention Iraq in general or other places before Basra.[99] Al-Ṭabarī, for example, begins:

> Abū Jaʿfar [al-Ṭabarī] said: When Khālid was finished with the affair of al-Yamāma, Abū Bakr al-Ṣiddīq, may God have mercy on him, wrote to him while Khālid was still there—according to what ʿUbaydallāh b. Saʿd al-Zuhrī narrated to us, saying: my uncle reported to us; he said: Sayf b.

---

96 Wurtzel specifically mentions "Armenia and the Caucasus, the Maghrib, Anatolia, and India". See Wurtzel, *Khalifa ibn Khayyat's History* viii.

97 See Chapter 1. There is one report from the Battle of al-Qādisiyya in which al-Mughīra b. Shuʿba said: "We used to worship stones and idols; when we saw a finer stone, we threw away the old one and took another one. We did not know of any lord until God, the Mighty and Majestic, sent a Prophet to us from among ourselves. He called us to Islam and we became Muslims. He summoned us to fight our enemies from those who refused to accept Islam and informed us that those who are killed among us will enter the Garden." This report does not resemble the usual style of Khalīfa's conquest reports, but it may well have been transmitted as a separate *ḥadīth* or as a part of Khalīfa's *musnad*, not as a part of the *Tārīkh*. It is transmitted through ʿAbdallāh b. Muḥammad b. Nājiya and Muḥammad b. Yūsuf al-Turkī, rather than Mūsā al-Tustarī. Abū Nuʿaym al-Aṣbahānī, *Maʿrifat al-ṣaḥāba* 5:2583; al-Dhahabī, *Siyar* 4279–4280; Ṣaddām, *Tārīkh Khalīfa* 64.

98 Khalīfa b. Khayyāṭ, *Tārīkh* (1985) 117.

99 Al-Yaʿqūbī, *Tārīkh* 2:17; al-Ṭabarī, *Tārīkh* 1:2016.

> ʿUmar reported to us from ʿAmr b. Muḥammad from al-Shaʿbī that [Abū Bakr wrote,] "Go on toward Iraq until you enter it. Begin with the gateway to India (*farj al-Hind*), which is al-Ubulla. Render the people of Persia and those nations under their rule peaceable."
>
> ʿUmar b. Shabba narrated to me; he said: ʿAlī b. Muḥammad narrated to us with the aforementioned *isnād* from those mentioned therein: Abū Bakr, may God have mercy on him, sent Khālid b. al-Walīd to the land of Kufa, in which was al-Muthannā b. Ḥāritha al-Shaybānī. Khālid departed in al-Muḥarram 12/633, going by way of Basra, where Quṭba b. Qatāda al-Sadūsī was.
>
> Abū Jaʿfar said: As for al-Wāqidī, he said: There is a difference of opinion about the matter of Khālid b. al-Walīd. Some say that he went straight from al-Yamāma to Iraq. Others say that he returned from al-Yamāma to Medina and then went to Iraq from Medina by way of Kufa until he reached al-Ḥīra.
>
> Ibn Ḥumayd narrated to us; he said: Salama narrated to us from Ibn Isḥāq from Ṣāliḥ b. Kaysān: Abū Bakr, may God have mercy on him, wrote to Khālid ordering him to go to Iraq. Khālid went on his way toward Iraq until he stopped at certain towns in al-Sawād called Bāniqyā, Bārūsmā and Ullays. Their people made a peace treaty with him.[100]

In light of these different views, Khalīfa's notion that Khālid was first sent to "the land of Basra" seems to reflect his special concern for Basra in the *Tārīkh*. As for the conquests during ʿUmar's reign, which reached Persia, Syria and Egypt, Khalīfa provides most information about the eastern conquests such as the campaigns of Abū ʿUbayd al-Thaqafī (13/634–635), the conquests of the regions around Basra (14/635–636), the Battle of al-Qādisiyya and the conquest of al-Madā'in (15/636–637), the campaigns of Abū Mūsā al-Ashʿarī and the Battle of Jalūlāʾ (17/638–639), the Battle of Tustar (20/641) and the Battle of Nihāwand (21/642).[101] Although Khalīfa's *Tārīkh* covers a wide range of regions and provides a considerable amount of detail, including on Syria and Egypt,[102] the most detailed conquest accounts pertain to Iraq and the East, which probably reflect Khalīfa's access to sources (mainly Basran transmitters) and his concerns as a Basran scholar.

---

100 Al-Ṭabarī, *Tārīkh* 1:2016–2017. Modified version of Blankinship's translation in al-Ṭabarī, *History* 11:1–3.

101 Khalīfa b. Khayyāṭ, *Tārīkh* (1985) 124–125, 127–129, 131–138, 144–149.

102 E.g. Khalīfa's *Tārīkh* (1985) 119–120, 125–127, 129–131, 142–144, 150, 152.

The conquests continue under ʿUthmān, reaching North Africa, Cyprus, Abyssinia, Khurāsān, Sijistān and other regions, until they are interrupted by internal conflicts from the end of ʿUthmān's reign. They are then resumed under Muʿāwiya and continue throughout the Umayyad period, apart from periods of uprisings and civil wars, when Khalīfa's narrative, like other early histories, focuses more on internal than external politics. Military expeditions are also reported in the ʿAbbāsid period, but they are more or less limited to suppression of revolts and short accounts of encounters with the Romans such as the annual summer campaigns.[103] Altogether, Khalīfa's conquest narrative resembles the wider tradition in terms of general content, although, as Wurtzel points out, it contains some unique details about certain military expeditions, especially concerning Armenia, Caucasus, Maghrib, Anatolia and India.[104]

The main difference to many other historians is the relative brevity of Khalīfa's accounts and his overall focus on basic facts of when, where and how the conquest occurred, as well as the names of commanders and occasionally other individuals involved. To illustrate this, we may briefly compare Khalīfa's account of the conquest of Damascus with the accounts of a few other early historians.[105] In the section for 14/635, Khalīfa begins:

> In it: Damascus was conquered. Abū ʿUbayda b. al-Jarrāḥ set out accompanied by Khālid b. al-Walīd. He besieged them and they made a treaty with him and then opened the Jābiya Gate for him. Khālid opened another gate by force and Abū ʿUbayda included them in the treaty.
>
> Al-Walīd b. Hishām narrated to me from his father from his grandfather; he said: Khālid led the people and began negotiating with them. He did not finish the treaty until he was replaced by Abū ʿUbayda, who enforced Khālid's treaty without changing the document. Their document was thus written in Khālid's name.

---

103 E.g. Khalīfa b. Khayyāṭ, *Tārīkh* (1985) 410, 417, 419, 421–423, 428, 432–438, 443–445, 448–456.

104 One of the main transmitters of this material is Abū Khālid al-Samtī (d. 190/805), whose information Wurtzel describes as unique to Khalīfa and without parallels in other sources. Wurtzel, *Khalifa ibn Khayyat's History* viii, 33.

105 Khalīfa's Damascus account is also discussed by Scheiner in *Die Eroberung* 13–16, 62–66, 182–187, 203–214, 380–383, 419–422. On Damascus, see also Noth, *Futūḥ* history; Khalek, *Damascus*. Ṣaddām's list of missing material in Baqī's recension contains only one short notice about the conquest of Damascus: "Khalīfa said: Then, after Syria had been conquered, Abū ʿUbayda appointed Khālid over Damascus." Al-Dhahabī, *Tārīkh al-Islām* 3:232; Ṣaddām, *Tārīkh Khalīfa* 62.

> This is a mistake because ʿUmar dismissed Khālid as soon as he became caliph.[106]
>
> ʿAbdallāh b. al-Mughīra narrated to us from his father; he said: Abū ʿUbayda made a treaty, stipulating that they will hand over half of their churches and houses and pay the head tax, and that they will not be prevented from their festivities and that nothing of their churches will be destroyed. These were the conditions that he concluded with the people of the city. The rest of the region was taken by force.
>
> Ibn al-Kalbī said: The treaty was concluded on a Sunday in the middle of Rajab in year 14/635. Abū ʿUbayda b. al-Jarrāḥ concluded it with them.
>
> Bakr narrated to me from Ibn Isḥāq; he said: Abū ʿUbayda concluded the treaty with them in Rajab.[107]

In comparison to the lengthy accounts of the conquest of Damascus found in many other histories, Khalīfa's account is very brief and lacks some events mentioned in other works.[108] Hence it is not the information that is unique to Khalīfa's *Tārīkh*—similar material is found in other histories[109]—but rather the concise way of presenting it. The citations of Ibn Isḥāq and Ibn al-Kalbī also show that Khalīfa had access to similar sources as other historians compiling lengthier works. In comparison to these other works, it is striking that the *Tārīkh* lacks narrative features—such as direct speech, graphic descriptions, anecdotes, citations of complete documents, details about the *jizya* and information about buildings in the city—that are found in the wider historical tradition.[110] This illustrates Khalīfa's focus on core facts such as chronology, main participants and the question of conquest by force or treaty. It is possible that some of Khalīfa's conquest material was abridged in the course of transmission, but he must have been responsible for at least the general form and content of these accounts, since most of the preserved material from al-Tustarī's recension corresponds to Baqī's extant recension.[111]

---

106 After narrating this report, al-Dhahabī notes that this sentence ("This is a mistake …") is Khalīfa's words by saying, "Khalīfa b. Khayyāṭ said this (*qālahu Khalīfa b. Khayyāṭ*)." See al-Dhahabī, *Tārīkh al-Islām* 3:123.

107 Khalīfa b. Khayyāṭ, *Tārīkh* (1985) 125–126.

108 See Scheiner's summary of the structures, main events and motifs in the Damascus accounts of al-Azdī, (pseudo-)al-Wāqidī and Ibn Aʿtham. Scheiner, Writing the history of the *futūḥ* 157–165.

109 See e.g. al-Balādhurī, *Futūḥ* 165–172; al-Ṭabarī, *Tārīkh* 1:2145–2155.

110 See Scheiner, Writing the history of the *futūḥ*; al-Balādhurī, *Futūḥ* 165–172; al-Ṭabarī, *Tārīkh* 1:2145–2155.

111 See Chapter 1.

Another distinct feature of Khalīfa's conquest narrative as a whole is that there are few anecdotes and little information about the conquered peoples, before or after the conquests—in contrast to the histories of al-Yaʿqūbī, al-Dīnawarī, al-Ṭabarī and al-Masʿūdī.[112] Instead, Khalīfa expresses the Muslim hegemony by his silence about the conquered peoples, who have almost no identity or agency in his *Tārīkh*.[113] Apart from encounters in battles, there are almost no accounts of interaction between the Muslims and the conquered peoples, accounts that are found elsewhere in the historical tradition—for instance, the numerous accounts of 'invitations to Islam' (*daʿwa*) offered by the Muslims to the leaders of their non-Muslim opponents.[114] The only accounts of non-Muslim leaders in Khalīfa's *Tārīkh* are the short notices about the succession of Persian kings during the Prophetic period and occasional remarks about enemy commanders in battles—for example, at al-Yarmūk, when the Romans, according to Ibn al-Kalbī, "numbered three hundred thousand under the command of Bāhān, a man from the Persians who had become Christian and joined the Romans."[115] Apart from that, Khalīfa is not concerned with the political or cultural history of the peoples incorporated in the caliphate, something that would interest many later 'universal' historians.[116] Thus Khalīfa's main concern in the *Tārīkh* is the internal affairs of the Muslim polity; external, or non-Muslim, affairs are mentioned only if they pertain directly to the history of the caliphate.

This might reflect Khalīfa's historical interests as an early *ḥadīth* scholar and historian of Arab descent: not so much the history of earlier non-Muslim

112 See Savant, *New Muslims* 90–129.

113 Savant discusses how some accounts of the conquests of Persia in third/ninth- and fourth/tenth-century histories "transform and diminish the identities of the losing side, namely, Sasanian soldiers, religious communities, and elite families." However, unlike some of these other historians (e.g. al-Yaʿqūbī, al-Ṭabarī and Ibn Aʿtham), Khalīfa narrates very little about the conquered peoples. Savant, *New Muslims* 198–229.

114 Noth and Conrad, *Early Arabic* 146–167; Savant, *New Muslims* 201–205. See e.g. al-Ṭabarī's lengthy passages about the interactions between Muslim delegations and the Persians in his *Tārīkh* 1:2239–2244, 2267–2274, 2280–2285, 2352–2353. There is one short report of this kind in Ṣaddām's list of missing material in Baqī's recension, but it was probably transmitted as an individual *ḥadīth* or as a part of Khalīfa's *musnad*, not as a part of the *Tārīkh*. Moreover, this report only describes the transformation of the Arabs through Islam and contains no information about the Persians. See Abū Nuʿaym al-Aṣbahānī, *Maʿrifat al-ṣaḥāba* 5:2583; al-Dhahabī, *Siyar* 4279–4280; Ṣaddām, *Tārīkh Khalīfa* 64.

115 Khalīfa b. Khayyāṭ, *Tārīkh* (1985) 79, 93–94, 130.

116 On the scope of these universal chronicles, see Donner, *Narratives* 127–138; Robinson, *Islamic historiography* 134–138.

peoples, nor the relations between the Muslims and others, but mainly the chronology and political-administrative history of the caliphate—the central political institution of the Muslim community. The focus on the political history of the Muslim community, rather than on non-Muslim history or interreligious polemics, is also found in the sections on *maghāzī* and post-Prophetic history in some early *ḥadīth* collections.[117] It is also the case for Abū Zurʿa's *Tārīkh* and to some extent al-Fasawī's *al-Maʿrifa wa-l-tārīkh*, although it is possible that the latter contained more material on non-Muslim peoples.[118] The history of events, personalities and appointments in different regions of the caliphate was important to *ḥadīth* scholars when analysing *isnāds*, acquiring information about transmitters and contextualising material—besides its role in understanding historical developments and clarifying certain understandings of the past.[119]

Khalīfa's particular concerns as a *ḥadīth* scholar can also be seen in the names of captives taken during the early conquests (some 25 names in total); most of them or their descendants later became prominent scholars. Among these scholars (whose ancestors or who themselves had been taken as captives) are Muḥammad b. Sīrīn, Muḥammad b. Isḥāq, ʿAbdallāh b. ʿAwn, al-Shaʿbī, ʿAbdallāh b. Abī Isḥāq al-Ḥaḍramī, Yaḥyā b. Abī Isḥāq al-Ḥaḍramī, Ḥammād b. Abī Sulaymān, Nāfiʿ b. Abī Nuʿaym, Makḥūl al-Shāmī, Ayyūb al-Sakhtiyānī, Nāfiʿ the *mawlā* of ʿAbdallāh b. ʿUmar and Ḥumayd al-Ṭawīl.[120] Many of the captives that Khalīfa mentions are from Basra or elsewhere in Iraq, and they are often named in his *isnāds*, which, along with their status as scholars, explains why they are mentioned.[121] This indicates what Khalīfa considered most important to include about the conquered peoples: those who had direct impact on the Muslim community and, more specifically, on the scholarly fields in which he was active.

4.3 *Caliphate*

The theme of caliphate is important in Khalīfa's *Tārīkh*, as it is in the historical tradition in general.[122] This theme treated the later continuation of the Muslim hegemony that had been established during the conquest period, in particular

117 ʿAbd al-Razzāq, *Muṣannaf* 5:313–492; Ibn Abī Shayba, *Muṣannaf* 13:196–503, 14:5–309.

118 Abū Zurʿa al-Dimashqī, *Tārīkh* 1:141–209; al-Fasawī, *Maʿrifa* 1:115–213, 3:365–454.

119 For various statements by *ḥadīth* scholars about the benefits of historical studies, see al-Sakhāwī, *al-Iʿlān* 19–81.

120 Khalīfa b. Khayyāṭ, *Tārīkh* (1985) 118, 128, 138, 151, 162, 206.

121 E.g. Khalīfa b. Khayyāṭ, *Tārīkh* (1985) 51, 54, 108, 118, 122, 136, 140, 162.

122 Donner, *Narratives* 182–183; Noth and Conrad, *Early Arabic* 37.

by examining and demonstrating the continuity of the caliphate and its legitimacy. As noted above, the annalistic and caliphal structure of the *Tārīkh*, especially the regular list sections concluding each caliph's reign, affirms the continuity of the Muslim polity from its origins in Medina at the time of the Prophet and the first caliphs to the later Umayyad and ʿAbbāsid dynasties. Despite recurring civil wars and periods of poor leadership, which Khalīfa acknowledges, the authority and legitimacy of the caliphate remain throughout his *Tārīkh*. This is evident in his narration of the early intra-Muslim conflicts, as discussed in Chapter 8. However, one of the most striking differences from other histories is the scarcity of information about the caliphs themselves in Khalīfa's *Tārīkh*.[123] The only information Khalīfa provides consists of brief notes about their genealogies, births and deaths—for example, at the beginning and end of Muʿāwiya's reign:

> The people united under Muʿāwiya [in 41/661]. His mother was Hind bt. ʿUtba b. Rabīʿa b. ʿAbd Shams b. ʿAbd Manāf.[124]

> In it [59/679]: Muʿāwiya died in Damascus on Thursday when eight days remained of Rajab. His son, Yazīd b. Muʿāwiya, led the funeral prayer for him. It is also said that Yazīd was not present and that al-Ḍaḥḥāk b. Qays led the prayer. Muʿāwiya died at the age of 82. Some say that he was 80 and others say 86. His reign lasted 19 years, 3 months and 20 days. He was born in Mecca in the house of Abū Sufyān b. Ḥarb. Some say in the house of ʿUtba b. Rabīʿa.[125]

There are no descriptions of their physical appearance, manners, clothing, moral qualities or characterising anecdotes of words and deeds in particular situations,[126] which one may find in other histories—including the works of, for example, Ibn Ḥabīb and probably also al-Fasawī.[127] In the wider tradition, this biographical material about the caliphs served the purpose not only of personal characterisation but also of moral evaluation, which links it to the theme of

---

123 This is also the case for the preserved material from al-Tustarī's recension that is missing in Baqī's recension, as collected by Ṣaddām in *Tārīkh Khalīfa*. See Chapter 1.

124 Khalīfa b. Khayyāṭ, *Tārīkh* (1985) 203.

125 Khalīfa b. Khayyāṭ, *Tārīkh* (1985) 226.

126 This is also the case for Khalīfa's material preserved in later sources, but missing in Baqī's recension. See Ṣaddām, *Tārīkh Khalīfa* 60–133.

127 Noth and Conrad, *Early Arabic* 37. See the sections for the Rāshidūn caliphs in Ibn Ḥabīb, *Tārīkh* 98–116; al-Fasawī, *Maʿrifa* 3:388–394, 399, 408–409.

leadership examined in Chapter 8.[128] Khalīfa's general approach to leadership is to avoid evaluations of personalities in favour of relatively straightforward outlines of events. In this case, he leaves out the details of the caliphs' biographies, focusing instead on the chronology and political-administrative history of their reigns. The prevalence of reports on, for example, the virtues of the Rāshidūn caliphs in the early *ḥadīth* and *ṭabaqāt* collections shows that such material about the caliphs was circulating among *ḥadīth* scholars and historians like Khalīfa.[129] The apparent reason for the absence is that such biographical material and individual anecdotes did not fit the format of the *Tārīkh* and its strictly chronological and political-administrative scope. At the same time, it illustrates how Khalīfa's *Tārīkh* is not a history of the individuals of the Muslim community and their separate lives, but a history of the community as one entity, represented by its central political institution: the caliphate.

5 Conclusion

Khalīfa treats many subjects that are important in the wider historical tradition, but his approach often differs from many other historians—even in important respects from other *ḥadīth* scholars compiling chronography. His take on the themes of prophethood, community and hegemony, as discussed in this chapter, is largely distinguished and determined by (1) the relatively concise annalistic-caliphal format of the *Tārīkh*, on the basis of which certain subjects and materials are included or excluded; (2) Khalīfa's strict focus on chronological and political-administrative aspects of these themes at the expense of many other popular subjects in the historical tradition, including biographical details, moral evaluations and typical *ḥadīth* material relating to law and belief; (3) the caliphal and community-centred perspective, which focuses on events pertaining to the caliphate and the post-*hijra* Muslim community as a collective rather than on specific individuals or groups within it (except the additional information about the dates of *ḥadīth* transmitters' deaths), and which more or less ignores the non-Muslim populations; and (4) the underlying Basran and early Sunnī outlook, which focuses particularly on information relating to Basra or Iraq in general and which, among other things, asserts the continuity of the caliphate and upholds the probity of the Compan-

128 Donner, *Narratives* 183.

129 E.g. Ibn Abī Shayba, *Muṣannaf* 11:100–156; Ibn Sa'd, *Ṭabaqāt* 3:17–38, 51–79, 155–195, 245–349; Ibn Ḥanbal, *Faḍā'il al-ṣaḥāba* 65–728.

ions of the Prophet. These points, especially the fourth—regarding Khalīfa's early Sunnī perspective—will be discussed further in Chapter 8, on the themes of leadership and civil wars.

CHAPTER 8

Themes II: Leadership and Civil War

1 Introduction

This chapter examines two of the central themes in the early historical tradition: leadership and civil war (*fitna*). There are many studies on historians' approaches to the early successions of caliphs and civil wars, but Khalīfa's *Tārīkh* has hitherto been somewhat neglected.[1] This chapter seeks to demonstrate how Khalīfa's early Sunnī outlook is reflected in his narration of these conflicts and how it differs from other early histories—thereby highlighting this often overlooked source of early Sunnī historical thought. It is suggested that Khalīfa's narration corresponds to positions taken by many early *ḥadīth* scholars with respect to matters such as the ranking of the Rāshidūn caliphs, the probity of the Companions and the importance of communal unity. It also resembles the views in some early *ḥadīth* collections and in later historical works by Sunnī scholars and *ḥadīth* specialists such as Abū Bakr b. al-ʿArabī, Ibn ʿAsākir, Ibn Kathīr and al-Dhahabī.[2]

The analysis is divided into the Rāshidūn, Umayyad and ʿAbbāsid periods. The examined events are selected based on their prominence in Khalīfa's *Tārīkh* and the wider tradition. For the Rāshidūn period, the chapter covers the succession of all four caliphs, the assassination of ʿUthmān and the civil wars during ʿAlī's caliphate. For the Umayyad period, it covers the succession of Muʿāwiya and Yazīd b. Muʿāwiya, al-Ḥusayn's martyrdom, the Battle of al-Ḥarra, the Zubayrid–Umayyad conflict, Ibn al-Ashʿath's revolt and the fall of the Umayyad caliphate. For the ʿAbbāsid period, it covers the succession dispute between al-Amīn and al-Maʾmūn, which is one of the few detailed events in Khalīfa's section on the ʿAbbāsid period. Similar to Chapter 7, this analysis is based on the notion of Khalīfa being responsible for at least the general form and content of Baqī b. Makhlad's extant recension of the *Tārīkh*, which also means acknowl-

1 E.g. Petersen, *ʿAlī and Muʿāwiya*; Shoshan, *Poetics* 157–252; El-Hibri, *Parable and politics*; Judd, Narratives, Reinterpreting al-Walīd b. Yazīd; Anthony, *Caliph and the heretic*; Keaney, Confronting the caliph; Hagler, Repurposed narratives. Two exceptions that briefly examine Khalīfa's work are Roberts, *Early Islamic historiography* 68–80; Keaney, *Medieval Islamic historiography* 21–46.

2 On these later scholars and their use of Khalīfa's *Tārīkh*, see Chapter 2.

 | DOI:10.1163/9789004383173_010

edging the possibility that some material was omitted, abridged or otherwise altered (by Baqī or someone else) in the course of transmission.

2 The Rāshidūn Period

2.1 *Succession of Caliphs*

The succession of the first four caliphs—known as the rightly-guided caliphs (*al-khulafāʾ al-rāshidūn*) in Sunnī scholarship—after the Prophet's death in 11/632 is an intensely debated topic in the historical tradition.[3] It includes the pledge of allegiance to Abū Bakr at the *saqīfa* ('shelter') of Banū Sāʿida, Abū Bakr's appointment of ʿUmar as successor, the *shūrā*-election of ʿUthmān and the pledge of allegiance to ʿAlī after ʿUthmān's assassination. By the second/eighth century, these events and the different approaches to them had become a clear dividing line between the different scholarly traditions. Broadly speaking, Shīʿīs upheld the exclusive right of ʿAlī (and his descendants) to the caliphate, while the early Sunnī scholars emphasised the legitimacy and special status of the first four caliphs. In contrast to most other historical compilers on this subject, Khalīfa completely avoids the details of the early successions.[4] However, his silence about the events underscores in itself the legitimacy of the succession of the Rāshidūn caliphs.

The disagreement following the death of the Prophet in 11/632 is a central episode in most early histories.[5] These accounts usually reflect support for either Abū Bakr's actual succession or the idea that ʿAlī should have succeeded

---

3 The fifth caliph, al-Ḥasan b. ʿAlī, is sometimes also included among the Rāshidūn caliphs, although his reign was turbulent and only lasted for about half a year. The Rāshidūn caliphs are, moreover, referred to in *ḥadīth*s such as the Prophet's words, "Those of you who live after me will see many disagreements, so you must hold to my *sunna* and the *sunna* of the rightly-guided, upright caliphs (*al-khulafāʾ al-mahdiyīn al-rāshidīn*)," and, "The caliphate (*khilāfa*) in my community will last 30 years. After that, there will be kingship (*mulk*)." See Abū Dāwūd, *Sunan* 7:16–17 (*kitāb al-sunna, bāb fī luzūm al-sunna*); al-Tirmidhī, *al-Jāmiʿ* 4:82 (*abwāb al-fitan, bāb mā jāʾa fī l-khilāfa*), 4:408 (*abwāb al-ʿilm, bāb mā jāʾa fī l-akhdh bi-l-sunna* …); Ibn Ḥanbal, *Musnad* 28:367–375 (*al-ʿIrbāḍ b. Sāriya*), 36:248 (*Safīna*); al-Ṭayālisī, *Musnad* 2:430–431 (*Safīna*).

4 There are no reports about the succession of the Rāshidūn caliphs in Ṣaddām's collection of material that later historians transmit from Khalīfa via al-Tustarī and others. See Ṣaddām, *Tārīkh Khalīfa* 60–75.

5 E.g. Ibn Hishām, *Sīra* 4:308–313; Ibn Ḥabīb, *Tārīkh* 96–97; al-Fasawī, *Maʿrifa* 3:365–366; al-Balādhurī, *Ansāb* 2:259–275; al-Yaʿqūbī, *Tārīkh* 2:7–11; al-Ṭabarī, *Tārīkh* 1:1820–1830, 1837–1845; al-Masʿūdī, *Murūj* 2:301–302; Ibn Aʿtham al-Kūfī, *Futūḥ* 1:3–14.

first.[6] Among the works in favour of ʿAlī's succession are the works of al-Yaʿqūbī and al-Masʿūdī. The latter summarises the events as follows:

> After the oath of allegiance was given to Abū Bakr on the day of the *saqīfa* and then renewed with the common people on Tuesday, ʿAlī came forth and said, "You have corrupted our affairs. You did not seek consultation and you did not respect our rights." Abū Bakr replied, "Indeed, but I feared sedition (*fitna*)." There was a lengthy affair and contention for the leadership (*al-imāma*) between the Muhājirūn and the Anṣār on the day of the *saqīfa*. Saʿd b. ʿUbāda left and did not pledge allegiance. He went to Syria where he was killed in year 15/636. However, this book is not the place for the story of how he was killed. No one from Banū Hāshim pledged allegiance [to Abū Bakr] until Fāṭima died, may God be pleased with her.[7]

In contrast, al-Ṭabarī provides a more complicated picture, with reports from various transmitters (through Abū Mikhnaf and Sayf b. ʿUmar), which altogether asserts the legitimacy of Abū Bakr's succession.[8] Many early *ḥadīth* collections also contain material on Abū Bakr's succession that emphasises his legitimacy.[9] Unlike all these works, however, Khalīfa completely ignores the *saqīfa* events. Instead, there is simply a segue from the Prophet's administrative appointments to the beginning of Abū Bakr's caliphate, about which Khalīfa says, "In year 11/632, Abū Bakr was given the general oath of allegiance on Tuesday, the day after the death of the Messenger of God (ṣ)."[10]

It is unlikely that a *saqīfa* account was lost in transmission, since Khalīfa similarly avoids the successions of ʿUmar, ʿUthmān and ʿAlī, which were also contentious subjects in the historical tradition.[11] By contrast, he narrates significant detail about other controversies in the Rāshidūn period, such as ʿUthmān's assassination and the civil wars during ʿAlī's caliphate. It is not until Muʿāwiya's appointment of his son, Yazīd, that Khalīfa details the issues of succession. This consistent silence on the succession of the first caliphs suggests a conscious

6 See El-Hibri, *Parable and politics* 42–61; Madelung, *Succession* 28–56.

7 Al-Masʿūdī, *Murūj* 2:301. See also Anthony's discussion of al-Yaʿqūbī's Shīʿī narrative of these events in Was Ibn Wāḍiḥ a Shiʿite historian? 28–30.

8 Al-Ṭabarī, *Tārīkh* 1:1820–1830, 1837–1848.

9 See Zaman, *Maghāzī* and the *muḥaddithūn* 10–11; Lucas, *Constructive critics* 255–266.

10 Khalīfa b. Khayyāṭ, *Tārīkh* (1985) 100.

11 Khalīfa b. Khayyāṭ, *Tārīkh* (1985) 122, 156, 180. See Madelung, *Succession* 54–56, 70–77, 141–151; El-Hibri, *Parable and politics* 66–76, 90–94, 105–108, 208–209, 269–278. Moreover, there are no indications in later sources, transmitting from al-Tustarī's recension, that Baqī would have omitted material about these successions. See Chapter 1.

avoidance, which is noteworthy for a couple of reasons. First, it reflects a support for the actual order of succession. By passing over the disagreements and attenuating the surrounding controversies reported elsewhere, Khalīfa naturalises the sequence of the first four caliphs and thereby asserts their legitimacy. The ranking of the first caliphs is further stressed in Khalīfa's section on Yazīd b. Muʿāwiya's succession—most explicitly by Ibn al-Zubayr, who asserts the legitimacy of the succession of the early caliphs and states that Abū Bakr is the best of the community after the Prophet and that ʿUmar is the best after Abū Bakr.[12] Second, the avoidance of the succession disputes (as reported elsewhere) illustrates Khalīfa's straightforward narrative style, focusing on well-established events of political or administrative significance—without leaving much room for doubt or uncertainty about the events or their meanings. Needless to say, this style is also a function of the relatively condensed format of the *Tārīkh*, but the complete absence of material on the succession of the Rāshidūn caliphs is nonetheless remarkable.

2.2 *The Assassination of ʿUthmān*

The assassination of ʿUthmān b. ʿAffān in 35/656 is a central episode in the historical tradition.[13] His initially prosperous reign ended in unrest, and ultimately in his assassination after a siege of his house in Medina, which initiated a period of civil war known as the first *fitna* or the great *fitna* (*al-fitnat al-kubrā*). Some early *akhbār* histories reflect Shīʿī stances on ʿUthmān's assassination and the other intra-Muslim conflicts.[14] Others reflect the broad spectra of early Sunnī perspectives, such as the works of Sayf b. ʿUmar, Ibn Saʿd, Ibn Abī Shayba, Ibn Ḥabīb, al-Fasawī, ʿAbdallāh b. Aḥmad b. Ḥanbal and al-Ṭabarī.[15] Similarly to these latter works, Khalīfa presents ʿUthmān as a martyr, exonerates the Companions and presents the assassination as the inception of intra-communal fighting, although his concise narrative style and arrangement differ in some respects.[16] In contrast to other compilers, Khalīfa

12 See also Ibn ʿUmar's praise of the earlier caliphs. Khalīfa b. Khayyāṭ, *Tārīkh* (1985) 213–214, 216.

13 See Keaney, *Medieval Islamic historiography* 1–20.

14 E.g. al-Yaʿqūbī, *Tārīkh* 2:55–73; al-Masʿūdī, *Murūj* 2:329–346; Ibn Aʿtham al-Kūfī, *Futūḥ* 2:388–431.

15 Sayf b. ʿUmar, *Kitāb al-Ridda* 10–213; Ibn Saʿd, *Ṭabaqāt* 3:61–79; Ibn Abī Shayba, *Muṣannaf* 14:183–214; ʿAbdallāh b. Aḥmad b. Ḥanbal (narrating from his father), *Faḍāʾil ʿUthmān*; Ibn Ḥabīb, *Tārīkh* 113–114; al-Fasawī, *Maʿrifa* 3:398–399; al-Ṭabarī, *Tārīkh* 1:2941–3025.

16 On this image in the other works, see Keaney, *Medieval Islamic historiography* 21–46. There is one report about the killing of ʿUthmān in Ṣaddām's collection of material that later

bases his account almost exclusively on Basran sources, which distinguishes it as a Basran early Sunnī narration of ʿUthmān's assassination. He also avoids material that is in some way critical of ʿUthmān, which can be found in the works of Ibn Saʿd, al-Balādhurī and al-Ṭabarī.[17]

Khalīfa's account of ʿUthmān's caliphate (r. 23–35/644–656) in Baqī's recension is dedicated mostly to military campaigns. No internal conflicts are mentioned until 33/653–654, when Khalīfa briefly notes that some people began to criticise ʿUthmān: "ʿĀmir b. Rabīʿa died when the people set about the opposition against ʿUthmān, may God be pleased with him."[18] There are, however, no allusions to 'six good years and six bad years' or any details about controversial policies.[19] He lists the names of the relatives whom ʿUthmān appointed to key posts in the caliphate but does not explicitly highlight this point, let alone criticise it.[20] Moreover, Khalīfa makes no mention of the conspiracy of ʿAbdallāh b. Sabaʾ (Ibn Sawdāʾ), which Sayf b. ʿUmar, in particular, popularised as an interpretation of ʿUthmān's assassination and the subsequent *fitna*.[21] Khalīfa's account of the assassination of ʿUthmān consists of 47 reports from the following direct transmitters:[22]

historians transmit from Khalīfa via al-Tustarī and others, but the same information and more or less the same wording is found in Baqī's recension. See Khalīfa b. Khayyāṭ, *Tārīkh* (1985) 174–175; Ṣaddām, *Tārīkh Khalīfa* 69. There is also another report from before the assassination, according to which ʿUthmān sent a message to ʿAlī, saying, "Your cousin will be killed and you will be deprived [of the caliphate] (*maslub*)." This report might have been lost in transmission, but it is also possible that it was never a part of the *Tārīkh* as Baqī received it from Khalīfa. Moreover, there is no particular reason to think that Baqī deliberately omitted it from his recension because of its content. See Ibn ʿAsākir, *Tārīkh madīnat Dimashq* 39:366; Ṣaddām, *Tārīkh Khalīfa* 68. Many of the reports about ʿUthmān in Baqī's recension are also transmitted by al-Tustarī in Ibn ʿAsākir's *Tārīkh madīnat Dimashq* 39:321–324, 337–339, 346–348, 356–357, 391–398, 403–404, 408, 411, 414, 486–487, 514–515, 523–524.

17 Ibn Saʿd, *Ṭabaqāt* 3:60–68; al-Balādhurī, *Ansāb* 6:133–189, 208–209; al-Ṭabarī, *Tārīkh* 1:2927–2980.

18 Khalīfa b. Khayyāṭ, *Tārīkh* (1985) 168, 180.

19 E.g. Ibn Saʿd, *Ṭabaqāt* 3:60; al-Balādhurī, *Ansāb* 5:133–138; El-Hibri, *Parable and politics* 126–127, 133–147.

20 Khalīfa b. Khayyāṭ, *Tārīkh* (1985) 178. On these controversies (from a Shīʿī perspective), see Madelung, *Succession* 81–113.

21 See Anthony, *Caliph and the heretic* 19–103. See also al-ʿAwd, *ʿAbdallāh b. Sabaʾ*.

22 One report is narrated with double *isnād*. Khalīfa's account also contains three lines of poetry from al-Farazdaq, Nābigha al-Jaʿdī and al-Qāsim b. Umayya b. Abī l-Ṣalt, which are not included in the list since they were not direct transmitters. Khalīfa b. Khayyāṭ, *Tārīkh* (1985) 177.

TABLE 10 Khalīfa's sources on the assassination of ʿUthmān

Name		Reports	Location
1.	Kahmas b. al-Minhāl	7	Basra
2.	Muʿtamir b. Sulaymān	7	Basra
3.	Ismāʿīl b. ʿUlayya	5	Basra
4.	Al-Madāʾinī	3	Basra/Baghdad
5.	ʿAbd al-Raḥmān b. Mahdī	2	Basra
6.	Abū Dāwūd al-Ṭayālisī	2	Basra
7.	Ghundar	2	Basra
8.	Khālid b. al-Ḥārith	2	Basra
9.	Muʿādh b. Hishām	2	Basra
10.	Yaḥyā b. Muḥammad al-Kaʿbī	2	Basra/Medina
11.	ʿAbd al-Aʿlā b. ʿAbd al-Aʿlā	1	Basra
12.	ʿAbd al-Wahhāb b. ʿAbd al-Majīd	1	Basra
13.	Abū ʿĀṣim al-Ḍaḥḥāk b. Makhlad	1	Basra
14.	Abū Bakr al-Kalbī	1	Basra
15.	Abū Qutayba Salm b. Qutayba	1	Basra
16.	Abū l-Yaqẓān	1	Basra
17.	Rawḥ b. ʿUbāda	1	Basra
18.	ʿUbaydallāh b. ʿAbdallāh b. ʿAwn	1	Basra
19.	ʿUmar b. Abī Khalīfa	1	Basra
20.	Yaḥyā b. Abī l-Ḥajjāj al-Khāqānī	1	Basra
21.	Yazīd b. Hārūn	1	Wāsiṭ
22.	ʿAbd al-Aʿlā b. al-Haytham	1	–
23.	Muḥammad b. ʿAmr	1	–
24.	Anonymous (from al-Aʿmash)	1	–

Many of these transmitters were considered reliable (*thiqa*), which indicates the importance that Khalīfa attached to the event.[23] This Basran selection of transmitters differs from al-Ṭabarī's heavy reliance (through intermediate transmitters) on Sayf b. ʿUmar and al-Wāqidī.[24] Al-Balādhurī cites some of Khalīfa's Basran transmitters, but also other non-Basrans.[25] This shows that

23 Ibn Saʿd, for example, mentions eleven of them in his *Ṭabaqāt* and declares ten of them reliable (*thiqa*). See Chapter 5.

24 Al-Ṭabarī, *Tārīkh* 1:2941–3025.

25 Al-Balādhurī, *Ansāb* 6:208–229.

non-Basran material circulated in Khalīfa's time, although it is unclear if Khalīfa had access to it.

Khalīfa's account of the assassination begins with the delegations that came to Medina from Egypt, Basra and Kufa to raise their complaints to ʿUthmān. This is the only time Khalīfa specifies the grievances against ʿUthmān, apart from the implicit references in the treaty that ʿAlī then negotiated with the rebels on behalf of ʿUthmān, which resulted in five conditions: (1) returning the exiled, (2) giving to the deprived, (3) distributing the conquest revenue (*fayʾ*) in full, (4) allocating it justly and (5) appointing trustworthy and resolute governors, including reappointing Ibn ʿĀmir over Basra and Abū Mūsā al-Ashʿarī over Kufa.[26] In response to the rebels' allegations, however, Khalīfa presents ʿUthmān's refutations in order to show that the allegations against him were baseless. For example, when the Egyptians censure ʿUthmān for reserving grazing pastures and cite a Qurʾānic verse to support their argument (10:59), ʿUthmān explains:

> Continue the verse; it was revealed about such-and-such. As for the pastures, ʿUmar reserved them specifically for the *ṣadaqa* camels [i.e. camels collected as *zakāt*] before me. When I was appointed, the *ṣadaqa* camels increased, so I increased the pastures because of the increased number of camels.[27]

Although Khalīfa does not refute all allegations, he lets the subsequent course of events speak for itself and lets it do so in favour of ʿUthmān. He narrates the famous story that the Egyptians, on return from Medina after the agreement with ʿUthman, found a messenger with a letter written in ʿUthmān's name, ordering the Egyptian governor to kill them.[28] Similar to Ibn Saʿd, Ibn Abī Shayba and Aḥmad b. Ḥanbal (as narrated by his son), Khalīfa accepts ʿUthmān's denial of having written the letter, which stresses his innocence and the baselessness of the subsequent attack on his house.[29] This differs from al-

26 Khalīfa b. Khayyāṭ, *Tārīkh* (1985) 169–170. On these criticisms, see Ibn al-ʿArabī, *al-ʿAwāṣim* 280–300; Madelung, *Succession* 81–113.

27 Khalīfa b. Khayyāṭ, *Tārīkh* (1985) 169. See also Ibn al-ʿArabī, *al-ʿAwāṣim* 289. Ibn ʿAsākir narrates the same report via al-Tustarī in *Tārīkh madīnat Dimashq* 39:323–324.

28 Khalīfa b. Khayyāṭ, *Tārīkh* (1985) 169. On this story elsewhere, see Madelung, *Succession* 112–113; El-Hibri, *Parable and politics* 186–187; Keaney, *Medieval Islamic historiography* 40; al-Yaʿqūbī, *Tārīkh* 2:72; al-Ṭabarī, *Tārīkh* 1:2964–2965; al-Masʿūdī, *Murūj* 2:344; Ibn al-ʿArabī, *al-ʿAwāṣim* 293–294.

29 On Ibn Saʿd and Aḥmad b. Ḥanbal, see Keaney, *Medieval Islamic historiography* 40. On Ibn Abī Shayba, see his *Muṣannaf* 14:200–201, 205–206. In one of Ibn Abī Shayba's reports

Balādhurī, who narrates that Marwān b. al-Ḥakam had written the letter, and from al-Ṭabarī, who narrates from al-Wāqidī that the besiegers remarked that ʿUthmān should have left the office even if Marwān had forged the letter in ʿUthmān's name, and from Sayf b. ʿUmar, who narrates that it was a part of the Sabaʾiyya plot.[30] Khalīfa also emphasises ʿUthmān's righteousness by narrating that he told the Egyptians, in line with Islamic law, either to accept his oath that he did not write it or to bring two witnesses, which they refused to do, declaring instead his blood permissible to shed—before besieging his house.[31] The report thereby suggests that they had not come to accept the truth of the matter or refer to the Islamic law, but either to depose ʿUthmān or shed his blood.[32] This is further accentuated by another report, in which ʿUthmān met with Mālik b. al-Ḥārith al-Nakhaʿī al-Ashtar, the leader of the Kufan opposition:

> Ibn ʿUlayya reported to me; he said: Ibn ʿAwn narrated to me from al-Ḥasan; he said: Waththāb informed me; he said: ʿUthmān sent me and I summoned al-Ashtar. ʿUthmān said, "What do the people want from me?" Al-Ashtar said, "You have to choose one of three things." He said, "What are they?" He said, "They give you the choice [between the following]. You may turn the affair over to them and say, 'This is your affair, choose whomever you will for it.' Or you may have yourself punished as retaliation. If you reject these two alternatives, they will kill you." ʿUthmān said, "Do I really have to choose one of these?" Al-Ashtar replied, "You have to choose one of these." He said, "As for turning the affair over to them, I will not throw off a robe that God has placed upon me. (He said that someone other than al-Ḥasan narrated:) By God, it would be dearer to me to have my neck struck off than leaving the community of Muḥammad [in animosity] against each other. As for having myself punished as retaliation, by God, I know that my two companions before me also punished [without having themselves punished] and my body cannot endure pun-

ʿUthmān seems to suspect ʿAlī for involvement in the affair of the letter, but the other report stresses that it was fabricated against both of them. See also Ibn al-ʿArabī, *al-ʿAwāṣim* 290–291.

30 Keaney, *Medieval Islamic historiography* 40; al-Balādhurī, *Ansāb* 6:184; al-Ṭabarī, *Tārīkh* 1: 2954–2958, 2992–2993.

31 Khalīfa b. Khayyāṭ, *Tārīkh* (1985) 169.

32 As Abū Bakr b. al-ʿArabī states, "They did not accept that [i.e. ʿUthmān's oath or bringing two witnesses] from him and broke their agreement with him and besieged him." *Al-ʿAwāṣim* 294.

ishment. As for your killing me, by God, if you kill me you will never again have love for each other and you will never again pray united and you will never again fight an enemy united."[33]

In the subsequent series of reports about the siege, Khalīfa presents ʿUthmān as the unjustly killed caliph and his assassination as the inception of *fitna* in the Muslim community. Some reports mention that ʿUthmān admonished the rebels besieging his house by mentioning the Prophet's praise of him and description of him as a martyr (*shahīd*) as well as other merits, which is said to have made some of the rebels hesitate. Khalīfa also repeats ʿUthmān's refusal to relinquish the caliphate for which God had made him responsible: "I will not throw off a robe that God has placed upon me." Similar ideas are evoked in ʿAbdallāh b. ʿUmar's advice to ʿUthmān, "I don't see any reason for you to throw off a shirt that God placed upon you and thereby make it a custom (*sunna*): every time a people dislike their caliph or leader, they kill him."[34] These reports correspond to Khalīfa's early Sunnī perspective on leadership and justify ʿUthmān's defence of the caliphate. Such reports are also narrated by Ibn Saʿd, Ibn Abī Shayba, Ibn Ḥabīb, ʿAbdallāh b. Aḥmad b. Ḥanbal and al-Ṭabarī in different variations.[35] ʿUthmān is likewise said to have told the rebels, similar to the lengthy report cited above, "Do not kill me, for, by God, if you kill me you will never again fight an enemy united and you will never again divide booty united and you will never again pray united." Khalīfa also adds that al-Ḥasan al-Baṣrī (d. 110/728) said, "By God, even if the people prayed united their hearts would still be disunited."[36] In this way, Khalīfa presents the caliphicide as the inception of *fitna* in the community.

A major issue for the early historical compilers was the role of the Companions in the assassination. Early Sunnī scholars exonerated the Companions and emphasised that ʿUthmān was unjustly killed at the hands of non-Medinan rebels, although they may admit that certain Companions had been critical of some of ʿUthmān's policies.[37] The historical tradition, especially works of Shīʿī-inclined historians, also contains some less harmonious material about the role

33 Khalīfa b. Khayyāṭ, *Tārīkh* (1985) 170. Ibn ʿAsākir narrates the same report via al-Tustarī in *Tārīkh madīnat Dimashq* 39:403–404.

34 Khalīfa b. Khayyāṭ, *Tārīkh* (1985) 170–172. Ibn ʿAsākir transmits the same report from Khalīfa via al-Tustarī in *Tārīkh madīnat Dimashq* 39:356–357.

35 Ibn Saʿd, *Ṭabaqāt* 3:62–66; Ibn Abī Shayba, *Muṣannaf* 14:184–186; ʿAbdallāh b. Aḥmad b. Ḥanbal, *Faḍāʾil ʿUthmān* 106–107; Ibn Ḥabīb, *Tārīkh* 113–114; al-Ṭabarī, *Tārīkh* 1:2990.

36 Khalīfa b. Khayyāṭ, *Tārīkh* (1985) 171. Ibn ʿAsākir narrates the same report via al-Tustarī in *Tārīkh madīnat Dimashq* 39:348.

37 See Keaney, *Medieval Islamic historiography* 38–46.

of certain Companions in the opposition against ʿUthmān.[38] In line with the early Sunnīs, Khalīfa frees the Companions of blame and presents ʿUthmān as a martyr, unjustly killed by non-Medinan rebels. He narrates, for instance, that one of the besiegers justified their actions by alluding to the Qurʾānic verses, "Permission to fight is given to those who are fought against because they have been wronged—truly God has the power to come to their support—those who were expelled from their homes without any right, merely for saying, 'God is our Lord'" (Q 22:39–40).[39] To this ʿUthmān replied:

> You have lied. You are not those [referred to in the verse], but we are. The people of Mecca expelled us and then God said, "Those who, if We establish them firmly on the earth, will establish the prayer and pay *zakāt*, and command what is right and forbid what is wrong." (Q 22:41) Praise preceded trial.[40]

This asserts the absence of Muhājirūn among the besiegers. Another report from al-Ḥasan al-Baṣrī explicitly states that there were no Muhājirūn or Anṣār among ʿUthmān's murderers, but merely Egyptian thugs (*aʿlāj*).[41] The usage of the pejorative term *aʿlāj* (sing. *ʿilj*)—often referring to non-Arab unbelievers or 'barbarians'—further frees the Companions of blame.[42] Khalīfa then makes clear that ʿUthmān forbade the Medinan Companions and Successors from spilling their blood for his sake and thereby initiating civil war among the Muslims. Many prominent Companions are reported to have offered to fight for ʿUthmān, among them Zayd b. Thābit (on behalf of the Anṣār), ʿAbdallāh b. ʿUmar, Abū Hurayra, al-Ḥasan b. ʿAlī, al-Ḥusayn b. ʿAlī and ʿAbdallāh b. al-Zubayr.[43] In one report, ʿUthmān specifically orders all those who hear and obey to put down their weapons, which presents the Companions' absence as a consequence of their loyalty and obedience to ʿUthmān.[44]

Another issue among the early historians was the alleged involvement of ʿĀʾisha in the uprising,[45] which some early Sunnīs responded to with reports

38 See Madelung, *Succession* 81–140.
39 Khalīfa b. Khayyāṭ, *Tārīkh* (1985) 171.
40 Khalīfa b. Khayyāṭ, *Tārīkh* (1985) 171. Ibn ʿAsākir narrates the same report via al-Tustarī in *Tārīkh madīnat Dimashq* 39:346–347.
41 Khalīfa b. Khayyāṭ, *Tārīkh* (1985) 176.
42 Lane, *Arabic-English lexicon* s.v. *ʿilj*.
43 Khalīfa b. Khayyāṭ, *Tārīkh* (1985) 173–174.
44 Khalīfa b. Khayyāṭ, *Tārīkh* (1985) 173.
45 For such material about ʿĀʾisha, see Madelung, *Succession* 100–103.

from ʿĀʾisha praising ʿUthmān, as well as condemning the rebels and disassociating herself from them.[46] Khalīfa narrates four statements from ʿĀʾisha condemning the murders and asserting ʿUthmān's innocence, thereby absolving her of blame. In one of them, ʿĀʾisha responds to the claim that she had written and encouraged the rebels, saying, "By the One in whom the believers believe and the unbelievers disbelieve, I did not write to them with black on white before taking this seat." One of the narrators, al-Aʿmash (d. 148/765), adds, "They thought that someone had forged it in her name."[47]

As for the actual killing, Khalīfa reports that ʿUthmān sat down with a copy of the Qurʾān, when a man entered and attacked him, cutting off "the first hand to write al-Mufaṣṣal."[48] The involvement of Muḥammad b. Abī Bakr—the son of the first caliph, born in the last year of the Prophet's life—is mentioned in a few reports, but he is said not to have been the actual killer. One report states that he left the house after an admonition from ʿUthmān ("You have taken a stance against me that your father would never have taken").[49] Other reports give different descriptions of those involved in the killing: (1) "a man from Banū Sadūs, known as the Black Death (*al-mawt al-aswad*)", (2) Kināna b. Bishr al-Tujībī, (3) "Rūmān, a man from Banū Asad b. Khuzayma", (4) Sūdān b. Ḥumrān and (5) "a man from Egypt known as Ḥimār." One report also describes how the intruders attacked ʿUthmān by turns until they killed him.[50] Similar information is found in other sources.[51] The importance of these reports is not so much that specific individuals are blamed but rather to emphasise the innocence of the Medinans in general and the Companions in particular. It is also reported that ʿUthmān's blood fell on the words in the Qurʾān, "God will be enough for you against them" (Q 2:137), which further accentuates his role as the unjustly killed caliph.[52]

Finally, Khalīfa mentions, in his own words, that "ʿUthmān, may God have mercy on him, was killed in it [35/656] on a Friday when a number of days remained of Dhū l-Ḥijja" and then provides various narrations about the exact

46 See e.g. Aḥmad b. Ḥanbal's reports from ʿĀʾisha about ʿUthmān in his *Faḍāʾil al-ṣaḥāba* 452, 455, 462–463, 467–468, 494–495, 499–501, 509, 521–522.

47 Khalīfa b. Khayyāṭ, *Tārīkh* (1985) 176. See also Ibn al-ʿArabī, *al-ʿAwāṣim* 296–297.

48 Khalīfa b. Khayyāṭ, *Tārīkh* (1985) 174.

49 Khalīfa b. Khayyāṭ, *Tārīkh* (1985) 174.

50 Khalīfa b. Khayyāṭ, *Tārīkh* (1985) 174–175.

51 Ibn Abī Shayba, *Muṣannaf* 14:202–203; Ibn Saʿd, *Ṭabaqāt* 3:69–71; Ibn Ḥabīb, *Tārīkh* 113–114; Abū Zurʿa al-Dimashqī, *Tārīkh* 1:187; al-Balādhurī, *Ansāb* 6:212–221; al-Ṭabarī, *Tārīkh* 1:3006–3007, 3021–3023.

52 Khalīfa b. Khayyāṭ, *Tārīkh* (1985) 175. Ibn ʿAsākir narrates the same report from Khalīfa via al-Tustarī in *Tārīkh madīnat Dimashq* 39:411.

date of the killing (10th, 12th, 17th and 18th). He also cites three lines of poetry from al-Farazdaq, Nābigha al-Jaʿdī and al-Qāsim b. Umayya b. Abī l-Ṣalt:

> (1) ʿUthmān, they killed him and violated his blood
> in the early dawn of the Night of Sacrifice (*laylat al-naḥr*).
>
> (2) And Ibn ʿAffān, a pure believer (*ḥanīf*) and Muslim,
> and the flesh of the sacrificial animals as it was taken away.
>
> (3) By my life, what an evil slaughter you took as sacrifice
> in opposition to the Messenger of God on the Day of Sacrifice.[53]

The purpose of these verses is, on the one hand, to confirm the date of the assassination in Dhū l-Ḥijja (alluded to in all three verses) and, on the other hand, to assert ʿUthmān's role as the unjustly killed caliph ("violated his blood", "a pure believer and Muslim" and "in opposition to the Messenger of God").

In summary, Khalīfa's account corresponds to the early Sunnī views of many third/ninth-century *ḥadīth* scholars: the emphasis on ʿUthmān's righteousness, his role as the unjustly killed caliph, the assassination as the beginning of intra-Muslim strife, the error of the rebels and the innocence of the Companions. Such perspectives can be found in, for example, Ibn Abī Shayba's *Muṣannaf* and ʿAbdallāh b. Aḥmad b. Ḥanbal's *Faḍāʾil ʿUthmān* (narrated from his father). Similar material reflecting early Sunnī ideas circulated in the wider tradition of *akhbār* history, but Khalīfa and these other *ḥadīth* scholars express these views more explicitly and largely avoid ambiguous and Shīʿī-inclined reports about ʿUthmān. The main difference from Ibn Abī Shayba and ʿAbdallāh b. Aḥmad b. Ḥanbal's material is Khalīfa's chronological arrangement of the events, the absence of *faḍāʾil* material about ʿUthmān and the almost total reliance on transmission from Basran *ḥadīth* scholars.

In addition, Sayf b. ʿUmar is an early *akhbārī* whose defence of ʿUthmān and assertion of the Companions' righteousness to some extent resemble Khalīfa's, but whose material, sources and narrative style differ. In contrast to Sayf's synthesised narrative based on longer reports, Khalīfa's narrative is restricted to short reports. Sayf also constructs a comprehensive theory of Ibn Sabaʾ and the Sabaʾiyya as the masterminds of the *fitna*, while Khalīfa limits his defence of ʿUthmān and the Companions to chronology, basic facts and some accounts of ʿUthmān's and the other Companions' actions. Moreover, in contrast to Sayf's

53 Khalīfa b. Khayyāṭ, *Tārīkh* (1985) 176–177.

limited number of sources—most of them unknown to both classical and modern scholars—Khalīfa narrates from a wide range of major *ḥadīth* authorities and *akhbār* historians.[54] Altogether, Khalīfa's perspective on the assassination of ʿUthmān resembles that of many other early *ḥadīth* scholars, while the chronological arrangement of his account bears more resemblance to the *akhbār* histories. In contrast to all these, however, Khalīfa's account is based almost exclusively on Basran sources, which sets it apart as a Basran early Sunnī narration of the assassination of ʿUthmān.

2.3 *Civil Wars during ʿAlī's Caliphate*

After the assassination of ʿUthmān at the end of 35/656, the Prophet's cousin ʿAlī b. Abī Ṭālib received the oath of allegiance in Medina. However, his reign was taken up by the civil wars known as the first *fitna* or the great *fitna*, including the Battle of the Camel (36/656) and the Battle of Ṣiffīn (37/657). The early historians compiled numerous works on these events. Some composed works on specific battles (e.g. Sayf b. ʿUmar and Naṣr b. Muzāḥim), while others included substantial sections in chronographies (e.g. Khalīfa and al-Ṭabarī) and occasionally in *ḥadīth* collections (e.g. Ibn Abī Shayba).[55] Similar to the assassination of ʿUthmān, the first *fitna* is one of the key subjects in early *akhbār* history and was important to the formation and articulation of religio-political identities.

2.3.1 The Battle of the Camel (36/656)

Khalīfa's section on the Battle of the Camel is the most detailed section in his account of the first *fitna* in Baqī's recension. It comprises roughly half of the section on ʿAlī's caliphate and contains 44 reports (one with double *isnād*), in contrast to the 12 reports on the Battle of Ṣiffīn.[56] However, later historians preserve other reports from Khalīfa on the Battle of Ṣiffīn that were presumably found in Mūsā al-Tustarī's recension of the *Tārīkh*. Ṣaddām collects 14 reports from al-Tustarī's recension preserved in later works, although 7 of these reports seem to be the same report from Abū ʿUbayda Maʿmar b. al-Muthannā divided

---

54 On these aspects of Sayf's narrative, see Anthony, *Caliph and the heretic* 21–24, 107–109, 116.

55 Sayf b. ʿUmar, *Kitāb al-Ridda* 239–372; Naṣr b. Muzāḥim, *Waqʿat Ṣiffīn*; Ibn Abī Shayba, *Muṣannaf* 14:232–309; Khalīfa b. Khayyāṭ, *Tārīkh* (1985) 180–197; al-Fasawī, *Maʿrifa* 3:401–407; al-Dīnawarī, *al-Akhbār al-ṭiwāl* 145–199; al-Yaʿqūbī, *Tārīkh* 2:78–91; al-Ṭabarī, *Tārīkh* 1:3106–360. See also Ibn al-ʿArabī, *al-ʿAwāṣim* 300–324.

56 One report on the Battle of the Camel in Ṣaddām's collection of material is missing in Baqī's recension, but exactly the same information is found in several reports in Baqī's recension. Ṣaddām, *Tārīkh Khalīfa* 69.

into different parts.[57] It is thus possible that Baqī b. Makhlad or someone else omitted these reports on Ṣiffīn (or some of them) in the course of transmission, but it is also possible that these reports were not a part of the *Tārīkh*, as Baqī received it from Khalīfa, and that he transmitted slightly different versions at different times. In other words, Khalīfa clearly transmitted more material on Ṣiffīn than what is found in Baqī's recension, but this material might not have been a part of the version of the *Tārīkh* that he transmitted to Baqī. As discussed below, the preponderance of reports on the Battle of the Camel can be explained by Khalīfa's concern for Basran history since it took place outside Basra, in contrast to the Battle of Ṣiffīn, which took place near al-Raqqa in upper Mesopotamia, and perhaps also by the greater prevalence of such reports in the *ḥadīth* circles of Basra. Khalīfa's main direct transmitters on the Battle of the Camel in Baqī's recension are listed in Table 11.

The list contains many prominent *ḥadīth* scholars, such as ʿAbd al-Raḥmān b. Mahdī, Bishr b. al-Mufaḍḍal, Abū Dāwūd al-Ṭayālisī and Wahb b. Jarīr.[58] Similar to Khalīfa's accounts of many other events, reports from *akhbārīyūn* such as Abū l-Yaqẓān and al-Madāʾinī outline the basic narrative (locations, chronology and relation between events), while reports from major *ḥadīth* scholars provide details, glimpses and views of Companions or Successors.[59] Khalīfa's sources differ from those of al-Balādhurī and al-Ṭabarī, who rely quite heavily on early *akhbārīyūn* such as Abū Mikhnaf and Sayf b. ʿUmar, although they have some sources in common (such as al-Madāʾinī and Wahb b. Jarīr).[60] It shows, however, that alternative accounts and transmissions circulated in the early third/ninth century.

Khalīfa begins year 36/656–657 by noting that ʿAlī received the oath of allegiance as successor to ʿUthmān. He then outlines the Battle of the Camel in two parts: the first part briefly summarises the battle alongside other events in 36/656–657, and the second part presents it in more detail. In the first section, Khalīfa summarises, in his own words, that al-Zubayr b. al-ʿAwwām, Ṭalḥa b. ʿUbaydallāh and ʿĀʾisha bt. Abī Bakr departed to Basra, where they fought against Ḥukaym b. Jabala al-ʿAbdī, who had been sent by ʿUthmān b. Ḥunayf (the governor of Basra under ʿAlī) and who, according to Khalīfa, had been the

57 Ṣaddām, *Tārīkh Khalīfa* 70–75. These reports pertain to the generals in the two armies, the fighting for the watering place at the Euphrates before the battle, the name of the one who killed ʿAmmār b. Yāsir, Abū l-ʿĀliya's avoidance of fighting and the deaths of Khuzayma b. Thābit, Qays b. Makshūḥ al-Murādī and Ḥābis b. Saʿd al-Ṭāʾī.

58 See Chapter 4.

59 E.g. Ghundar's three reports in Khalīfa b. Khayyāṭ, *Tārīkh* (1985) 184, 191.

60 Al-Balādhurī, *Ansāb* 3:21–42; al-Ṭabarī, *Tārīkh* 1:3106–256.

TABLE 11 Khalīfa's sources on the Battle of the Camel

	Name	Reports	Location
1.	Abū l-Yaqẓān	11	Basra
2.	Al-Madā'inī	5	Basra
3.	Ghundar	3	Basra
4.	'Alī b. 'Āṣim	3	Wāsiṭ
5.	Abū 'Abd al-Raḥmān al-Qurashī	3	–
6.	Anonymous	3	–
7.	Abū Bakr al-Kalbī	2	Basra
8.	Abū 'Ubayda Ma'mar b. al-Muthannā	2	Basra
9.	Ḥātim b. Muslim	2	Basra
10.	Mu'ādh b. Hishām	2	Basra
11.	Wahb b. Jarīr	2	Basra
12.	'Abd al-Raḥmān b. Mahdī	1	Basra
13.	Abū Dāwūd al-Ṭayālisī	1	Basra
14.	Ashhal b. Ḥātim	1	Basra
15.	Bishr b. al-Mufaḍḍal	1	Basra
16.	Kahmas b. al-Minhāl	1	Basra
17.	Abū Ghassān Mālik b. Ismā'īl	1	Kufa
18.	'Ubaydallāh b. Mūsā	1	Kufa

leader of the Basran opposition against 'Uthmān.[61] He then mentions that 'Alī left Medina, sent al-Ḥasan b. 'Alī b. Abī Ṭālib and 'Ammār b. Yāsir to mobilise the Kufans, and headed to Basra, where the battle took place "on a Friday ten days into Jumādā al-Ākhira in year 36/656."[62] He notes in the first part that Marwān b. al-Ḥakam killed Ṭalḥa during the battle and that 'Amr (or 'Umayr) b. Jurmūz killed al-Zubayr as he was leaving the battlefield. He also mentions that Mujāshi' b. Mas'ūd al-Sulamī and Ḥukaym b. Jabala were killed in the aforementioned fighting before the battle and that Muḥammad b. Ṭalḥa b. 'Ubaydallāh and 'Abd al-Raḥmān b. 'Attāb b. Asīd were killed in actual battle. Thereafter Khalīfa summarises other events in 36/656–657 that occurred after the battle.

In this first 'introductory' section, as Roberts has pointed out, "the actions and deaths of Ṭalḥa and al-Zubayr are as noteworthy and important as the bat-

61 Khalīfa b. Khayyāṭ, *Tārīkh* (1985) 168, 180–181.

62 Khalīfa b. Khayyāṭ, *Tārīkh* (1985) 181.

tle."[63] Khalīfa's straightforward style, without details about intrigues and personal motives, attenuates the responsibility and potential blame of the Companions involved in the opposition against ʿAlī (Ṭalḥa, al-Zubayr and ʿĀʾisha). Moreover, by referring to ʿAlī's oath of allegiance in the passive form (*būyiʿa*—'he received the oath of allegiance') rather than the active (*bāyaʿa*—'so-and-so pledged allegiance'), Khalīfa avoids the issues regarding who pledged allegiance and what the circumstances were.[64] While it does not question ʿAlī's legitimacy as caliph, it also does not question the characters of Ṭalḥa and al-Zubayr by suggesting that they had violated their oaths.[65]

In the detailed second part, Khalīfa provides a slightly different take on the battle, which underlines the legitimacy of ʿAlī's caliphate and provides more details about the actions of Ṭalḥa, al-Zubayr and ʿĀʾisha during the conflict. He describes the arrival of ʿĀʾisha's coalition in Basra, but also the hostility that they faced from the city's population. They then met ʿUthmān b. Ḥunayf, ʿAlī's governor in Basra, at al-Zābūqa, and a brief pitched battle took place between them, after which they negotiated a truce stipulating that ʿUthmān b. Ḥunayf would maintain control of the city, that Ṭalḥa and al-Zubayr could stay wherever they wished in Basra and that they would not interfere with one another until ʿAlī arrived. However, Khalīfa reports from al-Madāʾinī that when ʿAbdallāh b. al-Zubayr set off the next day with some of his companions to find provisions, they were encountered by seven hundred men led by Ḥukaym b. Jabala.[66] This is the specific context for battle that Khalīfa summarised at the beginning of 36/656–657, which is here presented as the result of a failed truce between the two sides. Unlike the Shīʿī Abū Mikhnaf, who explicitly blames Ṭalḥa and al-Zubayr for the fighting, and the ʿUthmānī Sayf b. ʿUmar, who blames Ḥukaym,[67] Khalīfa straightforwardly recounts that fighting occurred outside Basra after ʿAbdallāh b. al-Zubayr's search for provisions, avoiding details of the motives behind the fighting.[68]

---

63 Roberts, *Early Islamic historiography* 74.

64 On these controversies, see Ibn Ḥabīb, *Tārīkh* 114–115; Ibn Qutayba, *al-Maʿārif* 208–209; al-Balādhurī, *Ansāb* 3:7–19; al-Yaʿqūbī, *Tārīkh* 2:75–78; al-Ṭabarī, *Tārīkh* 1:3066–3086. See also Ibn al-ʿArabī, *al-ʿAwāṣim* 299–300; Madelung, *Succession* 141–148.

65 Roberts, *Early Islamic historiography* 75.

66 Khalīfa b. Khayyāṭ, *Tārīkh* (1985) 168.

67 Sayf b. ʿUmar, *Kitāb al-Ridda* 282–292; al-Balādhurī, *Ansāb* 3:26–27; al-Ṭabarī, *Tārīkh* 1:3115–3126; Anthony, *Caliph and the heretic* 121–126.

68 Khalīfa b. Khayyāṭ, *Tārīkh* (1985) 181–183. Khalīfa's report (from al-Madāʾinī) states that "Ibn al-Zubayr set off in the morning towards al-Zābūqa, which was the place of provision, in order to find provisions for his companions. Then Ḥukaym b. Jabala al-ʿAbdī arrived with 700 men from ʿAbd al-Qays and Bakr b. Wāʾil, and they fought against each other. Ḥukaym b. Jabala was killed alongside his brother al-Riʿl b. Jabala and his son al-Ashraf b. Ḥukaym."

It is then reported that ʿAlī sent his son, al-Ḥasan, and ʿAmmār b. Yāsir to mobilise the Kufans, which is the context of ʿAmmār's famous words, "By God, I know that she [ʿĀʾisha] is the Prophet's wife in this world and the next, but God has tested you, through her, whether you follow him or her."[69] The report is narrated from the Basran *ḥadīth* authority, Ghundar, and complements the chronology by describing how the events were viewed in ʿAlī's ranks.[70] It also affirms ʿĀʾisha's special merit, despite her stance against ʿAlī, and provides a rationale for the stance taken by ʿAlī's side. About 6,000–7,000 Kufans and 4,000 Medinans are reported to have joined ʿAlī, including 800 Anṣār and 400 who had been present with the Prophet at the Pledge of Good-Pleasure (*bayʿat al-riḍwān*). Khalīfa thereby makes clear that ʿAlī had support from numerous Companions, which indicates that ʿAlī and his side were correct in defending his rule. Khalīfa also lists the generals in the two armies, which makes clear that many prominent Companions participated, although the only other Badr veterans were ʿAlī, ʿAmmār, Ṭalḥa and al-Zubayr.[71]

Khalīfa's battle account begins with a short report from al-Madāʾinī specifying the date and location: the two armies met on a Thursday in the middle of Jumādā al-Ākhira 36/656 near the palace of ʿUbaydallāh b. Ziyād, and the battle took place the following day. The first battle scene is that of the Basran judge Kaʿb b. Sawwar, who was killed before the battle as he came out with a copy of the Qurʾān (*muṣḥaf*) between the two armies, imploring them to avoid fighting.[72] This report alludes to the 'third stance' of striving to avoid, and staying away from, *fitna* and intra-Muslim fighting, which reappears throughout Khalīfa's *fitna* accounts.[73] It is also one of the few proper battle scenes besides the

69 Khalīfa b. Khayyāṭ, *Tārīkh* (1985) 184.

70 Ghundar's narration (not through Khalīfa) is found in al-Bukhārī, *Ṣaḥīḥ* 5:29; Aḥmad b. Ḥanbal, *Faḍāʾil al-ṣaḥāba* 876–877. A similar report is also found (with a different *isnād*) in Ibn Abī Shayba's *Muṣannaf* 14:246.

71 Khalīfa b. Khayyāṭ, *Tārīkh* (1985) 184, 186.

72 Khalīfa b. Khayyāṭ, *Tārīkh* (1985) 185. Also in al-Fasawī, *Maʿrifa* 3:401; Ibn Abī Shayba, *Muṣannaf* 14:254. The same event is narrated in Sayf's corpus, but here it is ʿĀʾisha who, in Anthony's summary, "hands a Qurʾān to Kaʿb ibn Sūr commanding him to approach ʿAlī's forces calling for arbitration. The Sabaʾiyya, unrelenting in their efforts to thwart peace, swiftly shot Kaʿb through with a flurry of arrows, Qurʾān in hand." Anthony, *Caliph and the heretic* 130.

73 See e.g. Ibn ʿUmar's stance on Yazīd, and Abū Saʿīd al-Khudrī's stance in the Battle of al-Ḥarra. Khalīfa b. Khayyāṭ, *Tārīkh* (1985) 217, 239. Regarding this, al-Shawkānī says, "Al-Qurṭubī said, 'The early generations of Muslims (*al-salaf*) had different opinions regarding that [i.e. fighting in times of *fitna*]. Saʿd b. Abī Waqqāṣ, ʿAbdallāh b. ʿUmar, Muḥammad b. Maslama and others held that it is obligatory to refrain from fighting. Some of them

killings of Ṭalḥa and al-Zubayr, and the fighting around ʿĀʾisha's camel. Instead, Khalīfa is concerned mainly with context, chronology, locations and the individuals involved rather than with details, motives and graphic descriptions of events, as many other historians were. The only one explicitly presented negatively is the Successor and future Umayyad caliph Marwān b. al-Ḥakam. Four reports describe how Marwān killed Ṭalḥa and then, according to one of them, turned to ʿUthmān's son, Abān, saying, "Now we have sorted out one of your father's murderers for you."[74] Ṭalḥa's statements at the same scene are slightly more ambiguous: when hit by the arrow, he said, "O God, take from me for ʿUthmān until You are pleased," and, in another report, "Leave it, for it is an arrow sent by God."[75] The reports seem to indicate regret about some involvement in the events at the end of ʿUthmān's reign or about not doing more to defend ʿUthmān, although Khalīfa does not elaborate on this. He simply notes that Ṭalḥa repented and sacrificed himself to redress the situation after the uprising

---

said that it is obligatory to remain in one's house. One group said that it is obligatory to completely relocate from the region of *fitna*. Others said that a person must avoid fighting so that even if they intend to kill him, he should not fight to defend himself. Others said that such a person should defend himself as well as his property and his family, and that he is excused if he kills or is killed. However, the majority of the Companions and the Successors maintained that it is obligatory to support the truth and fight the wrongdoers (*al-bāghīn*).' Al-Nawawī said the same and added that this is the view (*madhhab*) of the majority of the scholars of Islam and they base this on the words of God Most High, '[But if one of them attacks the other unjustly,] then fight the attackers until they return to God's command.' (49:9) Al-Nawawī said, 'This is the correct position and the *ḥadīth*s [about avoiding *fitna*] are understood as referring to either someone who is not sure about who is in the right or two unjust parties who both lack a legitimate claim.' He said, 'If it was like the first ones said [that it is obligatory in all situations to avoid fighting in times of *fitna*] then corruption would prevail and the rebels (*ahl al-baghy*) and purveyors of falsehood (*mubṭilūn*) would become overbearing.' Some scholars elaborated on the issue as follows: if the fighting occurs between two parties, none of whom have a legitimate leader (*imām*), then [participating in the] fighting is forbidden and the *ḥadīth*s are understood as referring to this. This is the position of al-Awzāʿī as previously mentioned. Al-Ṭabarī said, 'Forbidding the wrong (*inkār al-munkar*) is obligatory upon the one who is able to do it, for the one supporting the rightful one is doing the right thing and the one supporting the mistaken one is mistaken. If the matter is unclear, then this is the situation to which the prohibition against fighting [in times of *fitna*] refers.'" See al-Shawkānī, *Nayl al-awṭār* 7:239–240. The subject is discussed in Crone, *God's rule* 135–139.

74 Khalīfa b. Khayyāṭ, *Tārīkh* (1985) 181, 185. See also Ibn al-ʿArabī, *al-ʿAwāṣim* 304; Ibn Kathīr, *al-Bidāya* 10:476.

75 Khalīfa b. Khayyāṭ, *Tārīkh* (1985) 185–186. Also narrated in Ibn Abī Shayba, *Muṣannaf* 14:257–258.

against ʿUthmān. In relation to this, Khalīfa also mentions in one narration that al-Zubayr was killed by ʿAmr (or ʿUmayr) b. Jurmūz at Wādī al-Sibāʿ as he was leaving the battlefield.[76]

According to four different reports, 7,000, 13,000 or 20,000 (two reports) were killed in the battle, the most prominent of whom Khalīfa names in a separate list. He also notes that 2,500 Basrans from al-Azd and 800 from Banū Ḍabba were killed as well as 400–500 from ʿAlī's companions.[77] Interestingly, Khalīfa corroborates the number of fallen Basrans by a statement of Abū Labīd Limāza b. Zabbār al-Jahḍamī—a Successor known for anti-ʿAlid (*nāṣibī*) tendencies—as he was asked whether he loves ʿAlī: "How could I love a man [i.e. ʿAlī] who killed 2,500 of my people while the sun moved from here to here?"[78] Khalīfa's affirmation of ʿAlī's rightness and legitimacy as caliph, the absence of anti-ʿAlid sentiment in the *Tārīkh* and the placement of the report indicate that the purpose of the report was to corroborate the number of fallen Basrans from al-Azd and perhaps also to illustrate the bitterness among some of those who lost the battle.[79] Right after the list of those who were killed in the battle, Khalīfa also adds some reports about the fighting around ʿĀʾisha's camel, which was the reason for the name of the battle.

The account concludes with two important reports about the memory of the battle, which Ibn Abī Shayba also narrates in his *Muṣannaf*.[80] The first recounts a discussion about the battle between al-Ḥārith b. Suwayd, who was on Ṭalḥa and al-Zubayr's side, and ʿAbdallāh b. Salama, who was on ʿAlī's—the former regretting his participation and the latter taking pride in fighting for ʿAlī's side.[81] The second report forcefully illustrates the tragic memory of the battle as a fight between two Muslim camps that used to be one:

> ʿUbaydallāh b. Mūsā narrated to us; he said: Misʿar narrated to us from ʿAmr b. Murra from al-Ḥārith b. Jumhān al-Juʿfī; he said: On the day of the Camel, we pointed our spears at their breasts and they pointed theirs at

76 Khalīfa b. Khayyāṭ, *Tārīkh* (1985) 186.

77 Khalīfa b. Khayyāṭ, *Tārīkh* (1985) 186–190.

78 Khalīfa b. Khayyāṭ, *Tārīkh* (1985) 186; al-Dhahabī, *Mīzān* 3:412; Ibn Ḥajar, *Tahdhīb* 3:480. Ibn ʿAsākir narrates the same report from Khalīfa via al-Tustarī in *Tārīkh madīnat Dimashq* 50:306.

79 Roberts also notes that Khalīfa portrays ʿAlī and his caliphate "in a generally positive light" and "consistently supports the legitimacy of ʿAlī's rule." Roberts, *Early Islamic historiography* 76–77.

80 Ibn Abī Shayba, *Muṣannaf* 14:241, 247–248.

81 Khalīfa b. Khayyāṭ, *Tārīkh* (1985) 191.

our breasts, so the men could have walked on the spears if they wished. And I heard these ones shout, "There is no god but God! God is greater!" and the others, "There is no god but God! God is greater!"[82]

It recalls ʿUthmān's words during the siege, "If you kill me you will never again fight an enemy united."[83] By this conclusion, Khalīfa asserts that both sides were Muslims fighting for what they understood to be God's sake, but regrettably against each other. This approach corresponds to that of many early *ḥadīth* scholars and early Sunnīs in general, who recognised the reality of the conflict but insisted that both sides fought based on *ijtihād* and died as Muslims—in contrast to the different approaches of the Shīʿa, the Muʿtazila, the Murjiʾa and the 'hard' ʿUthmāniyya.[84] Although these early Sunnīs generally considered ʿAlī to have been in the right, the Companions on both sides in the conflict were excused since they had all exercised *ijtihād* and striven to do the right thing based on their interpretations of the situation.[85] However, it is noteworthy that Khalīfa provides no information about the motivations behind Ṭalḥa, al-Zubayr and ʿĀʾisha's opposition to ʿAlī, which some other compilers used to explain their stance.[86] This illustrates Khalīfa's systematic avoidance of intrigues, conspiracies and personal motives, although his detached style and non-judgmental approach reflect, as we have seen elsewhere, his early Sunnī perspective.[87]

Similar to many other early historians, Khalīfa stresses the legitimacy of ʿAlī's rule and indicates the rightness of his opposition to the coalition of Ṭalḥa, al-Zubayr and ʿĀʾisha.[88] At the same time, however, he shifts focus from the motives and faults of individuals—except Marwān b. al-Ḥakam, who killed

---

82 Khalīfa b. Khayyāṭ, *Tārīkh* (1985) 191.

83 Khalīfa b. Khayyāṭ, *Tārīkh* (1985) 171.

84 Anthony, *Caliph and the heretic* 106–107.

85 As Ibn Ḥajar summarised, "The *ahl al-sunna* have agreed upon the obligation to refrain from accusing anyone among the Companions because of that which occurred between them, even if one knows who was in the right. The reason is that they did not fight in those wars except on the basis of *ijtihād* and God has pardoned the one who is mistaken in his *ijtihād*—in fact, it has been established that he is rewarded once, while the one who is correct is rewarded twice." Ibn Ḥajar, *Fatḥ al-Bārī* 13:37. See also Ibn Rushd, *al-Bayān* 16:361, 18:175–177; Ibn al-ʿArabī, *Aḥkām al-Qurʾān* 4:149–151; Ibn Juzayy, *al-Qawānīn* 39–40; Abou El Fadl, *Rebellion* 32–47.

86 See e.g. Sayf b. ʿUmar, *Kitāb al-Ridda* 284–287; Ibn Abī Shayba, *Muṣannaf* 14:242, 246, 253; al-Dīnawarī, *al-Akhbār al-ṭiwāl* 145–146.

87 Cf. Wurtzel's notion of "detached neutrality and objectivity" in *Khalifa ibn Khayyat's History* 24.

88 See Roberts, *Early Islamic historiography* 289–292.

Ṭalḥa, and ʿAmr b. Jurmūz, who killed al-Zubayr—to general information such as chronology, participants, locations and the memory of the battle. A similar account in terms of historical views is Ibn Abī Shayba's *Kitāb al-Jamal* in his *Muṣannaf*.[89] His early Sunnī perspective resembles Khalīfa's: like Khalīfa, he affirms ʿAlī's rightness and legitimacy, without maligning the other Companions, and asserts that both sides fought as Muslims, although the arrangement and type of material differ on four main points.

First, Ibn Abī Shayba's section is not as chronological as Khalīfa's; some events are narrated chronologically, but other events that occurred before or after are mixed with reports about the battle. Second, Ibn Abī Shayba's account contains a few lengthy reports (several pages in the modern edition) the like of which are absent in Khalīfa's *Tārīkh*.[90] Third, Ibn Abī Shayba includes many statements by ʿAlī, emphasising that both sides were Muslims and describing the opponents as "our brothers who transgressed against us (*ikhwānunā baghaw ʿalaynā*)."[91] Fourth, unlike Khalīfa, Ibn Abī Shayba occasionally interpolates Prophetic *ḥadīth*s in some way relating to the events—such as the Prophet's words that "a people who appoint a woman as their leader will never succeed."[92] These differences seem to reflect Ibn Abī Shayba's different purpose behind the compilation of the *Muṣannaf*: to collect and topically arrange individual reports of relevance in *fiqh, ʿaqīda, maghāzī-sīra* and other related subjects, rather than to establish chronology or place events in their broader historical context as Khalīfa.

2.3.2 Battle of Ṣiffīn (37/657)

The early historical accounts of the Battle of Ṣiffīn reflect the debates about the ʿAlī–Muʿāwiya conflict in the second/eighth and third/ninth centuries.[93] Shīʿī-inclined historians used the Ṣiffīn story to accentuate ʿAlī's special claim to the caliphate, vilify Muʿāwiya and criticise the Umayyads' seizure of the caliphate.[94] By contrast, early Sunnī scholars such as Khalīfa and Ibn Abī Shayba avoid vilification and make clear that both sides fought based on *ijtihād* and died as Muslims, although ʿAlī was right and the legitimate caliph.[95]

89 Ibn Abī Shayba, *Muṣannaf* 14:232–268.

90 Ibn Abī Shayba, *Muṣannaf* 14:232–239, 251–255.

91 Ibn Abī Shayba, *Muṣannaf* 14:239–241, 245–246, 248, 258, 262–264.

92 Ibn Abī Shayba, *Muṣannaf* 14:242, 247, 260, 264.

93 See Petersen, *ʿAlī and Muʿāwiya*; Madelung, *Succession* 184–310; El-Hibri, *Parable and politics* 219–261. See also Ibn al-ʿArabī, *al-ʿAwāṣim* 305–313.

94 Hagler, Repurposed narratives 1.

95 Ibn Abī Shayba, *Muṣannaf* 14:268–282. See also Ibn al-ʿArabī, *al-ʿAwāṣim* 305–313, *Aḥkām al-Qurʾān* 4:149–151; Ibn Rushd, *al-Bayān* 16:361, 18:175–177; Ibn Juzayy, *al-Qawānīn* 39–40.

Their accounts also anticipate later Sunnī histories that present similar views.[96] This tendency is also clearer in Khalīfa's account than in the narratives of al-Balādhurī and al-Ṭabarī, which contain much material from Shīʿī sources such as Abū Mikhnaf and Hishām b. al-Kalbī.[97] This is likewise the case for the material on the Battle of Ṣiffīn in al-Tustarī's recension of Khalīfa's *Tārīkh*, as preserved partially in later sources, which reflect the same historical perspective as Baqī's recension. Al-Tustarī narrates, for example, one report from Khalīfa that asserts that both sides fought as Muslims:

> Khalīfa b. Khayyāṭ narrated to us: Abū Dāwūd and others narrated to us from Abū Khalda from Abū l-ʿĀliya, who said: In the days of ʿAlī and Muʿāwiya, I came to them and found two ranks of inestimable sizes. When one side glorified God, the other side glorified God. And when one side perished, the other side perished. I said [to myself], "Which of the two do you think is the disbelieving side and which do you think is the believing side?" Then I went back before the evening.[98]

In Baqī's recension, Khalīfa introduces the Battle of Ṣiffīn in 37/657–658 but saves the details of the battle for 38/658–659. He thereby gives a brief account of the post-battle arbitration (*taḥkīm*) in 37/657–658, before returning with the details of the battle itself:

> In it [year 37/658]: The two arbiters met—Abū Mūsā al-Ashʿarī for ʿAlī and ʿAmr b. al-ʿĀṣ for Muʿāwiya—at Dūmat al-Jandal in the month of Ramaḍān. It is also said at Adhruḥ, which is near Dūmat al-Jandal. ʿAlī sent Ibn ʿAbbās and did not attend himself, but Muʿāwiya was present. The two arbiters could not agree on anything and the people dispersed. Then the Syrians pledged allegiance to Muʿāwiya for the caliphate in Dhū l-Qaʿda of year 37/658.[99]

---

96 E.g. Ibn ʿAsākir's (d. 571/1176) *Tārīkh madīnat Dimashq*, Ibn al-Athīr's (d. 630/1233) *al-Kāmil fī l-tārīkh* and Ibn Kathīr's (d. 774/1373) *al-Bidāya wa-al-nihāya*. See Hagler, Repurposed narratives 2.

97 Al-Balādhurī, *Ansāb* 3:65–115; al-Ṭabarī, *Tārīkh* 1:3274–3349.

98 Ibn ʿAsākir, *Tārīkh madīnat Dimashq* 18:182; Ṣaddām, *Tārīkh Khalīfa* 75. The other reports from Abū l-ʿĀliya (not via Khalīfa) confirm that the reason he left and avoided fighting was that both sides were Muslims. See Ibn ʿAsākir, *Tārīkh madīnat Dimashq* 18:181–182; Ibn Saʿd, *Ṭabaqāt* 9:113.

99 Khalīfa b. Khayyāṭ, *Tārīkh* (1985) 191–192. Ibn ʿAsākir narrates the same report via al-Tustarī in *Tārīkh madīnat Dimashq* 23:67.

TABLE 12 Khalīfa's sources on the Battle of Ṣiffīn

Name	Reports	Locations
1. Al-Madāʾinī	3	Basra/Baghdad
2. Abū Ghassān Mālik b. Ismāʿīl	2	Kufa
3. Abū ʿAbdallāh	2	–
4. Abū ʿUbayda Maʿmar b. al-Muthannā	1	Basra
5. ʿAbd al-Aʿlā b. ʿAbd al-Aʿlā	1	Basra
6. Abū Nuʿaym al-Faḍl b. Dukayn	1	Kufa
7. Yaḥyā b. Arqam	1	–
8. Unknown (from Shuʿba)	1	–

This is Khalīfa's only mention of the arbitration, which can be contrasted with the lengthy accounts of rivalry and trickery elsewhere.[100] Instead of delving into such controversies, Khalīfa laconically recounts the failure to reach an agreement and the Syrians' pledge of allegiance to Muʿāwiya as caliph. Khalīfa also notes the 20,000 men who joined the Ḥarūriyya—whom he identifies as Khawārij—under Shabath b. Ribʿī right after the arbitration.[101] The main Ṣiffīn account in Baqī's recension consists of a few short summaries by Khalīfa and twelve reports from the transmitters listed in Table 12.

There are fewer reports on the Battle of Ṣiffīn than on ʿUthmān's assassination and the Battle of the Camel. The proportion of Basrans and major *ḥadīth* authorities is also lower, although Abū Nuʿaym, ʿAbd al-Aʿlā and Abū Ghassān were prominent ones.[102] Al-Tustarī's recension of Khalīfa's *Tārīkh* must have contained more reports on the Battle of Ṣiffīn than Baqī's extant recension; Ṣaddām collects 14 narrations preserved in later works that are not found in Baqī's recension, although 7 of them seem to be the same report divided into different parts. It is, however, hard to determine if these narrations were omitted in the course of transmission or if they were simply not a part of the version of the *Tārīkh* that Baqī received from Khalīfa. The lower number of reports, even with those from al-Tustarī's recension included, might suggest that fewer Ṣiffīn

100 E.g. al-Yaʿqūbī, *Tārīkh* 2:88–91; al-Balādhurī, *Ansāb* 3:110–122; al-Ṭabarī, *Tārīkh* 1:3329–3360. See also Ibn al-ʿArabī, *al-ʿAwāṣim* 308–313; Hinds, Ṣiffīn arbitration agreement; Petersen, *ʿAlī and Muʿāwiya*; Madelung, *Succession* 238–262; El-Hibri, *Parable and politics* 242–251; Marsham, Pact (*amāna*).

101 Khalīfa b. Khayyāṭ, *Tārīkh* (1985) 192, 197.

102 See Chapter 4.

reports were circulating in Khalīfa's circles in Basra.[103] It also corresponds to Khalīfa's special concern for Basran history; unlike the Battle of the Camel outside Basra, the Battle of Ṣiffīn took place in upper Mesopotamia near al-Raqqa.

Khalīfa opens with three accounts from al-Madā'inī about the numbers on each side. He then notes the story of Mu'āwiya's side preventing 'Alī's side from accessing the watering place by the Euphrates, after which 'Alī sent a force of 2,000 men who defeated 5,000 Syrians blocking the water.[104] Khalīfa's account is much briefer than other histories and avoids the negative material about Mu'āwiya and 'Amr b. al-'Āṣ, which can be found in the popular *Waq'at Ṣiffīn* of the Shī'ī *akhbārī* Naṣr b. Muzāḥim and other works.[105] By contrast, Khalīfa's *Tārīkh* simply notes the blockade and the subsequent fight without any evaluations or negative depictions.

Altogether, Khalīfa is more concerned with the chronology, locations and participants than with the details of the actual fighting. A large part of his account concerns the composition of the two armies, including their numbers, generals, tribal elements and Companions/Successors. This also seems to have been the case with al-Tustarī's recension. It thereby differs from the more detailed and graphic accounts in other early histories.[106] It also differs from Ibn Abī Shayba, who focuses more on the battle itself, as well as on the perspectives of the participants and the status of the people involved—such as 'Ammār b. Yāsir's statement, "Do not say that the Syrians have become unbelievers, but rather say that they have transgressed and acted wrongfully (*fasaqū wa-ẓalamū*)."[107] In that sense, Ibn Abī Shayba is more concerned with the legal and ideological implications of the battle than Khalīfa, who focuses on historical and chronological information.

Khalīfa concludes with a few accounts of the number of those killed in the battle (60,000–70,000). He notes that 'Alī was joined by 800 who had been present at the Pledge of Good-Pleasure (*bay'at al-riḍwān*), which is 400 more than in the Battle of the Camel.[108] This number might suggest that, in Khal-

103 Perhaps also indicated by al-Balādhurī's account, which is based on many Kufans, such as Abū Mikhnaf, al-Haytham b. 'Adī and Ibn al-Kalbī. See al-Balādhurī, *Ansāb* 3:65–115.

104 Ibn al-'Adīm transmits the same account with almost identical wording from Mūsā al-Tustarī's recension. Ibn al-'Adīm, *Bughyat al-ṭalab* 4:1912; Khalīfa b. Khayyāṭ, *Tārīkh* (1985) 193; Ṣaddām, *Tārīkh Khalīfa* 71.

105 Naṣr b. Muzāḥim, *Waq'at Ṣiffīn* 157–193; Hagler, Repurposed narratives 3–6; Madelung, *Succession* 226–227.

106 E.g. Naṣr b. Muzāḥim, *Waq'at Ṣiffīn*; al-Balādhurī, *Ansāb* 3:65–115; al-Ya'qūbī, *Tārīkh* 2:83–91; al-Dīnawarī, *al-Akhbār al-ṭiwāl* 156–199; al-Ṭabarī, *Tārīkh* 1:3256–360.

107 Ibn Abī Shayba, *Muṣannaf* 14:270.

108 Khalīfa b. Khayyāṭ, *Tārīkh* (1985) 184, 196.

īfa's understanding, ʿAlī's rightness and communal support was even stronger against Muʿāwiya at Ṣiffīn than against Ṭalḥa and al-Zubayr the year before. Khalīfa also lists about a dozen prominent individuals who were killed on both sides at Ṣiffīn, although there are many fewer names than in the lengthy list for the Battle of the Camel.[109] Moreover, the report traced back to the Companion ʿAbd al-Raḥmān b. Abzā, about the 800 men on ʿAlī's side who had been present at the Pledge of Good-Pleasure, mentions that "63 of us were killed, among them ʿAmmār b. Yāsir."[110] Apart from ʿAmmār b. Yāsir's close companionship with the Prophet, the singling out of his name among those who were killed might be an indirect reference to the famous Prophetic *ḥadīth*, "ʿAmmār will be killed by the unjust faction (*al-fiʾat al-bāghiya*)."[111] In that case, it would further indicate that, according to Khalīfa, ʿAlī was in the right and that Muʿāwiya was mistaken in his decision to oppose him, although the latter was excused because both sides in the conflict had exercised *ijtihād* and striven to do the right thing based on their judgements of the situation.[112]

Overall, Khalīfa's account follows the same pattern as other controversial events recounted in the *Tārīkh*; it lacks many details and stories of conspiracies, rivalries, personal motives and anecdotes known from the wider tradition,[113] focusing mainly on questions of chronology and participation. However, by this non-judgemental narrative style and limitation to well-established facts, Khalīfa presents an early Sunnī perspective that acknowledges ʿAlī's rightness—by, for example, his legitimate oath of allegiance and greater support from the Companions—without maligning Muʿāwiya and the Companions on his side.

---

109 Al-Dhahabī transmits from Khalīfa a list of 24 Companions, including seven Badr veterans (*badriyyūn*), who fought on ʿAlī's side at Ṣiffīn, which also suggests that al-Tustarī's recension contained a more detailed account of the Battle of Ṣiffīn. See al-Dhahabī, *Tārīkh al-Islām* 3:545. There are also a few other references to Khalīfa's lists of those who were killed on both sides in the preserved material from al-Tustarī, but they might refer to the short lists preserved in Baqī's recension, although one of the names is missing. See Khalīfa b. Khayyāṭ, *Tārīkh* (1985) 194; Ibn ʿAsākir, *Tārīkh madīnat Dimashq* 11:353; 49:497; Ṣaddām, *Tārīkh Khalīfa* 74.

110 Khalīfa b. Khayyāṭ, *Tārīkh* (1985) 196. See also Dhahabī, *Siyar* 417, *Tārīkh al-Islām* 3:545, in which the same sentence is rendered "63 of *them* were killed, among them ʿAmmār b. Yāsir." A report in al-Tustarī's recension mentions that Ḥuwayy b. Mäniʿ was the one who killed ʿAmmār. Ibn al-ʿAdīm, *Bughyat al-ṭalab* 6:2995.

111 Al-Bukhārī, *Ṣaḥīḥ* 4:21 (*bāb al-jihād wa-l-siyar, kitāb masḥ al-ghubār ʿan al-nās …*); Muslim, *Ṣaḥīḥ* 1333 (*kitāb al-fitan wa-ashrāṭ al-sāʿa, bāb lā taqūmu al-sāʿa ḥattā yamurra al-rajul bi-qabr al-rajul …*). It is also found in Ibn Abī Shayba's *Muṣannaf* 14:271–272, 281–282.

112 See the previous discussions about *ijtihād*.

113 For a collection of such material, see Madelung, *Succession* 184–238.

3 The Umayyad Period

About half of Khalīfa's *Tārīkh*, as transmitted by Baqī b. Makhlad, pertains to the Umayyad period. It includes detailed accounts of several intra-Muslim conflicts that were controversial in the early historical tradition. This section examines seven episodes that Khalīfa treats in some detail and which illustrate his historical perspective: (1) al-Ḥasan's transfer of the caliphate to Muʿāwiya, (2) Muʿāwiya's appointment of his son Yazīd, (3) al-Ḥusayn's martyrdom at Karbalāʾ, (4) the Battle of al-Ḥarra, (5) the second *fitna* between the Zubayrids and the Umayyads, (6) Ibn al-Ashʿath's revolt and (7) the fall of the Umayyads and the ʿAbbāsid Revolution.

3.1 *Al-Ḥasan's Transfer of the Caliphate to Muʿāwiya*

Khalīfa's account of al-Ḥasan b. ʿAlī's transfer of the caliphate to Muʿāwiya is comprised of the following summary in his own words, opening the section for year 41/661–662:

> In it: the year of unity (*sanat al-jamāʿa*). Al-Ḥasan b. ʿAlī b. Abī Ṭālib and Muʿāwiya reached an agreement. They met in Maskin, in the region of al-Sawād near al-Anbār, and made peace with each other. Al-Ḥasan surrendered [the caliphate] to Muʿāwiya. That was in the month of Rabīʿ al-Ākhir or Jumādā al-Ūlā 41/661.
>
> Al-Ḥasan b. ʿAlī's reign lasted seven months and seven days. He retained his father's governors. Al-Mughīra b. Shuʿba forged a letter of appointment in al-Ḥasan's name and led the pilgrimage in year 40/661. Al-Ḥasan died in Medina in 49/669. Saʿīd b. al-ʿĀṣ, then governor of Medina, led the funeral prayer for him. He died at the age of 46. He was born in Medina in year 3/625. His mother was Fāṭima, the daughter of the Messenger of God (ṣ). The people united under Muʿāwiya, whose mother was Hind bt. ʿUtba b. Rabīʿa b. ʿAbd Shams b. ʿAbd Manāf.[114]

114 Khalīfa b. Khayyāṭ, *Tārīkh* (1985) 203. See Wurtzel, *Khalifa ibn Khayyat's History* 53. Ibn ʿAsākir transmits the first passage ("In it: the year of unity" to "Jumādā al-Ūlā 41/661") from al-Tustarī in *Tārīkh madīnat Dimashq* 59:148–149 and cites different parts of the second passage elsewhere. See *Tārīkh madīnat Dimashq* 13:303, 60:45. Two reports about al-Ḥasan b. ʿAlī in Ṣaddām's collection of material from Khalīfa are missing in Baqī's recension. The first report, transmitted by al-Tustarī, is the same as in Baqī's recension, except that it dates al-Ḥasan's death to 50/670 instead of 49/669. The other report, transmitted by Aḥmad b. Sahl b. Ayyūb al-Ahwāzī (d. 291/904), mentions al-Ḥasan's giving away his wealth in charity, but it seems to be a separate report about al-Ḥasan's merits, not a part of the *Tārīkh*. This is indicated by both the transmitter, who is not known to have transmitted the *Tārīkh*

Khalīfa presents the year as the 'year of unity', similarly the Syrian *ḥadīth* scholar Abū Zurʿa al-Dimashqī, but the latter is otherwise much more explicit in asserting Muʿāwiya's legitimacy as caliph—for example, by listing prominent Companions and Successors who acknowledged his caliphate.[115] The term is also found in other early histories and became common in later Sunnī scholarship.[116] The rest of the account is straightforward, without notices of rivalries or conspiracies—perhaps apart from al-Mughīra b. Shuʿba's letter. This differs from the works of, for example, al-Balādhurī, al-Yaʿqūbī, al-Masʿūdī and Ibn Aʿtham, who to various degrees emphasise the conflict between al-Ḥasan and Muʿāwiya, as well as the strategies by which the latter obtained the caliphate.[117] Khalīfa's account emphasises the enduring legitimacy of the caliphate and the probity of the involved parties—partly a function of his straightforward, non-judgemental narrative style and avoidance of ambiguities, anecdotes and conspiracies.

3.2 *Muʿāwiya's Appointment of Yazīd*

In contrast to al-Ḥasan's resignation, Khalīfa treats Muʿāwiya's controversial appointment of his son, Yazīd, in great detail.[118] The account consists of three reports from Wahb b. Jarīr, two from ʿAbd al-Raḥmān b. Mahdī, one from Ismāʿīl b. Sinān and one from Ashhal b. Ḥātim—all of them Basran transmitters, and the first two major *ḥadīth* scholars. The three reports from Wahb b. Jarīr are unusually lengthy and provide a full narrative, while the other reports are shorter accounts of certain Companions' views on Yazīd's succession. The reason for all this detail might be its historical importance for Khalīfa and other early Sunnīs as the beginning of dynastic succession and the end of the earlier rightly guided model of the first four caliphs. In Khalīfa's narrative, Muʿāwiya's appointment is heavily criticised by major Medinan Companions without any

from Khalīfa, and the *faḍāʾil* content of the report, which does not resemble the usual content of Khalīfa's *Tārīkh*. See Ibn ʿAsākir, *Tārīkh madīnat Dimashq* 13:244, 303; Khalīfa b. Khayyāṭ, *Tārīkh* (1985) 203; Ṣaddām, *Tārīkh Khalīfa* 76. On the transmitter, Aḥmad b. Sahl b. Ayyūb, see al-Dhahabī, *Tārīkh al-Islām* 22:49.

115 Abū Zurʿa al-Dimashqī, *Tārīkh* 188–190.

116 Ibn Saʿd, *Ṭabaqāt* 6:26; al-Fasawī, *Maʿrifa* 3:409; al-Ṭabarī, *Tārīkh* 2:199. For its usage in later scholarship, see e.g. al-Dhahabī, who calls it *ʿām al-jamāʿa* and then cites Khalīfa's *Tārīkh*. Al-Dhahabī, *Tārīkh al-Islām* 4:5.

117 Al-Balādhurī, *Ansāb* 3:267–301; al-Yaʿqūbī, *Tārīkh* 2:121–123; al-Masʿūdī, *Murūj* 2:426–432; Ibn Aʿtham al-Kūfī, *Futūḥ* 4:284–299, 322. See also Madelung, *Succession* 311–333.

118 Khalīfa b. Khayyāṭ, *Tārīkh* (1985) 213–218. Twenty-three reports on Muʿāwiya's caliphate in Ṣaddām's collection of material are missing in Baqī's recension, but none of these concern the appointment of Yazīd. Ṣaddām, *Tārīkh Khalīfa* 75–83.

explicit attempts at defence, not even from Muʿāwiya himself. It suggests a view that Muʿāwiya's decision was not the best alternative and that it marked the end of the rightly-guided model of succession, but not the end of the legitimacy or the continuity of the caliphate itself, which, as Khalīfa's narrative emphasises, remained throughout the Umayyad and ʿAbbāsid periods.

Khalīfa's first report describes Muʿāwiya's attempt to make the people of al-Ḥijāz pledge allegiance to Yazīd during the pilgrimage in 51/671, after the Syrians had pledged allegiance to him the year before.[119] In Mecca, he meets ʿAbdallāh b. ʿUmar, ʿAbdallāh b. al-Zubayr and ʿAbd al-Raḥmān b. Abī Bakr—three of the most prominent living Companions, whose fathers had been among the closest men to the Prophet. Each of them criticises Muʿāwiya's idea of appointing Yazīd from different angles. These criticisms also correspond to the range of opinions in later Sunnī discourses about leadership.[120] First, Ibn ʿUmar tells Muʿāwiya that it diverts from the practice of the previous caliphs, who did not appoint their sons and who only acted in the best interest of the Muslims, but adds that he will be loyal to whomever the Muslim community agrees upon. Second, ʿAbd al-Raḥmān b. Abī Bakr says to Muʿāwiya that it must be decided by a council (*shūrā*) as before or else they will convene one against him. Third, Ibn al-Zubayr tells Muʿāwiya that they cannot pledge allegiance to two caliphs at the same time and that he has to resign if he wants to appoint Yazīd.[121] The report also mentions that the Syrians demanded from Muʿāwiya that the three of them pledge allegiance to Yazīd in public, but eventually seem to have accepted his word that they had already pledged allegiance. It thereby situates Muʿāwiya between the ideals of the Ḥijāzī Companions and the demands of the Syrian military, which highlights the Syrian context as a factor behind Yazīd's succession and thus perhaps indirectly explains Muʿāwiya's decision.

The second report mentions Muʿāwiya's alleged threat to kill Ibn ʿUmar if he refused to pledge allegiance. According to the report, when Ibn ʿUmar heard about it, he characteristically responded that patience is better than fighting.[122] It concludes with Muʿāwiya denying it, saying, "Me killing Ibn ʿUmar? By God,

---

119 Khalīfa b. Khayyāṭ, *Tārīkh* (1985) 211, 213–214. The historical tradition gives different dates for the *ḥajj* or *ʿumra* during which Muʿāwiya tried to secure Yazīd's succession, but Khalīfa places it in 51/671. See Marsham, *Rituals* 90; Mcmillan, *Meaning of Mecca* 51–54; al-Yaʿqūbī, *Tārīkh* 2:138; al-Ṭabarī, *Tārīkh* 2:173–177.

120 See e.g. al-Māwardī, *al-Aḥkām al-sulṭāniyya* 3–29.

121 Similar to what Khalīfa reports about Saʿīd b. al-Musayyib's refusal to pledge allegiance to ʿAbd al-Malik's two sons, al-Walīd and Sulaymān, since he would not pledge allegiance to two leaders. Saʿīd b. al-Musayyib is reported to have said, "If ʿAbd al-Malik wants me to pledge allegiance to al-Walīd, let him resign." Khalīfa b. Khayyāṭ, *Tārīkh* (1985) 289–290.

122 Khalīfa b. Khayyāṭ, *Tārīkh* (1985) 214–215. See also 213, 217.

I would never do that!"[123] The report is ambiguous—the two claims stand against each other—but the apparent sense is that Muʿāwiya made the threat and then took back his words.

The third and longest report describes the encounters in Mecca between Muʿāwiya, Ibn ʿUmar, Ibn al-Zubayr, Ibn Abī Bakr and al-Ḥusayn b. ʿAlī. Similar to the first report, it presents views that correspond to early Sunnī positions on leadership. Speaking on behalf of the people of al-Ḥijāz, Ibn al-Zubayr gives Muʿāwiya three alternatives: "If you wish, you may do what the Messenger of God (ṣ) did. Or, if you wish, you may do what Abū Bakr did, and he was the best of this community after the Messenger of God (ṣ). Or, if you wish, you may do what ʿUmar did, and he was the best of this community after Abū Bakr."[124] In that, the report gives precedence to the chronological ranking of the caliphs and the validity of the succession of Abū Bakr, ʿUmar and ʿUthmān. He then clarifies what each of them did:

> Ibn al-Zubayr said, "The Messenger of God (ṣ) died and did not designate or appoint anyone as his successor. The Muslims agreed upon Abū Bakr. So, if you wish, you can desist from this affair until God decides it and then the Muslims can choose for themselves." Muʿāwiya said, "But today there is no one among you like Abū Bakr. He was a man nobody would oppose. I fear for you the difference of opinions." Ibn al-Zubayr said, "You have indeed spoken the truth. By God, we do not want you to leave us in charge of his community, so do what Abū Bakr did." Muʿāwiya replied, "Fine. What did Abū Bakr do?" Ibn al-Zubayr said, "He selected a man of a distant branch of Quraysh, who was neither one of his father's sons nor one of his near relatives, and designated him as his successor. So, if you wish, you may consider any man of Quraysh, who is not from Banū ʿAbd Shams, and be content with him." Muʿāwiya said, "Fine. What is the third alternative?" Ibn al-Zubayr replied, "That you do what ʿUmar did." Muʿāwiya asked, "And what did ʿUmar do?" Ibn al-Zubayr replied, "He put the matter in the hands of a council (*shūrā*) composed of six men of Quraysh, among whom were none of his sons, brothers or near relatives." Muʿāwiya said, "Do you have anything else to suggest?" He said, "No." Muʿāwiya said [to the others], "And what about you?" They said, "Nor do we."[125]

123 Khalīfa b. Khayyāṭ, *Tārīkh* (1985) 215.
124 Khalīfa b. Khayyāṭ, *Tārīkh* (1985) 216.
125 Khalīfa b. Khayyāṭ, *Tārīkh* (1985) 216. See Wurtzel, *Khalifa ibn Khayyat's History* 71–72.

Muʿāwiya is then said to have threatened them and surrounded them with guards to prevent them from intervening during his public designation of Yazīd as successor, which, according to this report, explains why they did not publicly oppose Muʿāwiya's decision. Again, the report articulates some early Sunnī views on the caliphate in general and Muʿāwiya's appointment of Yazīd in particular, although the rather negative depiction of Muʿāwiya is noteworthy and unusual for Khalīfa's *Tārīkh*.[126] It is also striking that Muʿāwiya lacks responses to the second and third alternatives, which supports Ibn al-Zubayr's three alternatives over Muʿāwiya's dynastic model.

The fourth report is Ibn ʿUmar's words after Yazīd's succession: "If he is good, we will be content and if he turns out to be a trial, we must be patient."[127] This critical loyalty and concern for communal unity is also asserted in the fifth report, from an anonymous Companion,[128] who acknowledges Yazīd's shortcomings and the problem of his succession but states that communal unity is better than division.[129] The section concludes with two reports from ʿAbdallāh b. ʿAmr—another leading Companion, and a son of Muʿāwiya's close associate, ʿAmr b. al-ʿĀṣ—who said, "The king of the holy land is Muʿāwiya and his son."[130] In the other, he says to Ibn al-Zubayr, "I have found in the books that you will torment and be tormented, and that you will claim the caliphate without being the caliph. I find Yazīd b. Muʿāwiya to be the caliph."[131] ʿAbdallāh b. ʿAmr was known for his knowledge of prophecies and his ability to read Syriac scriptures.[132] His words seem to support the appointment of Yazīd and they also foreshadow Ibn al-Zubayr's later claim to the caliphate. The Umayyad dynasty as predicted in prophecies is well-known in the works of *ḥadīth* and *akhbār*—such as in the famous Prophetic *ḥadīth*, "The caliphate (*khilāfa*) in my community will last 30 years. After that, there will be kingship (*mulk*)."[133] Despite the reports from

126 These three reports were rejected by Abū Bakr b. al-ʿArabī in *al-ʿAwāṣim* 324–336, where he, among other things, points out that they contradict what al-Bukhārī narrates about Ibn ʿUmar in his *Ṣaḥīḥ* 5:110 (*kitāb al-maghāzī, bāb ghazwat al-khandaq*), 9:57 (*kitāb al-fitan, bāb idhā qāla ʿinda qawm shayʾan thumma kharaja fa-qāla bi-khilāfihi*).

127 Khalīfa b. Khayyāṭ, *Tārīkh* (1985) 217.

128 Abū Bakr b. al-ʿArabī notes that it most likely refers to Ibn ʿUmar in *al-ʿAwāṣim* 335–336.

129 Khalīfa b. Khayyāṭ, *Tārīkh* (1985) 217.

130 Ibn ʿAsākir transmits the same report from Khalīfa via al-Tustarī in *Tārīkh madīnat Dimashq* 65:408.

131 Khalīfa b. Khayyāṭ, *Tārīkh* (1985) 218. Ibn ʿAsākir transmits the same report from Khalīfa via al-Tustarī in *Tārīkh madīnat Dimashq* 68:81.

132 See e.g. Ibn Saʿd, *Ṭabaqāt* 5:82–90; Ibn Qutayba, *al-Maʿārif* 286–287; Ibn ʿAbd al-Barr, *al-Istīʿāb* 3:956–959; al-Dhahabī, *Siyar* 2448–2451.

133 Al-Ṭayālisī, *Musnad* 2:430–431 (*Safīna*); al-Tirmidhī, *al-Jāmiʿ* 4:82 (*abwāb al-fitan, bāb mā jāʾa fī l-khilāfa*); Ibn Ḥanbal, *Musnad* 36:248 (*Safīna*).

ʿAbdallāh b. ʿAmr, as a whole Khalīfa's account is more critical than supportive of Muʿāwiya's designation of Yazīd, although the importance of communal unity and avoidance of intra-Muslim conflicts is emphasised throughout—especially in Ibn ʿUmar's words and his stance, which is central to Khalīfa's account. Thus, in the light of the earlier reports, Khalīfa most likely cited ʿAbdallāh b. ʿAmr to illustrate different perspectives on Yazīd's succession among the Companions rather than to support it as the preferred option.

In summary, Khalīfa's account of Muʿāwiya's appointment of Yazīd raises a couple of important points regarding the form of the *Tārīkh* and Khalīfa's historical views. First, Wahb b. Jarīr's reports differ, in their length and detail, from the usual style of short and straightforward reports in the *Tārīkh*, but they resemble the type of material in lengthier narrative histories.[134] This suggests that Khalīfa found these events important enough to narrate in detail since Muʿāwiya's decision, as Khalīfa's reports suggest, marked the end of the rightly-guided model and the beginning of a new dynastic era.

Second, Khalīfa's accounts of Yazīd's succession reflect some early Sunnī ideas about the Rāshidūn caliphs, the Companions and caliphal succession, which is particularly clear in Ibn al-Zubayr's statements. They also reflect an attitude of critical loyalty to authorities and an emphasis on communal unity, as in Ibn ʿUmar's well-known stances with respect to these issues.[135] In this way, Khalīfa's selection of reports defines the legitimate spectra of historical views and the ideal modes of succession, which ended with the introduction of dynastic succession, although the caliphate remained as the political organisation of the community. As for Muʿāwiya's decision to appoint Yazīd, it would probably have been considered a matter of *ijtihād* (in which the one striving to judge correctly is excused if he is mistaken) among early Sunnīs like Khalīfa, although Khalīfa's account makes clear that Muʿāwiya's decision in this matter was criticised by several senior Companions who took different stances. He also includes some negative material about Muʿāwiya's actions, such as the reports about him threatening certain Companions and forcing them to comply with his appointment of Yazīd, which presents the other Companions' stances as much more favourable. In addition, Khalīfa's account of Yazīd's disastrous rule highlights that Muʿāwiya's decision to appoint him was, in retro-

---

134 E.g. al-Balādhurī, *Ansāb* 5:152–153; al-Ṭabarī, *Tārīkh* 2:173–178; Ibn al-Athīr, *al-Kāmil fī l-tārīkh* 3:349–355; al-Dhahabī, *Tārīkh al-Islām* 4:147–152. See also Ibn al-ʿArabī, *al-ʿAwāṣim* 324–336.

135 See e.g. Ibn Saʿd, *Ṭabaqāt* 4:133–175. See also Veccia Vaglieri, ʿAbd Allāh b. ʿUmar b. al-Khaṭṭāb; Abou El Fadl, *Rebellion* 41–42.

spect, clearly mistaken.[136] A critical account of Yazīd's succession, by another early Sunnī historian, is found in the *Tārīkh* of Ibn Ḥabīb. Unlike Khalīfa, however, Ibn Ḥabīb seems to partially defend Muʿāwiya by discussing how good deeds (like Muʿāwiya's many merits, in addition to his companionship with the Prophet) eliminate wrong deeds (like the appointment of Yazīd) and how God repays good deeds tenfold but wrong deeds only once.[137] A quite different approach is found in the *Tārīkh* of Abū Zurʿa al-Dimashqī, who mentions that Yazīd led several Companions in the first siege of Constantinople and that major Companions/Successors acknowledged Muʿāwiya as caliph, before simply noting that Yazīd succeeded him.[138] In that sense, the Syrian Abū Zurʿa's account appears pro-Umayyad (or at least pro-Muʿāwiya) and, unlike Khalīfa, does not emphasise that the appointment was a break with the earlier rightly-guided model.

3.3 *Al-Ḥusayn's Martyrdom*

One of the most controversial events in the historical tradition is the martyrdom of al-Ḥusayn b. ʿAlī b. Abī Ṭālib at Karbalāʾ on the 10th of al-Muḥarram 61/680. It followed Yazīd's succession, when large parts of the community, especially in al-Ḥijāz and Iraq, refused to accept his authority—among them al-Ḥusayn and ʿAbdallāh b. al-Zubayr. The early histories report extensively how al-Ḥusayn departed to Kufa, after having been invited to take action against Yazīd, and was killed along with his family and companions—although the interpretations and details may differ.[139] These works show the centrality of al-Ḥusayn's martyrdom in the memory of the Muslim community. This is also evident in Khalīfa's commemoration of the Karbalāʾ martyrs and in his praise of al-Ḥusayn and his family in the *Tārīkh*. Unlike the detailed and dramatic material elsewhere, Khalīfa's account is characteristically concise and straightforward, but it nonetheless shows what he considered most important to record from Karbalāʾ.

---

136 Muʿāwiya's appointment of Yazīd is, therefore, one of the accounts in Baqī b. Makhlad's extant recension that challenge Ṣaddām's claim that Baqī omitted negative material about the Umayyads. Ṣaddām, *Tārīkh Khalīfa* 21–22.

137 Ibn Ḥabīb, *Tārīkh* 125–126.

138 Abū Zurʿa al-Dimashqī, *Tārīkh* 1:188–191.

139 E.g. Ibn Saʿd, *Ṭabaqāt* 6:421–460; al-Yaʿqūbī, *Tārīkh* 2:155–169; al-Dīnawarī, *al-Akhbār al-ṭiwāl* 231–260; al-Ṭabarī, *Tārīkh* 2:272–390; al-Masʿūdī, *Murūj* 3:54–63; Ibn Aʿtham al-Kūfī, *Futūḥ* 5:29–157. See also Veccia Vaglieri, al-Ḥusayn b. ʿAlī b. Abī Ṭālib; Haider, al-Ḥusayn b. ʿAlī b. Abī Ṭālib; Howard, Ḥusayn the martyr; Shoshan, *Poetics* 233–252; Hylén, Ḥusayn the mediator; Borrut, Remembering Karbalāʾ.

The background to the event is given in 60/679–680: al-Ḥusayn sent his cousin, Muslim b. ʿAqīl, to take the oath of allegiance from the Kufans, but Muslim was eventually captured and killed by Yazīd's governor, ʿUbaydallāh b. Ziyād. At this point, Khalīfa narrates, al-Ḥusayn left Mecca and went towards Kufa:

> Al-Farazdaq said: I went out intending to make the pilgrimage. When I reached Dhāt ʿIrq, I saw some tents that had been set up. I asked to whom they belong and they replied, "To al-Ḥusayn b. ʿAlī." I went to al-Ḥusayn and said, "Son of the Prophet (ṣ), what has made you hasten away from the pilgrimage?" He replied, "These people—meaning the Kufans—wrote to me about their situation." Then he asked me, "How did you leave the people behind you?" I said, "May my father and mother be your ransom, I left the hearts with you, the swords with Banū Umayya and the victory in heaven."[140]

The report foreshadows al-Ḥusayn's death at Karbalāʾ and reflects a clear view on the events: al-Ḥusayn was more righteous and beloved, but the Umayyads possessed the political and military power. It also recalls Ibn ʿUmar's words, "If he [Yazīd] is good, we will be content and if he turns out to be a trial, we must be patient."[141] Along with the Battle of al-Ḥarra, as discussed below, it might suggest an interpretation that the troubles under Yazīd were foremost caused by his oppressive and deficient leadership but that at the same time, in retrospect, they were exacerbated by the attempts to take action against him. Similar to the Battle of al-Ḥarra, Khalīfa commemorates al-Ḥusayn and his family by listing those who were killed at Karbalāʾ. He also provides names of the mothers of those who were killed, which is otherwise limited in the *Tārīkh* to the caliphs. Two reports, in particular, venerate the martyrs:

> Muḥammad b. Muʿāwiya narrated to us from Sufyān from Abū Mūsā; he said: I heard al-Ḥasan al-Baṣrī say: Sixteen men of al-Ḥusayn's family were killed with him. On that day, there was no family on the face of the earth with men like them.

---

140 Khalīfa b. Khayyāṭ, *Tārīkh* (1985) 231. See Wurtzel, *Khalifa ibn Khayyat's History* 92–93. Khalīfa adds in a later report that Ibn al-Zubayr had met al-Ḥusayn in Mecca before his departure to Kufa and told him, "What is keeping you from your partisans and the partisans of your father? If I had partisans like yours I would certainly go to them." Khalīfa b. Khayyāṭ, *Tārīkh* (1985) 233.

141 Khalīfa b. Khayyāṭ, *Tārīkh* (1985) 217.

> Al-Ḥasan b. Abī ʿAmr narrated to us; he said: I heard Fiṭr b. Khalīfa; he said: I heard Mundhir al-Thawrī [transmitting] from Ibn al-Ḥanafiyya; he said: Seventeen men were killed with al-Ḥusayn, all of whom had moved in Fāṭima's womb.[142]

This is one of the few instances in the *Tārīkh* where Khalīfa reports explicit praise for individuals. Similar praise is found in works by other *ḥadīth* scholars, such as Ibn Abī Shayba's *Muṣannaf* and Aḥmad b. Ḥanbal's *Faḍā'il al-ṣaḥāba*.[143] Although Khalīfa pays relatively little attention to ʿAlid uprisings in the *Tārīkh*, the image of the Prophetic household is not unfavourable: al-Ḥusayn, in this case, is portrayed as a beloved martyr, and his family as uniquely virtuous. This reflects the importance of the Prophetic household in the early *ḥadīth* circles. It also shows that, even if patience and avoiding *fitna* was generally viewed as the proper response to oppressive governance, active opposition could be justified in certain circumstances, and not all individuals who took action against rulers were considered 'rebels' (*bughāt*)—certainly not Companions.[144] Rather, in the case of Ṭalḥa, al-Zubayr, Muʿāwiya, al-Ḥusayn and Ibn al-Zubayr, their actions seem to have been viewed as exercises in qualified independent judgement (*ijtihād*). This perspective may explain Khalīfa's non-judgemental approach to the actions of Companions (such as al-Ḥusayn and Ibn al-Zubayr, but *not* Yazīd) in the conflicts of the late Rāshidūn and early Umayyad periods. For Khalīfa, there seem to have been no doubt about al-Ḥusayn's virtue or the validity of his actions and his *ijtihād*, although his overall narrative might indicate a preference for Ibn ʿUmar's approach of patience to avoid further *fitna*. At the end of the section on the Karbalā' events, Khalīfa also notes that "the person responsible for killing al-Ḥusayn was Shamir (or Shimr) b. Dhī l-Jawshan and the leader of the army was ʿUmar b. Saʿd b. Mālik."[145] Overall, Khalīfa's account is considerably less dramatic than many accounts of other *akhbār* historians—including early Sunnīs such as Ibn Saʿd and al-Ṭabarī—but nonetheless reflects a special veneration for al-Ḥusayn and the Karbalā' martyrs, which at the same time highlights the error and brutal transgression of those who attacked and killed them.[146]

142 Khalīfa b. Khayyāṭ, *Tārīkh* (1985) 235. Ibn al-Ḥanafiyya's words probably refer to Fāṭima bt. Asad, the mother of ʿAlī b. Abī Ṭālib, since not all of those killed with al-Ḥusayn were descendants of Fāṭima, the daughter of the Prophet.

143 Ibn Abī Shayba, *Muṣannaf* 11:162–167; Ibn Ḥanbal, *Faḍā'il al-ṣaḥāba* 766–789.

144 See Abou El Fadl, *Rebellion* 32–47, 65–68.

145 Khalīfa b. Khayyāṭ, *Tārīkh* (1985) 235.

146 Ibn Saʿd, *Ṭabaqāt* 6:421–460; al-Ṭabarī, *Tārīkh* 2:272–390. The only report about al-Ḥusayn in Ṣaddām's collection of preserved material from Khalīfa that is missing in Baqī's recen-

Al-Ḥusayn's death is one of few ʿAlid martyrdoms or uprisings narrated in detail in Baqī's recension, besides some reports on the uprising of ʿAbdallāh b. Muʿāwiya (described as a revolt of "some people from the Shīʿa") in the late Umayyad period and that of Muḥammad al-Nafs al-Zakiyya and his brother Ibrāhīm in 145/762–763.[147] This can be contrasted with his lengthy accounts of the Battle of al-Ḥarra, Ibn al-Ashʿath's revolt and the Khārijī revolts in the late Umayyad period. Later sources preserve a bit more material on the revolts of al-Mukhtār, Zayd b. ʿAlī and Ibrāhīm b. ʿAbdallāh (the brother of Muḥammad al-Nafs al-Zakiyya) from al-Tustarī's recension.[148] Baqī or someone else possibly omitted this material, but it is just as possible that Khalīfa transmitted slightly different versions of the *Tārīkh* at different times and that this material was not a part of the *Tārīkh* as Baqī received it. However, the scarcity of information about the ʿAlids and their uprisings remains a distinct feature of Khalīfa's *Tārīkh*, even if one takes into consideration the additional material from al-Tustarī's recension.[149] This might suggest that Khalīfa considered these events less important to the political-administrative affairs of the caliphate (than, for example, the Battle of al-Ḥarra and the Khārijī revolts) and/or that he deliberately avoided the historiographical territories of the Shīʿīs. It also corresponds to Khalīfa's avoidance of rivalries and stories of individuals, and perhaps his Basran early Sunnī historical perspective, which might have led him to tone down somewhat the special role of the ʿAlid uprisings and martyrdoms.

3.4 *The Battle of al-Ḥarra*

The Battle of al-Ḥarra is another event that receives a detailed treatment in Khalīfa's *Tārīkh*, similar to the wider historical tradition.[150] The battle took place in 63/683 on the outskirts of Medina, where the people of al-Ḥijāz who had renounced Yazīd were brutally crushed by the Syrian forces sent by Yazīd. The historical tradition mainly remembers it for the great number of Companions and Successors who were killed or abused when the Syrian army sacked Medina. The battle seems to have been particularly important in the

sion is a short notice about al-Ḥusayn's birth in year 4/626. Ibn ʿAsākir, *Tārīkh madīnat Dimashq* 14:115; Ṣaddām, *Tārīkh Khalīfa* 58.

147 Khalīfa b. Khayyāṭ, *Tārīkh* (1985) 375, 387, 391, 421–422.

148 See Chapter 1.

149 See also Wurtzel, *Khalifa ibn Khayyat's History* 29.

150 E.g. Khalīfa b. Khayyāṭ, *Tārīkh* (1985) 236–250; al-Balādhurī, *Ansāb* 5:337–355; al-Yaʿqūbī, *Tārīkh* 164–167; al-Ṭabarī, *Tārīkh* 2:400–423; Ibn Aʿtham al-Kūfī, *Futūḥ* 5:172–191. See also Kister, Battle of the Harra. There is only one report that briefly mentions the Battle of al-Ḥarra in Ṣaddām's collection of preserved material from Khalīfa that is missing in Baqī's recension, but it mainly pertains to the governors under Yazīd. Ṣaddām, *Tārīkh Khalīfa* 84.

early *ḥadīth* circles, where these Companions and Successors were constantly evoked as transmitters of the Prophet's legacy.[151] This is reflected in Khalīfa's *Tārīkh*: seven of twelve reports in Baqī's recension are narrated on the authority of Wahb b. Jarīr—a Basran *ḥadīth* authority whom Aḥmad b. Ḥanbal described as *ṣāḥib sunna*.[152] Khalīfa also cites Abū l-Yaqẓān thrice and al-Madā'inī twice—both Basran *akhbār* experts. Al-Balādhurī likewise transmits some material from Wahb b. Jarīr and al-Madā'inī on these events, but also, similar to al-Ṭabarī, relies on al-Wāqidī, ʿAwāna b. al-Ḥakam, Hishām b. al-Kalbī, Abū Mikhnaf and others, which confirms that non-Basran material about these events circulated widely.[153]

Khalīfa begins with the events leading up to the battle: after the pilgrimage in 62/682, a Medinan delegation led by ʿAbdallāh b. Ḥanẓala was sent to Yazīd, who tried to persuade them to pledge allegiance. Upon their return, the delegation publicly renounced Yazīd, and the Medinans elected (by *shūrā*) their own leaders over Quraysh and the Anṣār. Here Khalīfa interpolates a report from Ibn ʿAbbās, who responded to the election of two leaders: "Two leaders: the people are doomed."[154] This conforms to the standard view among the early Sunnīs (and others) that there should be only one leader, in line with the Companions' rejection of separate leaders for the Muhājirūn and the Anṣār after the death of the Prophet.[155] It also partially explains the failure of the Medinan uprising and draws a lesson from it.

Khalīfa straightforwardly recounts how Yazīd prepared an army that brutally defeated the Medinans after Banū Ḥāritha had allowed the Syrians to pass through and attack from behind. Afterwards, the Syrian general Muslim b. ʿUqba entered the city and called the people to pledge allegiance to Yazīd as slaves (*khawal*) "whose families, lives and property he may deal with as he wishes."[156] This is not the only place Khalīfa depicts Muslim b. ʿUqba as the instigator of slaughter and abuse: in another report, he executes the Companion ʿAbdallāh b. Zamʿa and his son Yazīd—the latter simply for saying, "I pledge allegiance to you on the basis of the Book of God and the Sunna of His

151 E.g. Ibn Saʿd, *Ṭabaqāt* 7:79, 81, 83–84, 89, 167, 169, 209, 241, 247, 251, 255–257, 259–262, 266, 270–271, 273–274, 276, 279, 294, 403, 498; al-Fasawī, *Maʿrifa* 3:423–428. For later Sunnī accounts, see Ibn al-Athīr, *al-Kāmil fī l-tārīkh* 3:455–462; al-Dhahabī, *Tārīkh al-Islām* 5:23–32; Ibn Kathīr, *al-Bidāya* 11:614–632.

152 See Chapter 4.

153 Al-Balādhurī, *Ansāb* 5:337–355; al-Ṭabarī, *Tārīkh* 2:400–423.

154 Khalīfa b. Khayyāṭ, *Tārīkh* (1985) 237.

155 See al-Māwardī, *al-Aḥkām al-sulṭāniyya* 10; Abū Yaʿlā b. al-Farrāʾ, *al-Aḥkām al-sulṭāniyya* 25. Also discussed in Crone, *God's rule* 272–275.

156 Khalīfa b. Khayyāṭ, *Tārīkh* (1985) 239.

Prophet."[157] Ibn ʿUqba is also the only person who is cursed in Khalīfa's *Tārīkh*: "In this year [64/684], Muslim b. ʿUqba al-Murrī died, may God show him no mercy and may He curse him."[158]

An important report that corresponds to early Sunnī attitudes to uprisings and the ideal of avoiding intra-Muslim conflicts as far as possible is narrated on Wahb's authority from Zaynab bt. Abī Salama, the wife of ʿAbdallāh b. Zamʿa. Her two sons were killed, and when their bodies were brought to her, she said, "My grief for this one is greater than my grief for that one. This one came forward and fought until he was killed; I fear for him. But that one held himself back until he was killed; I hope for him."[159] Ibn ʿAbd al-Barr narrates a longer version of the report (not through Khalīfa) that explicitly states that Zaynab was not sure that the son who had joined the uprising and fought had done the right thing, whereas the one who held back was certainly killed unjustly.[160] In both cases, however, the report highlights the regrettable outcome of the uprising and the retrospective uncertainty among some Medinans about its rightness—without in any way excusing the crimes and transgressions of Ibn ʿUqba and the Syrian army.

Similar to the Battle of the Camel, Khalīfa's concluding report provides a perspective on the events. In the case of al-Ḥarra, it is Wahb b. Jarīr's account of the Companion Abū Saʿīd al-Khudrī, who went into a cave on the day of the battle. When one of the Syrians found his hideout and entered, Abū Saʿīd put down his sword and said, "Take on my sin and your sin and so become one of the companions of the Fire. That is the repayment of the wrongdoers."[161] Realising that it was Abū Saʿīd al-Khudrī, the Syrian begged him to ask God to forgive him, and Abū Saʿīd replied, "May God forgive you."[162] The report alludes to the ideal among many early Sunnīs of staying away from *fitna*, as in the famous *ḥadīth*, "Whoever finds a place of refuge or protection [from *fitna*] should seek refuge in it."[163] The words of Abū Saʿīd refer to the Qurʾānic story of Cain and

157 Khalīfa b. Khayyāṭ, *Tārīkh* (1985) 239.
158 Khalīfa b. Khayyāṭ, *Tārīkh* (1985) 254.
159 Khalīfa b. Khayyāṭ, *Tārīkh* (1985) 239.
160 Ibn ʿAbd al-Barr, *al-Istīʿāb* 4:1855–1856.
161 Referring to Q 5:29.
162 Khalīfa b. Khayyāṭ, *Tārīkh* (1985) 239. Ibn ʿAsākir narrates the same report from Khalīfa via al-Tustarī in *Tārīkh madīnat Dimashq* 20:394.
163 The whole *ḥadīth* reads, "There will be afflictions (*fitan*) during which the sitting person will be better than the standing one, and the standing one will be better than the walking one, and the walking one will be better than the running one. Whoever exposes himself to these afflictions, they will destroy him. So whoever finds a place of refuge or protection should seek refuge in it." Al-Bukhārī, *Ṣaḥīḥ* 9:51 (*kitāb al-fitan, bāb takūnu fitna al-qāʿid*

Abel (Q 5:27–30), which is here put in the context of intra-Muslim conflict. Khalīfa's conclusion with this report underlines the transgression of the Syrians and presents Abū Saʿīd al-Khudrī's stance as favourable, especially in light of the disastrous outcome of the conflict. Khalīfa highlights this outcome by an extensive list of Medinans who were killed: in total 306 men from Quraysh and the Anṣār.[164] In this way, the Medinan Companions and Successors are commemorated, similar to those who were killed in the Battle of the Camel and at Karbalāʾ.

3.5 *The Second* Fitna*: Zubayrids vs Umayyads*

The second *fitna* refers to the Zubayrid–Umayyad conflict between 64/684, when ʿAbdallāh b. al-Zubayr established his caliphate in Mecca, and 73/692, when he was defeated. The second *fitna* is a major subject in the early historical tradition, but it is less ideologically loaded than the first *fitna*, during ʿAlī's caliphate.[165] Surely, Ibn al-Zubayr was a prominent Companion, but the second *fitna* did not involve senior Companions on both sides, as the previous one had. Nonetheless, the memory of Ibn al-Zubayr's caliphate was important in Sunnī historical thought: Ibn al-Zubayr represented, on the one hand, a legitimate opposition to Umayyad oppression and, on the other hand, a successful repression of the Khawārij and al-Mukhtār's Shīʿī movement.[166] This is also reflected in Khalīfa's *Tārīkh*, where Ibn al-Zubayr is presented as a valid claimant to the caliphate in the absence of an agreed-upon caliph after the chaotic reign of Yazīd b. Muʿāwiya, and as more favourable than his two opponents, Marwān b. al-Ḥakam and ʿAbd al-Malik b. Marwān.[167]

---

fīhā khayr min al-qāʾim); Muslim b. al-Ḥajjāj, *Ṣaḥīḥ* 1319 (*kitāb al-fitan wa-ashrāṭ al-sāʿa, bāb nuzūl al-fitan …*).

164 Khalīfa b. Khayyāṭ, *Tārīkh* (1985) 250.

165 E.g. Ibn Saʿd, *Ṭabaqāt* 6:477–518; Ibn Ḥabīb, *Tārīkh* 127–128; al-Balādhurī, *Ansāb* 5:319–327, 357–376, 6:341–361, 7:7–28, 83–141; Abū Zurʿa al-Dimashqī, *Tārīkh* 1:191–193; al-Dīnawarī, *al-Akhbār al-ṭiwāl* 260–264, 301–306; al-Yaʿqūbī, *Tārīkh* 2:170–187; al-Ṭabarī, *Tārīkh* 2:429–852.

166 See Campbell, ʿAbdallāh b. al-Zubayr; Abou El Fadl, *Rebellion* 68–70.

167 Al-Tustarī narrates some ten reports about the Zubayrid–Umayyad conflict that are not found in Baqī's recension, which provide some additional details about ʿAbdallāh b. al-Zubayr's governors, ʿAmr b. al-Zubayr attack against his brother and, in particular, the fighting between the armies of ʿAbd al-Malik and Muṣʿab b. al-Zubayr. Al-Tustarī also narrates five reports pertaining to al-Mukhtār's revolt that occurred during Ibn al-Zubayr's caliphate. Whether or not this material was a part of the *Tārīkh* as Baqī received it from Khalīfa, it reflects the same historical perspective as the material in the Baqī's recension. See Ṣaddām, *Tārīkh Khalīfa* 88–96.

As noted above, Khalīfa reports that Ibn al-Zubayr had been one of the leading Companions who opposed Yazīd's succession and urged Muʿāwiya to follow the practice of the Prophet, Abū Bakr and ʿUmar.[168] In 63/683, towards the end of Yazīd's reign (60–64/680–683), Ibn al-Zubayr maintained his rejection of Yazīd, whom he accused of drinking wine, abandoning the prayer and partaking in recreational hunting—despite Yazīd's attempts to persuade him with gifts and promises of governance.[169] In this way, Khalīfa illustrates Ibn al-Zubayr's unwavering opposition to Yazīd, based not only on the controversial succession but also on Yazīd's inadequacy for the caliphal office. Interestingly, one of Yazīd's delegates is said to have countered Ibn al-Zubayr's criticism of Yazīd, saying, "Your words are more apt for yourself than him." However, in light of Ibn al-Zubayr's reputation as a righteous man of devotion and strictness, the reply may be understood as a desperate, misinformed or perhaps even ironic reply.

Ibn al-Zubayr fortified himself at the Kaʿba in Mecca against the Syrian army. The siege lasted 50 days, until Yazīd's death in 64/683, when Ibn al-Zubayr received the oath of allegiance as caliph and began to extend his power. Khalīfa emphasises that Ibn al-Zubayr only claimed the caliphate after Yazīd's death and explains in his own words, "Before that, Ibn al-Zubayr had only been calling for a council (*shūrā*) among the members of the community. But three months after the death of Yazīd b. Muʿāwiya, he called for the oath of allegiance to himself and received the oath for the caliphate on the 9th of Rajab 64/684."[170] This association of Ibn al-Zubayr with *shūrā* is also noted in al-Balādhurī's *Ansāb al-ashrāf* but was ignored by al-Ṭabarī in his *Tārīkh* and, as Campbell puts it, "not well remembered in the dominant historical tradition."[171] Moreover, none of al-Dīnawarī, al-Yaʿqūbī and al-Masʿūdī transmit material about Ibn al-Zubayr's association with *shūrā*.[172] By mentioning the call to *shūrā*, Khalīfa contrasts Ibn al-Zubayr's accession to the caliphate with the dynastic succession of the Umayyads in general and of Yazīd in particular, although Ibn al-Zubayr eventually decided to call people to the oath of allegiance to himself.

Khalīfa also provides a brief account of the internal struggles in Syria after Yazīd's succession, which led to Marwān receiving the pledge of allegiance from

168 Khalīfa b. Khayyāṭ, *Tārīkh* (1985) 213–217.

169 Khalīfa b. Khayyāṭ, *Tārīkh* (1985) 251–252.

170 Khalīfa b. Khayyāṭ, *Tārīkh* (1985) 258. Al-Tustarī also narrates from Khalīfa that, "when the people of Medina renounced Yazīd b. Muʿāwiya, Ibn al-Zubayr called for Yazīd's deposition and for a council (*shūrā*) to solve the matter [of electing a leader]." Ibn ʿAsākir, *Tārīkh madīnat Dimashq* 11:415–416.

171 Campbell, *Telling memories* 156–165.

172 Campbell, *Telling memories* 165n124.

the Syrians with his two sons, ʿAbd al-Malik and ʿAbd al-ʿAzīz, as successors.[173] Khalīfa does not disqualify either of Ibn al-Zubayr and Marwān, but simply notes that both received the oath of allegiance and were considered caliphs by different groups. However, Ibn al-Zubayr's claim seems much more favourable in light of the earlier reports: he was the first child born among the Muhājirūn in Medina after the *hijra*, he defended ʿUthmān, urged Muʿāwiya to follow the rightly-guided model of succession and fought for *shūrā* until Yazīd's death, while Marwān defended ʿUthmān, but also treacherously murdered Ṭalḥa and instructed the Medinan governor, al-Walīd b. ʿUtba, to kill al-Ḥusayn b. ʿAlī and Ibn al-Zubayr as they refused to pledge allegiance to Yazīd.[174]

That said, Khalīfa's depiction of Ibn al-Zubayr's caliphate is far from idealistic: he is, for example, reported to have imprisoned Muḥammad b. al-Ḥanafiyya and a number of his companions (including Abū l-Ṭufayl ʿĀmir b. Wāthila) for not pledging allegiance to him. Ibn al-Zubayr's governor of Medina, Jābir b. al-Aswad, also flogged Saʿīd b. al-Musayyib for the same reason.[175] The division in the community under Zubayrid rule is illustrated by the pilgrimage in 66/686, which was divided between the Khārijī leader Najda b. ʿĀmir, the Hāshimī leader Ibn al-Ḥanafiyya and Ibn al-Zubayr. As Khalīfa narrates it, however, the majority of the people (*jamāʿat al-nās*) at ʿArafa remained with Ibn al-Zubayr.[176] It is worth noting that Khalīfa provides relatively little information about the Umayyads in Syria during the Zubayrid caliphate (64–73/684–692), which might explain why many of Baqī b. Makhlad's added reports pertain to the Umayyads in this period.[177]

In Baqī's recension, Khalīfa provides a very short account of the Shīʿī revolt of al-Mukhtār in Kufa (66–67/685–687), which was eventually defeated by Muṣʿab

173 Khalīfa b. Khayyāṭ, *Tārīkh* (1985) 254–261.

174 On Marwān's instruction to al-Walīd b. ʿUtba, see Khalīfa b. Khayyāṭ, *Tārīkh* (1985) 232–233. Moreover, the way Marwān defeated al-Ḍaḥḥāk b. Qays at Marj Rāhiṭ and took control of Syria is not presented in a particularly admirable way: "Ibn Ziyād said to Marwān, 'Al-Ḍaḥḥāk has a cavalry from Qays and we will not be able to harm them as we want except by employing a stratagem. So ask them to make peace and hold back from fighting, but prepare the cavalry. Then, when they put down their arms, unleash the cavalry against them.' The mediators went between them and al-Ḍaḥḥāk held back from fighting. Then Marwān attacked them with his cavalry and they retreated to their flag in disarray. Al-Ḍaḥḥāk was killed alongside many of his cavalry from Qays." Khalīfa b. Khayyāṭ, *Tārīkh* (1985) 259–260. See Wurtzel, *Khalifa ibn Khayyat's History* 116–117.

175 Khalīfa b. Khayyāṭ, *Tārīkh* (1985) 262, 265. Khalīfa also reports that Saʿīd b. al-Musayyib was later flogged for refusing to pledge allegiance to ʿAbd al-Malik's two sons, al-Walīd and Sulaymān. *Tārīkh* (1985) 289–290.

176 Khalīfa b. Khayyāṭ, *Tārīkh* (1985) 263–264.

177 See Chapter 1.

b. al-Zubayr, who governed Iraq for his brother. In contrast to the lengthy accounts elsewhere, Khalīfa only makes some brief points about chronology and individuals who were killed.[178] Al-Tustarī transmits some additional reports and details about al-Mukhtār's revolt, which might or might not have been a part of the version of the *Tārīkh* that Khalīfa transmitted to Baqī. However, they fit the historical perspective in Baqī's recension.[179] In 70/689–690, Khalīfa notes that ʿAmr b. Saʿīd b. al-ʿĀṣ staged a coup against ʿAbd al-Malik after his succession and that they made a treaty, after which ʿAbd al-Malik had him killed. At this point, events begin to turn in favour of the Umayyads, and the Zubayrids are defeated in the provinces. In 72/691–692 ʿAbd al-Malik sent al-Ḥajjāj b. Yūsuf, who besieged Ibn al-Zubayr in Mecca and raised war engines against the Sacred Mosque. Ibn al-Zubayr was eventually defeated and killed on the 17th of Jumādā al-Ākhira 73/692 and, as Khalīfa puts it, "the people agreed upon ʿAbd al-Malik [as caliph]."[180]

Khalīfa's account of the Zubayrid–Umayyad conflict is not an idealised pro-Zubayrid or pro-Umayyad story, although Ibn al-Zubayr's claim to the caliphate seems more favourable in Khalīfa's narrative. Instead, it is a straightforward outline that locates the caliphate with the political authority over the majority community: first Ibn al-Zubayr, then ʿAbd al-Malik. Accordingly, Khalīfa does not count ʿAbd al-Malik's caliphate from Marwān's death and the time he received the oath of allegiance—as the Andalusian Ibn Ḥabīb and the Syrian Abū Zurʿa, for example—but from the death of Ibn al-Zubayr.[181] He also concludes Ibn al-Zubayr's reign with the standard details of the length of his reign and his date and place of birth, similar to other caliphs.[182] This treatment is characteristic of Khalīfa's perspective on the circulation of political power in the *Tārīkh*: Ibn al-Zubayr was not only a venerated Companion but also, for almost ten years, the strongest and most capable political leader of the community—before events turned in favour of the Umayyads under ʿAbd al-Malik.[183]

---

178 Khalīfa b. Khayyāṭ, *Tārīkh* (1985) 263–264. For other historians' accounts, see al-Balādhurī, *Ansāb* 6:375–455; al-Dīnawarī, *al-Akhbār al-ṭiwāl* 282–301; al-Yaʿqūbī, *Tārīkh* 2:174–176, 181–182; al-Ṭabarī, *Tārīkh* 2:642–750.

179 See Ṣaddām, *Tārīkh Khalīfa* 88–91.

180 Khalīfa b. Khayyāṭ, *Tārīkh* (1985) 269.

181 Khalīfa b. Khayyāṭ, *Tārīkh* (1985) 299; Ibn Ḥabīb, *Tārīkh* 130; Abū Zurʿa al-Dimashqī, *Tārīkh* 1:193.

182 Khalīfa b. Khayyāṭ, *Tārīkh* (1985) 269–270.

183 Cf. Robinson's discussion of "the caliphate of Ibn al-Zubayr" and the "rebellion of ʿAbd al-Malik" in *ʿAbd al-Malik* 31–48.

3.6 *Ibn al-Ashʿath's Revolt*

An event that receives much attention in Khalīfa's *Tārīkh* is the revolt of ʿAbd al-Raḥmān b. Muḥammad b. al-Ashʿath (known as Ibn al-Ashʿath) in 81–83/700–702 against the Umayyad governor of Iraq, al-Ḥajjāj b. Yūsuf (r. 75–95/694–714). Detailed accounts are found in other sources, but Khalīfa's special attention to this, not other, failed revolts is noteworthy.[184] The reason is probably the Basran connection and the involvement of many *qurrāʾ* from Iraq—literally Qurʾān reciters, but in Khalīfa's understanding probably referring to learned people in general.[185] Khalīfa seems to express a view that the uprising might have been justifiable because of al-Ḥajjāj's oppression and the participation of leading Muslims, but that the disastrous outcome nonetheless reinforces the idea of striving to avoid intra-Muslim fighting as far as possible—similar to the Battle of al-Ḥarra. The account of Ibn al-Ashʿath's revolt consists of 27 reports (some with double *isnāds*) from the direct transmitters listed in Table 13.

All of the known transmitters are Basrans, and a number of them are prominent *ḥadīth* scholars. In addition to the high number of reports, this shows Khalīfa's concern for Ibn al-Ashʿath's revolt as a key event in the Umayyad period—especially for the Iraqi scholarly community. The Kufan sources cited by al-Balādhurī and al-Ṭabarī also confirm that non-Basran accounts of Ibn al-Ashʿath's revolt circulated in Khalīfa's time, which makes his Basran selection even more distinctive.[186]

Khalīfa's narrative is straightforward: al-Ḥajjāj had dispatched Ibn al-Ashʿath in command of an army to Sijistān, but in 81/700 Ibn al-Ashʿath renounced al-Ḥajjāj and marched against him with the army and the *qurrāʾ* who joined him. After Ibn al-Ashʿath's initial success, al-Ḥajjāj won a series of battles in 82/701, in which many of the *qurrāʾ* were killed. The remnants of Ibn al-Ashʿath's army were later defeated in Khurāsān, and Ibn al-Ashʿath eventually committed suicide after being captured by al-Ḥajjāj's men. Similar to most historians, Khalīfa depicts al-Ḥajjāj as a tyrant who bombarded the Kaʿba and executed many great men, but he provides relatively few details of al-Ḥajjāj's notori-

---

184 See al-Balādhurī, *Ansāb* 7:303–374; al-Yaʿqūbī, *Tārīkh* 2:198–201; al-Ṭabarī, *Tārīkh* 2:1052–1125. See also Abou El Fadl, *Rebellion* 70–72. Ṣaddām's list of missing material in Baqī's recension contains no reports about Ibn al-Ashʿath's revolt. See Ṣaddām, *Tārīkh Khalīfa* 89–105.

185 See Khalīfa's list of *qurrāʾ*, which consists exclusively of Iraqi scholars, in *Tārīkh* (1985) 286–287. Ibn Kathīr also states that the *qurrāʾ* are the *ʿulamāʾ* in *al-Bidāya* 12:317. See also Veccia Vaglieri, Ibn al-Ashʿath; Hinds, Kufan political alignments; Juynboll, *Qurrāʾ*, Position of Qurʾān recitation, Qurʾān reciter; Calder, Qurrāʾ; Shah, Quest for the origins.

186 Al-Balādhurī, *Ansāb* 7:303–374; al-Ṭabarī, *Tārīkh* 2:1052–1125.

TABLE 13 Khalīfa's sources on Ibn al-Ashʿath's revolt

	Name	Reports	Location
1.	Al-Madāʾinī	6	Basra/Baghdad
2.	Abū l-Yaqẓān	4	Basra
3.	Umayya b. Khālid al-Qaysī	4	Basra
4.	Anonymous	3	–
5.	Ghundar	2	Basra
6.	ʿĀmir b. Ṣāliḥ b. Rustam	2	Basra
7.	Al-Aṣmaʿī	1	Basra
8.	Abū ʿUbayda Maʿmar b. al-Muthannā	1	Basra
9.	ʿAbd al-Raḥmān b. Mahdī	1	Basra
10.	Muḥammad b. Muʿādh	1	Basra
11.	Salm b. Qutayba	1	Basra
12.	Sulaymān b. Ḥarb	1	Basra
13.	ʿAlī b. ʿAbdallāh (b. al-Madīnī?)	1	Basra?
14.	Yaḥyā b. Muḥammad	1	Medina/Basra

ous rule. Al-Ḥajjāj's execution of Saʿīd b. Jubayr in 95/713–714, for example, is only given one line in the *Tārīkh*—in contrast to the lengthy accounts by Ibn Saʿd, al-Balādhurī and al-Ṭabarī.[187] Al-Tustarī transmits from Khalīfa an account of al-Ḥajjāj's inaugural *khuṭba* in Iraq, which is not found in Baqī's recension, and another report, according to which Mālik b. Dīnār al-Baṣrī (d. 130/748) said, "I saw al-Ḥasan and Saʿīd, the two sons of Abū l-Ḥasan. Saʿīd was inciting against al-Ḥajjāj, but al-Ḥasan said, 'Al-Ḥajjāj is a punishment that God Most High has inflicted upon you, so do not respond to God's punishment with your swords, but rather respond to it with supplication (*duʿāʾ*) and humble entreaty (*taḍarruʿ*).'"[188] Although al-Ḥasan al-Baṣrī's words in the second report clearly describe al-Ḥajjāj's rule as a punishment, at the same time they give preference to avoiding armed revolt, which corresponds to the historical perspective on Ibn al-Ashʿath's revolt in Baqī's recension.

Khalīfa does not explicitly evaluate Ibn al-Ashʿath's revolt, but it appears at least justifiable because of the support from the *qurrāʾ* and al-Ḥajjāj's bru-

187 Khalīfa b. Khayyāṭ, *Tārīkh* (1985) 307; Ibn Saʿd, *Ṭabaqāt* 8:382–385; al-Balādhurī, *Ansāb* 7:363–374; al-Ṭabarī, *Tārīkh* 2:1261–1266.

188 Ibn ʿAsākir, *Tārīkh madīnat Dimashq* 12:127, 177.

tality, including executions of many prominent individuals.[189] About 500 *qurrāʾ* are said to have fought on the side of Ibn al-Ashʿath, which Khalīfa highlights with a list of 25 *qurrāʾ* who joined the revolt—all of them Basran and Kufan *ḥadīth* transmitters.[190] Khalīfa notes that Ibn Ashʿath and his army, in 81/700–701, "marched in revolt against al-Ḥajjāj, but making no mention of revolt against ʿAbd al-Malik," which presents the beginning of the uprising as a grievance against al-Ḥajjāj, not the caliph, ʿAbd al-Malik, although the latter is reported to have described the rebellion as an act of disbelief (*kufr*) in a letter to al-Ḥajjāj.[191] By contrast, al-Ṭabarī narrates from Abū Mikhnaf that Ibn al-Ashʿath's people explicitly said in 81/700–701, "If we disavow al-Ḥajjāj, ʿAbd al-Malik's governor, then we have disavowed ʿAbd al-Malik," before pledging allegiance to Ibn al-Ashʿath.[192] However, Khalīfa narrates no praise for Ibn al-Ashʿath as an individual, depicting him simply as a commander who mutinied and mobilised the discontented Iraqis but who eventually failed and apparently committed suicide.[193]

Moreover, there is no praise for the revolt as such: al-Ḥasan al-Baṣrī, for example, is said to have been "forced to revolt (*ukhrija karhan*)" after Ibn al-Ashʿath was told that, "If you want them to be killed around you as they were killed around ʿĀʾisha's camel, make al-Ḥasan join the revolt."[194] Although many Successors participated willingly, the result was, as one report puts it, that "there were none of Ibn al-Ashʿath's companions who fell whose death was not regretted and there were none of those who survived who did not praise God who saved him."[195] Thereby Khalīfa presents Ibn al-Ashʿath's revolt as perhaps justifiable due to al-Ḥajjāj's oppressive rule and the support by prominent Muslims,[196] but nonetheless regrettable in terms of the outcome. Similar to the earlier civil wars, Khalīfa concludes with a summarising report. In this case, it is the dialogue after Ibn al-Ashʿath's defeat between al-Ḥajjāj and the leading Successor, ʿĀmir al-Shaʿbī, who had participated in the uprising:

---

189 In a similar way, al-Azdī narrates three reports from Khalīfa about various scholars supporting the uprising of Ibrāhīm b. ʿAbdallāh (the brother of Muḥammad al-Nafs al-Zakiyya) in Basra at the time of al-Manṣūr. Al-Azdī, *Tārīkh al-Mawṣil* 188–189.

190 Khalīfa b. Khayyāṭ, *Tārīkh* (1985) 286–287.

191 Khalīfa b. Khayyāṭ, *Tārīkh* (1985) 280, 282.

192 Al-Ṭabarī, *Tārīkh* 2:1057–1058.

193 Khalīfa reports that Ibn al-Ashʿath threw himself off a castle at al-Rukhkhaj. *Tārīkh* (1985) 289. See also al-Ṭabarī, *Tārīkh* 2:1132–1136.

194 Khalīfa b. Khayyāṭ, *Tārīkh* (1985) 287.

195 Khalīfa b. Khayyāṭ, *Tārīkh* (1985) 287.

196 Similar to the uprising of Muḥammad al-Nafs al-Zakiyya and his brother Ibrāhīm b. ʿAbdallāh at the time of al-Manṣūr. See Khalīfa's three reports in al-Azdī, *Tārīkh al-Mawṣil* 188–189.

> Al-Aṣmaʿī said: ʿUthmān al-Shaḥḥām narrated to me; he said: When al-Shaʿbī was brought before al-Ḥajjāj, he scolded him. Al-Shaʿbī said, "Our land has become dry and our abode rugged. We are in constant fear. We have been afflicted with a civil war (*fitna*) with respect to which we were neither innocent and pious, nor wicked and strong." Al-Ḥajjāj replied to him, "Well said."[197]

Al-Shaʿbī's words suggest that the Iraqis had lived under oppression, which may explain the revolt, but when the *fitna* of intra-Muslim fighting actually occurred, the lines between righteousness and wickedness began to blur. This, again, alludes to the position of avoiding and seeking refuge from *fitna*. Thus Khalīfa's accounts of the Battle of al-Ḥarra and the revolt of Ibn al-Ashʿath are examples of early Sunnī views on *fitna*, in the sense of revolt and intra-Muslim fighting.[198] Ibn Ḥajar (d. 852/1449) says regarding those early scholars who believed in armed revolt against oppressive rulers (*a'immat al-jawr*):

> This was an old view (*madhhab qadīm*) among some of the early generations (*al-salaf*). However, the issue settled [among the scholars] upon avoiding it, because they saw it leading to greater harm. The events of al-Ḥarra, Ibn al-Ashʿath and others are warning examples for those who reflect.[199]

Khalīfa's perspective on both the Battle of al-Ḥarra and Ibn al-Ashʿath's revolt seems to agree with Ibn Ḥajar's outline. His accounts reflect an early Sunnī ideal of speaking the truth and criticising corrupt leaders,[200] but as far as possible remaining patient and avoiding political insurrection because of the greater harm it often leads to—as the Battle of al-Ḥarra and the revolt of Ibn al-Ashʿath were taken to illustrate. Khalīfa shared this perspective with many other early Sunnī scholars, for whom the Muslim community was in some sense independent of its ruler (although he should be obeyed in political matters as long as it did not involve disobedience to God) and instead meant to unite around a common scheme of law and belief.[201] Perhaps for this reason, the early Sunnīs

197 Khalīfa b. Khayyāṭ, *Tārīkh* (1985) 287–288. See Wurtzel, *Khalifa ibn Khayyat's History* 153.

198 See also what al-Bukhārī narrates about the subject in his *Ṣaḥīḥ* 9:46–61 (*kitāb al-fitan*), and Muslim in his *Ṣaḥīḥ* 1316–1352 (*kitāb al-fitan wa-ashrāṭ al-sāʿa*).

199 Ibn Ḥajar, *Tahdhīb* 1:399. See also Ibn Taymiyya's similar discussion about revolts against oppressive rulers, including the Battle of al-Ḥarra and the revolt of Ibn al-Ashʿath, in *Minhāj al-sunna* 4:527–531.

200 See above regarding Khalīfa's accounts of Yazīd's succession and the second *fitna*.

201 See Melchert, *Ahmad* 93.

did not consider reprobate rulers (Umayyads or ʿAbbāsids) as catastrophic as the Khawārij and the Shīʿī groups did—neither in history nor in contemporary politics.

3.7 *The Fall of the Umayyads and the ʿAbbāsid Revolution*

The fall of the Umayyads and the ʿAbbāsid Revolution (c. 129–132/147–50) receive much attention from the early historians, but Khalīfa's *Tārīkh* remains the earliest surviving chronological account.[202] Hence it provides an important addition to the discussion of how third/ninth-century historians interpreted the transition from Umayyad to ʿAbbāsid rule.[203] In a comparison between al-Balādhurī and al-Ṭabarī, Judd points out that al-Balādhurī focuses mainly on moral and religious corruption as the cause for the Umayyads' demise, while al-Ṭabarī emphasises personal greed and tribal strife.[204] This section suggests that Khalīfa, by largely avoiding questions of religio-political claims and personal motives, presents the fall of the Umayyads as a more general process of (1) increasing revolts throughout the caliphate, (2) unsuccessful battles in the East and (3) internal conflicts in the Umayyad family. Thus Khalīfa's interpretation is less thematic than al-Balādhurī's and al-Ṭabarī's, but it still provides a coherent narrative of the events and developments that paved the way for the ʿAbbāsid dynasty.

In contrast to other historians' material about the ʿAbbāsid propaganda campaign in Iraq and Khurāsān leading up to the revolution, Khalīfa only first mentions the ʿAbbāsid movement with the appearance of Abū Muslim al-Khurāsānī in Ramaḍān 129/747.[205] Instead, he focuses on the increasing political and military problems within the caliphate that weakened the Umayyad authority, especially after Hishām b. ʿAbd al-Malik's death in 125/743. His successor, al-Walīd (II) b. Yazīd, is arguably the most vilified Umayyad caliph in the historical tradition alongside Yazīd b. Muʿāwiya. The historical tradition remembers him as the personification of Umayyad tyranny, depravity and impiety, as well as a "hopelessly romantic, drunken poet."[206] Because of Khalīfa's exclusive focus on politics and administration, this is less prominent than in, for example, the accounts of al-Balādhurī and al-Ṭabarī.[207] It is also noteworthy

202 E.g., al-Balādhurī, *Ansāb* 9:217–335; al-Yaʿqūbī, *Tārīkh* 2:268–282; al-Dīnawarī, *al-Akhbār al-ṭiwāl* 334–351; al-Ṭabarī, *Tārīkh* 2:1890–2017, 3:1–23.

203 Humphreys, *Islamic history* 111–116; Judd, Narratives, Medieval explanations.

204 Judd, Narratives 210, Medieval explanations 91–94.

205 Wurtzel, *Khalifa ibn Khayyat's History* 30. See also Humphreys, *Islamic history* 111–116.

206 Judd, Narratives 214, Reinterpreting al-Walīd b. Yazīd 439–441.

207 Al-Balādhurī, *Ansāb* 9:145–187; al-Ṭabarī, *Tārīkh* 2:1740–1825. Al-Tustarī narrates four re-

that Khalīfa does not narrate from his main source, al-Madāʾinī, about al-Walīd, while al-Balādhurī and al-Ṭabarī base their accounts mainly on al-Madāʾinī.[208] Instead, Khalīfa transmits from different transmitters, but mainly from Ismāʿīl b. Ibrāhīm regarding the assassination of al-Walīd.

In relation to the assassination in 126/744, Khalīfa routinely notes the date of al-Walīd's death, age, birthplace and the length of his reign.[209] He also notes that the assassination was led by Yazīd b. al-Walīd b. ʿAbd al-Malik and took place at the desert castle of al-Bakhrāʾ. There are no references to Yazīd b. al-Walīd's support from the Qadariyya of Mizza (as al-Balādhurī narrates it) or the Kalbī tribesmen of Mizza (as al-Ṭabarī narrates it).[210] As with other intra-Muslim conflicts, Khalīfa is not particularly concerned with the doctrinal, moral or tribal motives behind the intra-Umayyad conflicts. The only explicit indication of al-Walīd's wickedness is a report about the assassination according to which the killers shouted, "Kill the sodomite as the people of Lot were killed!"[211] A second report mentions that al-Walīd held a copy of the Qurʾān, saying, "I shall be killed in the same way as my paternal cousin ʿUthmān was killed."[212] Thereby Khalīfa records both the standard accusation of sodomy and al-Walīd's own claim to be the second 'unjustly killed caliph,' which creates a somewhat ambiguous image. It resembles al-Balādhurī's narration that Marwān (II) b. Muḥammad saw al-Walīd as the unjustly killed caliph (*al-khalīfat al-maẓlūm*) and himself in Muʿāwiya's role of seeking vengeance for ʿUthmān's death.[213] The report also alludes to the similar outcomes of ʿUthmān's and al-Walīd's deaths: both caliphicides preceded civil wars that led to the collapse of, first, the rightly-guided model of governance and, second, the Umayyad dynasty.

It is not until Yazīd b. al-Walīd's inaugural *khuṭba* in 126/744 that Khalīfa mentions any motivation for the mutiny against al-Walīd.[214] His *khuṭba* con-

ports from Khalīfa that are not found in Baqī's recension, but they contain no information about al-Walīd b. Yazīd's character and only pertain to the leaders of the pilgrimage, the date of Sulaymān b. Ḥabīb's death, the name of al-Walīd b. Yazīd's chamberlain (*ḥājib*) and the date of Khālid al-Qasrī's death. See Ibn ʿAsākir, *Tārīkh madīnat Dimashq* 16:162, 22:212, 45:115, 48:6; Ṣaddām, *Tārīkh Khalīfa* 110–111.

208 Judd, Narratives 211.

209 Khalīfa b. Khayyāṭ, *Tārīkh* (1985) 363.

210 Judd, Narratives 217–218. See also Judd, Medieval explanations 92–94.

211 Khalīfa b. Khayyāṭ, *Tārīkh* (1985) 364.

212 Khalīfa b. Khayyāṭ, *Tārīkh* (1985) 365.

213 Al-Balādhurī, *Ansāb* 9:199; Judd, Narratives 221.

214 Khalīfa b. Khayyāṭ, *Tārīkh* (1985) 365. See also al-Balādhurī, *Ansāb* 9:191–192; al-Ṭabarī, *Tārīkh* 2:1834–1835. The same narration from Khalīfa is found in al-Azdī, *Tārīkh al-Mawṣil* 57–58.

tains pious critique of al-Walīd as a tyrant, during whose reign "the signposts of guidance were obliterated and the light of the godfearing people was extinguished." Yazīd describes al-Walīd as "permitting the prohibited, engaging in innovations and altering the Sunna," which necessitated action against him to restore justice based on "the Book of God and the Sunna of His Prophet." By citing this critique against al-Walīd and the old Umayyad ways, Khalīfa highlights the motive for overthrowing al-Walīd, although the outcome, like other revolts in the *Tārīkh*, did not match the glorious expectations beforehand and only created further intra-Muslim fighting.

In the aftermath of Yazīd b. al-Walīd's death, Marwān (II) b. Muḥammad eventually seized the caliphate in 127/744. From this point, Khalīfa focuses on the escalating revolts throughout the caliphate—especially the Khawārij in al-Jazīra, Iraq, North Africa and Yemen.[215] Khalīfa's accounts of Khārijī revolts are generally straightforward and non-judgemental, in line with his usual narrative style.[216] However, some reports clearly undermine the Khārijī cause, such as the conclusion to the Battle of al-Nahrawān (38/658), in which 'Alī's army defeated the first Khawārij, known as al-Ḥarūriyya:

> Al-Muʿtamir b. Sulaymān said: I heard from my father that Anas said: Shabath b. Ribʿī said, "I was the first to organise the Ḥarūriyya [i.e. the Khawārij]." A man told him, "That is nothing to be proud of."[217]

Other examples are the uprisings during Muʿāwiya's reign, including the atrocities and indiscriminate political massacring (*istiʿrāḍ*) of Qurayb and Zaḥḥāf.[218] However, the narrative function of the Khawārij in the late Umayyad and early 'Abbāsid period is slightly different. They are still presented as extreme anti-caliphal rebels and contributors to the Umayyad decline, but Khalīfa also cites some of their anti-government rhetoric. The clearest example is Abū Ḥamza's *khuṭba* after the Khārijī occupation of Mecca in 129/746–747.[219] On the one hand, Abū Ḥamza's *khuṭba* confirms the historical image of the Khawārij as

215 Khalīfa b. Khayyāṭ, *Tārīkh* (1985) 375–395.

216 Wurtzel, *Khalifa ibn Khayyat's History* 30.

217 Khalīfa b. Khayyāṭ, *Tārīkh* (1985) 192. Khalīfa identifies the Ḥarūriyya as Khawārij on p. 197.

218 Khalīfa b. Khayyāṭ, *Tārīkh* (1985) 219–222. Khalīfa reports, for example, that "Wahb said: I heard Ghassān b. Muḍar say: I heard Saʿīd b. Yazīd say that Abū Bilāl [Mirdās b. Udayya] said, 'Qurayb—may God not draw him near (*lā qarrabahu Allāh*)! I swear by God, I would rather fall from the sky to the earth than do what he did,' referring to the indiscriminate massacring (*al-istiʿrāḍ*)."

219 Khalīfa b. Khayyāṭ, *Tārīkh* (1985) 385–387. Also in al-Balādhurī, *Ansāb* 9:290–294; al-Ṭabarī, *Tārīkh* 2:2008–2012; Crone and Hinds, *God's caliph* 129–132.

young idealists (*shabāb*) going to extremes in worship and warfare, declaring war against all tyrants and anyone who supports them, and thereby causing bloodshed and strife within the Muslim community.[220] On the other hand, it also criticises the late Umayyads' despotic rule, unlawful seizure of wealth and governance without regard for the revealed law. In the section on the early ʿAbbāsid period, Khalīfa cites a letter from ʿAbd al-Salām al-Yashkurī criticising the caliph al-Mahdī in a similar way.[221] The main purpose of these accounts was probably to show the sentiments among the Khawārij in the late Umayyad and early ʿAbbāsid period. However, the Khawārij might also have been used to airing criticism against some later caliphs, without supporting the Khawārij or criticising the caliphate per se—al-Mahdī, for instance, is clearly affirmed as the Commander of the Believers.[222]

A longer version of Abū Ḥamza's *khuṭba*—containing specific criticism against ʿUthmān, ʿAlī and the Umayyad caliphs—is narrated from Khalīfa in al-Azdī's *Tārīkh al-Mawṣil*.[223] Al-Azdī does not specify from whom he received the report, but it might be Ibn Muḥammad b. Isḥāq, whom he cites elsewhere as the source for Khalīfa's material.[224] Al-Azdī might have received a copy of Khalīfa's *Tārīkh* from Ibn Muḥammad b. Isḥāq, but it is also possible that he only had access to some individual reports from Khalīfa, not the entire *Tārīkh*. Accordingly, Baqī or someone else possibly omitted this report, but it is also possible that it was never a part of Khalīfa's *Tārīkh* (whether in Baqī's recension or al-Tustarī's) and that Khalīfa transmitted it separately from his *Tārīkh*. Whether or not it was a part of the *Tārīkh*, Khalīfa's transmission of the longer version shows that he was not opposed in principle to transmitting accusations against the Umayyads or other types of negative material about them. This is also confirmed by many reports in Baqī's recension of the *Tārīkh*.[225] At the same time, Khalīfa clearly agreed neither with Abū Ḥamza's accusations of unbelief (*takfīr*) nor with his general historical views—especially on the Companions ʿUthmān, ʿAlī and Muʿāwiya—which suggests that he transmitted the *khuṭba* as a historical document of Khārijism in the late Umayyad period, not to criticise the caliphs of the past.

220 On this image, see Hagemann, *History and memory* 73–101.
221 Khalīfa b. Khayyāṭ, *Tārīkh* (1985) 443–445.
222 Khalīfa b. Khayyāṭ, *Tārīkh* (1985) 439.
223 Al-Azdī, *Tārīkh al-Mawṣil* 103–106. See also Chapter 1.
224 Al-Azdī, *Tārīkh al-Mawṣil* 188–189.
225 See the above discussions about, for example, the accounts of Muʿāwiya, Yazīd b. Muʿāwiya and Marwān b. al-Ḥakam.

Abū Ḥamza and his Khārijī movement went on from Mecca to slaughter numerous Medinans (including twelve from the family of al-Zubayr b. al-ʿAwwām) in the Battle of Qudayd (130/747–748), which Khalīfa commemorates with a list of fallen Medinans—thereby taking the side of the Medinans against the Khawārij.[226] Khalīfa's particular focus on this and other Khārijī revolts in the late Umayyad period foregrounds the Khawārij as a major cause of the Umayyad demise.

It is not until Ramaḍān 129/747 that Khalīfa introduces Abū Muslim's movement that brought the ʿAbbāsids to power.[227] Khalīfa's narrative of the last five years of Umayyad rule is fairly detailed, but it focuses as usual on chronology, locations and participants in events, without paying too much attention to personal motives, conspiracies or religious or tribal interests. The ʿAbbāsid victory is depicted as a result of successful military campaigns (led by Abū Muslim, Qaḥṭaba b. Shabīb and ʿAbdallāh b. ʿAlī) and of shrewd navigation through a time when the Umayyad authority was worn down by wars, revolts and internal disputes. Introducing the new dynasty, Khalīfa narrates that Abū l-ʿAbbās—known as al-Saffāḥ (meaning 'the blood-shedder' or perhaps 'the generous')—received the pledge of allegiance in Kufa in 132/749 and led the Friday prayer. However, the choice of report gives an ambiguous image of the new dynasty, perhaps illustrating the transformation of the ʿAbbāsid revolution from an idealistic mission into the imposition of another dynasty:

> ʿAbdallāh b. al-Mughīra narrated to me from his father; he said: I saw Abū l-ʿAbbās when he went to the Friday prayer, riding a small grey horse, between his paternal uncle, Dāwūd b. ʿAlī, and his brother, Abū Jaʿfar. He was a handsome young man, but pallid. He reached the mosque, ascended the *minbar* and began to speak. Dāwūd b. ʿAlī ascended and stood two steps up on the *minbar*. He praised God and said, "People! No one has ascended this *minbar* of yours as caliph since ʿAlī b. Abī Ṭālib, other than this nephew of mine." He made promises to the people and raised their hopes.
>
> My father added: Then I saw him the next Friday. His face seemed like a shield and his neck like a silver pitcher. The pallor had disappeared. By God, only a week had passed.[228]

226 Khalīfa b. Khayyāṭ, *Tārīkh* (1985) 392–393.

227 Khalīfa b. Khayyāṭ, *Tārīkh* (1985) 387.

228 Khalīfa b. Khayyāṭ, *Tārīkh* (1985) 409–410. See Wurtzel, *Khalifa ibn Khayyat's History* 312–313. Ibn ʿAsākir transmits the same report via al-Tustarī in *Tārīkh madīnat Dimashq* 32:287.

Al-Saffāḥ quickly learned the requirements of governance and immediately, as Khalīfa goes on to mention, began to eliminate his political opponents.[229] In this way, Khalīfa treats the ʿAbbāsid dynasty similarly to their Umayyad predecessors: although they did not represent ideal government, they were after all a Qurashī dynasty of superior political authority and military power that possessed the caliphate through the oath of allegiance. Khalīfa's account of al-Saffāḥ's *khuṭba* is shorter than the accounts of al-Balādhurī, al-Yaʿqūbī and al-Ṭabarī.[230] Moreover, Khalīfa mentions no details of the ʿAbbāsids' special religious and hereditary claims to the caliphate, apart from Dāwūd b. ʿAlī's assertion that al-Saffāḥ was the first real caliph since their Hāshimī ancestor, ʿAlī b. Abī Ṭālib. By avoiding the issues of religio-political legitimacy in relation to the ʿAbbāsid takeover, Khalīfa de-emphasises the dynastic change to a larger extent than some other historians who are more concerned with the ʿAbbāsid claims to authority.[231] Khalīfa also foregrounds the continuity of the caliphate and its offices by the administrative list sections, which, apart from the names of the appointees, remain the same throughout the Umayyad and ʿAbbāsid periods. Thus he takes no clear stance in the Umayyad–ʿAbbāsid conflict, which suggests a pragmatic acceptance of the ʿAbbāsids in light of the interests of avoiding *fitna* and upholding the political unity of the Muslim community.

4 The ʿAbbāsid Period

Khalīfa's section for the ʿAbbāsid period (132–232/750–847) in the *Tārīkh*, as transmitted by Baqī b. Makhlad, is substantially shorter than the other sections (about a sixth of the work in total). He treats the succession of caliphs and the

229 Khalīfa b. Khayyāṭ, *Tārīkh* (1985) 402, 404, 410. In relation to this, Khalīfa also narrates that "ʿAbdallāh b. ʿAlī executed some 80 men from Banū Umayya" after entering Damascus in 132/750. *Tārīkh* (1985) 404. On this event, see Borrut, Future of the past 285–287. Al-Azdī transmits from Khalīfa an account of ʿAbdallāh b. ʿAlī's exhumation of the Umayyad caliphs that is not found in Baqī's recension, but he does not mention from whom he received this report, and it might not have been a part of Khalīfa's *Tārīkh*. As with Abū Ḥamza's *khuṭba*, it is possible that al-Azdī received a copy of Khalīfa's *Tārīkh* from Ibn Muḥammad b. Isḥāq, whom he cites elsewhere, but it is also possible that al-Azdī only had access to a number of individual reports from Khalīfa and that this account was not a part of the *Tārīkh* (whether in Baqī's transmission or al-Tustarī's). Al-Azdī, *Tārīkh al-Mawṣil* 138. See also Chapter 1.

230 Al-Balādhurī, *Ansāb* 4:185–186; al-Yaʿqūbī, *Tārīkh* 2:284; al-Ṭabarī, *Tārīkh* 3:29–33. See also al-Dīnawarī, *al-Akhbār al-ṭiwāl* 351; al-Masʿūdī, *Murūj* 3:256.

231 E.g. al-Balādhurī, *Ansāb* 4:173–178, 209–219; al-Yaʿqūbī, *Tārīkh* 2:282–284; al-Ṭabarī, *Tārīkh* 3:23–34.

intra-Muslim conflicts in much less detail than the earlier periods. Some of the controversial events that Khalīfa deals with laconically in a couple of sentences include ʿAbdallāh b. ʿAlī's opposition to al-Manṣūr, the execution of Abū Muslim, al-Manṣūr's designation of al-Mahdī instead of ʿĪsā b. Mūsā, al-Maʾmūn's appointment of ʿAlī al-Riḍā, the death of ʿAlī al-Riḍā, and al-Muʿtaṣim's succession to al-Maʾmūn.[232] A bit more detail is provided on Muḥammad al-Nafs al-Zakiyya's uprising and a few Khārijī revolts, but, as usual, Khalīfa leaves it more or less at the basic sequence of events.[233] A major episode that receives a bit more detailed treatment is the fourth *fitna*, between al-Amīn and al-Maʾmūn, which is examined below. Khalīfa's account of this episode illustrates how his ʿAbbāsid narrative upholds the legitimacy of the dynasty and, more generally, the continuity of the caliphate. It is also significant that Khalīfa's image of the ʿAbbāsids is limited to their political roles without focus on their religious claims or policies—perhaps understandable since they often must have clashed with Khalīfa's own.[234]

4.1 *The Fourth* Fitna*: Al-Amīn and al-Maʾmūn*

The succession dispute and civil war from 196/811 to 198/813 between Hārūn al-Rashīd's sons, al-Amīn and al-Maʾmūn, receives a fairly detailed treatment in Khalīfa's *Tārīkh*, although considerably shorter than elsewhere.[235] The origin of the conflict is introduced in year 186/802:

> The Commander of the Believers, Hārūn, led the pilgrimage. He renewed the oath of allegiance for his two sons, Muḥammad al-Makhlūʿ ('the Deposed') and ʿAbdallāh al-Maʾmūn. He wrote out certain conditions between them and hung the contract in the Kaʿba.[236]

---

232 Khalīfa b. Khayyāṭ, *Tārīkh* (1985) 415–416, 423–424, 470–471, 475. This is also the case for the material in Ṣaddām's collection of reports from Khalīfa that are missing in Baqī's recension. Ṣaddām, *Tārīkh Khalīfa* 118–130.

233 Khalīfa b. Khayyāṭ, *Tārīkh* (1985) 421–422, 443–445, 451–456. As discussed in Chapter 1, al-Azdī also transmits three reports from Khalīfa on the Basran uprising of Ibrāhīm b. ʿAbdallāh (the brother of Muḥammad al-Nafs al-Zakiyya) that are not found in Baqī's recension. Al-Azdī, *Tārīkh al-Mawṣil* 188–189.

234 See Chapter 3.

235 E.g. al-Yaʿqūbī, *Tārīkh* 2:383–396; al-Ṭabarī, *Tārīkh* 3:764–974. On the fourth *fitna* in the early histories (especially al-Ṭabarī's *Tārīkh*), see El-Hibri, *Reinterpreting* 59–94, 143–177. There are no reports on this in Ṣaddām's list of material transmitted from Khalīfa that is missing in Baqī's recension. See Ṣaddām, *Tārīkh Khalīfa* 128–130.

236 Khalīfa b. Khayyāṭ, *Tārīkh* (1985) 457.

Thereby Khalīfa describes al-Amīn as al-Makhlūʿ even before his succession to the caliphate in 193/809—in contrast to al-Ṭabarī, who begins to designate al-Amīn as al-Makhlūʿ from 195/810–811, when al-Maʾmūn began to claim the caliphate.[237] Khalīfa notes that the summons to accept al-Maʾmūn as the new caliph began in 195/810–811 in Khurāsān and the following year in Mecca, Medina and Iraq, but he refers to him as 'Commander of the Believers' before that. For example, Khalīfa narrates in his own words that, "In it [194/809–810]: Rāfiʿ b. Layth surrendered to the Commander of the Believers, al-Maʾmūn, and went to him, and that was before al-Makhlūʿ was killed."[238] He thereby presents al-Maʾmūn as the real Commander of the Believers already at the beginning of al-Amīn's reign. Khalīfa summarises the armed conflict during the *fitna*, which led to the defeat and death of al-Amīn, and concludes:

> Al-Makhlūʿ was born in Baghdad in year 170/787 and killed in Baghdad in al-Muḥarram in year 198/813 at the age of 28. His reign lasted two years until he was renounced and al-Maʾmūn was named caliph in Khurāsān. Two years later he was renounced in Iraq and al-Ḥijāz. Thus, his reign lasted four years and eight months until he was killed. Then things were consolidated under the Commander of the Believers, ʿAbdallāh al-Maʾmūn, the son of the Commander of the Believers.[239]

In this way, Khalīfa summarises the events in favour of al-Maʾmūn and presents the civil war entirely from the victor's perspective. This illustrates the caliphate-centred tendency in Khalīfa's narrative: events are often considered from the vantage point of the victorious caliphs. Khalīfa's account might also reflect his own political and scholarly context. Declaring al-Amīn deposed from the beginning of his reign seems to have been a way of justifying al-Maʾmūn's opposition to him, which is consistent with Khalīfa's emphasis on the continuing legitimacy of the caliphate and its institutions. Although Khalīfa did not agree with the ʿAbbāsid official ideology, he seems to have accepted their political authority—for instance, by entitling them Commanders of the Believers and by casting some of their opponents as illegitimate. In the case of the fourth *fitna*, Khalīfa reproduces a prevailing Maʾmūnid narrative. The era of al-Maʾmūn and his immediate successors was a time when the ʿAbbāsids patron-

237 Al-Ṭabarī, *Tārīkh* 3:826, 830–831. He is also described as al-Makhlūʿ in the material that Ibn ʿAsākir transmits from Khalīfa via al-Tustarī in *Tārīkh madīnat Dimashq* 56:214.

238 Khalīfa b. Khayyāṭ, *Tārīkh* (1985) 466.

239 Khalīfa b. Khayyāṭ, *Tārīkh* (1985) 468.

ised historical writing, which may have shaped the historical tradition in some ways and the image of the early ʿAbbāsids, as reflected in later third/ninth-century histories.[240] Al-Amīn is also one of the few caliphs criticised through reports or negative representations in the *Tārīkh*—in his case, by consistently being referred to as al-Makhlūʿ—alongside Yazīd b. Muʿāwiya, Marwān b. al-Ḥakam and al-Walīd (II) b. Yazīd, as well as, to some extent, Muʿāwiya b. Abī Sufyān. Considering the political climate of Khalīfa's day, at a time when the ʿAbbāsid caliphs still maintained the Ma'mūnid line, criticism or negative depiction of al-Amīn was probably common discourse.

Finally, it is noteworthy that Khalīfa does not mention the *miḥna* in Baqī's recension. The *Tārīkh* was transmitted to Baqī at a time when al-Ma'mūn's policies, including the *miḥna*, were still upheld; the last year in the *Tārīkh* is 232/847, which is the earliest date given for al-Mutawakkil's gradual ending of the *miḥna*.[241] It was, however, most likely mentioned in al-Tustarī's recension, which was transmitted later; the last date in what Ibn ʿAsākir transmits from al-Tustarī is 238/853.[242] Al-Dhahabī transmits that Khalīfa said, "Al-Mutawakkil succeeded as caliph and affirmed the Sunna. He spoke about it at his court and wrote to the different regions about lifting the *miḥna*, spreading the Sunna and supporting its people."[243] This report, probably from al-Tustarī's recension of the *Tārīkh*, which most likely was al-Dhahabī's source for Khalīfa's material, clearly illustrates Khalīfa's early Sunnī orientation. The silence on the *miḥna* in Baqī's recension can thus be explained by the political climate at the time—the *miḥna* was still under way. Khalīfa is reported to have accompanied the Basran judge Aḥmad b. Riyāḥ, accused by the Muʿtazila, to the court of al-Wāthiq (r. 227–232/842–847),[244] which suggests that the *miḥna* reached him personally and that it might have contributed to his avoiding the subject. It does, however, also correspond to Khalīfa's general avoidance of doctrinal issues in the *Tārīkh* in favour of politics and administration.

240 On the historiographical image of al-Ma'mūn, see El-Hibri, *Reinterpreting Islamic historiography* 95–177; Cooperson, *Classical Arabic biography* 24–69. See also Kennedy, Caliphs and their chroniclers.

241 See Chapter 3.

242 Ibn ʿAsākir, *Tārīkh madīnat Dimashq* 8:140. The other later dates in Ibn ʿAsākir's transmission from al-Tustarī are 233/847–848, 234/848–849, 236/850–851. See Chapter 1.

243 Al-Dhahabī, *Siyar* 1316. See Chapter 1.

244 Wakīʿ, *Akhbār al-quḍāt* 347.

5 Conclusion

This chapter has examined Khalīfa's accounts of leadership in the *Tārīkh*, as transmitted by Baqī b. Makhlad, focusing on the successions and civil wars in the Rāshidūn, Umayyad and ʿAbbāsid periods in an attempt to show how they reflect his early Sunnī perspective. It has been suggested that Khalīfa's *Tārīkh*, in both form and content, resonates with early Sunnī views such as the chronological ranking of the first four caliphs, the probity of the Companions, the importance of communal unity and the idea of critical loyalty to political leaders. It has also demonstrated that, while one of the main purposes of the *Tārīkh* was to determine chronology, Khalīfa also sought to clarify and provide a perspective on certain historical episodes. His approach to the theme of leadership can be summarised in ten points.

First, Khalīfa smooths over the issues of succession in the early community, sometimes by de-emphasising them and sometimes by omitting episodes altogether—most notably the successions of Abū Bakr, ʿUmar, ʿUthmān and ʿAlī. It is not until the Umayyad period, with the succession of Yazīd b. Muʿāwiya, that Khalīfa details the issues of succession, which indicates the special status and unquestionable order of the first four Rāshidūn caliphs. In this way, Khalīfa naturalises the succession of the early caliphs and establishes their legitimacy.

Second, the successions and civil wars in the *Tārīkh* are considered by their outcomes, rather than alternative courses of history. In other words, Khalīfa is more concerned with what actually happened than what 'should' or 'could' have happened. In some cases, this retrospective narrative mode contributes to legitimising the actual sequence of succession by excluding 'alternative histories' or uncertainties (as in the succession of the first four caliphs). It also provides historical examples of the dangers of communal disunity and political insurrection; none of the civil wars, as Khalīfa presents them, had any immediately positive results, although each time the caliphate and the community recovered.

Third, Khalīfa's accounts of leadership and civil war, as with the *Tārīkh* in general, are characterised by his overall concise reports and straightforward, realistic narrative style. He avoids the moral evaluations and embellished narrations about political motives, rivalries and conspiracies that are found in many other histories. Instead, he focuses mainly on basic facts (such as chronology, location and participants) regarding well-established events. Accordingly, Khalīfa seems to have compiled the *Tārīkh* as a critical chronological collection of historical material for his fellow *ḥadīth* and *akhbār* scholars, many of whom already shared his early Sunnī perspective and his view on the importance of chronological information.

Fourth, Khalīfa's general narrative articulates early Sunnī religio-political stances, and some of his reports explicitly establish Sunnī perspectives on issues of succession and *fitna*. This is most evident in the assassination of ʿUthmān and the succession of Yazīd, where Companions present different views that were later incorporated in Sunnī political thought. A number of statements also correspond to later Sunnī notions of avoiding political insurrection because of its often more harmful consequences—for example, in relation to the Battle of al-Ḥarra and Ibn al-Ashʿath's revolt.

Fifth, Khalīfa upholds the probity of the Companions and absolves them of blame in the intra-Muslim conflicts, or at least avoids judging them—even if some of their actions, such as Muʿāwiya's appointment of Yazīd, are criticised in the reports. Regarding the assassination of ʿUthmān, for example, Khalīfa makes clear that Egyptian thugs were responsible and that the Companions were absent only because ʿUthmān had ordered them to stay away. Khalīfa also deals with specific issues such as ʿĀʾisha's alleged involvement and narrates four reports absolving her of responsibility. In this way, Khalīfa's view on the Companions' general probity corresponds to what is known from other early Sunnī scholars of his time.

Sixth, Khalīfa's narrative articulates a rather inclusive approach to revolts. His accounts of revolts against oppressive leaders—such as Yazīd and al-Ḥajjāj—illustrate the dangers of political insurrection and the greater harm they might cause. However, his narrative also seems to justify some revolts in light of the oppressive leadership and the number of righteous Muslims involved (e.g. the Medinans' opposition to Yazīd and Ibn al-Ashʿath's revolt against al-Ḥajjāj). In this way, Khalīfa's narrative seems to give precedence to steadfastness and the avoidance of political insurrection, but it also accommodates the uprisings of some Companions and Successors, despite the regrettable outcomes.

Seventh, scholars and *ḥadīth* narrators are prominent in Khalīfa's narrative; besides his great concern with the dates of *ḥadīth* transmitters' deaths, Khalīfa also pays attention to their involvement in the political conflicts. This is particularly evident in his accounts of the Battle of al-Ḥarra and Ibn al-Ashʿath's revolt. Those fallen in these battles are commemorated with lengthy lists of well-known names in *ḥadīth* scholarship, which reflect the interests of Khalīfa and his fellow scholars.

Eighth, Khalīfa's narrative reflects a pragmatic view on politics and authority. Khalīfa avoids explicit evaluations of the virtues or vices of particular caliphs—apart from where he depicts positively the first four caliphs and, occasionally, depicts negatively later ones. In particular, the relative sparsity of negative material about the Umayyads distinguishes Khalīfa's *Tārīkh* from many other early histories, although there is, as Wurtzel points out, "very little that could be interpreted as positively pro-Umayyad other than by inference."[245] Instead of evaluating the caliphs or dynasties, Khalīfa pragmatically focuses on the circulation of political power and recounts the events pertaining to those who actually ruled the majority community—whether senior Companions, Umayyads, Zubayrids or ʿAbbāsids. In this way, there are no major breaks between the caliphates in terms of politics and administration, except the mode of succession, which changed after Muʿāwiya. This highlights the continuity of the caliphal institution and its legitimacy over time, while still distinguishing the Rāshidūn caliphs and their special status from the later dynasties.

Ninth, religious claims and movements are not prominent in Khalīfa's narrative, and Khalīfa provides very little information about the stances of the caliphs. Some exceptions are Ibn al-Zubayr's criticism of Yazīd's succession, and the *khuṭba* of Yazīd b. al-Walīd. Khalīfa also mentions a few religio-political claims of movements (mainly the Khawārij) against the caliphate—including clear statements such as the *khuṭba* of Abū Ḥamza and the letter of ʿAbd al-Salām al-Yashkurī—but otherwise such claims are unusual. In particular, Khalīfa pays comparatively little attention to the various ʿAlid movements and their claims to religious and political authority. Instead, his narrative remains focused on key political-administrative events pertaining to the Muslim community in general and the caliphate in particular.

Tenth, Khalīfa relies heavily on transmission from Basran *ḥadīth* scholars, in addition to a few major *akhbār* compilers such as al-Madāʾinī and Abū l-Yaqẓān, for information about the intra-Muslim conflicts. His selection of sources differs from the geographically less limited selection in later histories such as those of al-Ṭabarī and al-Balādhurī, who also make more extensive use of popular, but criticised *akhbār* transmitters such as Abū Mikhnaf and Sayf b. ʿUmar. Thus, by relying on material that he received directly from these Basran transmitters, Khalīfa produced a narrative of the early intra-Muslim conflicts from a Basran, early Sunnī perspective.

These ten points illustrate the main features of Khalīfa's *Tārīkh* that to various degrees distinguish it from other early historical works. They may also help

245 Wurtzel, *Khalifa ibn Khayyat's History* 27. As discussed above, it is possible that some anti-Umayyad material was omitted in the course of transmission, such as Abū Ḥamza's *khuṭba* or the report about the exhumation of the Umayyad caliphs, but it is also possible that Khalīfa transmitted slightly different accounts to different students at different times and that these reports were not a part of the version of the *Tārīkh* that Khalīfa transmitted to Baqī b. Makhlad. Moreover, some negative material about Umayyad caliphs was nonetheless preserved in Baqī's recension (e.g. about Muʿāwiya, Yazīd b. Muʿāwiya, Marwān b. al-Ḥakam and al-Walīd b. Yazīd). See Chapter 1.

to explain the later circulation of the *Tārīkh* among classical Sunnī scholars and *ḥadīth* experts such as Ibn ʿAbd al-Barr, Abū Bakr b. al-ʿArabī, Ibn ʿAsākir, al-Dhahabī and Ibn Kathīr, who seem to have understood and appreciated Khalīfa's *ḥadīth*-minded, early Sunnī compilation of chronological history.

Conclusion

1 Overview

In comparison to the core subjects of *ḥadīth* scholarship—such as jurisprudence (*fiqh*) and credal beliefs (*ʿaqīda*)—chronological history (*tārīkh*) was not one of the main concerns of the early *ḥadīth* scholars. However, a few third/ninth-century *ḥadīth* scholars compiled chronological history for an audience of like-minded early Sunnī scholars, often in close relation to the biographical study and evaluation of *ḥadīth* transmitters (*ʿilm al-rijāl*). These works have hitherto been largely neglected in the modern study of Islamic historical writing. This book therefore set out to examine the earliest surviving chronography of this type—the *Tārīkh* of the Basran *ḥadīth* scholar and *akhbār* historian Khalīfa b. Khayyāṭ, as transmitted by the Andalusian *ḥadīth* master Baqī b. Makhlad al-Qurṭubī—by analysing both the text and the context of its compilation. Throughout its eight chapters, the book has provided a complete picture of how Khalīfa worked as a historian in terms of his scholarly affiliations, social and intellectual context, sources, methods, arrangement of material and narration of key themes in the historical tradition. In so doing, the book has addressed three main areas of inquiry with wider implications for the study of early Islamic historical writing: (1) the methods, concerns and contexts of individual historians; (2) the study of chronography among the early *ḥadīth* scholars; and (3) articulations of pre-classical Sunnī views in the early historical tradition.

2 Methods, Concerns and Contexts of the Early Historians

The book highlights the importance of detailed studies on the methods and concerns of individual historians as well as their scholarly and social contexts—both for historiographical studies on the development of early Islamic historical writing and for the use of these sources in historical scholarship on early Islam. Each chapter has examined aspects of Khalīfa's context, methods and concerns that to various extents distinguish his *Tārīkh* from other historical texts. Some aspects, such as Khalīfa's Sunnī orientation and straightforward narrative style, have been noted briefly in previous studies on the *Tārīkh*, but this book has examined in detail how these aspects are reflected in the work. It has also highlighted other aspects that have been overlooked in previous studies, such as the transmission of the *Tārīkh* in its different recensions,

 | DOI:10.1163/9789004383173_011

Khalīfa's scholarly network, his methods of compilation and the similarities between his *Tārīkh* and other historical works compiled by early *ḥadīth* scholars. After outlining the history of the transmission of Khalīfa's *Tārīkh*, with a focus on Baqī b. Makhlad's extant recension (Chapter 1), the book located Khalīfa among the Basran *ḥadīth* scholars of the late second/eighth and early third/ninth centuries, in particular the 'Proponents of Ḥadīth' (*ahl al-ḥadīth*), with whom many of his students and teachers were affiliated (Chapters 2–3). The subsequent chapters then showed how Khalīfa's early Sunnī perspective, his affiliation with the Basran *ḥadīth* scholars and his concern for compiling a critical and relatively concise chronology of Islamic history are reflected in the form and content of the *Tārīkh*:

- In his sources: Khalīfa received most of his material from Basran transmitters, many of whom were prominent *ḥadīth* authorities (Chapter 4).
- In his methods: Khalīfa shared the transmission-centred approach of the *ḥadīth* scholars, employed different levels of strictness in selecting reports and transmitters, depending on the importance or controversy of the issue at hand, and likewise used different types of transmission formulas depending on the subject (Chapter 5).
- In his arrangement of material: Khalīfa's particular combination of annalistic and caliphal chronography in the year and list sections fits, foremost, the chronological and political-administrative scope of the *Tārīkh*, but it also corresponds to his early Sunnī perspective by foregrounding the continuity of the caliphate and its institutions. The content of the year sections also shows a particular concern with recording the dates of *ḥadīth* transmitters' deaths (Chapter 6).
- In his narrative of key themes: Khalīfa's approach to the themes of prophethood, community, hegemony and leadership is distinguished and determined by his strict chronological format, his early Sunnī outlook, his nearly exclusive focus on politics and administration, and his caliphate-centred perspective. Especially his approach to leadership, including successions and civil wars, corresponds to positions taken by many early Sunnī scholars, such as the special status of the first four caliphs, the general probity of the Companions and the importance of communal unity (Chapters 7–8).

Taken together, these aspects suggest that Khalīfa foremost compiled the *Tārīkh* as a critical chronological handbook of Islamic history for his fellow *ḥadīth* scholars, who shared his transmission-based approach to historical knowledge and his early Sunnī perspective on the history of the Muslim community.

Besides illustrating Khalīfa's specific methods and concerns, the book has also highlighted how these differ from those of many other historical compilers. The main explanation for the distinct characteristics of Khalīfa's *Tārīkh* has been sought in his own scholarly context: Khalīfa was closely affiliated with the Basran *ḥadīth* scholars, many of whom are known to have shared his early Sunnī perspective and, of course, his transmission-based approach to the Islamic sciences. This context has helped to explain many aspects of Khalīfa's *Tārīkh*, such as his methods, selection of sources and concerns when presenting events. It has highlighted the importance of taking into consideration the scholarly and social contexts in which the early histories were compiled in order to understand the specific approaches of individual historians. Thus, rather than speaking of local historiographical schools to explain the different types of historiography that were compiled in different places during first three centuries AH, it might be more useful to discuss them in terms of different scholarly traditions and networks (located in urban centres, but not necessarily limited to them) in addition to local concerns that shaped the specific historiographical expressions of these scholarly traditions. This also helps to explain the similarities between Khalīfa's *Tārīkh* and other historical works compiled by early *ḥadīth* scholars. Altogether, this book has shown that Khalīfa's *Tārīkh* is significant not only because of its early date but also because the methods, concerns and context of compilation differ in many respects from the wider historical tradition and because these differences help us to better understand the development of Islamic historical writing.

3 Chronography among the Early *Ḥadīth* Scholars

The book has situated Khalīfa's *Tārīkh* in the wider context of historical works compiled by early *ḥadīth* scholars, such as al-Fasawī, Ibn Abī Khaythama and Abū Zur'a al-Dimashqī. It has highlighted certain commonalities in form, content and religio-political (early Sunnī) views, which are more common and more clearly articulated in these works than the wider *akhbār* tradition of the second/eighth and third/ninth centuries. Similar early Sunnī historical perspectives, but in a different format, can also be found in the sections on *faḍā'il*, *maghāzī* and post-Prophetic history in the early *ḥadīth* collections. This book has shown that, although chronography was unusual in the *ḥadīth* circles, it was compiled by some *ḥadīth* scholars for an audience of primarily other *ḥadīth* scholars (as indicated by the sources, methods, arrangement and narrative approach of these compilers).

The question of audience was also corroborated by the fact that a number of surviving chronographical texts of third/ninth-century *ḥadīth* scholars were combined with, or transmitted/compiled alongside, biographical material on *ḥadīth* transmitters (often in the *ṭabaqāt* format)—clearly compiled for an audience of *ḥadīth* scholars. In contrast to the notion in some previous studies that *ḥadīth* scholars completely avoided history in general and chronography in particular, this book has suggested that chronography had a place in the *ḥadīth* circles, although it was not one of the main subjects, and that it was linked to *ʿilm al-rijāl* and *ṭabaqāt* compilation. Although Khalīfa divided his *tārīkh* and *ṭabaqāt* material into two works, they seem to have been compiled in close relation to each other and were transmitted as a pair by both Baqī b. Makhlad and Mūsā b. Zakariyyā al-Tustarī. For this reason, Khalīfa's *Ṭabaqāt* also deserves a more detailed treatment and comparison to other works in the same genre, which would complement the results of this book and further elucidate Khalīfa's specific methods and concerns in compiling the *Ṭabaqāt*.

4 Articulations of Sunnī Views in the Early Historical Tradition

With a focus on Khalīfa's *Tārīkh*, this book has explored early articulations of Sunnī views in the historical tradition. The term 'early Sunnī' has referred to those second/eighth- and third/ninth-century scholarly groups that were overall characterised by a transmission- and text-based approach to *fiqh* and *ʿaqīda*, in addition to a firm commitment to the collective authority of the Prophet's Companions and the special merit of the first four caliphs. The book has shown how Khalīfa's early Sunnī orientation is expressed in his selection of sources, structuring of the work and presentation of historical events. It has also highlighted similarities in historical views between Khalīfa and many other early *ḥadīth* scholars, whether they compiled *tārīkh, ṭabaqāt* or *faḍāʾil* works or included Prophetic and post-Prophetic history in larger *ḥadīth* collections. Although the disciplines of *ḥadīth, fiqh* and *ʿaqīda* were far more important in the articulation of early Sunnism than the collection of historical reports (*akhbār*), there were early Sunnī scholars, like Khalīfa, who compiled *akhbār* histories articulating such ideas.

Khalīfa's *Tārīkh* is one of the earliest surviving chronographies that coherently present early Sunnī historical perspectives in a way that resembles later classical scholars. The main explanation for this, as this book has outlined, is Khalīfa's own background in *ḥadīth* scholarship and his affiliation with the *ḥadīth* scholars of the late second/eighth and early third/ninth centuries, who were fundamental in the articulation of early Sunnism. Khalīfa seems to have articulated many of their ideas in the form of chronography, and his *Tārīkh* is, therefore, a valuable source in the study of pre-classical Sunnī historical thought and compilation. That said, this book has focused on Khalīfa's *Tārīkh*; more studies are needed on the wider early Sunnī historical tradition, including the other surviving chronographies, as well as the *ḥadīth* collections and *faḍā'il* works. This will improve our understanding of the development of Sunnī historical thought by taking into consideration works from different genres of history (such as *ṭabaqāt, faḍā'il* and *maghāzī*-sections in *ḥadīth* collections), which were just as important as chronography (*tārīkh*) for articulating certain interpretations and historical understandings.

In summary, discussion of these three themes highlights the significance of Khalīfa's *Tārīkh* for understanding the development of early Islamic historical writing and thought—in particular, historical compilation among the early *ḥadīth* scholars. However, more work is needed on the significance of Khalīfa's *Tārīkh* for scholarship on the actual political and administrative history of early Islam. Although this book provides material that can be used for evaluating the utility of the *Tārīkh* in historical scholarship, the approach has been strictly historiographical, in the sense of studying how history is written; the purpose has been not to evaluate the historical accuracy of Khalīfa's material but to show how Khalīfa worked as a Basran early Sunnī historian at the beginning of the third/ninth century and how his *Tārīkh* relates to the wider context of historical works compiled by early *ḥadīth*-minded scholars. Hence the book provides an understanding of Khalīfa's *Tārīkh* in relation to the social and political world in which he worked, the scholarly tradition in which he stood and the textual environment in which he compiled his chronicle. It has shown that the *Tārīkh* of Khalīfa b. Khayyāṭ is indeed an important early historical work—especially for historiographical studies—that can tell us much that we do not otherwise know from the wider historical tradition.

Appendix: Citations of Khalīfa in al-Bukhārī's *al-Jāmiʿ al-ṣaḥīḥ*

1 Book of the Funerals—Chapter on the Dead Hearing the Tread of Sandals

ʿAyyāsh narrated to us: ʿAbd al-Aʿlā narrated to us: Saʿīd narrated to us—**and Khalīfa said to me (*qāla lī*)**: Ibn Zurayʿ narrated to us: Saʿīd narrated to us—from Qatāda from Anas, may God be pleased with him: The Prophet (ṣ) said, "When a human is placed in his grave and his companions return and he even hears the tread of their sandals, two angels come to him and make him sit and ask him, 'What did you use to say about this man, Muḥammad (ṣ)?' He will say, 'I testify that he is the slave of God and His Messenger.' It will be said, 'Look at your place in the Fire. God has given you a place in the Garden instead of it.'" The Prophet (ṣ) added, "He will see both places. But an unbeliever or hypocrite will say [to the two angels], 'I do not know. I used to say what everyone else said.' He will be told, 'Neither did you know nor did you follow the guidance.' Then he will be struck between his ears with an iron hammer and he will cry out with a cry that is heard by everything near him except humans and jinns."[1]

2 Book of the Pilgrimage (*ḥajj*)—Chapter on a Menstruating Woman Performing All the Rites Except the Circumambulation (*ṭawāf*) of the House

Muḥammad b. al-Muthannā narrated to us: ʿAbd al-Wahhāb narrated to us—**and Khalīfa said to me (*qāla lī*)**: ʿAbd al-Wahhāb narrated to us—that Ḥabīb al-Muʿallim narrated to us from ʿAṭāʾ from Jābir b. ʿAbdallāh, may God be pleased with him and his father: The Prophet (ṣ) and his Companions entered *iḥrām* for the pilgrimage and none except the Prophet (ṣ) and Ṭalḥa had sacrificial animals with them. ʿAlī arrived from Yemen with sacrificial animals. He said, "I have entered *iḥrām* for what the Prophet (ṣ) has entered *iḥrām*." The Prophet (ṣ) ordered his Companions to make it an *ʿumra* and perform the circumambulation (*ṭawāf*) and then to cut their hair short and to leave the state of *iḥrām*—except those who had sacrificial animals with them. They said, "How can we proceed to Minā when some of us have just had a seminal discharge?" That reached the Prophet (ṣ) and he said, "If I had known at the start of this affair what

1 Al-Bukhārī, *Ṣaḥīḥ* 2:90 (*kitāb al-janāʾiz, bāb al-mayyit yasmaʿu khafq al-niʿāl*).

 | DOI:10.1163/9789004383173_012

I know at the end, I would not have brought a sacrificial animal with me. If I did not have a sacrificial animal with me, I would have come out of the state of *iḥrām*." ʿĀʾisha got her menstrual period and performed all the rites except the circumambulation of the House. When she became clean, she did the circumambulation of the House and said, "Messenger of God, you are all returning with both the pilgrimage and the *ʿumra* and I am only returning with the pilgrimage." So he ordered ʿAbd al-Raḥmān b. Abī Bakr to accompany her to al-Tanʿīm and she performed an *ʿumra* after the pilgrimage.[2]

3 Book of the Beginning of Creation—Chapter regarding the Angels

Hudba b. Khālid narrated to us: Hammām narrated to us from Qatāda—**and Khalīfa said to me (*qāla lī*)**: Yazīd b. Zurayʿ narrated to us: Saʿīd and Hishām narrated to us; they both said: Qatāda narrated to us—that Anas b. Mālik narrated to us from Mālik b. Ṣaʿṣaʿa, may God be pleased with both of them: The Prophet (ṣ) said, "While I was at the House, somewhere between sleep and wakefulness, between two men, a golden tray filled with wisdom and belief was brought to me. My chest was opened from its upper part to the lower abdomen and then my abdomen was washed with Zamzam water and then filled with wisdom and belief. I was brought a white animal, smaller than a mule and bigger than a donkey: al-Burāq. I went with Gabriel until we reached the lowest heaven. It was said, 'Who is this?' He replied, 'Gabriel.' It was said, 'Who is with you?' He replied, 'Muḥammad.' It was said, 'Has he been sent for?' He said, 'Yes.' It was said, 'Welcome to him! What an excellent visitor has come!' I came to Adam and greeted him. He said, 'Welcome to you, a son and a Prophet!' We reached the second heaven and it was said, 'Who is this?' He replied, 'Gabriel.' It was said, 'Who is with you?' He replied, 'Muḥammad.' It was said, 'Has he been sent for?' He replied, 'Yes.' It was said, 'Welcome to him! What an excellent visitor has come!' I came to Jesus and John (Yaḥyā) and they said, 'Welcome to you, a brother and a Prophet!' We reached the third heaven and it was said, 'Who is this?' He said, 'Gabriel.' It was said, 'Who is with you?' He said, 'Muḥammad.' It was said, 'Has he been sent for?' He said, 'Yes.' It was said, 'Welcome to him! What an excellent visitor has come!' I came to Joseph and greeted him and he said, 'Welcome to you, a brother and a Prophet!' We reached the fourth heaven and it was said, 'Who is this?' He replied, 'Gabriel.' It was said, 'Who is with you?' He replied, 'Muḥammad.' It was said, 'Has he been sent for?' He replied, 'Yes.' It was said, 'Welcome to him! What an excellent visitor has come!' I came to Idrīs and greeted him, and he said, 'Welcome to you, a brother and a Prophet!' We reached the fifth heaven and it

---

2 Al-Bukhārī, *Ṣaḥīḥ* 2:159–160 (*kitāb al-ḥajj, bāb taqḍī al-ḥāʾiḍ al-manāsik kullahā illā al-ṭawāf bi-l-bayt*).

was said, 'Who is this?' He replied, 'Gabriel.' It was said, 'Who is with you?' He said, 'Muḥammad.' It was said, 'Has he been sent for?' He replied, 'Yes.' It was said, 'Welcome to him! What an excellent visitor has come!' We came to Aaron and I greeted him and he said, 'Welcome to you, a brother and a Prophet!' We reached the sixth heaven and it was said, 'Who is this?' He replied, 'Gabriel.' It was said, 'Who is with you?' He replied, 'Muḥammad.' It was said, 'Has he been sent for?' He replied, 'Yes.' It was said, 'Welcome to him! What an excellent visitor has come!' I came to Moses and greeted him and he said, 'Welcome to you, a brother and a Prophet!' When I moved on, he wept. He was asked, 'Why are you weeping?' He said, 'O Lord, the community of this youth who was sent after me will enter the Garden in greater numbers than my community!' We reached the seventh heaven, and it was said, 'Who is this?' He replied, 'Gabriel.' It was said, 'Who is with you?' He said, 'Muḥammad.' It was said, 'Has he been sent for?' [It was said,] 'Welcome to him! What an excellent visitor has come!' I came to Abraham and greeted him. He said, 'Welcome to you, a son and a Prophet!' The Much-Frequented House (*al-bayt al-maʿmūr*) was shown to me and I asked Gabriel, who said, 'This is the Much-Frequented House. Every day 70,000 angels pray in it and when they leave, they never return to it. It is the last time they enter.' Then I was shown the Tree of the Furthest Limit (*sidrat al-muntahā*) and its fruits were like the pots of Hajar, and its leaves were like elephant ears. At its root spring four rivers: two hidden rivers and two visible rivers. I asked Gabriel and he said, 'The two hidden ones are in the Garden, and the two visible ones are the Nile and the Euphrates.' Then 50 prayers were made obligatory for me. I descended until I came to Moses, who said, 'What have you done?' I said, 'Fifty prayers were made obligatory for me.' He said, 'I know the people better than you because I had the hardest experience dealing with the Children of Israel. Your community will not be able to do it. Go back to your Lord and ask Him.' I went back and asked and He made it 40. Then the like of it happened, and it was made 30, and then the like of it and He made it 20, and then the like of it and He made it 10. Then I went to Moses and he said the same thing. Then He made it 5. I went to Moses and he said, 'What have you done?' I said, 'He made it 5.' He said the same thing, but I said, 'I have submitted to what is good.' Then there was a call, 'I have decreed My obligation and I have reduced the burden on My slaves and I will reward a single good deed tenfold.'"[3]

3 Al-Bukhārī, *Ṣaḥīḥ* 4:109–111 (*kitāb badʾ al-khalq, bāb dhikr al-malāʾika*).

4 Book of the Beginning of Creation—Chapter on When One of You Says *āmīn,* as Do the Angels in the Heaven, and They Coincide with One Another, He Will Be Forgiven His Past Wrong Actions

Muḥammad b. Bashshār narrated to us: Ghundar narrated to us: Shuʿba narrated to us from Qatāda—**and Khalīfa said to me (*qāla lī*)**: Yazīd b. Zurayʿ narrated to us: Saʿīd narrated to us from Qatāda—from Abū l-ʿĀliya: The paternal cousin of your Prophet, meaning Ibn ʿAbbās, may God be pleased with him and his father, narrated to us that the Prophet (ṣ) said, "On the night of my Night Journey (*isrāʾ*) I saw Moses, a tall, brown, curly-haired man, like one of the men of Shanūʾa. And I saw Jesus, a man of medium height and moderate complexion, tending to redness and whiteness, and straight hair. I saw Mālik, the guardian of the Fire. The Dajjāl was also among the signs that God showed me. 'Be in no doubt about the meeting with him [i.e. Moses].'" (Q 32:23) Anas and Abū Bakra narrated that the Prophet (ṣ) said, "The angels will guard Medina against the Dajjāl."[4]

5 Book of Virtues—Chapter on the Idolaters' Asking the Prophet (ṣ) to Show Them a Sign after Which He Showed Them the Splitting of the Moon

ʿAbdallāh b. Muḥammad narrated to me: Yūnus narrated to us: Shaybān narrated to us from Qatāda from Anas b. Mālik—**and Khalīfa said to me (*qāla lī*)**: Yazīd b. Zurayʿ narrated to us: Saʿīd narrated to us from Qatāda from Anas b. Mālik, may God be pleased with him, who said: The people of Mecca asked the Messenger of God (ṣ) to show them a sign and he showed them the splitting of the moon.[5]

6 Book of the Virtues of the Prophet's Companions—Chapter on the Merits of ʿUmar b. al-Khaṭṭāb Abū Ḥafṣ al-Qurashī al-ʿAdawī

Musaddad narrated to us: Yazīd b. Zurayʿ narrated to us: Saʿīd narrated to us—**and Khalīfa said to me (*qāla lī*)**: Muḥammad b. Sawāʾ and Kahmas b. al-Minhāl narrated to us; they both said: Saʿīd narrated to us—from Qatāda from Anas b. Mālik, may God be pleased with him, who said: The Prophet (ṣ) ascended the mountain of Uḥud accom-

---

4 Al-Bukhārī, *Ṣaḥīḥ* 4:116 (*kitāb badʾ al-khalq, bāb idhā qāla aḥadukum āmīn*).

5 Al-Bukhārī, *Ṣaḥīḥ* 4:206–207 (*kitāb al-manāqib, bāb suʾāl al-mushrikīn an yuriyahum al-nabī ṣallā Allāhu ʿalayhi wa-sallam āyatan fa-arāhum inshiqāq al-qamar*).

panied by Abū Bakr, ʿUmar and ʿUthmān. The mountain shook beneath them. The Prophet hit it with his foot and said, "Be firm, Uḥud, there is no one on you but a Prophet, a truthful one (*ṣiddīq*) and two martyrs."[6]

7 Book of Military Expeditions—Chapter

Khalīfa narrated to me (*ḥaddathanī*): Muḥammad b. ʿAbdallāh al-Anṣārī narrated to us: Saʿīd narrated to us from Qatāda from Anas, may God be pleased with him, who said: Abū Zayd died without leaving any offspring and he was one of those who fought at Badr.[7]

8 Book of Military Expeditions—Chapter of "Then He Sent Down to You, after the Distress, Security, Restful Sleep Overtaking a Group of You …" (Q 3:154)

Khalīfa said to me (*qāla lī*): Yazīd b. Zurayʿ narrated to us: Saʿīd narrated to us from Qatāda from Anas from Abū Ṭalḥa, may God be pleased with both of them, who said: I was one of those overcome by slumber on the day of Uḥud so that my sword fell from my hand several times. The sword fell and I picked it up and it fell again and I picked it up.[8]

9 Book of Military Expeditions—Chapter on the Expedition of al-Rajiʿ, Riʿl, Dhakwan and Biʾr Maʿūna

Khalīfa added (*zāda*): Ibn Zurayʿ narrated to us: Saʿīd narrated to us from Qatāda: Anas narrated to us that those 70 men of the Anṣār were killed at Biʾr Maʿūna.[9]

---

6 Al-Bukhārī, *Ṣaḥīḥ* 5:11–12 (*kitāb faḍāʾil aṣḥāb al-nabī, bāb manāqib ʿUmar b. al-Khaṭṭāb*).

7 Al-Bukhārī, *Ṣaḥīḥ* 5:81 (*kitāb al- maghāzī, bāb*).

8 Al-Bukhārī, *Ṣaḥīḥ* 5:99 (*kitāb al- maghāzī, bāb thumma anzala ʿalaykum min baʿd al-ghamm amanatan nuʿāsan*).

9 Al-Bukhārī, *Ṣaḥīḥ* 5:105 (*kitāb al-maghāzī, bāb ghazwat al-Rajīʿ wa-Riʿl wa-Dhakwān wa-Biʾr Maʿūna*).

10 Book of Military Expeditions—Chapter on the Prophet's (ṣ) Return from al-Aḥzāb and His Going Out to Banū Qurayẓa and Laying Siege to Them

Ibn Abī l-Aswad narrated to us: Muʿtamir narrated to us—**and Khalīfa narrated to me (*ḥaddathanī*):** Muʿtamir narrated to us—he said: I heard my father [transmit] from Anas, may God be please with him, who said: Some people used to assign date palms to the Prophet (ṣ) until Qurayẓa and al-Naḍīr were conquered. My people told me to go to the Prophet (ṣ) and ask him to return some or all that they had given to him, but the Prophet (ṣ) had given those trees to Umm Ayman. Umm Ayman came and put the garment around my neck and said, "No, by the One who is the only God, he will not give them to you as he has given them to me," or words to that effect. The Prophet (ṣ) said [to her], "You will have this-and-that instead." But she said, "No, by God," until he gave her (I think he said) ten times the number of them, or words to that effect.[10]

11 Book of Marriage—Chapter on Marrying Several Women

Musaddad narrated to us: Yazīd b. Zurayʿ narrated to us: Saʿīd narrated to us from Qatāda from Anas, may God be pleased with him, that the Prophet (ṣ) used to go around to his wives in one night and he had nine wives. **And Khalīfa said to me (*qāla lī*):** Yazīd b. Zurayʿ narrated to us: Saʿīd narrated to us from Qatāda that Anas narrated this *ḥadīth* to them about the Prophet (ṣ).[11]

12 Book of Drinks—Chapter on the Prophet (ṣ) Allowing the Use of Bowls and Containers after Forbidding Them

Yūsuf b. Mūsā narrated to us: Muḥammad b. ʿAbdallāh Abū Aḥmad al-Zubayrī narrated to us: Sufyān narrated to us from Manṣūr from Sālim from Jābir, may God be pleased with him, who said: The Messenger of God (ṣ) forbade the use of certain containers, but the Anṣār said, "We cannot dispense with them." He said, "If so, then use them." **And Khalīfa said (*qāla*):** Yaḥyā b. Saʿīd narrated to us: Sufyān narrated this *ḥadīth* to us from Manṣūr from Sālim b. Abī l-Jaʿd from Jābir.[12]

---

10 Al-Bukhārī, *Ṣaḥīḥ* 5:112 (*kitāb al-maghāzī, bāb marjaʿ al-nabī ṣallā Allāhu ʿalayhi wa-sallam min al-aḥzāb*).

11 Al-Bukhārī, *Ṣaḥīḥ* 7:3 (*kitāb al-nikāḥ, bāb kathrat al-nisāʾ*).

12 Al-Bukhārī, *Ṣaḥīḥ* 7:106–107 (*kitāb al-ashriba, bāb tarkhīṣ al-nabī ṣallā Allāhu ʿalayhi wa-sallam fī l-awʿiya wa-l-ẓurūf baʿd al-nahy*).

13 Book of Good Manners—Chapter on Smiling and Laughing

Muḥammad b. Maḥbūb narrated to us: Abū ʿAwāna narrated to us from Qatāda from Anas—**and Khalīfa said to me (*qāla lī*):** Yazīd b. Zurayʿ narrated to us: Saʿīd narrated to us from Qatāda from Anas, may God be pleased with him, who said: A man came to the Prophet (ṣ) on a Friday while he was delivering the *khuṭba* in Medina. He said, "There is a lack of rain, so ask your Lord for rain." The Prophet (ṣ) looked at the sky and we could not see any clouds. He prayed for rain and the clouds gathered together and it rained until the valleys of Medina started flowing with water. It continued raining until the next Friday. Then that man or another man stood up while the Prophet (ṣ) was delivering the *khuṭba* and said, "We are drowning. Ask your Lord to make it stop for us." The Prophet smiled and said two or three times, "O God, let it rain around us but not on us." The clouds began to disperse from Medina to the right and left and it rained around Medina, but not upon it. God showed them the miracle of His Prophet (ṣ) and His response to his supplication.[13]

14 Book of Supplications—Chapter on Every Prophet Having a Supplication That Is Answered

Ismāʿīl narrated to us; he said: Mālik narrated to me from Abū l-Zinād from al-Aʿraj from Abū Hurayra that the Prophet (ṣ) said, "Every Prophet has a [special] supplication that he makes and I want to keep my supplication as intercession for my community in the Hereafter." **And Khalīfa said to me (*qāla lī*):** Muʿtamir said that he heard his father [transmit] from Anas that the Prophet (ṣ) said, "Every Prophet will ask for something …" or he said, "Every Prophet has a supplication that he makes which will be answered. I have made my supplication intercession for my community on the Day of Rising."[14]

15 Book of the Limits and Punishments Set by God (*ḥudūd*)—Chapter on the Virtue of the One Who Abandons Indecencies

Muḥammad b. Abī Bakr narrated to us: ʿUmar b. ʿAlī narrated to us—**and Khalīfa narrated to me (*ḥaddathanī*):** ʿUmar b. ʿAlī narrated to us—Abū Ḥāzim narrated to us

13 Al-Bukhārī, *Ṣaḥīḥ* 8:24–25 (*kitāb al-adab, bāb al-tabassum wa-l-ḍaḥik*).
14 Al-Bukhārī, *Ṣaḥīḥ* 8:67 (*kitāb al-daʿawāt, bāb li-kulli nabī daʿwa mustajāba*).

from Sahl b. Saʿd al-Sāʿidī, who said: The Prophet (ṣ) said, "Whoever guarantees me the chastity of what is between his legs and what is between his jaws, I will guarantee him the Garden."[15]

16 Book of Dream Interpretation—Chapter on Holding Onto a Handle or a Ring

ʿAbdallāh b. Muḥammad narrated to me: Azhar narrated to us from Ibn ʿAwn—**and Khalīfa narrated to me (*ḥaddathanī*):** Muʿādh narrated to us: Ibn ʿAwn narrated to us—from Muḥammad [who said]: Qays b. ʿUbād narrated to us from ʿAbdallāh b. Salām, who said: I dreamt that I was in a meadow and there was a pillar in the middle of it and a handle on the top of the pillar. I was told, "Climb it." I said, "I cannot." Then a servant came and lifted up my garment and I climbed up and took hold of the handle. I woke up while still holding on to it. I recounted it to the Prophet (ṣ) and he said, "That meadow is the meadow of Islam. That pillar is the pillar of Islam. That handle is the firmest handle (*al-ʿurwat al-wuthqā*) and you will continue to hold on to Islam firmly until you die."[16]

17 Book of Trials (*fitan*)—Chapter on Seeking Refuge with God from the Trials

And Khalīfa said to me (*qāla lī*): Yazīd b. Zurayʿ narrated to us: Saʿīd narrated to us, and Muʿtamir from his father, from Qatāda that Anas narrated this [aforementioned] *ḥadīth* from the Prophet (ṣ) with the wording, "… seeking refuge with God from the evil of the trials (*al-fitan*)."[17]

18 Book of God's Oneness—Chapter on God's Words "And He Is the Almighty, the All-Wise" (Q 14:4)

Ibn Abī l-Aswad narrated to us: Ḥaramī narrated to us: Shuʿba narrated to us from Qatāda from Anas that the Prophet (ṣ) said, "… thrown into the Fire …" **And Khalīfa said to me (*qāla lī*):** Yazīd b. Zurayʿ narrated to us: Saʿīd narrated to us from Qatāda from Anas and [Khalīfa also narrated] from Muʿtamir who said that he heard his father

15 Al-Bukhārī, *Ṣaḥīḥ* 8:164 (*kitāb al-ḥudūd, bāb faḍl man taraka al-fawāḥish*).
16 Al-Bukhārī, *Ṣaḥīḥ* 9:37 (*kitāb al-taʿbīr, bāb al-taʿlīq bi-l-ʿurwa wa-l-ḥalqa*).
17 Al-Bukhārī, *Ṣaḥīḥ* 9:53 (*kitāb al-fitan, bāb al-taʿawwudh min al-fitan*).

[transmit] from Qatāda from Anas that the Prophet (ṣ) said, "People will continue to be thrown into the Fire and it will keep on saying, 'Is there any more?' until the Lord of all the worlds places His Foot over it (*ḥattā yaḍaʿa fīhā rabb al-ʿālamīn qadamahu*) and its sides will come together. Then it will say, 'Enough! Enough! By Your might and generosity!' The Garden will remain spacious enough to accommodate more people until God creates some more people and let them dwell in the spare space of the Garden."[18]

19 Book of God's Oneness—Chapter on God's Words "They Want to Change God's Words" (Q 48:15)

Khalīfa said (*qāla*): Muʿtamir narrated to us regarding "… did not store up (*lam yabtaʾiz*)" and said that Qatāda explained that it meant, "did not store up (*lam yaddakhir*)."[19]

20 Book of God's Oneness—Chapter on What the Prophet (ṣ) Mentioned and Narrated from His Lord

Ḥafṣ b. ʿUmar narrated to us: Shuʿba narrated to us from Qatāda—**and Khalīfa said to me (*qāla lī*):** Yazīd b. Zurayʿ narrated to us from Saʿīd from Qatāda—from Abū l-ʿĀliya from Ibn ʿAbbās, may God be pleased with him and his father, from the Prophet (ṣ) who related that his Lord said, "It is not befitting for a slave to say that he is better than Jonah the son of Mattā (Yūnus b. Mattā)," ascribing him to his father.[20]

21 Book of God's Oneness—Chapter on God's Words "It Is Indeed a Glorious Qurʾān on a Preserved Tablet" (Q 85:21–22)

And Khalīfa b. Khayyāṭ said to me (*wa-qāla lī*): Muʿtamir narrated to us, saying that he heard his father [transmit] from Qatāda from Abū Rāfiʿ from Abū Hurayra that the

18 Al-Bukhārī, *Ṣaḥīḥ* 9:117 (*kitāb al-tawḥīd, bāb qawl Allāh taʿālā wa-huwa al-ʿAzīz al-Ḥakīm*). See also Ibn Ḥajar's commentary on the words "until the Lord of all the worlds places His Foot over it (*ḥattā yaḍaʿa fīhā rabb al-ʿālamīn qadamahu*)" in *Fatḥ al-Bārī* 8:471–472, 13:383.

19 Al-Bukhārī, *Ṣaḥīḥ* 9:146 (*kitāb al-tawḥīd, bāb qawl Allāh taʿālā yurīdūna an yubaddilū kalām Allāh*).

20 Al-Bukhārī, *Ṣaḥīḥ* 9:157 (*kitāb al-tawḥīd, bāb dhikr al-nabī ṣallā Allāhu ʿalayhi wa-sallam wa-riwāyatihi ʿan rabbihi*).

Prophet (ṣ) said, "When God created the creation, He wrote in a book that is with Him, 'My mercy has overcome (or preceded) My anger.' It is with Him above the throne (*fa-huwa ʿindahu fawqa al-ʿarsh*)."[21]

21 Al-Bukhārī, *Ṣaḥīḥ* 9:160 (*kitāb al-tawḥīd, bāb qawl Allāh taʿālā bal huwa qurʾān majīd fī lawḥ maḥfūẓ*).

Bibliography

Abbott, N., *Studies in Arabic literary papyri*, 1: *Historical texts*, Chicago 1957.

Abbott, N., *Studies in Arabic literary papyri*, 2: *Qur'anic commentary and tradition*, Chicago 1967.

ʿAbdallāh b. Aḥmad b. Ḥanbal, *Faḍāʾil ʿUthmān b. ʿAffān*, ed. Ṭalʿat b. Fuʾād al-Ḥulwānī, Jeddah 2000.

ʿAbd al-Razzāq al-Ṣanʿānī, *al-Muṣannaf*, ed. Ḥabīb al-Raḥmān al-Aʿẓamī, 12 vols., Beirut 1983.

ʿAbd al-Wahhāb al-Baghdādī, *Sharḥ ʿaqīdat Mālik al-ṣaghīr Ibn Abī Zayd al-Qayrawānī*, ed. Muḥammad Būkhubza and Badr al-ʿAmrānī, Rabat 2014.

Abou El Fadl, K., *Rebellion and violence in Islamic law*, Cambridge 2001.

Abū Dāwūd al-Sijistānī, *Sunan*, ed. Shuʿayb al-Arnāʾūṭ and Muḥammad Kāmil Qurrah Balalī, 7 vols., Damascus 2009.

Abū Nuʿaym al-Aṣbahānī, *Dhikr akhbār Aṣbahān*, ed. S. Dedering, 2 vols., Leiden 1931.

Abū Nuʿaym al-Aṣbahānī, *Ḥilyat al-awliyāʾ*, 10 vols., Beirut 1996.

Abū Nuʿaym al-Aṣbahānī, *Maʿrifat al-ṣaḥāba*, ed. ʿĀdil b. Yūsuf al-Ghazāzī, 7 vols., Riyadh 1998.

Abū l-Shaykh al-Aṣbahānī, *Ṭabaqāt al-muḥaddithīn bi-Aṣbahān wa-l-wāridīn ʿalayhā*, ed. ʿAbd al-Ghafūr ʿAbd al-Ḥaqq Ḥusayn al-Balūshī, 4 vols., Beirut 1992.

Abū ʿUbayd al-Qāsim b. Sallām, *Kitāb al-Amwāl*, ed. Muḥammad ʿImāra, Beirut 1989.

Abū ʿUbayd al-Qāsim b. Sallām, *Kitāb al-Īmān*, ed. Muḥammad Nāṣir al-Dīn al-Albānī, Riyadh 2000.

Abū Yaʿlā b. al-Farrāʾ, *al-Aḥkām al-sulṭāniyya*, ed. Muḥammad Ḥāmid al-Faqī, Beirut 2000.

Abū Yaʿlā b. al-Farrāʾ, *al-ʿUdda fī uṣūl al-fiqh*, ed. Aḥmad b. ʿAlī Sīr al-Mubārakī, 5 vols., Riyadh 1993.

Abū Yaʿlā al-Mawṣilī, *Musnad Abī Yaʿlā al-Mawṣilī*, ed. Ḥusayn Salīm Asad, 16 vols., Damascus/Beirut 1989.

Abū Yūsuf, Yaʿqūb b. Ibrāhīm, *Kitāb al-Kharāj*, Beirut 1979.

Abū Zurʿa al-Dimashqī, *Tārīkh Abī Zurʿa al-Dimashqī*, ed. Shukrallāh al-Qawjānī, 2 vols., Damascus 1980.

Adang, C., *Muslim writers on Judaism and the Hebrew Bible from Ibn Rabban to Ibn Hazm*, Leiden 1996.

Agius, D.A., *Classic ships of Islam: From Mesopotamia to the Indian Ocean*, Leiden 2008.

Ahmed, A.Q., *The religious elite of the early Islamic Hijaz: Five prosopographical case studies*, Oxford 2011.

Andersson, T. and A. Marsham, The first Islamic chronicle: The Chronicle of Khalīfa b. Khayyāṭ (d. AD 854), in M. Campopiano and H. Bainton (eds.), *Universal chronicles in the High Middle Ages*, York 2017, 19–41.

Anthony, S.W., *The caliph and the heretic: Ibn Sabaʾ and the origins of Shīʿism*, Leiden 2011.

Anthony, S.W., Was Ibn Wāḍiḥ al-Yaʿqūbī a Shiʿite historian? The state of the question, in *al-ʿUṣūr al-Wusṭā* 24 (2016), 15–41.

ʿĀṣī, Ḥusayn, *Khalīfa b. Khayyāṭ fī tārīkhihi wa-ṭabaqātihi*, Beirut 1993.

Atallah, W., al-Kalbī, in *EI*².

Atassi, A.N., The transmission of Ibn Saʿd's biographical dictionary *Kitāb al-Ṭabaqāt al-kabīr*, in *Journal of Arabic and Islamic Studies* 12 (2012), 56–80.

Ávila, M.L., Baqī b. Makhlad, in *EI*³.

Ávila, M.L., Nuevos datos para la biografía de Baqī b. Majlad, in *Qanṭara* 6 (1985), 321–368.

al-ʿAwd, Sulaymān b. Fahd, *ʿAbdallāh b. Sabaʾ wa-atharuhu fī aḥdāth al-fitna fī ṣadr al-Islām*, Riyadh 1991–1992.

al-ʿAwnī, Ḥātim b. ʿĀrif, *al-Yaqīnī wa-l-ẓannī min al-akhbār*, Beirut 2013.

Aʿẓamī, M.M., *Studies in early ḥadīth literature*, Indianapolis 1978.

al-Aʿẓamī, ʿAlī, *Mukhtaṣar tārīkh al-Baṣra*, Baghdad 1927.

al-Azdī, Muḥammad b. ʿAbdallāh, *Futūḥ al-Shām*, ed. ʿIṣām Muṣṭafā ʿUqla and Yūsuf Aḥmad Banī Yāsīn, Irbid 2004.

al-Azdī, Yazīd b. Muḥammad, *Tārīkh al-Mawṣil*, ed. ʿAlī Ḥabība, Cairo 1967.

al-Azharī, Abū Manṣūr, *Tahdhīb al-lugha*, ed. ʿAbd al-Salām Hārūn et al., 15 vols., Cairo 1966.

al-Azmeh, A., *Arabic thought and Islamic societies*, London 1986.

al-Bājī, Abū l-Walīd, *al-Taʿdīl wa-l-tajrīḥ li-man kharaja ʿanhu al-Bukhārī fī l-jāmiʿ al-ṣaḥīḥ*, ed. Aḥmad Labzār, 3 vols., Rabat 1991.

al-Balādhurī, Aḥmad b. Yaḥyā, *Ansāb al-ashrāf*, ed. Suhayl Zakkār and Riyāḍ Ziriklī, 13 vols., Beirut 1996.

al-Balādhurī, Aḥmad b. Yaḥyā, *Futūḥ al-buldān*, ed. ʿAbdallāh Anīs al-Ṭabbāʿ and ʿUmar Anīs al-Ṭabbāʿ, Beirut 1987.

Bayhom-Daou, T., al-Maʾmūn's alleged apocalyptic beliefs: A reconsideration of the evidence, in *BSOAS* 71 (2008), 1–24.

Bazmee Ansari, A.S., Djāṭ, in *EI*².

Beaumont, D., Hard-boiled: Narrative discourse in early Muslim traditions, in *SI* 83 (1996), 5–31.

Becker, C.H. and F. Rosenthal, al-Balādhurī, in *EI*².

al-Bīrūnī, Abū Rayḥān, *Kitāb al-Āthār al-bāqiya ʿan al-qurūn al-khāliya*, ed. E. Sachau, Leipzig 1878.

Bonner, M., The waning of empire, 861–945, in C.F. Robinson (ed.), *The new Cambridge history of Islam volume 1: The formation of the Islamic world sixth to eleventh centuries*, Cambridge 2010, 305–359.

Bonner, M.R.J., *An historiographical study of Abū Ḥanīfa Aḥmad ibn Dāwūd b. Wanand al-Dīnawarī's Kitāb al-Akhbār al-ṭiwāl*, PhD thesis, University of Oxford 2014.

Borrut, A., *Entre mémoire et pouvoir: L'espace syrien sous les derniers Omeyyades et les premiers Abbassides (v. 72–193/692–809)*, Leiden 2011.

Borrut, A., The future of the past: Historical writing in early Islamic Syria and Umayyad memory, in A. George and A. Marsham (eds.), *Power, patronage and memory in early Islam: Perspectives on Umayyad elites*, Oxford 2018, 275–300.

Borrut, A., Remembering Karbalāʾ: The construction of an early Islamic site of memory, in JSAI 42 (2015), 249–282.

Borrut, A., Vanishing Syria: Periodization and power in early Islam, in *Der Islam* 91 (2014), 37–68.

Bosworth, C.E., al-Zuṭṭ, in *EI*².

Bray, J., Lists and memory: Ibn Qutayba and Muḥammad b. Ḥabīb, in F. Daftary and J.W. Meri (eds.), *Culture and memory in medieval Islam: Essays in honour of Wilferd Madelung*, London 2003, 210–231.

Brown, J., *The canonization of al-Bukhārī and Muslim: The formation and function of the Sunnī ḥadīth canon*, Leiden 2007.

Brown, J., Did the Prophet say it or not? The literal, historical, and effective truth of *ḥadīths* in early Sunnism, in *JAOS* 129 (2009) 259–285.

Brown, J., Even if it's not true it's true: Using unreliable ḥadīths in Sunni Islam, in *Islamic Law and Society* 18 (2011), 1–52.

Brown, J., *Hadith: Muhammad's legacy in the medieval and modern world*, Oxford 2009.

Brown, J., How we know early ḥadīth critics did *matn* criticism and why it's so hard to find, in *Islamic Law and Society* 15 (2008), 143–184.

al-Bukhārī, Muḥammad b. Ismāʿīl, *al-Jāmiʿ al-ṣaḥīḥ*, ed. Muḥammad Zuhayr b. Nāṣir al-Nāṣir, 9 vols., Beirut 2001.

al-Bukhārī, Muḥammad b. Ismāʿīl, *Kitāb al-Ḍuʿafāʾ al-ṣaghīr*, ed. Maḥmūd Ibrāhīm Zāyid, Beirut 1986.

al-Bukhārī, Muḥammad b. Ismāʿīl, *al-Tārīkh al-kabīr*, 9 vols., Hyderabad 1958.

Bulliet, R., Sedentarization of nomads in the seventh century: The Arabs in Basra and Kufa, in P.C. Salzman (ed.), *When nomads settle: Processes of sedentarization as adaptation and response*, New York 1980, 35–47.

Calder, N., The Qurrāʾ and the Arabic lexicographical tradition, in *JSS* 36 (1991), 297–307.

Campbell, S., ʿAbdallāh b. al-Zubayr, in *EI*³.

Campbell, S., *Telling memories: The Zubayrids in Islamic historical memory*, PhD thesis, University of California 2003.

Chejne, A.G., *Succession to the rule in Islam with special reference to the early ʿAbbasid period*, Lahore 1960.

Chokr, M., *Zandaqa et zindīqs en islam au second siècle de l'Hégire*, Damascus 1993.

Clarke, N., *The Muslim conquest of Iberia: Medieval Arabic narratives*, London/New York 2012.

Cobb, P.M., Al-Mutawakkil's Damascus: A new ʿAbbāsid capital? in *JNES* 58 (1999), 241–257.

Cook, M., The opponents of the writing of tradition in early Islam, in *Arabica* 44 (1997), 437–530.

Cooperson, M., *Classical Arabic biography: The heirs of the prophets in the age of al-Ma'mun*, Cambridge 2000.

Crone, P., *God's rule: Government and Islam*, New York 2004.

Crone, P., Muhallabids, in *EI*².

Crone, P., Review of Samarrai's edition of Sayf b. ʿUmar's *Kitāb al-Ridda wa-l-futūḥ*, in *JRAS* 6 (1996), 237–240.

Crone, P., ʿUthmāniyya, in *EI*².

Crone, P. and M. Hinds, *God's caliph: Religious authority in the first centuries of Islam*, Cambridge 1986.

Cubitt, C., Introduction: Writing true stories: A view from the West, in A. Papaconstantinou, M. Debié, and H. Kennedy (eds.), *Writing "true stories": Historians and hagiographers in the late antique and medieval Near East*, Turnhout 2010, 1–12.

al-Ḍabbī, Abū Jaʿfar, *Bughyat al-multamis fī tārīkh rijāl ahl al-Andalus*, ed. Ibrāhīm al-Abyārī, Cairo/Beirut 1989.

al-Daʿjānī, Ṭ.S., *Mawārid Ibn ʿAsākir fī Tārīkh Dimashq*, Medina 2004.

De Blois, F.C., et al., Ta'rīkh, in *EI*².

De la Vaissière, É., *Sogdian traders: A history*, trans. J. Ward, Leiden 2005.

Debié, M., Syriac historiography and identity formation, in *Church History and Religious Culture* 89 (2009), 93–114.

al-Dhahabī, Shams al-Dīn, *Mīzān al-iʿtidāl fī naqd al-rijāl*, ed. Muḥammad Riḍwān ʿIrqsūsī et al., 5 vols., Damascus 2009.

al-Dhahabī, Shams al-Dīn, *al-Mughnī fī l-ḍuʿafā'*, ed. Nūr al-Dīn ʿItr, 2 vols., Qatar n.d.

al-Dhahabī, Shams al-Dīn, *al-Mūqiẓa fī ʿilm muṣṭalaḥ al-ḥadīth*, ed. ʿAbd al-Fattāḥ Abū Ghudda, Aleppo 1991–1992.

al-Dhahabī, Shams al-Dīn, *Siyar aʿlām al-nubalā'*, ed. Ḥassān ʿAbd al-Mannān, Riyadh 2004.

al-Dhahabī, Shams al-Dīn, *Tadhkirat al-ḥuffāẓ*, Hyderabad 1958.

al-Dhahabī, Shams al-Dīn, *Tārīkh al-Islām wa-wafayāt al-mashāhīr wa-l-aʿlām*, ed. ʿUmar ʿAbd al-Salām Tadmurī, 53 vols., Beirut 1989.

Di Branco, M., A rose in the desert? Late antique and early Byzantine chronicles and the formation of Islamic universal historiography, in P. Liddel and A. Fear (eds.), *Historiae mundi: Studies in universal historiography*, London 2010, 189–206.

Dickinson, E., *The development of early Sunnite* hadith *criticism: The* Taqdima *of Ibn Abī Ḥātim al-Rāzī* (240/854–327/938), Leiden 2001.

al-Dīnawarī, Abū Ḥanīfa, *al-Akhbār al-ṭiwāl*, ed. Muḥammad Saʿīd al-Rāfiʿī, Cairo 1912.

Donner, F. Basra, in *EIr*.

Donner, F., *The early Islamic conquests*, Princeton 1981.

Donner, F., *Narratives of Islamic origins: The beginnings of Islamic historical writing*, Princeton 1998.

Dūrī, ʿAbd al-ʿAzīz, *The rise of historical writing among the Arabs*, trans. L.I. Conrad, Princeton 1983.

Dutton, Y., Orality, literacy and the 'seven *aḥruf*' *ḥadīth*, in *JIS* 23 (2012), 1–49.

Ed., Yazīd b. Zurayʿ, in *EI²*.

El Shamsy, A., *The canonization of Islamic law: A social and intellectual history*, Cambridge 2013.

Elad, A., *The rebellion of Muḥammad al-Nafs al-Zakiyya in 145/762: Ṭālibīs and early ʿAbbāsids in conflict*, Leiden 2015.

El-Hibri, T., The empire in Iraq, 763–861, in C.F. Robinson (ed.), *The new Cambridge history of Islam volume 1: The formation of the Islamic world sixth to eleventh centuries*, Cambridge 2010, 269–304.

El-Hibri, T., *Parable and politics in early Islamic history: The Rashidun caliphs*, New York 2010.

El-Hibri, T., *Reinterpreting Islamic historiography: Harun al-Rashid and the narrative of the Abbasid caliphate*, Cambridge 1999.

El-Hibri, T., The unity of Tabari's chronicle, in N. Yavari (ed.) *Views from the edge: Essays in honor of Richard W. Bulliet*, New York 2004, 63–69.

Ess, J. van, *Theologie und Gesellschaft im 2. und 3. Jahrhundert Hidschra: eine Geschichte des religiösen Denkens im frühen Islam*, 6 vols., Berlin/New York 1991.

al-Faruque, M., The revolt of ʿAbd al-Raḥmān ibn al-Ashʿath: Its nature and causes, in *Islamic Studies* 25 (1986), 289–304.

al-Fasawī, Abū Yūsuf Yaʿqūb b. Sufyān, *Kitāb al-Maʿrifa wa-l-tārīkh*, ed. Akram Ḍiyāʾ al-ʿUmarī, 4 vols., Medina 1989.

Fierro, M.I., The Introduction of hadith in al-Andalus (2nd/8th–3rd/9th centuries), in *Der Islam* 66 (1989), 68–93.

Fisher, A., and A.K. Irvine, Kaḥṭān, in *EI²*.

Fornara, C., *The nature of history in ancient Greece and Rome*, Berkeley/Los Angeles 1983.

Fück, J.W., Ibn Khallikān, in *EI²*.

Gabrieli, F., *al-Maʾmūn e gli ʿAlidi*, Leipzig 1929.

Gaiser, A., Source-critical methodologies in recent scholarship on the Khārijites, in *History Compass* 7 (2009), 1376–1390.

Gerhard, C., Das Kitāb al-Ṭabaqāt des Abū Zurʿa al-Dimašqī (–281 H.). Anmerkungen zu einem unbekannten frühen riǧāl-Werk, in WO 20/21 (1989), 167–226.
al-Ghawrī, Sayyid ʿAbd al-Mājid, *Muʿjam alfāẓ wa-ʿibārāt al-jarḥ wa l-taʿdīl al-mashhūra wa-l-nādira*, Beirut 2011.
Gilliot, C., Ṭabakāt, in EI[2].
Gilliot, C., Yāqūt al-Rūmī, in EI[2].
Gimaret, D., Muʿtazila, in EI[2].
Given-Wilson, C., *Chronicles: The writing of history in medieval England*, London/New York 2004.
Gordon, M., *The breaking of a thousand swords: A history of the Turkish military of Samarra (A.H. 200–275/815–889 C.E.)*, New York 2001.
Görke, A., The relationship between *maghāzī* and *ḥadīth* in early Islamic scholarship, in BSOAS 74 (2011), 171–185.
Görke, A., and G. Schoeler., *Die ältesten Berichte über das Leben Muhammads: Das Korpus ʿUrwa ibn az-Zubair*, Princeton 2008.
Guillaume, A., *The life of Muḥammad: A translation of Ibn Isḥāq's* Sīrat Rasūl Allāh, Oxford/New York 1955.
Günther, S., *Maqātil* literature in medieval Islam, in JAL 25 (1994), 192–212.
Haddad, G.F., Enduring myths of Orientalism: Book review of *The oral and the written in early Islam* by Gregor Schoeler, in *The Muslim World Book Review* 27 (2007), 24–29.
Hagemann, H., *History and memory: Khārijism in early Islamic historiography*, PhD thesis, University of Edinburgh 2014.
Hagler, A.M., Repurposed narratives: The battle of Ṣiffīn and the historical memory of the Umayyad dynasty, in *Mathal/Mashal* 3 (2013), 1–27.
Haider, N.I., al-Ḥusayn b. ʿAlī b. Abī Ṭālib, in EI[3].
al-Ḥākim al-Naysābūrī, *Al-Mustadrak ʿalā al-ṣaḥīḥayn*, ed. Muṣṭafā ʿAbd al-Qādir ʿAṭā, 5 vols., Beirut 1990.
Hallaq, W., *The origins and evolution of Islamic law*, Cambridge 2005.
Hawting, G.R., *The first dynasty of Islam: The Umayyad caliphate AD 661–750*, London 2000.
Hinds, M., Kufan political alignments and their background in the mid-seventh century A.D., in IJMES 2 (1971), 346–367.
Hinds, M., Miḥna, in EI[2].
Hinds, M., The Ṣiffīn arbitration agreement, in JSS 17 (1972), 93–129.
Hirschler, K., *Medieval Arabic historiography: Authors as actors*, London 2006.
Hodgson, M.G.S., *The venture of Islam*, 1: *The classical age of Islam*, Chicago 1974.
Horovitz, J., *The earliest biographies of the Prophet and their authors*, trans. L.I. Conrad, Princeton 2002.
Howard, I.K.A., Ḥusayn the martyr: A commentary on the accounts of the martyrdom

in Arabic sources, in *Al-Serāt* (Papers from the Imam Ḥusayn conference in London, July 1984) 12 (1986), 124–142.

Hoyland, R., Arabic, Syriac and Greek historiography in the first Abbasid century: An inquiry into inter-cultural traffic, in *ARAM* 3 (1991), 211–233.

Hoyland, R., History, fiction and authorship in the first centuries of Islam, in J. Bray (ed.), *Writing and representation in medieval Islam: Muslim horizons*, London 2006, 16–46.

al-Ḥumaydī, *Jadhwat al-muqtabis fī tārīkh ʿulamāʾ al-Andalus*, ed. Bashshār ʿAwwād Maʿrūf and Muḥammad Bashshār ʿAwwād, Tunis 2008.

Humphreys, R.S., *Islamic history: A framework for inquiry*, London 1991.

Hylén, T., *Ḥusayn the mediator: A structural analysis of the Karbalāʾ drama according to Abū Jaʿfar Muḥammad b. Jarīr al-Ṭabarī (d. 310/923)*, PhD thesis, University of Uppsala 2007.

Ibn ʿAbd al-Barr, Abū ʿUmar Yūsuf b. ʿAbdallāh, *al-Istīʿāb fī maʿrifat al-aṣḥāb*, ed. ʿAlī b. Muḥammad al-Bajāwī, 4 vols., Beirut 1992.

Ibn ʿAbd Rabbih, *al-ʿIqd al-farīd*, ed. Mufīd Muḥammad Qumayḥa, 9 vols., Beirut 1983.

Ibn Abī Ḥātim, *al-Jarḥ wa-l-taʿdīl*, 9 vols., Hyderabad 1952.

Ibn Abī l-ʿIzz, ʿAlī b. ʿAlī, *Sharḥ al-ʿaqīdat al-Ṭaḥāwiyya*, ed. ʿAbdallāh b. ʿAbd al-Muḥsin al-Turkī and Shuʿayb al-Arnāʾūṭ, Beirut 1990.

Ibn Abī Khaythama, Abū Bakr Aḥmad, *al-Tārīkh al-kabīr*, ed. Ṣalāḥ b. Fatḥī Halal, 4 vols., Cairo 2004.

Ibn Abī Shayba, Abū Bakr, *al-Muṣannaf*, ed. Ḥamad b. ʿAbdallāh al-Jumʿa and Muḥammad b. Ibrāhīm al-Laḥīdān, 16 vols., Riyadh 2004.

Ibn Abī Yaʿlā, *Ṭabaqāt al-ḥanābila*, ed. ʿAbd al-Raḥmān b. Sulaymān al-ʿUthaymīn, 3 vols., Riyadh 1999.

Ibn ʿAdī, Abū Aḥmad ʿAbdallāh, *al-Kāmil fī ḍuʿafāʾ al-rijāl*, 7 vols., Beirut 1984.

Ibn al-ʿAdīm, *Bughyat al-ṭalab fī tārīkh Ḥalab*, ed. Suhayl Zakkār, 12 vols., Beirut 1988.

Ibn al-ʿArabī, Abū Bakr, *Aḥkām al-Qurʾān*, ed. Muḥammad ʿAbd al-Qādir ʿAṭā, 4 vols., Beirut 2003.

Ibn al-ʿArabī, Abū Bakr, *al-ʿAwāṣim min al-qawāṣim*, ed. ʿAmmār al-Ṭālibī, Cairo 1997.

Ibn ʿAsākir, ʿAlī b. al-Ḥasan, *Tārīkh madīnat Dimashq*, ed. ʿUmar b. Gharāma al-ʿAmrawī, 80 vols., Beirut 1995.

Ibn Aʿtham al-Kūfī, *al-Futūḥ*, 8 vols., Beirut 1986.

Ibn al-Athīr, ʿIzz al-Dīn, *al-Kāmil fī l-tārīkh*, ed. Abū l-Fidāʾ ʿAbdallāh al-Qāḍī and Muḥammad Yūsuf al-Daqqāq, 10 vols., Beirut 1987.

Ibn al-Athīr, ʿIzz al-Dīn, *al-Lubāb fī tahdhīb al-ansāb*, 3 vols., Baghdad n.d.

Ibn al-Faraḍī, *Tārīkh ʿulamāʾ al-Andalus*, ed. Bashshār ʿAwwād Maʿrūf, 2 vols., Tunis 2008.

Ibn Ḥabīb, ʿAbd al-Malik, *Kitāb al-Tārīkh*, ed. J. Aguadé, Madrid 1990.

Ibn Ḥajar, al-ʿAsqalānī, *Fatḥ al-Bārī*, ed. ʿAbd al-Qādir Shaybat al-Ḥamd, 13 vols., Riyadh 2001.

Ibn Ḥajar, al-ʿAsqalānī, *Lisān al-mīzān*, ed. ʿAbd al-Fattāḥ Abū Ghudda, 10 vols., Beirut 2002.

Ibn Ḥajar, al-ʿAsqalānī, *al-Muʿjam al-mufahras*, ed. Muḥammad Shakkūr al-Mayādīnī, Beirut 1998.

Ibn Ḥajar, al-ʿAsqalānī, *al-Nukat ʿalā kitāb Ibn al-Ṣalāḥ*, ed. Rabīʿ b. Hādī ʿUmayr, 2 vols., Medina 1984.

Ibn Ḥajar, al-ʿAsqalānī, *Nuzhat al-naẓar fī tawḍīḥ nukhbat al-fikar fī muṣṭalaḥ ahl al-athar*, ed. Muḥammad Murābī, Damascus/Beirut 2015.

Ibn Ḥajar, al-ʿAsqalānī, *Tahdhīb al-tahdhīb*, ed. Ibrāhīm al-Zaybaq and ʿĀdil Murshid, 4 vols., Beirut 1996.

Ibn Ḥajar, al-ʿAsqalānī, *Taqrīb al-tahdhīb*, ed. Abū l-Ashbāl Ṣaghīr Aḥmad Shāghif al-Bākistānī, Riyadh 2000.

Ibn al-Ḥājib, Abū ʿAmr ʿUthmān b. ʿUmar, *Mukhtaṣar muntahā l-suʾl wa-l-amal fī ʿilmay al-uṣūl wa-l-jadal*, ed. Nadhīr Ḥamādū, 2 vols., Beirut 2006.

Ibn Ḥanbal, Aḥmad, *Faḍāʾil al-ṣaḥāba*, ed. Waṣīallāh b. Muḥammad ʿAbbās, Mecca 1983.

Ibn Ḥanbal, Aḥmad, *Mawsūʿat aqwāl al-imām Aḥmad b. Ḥanbal*, ed. Abū l-Maʿāṭī al-Nūrī, Aḥmad ʿAbd al-Razzāq ʿĪd and Maḥmūd Muḥammad Khalīl, 4 vols., Beirut 1997.

Ibn Ḥanbal, Aḥmad, *Musnad*, ed. Shuʿayb al-Arnāʾūṭ et al., 50 vols., Beirut 1999.

Ibn Ḥazm, *al-Fiṣal fī l-milal wa-l-ahwāʾ wa-l-niḥal*, ed. Muḥammad Ibrāhīm Naṣr and ʿAbd al-Raḥmān ʿUmayra, 5 vols., Beirut 1996.

Ibn Ḥibbān, Muḥammad, *al-Iḥsān fī taqrīb Ṣaḥīḥ Ibn Ḥibbān* (arranged by ʿAlāʾ al-Dīn ʿAlī b. Balbān al-Fārisī), ed. Shuʿayb al-Arnāʾūṭ, 18 vols., Beirut 1988.

Ibn Ḥibbān, Muḥammad, *Kitāb al-Thiqāt*, 9 vols., Hyderabad 1973.

Ibn Hishām, *al-Sīrat al-nabawiyya*, ed. ʿUmar ʿAbd al-Salām Tadmurī, 4 vols., Beirut 1990.

Ibn al-Jawzī, Abū l-Faraj, *al-Muntaẓam fī tārīkh al-mulūk wa-l-umam*, ed. Muḥammad ʿAbd al-Qādir ʿAṭāʾ and Muṣṭafā ʿAbd al-Qādir ʿAṭāʾ, 18 vols., Beirut 1992.

Ibn al-Jazarī, *Ghāyat al-nihāya fī ṭabaqāt al-qurrāʾ*, ed. G. Bergstraesser, 2 vols., Beirut 2006.

Ibn al-Junayd al-Khuttalī, ʿAbdallāh b. Ibrāhīm, *Suʾālāt Ibn al-Junayd li-Yaḥyā b. Maʿīn*, ed. Aḥmad Muḥammad Nūr Sayf, Medina 1988.

Ibn Juzayy, Muḥammad b. Aḥmad, *al-Qawānīn al-fiqhiyya*, ed. Mājid al-Ḥamawī, Beirut 2013.

Ibn Kathīr, Ismāʿīl b. ʿUmar, *al-Bidāya wa-l-nihāya*, ed. ʿAbdallāh b. ʿAbd al-Muḥsin al-Turkī, 21 vols., Cairo 1997.

Ibn Khallikān, Aḥmad b. Muḥammad, *Wafayāt al-aʿyān wa-anbāʾ abnāʾ al-zamān*, ed. Iḥsān ʿAbbās, 8 vols., Beirut 1994.

Ibn Manẓūr, *Lisān al-ʿarab*, 15 vols., Beirut 1955.
Ibn Maʿīn, Yaḥyā, *al-Tarīkh*, ed. Aḥmad Muḥammad Nūr Sayf, 4 vols., Mecca 1979.
Ibn al-Nadīm, *Kitāb al-Fihrist*, ed. Ayman Fu'ād Sayyid, 2 vols., London 2009.
Ibn Qāniʿ, *Muʿjam al-ṣaḥāba*, ed. Ṣalāḥ al-Dīn b. Sālim al-Miṣrātī, Medina 1997.
Ibn Qutayba, *al-Maʿārif*, ed. Tharwat ʿUkāsha, Cairo 1969.
Ibn Qutayba, *Ta'wīl mukhtalif al-ḥadīth*, ed. Salīm b. ʿĪd al-Hilālī, Cairo 2009.
Ibn Rushd, Abū l-Walīd, *al-Bayān wa-l-taḥṣīl*, ed. Muḥammad Ḥajjī, 20 vols., Beirut 1988.
Ibn al-Ṣalāḥ, *Fatāwā wa-masā'il Ibn al-Ṣalāḥ*, ed. ʿAbd al-Muʿṭī Qalʿajī, 2 vols., Beirut 1986.
Ibn al-Ṣalāḥ, *ʿUlūm al-ḥadīth*, ed. Nūr al-Dīn ʿIṭr, Beirut 1986.
Ibn Saʿd, *Kitāb al-Ṭabaqāt al-kabīr*, ed. ʿAlī Muḥammad ʿUmar, 11 vols., Cairo 2001.
Ibn Sayyid al-Nās, Muḥammad, *ʿUyūn al-athar fī funūn al-maghāzī wa-l-shamā'il wa-l-siyar*, ed. Muḥammad al-ʿĪd al-Khaṭrāwī and Muḥyī al-Dīn Matū, 2 vols., Beirut n.d.
Ibn Shabba, Abū Zayd ʿUmar, *Tārīkh al-Madīnat al-Munawwara*, ed. Fahīm Muḥammad Shaltūt, 4 vols., Mecca 1979.
Ibn Taghrībirdī, Yūsuf, *al-Nujūm al-zāhira fī muluk Miṣr wa-l-Qāhira*, ed. Muḥammad Ḥusayn Shams al-Dīn, Beirut 1992.
Ibn Taymiyya, *al-ʿAqīdat al-Wāsiṭiyya*, ed. Abū Muḥammad Ashraf b. ʿAbd al-Maqṣūd, Riyadh 1999.
Ibn Taymiyya, *Minhāj al-sunnat al-nabawiyya*, ed. Muḥammad Rashād Sālim, 9 vols., Riyadh 1986.
al-ʿIjlī, Aḥmad b. ʿAbdallāh, *Maʿrifat al-thiqāt*, ed. ʿAbd al-ʿAlīm al-Bastawī, 2 vols., Medina 1985.
Ismāʿīl Pāshā al Baghdādī, *Hadiyyat al-ʿārifīn asmā' al-mu'allifīn wa-āthār al-muṣannifīn*, 2 vols., Beirut n.d.
ʿItr, Nūr al-Dīn, *Manhaj al-naqd fī ʿulūm al-ḥadīth*, Beirut 1979.
ʿIyāḍ b. Mūsā al-Yaḥṣubī, *al-Shifā bi-taʿrīf ḥuqūq al-Muṣṭafā*, ed. ʿAlī Muḥammad al-Bajāwī, 2 vols, Beirut 1984.
ʿIyāḍ b. Mūsā al-Yaḥṣubī, *Tartīb al-madārik wa-taqrīb al-masālik li-maʿrifat aʿlām madhhab Mālik*, ed. Muḥammad b. Tāwīt al-Ṭanjī et al., 8 vols., Rabat 1981.
al-Jāḥiẓ, Abū ʿUthmān, *al-Bayān wa-l-tabyīn*, ed. ʿAbd al-Salām Hārūn, 4 vols., Cairo 1998.
al-Jāḥiẓ, Abū ʿUthmān, *Kitāb al-ʿUthmāniyya*, ed. ʿAbd al-Salām Hārūn, Beirut 1991.
al-Jāḥiẓ, Abū ʿUthmān, *Rasā'il*, ed. ʿAbd al-Salām Hārūn, 4 vols., Cairo, 1964.
al-Jahshiyārī, Muḥammad b. ʿAbdūs, *Kitāb al-Wuzarā' wa-l-kuttāb*, ed. Ḥasan al-Zayn, Beirut 1988.
Jarrar, M., *Die Prophetenbiographie im Islamischen Spanien. Ein Beitrag zur Überlieferungs- und Redaktionsgeschichte*, Frankfurt am Main 1989.
Jones, J.M.B., The chronology of the *maghāzī*: A textual survey, in *BSOAS* 19 (1957), 245–280.

Jones, J.M.B., The *maghāzī* literature, in A.F.L. Beeston et al. (eds.), *The Cambridge history of Arabic literature: Arabic literature to the end of the Umayyad period*, Cambridge 1983, 344–351.

Judd, S., Abū Zurʿa al-Dimashqī, in *EI*³.

Judd, S., Ibn ʿAsākir's sources for the late Umayyad period, in J.E. Lindsay (ed.), *Ibn ʿAsākir and early Islamic history*, Princeton 2001, 78–99.

Judd, S., Medieval explanations for the fall of the Umayyads, in A. Borrut and P. Cobb (eds.), *Umayyad legacies: Medieval memories from Syria to Spain*, Leiden 2010, 89–104.

Judd, S., Narratives and character development: al-Tabari and al-Baladhuri on late Umayyad history, in S. Günther (ed.), *Ideas, images, and methods of portrayal: Insights into classical Arabic literature and Islam*, Leiden 2005, 209–226.

Judd, S., Reinterpreting al-Walīd b. Yazīd, in *JAOS* 128 (2008), 439–458.

Judd, S., *Religious scholars and the Umayyads: Piety-minded supporters of the Marwanid caliphate*, London 2014.

Juynboll, G.H.A., The position of Qur'ān recitation in early Islam, in *JSS* 19 (1974), 240–251.

Juynboll, G.H.A., The *qurrā'* in early Islamic history, in *JESHO* 16 (1973), 113–129.

Juynboll, G.H.A., The Qur'ān reciter on the battlefield and concomitant issues, in *Zeitschrift Der Deutschen Morgenländischen Gesellschaft* 125 (1975), 11–27.

Juynboll, G.H.A., Sunna, in *EI*².

Keaney, H.N., Confronting the caliph: ʿUthmān b. ʿAffān in three ʿAbbasid chronicles, in *SI, New Series* 1 (2011), 37–65.

Keaney, H.N., *Medieval Islamic historiography: Remembering rebellion*, London/New York 2013.

Kennedy, H., *al-Ṭabarī: A medieval Muslim historian and his work*, Princeton 2008.

Kennedy, H., Caliphs and their chroniclers in the middle Abbasid period (third/ninth century), in C.F. Robinson (ed.), *Texts, documents and artefacts: Islamic studies in honour of D.S. Richards*, Leiden 2003, 17–35.

Kennedy, H., The decline and fall of the first Muslim empire, in *Der Islam* 81 (2004), 3–30.

Kennedy, H., *The early Abbasid caliphate: A political history*, London/Sydney 1981.

Kennedy, H., The feeding of the five hundred thousand: Cities and agriculture in early Islamic Mesopotamia, in *Iraq* 73 (2011), 177–199.

Kennedy, H., *The Prophet and the age of caliphates: The Islamic Near East from the 6th to the 11th century*, Harlow 2004.

Kennedy, H., The reign of al-Muqtadir (295–320/908–932): A history, in M. van Berkel et al. (eds.), *Crisis and continuity at the Abbasid court*, Leiden 2013, 13–47.

Keller, Nuh Ha Mim, *Reliance of the traveller: A classic manual of Islamic sacred law* [translation of *ʿUmdat al-sālik* by Aḥmad b. al-Naqīb al-Miṣrī], Beltsville 1994.

Khalek, N., *Damascus after the Muslim conquest: Text and image in early Islam*, Oxford 2011.

al-Khallāl, Abū Bakr, *al-Sunna*, ed. ʿAṭiyya al-Zahrānī, 5 vols., Riyadh 1989.

Khalidi, T., *Arabic historical thought in the classical period*, Cambridge 1994.

Khalidi, T., *Islamic historiography: The histories of al-Masʿūdī*, New York 1975.

Khalīfa b. Khayyāṭ, *Kitāb al-Ṭabaqāt*, ed. Akram Ḍiyāʾ al-ʿUmarī, Baghdad 1967.

Khalīfa b. Khayyāṭ, *Kitāb al-Ṭabaqāt*, ed. Suhayl Zakkār, Beirut 1993.

Khalīfa b. Khayyāṭ, *Tārīkh*, ed. Akram Ḍiyāʾ al-ʿUmarī, Riyadh 1985.

Khalīfa b. Khayyāṭ, *Tārīkh*, ed. Suhayl Zakkār, Beirut 1993.

al-Khaṭīb al-Baghdādī, *Kitāb al-Kifāya fī ʿilm al-riwāya*, Hyderabad 1938.

al-Khaṭīb al-Baghdādī, *Tārīkh Madīnat al-Salām* [*Tārīkh Baghdād*], ed. Bashshār ʿAwwād Maʿrūf, 17 vols., Beirut 2001.

Khoury, R.G., *ʿAbd Allāh ibn Lahīʿa (97–174/715–790)*, Wiesbaden 1986.

Kimber, R.A., al-Maʾmūn and Baghdad: The nomination of ʿAlī al-Riḍā, in C. Vázquez de Benito and M.A. Manzano Rodriguez (eds.), *Actas XVI Congreso UEAI*, Salamanca 1995, 275–280.

al-Kindī, Muḥammad b. Yūsuf, *Kitāb al-Wulāt wa-kitāb al-quḍāt*, ed. R. Guest, Beirut 1908.

Kister, M.J., The battle of the Harra: Some socio-economic aspects, in M. Rosen-Ayalon (ed.), *Studies in memory of Gaston Wiet*, Jerusalem 1977, 33–49.

Kister, M.J., The *sīrah* literature, in A.F.L. Beeston et al. (eds.), *The Cambridge history of Arabic literature: Arabic literature to the end of the Umayyad period*, Cambridge 1983, 352–367.

al-Laknawī, ʿAbd al-Ḥayy, *al-Rafʿ wa-l-takmīl fī l-jarḥ wa-l-taʿdīl*, ed. ʿAbd al-Fattāḥ Abū Ghudda, Cairo 2000.

al-Lālakāʾī, Abū l-Qāsim, *Sharḥ uṣūl iʿtiqād ahl al-sunna wa-l-jamaʿa*, ed. Aḥmad b. Saʿd b. Ḥamdān, 4 vols., Riyadh 1991.

Landau-Tasseron, E., Sayf ibn ʿUmar in medieval and modern scholarship, in *Der Islam* 67 (1990), 1–26.

Lane, E.W., *An Arabic-English lexicon*, London 1863.

Lecker, M., Biographical notes on Abū ʿUbayda Maʿmar b. al-Muthannā, in *SI* 81 (1995), 71–100.

Leder, S., *Das Korpus al-Haiṯam ibn ʿAdī (st. 207/822): Herkunft, Überlieferung, Gestalt früher Texte der aḫbār Literatur*, Frankfurt am Main 1991.

Leder, S., The literary use of the *khabar*: A basic form of historical writing, in L.I. Conrad and A. Cameron (eds.), *The Byzantine and early Islamic Near East*, 1: *Problems in the literary source material*, Princeton 1992, 277–315.

Levi Della Vida, G., Khāridjites, in *EI*².

Lewin, B., al-Aṣmaʿī, in *EI*².

Lewin, B., al-Dīnawarī, in *EI*².

Lewinstein, K., The Azāriqa in Islamic heresiography, in *BSOAS* 54 (1991), 251–268.

Lewinstein, K., Making and unmaking a sect: The heresiographers and the Ṣufriyya, in *SI* 76 (1992), 75–96.

Lewinstein, K., *Studies in Islamic heresiography: The Khawārij in two* firaq *traditions*, PhD thesis, Princeton University 1989.

Lindstedt, I., The life and deeds of ʿAlī b. Muḥammad al-Madāʾinī, in *Zeitschrift Für Geschichte Der Arabisch-Islamischen Wissenschaften* 20–21 (2014), 235–270.

Lindstedt, I., The role of al-Madāʾinī's students in the transmission of his material, in *Der Islam* 91 (2014), 295–340.

Lindstedt, I., *The transmission of al-Madāʾinī's material: Historiographical studies*, PhD thesis, University of Helsinki 2013.

Lucas, S.C., *Constructive critics: Ḥadīth literature and the articulation of Sunnī Islam*, Leiden 2004.

Lucas, S.C., Principles of traditionist jurisprudence reconsidered, in *MW* 100 (2010), 145–156.

Lucas, S.C., Where are the legal ḥadīth? A study of the *Muṣannaf* of Ibn Abī Shayba, in *Islamic Law and Society* 15 (2008), 283–314.

Madelung, W., New documents concerning al-Maʾmūn, al-Faḍl b. Sahl, and ʿAlī al-Riḍā, in W. al-Qāḍī (ed.), *Studia Arabica et Islamica: Festschrift for Iḥsān ʿAbbās on his sixtieth birthday*, Beirut 1981, 333–346.

Madelung, W., *The succession to Muḥammad: A study of the early caliphate*, Cambridge 1997.

Madelung, W., The Sufyānī between tradition and history, in *SI* 63 (1986), 5–48.

Mahmood, I., Religious inquisition as social policy: The persecution of the Zanādiqa in the early ʿAbbāsid caliphate, in *Arab Studies Quarterly* 16 (1994), 53–73.

Makdisi, G., Ashʿarī and the Ashʿarites in Islamic religious history I: The Ashʿarite movement and Muslim orthodoxy, in *SI* 17 (1962), 37–80.

Makdisi, G., Ṭabaqāt-biography: law and orthodoxy in classical Islam, in *Islamic Studies* 32 (1993), 371–396.

Mālik b. Anas, *al-Muwaṭṭaʾ*, ed. Bashshār ʿAwwād Maʿrūf, 2 vols., Tunis 1996.

al-Mālikī, Abū Bakr ʿAbdallāh b. Muḥammad, *Kitāb Riyāḍ al-nufūs fī ṭabaqāt ʿulāmāʾ al-Qayrawān wa-Ifrīqiya*, ed. Ḥusayn Muʾnis, Cairo 1951.

Marín, M., Baqī b. Majlad y la introducción del estudio del *ḥadīth* en al-Andalus, in *Qanṭara* 1 (1980), 165–208.

Marsham, A., The pact (*amāna*) between Muʿāwiya ibn Abī Sufyān and ʿAmr ibn al-ʿĀṣ (656 or 658 CE): 'Documents' and the Islamic historical tradition, in *JSS* 57 (2012), 69–96.

Marsham, A., *Rituals of Islamic monarchy: Accession and succession in the first Muslim empire*, Edinburgh 2009.

Marsham, A., Universal histories in Christendom and the Islamic world, c. 700–c. 1400, in C.F. Robinson and S. Foot (eds.), *The Oxford history of historical writing, 2: 400–1400*, Oxford 2012, 431–455.

Mårtensson, U., Discourse and historical analysis: The case of al-Ṭabarī's History of the Messengers and the Kings, in *JIS* 16 (2005), 287–331.

Mårtensson, U., *Tabari*, Oxford 2009.

al-Masʿūdī, Abū l-Ḥasan, *Murūj al-dhahab wa-maʿādin al-jawhar*, ed. Yūsuf Asʿad Dāghir, 4 vols., Beirut 1978.

al-Māwardī, Abū l-Ḥasan ʿAlī b. Muḥammad, *al-Aḥkām al-sulṭāniyya wa-l-wilāyāt al-dīniyya*, ed. Aḥmad Mubārak al-Baghdādī, Kuwait 1989.

Mcmillan, M.E., *The meaning of Mecca: The politics of pilgrimage in early Islam*, London 2011.

Melchert, C., *Ahmad ibn Hanbal*, Oxford 2006.

Melchert, C., al-Fasawī, Yaʿqūb b. Sufyān, in *EI*³.

Melchert, C., *The formation of the Sunni schools of law: 9th–10th centuries C.E.*, Leiden 1997.

Melchert, C., How Ḥanafism came to originate in Kufa and traditionalism in Medina, in *Islamic Law and Society* 6 (1999), 318–347.

Melchert, C., Religious policies of the caliphs from al-Mutawakkil to al-Muqtadir, AH 232–295/AD 847–908, in *Islamic Law and Society* 3 (1996), 316–342.

Melchert, C., The traditionist-jurisprudents and the framing of Islamic law, in *Islamic Law and Society* 8 (2001), 383–406.

al-Mizzī, Abū l-Ḥajjāj Yūsuf, *Tahdhīb al-kamāl fī asmāʾ al-rijāl*, ed. Bashshār ʿAwwād Maʿrūf, 35 vols., Beirut 1980.

Montgomery Watt, W., Djahmiyya, in *EI*²

Morony, M.G., *Iraq after the Muslim conquest*, New Jersey 2005.

Motzki, H., *The origins of Islamic jurisprudence: Meccan fiqh before the classical schools*, Leiden 2002.

Mughalṭāy, ʿAlāʾ al-Dīn, *Ikmāl tahdhīb al-kamāl fī asmāʾ al-rijāl*, ed. Abū ʿAbd al-Raḥmān ʿĀdil b. Muḥammad and Abū Muḥammad Usāma b. Ibrāhīm, 12 vols., Cairo 2001.

Muḥammad Makhlūf, *Shajarat al-nūr al-zakiyya fī ṭabaqāt al-mālikiyya*, ed. ʿAbd al-Majīd Khayālī, Beirut 2003.

Muranyi, M., ʿAbd al-Malik b. Ḥabīb, in *EI*³.

Muslim b. al-Ḥajjāj, *al-Ṭabaqāt*, ed. Abū ʿUbayda Mashhūr b. Ḥasan, 2 vols., Riyadh 1991.

Muslim b. al-Ḥajjāj, *Ṣaḥīḥ Muslim*, ed. Naẓar b. Muḥammad al-Fāriyābī, 2 vols., Riyadh 2006.

Nagel, T., *Rechtleitung und Kalifat: Versuch über eine Grundfrage der islamischen Geschichte*, Bonn 1975.

Naṣr b. Muzāḥim, *Waqʿat Ṣiffīn*, ed. ʿAbd al-Salām Muḥammad Hārūn, Beirut 1990.

Nawas, J.A., An early Muslim philosopher of history: Khalīfa b. Khayyāt (d. 240 A.H./

854 A.D.) and the encyclopedic tradition of Islamic historiography, in *Orientalia lovaniensia periodica* 26 (1995), 163–170.
al-Nawawī, Yaḥyā b. Sharaf, *Tahdhīb al-asmā' wa l lughāt*, 4 vols., Beirut n.d.
Noth, A., Der Charakter der ersten großen Sammlungen von Nachrichten zur frühen Kalifenzeit, in *Der Islam* 47 (1971), 168–199.
Noth, A., *Futūḥ* history and *futūḥ* historiography: The Muslim conquest of Damascus, in *Qanṭara* 10 (1990), 453–462.
Noth, A., Zum Verhältnis von Kalifater Zentralgewalt und Provinzen in Umayyadischer Zeit. Die '*Ṣulḥ*'-'*Anwa*'-Traditionen für Ägypten und den Iraq, in *WI* 14 (1973), 150–162.
Noth, A., and L.I. Conrad., *The early Arabic historical tradition: A source-critical study*, Princeton 1994.
Nūrī, Muʿammar, *Muḥammad b. Waḍḍāḥ al-Qurṭubī: Mu'assis madrasat al-ḥadīth bi-l-Andalus maʿa Baqī b. Makhlad*, Rabat 1983.
Palmer, A., *The seventh century in the West-Syrian chronicles*, Liverpool 1993.
Pellat, C., al-Baṣra, in *EI*².
Pellat, C., al-Masʿūdī, in *EI*².
Pellat, C., *Le milieu basrien et la formation de Gahiz*, Paris 1953.
Pellat, C., Nābita, in *EI*².
Pellat, C., and S.H. Longrigg, Baṣra, in C.E. Bosworth (ed.), *Historic cities of the Islamic world*, Leiden 2007, 49–53.
Petersen, E.L., *'Alī and Muʿāwiya in early Arabic tradition: Studies on the genesis and growth of Islamic historical writing until the end of the ninth century*, Copenhagen 1964.
Picken, G., *Spiritual purification and Islam: The life and works of al-Muḥāsibī*, London 2011.
Popper, W., Abū 'l-Maḥāsin Djamāl al-Dīn Yūsuf b. Taghrībirdī, in *EI*².
al-Qāḍī, W., Biographical dictionaries: Inner structure and cultural significance, in G.N. Atiyeh (ed.), *The book in the Islamic world: The written word and communication in the Middle East*, New York 1995, 93–122.
al-Qāḍī, W., The earliest "Nābita" and the paradigmatic "Nawābit", in *SI* 78 (1993), 27–61.
Radtke, B., *Weltgeschichte und Weltbeschreibung im mittelalterlichen Islam*, Beirut/Stuttgart 1992.
Rahman, F., *Revival and reform in Islam: A study of Islamic fundamentalism*, ed. Ebrahim Moosa, Oxford 1999.
Raisuddin, A.N.M., Baqī b. Makhlad al-Qurtubī (201–276/818–889) and his contribution to the study of *ḥadīth* literature in Muslim Spain, in *Islamic Studies* 27 (1988), 161–168.
Raven, W., Saʿīd b. Abī 'Arūba, in *EI*².
Roberts, J.B., *Early Islamic historiography: Ideology and methodology*, PhD thesis, Ohio State University 1986.

Robinson, C.F., *'Abd al-Malik*, London 2005.

Robinson, C.F., *Empire and elites after the Muslim conquest: The transformation of northern Mesopotamia*, Cambridge 2000.

Robinson, C.F., *Islamic historiography*, Cambridge 2003.

Robinson, C.F., A local historian's debt to al-Ṭabarī: The case of al-Azdī's *Ta'rīkh al-Mawṣil*, in *JAOS* 126 (2006), 521–535.

Robson, J., Ibn al-ʿArabī, in *EI*^{2}.

Rosenthal, F., Abū Nuʿaym al-Faḍl b. Dukayn al-Mulāʾī, in *EI*^{2}.

Rosenthal, F., Awāʾil, in *EI*^{2}.

Rosenthal, F., al-Azdī, in *EI*^{2}.

Rosenthal, F., *A history of Muslim historiography*, Leiden 1968.

Rosenthal, F., Ibn al-Athīr, in *EI*^{2}.

Rubin, U., *The eye of the beholder: The life of Muḥammad as viewed by the early Muslims*, Princeton 1995.

Ṣaddām, R.F., *Tārīkh Khalīfa b. Khayyāṭ (al-qism al-ḍāʾiʿ)*, Baghdad 2016.

al-Sakhāwī, Muḥammad b. ʿAbd al-Raḥmān, *al-Iʿlān bi-l-tawbīkh li-man dhamma ahl al-tārīkh*, ed. Ṣāliḥ Aḥmad al-ʿIly, Beirut 1986.

al-Sakhāwī, Muḥammad b. ʿAbd al-Raḥmān, *Fatḥ al-Mughīth bi-sharḥ alfiyyat al-ḥadīth*, ed. ʿAbd al-Karīm al-Khuḍayr and Muḥammad b. ʿAbdallāh Āl Fuhayd, 5 vols., Riyadh 2005.

al-Samʿānī, ʿAbd al-Karīm, *al-Ansāb*, ed. ʿAbd al-Raḥmān al-Muʿallimī al-Yamānī et al., 12 vols., Cairo 1976.

al-Samuk, S.M., *Die historischen Überlieferungen nach Ibn Isḥāq. Eine synoptische Untersuchung*, PhD thesis, Johann Wolfgang Goethe Universität 1978.

Savant, S.B., *The new Muslims of post-conquest Iran: Tradition, memory, and conversion*, Cambridge 2013.

Sayf b. ʿUmar, *Kitāb al-Ridda wa-l-futūḥ wa-kitāb al-jamal wa-masīr ʿĀʾisha wa-ʿAlī*, ed. Qasim al-Sāmarrāʾī, Leiden 1995.

Schacht, J., The *Kitāb al-tārīḫ* of Ḫalīfa b. Ḫayyāṭ, in *Arabica* 16 (1969), 79–81.

Schacht, J., *The origins of Muhammadan jurisprudence*, Oxford 1950.

Scheiner, J., *Die Eroberung von Damaskus: Quellenkritische Untersuchung zur Historiographie in klassisch-islamischer Zeit*, Leiden 2010.

Scheiner, J., Grundlegendes zu al-Azdīs *Futūḥ aš-Šām*, in *Der Islam* 84 (2007), 1–16.

Scheiner, J., Writing the history of the *futūḥ*: The *futūḥ*-works by al-Azdī, Ibn Aʿtham, and al-Wāqidī, in P. Cobb (ed.), *The lineaments of Islam: Studies in honor of Fred McGraw Donner*, Leiden 2012, 151–176.

Schoeler, G., *The biography of Muḥammad: Nature and authenticity*, ed. J.E. Montgomery, trans. U. Vagelpohl, London/New York 2011.

Schoeler, G., *The genesis of literature in Islam: From the aural to the read*, Edinburgh 2009.

Schoeler, G., *The oral and the written in early Islam*, ed. J.E. Montgomery, trans. U. Vagelpohl, London/New York 2006.

Sellheim, R., Kitāb, in *EI*².

Sellheim, R., Prophet, Chalif und Geschichte: Die Muhammed-Biographie des Ibn Isḥāq, in *Oriens* 18–19 (1967), 33–91.

Sezgin, F., *Geschichte des arabischen Schritums I*, Leiden 1967.

Sezgin, U., *Abū Mikhnaf: Ein Beitrag zur Historiographie der umaiyadischen Zeit*, Leiden 1971.

Shah, M., The quest for the origins of the *qurrā'* in the classical Islamic tradition, in *JQS* 7 (2005), 1–35.

Sharon, M., *Black banners from the East: The establishment of the 'Abbāsid state—Incubation of a revolt*, Jerusalem 1983.

Sharon, M., *Revolt: The social and military aspects of the 'Abbāsid Revolution*, Jerusalem 1990.

al-Shawkānī, Muḥammad b. 'Alī, *Irshād al-fuḥūl ilā taḥqīq al-ḥaqq min 'ilm al-uṣūl*, ed. Abū Ḥafṣ Sāmī b. al-'Arabī al-Atharī, 2 vols., Riyadh 2000.

al-Shawkānī, Muḥammad b. 'Alī, *Nayl al-awṭār*, ed. Abū Mu'ādh Ṭāriq b. 'Iwaḍallāh b. Muḥammad, 12 vols., Riyadh/Cairo 2005.

Shboul, A., *al-Mas'ūdī and his world: A Muslim humanist and his interest in non-Muslims*, London 1979.

Shoshan, B., *Poetics of Islamic historiography: Deconstructing al-Ṭabarī's History*, Leiden 2004.

Shoufani, E., *al-Riddah and the Muslim conquest of Arabia*, Toronto 1973.

Sourdel, D., La politique religieuse du calife 'Abbaside al-Ma'mūn, in *Revue des études islamiques* 30 (1962), 27–48.

Spectorsky, S.A., *Ḥadīth* in the responses of Isḥāq b. Rāhawayh, in *Islamic Law and Society* 8 (2001), 407–431.

Stowasser, B., *The day begins at sunset: Perceptions of time in the Islamic world*, London 2014.

al-Suyūṭī, Jalāl al-Dīn, *History of the Umayyad caliphs: From the* Tārīkh al-Khulafā', trans. T. Andersson, London 2015.

al-Suyūṭī, Jalāl al-Dīn, *Tārīkh al-khulafā'*, Qatar 2013.

al-Ṭabarānī, Abū l-Qāsim, *al-Mu'jam al-ṣaghīr*, Beirut 1983.

al-Ṭabarī, Abū Ja'far Muḥammad b. Jarīr, *Tahdhīb al-āthār*, ed. Maḥmūd Muḥammad Shākir, 5 vols., Cairo 1982.

al-Ṭabarī, Abū Ja'far Muḥammad b. Jarīr, *The History of al-Ṭabarī*, 1: *General introduction and from the Creation to the Flood*, trans. F. Rosenthal, Albany NY 1989.

al-Ṭabarī, Abū Ja'far Muḥammad b. Jarīr, *The History of al-Ṭabarī*, 11: *The challenge to the empires*, trans. K.Y. Blankinship, Albany NY 1993.

al-Ṭabarī, Abū Ja'far Muḥammad b. Jarīr, *Tārīkh al-rusul wa-l-mulūk*, ed. M. de Goeje, 15 vols., Leiden 1879.

al-Ṭaḥāwī, Abū Jaʿfar, *al-ʿAqīdat al-Ṭaḥāwiyya*, Beirut 1995.

al-Ṭayālisī, Abū Dāwūd, *Musnad*, ed. Muḥammad b. ʿAbd al-Muḥsin al-Turkī, 4 vols., Giza 1999.

Thucydides, *The Peloponnesian war*, trans. J.F. Finley, New York 1951.

al-Tirmidhī, Abū ʿĪsā, *al-Jāmiʿ al-kabīr*, ed. Bashshār ʿAwwād Maʿrūf, 6 vols., Beirut 1996.

Toorawa, S.M., *Ibn Abi Tahir Tayfur and Arabic writerly culture: A ninth-century bookman in Baghdad*, London 2010.

Tor, D.G., An historiographical re-examination of the appointment and death of ʿAlī al-Riḍā, in *Der Islam* 78 (2001), 103–128.

Troupeau, G., Abū ʿAmr al-Shaybānī, in EI².

Tsafrir, N., *The history of an Islamic school of law: The early spread of Hanafism*, Cambridge, Mass. 2004.

Turner, J.P., *Inquisition in early Islam: The competition for political and religious authority in the Abbasid empire*, London 2013.

al-ʿUmarī, Akram Ḍiyāʾ, *Baqī b. Makhlad al-Qurṭubī wa-muqaddimat musnadihi*, Beirut 1984.

al-ʿUqaylī, Abū Jaʿfar Muḥammad b. ʿAmr, *Kitāb al-Ḍuʿafāʾ al-kabīr*, ed. ʿAbd al-Muʿṭī Amīn Qalʿajī, 4 vols., Beirut 1984.

Veccia Vaglieri, L., ʿAbd Allāh b. ʿUmar b. al-Khaṭṭāb, in EI².

Veccia Vaglieri, L., al-Ḥusayn b. ʿAlī b. Abī Ṭālib, in EI².

Veccia Vaglieri, L., Ibn al-Ashʿath, in EI².

Wakīʿ, Muḥammad b. Khalaf b. Ḥayyān, *Akhbār al-quḍāt*, ed. Saʿīd Muḥammad al-Laḥḥām, Beirut n.d.

al-Wāqidī, Muḥammad b. ʿUmar, *Kitāb al-Maghāzī*, ed. M. Jones, 3 vols., Beirut 1984.

Ward, A., *History and chronicles in late medieval Iberia: Representations of Wamba in late medieval narrative histories*, Leiden 2011.

Watt, M., *The formative period of Islamic thought*, Edinburgh 1973.

Watt, M., The materials used by Ibn Isḥāq, in B. Lewis and P.M. Holt (eds.), *Historians of the Middle East*, London 1962, 23–34.

Watt, M., The reliability of Ibn Isḥāq's sources, in T. Fahd (ed.), *La vie du Prophète Mahomet: Colloque de Strasbourg (octobre 1980)*, Paris 1983.

Webb, P.A., *Creating Arab origins: Muslim constructions of al-Jāhiliyya and Arab history*, PhD thesis, School of Oriental and African Studies 2014.

Wellhausen, J., *The Arab kingdom and its fall*, trans. M.G. Weir, Calcutta 1927.

Wellhausen, J., Prolegomena zur ältesten Geschichte des Islams, in *Skizzen und Vorarbeiten: Prolegomena zur ältesten Geschichte des Islams*, Berlin 1899, 6:1–160.

Wellhausen, J., *The religio-political factions in early Islam*, trans. R.C. Ostle and S.M. Walzer, Amsterdam 1975.

Wilkinson, J.C., *Ibâḍism: Origins and early development in Oman*, Oxford 2010.

Wuld Abāh, Muḥammad al-Mukhtār, *Madkhal ilā uṣūl al-fiqh al-mālikī*, Beirut 2011.

Wurtzel, C., *Khalifa ibn Khayyat's History on the Umayyad dynasty (660–750)*, ed. R.G. Hoyland, Liverpool 2015.

Wurtzel, C., *The Umayyads in the "History" of Khalīfa b. Khayyāṭ*, PhD thesis, Yale University 1977.

Wymann-Landgraf, U.F.A., *Mālik and Medina: Islamic legal reasoning in the formative period*, Leiden 2013.

Yaḥyā b. Ādam, *Kitāb al-Kharāj*, ed. Ḥusayn Mu'nis, Cairo 1998.

al-Yaʿqūbī, Aḥmad, *Kitāb al-Buldān*, ed. M.J. de Goeje, Leiden 1892.

al-Yaʿqūbī, Aḥmad, *Tārīkh al-Yaʿqūbī*, ed. ʿAbd al-Amīr Mihnā, 2 vols., Beirut 2010.

Yāqūt al-Ḥamawī, *Muʿjam al-udabāʾ*, ed. Iḥsān ʿAbbās, 7 vols., Beirut 1993.

Yusuf, H., *The creed of Imam al-Ṭaḥāwī*, Berkeley CA 2007.

Zahniser, M., Insights from the ʿUthmāniyya of al-Jāḥiẓ into the religious policy of al-Ma'mūn, in *MW* 69 (1979), 8–17.

Zakkār, S., Ibn Khayyāṭ al-ʿUṣfurī, in *EI*².

Zaman, M.Q., *Maghāzī* and the *muḥaddithūn*: Reconsidering the treatment of "historical" materials in early collections of hadith, in *IJMES* 28 (1996), 1–18.

Zaman, M.Q., *Religion and politics under the early ʿAbbāsids: The emergence of the proto-Sunnī elite*, Leiden 1997.

Zaman, M.Q., al-Yaʿqūbī, in *EI*².

al-Zuḥaylī, Wahba, *Uṣūl al-fiqh al-Islāmī*, 2 vols., Damascus/Beirut 2013.

Index

Abān b. ʿUthmān 35, 242
ʿAbbāsid politics 68–70
ʿAbbāsid religious policies 71–74, 276–278
ʿAbbāsid Revolution 76, 116, 270–275
ʿAbd al-Aʿlā b. ʿAbd al-Aʿlā 19, 49, 119, 161, 170, 230, 247
ʿAbdallāh b. Aḥmad b. Ḥanbal 51–52, 228, 233, 236
ʿAbdallāh b. ʿAlī 39, 274, 275n229, 276
ʿAbdallāh b. ʿAmr b. al-ʿĀṣ 254–255
ʿAbdallāh b. ʿAwn 41, 85, 129, 221, 232
ʿAbdallāh b. Ḥanẓala 260
ʿAbdallāh b. Lahīʿa 130, 137, 160
ʿAbdallāh b. Maslama al-Qaʿnabī 49, 122–123, 170
ʿAbdallāh b. Muʿāwiya 259
ʿAbdallāh b. al-Mughīra 49, 111, 127, 136–137, 174, 208, 219, 274
ʿAbdallāh b. Sabaʾ 229, 236, *see also* Sabaʾiyya
ʿAbdallāh b. Salām 157, 204n40, 296
ʿAbdallāh b. Salama 243
ʿAbdallāh b. Shaqīq al-ʿUqaylī 85
ʿAbdallāh b. ʿUmar 233–234, 252–255, 257–258
ʿAbdallāh b. Zamʿa 260–261
ʿAbdallāh b. al-Zubayr 20, 33–34, 76, 189, 228, 234, 240, 252–256, 258, 262–265, 281
ʿAbd al-ʿAzīz b. ʿImrān 129
ʿAbd al-Malik b. Ḥabīb 1n1, 3, 7, 55n43, 69, 90, 93, 96–97, 99–103, 124, 176, 199, 202–203, 207, 222, 228, 233, 256, 265
ʿAbd al-Malik b. Marwān 20, 33–34, 163, 188, 192–193, 262, 264–265, 268
ʿAbd al-Raḥmān b. Abī Bakr 252, 290
ʿAbd al-Raḥmān b. Abzā 249
ʿAbd al-Raḥmān b. ʿAttāb b. Asīd 239
ʿAbd al-Raḥmān b. Mahdī 49, 106, 115, 149–150, 161, 210, 212, 230, 238–239, 251, 267
ʿAbd al-Salām al-Yashkurī 273, 281
ʿAbd al-Wahhāb b. ʿAbd al-Majīd 49, 113–114, 148, 161, 210, 230
ʿAbd al-Wārith b. Saʿīd b. Dhakwān 42
Abraham, the Prophet 169, 198, 199n19, 291
Abū l-ʿAbbās al-Saffāḥ (ʿAbbāsid caliph) 39–40, 274–275
Abū ʿAmr al-Shaybānī 122, 124, 160
Abū ʿĀṣim al-Ḍaḥḥāk b. Makhlad 48, 115, 161, 230
Abū Bakr b. al-ʿArabī 58, 61, 64, 225, 282
Abū Bakr al-Ṣiddīq 29, 79–80, 83–84, 157, 187–188, 190, 211–217, 226–228, 253, 293
Abū Dāwūd al-Ṭayālisī 48, 106, 114, 129, 161, 230, 238–239
Abū l-Dhayyāl Zuhayr b. Hunayd 39, 118
Abū Ghassān Mālik b. Ismāʿīl 49, 122, 239, 247
Abū Ḥamza al-Azdī 37–39, 272–274, 281
Abū Ḥanīfa 41, 81, 98
Abū Ḥātim al-Rāzī 51–53, 56, 110, 116, 118, 120
Abū Hurayra 180, 234, 295, 297
Abū Jaʿfar al-Manṣūr (ʿAbbāsid caliph) 40, 69, 126, 130, 189, 276
Abū Khālid al-Baṣrī 110, 160, 182, 218n104
Abū Labīd Limāza b. Zabbār al-Jahḍamī 243
Abū Manṣūr al-Azharī 26
Abū Maʿshar 92, 130–131, 176
Abū Mikhnaf 10, 12, 92, 100–102, 134, 159, 176, 208, 215, 227, 238, 240, 246, 260, 268, 281
Abū Mūsā al-Ashʿarī 170, 217, 231, 246
Abū Muslim al-Khurāsānī 40, 270, 274, 276
Abū Nuʿaym al-Faḍl b. Dukayn 49, 117, 133, 247
Abū l-Qāsim Aḥmad b. ʿAbdallāh 18, 39
Abū Qutayba Salm b. Qutayba 120, 161, 230
Abū Saʿīd al-Khudrī 261–262
Abū l-Sarāyā 77, 79
Abū ʿUbayda b. al-Jarrāḥ 156, 208, 218–219
Abū ʿUbayda Maʿmar b. al-Muthannā 89n117, 109, 116–117, 124, 128, 136–137, 160, 198, 237, 239, 247, 267
Abū Wahb ʿAbdallāh b. Bakr al-Sahmī 49, 127
Abū l-Yaqẓān 35, 50, 108, 130, 136, 152, 160–161, 230, 238–239, 260, 267, 281
Abū Zurʿa al-Dimashqī 3, 7, 90, 93, 98–103, 150, 167, 176, 221, 251, 256, 265, 285

Abū Zurʿa al-Rāzī 51–52, 56, 118–120
Adam, the Prophet 169, 198, 290
ahl al-ḥadīth 5–6, 17, 52, 54–55, 65, 67, 78, 80–89, 100, 103, 284
ahl al-raʾy 81, 87–89
Aḥmad b. Ḥanbal 17, 44, 81, 98–99, 111, 124, 127, 231, 236, 258, 260
Aḥmad b. Riyāḥ 47, 73, 278
Aḥmad b. Sahl b. Ayyūb 32n92, 250n114
ʿĀʾisha bt. Abī Bakr 120, 132, 201, 212, 234–235, 238, 240–244, 268, 280, 290
akhbār history 90–93, 139–151, 167
Alexander the Great 169, 198
ʿAlī b. Abī Ṭālib 30, 38, 79–81, 83–85, 99, 187–189, 201, 226–227, 231, 237–249, 273–275, 289
ʿAlī b. al-Madīnī 49, 56–57
ʿAlī al-Riḍā 72, 276
al-Aʿmash 41, 161, 230, 235
al-Amīn (ʿAbbāsid caliph) 42, 73, 189, 276–278
ʿAmmār b. Yāsir 30, 239, 241, 248–249
ʿAmr b. al-ʿĀṣ 30–31, 155, 157, 181, 208, 246, 248
ʿAmr (or ʿUmayr) b. Jurmūz 239, 243, 245
ʿAmr b. Saʿīd b. al-ʿĀṣ 265
ʿAmr b. Tammām 39
al-Andalus 1, 12–13, 17–18, 21–22, 28, 37, 39, 59–61, 69, 93, 96
ʿaqīda 3, 4, 6, 80–83, 86–89, 91, 100, 103, 145, 149–150, 245, 283, 286
ʿarḍ 23, 27
al-Aṣbahānī, Abū Bakr b. al-Muqriʾ 16n7
al-Aṣbahānī, Abū Nuʿaym 60
al-Aṣbahānī, Abū l-Shaykh 60
aṣḥāb al-ḥadīth *see ahl al-ḥadīth*
al-Ashʿarī, Abū l-Ḥasan 151
al-Ashʿarī, Aḥmad b. Muḥammad 13, 18
Ashhal b. Ḥātim 48, 121, 129, 239, 251
al-Ashnānī, Abū l-Ḥasan Aḥmad 17
al-Ashtar, Mālik b. al-Ḥārith 30, 232
al-Aṣmaʿī 49, 119, 124, 160, 267, 269
atbāʿ al-tābiʿīn *see* Successors of the Successors
aural transmission 22–24
awāʾil 205–206
ʿAwāna b. al-Ḥakam 260
al-Awzāʿī 98–99
al-Azdī, Muḥammad b. ʿAbdallāh 215
al-Azdī, Yazīd b. Muḥammad 37–42, 60, 99, 273

Baghdad 47, 69, 73–75, 77, 82, 132, 277
Bakkār b. ʿAbdallāh 19
Bakr b. Sulaymān 48, 109–110, 125
al-Balādhurī 10, 73, 101, 124, 162, 208–209, 211, 215, 229–230, 232, 238, 246, 251, 260, 263, 266–267, 270–271, 275, 281
Baqī b. Makhlad 1, 5–6, 11–12, 15–44, 46, 51–52, 55, 59–61, 70, 73–74, 96, 103, 167, 179, 206, 216, 219, 238, 246–247, 259, 264–265, 273, 278, 286
Basra 1, 5–7, 17, 38–39, 41, 46–47, 50, 54–55, 65, 74–80, 82–85, 105, 131–133, 135–137, 151, 159, 165, 187–189, 191, 216–217, 221, 223, 238–240, 248, 266, 281, 284
Bayhas b. Ḥabīb 116, 136
Bishr b. al-Mufaḍḍal 48, 85, 121, 123, 185, 238–239
al-Bukhārī 29, 45–46, 50, 52, 56–58, 65, 87, 94, 116, 131, 166, 197, 289–298

calendar systems 169, 198–199, *see also* Hijrī calendar
caliphate, theme of 221–223
Camel, Battle of 12, 75–76, 85, 161, 181–182, 237–245
Christian historiography 169
chronography *see tārīkh*
chronology 172–186, 193–194, *see also tārīkh*
civil war *see fitna*
Companions of the Prophet 4, 9, 31, 53, 81–82, 102, 132, 152–153, 173–174, 183–184, 213–215, 225, 228, 233–236, 238, 240–241, 244–245, 248–249, 251–256, 258–262, 279–280, 284, 286
conquests 167, 181, 200, 202, 204, 208–210, 215–221

al-Ḍaḥḥāk b. Qays 222, 264n174
Damascus 20, 39, 62–63, 132, 156, 218–219
dates, dating 12, 97, 102, 147, 166–172, 179–186, 193, 198–199, 280, 284
Dāwūd b. Abī Hind 130
Dāwūd b. ʿAlī 274–275

al-Dhahabī 4, 16, 43, 59, 63–64, 73, 225, 278, 282
al-Dīnawarī 93, 100, 102, 199, 207, 210, 220, 263

Egypt 21, 30–31, 59, 61–64, 130, 155, 217, 231–232, 234–235
emigration *see hijra*
exhumation of Umayyad caliphs 37, 39–40, 275n229

faḍā'il 167, 236, 285–287
al-Farazdaq 236, 257
al-Fasawī 3, 7, 90, 93–94, 97–103, 150, 167, 176, 202–203, 207, 221–222, 228, 285
Fāṭima bt. Asad 258
Fāṭima, the Prophet's daughter 29, 72, 201, 227, 250
fiqh 3–6, 23, 47, 71, 80–83, 86–89, 91, 100, 103, 145, 149–150, 185, 245, 283, 286
first *fitna* 228, 237–249, 262
fitna 9, 83, 96, 102, 135, 167, 178, 225, 227–229, 233, 236–249, 258, 261–265, 269, 275–281, 284, 296
fourth *fitna* 68–69, 73, 76–78, 276–278
fuqahā' 3, 5–6, 17–18, 54–55, 65, 67, 71, 80–81, 85–87, 90, 93–94, 96–97, 176, 190, 200
futūh *see* conquests

ghulāt 80
Ghundar, Muḥammad b. Ja'far 49, 106, 113, 129, 161, 230, 239, 241, 267, 292
governors 27, 75–76, 154–155, 173–174, 176, 178, 187–192, 205–208

al-Hādī, Mūsā ('Abbāsid caliph) 189
ḥadīth scholars, *ḥadīth* transmitters 3–9, 13, 17–18, 21, 47–68, 70–71, 75, 80–87, 90–106, 112, 123–125, 133–151, 158–162, 164–167, 171, 179, 183–185, 193–194, 196, 200, 210, 221, 223, 225, 236–238, 244, 247, 251, 258, 260, 266, 268, 279–287
ḥajj *see* pilgrimage
al-Ḥajjāj b. Yūsuf 75, 155, 265–269, 280
al-Ḥākim al-Naysābūrī 16
Ḥammād b. Salama 48, 108, 128, 202
Ḥammād b. Zayd 41, 85
Ḥanafiyya 87–88
al-Ḥārith b. Suwayd 243
al-Ḥarra, Battle of 155, 161, 257, 259–262, 266, 269, 280
Hārūn al-Rashīd ('Abbāsid caliph) 42, 68, 71–72, 76–77, 185, 189, 276
al-Ḥarūriyya 76, 206, 247, 272, *see also* Khawārij
al-Ḥasan b. 'Alī 32, 226n3, 234, 239, 250–251
al-Ḥasan al-Baṣrī 233–234, 257, 267–268
al-Ḥasan b. Sahl 77
Ḥātim b. Muslim 48, 127, 160, 175, 239
al-Haytham b. 'Adī 92, 100, 176
al-Ḥijāz 252–253, 256, 259, 277
hijra 169–171, 198–200, 203
Hijrī calendar 1, 168–172, 183, 188, 198–200
Hishām b. 'Abd al-Malik 35, 39, 270
Hishām b. Ḥassān 41
Hishām b. al-Kalbī 10, 12, 100–101, 110–111, 133–134, 136–137, 157, 160, 176, 219–220, 246, 260
Hishām b. Qaḥdham 126
historiographical themes 8–9, 195
Ḥukaym b. Jabala al-'Abdī 238–240
al-Ḥusayn b. 'Alī b. Abī Ṭālib 155, 234, 253, 256–259, 264

Ibn 'Abbās 148, 246, 260, 292, 297
Ibn 'Abd al-Barr 30–31, 58, 60–61, 64, 261, 282
Ibn 'Abd Rabbih 38, 60
Ibn Abī Ḥātim 52, 56
Ibn Abī Khaythama 3, 7, 58, 90, 93–94, 98–103, 167, 176, 202–203, 205, 207, 285
Ibn Abī Shayba 17, 90, 150, 167, 205, 228, 231, 233, 236–237, 243, 245, 248, 258
Ibn Abī Zayd al-Qayrawānī 214n91
Ibn 'Adī 52, 57–58, 108, 116, 130
Ibn al-'Adīm 35
Ibn 'Āmir, 'Abdallāh 182, 191, 231
Ibn 'Asākir 4, 11, 16–17, 21–22, 25, 27, 35–36, 43, 61–62, 64–65, 216, 225, 278, 282
Ibn al-Ash'ath 41, 76, 155, 161, 163–164, 266–270, 280
Ibn A'tham 215, 251
Ibn al-Athīr 58, 62

Ibn Ḥajar 56, 59, 63–64, 269
Ibn al-Ḥanafiyya, Muḥammad 258, 264
Ibn Ḥibbān 57–58, 99, 109, 116, 118, 126
Ibn Isḥāq 10, 12, 92, 105–106, 125–126, 137, 148, 152–153, 176, 179, 200, 202, 204, 207, 210, 213, 215, 217, 219, 221
Ibn Kathīr 4, 16, 63–64, 225, 282
Ibn Khallikān 58, 62–63
Ibn Mufarrij, Abū ʿAbdallāh Muḥammad 18
Ibn Muḥammad b. Isḥāq 37, 41, 60n75, 273, 275n229
Ibn al-Nadīm 52, 55, 65, 86
Ibn Qāniʿ 16
Ibn Qutayba 205
Ibn Saʿd 53, 85, 94–95, 99–103, 111, 113, 119, 121, 123–124, 129, 131, 158, 160–161, 207, 228–229, 231, 233, 258, 267
Ibn Shabba 26, 217
Ibn Ṭabāṭabā 77, 79
Ibn Taghrībirdī 64
Ibrāhīm b. ʿAbdallāh 40–41, 76, 79, 259
al-ʿIjlī 83n89, 111, 119
ijtihād 214, 244–245, 249, 255, 258
ʿilm al-rijāl 3, 7, 53–54, 58, 94–96, 99, 102–103, 283, 286
inquisition *see miḥna*
Iraq 5–6, 72, 74–79, 81–82, 87–88, 136, 153–155, 174, 186, 189, 207, 216–217, 221, 223, 256, 265–267, 270, 272, 277
ʿĪsā b. Mūsā 276
Ishmael, the Prophet 169, 198–199
Ismāʿīl b. ʿAyyāsh 19
Ismāʿīl b. Ibrāhīm al-Shuʿayrāwī 112, 119, 271
Ismāʿīl b. Isḥāq 119
Ismāʿīl b. Sinān 48, 121, 128, 251
Ismāʿīl b. ʿUlayya 48, 106, 117, 128–129, 137, 161, 210, 230, 232
isnād 4n21, 26, 90–91, 93–95, 143–154, 157–165, 172

al-Jāḥiẓ 38, 85–86
Jahmiyya 88–89
jamāʿī 4, 89
Jarīr b. Ḥāzim 127
jizya 208–209, 219
judges 32–33, 71, 137, 154–155, 174, 178, 187–189, 191–192, 205, 207
jurists, jurisprudents see *fuqahāʾ*
Juwayriya b. Asmāʾ 35, 108, 111

Kaʿb b. Sawwar 241
Kahmas b. al-Minhāl 49, 115–116, 128, 161, 230, 239, 292
Khālid b. al-Ḥārith 48, 121, 123, 161, 230
Khālid al-Qasrī 75
Khālid b. al-Walīd 156–157, 180, 213–219
Khalīfa b. Khayyāṭ, Abū ʿAmr
- on the ʿAbbāsid Revolution 270–275
- on the ʿAbbāsids 175, 177–178, 207, 275–278, 281
- on administration 207–208
- on administrative offices 154–155, 174, 176–178, 187–193, 205–208
- on ʿAlid uprisings 36, 258–259, 281
- annalistic chronology in his *Tārīkh* 173–174, 193
- audience of his *Tārīkh* 7, 67, 104, 151, 171
- Basra in his *Tārīkh* 136, 206, 216–217, 221, 223, 238, 248, 266, 281
- on the Battle of the Camel 237–245
- on the Battle of al-Ḥarra 259–262
- on the Battle of Ṣiffīn 245–249
- birth 46, 68
- caliphal chronology in his *Tārīkh* 174–176, 193
- on caliphate 221–223
- on conquests 215–221
- death 43n139, 46–47, 68
- education 47–50
- epistemology 140–151
- on the first *fitna* 237–249
- on the foundation of the Muslim community 203–204
- on the fourth *fitna* 276–278
- genealogy 45–46
- on al-Ḥasan's transfer of the caliphate 250–251
- on al-Ḥusayn's martyrdom 256–259
- on Ibn al-Ashʿath's revolt 266–270
- introductory section in his *Tārīkh* 167–172
- *isnād*, use of 8, 151–164
- on the Khawārij 247, 272–274, 281
- in later scholarship 59–65
- on law and legal rulings 205–206
- lists in his *Tārīkh* 94, 154–155, 174–178, 187–194
- methods 139–165
- and the *miḥna* 47, 73–74, 278

on Muʿāwiya's appointment of Yazīd 251–256
name 45–46
on non-Muslims 102, 204, 220–221, 223
on Prophets and prophethood 196–203
on the Rāshidūn caliphs 9, 86, 188, 207, 223, 225–228, 251–256, 279–281, 284
reputation 55–59
on the *ridda* wars 210–215
on the second *fitna* 262–265
sources in his *Tārīkh* 105–138
structure of his *Tārīkh* 166–194
students 50–52
on succession 9, 225–228, 251–256, 276–277, 279–280
system of reference *see isnād*
Ṭabaqāt, Kitāb al- 3, 7, 14, 16, 52–54, 57–58, 61–66, 90, 95–96, 104, 124, 143, 151, 158, 167, 178, 179–180, 183–185, 212, 286
on taxation 208–209
teachers 47–50
title of his *Tārīkh* 166–167
transmission of his *Tārīkh* 15–44
transmitter criticism 158–162
on the Umayyads 38–40, 175, 177–178, 206–207, 250–275, 280–281
on ʿUthmān's assassination 228–237
works 52–55
Khalīfa b. Khayyāṭ, Abū Hubayra 46
kharāj 208–209
al-Khaṭīb al-Baghdādī 46–47
Khawārij 76, 78–79, 89, 109, 206, 247, 259, 262, 264, 270, 272–274, 276, 281
Khayyāṭ b. Khalīfa 46
Khurāsān 72, 77, 187, 189, 192–193, 218, 266, 270, 277
khuṭba 34, 37–39, 267, 271–275, 281, 295
Kināna b. Bishr al-Tujībī 235
kitāba 24
Kufa 35–36, 74–76, 79–80, 82, 84, 132–136, 159, 241, 256–257, 274

al-Layth b. Saʿd 20
lecture notes 22–25
lists in Islamic historiography 94, 175–176, 190–191
local historiographical schools 135–136, 285
al-Madāʾinī 49, 92, 100–101, 106–108, 136–137, 152–153, 179, 204, 210, 213, 230, 238–241, 247–248, 260, 267, 271, 281
maghāzī-sīra 96, 150, 167, 171, 179, 196, 199–204, 285–287
al-Mahdī (ʿAbbāsid caliph) 42, 69, 71–72, 189, 273, 276
Mālik b. Dīnār 184, 267
al-Mālikī, Abū Bakr 60
Mālik b. Nuwayra 213–214
al-Maʾmūn (ʿAbbāsid caliph) 42, 68–69, 72–73, 76–77, 156, 189, 276–278
Manṣūr b. al-Mahdī 42, 76
maqātil 135, 167, 178, 259
Marwān b. al-Ḥakam 20, 30, 33, 38, 157, 191, 232, 239, 242, 244, 262–264, 278
Marwān (II) b. Muḥammad 36, 271–272
Marwān b. Muḥammad al-Ṭāṭarī 19
Maslama b. ʿAbd al-Malik 39
Maslama b. al-Qāsim al-Andalusī 57
al-Masʿūdī 93, 100, 102, 208, 210, 220, 227, 251, 263
matn 90
al-Māwardī, Abū Ghālib Muḥammad 17
Maysara b. Bakr 41
Mecca 171, 200, 202, 252–253, 262–265, 272, 292
Medina 1, 132, 171, 187, 200, 203, 231, 259–262, 274, 292, 295
miḥna 43–44, 47, 70–74, 88, 117, 278
al-Mizzī 48, 50, 59
Moses, the Prophet 169, 291–292
Muʿādh b. Muʿādh 50, 121, 123, 129, 210
Muʿāwiya b. Abī Sufyān 21, 32–33, 38–39, 99, 156–157, 191–192, 206, 222, 227, 245–256, 258, 278, 280–281
Muʿāwiya (II) b. Yazīd 33
Mughalṭāy b. Qalīj 59
al-Mughīra, Abū ʿAbdallāh 127
al-Mughīra b. Shuʿba 216n97, 250–251
muḥaddithūn see *ḥadīth* scholars
al-Muhallab b. Abī Ṣufra 20, 34
Muḥammad, the Prophet 1, 8, 29, 53–54, 87, 96–99, 147–148, 152–153, 155, 170, 179–180, 187, 190, 196–204, 206–207, 214, 241, 245, 249, 253, 289–298

Muḥammad b. ʿAbdallāh al-Anṣārī 49, 117–118, 129, 137, 293
Muḥammad b. ʿAbdallāh b. Numayr 20
Muḥammad b. ʿAbd al-Raḥmān 22, 28
Muḥammad b. Abī Bakr 30, 235
Muḥammad b. Abī Ḥudhayfa 30–31
Muḥammad b. ʿĀʾidh al-Dimashqī 19
Muḥammad b. Muʿāwiya 49, 109, 116–117, 160, 198, 257
Muḥammad b. Sīrīn 4n21, 170, 221
Muḥammad b. Ṭalḥa b. ʿUbaydallāh 239
Muḥammad b. Yūnus al-Kudaymī 57
Mujāshiʿ b. Masʿūd al-Sulamī 239
al-Mukhtār al-Thaqafī 33–34, 36, 259, 262, 264–265
Murjiʾa 82, 87–88, 244
Muṣʿab b. al-Zubayr 34, 264–265
Mūsā b. Ismāʿīl al-Tabūdhakī 50, 120, 128, 210
muṣannaf 3, 18, 90, 128
Mūsā b. ʿUqba 110
Muslim b. ʿAqīl b. Abī Ṭālib 155–156, 257
Muslim b. al-Ḥajjāj 94, 99, 158, 172
Muslim b. Ibrāhīm al-Farāhīdī 122–123
Muslim b. ʿUqba 260–261
musnad 3, 18, 52–53, 90, 94, 114, 124
Muʿtamir b. Sulaymān 50, 118, 161, 185, 230, 272
al-Muʿtaṣim (ʿAbbāsid caliph) 68–70, 77, 189, 276
al-Mutawakkil (ʿAbbāsid caliph) 42–43, 65, 68, 70, 73–74, 278
Muʿtazila 47, 72–73, 82, 86–89, 119, 151, 244, 278

Nābigha al-Jaʿdī 236
Nābita 85–86
al-Nafs al-Zakiyya, Muḥammad 41, 71, 76, 79, 82, 259, 276
al-Nahrawān, Battle of 76, 182, 272
Najda b. ʿĀmir 264
al-Nasāʾī 20, 131
Naṣr b. Muzāḥim 10, 12, 100–102, 176, 208, 237, 248
al-Nawawī 58, 62–64
al-Nihāwandī, Abū ʿAbdallāh Aḥmad 17
Noah, the Prophet 169, 198
North Africa 17, 21, 59–60, 62, 69, 188, 218, 272

Persian history 169, 180, 197–198, 220
pilgrimage 20, 154–155, 168, 183, 190, 205, 252, 264, 276, 289–290
poetry 91, 236
pre-Islamic Arabia 169, 197–199
prophethood 169, 196–203
Prophets before Muḥammad 196–199

Qadariyya 88, 98, 116, 119, 126, 128, 271
Qaḥdham b. Sulaymān b. Dhakwān 108, 126
Qaḥṭaba b. Shabīb 274
al-Qāsim b. Umayya b. Abī l-Ṣalt 236
qibla 147–148, 201
qirāʾa 23
Qudayd, Battle of 155, 186, 274
Qurʾān 4, 18, 50–52, 72, 83, 88–89, 91, 95, 168–169, 171, 196–198, 211–212, 231, 234–235, 241, 261–262, 266, 271
Qurayb b. Murra 272
qurrāʾ 266–268
quṣṣāṣ 150

Rāfiʿ b. Layth 277
Raqqa 132, 238, 248
Rāshidūn caliphs 4, 9, 29–32, 71, 80, 82–86, 99, 153, 180–182, 187–188, 207, 225–228, 253, 279, 281
Rawḥ b. ʿUbāda 48, 122–123, 161, 230
ridda wars 210–215
rightly-guided caliphs *see* Rāshidūn caliphs

Sabaʾiyya 141, 229, 232, 236
ṣaḥāba *see* Companions of the Prophet
ṣāḥib sunna 82, 111, 127, 260
Saʿīd b. Abī ʿArūba 41, 115–116, 128
Saʿīd b. Jubayr 267
Saʿīd b. al-Musayyib 132, 148, 170, 184, 202, 252n121, 264
samāʿ 22–23, 27, 48n20, 107n4
Samarra 47, 68–69
Sayf b. ʿUmar 10, 92, 100–102, 134, 141, 159, 176, 206–208, 227–230, 232, 236–238, 240, 281
second *fitna* 20–21, 78, 262–265
Shabath b. Ribʿī 247, 272
al-Shaʿbī, ʿĀmir 215, 268–269
Shamir (or Shimr) b. Dhī l-Jawshan 258
al-Shawkānī 241n73

Shīʿa 78–80, 89, 259
Imāmiyya, Rāfiḍa 80, 89
Zaydiyya 79, 89
Shīʿī historians 9, 102, 133–135, 178, 191, 215, 228, 233–234, 244–246, 259
Shuʿba b. al-Ḥajjāj 41, 108, 113, 128–129, 148, 292, 296–297
shūrā 226, 252–253, 260, 263–264
Ṣiffīn, Battle of 76, 85, 161, 182, 237–238, 245–249
sīra *see maghāzī-sīra*
al-Sīrāfī, Abū l-Ḥasan Muḥammad 17
storytellers *see quṣṣāṣ*
Successors 4, 53–54, 81, 132, 152–153, 173–174, 183–184, 234, 238, 251, 256, 259–260, 262, 268, 280
Successors of the Successors 153
Sūdān b. Ḥumrān 235
Sulaymān b. ʿAbd al-Malik 35, 39, 174–175
Sulaymān b. Ḥarb 48, 122–123, 267
ṣulḥ *see* treaty
Sunna 43, 73–74, 83, 119, 207, 260, 272, 278
Sunnism (early) 2, 4–5, 9, 80–87, 89, 102, 133–135, 177–178, 225–228, 233–236, 244–246, 252–255, 269–270, 279–280, 286–287
al-Suyūṭī 64
Syria 20–21, 26, 58–59, 61–65, 98, 217, 246–248, 252, 259–265
Syriac historiography 92

ṭabaqāt (genre) 3, 7, 53, 67–68, 90, 93–104, 167, 285–287
Ṭabaqāt of Khalīfa b. Khayyāṭ *see* Khalīfa b. Khayyāṭ, Abū ʿAmr
al-Ṭabarānī 16
al-Ṭabarī 10, 62, 65, 93, 100–103, 124, 134, 143, 171–172, 176, 178, 187, 193, 199, 207–208, 210–211, 214–217, 220, 227–230, 232–233, 237–238, 246, 258, 260, 263, 266–268, 270–271, 275, 277, 281
tābiʿūn *see* Successors
tafsīr 18, 196–197
al-Ṭaḥāwī 89n115, 177n45
al-Ṭalamankī, Abū ʿUmar Aḥmad 18
Ṭalḥa b. ʿUbaydallāh 30, 238–245, 249, 258, 264, 289
tārīkh (genre) 2–3, 7, 67–68, 90–93, 96–104, 166–172, 177–178, 193, 283, 285–287
Tārīkh of Khalīfa b. Khayyāṭ *see* Khalīfa b. Khayyāṭ, Abū ʿAmr
tashayyuʿ 80, 84, 117, 126, 130, 135n113
taxation 208–209
Thucydides 146
transmission formulas 8, 162–164, 284
treaty 156, 179–180, 204–205, 208–209, 217–219
al-Tustarī, Mūsā b. Zakariyyā 5, 12, 14–44, 51, 53, 59, 61, 73, 96, 103, 167, 175, 206, 216, 219, 237, 246–248, 259, 265, 267, 273, 278, 286

ʿUbaydallāh b. Ziyād 75, 156, 241, 257
ʿUmar (II) b. ʿAbd al-ʿAzīz 35, 38, 174–175
ʿUmar b. Aḥmad al-Ahwāzī 14, 16n7
ʿUmar b. al-Khaṭṭāb 29, 79–80, 83–84, 169–170, 187–188, 190, 205, 214, 226–228, 253, 292–293
ʿUmar b. Saʿd b. Mālik 258
Umayya b. Khālid 118, 129, 267
al-ʿUqaylī, Abū Jaʿfar 56
ʿUrwa b. al-Zubayr 152, 184, 196
ʿUthmān b. ʿAffān 29–31, 38, 79–80, 83–85, 160–163, 188, 206, 226–237, 242, 244, 253, 271, 273, 279–280, 293
ʿUthmān b. Ḥunayf 183, 238, 240
ʿUthmāniyya 28, 83–85, 113, 129, 244

Wahb b. Jarīr 50, 106, 111–112, 125, 127, 238–239, 251, 255, 260–261
Wakīʿ b. al-Jarrāḥ 50, 122–123
al-Walīd b. ʿAbd al-Malik 35, 39, 137
al-Walīd b. Hishām al-Qaḥdhamī 50, 108–109, 126, 129, 136, 156, 160, 174, 218
al-Walīd b. Muslim al-Dimashqī 19
al-Walīd (II) b. Yazīd 36, 38, 270–272, 278
al-Wāqidī 19, 49, 92, 101, 122–124, 157, 159, 162, 176, 207, 217, 230, 232, 260
al-Waqqashī, Abū l-Walīd Hishām 18
Wāsiṭ 75, 132
al-Wāthiq (ʿAbbāsid caliph) 47, 73, 189, 278
wijāda 24

Yaḥyā b. ʿAbdallāh b. Bukayr 19–20
Yaḥyā b. Maʿīn 42, 46, 56, 84, 98, 111, 116, 119–120, 129, 131
Yaḥyā b. Muḥammad al-Kaʿbī 50, 114, 129, 161, 230, 267

Yaḥyā b. Saʿīd al-Qaṭṭān 50, 106, 114–115, 160, 294
al-Yamāma, Battle of 186, 210–212, 216
al-Yaʿqūbī 73, 93, 100, 102, 176, 178, 187, 190–191, 193–194, 199, 207–208, 210, 215–216, 220, 227, 251, 263, 275
Yāqūt al-Ḥamawī 62
Yazdajird b. Shahrayār 169, 198
Yazīd b. ʿAbdallāh b. Zamʿa 260–261
Yazīd (II) b. ʿAbd al-Malik 35
Yazīd b. Hārūn 50, 122–123, 161, 230
Yazīd b. Muʿāwiya 20, 33, 38–39, 155, 163, 222, 251–260, 262–264, 278–281
Yazīd b. al-Muhallab 76, 155
Yazīd (III) b. al-Walīd 36, 271–272, 281
Yazīd b. Zurayʿ 50, 85, 106, 112–113, 128, 148, 168, 289–290, 292–297
Yūsuf b. ʿUmar al-Thaqafī 35, 75, 108, 126, 136

Zaḥḥāf b. Zaḥr 272
zandaqa, zanādiqa 71–72
Zayd b. ʿAlī b. al-Ḥusayn 35–36, 259
Zayd b. Thābit 234
Zaynab bt. Abī Salama 261
Ziyād b. Abīhi 75, 155
al-Zubayr b. al-ʿAwwām 238–245, 249, 258, 274
al-Zuhrī 132, 152–153, 179, 196, 202, 213, 216
Zuṭṭ 77

Printed in the United States
By Bookmasters